INTERNATIONAL LAW AND
HUMAN RIGHTS

INTERNATIONAL LAW
AND
HUMAN RIGHTS

BY

H. LAUTERPACHT
K.C., LL.D., F.B.A.

Whewell Professor of International Law in the University of Cambridge; Fellow of Trinity College, Cambridge; Associate of the Institute of International Law

ARCHON BOOKS
1968

First published 1950
Reprinted 1968 with permission
Stevens & Sons Limited
in an unaltered and unabridged edition

Library of Congress Catalog Card Number: 68-20373
Printed in the United States of America

To

R. L.

PREFACE

Since the publication, in 1945, of my book entitled *An International Bill of the Rights of Man,* I have been devoting further study and reflection to the question of an international bill of human rights and, generally, of the international protection of the rights of man. Much of what at the beginning of 1945 was in the nature of proposals has subsequently either become part of the law enshrined in the Charter of the United Nations or has loomed large in the discussions concerned with making the obligations of the Charter more tangible and effective through the adoption of an international bill of human rights and otherwise.

Accordingly, one of the three main purposes of the present book is to analyse the legal effects of the provisions of the Charter in the matter and the practice of the organs of the United Nations concerned with the interpretation and application of those provisions. Its second object is to re-examine the question of the international bill of the rights of man in the light of the efforts made in the initial stage of the United Nations to give substance to an idea which must be regarded as inherent in the Charter. Thirdly, it appeared to me that any discussion of the international protection of human rights either in general or through the Charter of the United Nations and a Bill of Rights adopted in pursuance thereof must be deficient unless it takes place against the wider background of the problem of the subjects of international law and of the interaction of the law of nations and the law of nature in relation to the enduring issue of human government—the securing of the natural and inalienable rights of man. With regard to the latter question I have drawn to some extent upon my previous book, referred to above, which is out of print and not likely to be reprinted. I have also thought it desirable to discuss in a general way the attempts at a regional solution of the problem such as embodied in the proposed European Court and Commission of Human Rights.

I am indebted to the various bodies and Editorial Committees

vii

for permission to reproduce, in a modified or expanded form, articles or lectures which I have published under their auspices. These include the Hague Academy of International Law, the Grotius Society, the International Law Association, *The Law Quarterly Review*, and *The British Year Book of International Law*.

I wish to express my warm thanks to Miss Felice Morgenstern, B.A., Whewell Scholar of International Law in the University of Cambridge, for reading the proof and checking references; to Mrs. Gladys Lyons, B.Sc.(Econ.), for revising the proof, for secretarial assistance, and for compiling the Table of Cases; to my son, Mr. E. Lauterpacht, B.A., of Trinity College, Cambridge, for the care bestowed upon reading the proof of Part One of the book; to Mr. A. B. Lyons, M.A., LL.B., for undertaking at high pressure the arduous task of preparing the Index; and to Mrs. E. E. Jansen and Mr. C. J. Staines, of the Squire Law Library, Cambridge, for copying large portions of an unattractive manuscript.

Various members of the Division of Human Rights of the United Nations, in particular Professor John P. Humphrey, the Director, Dr. Egon Schwelb, the Deputy-Director, and Dr. K. Das, have assisted me by placing at my disposal the non-confidential documents and records connected with their work. I am much indebted to them. They have not always been able to concur in my views, but I am confident that we are in agreement as to the ultimate objective.

I have been fortunate in enlisting the courteous and most efficient collaboration of the Publishers, and I desire to express my sincere thanks to them and to their Printers.

H. LAUTERPACHT.

Trinity College,
Cambridge.
February 1950.

TABLE OF CONTENTS

PART ONE

THE RIGHTS OF MAN AND THE LAW OF NATIONS

SECTION I

THE SUBJECTS OF THE LAW OF NATIONS

ix

SECTION II

THE LAW OF NATURE AND THE RIGHTS OF MAN

PART TWO

HUMAN RIGHTS UNDER THE CHARTER OF THE UNITED NATIONS

SECTION I

THE LAW OF THE CHARTER

PART THREE

*THE INTERNATIONAL BILL OF THE RIGHTS
OF MAN*

SECTION I

THE PROBLEM OF THE BILL OF RIGHTS

SECTION II

THE PRINCIPLES OF AN INTERNATIONAL BILL OF THE RIGHTS OF MAN

SECTION III

THE UNIVERSAL DECLARATION AND THE EUROPEAN COURT

TABLE OF CASES

PART ONE

THE RIGHTS OF MAN AND THE LAW OF NATIONS

CHAPTER 1

THE TRADITIONAL DOCTRINE AND THE PRACTICE OF STATES

1. INTRODUCTORY: THE SIGNIFICANCE OF THE PROBLEM OF THE SUBJECTS OF INTERNATIONAL LAW

THIS book is devoted to two main objects. The first is the exposition of the existing law, as enshrined in the Charter of the United Nations, relating to the international recognition and protection of human rights and fundamental freedoms. The second is the consideration of the problems arising out of the proposals made for the extension of the existing law, as embodied in the Charter, through the adoption of an International Bill of the Rights of Man. Both these questions are intimately connected with the more general problem of the position of the individual as a subject of the law of nations. Thus, in the first instance, if the provisions of the Charter relating to human rights are to be adequately interpreted, they must be read against the broad background of the position of the individual in international law. If we remain hidebound by the traditional approach to that question we shall be inclined to see in the Articles of the Charter bearing upon human rights an artificial innovation altogether divorced from previous practice and out of keeping with the natural framework of international law. Our interpretation will accordingly be hesitant and restrictive. If, on the other hand, we contemplate these Articles of the Charter, fundamental and epoch-making as they are, as rooted in a substantial body of practice and as not inconsistent with the essential structure of international law, we shall have removed an obstacle of some importance in the way of giving full scope to a crucial purpose

3

of the Charter of the United Nations. The interpretation of
the Charter in that matter depends to a substantial degree upon
the realisation that there is no rule of international law which
definitely precludes individuals and bodies other than States from
acquiring directly rights under or being bound by duties imposed
by customary or conventional international law, and that the
developments of the last quarter of a century have translated that
capacity, in many fields and in respect of both rights and duties,
into part of positive law. As a result of the Charter of the
United Nations—as well as of other changes in international law
—the individual has acquired a status and a stature which have
transformed him from an object of international compassion
into a subject of international right. For in so far as international
law as embodied in the Charter and elsewhere recognises fundamental rights of the individual independent of the law of the State,
to that extent it constitutes the individual a subject of the law
of nations. There is nothing in what is often referred to as the
structure of international law which prevents that result from
being achieved.

Similarly, the consideration and the proposed solutions of the
questions involved in the contemplated International Bill of the
Rights of Man must, to a large extent, depend upon or be influenced by our view as to the substance, the nature and the flexi-
bility of the rules of international law in the matter of the status
of the individual. Admittedly, the Bill of Rights, if it is to attain
the significance which has been attached to it, must go beyond
the existing law. But the distance which it will traverse in that
direction will in some measure be determined by our judgment
as to the content and the adaptability, in this field, of the system
of international law as it has evolved in the last century. Thus
the idea of an effective right of petition exercised at the instance
of the individual—to the point, if need be, of conceding to him
an independent right of access to an international tribunal—must
be influenced by our notions of the status of the individual in
international society. If ' the very structure of international law '
renders the idea of any such departure heretical and impracticable, then we must temper our reformatory zeal accordingly. If
what is occasionally described as ' the very structure of
international law ' on the subject is no more than a form of words
—or, at most, a generalisation of a past period of immaturity—

then the way is open, in this respect, to such beneficent changes as the moral sense of mankind, the necessities of international peace and the enduring purposes of the law of nations may require. For these reasons it has been deemed proper to devote the opening Chapters of this book to a doctrinal examination of the question of the subjects of international law and to an analysis of the practice of States in this sphere.

The question of the subjects of international law has been discussed in the past largely from two aspects. It has been debated, in the first instance, as part of the controversy whether not only States but also individuals are subjects of the law of nations. With regard to individuals, the discussion has centred largely on the question whether they possess or can possess rights given to them directly by customary international law and treaties. In particular, much attention has been devoted to the problem of the direct access of individuals to international tribunals and other international agencies. The issue of the so-called fundamental rights of the individual recognised and protected by international law as against the sovereign power of the State has underlain, though in a somewhat inarticulate form, much of the discussion.

All these are questions of significance. But there have been other factors which have imparted to the discussion a degree of urgency unusual in a seemingly theoretical controversy. One of them has been the position of individuals as subjects of international duties. In the first instance, the proposition that individuals can be subjects of international rights necessarily involves the corollary that they can be subjects of international duties; the cogency of the claim to the former gains by an admission of the latter. Secondly, to assert that duties prescribed by international law are binding upon the impersonal entity of States as distinguished from the individuals who compose them and who act on their behalf is to open the door wide for the acceptance, in relation to States, of standards of morality different from those applying among individuals. Experience has shown that 'different' standards mean, in this connexion, standards which are lower and less exacting. Thirdly, upon final analysis it is difficult to escape the conclusion that unless legal duties are accepted as resting upon the individual being, they do not in practice—nor, to some extent, in law—obligate anyone. These apparently theoretical considerations received illuminating comment in the Judgment given on 30 September, 1946, by the International Military Tribunal established by the Four-Power Agreement, and the Charter annexed thereto, of 6 August, 1945. The Tribunal said:

> ' It was submitted that international law is concerned with the actions of sovereign States, and provides no punishment for individuals . . . these submissions must be rejected. . . . Crimes against international law are committed by men, not by abstract entities, and only by punishing individuals who commit such crimes can the provisions of international law be enforced.' [1]

This statement was in the nature of an explanatory gloss upon the provision of Article 6 of the Charter which laid down that there shall be individual responsibility of the defendants for the acts within the jurisdiction of the Tribunal. The joint effect of the Charter and the Judgment was to bring to mind with particular emphasis the fact that the question of the subjects of international law is not one of mere theory. However, this is only one aspect of the wider problem which it is intended to discuss in the present Section. It will be submitted: (a) that the doctrine that States are the only subjects of international law is not an accurate statement of the actual legal position; (b) that the modern development of international law, from a system of procedural and ceremonial rules regulating the external intercourse of States and delimiting their jurisdiction, to a body of law concerned with substantive interests of States and their nationals, has rendered the traditional positivist doctrine on the subject obsolete and unworkable; and (c) that the time is now ripe for assessing the significance of these changes in the substantive law and in the functioning of organised international society.

2. THE POSITIVIST DOCTRINE

The orthodox positivist doctrine has been explicit in the affirmation that only States are subjects of international law. [2]

---

[1] *Transcript of the Proceedings*, p. 16,878.

[2] That traditional doctrine is now rejected by the great majority of those who have devoted special study to the matter—though it continues to linger in some repetitious statements in textbooks. Dr. Knubben, in the most exhaustive work yet published on the subjects of international law—*Die Subjekte des Völkerrechts* (1928)—reaches the conclusion that the traditional view is antiquated and no longer tenable. He defines international law as ' a law regulating the mutual relations of States and the international relations

In those cases in which individuals seem to derive benefits under international law, the predominant view has been that such benefits are enjoyed not by virtue of a right which international law gives to the individual, but by reason of a right appertaining to the State of which the individual is a national. The right is a right of the State; the individual is the object of that right. Thus, while it is an established principle acted upon by international tribunals that the alien resident within the territory of a State is entitled to be treated in accordance with a minimum standard of civilisation, the traditional theory has been that, in strict law, it is not the alien who is thus ' entitled ', but only his State. His membership of the State—his nationality—is an essential condition of the jurisdiction of international tribunals when resorted to for the purpose of redressing wrongs alleged to have been suffered by him. Much of the existing practice, in the form of the rule of ' nationality of claims' and otherwise, seems to lend support to that view. When confronted with the so-called Calvo Clause, international tribunals have held that it is not competent for an alien to sign away, with an effect binding upon his Government and the tribunal, his right to appeal for the protection of his State in case of a denial of justice amounting to a violation of international law—the reason being that the faculty to vindicate the violated rule of international law is the right of

of other subjects, in particular those of States and of entities other than States ' (at p. 527). Professor Spiropoulos, in an important essay published in the same year and anticipating more recent developments such as an International Bill of Human Rights—*L'individu en droit international*— arrives at the same view. So, in 1927, did the author of this book: Lauterpacht, *Private Law Sources and Analogies of International Law* (1927), pp. 73-79; Politis, *Les nouvelles tendences du droit international* (1927), pp. 55-93; Segal, *L'individu en droit international* (1932); Ténékidès, *L'individu dans l'ordre juridique international* (1933); Siotto-Pintor, ' Les sujets du droit international autres que les Etats ', in *Hague Recueil*, 41 (1932) (iii), pp. 251-357. More recently, Professor Jessup has shown both the decisive inroads which practice has made upon the established doctrine and the further possible impacts of the change resulting from the fact that the individual—and, generally, persons and bodies other than States—have in many respects acquired a status in international law: see Jessup, ' Responsibility of States for Injuries to Individuals ', in *Columbia Law Review*, 46 (1946), pp. 903-928, ' The Subjects of a Modern Law of Nations ', in *Michigan Law Review*, 45 (1947), pp. 383-408, and ' Law of International Contractual Agreements ', in *American Journal of International Law*, 41 (1947), pp. 378-405. The substance of these articles is included in Jessup, *A Modern Law of Nations* (1948). In fact, what has been considered the established doctrine is no longer ' established '. From this affirmation of the position of the individual in international law there must be distinguished the general jurisprudential view advocated by Professor Scelle, according to which individuals only are the subjects of international law: *Manuel élémentaire de droit international public* (1943), p. vii. See also below, pp. 41, 65, 66.

his State, not a right of his own. For a similar reason the traditional theory has denied the possibility of any direct relation between international and municipal law. If individuals can never be subjects of international rights and duties then, according to that view, the rules of international law can have no immediate effect, without a previous act of transformation, upon the municipal law of the State. On that theory the classical English doctrine that the law of nations is part of the law of the land—a doctrine which has become part of the law of many States—is merely a deceptive and inaccurate form of words. For the same reason it has been asserted that so-called fundamental rights of the individual recognised by international law are not only non-existent but also impossible in principle as being inconsistent with the structure of international law conceived as a law between States only. Similarly, if individuals have no rights under international law, it seems to follow that they can have no *locus standi* before international tribunals and other international agencies, though occasionally it has been argued that they are not subjects of international law *because* of their procedural incapacity before international tribunals. Finally, it has been denied, for essentially the same reason, that international public bodies of a political and administrative character, created by agreements between States, possess an international juridical personality of their own and are as such subjects of international law in their own right.

This dualism of subjects, of international law and of municipal law respectively, has been stressed with particular emphasis by the exponents of the positivist school of thought. It is not surprising that this should have been so. In the first instance, in so far as the positivist doctrine is identified with the extreme assertion of State sovereignty, it is natural that it should have viewed with disapproval the notion of private persons, or even of public international bodies, being placed in the same elevated category as sovereign States. Secondly, inasmuch as the conception of fundamental rights of the individual represents him as a subject of international rights irrespective of the law of the State, it amounts to a rejection of the doctrine that the will of States is the exclusive source of international law. If, according to the positivist doctrine, States themselves can become subjects of international law only by virtue of recognition granted, with constitutive effect, by already existing States acting in the free and unfettered exercise of their discretion, this is much more so with regard to individuals and other persons. Even those positivist writers who have admitted the possibility of persons other than States being subjects of international law have insisted that this could be so only as the result of express agreement by States. It is thus probable that the criticism of the accepted doctrine in the matter of the subjects of international law cannot be separated from the challenge to the twin positivist doctrine of international law as emanating exclusively from the will of States.

3. THE PRACTICE OF STATES

Like various other tenets of the positivist creed, the doctrine that only States are subjects of international law is unable to stand the test of actual practice. This is so although some of the criticism directed against it under this head has been of controversial value and confined to matters of limited compass. Thus the rules of international law in the matter of piracy have often been referred to as confuting the predominant doctrine. It has been pointed out that inasmuch as every State is entitled to exercise jurisdiction over a pirate, piracy is a crime not only under municipal law but also under international law, and that, therefore, pirates are subjects of the law of nations. Yet it is possible that the rule in question amounts in effect to no more than a reciprocal concession of jurisdictional rights over an alien for a crime committed abroad, as is the case, for instance, in the matter of the jurisdiction over aliens conceded in the Convention of 1929 on the Suppression of Counterfeiting Currency[3] or in the (unratified) Convention of 1937 for the Prevention and Punishment of Terrorism.[4] For while some countries, such as Great Britain, in assuming jurisdiction over pirates refer to piracy as defined by the law of nations, others assume jurisdiction over piracy as defined by their own law. On the other hand, when—as in the Nyon Agreement of 1937 relating to piratical acts of submarines in the Mediterranean in the course of the Spanish Civil War of 1936-1939—States claim to assume jurisdiction over offenders of whatever nationality (and not only of the nationality of the

[3] Hudson, *International Legislation,* vol. 4, p. 2692.
[4] *Ibid.,* vol. 7, p. 862.

Contracting Parties), we are confronted with the direct subjection of individuals to international law in a manner which cannot be interpreted as a mutual concession of jurisdictional rights.

Similarly, it is controversial whether it can be accurately maintained that a blockade-runner penalised by a belligerent is a subject of the law of nations inasmuch as he is being punished for a violation of a rule of international law. There is probably no rule of international law prohibiting individuals from breaking a blockade or carrying contraband. The penalty for such acts is inflicted by the belligerent in conformity with his own law, though subject to an authorisation laid down and qualified by international law. The rules of international law in the matter of contraband and blockade are binding upon States in the sense that they circumscribe their freedom of action in interfering with and suppressing the activities of nationals of other States.

Somewhat strangely, insufficient attention has been paid, in this connexion, to the fact that the operation of the law of war constitutes a decisive refutation of the view that States only, and not individuals, are subjects of international duties. For it is an accepted principle of law that individual members of the armed forces of the belligerent are criminally responsible for violations of the law of war and that the enemy State is entitled to punish them for war crimes committed by them. The controversy, which is now somewhat unreal, whether they are thus liable for acting in obedience to superior orders is irrelevant in this connexion. For it is universally agreed that in any case persons who have ordered the commission of war crimes are liable to punishment for the violation of rules of warfare. It is clear that in this vital respect the apparently established doctrine breaks down altogether. The law declines, in this matter, to accept the artificial distinction between the State and those acting on its behalf. The fact that the offender acts on behalf of the State is irrelevant. He is bound personally by rules of international law whether he is acting in his personal capacity, in order to satisfy private greed or lust, or as an organ of the State.[5]

Neither can it be said that, in the criticism of the doctrine that only States are subjects of international law, full use—or, indeed, any use—has been made of the fact that according to the law of

[5] See below, pp. 39, 43, 44.

many States rules of international law form part of their domestic law. This is so in particular in Great Britain, in the United States, and in other common law countries where the doctrine of the incorporation of international law as part of the law of the land must be regarded as firmly established—at least with regard to customary international law. There has been occasional hesitation on the part of English courts in acknowledging the full operation of the doctrine of incorporation, but there ought to be no doubt as to its validity, its general effectiveness and its significance.[6] It constitutes perhaps the most important contribution of common law to the cause of the law of nations. It has been expressly adopted by a number of countries; it is probable that, without express adoption, it has been acted upon by others.[7] The principle that international law is, without an express act of transformation, part of municipal law means in effect that rights and duties created by international law are directly applicable to individuals through the instrumentality of municipal courts and that, to that extent, individuals are subjects of the law of nations. Writers of the positivist complexion have denied the operation of that principle by resorting to the device of begging the question. International law, they have maintained, cannot act directly in the municipal sphere for the reason that the subjects of the two systems of law are fundamentally different. Actually, the alleged difference of subjects is disproved by the fact that, according to the law of the majority of States, international law is a direct source of rights and obligations of

---

[6] See the writer's paper in *Transactions of the Grotius Society*, 25 (1939), pp. 77-84.

[7] For an emphatic affirmation of the doctrine of incorporation of international law, both customary and conventional, as part of Swiss law, see Guggenheim, *Lehrbuch des Völkerrechts*, Part I (1947), pp. 34-36. Swiss law goes further in this direction than that of Great Britain or the United States. In case of a conflict between a treaty and a subsequent Swiss law, the former prevails: *ibid.*, p. 36. Article 26 of the French Constitution of 1946 provides that 'diplomatic treaties duly ratified and published possess the force of law even if contrary to French municipal statutes'; Article 28 lays down that as such treaties are superior to French statutory law they cannot be abrogated, modified or suspended except by virtue of express denunciation. (See also below, p. 158, n. 31.) It will be noted that in the United States a statute can validly alter, in relation to municipal courts, the provisions of a binding treaty. For the provisions of other constitutions based on the doctrine of incorporation see Oppenheim, *International Law*, vol. I (7th ed. by Lauterpacht, 1948), p. 41. And see generally on the subordination of constitutions to rules of international law Blondeau in *Revue de droit public*, 1932, pp. 579 *et seq.* As to the position in Latin-America see Accioly, *Traité de droit international public* (translated by Goulé), vol. I (1940), pp. 18-20.

individuals enforceable by municipal courts. The wide acceptance of that practice has imparted to it a degree of generality
which has made it approximate to a customary rule of international law. For the uniformity of municipal law and legislation
in matters affecting international law is in itself evidence of
international custom.

4. PUBLIC INTERNATIONAL BODIES AS SUBJECTS OF INTERNATIONAL LAW

It is predominantly in international practice proper, as distinguished from municipal law, that we must look for guidance on
the question of subjects of international law—' predominantly ',
for there is no escape from the fact that, in this as in other matters,
certain principles follow from the very existence and the assumed
purposes of international society. International practice shows
that persons and bodies other than States are often made subjects
of international rights and duties; that such developments are not
inconsistent with the structure of international law; and that in
each particular case the question whether a person or a body is a
subject of international law must be answered in a pragmatic
manner by reference to actual experience and to the reason of the
law as distinguished from a preconceived notion as to who can
be subjects of international law. Before discussing the position
of public international bodies as subjects of international law,
brief reference may be made to some examples, occasionally
referred to by writers, of international legal capacity of bodies
other than States.

Thus, although insurgents recognised as belligerents are not
States, they are entitled to exercise belligerent rights in relation
to the recognising States and their nationals. They are bound
by the obligation to conduct hostilities in accordance with the
rules of international law. This, indeed, is an acknowledged
condition of recognition of belligerency. Moreover, substantial
practice supports what is probably the accurate view on the
subject, namely, that insurgents are entitled as a matter of law to
recognition of belligerency provided that the requisite conditions
of fact are present. This view has been frequently challenged
on the ground that insurgents, not being subjects of international

law, cannot possess a legal right to recognition. However, that challenge is based on the controversial assumption that unrecognised insurgents are not and cannot be subjects of international rights and duties, including the right to recognition of belligerency. There is no sufficient warrant for any such assumption. Moreover, it is also clear that unrecognised insurgents, without having acquired a specific status of belligerency, may be admitted to various forms of intercourse with outside States. Such intercourse, which involves the application of international law by and in relation to the insurgents, may include the conclusion of agreements, diplomatic and consular relations, and recognition of the insurgent authority as a government.[8] Of these possibilities the relations between Great Britain and the Nationalist Government of Spain in the concluding stages of the Spanish Civil War of 1936-1939 afford an interesting example. It would therefore appear that not only insurgents recognised as belligerents, but also insurgents not recognised as such, may be subjects of international rights and duties.[9]

The international position of the Holy See in the years 1871-1929, *i.e.*, in the period between the annexation of the Papal State by Italy in 1870 and the restoration of its temporal sovereignty in the Lateran Treaty of 1929, offers another example of a formal international status of an entity which is not a State. In that period the Holy See concluded treaties (in the form of concordats) and entertained diplomatic relations with the great majority of States. It was to that extent a subject of international law without being a State in the accepted sense of the term. It may be noted that, subsequent to the Lateran Treaty, the Holy See, henceforth fully restored to statehood, provides another instructive illustration of the potentialities of international personality. We are confronted here with an international organism invested with formal attributes of statehood but devoted to purposes differing fundamentally from those ordinarily served by States—a significant intimation of the wide range of international status.

Finally, while the present position of the Members of the

---

[8] It is occasionally maintained that a measure of intercourse on that scale constitutes implied recognition of belligerency. There is no warrant for that assertion.

[9] See Lauterpacht, *Recognition in International Law* (1947), pp. 270-278, 403-405.

British Commonwealth of Nations is indistinguishable from the full international status of normal statehood, their former status was instructive for the question under discussion. Prior to the developments after the First and Second World Wars the British Dominions were represented in the international sphere by Great Britain alone. In that period the Dominions exercised treaty-making powers and maintained diplomatic relations. Though not States, they were subjects of international law. This attribution of international rights and duties to States which are not fully sovereign entities was not a novel development. Thus the heads and Governments of protectorates and protected States have often been treated as entitled to the jurisdictional immunities which international law concedes to sovereign States. In general, protected States, though deprived of full international capacity, have been regarded as international persons—as subjects of international law—for some purposes.

It is now generally agreed that public international bodies created by agreement among States are capable of possessing an international personality distinct from that of the States which compose them. These bodies include the United Nations; the specialised agencies brought into relationship with the United Nations, such as the International Labour Organisation, the International Civil Aviation Organisation, the Food and Agriculture Organisation of the United Nations, the United Nations Educational, Scientific and Cultural Organisation, and the International Refugee Organisation; various other international administrative unions which have achieved a requisite degree of distinctness and cohesion; and a variety of other agencies ranging from the International River Commissions to—to mention a somewhat exotic example—the International Commission for the Cape Spartel Lighthouse.[10] Whether in any particular case the international public body in question does in fact possess a distinct international personality of its own is a matter of law as laid down in the relevant international agreements (although, as will be suggested, it is arguable that this also is a question of principle independent of any specific legal provision). Some of these bodies have been accorded a distinct legal personality under the municipal law of various States. Thus, in Great Britain under

[10] For a detailed bibliography on the international personality of these bodies see Jenks in *British Year Book of International Law*, 22 (1945), p. 267, n. 1.

the Diplomatic Privileges (Extension) Act, 1944, the Crown was given power to provide by Order in Council that an international organisation shall have the legal capacities of a body corporate. Various conventions creating international agencies stipulate that the contracting parties shall accord to the international agency in question a legal personality under their law.[11]

However, there has been hesitation in expressly conferring full international capacity upon these bodies. Thus, the Constitution of the Food and Agriculture Organisation of the United Nations provides that ' The Organisation shall have the capacity of a legal person to perform any legal act appropriate to its purpose which is not beyond the powers granted to it by this Constitution.'[12] The Constitution of the International Refugee Organisation, approved by the First General Assembly in December, 1946, lays down that ' The Organisation shall enjoy in the territory of each of its members such legal capacity as may be necessary for the exercise of its functions and the fulfilment of its objectives ' (Article 13).[13] It is arguable that these and similar provisions amount to the conferment of an international personality—some of the consequences of which must be implemented by municipal legislation, whenever necessary—upon these organisations and that they were not intended to be limited to the municipal sphere. But the hesitation, which is to a large extent the result of the traditional view that States only are the subjects of international law, is significant. It contrasts with the explicit language of other instruments, such as the Agreement of 1946 concerning the establishment of a European Central Inland Transport Organisation which, in addition to providing for the capacity to perform legal acts appropriate to the objects of the Organisation, includes the express undertaking by member States ' to recognise the international personality and legal capacity which the Organisation possesses '.[14] The contractual capacity of some of the international public bodies has been expressly

[11] For examples see Jenks, *loc. cit.*, p. 268, n. 2.
[12] Article XV (1).
[13] An identical wording was adopted in Article 66 of the Constitution of the World Health Organisation signed on 22 July, 1946.
[14] Article VIII (13). The Convention of 1944 on the Inter-American Institute of Agricultural Sciences contemplates the substitution of an international status for the previous incorporation of the Institute under the laws of the District of Columbia. And see Jenks, *loc cit.*, pp. 272 and 273, n. 1, for other examples.

recognised. They have made agreements with the United Nations, with one another, and with governments. Thus the International Labour Organisation has concluded an agreement with Switzerland defining the privileges and immunities of the Organisation in that country.[15] That Agreement is also conspicuous by reason of the fact that it provides for the submission to arbitration of disputes arising out of it. In the same category there must be included the Agreement of 17 July, 1948, between the World Health Organisation and the Swiss Federal Council. Moreover, some specialised agencies have been accorded a substantial degree of independent procedural capacity by being given authority to ask the International Court of Justice for an advisory opinion.[16] Even prior to the setting up of the United Nations the amended Statute of the Permanent Court of International Justice, following the rules of the Court previously enacted and applied in practice, permitted public international organisations to take part in the written and oral proceedings before the Court when acting in the exercise of its advisory jurisdiction.[17] In particular, on a number of

[15] Protocol of 11 March, 1946: U.N. Treaty Series, vol. 15, p. 378.

[16] Article 96 of the Charter provides that advisory opinions may be asked of the Court by the General Assembly or by the Security Council on any legal questions. Paragraph 2 of this Article lays down that ' other organs of the United Nations and Specialised Agencies, which may at any time be so authorised by the General Assembly, may also request advisory opinions of the Court on legal questions arising within the scope of their activities '. In 1946 the General Assembly authorised the Economic and Social Council (Assembly Doc. A/201), as one of the principal organs of the United Nations, to request advisory opinions on all legal questions within its scope, including legal questions concerning mutual relationships of the United Nations and the specialised agencies. As regards the specialised agencies, the General Assembly, in the same year, authorised the following to request advisory opinions of the Court: the International Labour Organisation (Assembly Doc. A/72), the United Nations Educational, Scientific and Cultural Organisation (*ibid.*, A/242), the Food and Agriculture Organisation (*ibid.*), and the International Civil Aviation Organisation (*ibid.*, A/106). Similar authorisation was given, by virtue of agreements with the United Nations approved by the General Assembly in 1947, to the International Bank for Reconstruction and Development, the International Monetary Fund, the International Telecommunications Union, and the World Health Organisation. In the case of the International Trade Organisation the significance of the provision in question is enhanced by the fact that the Advisory Opinion of the Court is declared to be binding upon the Organisation (Article 96 of the Havana Charter of 1948). In 1948 an authorisation of the same kind was granted to the Inter-governmental Maritime Consultative Organisation, the International Refugee Organisation and the Interim Committee of the General Assembly. And see generally on the status of international organisations in relation to the International Court of Justice, Jenks in *Transactions of Grotius Society,* 32 (1946), pp. 1-41.

[17] Article 73 of the Rules; Articles 66 and 67 of the Revised Statute.

occasions representatives of the International Labour Organisation addressed the Court.[18]   In the proceedings connected with the Advisory Opinion concerning the competence of the International Labour Organisation to propose legislation affecting the employer, notice of the proceedings was also sent to the International Organisation of Industrial Employers, the International Federation of Trade Unions, and the International Confederation of Christian Trade Unions—all of which made statements in the hearings before the Court.[19]   The two last-named Organisations similarly participated in the proceedings arising out of the request for an Advisory Opinion concerning the Employment of Women during the Night.[20]   In the course of proceedings arising out of the request for an Advisory Opinion on the Consistency of Certain Danzig Legislative Decrees with the Constitution of the Free City, the Court invited and received an ‘explanatory note’ from the petitioners, certain political parties in Danzig, who protested to the Council of the League of Nations against penal legislative decrees enacted by the Free City.[21]   Occasionally, public international bodies have been endowed with the capacity of resorting to tribunals of an international character.   Of these, the powers given to the Reparations Commission—a body the international legal personality of which has been asserted by writers of authority[22]—under the London Agreement of 1924 are conspicuous.   A number of important cases were decided under these provisions.[23]   Neither are instances lacking of international arbitral decisions in cases in which one of the parties has been a public or private corporation opposing a State.[24]

---

[18] See, for a detailed account, Hudson, *The Permanent Court of International Justice, 1920-1942* (1943), pp. 400-402.

[19] See *P.C.I.J.*, Series C, No. 12, pp. 259-262.

[20] *Ibid.*, Series A/B, No. 50, p. 367.

[21] *Ibid.*, Series A/B, No. 65, p. 43.

[22] See Sir John Fischer Williams in *British Year Book of International Law*, 13 (1932), pp. 9-38, and in *American Journal of International Law*, 24 (1930), p. 665.

[23] See *Dawes Plan Interpretation* (*Commissioner of Controlled Revenues*) *Case*, between Germany and the Reparations Commission: *Annual Digest, 1925-1926*, Case No. 151; *Social Insurance* (*Upper Silesia*) *Case*, between Germany and the Reparations Commission: *ibid.*, Case No. 264; *Standard Oil Company Tankers Case*, between the Reparations Commission and the United States: *ibid.*, Cases No. 169 and 353; *Reparations Commission* v. *German Government*: *ibid.*, 1923-1924, Cases No. 194 and 199.

[24] *Lena Goldfields Arbitration* (Lena Goldfields Corporation against Russia): *ibid.*, 1929-1930, Case No. 1; *Société des Quais de Smyrna* v. *Greek Govern-*

Finally, apart from express attribution of international personality or the implied conferment or acquisition thereof as the
result of actual exercise of rights in conformity with international
law, it is probable that the international personality of these
bodies follows from the fact of their being autonomous entities
created by international agreement and distinct from the States
which created them. Their separate personality is not in doubt.
It is only because of the aberrations of the doctrine of the
exclusive international personality of States that there has been
a tendency to question their separate international personality.
Yet to subject them to the law of any single State is, in effect,
to allow that State to assume jurisdiction over the States responsible for their creation. These were the reasons why the Italian
Court of Cassation, in holding in 1931 that the International
Institute of Agriculture was an ' international person . . . free . . .
from interference by the sovereign power of the States composing
the Union ', overruled the Court of Appeal of Rome, which held
that the Institute ' was not a subject of international law, seeing
that it did not exercise sovereignty over a fixed territory and a
population '.[25]

The international personality of international public bodies
not only constitutes additional evidence of the inaccuracy of the
traditional doctrine according to which States are the exclusive
subjects of international law. It shows its inadequacy in meeting
the developing needs of international society. A purely formal
international law concerned with war, with delimitation of jurisdictional competence and with ceremonial, could limit itself to the
narrow and selected circle of sovereign States. In modern international society the interests to be protected and regulated can
no longer be entrusted exclusively to States. These interests call
for the recognition of new subjects of rights and duties conceived
as the rational means of international social welfare. In this sense
the question whether international public bodies are subjects of
international law is not one of mere doctrine. Nor is it merely
a question of making them capable of enjoying jurisdictional

ment: *ibid.,* Case No. 291; *Sopron Köszeg Local Railway Co.* v. *Austria*:
ibid., Case No. 34; *Radio Corporation of America* v. *National Government
of China*: *ibid.,* 1935-1937, Case No. 12.
[25] *International Institute of Agriculture* v. *Profili*: *Annual Digest,* 1929-1930,
Case No. 254.

immunities,[26] or of securing for them the benefits of a uniform legal régime.[27]   The problem is rather one of not permitting the dead hand of an obsolete theory to continue to lie heavily upon the development of international organisation.   It is a question of meeting satisfactorily the requirements of an expanding and developing law not limited to the niceties of international intercourse but concerned with the well-being of the individuals as the ultimate units of human society and with the adequacy of the instruments which serve their needs.[28]   We can hope to gain an accurate approach to an understanding of the nature of modern international law only if we discard the notion that it regulates exclusively the relations of States and realise that it is concerned with interests which are in need of regulation on account of the existence of independent States constituting the international society.   These interests are not co-extensive with the external relations of States.

5.   The United Nations

The Charter of the United Nations is conspicuous for its restraint on the question of the international personality of the United Nations.   It provides, in Article 104, that ' the Organisation shall enjoy in the territory of each of its Members such legal capacity as may be necessary for the exercise of its functions '.   As suggested above, it is possible that the result of that Article is to confer upon the United Nations a legal personality the incidents of which are to be implemented by municipal legislation in those countries in which the provisions of the Charter are not self-executing.   Yet it appears from the history of the drafting of Article 104 that the omission of an express reference to *international* personality was not accidental.   It is stated in the official report to the President of the United States that ' The committee which discussed this matter was anxious to avoid any implication that the United Nations will be in any sense a

---

[26] For this result can be equally well achieved by the argument that the international public body, being a body of representatives of sovereign States, enjoys the jurisdictional immunities to which these States are entitled: see *Godman* v. *Winterton*, decided in 1940 by the English Court of Appeal—a case involving a claim against the Intergovernmental Committee for Refugees: *Annual Digest*, 1919-1942 (Supplementary Volume), Case No. 111.

[27] See on this point Friedmann in *Modern Law Review*, 6 (1943), pp. 203-205.

[28] See below, p. 68.

" superstate " '.[29]   It was not explained in what way the express conferment of international personality could have that effect.

Nevertheless, an international public body—such as the United Nations—may possess or acquire international personality by virtue of facts other than formal attribution of such capacity. Such result may be brought about by the fact of that body being entrusted with or exercising functions compatible with or implying international personality.   Thus the United Nations must be deemed to possess that quality by virtue of the treaty-making power conferred upon it by the Charter or otherwise actually exercised by it.[30]   Thus, for instance, the Convention of 26 June, 1947, between the United Nations and the United States concerning the headquarters of the United Nations is, with its provisions for ratification, registration, and settlement of disputes, hardly distinguishable from an ordinary treaty between two sovereign States.[31]   The same Agreement provided for settlement by arbitration of disputes arising between the United Nations and the United States concerning its interpretation or application. The Convention of 1946 on the Privileges and Immunities of the United Nations provides generally, in terms less restricted than the

[29] *The Charter of the United Nations, Hearings before the Committee on Foreign Relations,* 1945, p. 135. Moreover, the relevant Committee of the San Francisco Conference rejected a Belgian proposal that the Charter should recognise expressly that the United Nations possesses international personality (Doc. 524.IV/2/26). On the other hand, it appears from the report of the *Rapporteur* of that Committee that the fact of the non-acceptance of the Belgian proposal could not properly be regarded as a rejection of the view which underlay it. The Report described such express attribution of international personality as ' superfluous '—apparently in the sense that the nature of the personality of the United Nations ' will in effect, be determined by implication by reference to the entirety of the provisions of the Charter ' (Report of Committee IV.2,A., Doc. 803). Accordingly, the preparatory work of the Conference cannot be cited against the view adopted by the Court. Probably the justly great authority and persuasiveness of the unanimous pronouncement of the Court on this subject would have been enhanced by an examination—however negative in its conclusions—of the preparatory work of the Conference.

[30] See, *e.g.*, Article 43 of the Charter which provides for the conclusion of agreements between the Security Council and Members of the United Nations concerning the armed forces and other forms of assistance to be contributed by them for the maintenance of international peace and security; and Article 63 concerning agreements between the Economic and Social Council and specialised international agencies brought into relationship with the United Nations. Such agreements have been concluded in 1946 with the International Labour Organisation, the United Nations Educational, Scientific and Cultural Organisation, the Food and Agriculture Organisation, and the International Civil Aviation Organisation. And see above, p. 16, n. 16, as to agreements with other specialised agencies.

[31] For the text of the Convention see *United Nations, Treaty Series,* vol. 11, p. 11.

Charter, that ' the United Nations shall possess juridical personality'. The text of the Agreement between the United Nations and Switzerland of 14 December, 1946, concerning the Ariana site of the United Nations at Geneva is even more specific. It lays down, in Article 1, that the ' Swiss Federal Council recognises the international personality and the juridical capacity of the Organisation of the United Nations '.[32] The regulations adopted by the General Assembly concerning the registration and publication of treaties in accordance with Article 102 of the Charter provide for registration *ex officio* of every treaty or agreement to which the United Nations is a party.[33] Moreover, in the course of its activity the United Nations has concluded—and must do so on an increasing scale—various agreements with non-governmental agencies such as, for instance, the Carnegie Foundation for the use of the Peace Palace or the repayment of loans granted by the Dutch Government to the Carnegie Foundation for carrying out alterations in the premises of the Permanent Court of International Justice.[34] The United Nations may exercise jurisdictional and legislative powers with regard to such trust areas as, according to Article 81 of the Charter, may be placed under the administrative authority of the United Nations. Moreover, it is vested with residuary sovereignty over trust territories. For it is axiomatic that these territories are not under the sovereignty of the Trustee Powers. For similar—though not as strong[35]—reasons the League of Nations was considered to possess a distinct international personality of its own.

The Advisory Opinion of the International Court of Justice

[32] U.N. Doc. A/175, p. 23. See also *ibid*. for the Interim Arrangement of the same date on Privileges and Immunities of the United Nations concluded between the Swiss Federal Council and the Secretary-General of the United Nations.

[33] Article 4 of the Regulations adopted by the General Assembly on 14 December, 1946.

[34] Agreements of 21 February, 1946: International Court of Justice, *Year Book*, 1946-1947, pp. 94-98. See also the Agreement of 19 July, 1946, between the United Nations and the League of Nations concerning the execution of the transfer to the United Nations of certain assets of the League of Nations: General Assembly, First Session, *Journal* No. 75, Suppl. A-64, p. 899.

[35] As rightly pointed out by Dr. Feller, when presenting in 1949 before the International Court of Justice the case for the United Nations in connection with the Advisory Opinion referred to below (p. 22), while the Covenant of the League rarely refers to the League of Nations the Charter refers constantly to the United Nations as an entity: *Verbatim Record of the Proceedings,* 7 March, 1949, C.R. 49/7, p. 49. See, to the same effect, Brierly in *British Year Book of International Law,* 23 (1946), p. 85.

of 11 April, 1949, concerning reparation for injuries suffered in the service of the United Nations is a contribution of outstanding importance not only in the matter of the international personality —which the Court fully affirmed—of the United Nations, but also on the question of subjects of international law in general. Accordingly, it is proper to reproduce in full the relevant passages of the Opinion of the Court. It said:

> ' The subjects of law in any legal system are not necessarily identical in their nature or in the extent of their rights, and their nature depends upon the needs of the community. Throughout its history, the development of international law has been influenced by the requirements of international life, and the progressive increase in the collective activities of States has already given rise to instances of action upon the international plane by certain entities which are not States. This development culminated in the establishment in June 1945 of an international organisation whose purposes and principles are specified in the Charter of the United Nations. But to achieve these ends the attribution of international personality is indispensable ' (p. 178).

> ' In the opinion of the Court, the Organisation was intended to exercise and enjoy, and is in fact exercising and enjoying, functions and rights which can only be explained on the basis of the possession of a large measure of international personality and the capacity to operate upon an international plane. It is at present the supreme type of international organisation, and it could not carry out the intentions of its founders if it was devoid of international personality. It must be acknowledged that its Members, by entrusting certain functions to it, with the attendant duties and responsibilities, have clothed it with the competence required to enable those functions to be effectively discharged ' (p. 179).

The significance of the Opinion is not impaired—it is enhanced —by the reasoning which accompanies it. In arriving at the conclusion that the United Nations ' is an international person ', the Court attached importance to pointing out that its ruling did not amount to saying that the United Nations is a State ' which it certainly is not, or that its legal personality and rights and duties are the same as those of a State '.[36] Neither did it imply that ' all its rights and duties must be upon the international plane, any more than all the rights and duties of a State must be upon that

[36] At p. 179.

plane '. The ruling means, in the words of the Court, that the United Nations ' is a subject of international law and capable of possessing international rights and duties, and that it has capacity to maintain its rights by bringing international claims '.[37] It is probably in the express attribution of international personality to the United Nations, and not in the more controversial reason of making the Charter fully effective,[38] that lay the true basis of the answer given by the Court to the question put to it. In thus laying down, with emphatic clarity, that States are not the only subjects of international law the Court did as much for liberating international law from the shackles of an obsolete and retrogressive doctrine as did its predecessor in rejecting the view that individuals cannot directly acquire international rights under treaties.[39] The cumulative effect of these two pronouncements of the highest international tribunal, in exposing the negative pretentiousness of an entrenched tenet of the positivist creed, goes far beyond the immediate issues which gave rise to them.[40]

6. CONSULTATIVE STATUS OF PRIVATE INTERNATIONAL ORGANISATIONS

The Charter of the United Nations has not gone to the length of the significant innovation introduced by the Constitution of the International Labour Organisation which gives to the organisations of employers and employees a direct and formal share in the legislative and other activities of the Organisation—an innovation embodied in its tripartite character. However, in Article 71 the Charter authorised the Economic and Social Council to make

[37] *Ibid.*

[38] The Opinion of the Court was based partly on the view that unless the United Nations had an independent right to bring claims in respect of injuries done to its officials, Article 100 of the Charter would be lacking in full effectiveness. That Article laid down the principle of the international and independent character and status of the officials of the United Nations. However, it is controversial whether it is a legitimate function of interpretation to extract the largest possible element of effectiveness from international agreements. Parties often intend to endow an international instrument with a limited rather than a full measure of effectiveness. Article 100 might retain a measure of effectiveness—though possibly not of full effectiveness—even if the United Nations had no right to bring an international claim on behalf of its officials. The true basis of that right is the international personality of the United Nations, as authoritatively—almost solemnly—proclaimed by the International Court of Justice in what is bound to prove one of its most significant pronouncements.

[39] See below, p. 28.

[40] See Wright in *American Journal of International Law*, 43 (1949), pp. 95-104 and 509-516, and Liang, *ibid.*, pp. 460-478.

' suitable arrangements for consultation with non-governmental organisations which are concerned with matters within its competence '. The same Article lays down that such arrangements may be made with international organisations and, where appropriate, with national organisations after consultation with the member of the United Nations concerned. The Economic and Social Council has made full use of that authorisation. It has appointed a Standing Committee on Non-Governmental Organisations, composed of the President and five members of the Council, the task of which is: (1) to recommend to the Council what action should be taken on applications for consultative status submitted by non-governmental organisations, and (2) to consult with these organisations. The latter are divided into three groups of which the first, composed of more representative and important bodies, is entitled, on the same footing as members of the United Nations and specialised governmental agencies, to submit items for the inclusion in the provisional agenda of each regular session of the Council.[41] Representatives of these organisations are entitled, subject to the procedure laid down by the Council, to be present and to make observations to it, or its Committees, in connexion with any item placed on the agenda in pursuance of its requests. The significance of the status of the organisations in that group may be gauged from the fact that they have brought before some of the principal organs of the United Nations important questions which have received detailed study and consideration. Thus in 1948 the World Federation of Trade Unions brought on the agenda of the Economic and Social

---

[41] In 1949 the organisations in that category—' category (a) '—included the following: World Federation of Trade Unions, International Co-operative Alliance, American Federation of Labour, International Chamber of Commerce, International Federation of Agricultural Production, International Federation of Christian Trade Unions, International Parliamentary Union, International Organisation of Employers, and World Federation of United Nations Associations.. See Doc. E/940/Add. 4; Rule 78 of Rules of Procedure, Resolution of 8th Session, Doc. E/1310. See also *Rules of Procedure of Functional Commissions,* Docs. E/565 and E/777. A non-governmental organisation in category (b) desirous to be heard before the Council or its Committees must make a request to that effect to the Chairman of the Committee on non-governmental organisations which, after hearing a representative of the organisation concerned, transmits to the Council a recommendation concerning the request. Organisations in categories (b) and (c) may submit to the Secretariat written statements and suggestions on matters within their competence. The Secretariat circulates a list of these communications, briefly indicating their substance. Upon the request of a member of the Council such communications must be reproduced in full and circulated. See on the subject Bell in *Bulletin of State Department,* 20 (1949), pp. 739 *et seq.*

Council the question of equality of pay for women.[42] In the same year the same body carried before the Council a complaint of illegal violation of the right of association in certain countries.[43] The countries concerned gave full replies to these allegations—although some of them invoked emphatically the clause of domestic jurisdiction of Article 2(7) of the Charter.[44] States not represented on the Council were invited to participate in the discussion under Article 69 of the Charter. The Council adopted a Resolution containing a recommendation to member States drawing their attention to the importance of ensuring within their territories the full exercise of trade union rights.[45] In the same year the American Federation of Labour brought before the Council the question of forced labour in some countries. Prolonged discussion was devoted to the matter. The Council adopted a Resolution expressing the opinion that an impartial enquiry was desirable into the charges concerning forced labour.[46]

In addition, the constitutions of various specialised agencies provide for co-operation and consultation with private international organisations. Thus the constitution of the International Refugee Organisation provides that it may establish ' such effective relationships as may be desirable with other international organisations '[47] and that it is ' to consult with public and private organisations whenever it is deemed advisable, in so far as such organisations share the purpose of the organisation and observe the principles of the United Nations '.[48] The Constitution of the International Civil Aviation Organisation lays down that the Council may enter into agreements with other international bodies for the maintenance of common services and for common arrangements concerning personnel and that, with the approval of the Assembly, it may enter into other arrangements for facilitating the work of the Organisation.[49] The Organisation has granted

---

[42] See below, p. 339.

[43] E/822 and E/822/Add. 1.

[44] See below, p. 204.

[45] Resolution 194(VIII).   Doc. E/1236.   See also Resolution 199(VIII); the Memorandum of the Secretariat: E/CN.4/156 and E/CN.164; and the *Official Record* of the Eighth Session of the Council.

[46] E/1237. See also *Official Record* of the Eighth and Ninth Sessions of the Economic and Social Council and Resolution 195(VIII); E/1237. See also Secretariat Document E/CN.157.

[47] Art. 14(1).

[48] Art. 2(2f).

[49] Art. 65 of the Chicago Convention of 1944 on International Civil Aviation.

consultative status to a number of private organisations. The amended Constitution of the International Labour Organisation of 1946 [50] makes similar provision for suitable arrangements for consultation with recognised non-governmental international organisations, including 'international organisations of employers, workers, agriculturists and co-operators'. The constitutions of other specialised agencies of the United Nations contain provisions of the same nature.[51] These and similar provisions add little to the formal status and procedural capacity of the individual —and of the international non-governmental organisations created for the promotion of his interests and of international co-operation generally—in the international sphere. But they illustrate both the inadequacy of the hitherto predominant doctrine and the manner in which international practice may soften and eventually discard a rigid rule no longer in keeping with modern needs.

[50] Art. 12(3).

[51] See, for instance, Article 71 of the Constitution of the World Health Organisation as well as Articles 18(h), 33 and 41; Article 27—as well as Article 14, para. 3(2)—of the Constitution of the International Telecommunications Union; Article 87(2) of the Havana Charter of 1948 of the International Trade Organisation; Articles 4E(13) and 11(4) of the Constitution of the United Nations Educational, Scientific and Cultural Organisation. Although the Constitution of the Food and Agriculture Organisation—established prior to the United Nations—contains no reference to non-governmental organisations, provision to that effect was made at the first Session of the Conference of the Organisation in 1945. And see Article 26(b) of the Convention establishing the World Meteorological Organisation and Article 11(4) of the Constitution of the International Maritime Consultative Organisation.

CHAPTER 2

THE INDIVIDUAL AS A SUBJECT OF INTERNATIONAL RIGHTS AND DUTIES

1. Individuals as Subjects of Rights under Treaties

THE position of the individual as a subject of international law has often been obscured by the failure to observe the distinction between the recognition, in an international instrument, of rights enuring to the benefit of the individual and the enforceability of these rights at his instance. The fact that the beneficiary of rights is not authorised to take independent steps in his own name to enforce them does not signify that he is not a subject of the law or that the rights in question are vested exclusively in the agency which possesses the capacity to enforce them.[1] Thus, in relation to the current view that the rights of the alien within foreign territory are the rights of his State and not his own, the correct way of stating the legal position is not that the State asserts its own exclusive right but that it enforces, in substance, the right of the individual who, as the law now stands, is incapable of asserting it in the international sphere. Conversely, there seems to be no warrant for the disposition to allow the question of enforceability of rights to be influenced by the doctrine that individuals cannot be subjects of international law. The question whether individuals in any given case are subjects of international law and whether that quality extends to the capacity of enforcement must be answered pragmatically by reference to the given situation and to the relevant international instrument. That instrument may make them subjects of the law without conferring upon them procedural capacity; it may aim at, and achieve, both these objects.

The legal position in the matter is well illustrated by the question whether individuals can acquire rights directly by treaty

[1] See below, p. 54. The following observation of the Permanent Court of International Justice, made in a different connexion, may be noted: ' It is scarcely necessary to point out that the capacity to possess civil rights does not necessarily imply the capacity to exercise those rights oneself ' (*Peter Pázmány University Case*, Series A/B, No. 61, p. 231).

independently of municipal legislation. Prior to the Advisory
Opinion of the Permanent Court of International Justice in the
case concerning the *Jurisdiction of the Courts of Danzig* in the
matter of Danzig railway officials,[2] that question was generally
answered in the negative—though even then some caution would
have been indicated having regard to the law of some countries,
such as the United States, in which duly ratified treaties are a self-
executing part of municipal law.[3] Similarly, there had already
existed treaties—such as that establishing the Central American
Court of Justice, the provisions relating to the Mixed Arbitral
Tribunals in the Peace Treaties of 1919, and the Polish-German
Upper Silesian Convention[4]—which conferred upon individuals
direct rights of international action. However, it was the
Advisory Opinion, given in 1928, in the case concerning the
Jurisdiction of the Courts of Danzig,[5] which dealt a decisive blow
to the dogma of the impenetrable barrier separating individuals
from international law. In that case Poland contended that the
agreement between her and Danzig regulating the conditions of
employment of Danzig officials whom she had taken over into
her railway service was an international treaty which created
rights and obligations as between Poland and Danzig only; that
as that agreement had not been incorporated into Polish municipal law it did not create rights and obligations for individuals;
that Poland's responsibility was limited to that owed to Danzig;
and that therefore Danzig courts, before which the officials had
brought an action in the matter, had no jurisdiction. The Court
rejected this contention. It said: —

> ' It may be readily admitted that, according to a well
> established principle of international law, the *Beamtenabkommen,*
> being an international agreement, cannot, as such, create direct
> rights and obligations for private individuals. But it cannot be
> disputed that the very object of an international agreement,
> according to the intention of the contracting Parties, may be the

---

[2] See below, pp. 28, 29.
[3] Possibly it could have been argued, in reply, that this was so only by virtue
of municipal law and not of international law—an argument the relevance of
which is open to question. It could also have been said, with more justification, that in some of these countries, as in the United States, a subsequent
statute can make inoperative a conflicting treaty. This is not possible under
the new French Constitution: see above, p. 11, n. 7.
[4] See below, p. 50.
[5] Permanent Court of International Justice, Advisory Opinion No. 15: Series
B, No. 15, pp. 17-21.

adoption by the parties of some definite rules creating individual rights and obligations and enforceable by the national courts. That there is such an intention in the present case can be established by reference to the terms of the *Beamtenabkommen.*' [6]

This pronouncement is among the most important rendered by the Court. On the first occasion on which it was directly[7] confronted with the traditional argument, it rejected it—though with the courtesy due to a doctrine which for a long time enjoyed undisputed ascendancy.[8] It laid down, in effect, that no considerations of theory can prevent the individual from becoming the subject of international rights if States so wish. That affirmation by the Permanent Court of International Justice of the right of individuals to acquire rights directly under treaties was not an isolated event. It was followed—and the coincidence is significant—by other judicial decisions pointing in the same direction.[9]

2. INDIVIDUALS AS SUBJECTS OF INTERNATIONAL LAW IN THE MATTER OF JURISDICTION AND EXTRADITION

The way in which the Permanent Court of International Justice— and other courts—have clarified the rules of international law bearing upon conferment of rights upon individuals by treaty

---

[6] At p. 17.

[7] The Judgment of the Court in the *Mavrommatis Palestine Concessions* case (*P.C.I.J.,* Series A, No. 2) gave some indication of the possible attitude of the Court. In that case the Court attached decisive importance to the fact that although no negotiations had taken place between the Greek Government and Great Britain, negotiations sufficient for the purpose of the jurisdiction of the Court had taken place between Great Britain and the Greek national concerned.

[8] Less than a quarter of a century prior to the Opinion of the Court, Anzilotti— in 1927 a Judge of the Court—wrote: ' It is inconceivable that there should exist subjects of international rights and duties other than States ': *Il diritto internazionale nei giudizi interni* (1905), p. 44.

[9] See, *e.g.,* the decision of the District Court of Amsterdam of 16 October, 1925, in the *Wirbelauer* case, to the effect that the Hague Convention of 1905 concerning Procedure in Civil Cases conferred rights directly upon Russian nationals in Holland irrespective of recognition of the Soviet Government by Holland (*Annual Digest,* 1927-1928, Case No. 36, and the Note bearing on the subject); the judgment of the Amsterdam Court of Appeals of 13 March, 1928, in the *Papadopoulos* case to the effect that the Treaty of Lausanne was binding not only upon the parties thereto but also upon individuals (*ibid.,* Case No. 285); the decision of the German Reichsgericht of 29 March, 1928, in the *German Railways (Most-Favoured Treatment)* case laying down that the provisions of Article 365 of the Treaty of Versailles could be invoked ' without the necessity of further measures in the sphere of international or public law ' by German subjects against the Reich (*ibid.,* Case No. 280); the

suggests that in this and other matters the question is not one of reliance upon preconceived notions but of investigation whether positive international law as embodied in custom or treaty has that effect having regard to the intention of States or to the reason of the thing.   On some of these questions practice is still under the influence of traditional doctrine.   Thus, for instance, municipal courts have held occasionally that such protection as extradition treaties stipulate in favour of individuals is not based on rules of international law which they are entitled to invoke in

decisions of the Egyptian Summary Tribunal of Port Said in 1931 and 1932 in the *Noujaim* case to the effect that the protection of the International Telegraph Convention of 1875 enured to the benefit not only of the contracting parties but also of private companies (*ibid.*, 1931-1932, Case No. 217A); the decision of the Danzig High Court of 16 January, 1934, in the *Zoppot Streetcrossing* case, applying expressly the principle laid down by the Permanent Court of International Justice in its Advisory Opinion No. 12 (*ibid.*, 1933-1934, Case No. 104).   See, on the other hand, the decisions of the German Reichsgericht of 29 March, 1928, in the *Liquidation of German Property (Treaty of Versailles)* case (*ibid.*, 1927-1928, Case No. 281), and of 14 March, 1928, in the *High Treason (Treaty of Versailles) in Germany* case (*ibid.*, Case No. 5); the *Martini* case between Italy and Venezuela, 3 May, 1930 (*ibid.*, 1929-1930, Case No. 93 (I)).   See also *Civilian War Claimants' Association, Ltd.* v. *The King,* 46 T.L.R. 581; 47 T.L.R. 102; [1932] A.C. 14; *Annual Digest,* 1931-1932, Case No. 118.   In this case the Court held that in concluding a treaty the Crown is not acting as trustee or agent for the subject.   See *ibid.* for the observation of Lord Atkin that when the Crown is negotiating a treaty it is inconsistent with its sovereign position that it should be acting as agent for the nationals, but that there is nothing to prevent it from acting as agent or trustee if it chooses deliberately to do so.   See also *Administrator of German Property* v. *Knoop* [1933] Ch. 439.   But see the decision of the Anglo-German Mixed Arbitral Tribunal of 13 December, 1923, in *Lederer* v. *German State,* in which the Tribunal rejected the contention of the British Government that it was the sole beneficiary of the provisions of Article 297 of the Treaty of Versailles in the matter of compensation: *Recueil des Décisions des Tribunaux arbitraux mixtes,* 3 (1924), p. 762.   The Tribunal said: 'the right to compensation granted by the Treaty is granted as compensation to the national of an Allied and Associated Power.   It is granted to him as a facultative right, that is to say, a right of which he may or may not make use' (at p. 768).   Referring to the wording of Article 297 (h) (2), the Tribunal observed that the very fact that the individual nationals were mentioned, in the first instance, as the persons to whom proceeds of liquidation and cash assets were to be paid immediately, showed that these persons were actually those who were entitled to payment, and 'that the Government in such a case can only be an intermediary to receive and hand over the said proceeds of liquidation' (at p. 769).   As the result of a careful analysis the Tribunal refused to attach a literal interpretation to the wording of Article 297 (h) according to which the proceeds of liquidation were to be credited to the State of which the owner was a national through the Clearing Offices established by the Treaty.   And see *Sigwald* v. *Germany,* decided in 1926 by the French-German Mixed Arbitral Tribunal, where it was held that the right granted under Article 297 (e) of the Treaty of Versailles was an individual right belonging to the subjects of the Allied Powers which could be put forward against Germany directly by the individuals concerned without the interposition of their Governments—with the result that an express abrogation of that Article was necessary in order to deprive such individuals of the right in question: *Annual Digest,* 1925-1926, Case No. 255.

their own right.[10] Municipal courts have occasionally assumed jurisdiction over persons brought before them in disregard of existing extradition treaties.[11] The reasons for that practice do not lie exclusively in the influence of the traditional doctrine in the matter of subjects of international law, but it is probable that that doctrine has had some share in the result.[12] The same circumstance explains, to some extent, why the principle of non-extradition of political offenders, which has become a constant feature of modern international practice as expressed in treaties, is not as yet a principle of international law on which the individual can rely as a matter of course. This is also the explanation of the practice of the courts of some countries in the matter of their jurisdiction over persons brought before them in violation of international law.[13] Apparently in these cases the courts were not of the view that such persons are entitled to rely in their own right on rules of international law. Otherwise, it is difficult to see how courts could consider themselves entitled to exercise jurisdiction.

3. THE CHARTER OF THE UNITED NATIONS AND THE POSITION OF
THE INDIVIDUAL AS A SUBJECT OF INTERNATIONAL LAW.
HUMANITARIAN INTERVENTION

The position with regard to treaties, extradition, and jurisdiction acts as a reminder that the answer to the question of the status of the individual as a subject of rights under international law

[10] See, for instance, the decision of the German *Reichsgericht* of 8 May, 1929 (*Extradition (Germany and Italy)* case: *Annual Digest,* 1929-1930, Case No. 167). See also the decision of the Court of Appeal of Paris, 5 December, 1947, in *In re Colman: Revue critique de droit international privé,* 36 (1947), p. 435.

[11] See, *e.g., United States* v. *Insull,* 8 F. Supp. 310; *Annual Digest,* 1933-1934, Case No. 75.

[12] The main reason has probably been the fact that out of the two principal functions of the law of extradition—that of the protection of the accused and that of international co-operation in the suppression of crime—the latter has been more prominent. Witness, for instance, the way in which some courts construed the requirement of 'liberal interpretation' as implying a construction favouring the accused (*Valentine* v. *United States* (1936), 299 U.S. 5), while others considered 'liberal interpretation' as necessitating an interpretation favouring the effectiveness of international co-operation in the suppression of crime (*Factor* v. *Laubenheimer* (1933), 290 U.S. 276).

[13] See, *e.g., Ex parte Lopez,* 6 F. Supp. 342; *Annual Digest,* 1933-1934, Case No. 76. It is particularly difficult to follow the reasons for that practice in States, like the United States of America, which are committed to the doctrine of incorporation of international law as part of the law of the land. See, on the other hand, *Re Jolis,* decided in 1933 by a French court: *ibid.,* Case No. 77.

must be sought in the first instance by reference to the actual development of the law. This applies also to the question as to whether international law recognises fundamental rights of the individual independent of the law of his State. Prior to the Charter of the United Nations the question of the existence of such rights was controversial. Their international recognition manifested itself in the precarious doctrine of humanitarian intervention in cases in which a State maltreats its subjects in a manner which shocks the conscience of mankind. That doctrine, advocated by writers going back to Grotius,[14] was honoured in theoretical recognition rather than in practice. In the eyes of governments there was often deemed to exist a conflict between the defence of human rights through external intervention and the considerations of international peace threatened by such intervention. That conflict was, in the long run, more apparent than real. For, ultimately, peace is more endangered by tyrannical contempt for human rights than by attempts to assert, through intervention, the sanctity of human personality. However, governments are not invariably in the habit of taking a long-range view in matters involving the peace of the peoples entrusted to their care. Another reason for abstaining from intervention has often been the consideration that outside interference, far from improving the position of victims of persecution, may, by drawing upon them the wrath of their governments, achieve the contrary result. That consideration, although frequently described as realistic,[15] must be regarded as contrary to experience. The fury of persecution receives an impetus not only from foreign acquiescence,[16] but also from the hesitation and reserve of foreign

[14] *De Jure Belli ac Pacis,* Book II, ch. XXV, § VIII. 2; ch. XX, § XL.1. Among modern writers there may be mentioned Heffter, *Das europäische Völkerrecht der Gegenwart* (1888), p. 114; Bluntschli, *Das moderne Völkerrecht der zivilisierten Staaten* (3rd ed., 1878), p. 270; Stowell, *Intervention in International Law* (1921), pp. 51-58. For a more cautious statement of the right of intervention with regard to the harsh treatment of nationals see Hyde, *International Law,* vol. I (1945), § 72.

[15] See Jessup in *American Journal of International Law,* 32 (1938), pp. 116-119. See also Schwarzenberger in *The Review of Politics,* 10 (1948), pp. 174-178, for a survey of British practice from this point of view. And see Adler and Margalith, *With Firmness in the Right. American Diplomatic Practice Affecting Jews, 1840-1945* (1946)—a valuable study.

[16] A similar argument, of equally doubtful accuracy, has been occasionally adduced as militating against the application of sanctions against States guilty of aggression. Thus in the course of the invasion of Manchuria by Japan in 1931 and of Abyssinia by Italy in 1936 it was urged by some that the application of sanctions might, by rallying indignant national sentiment and solidarity round the guilty government, strengthen the position of the aggressor.

intercession coupled with courteous admission that there is no right of intercession.[17] Such intercession—or protests—have often taken place not in reliance upon any legal right of intervention for the sake of humanity, but for the reason that the measure of oppression, by bringing about the emigration, on a large scale, of the victims of the persecution, affects injuriously the interests of the protecting State. The cumulative result of that approach to the doctrine of humanitarian intervention has been not only to make it sporadic and infrequent but also to cast doubt upon its existence as a rule of international law. Yet there has been occasional recognition of some fundamental human rights in treaties providing for religious freedom and the cultural and political rights of minorities.[18] Of these, the Minorities Treaties concluded after the First World War provide an outstanding example.

It is in the Charter of the United Nations that the individual human being first appears as entitled to fundamental human rights and freedoms. We shall fail utterly to realise the full significance of that innovation if we permit our understanding of it to be blurred by the fact that these rights are not defined in detail or, so far as the Charter is concerned, that they are not fully enforceable at the instance either of the individual or of the

[17] That attitude has occasionally gone to the length of States abstaining from the protection of their own nationals caught in the meshes of foreign persecution. Thus when Czarist Russia adopted discriminatory measures against Russian Jews the British Government eventually acquiesced in the view that British Jews in Russia had no legal claim to be treated in a manner different from the treatment of Russian Jews: *State Papers*, vol. 79, pp. 833, 845. On that occasion the British Government relied on the Opinion of the Law Officers of the Crown of 6 May, 1862 (printed in McNair, *The Law of Treaties* (1938), pp. 250, 251), from which the crucial passage may be quoted: 'Russian subjects, being Jews, incur certain disabilities, and we think that the equality intended and provided for by the Treaty is not infringed by British subjects in Russia, who are Jews, whilst residing there, also sharing the same disabilities.' In 1881 the Law Officers, confronted with the same question, declined to subscribe to that view. They said: '. . . when we consider the consequences which such a construction of the Treaty involves, we cannot say that it is the correct one' (*ibid.*, p. 195). But they thought, for reasons which are not apparent, and which they did not attempt to particularise, that it was not open to the British Government to insist on an interpretation of the Treaty at variance with that placed upon it in 1862. In 1938 the British Government acted on the view, which cannot be described as sound, that the Anglo-German Treaty of Commerce and Navigation of December, 1924, did not secure to 'British subjects who are regarded as Jews under German law, any rights which are not enjoyed in Germany by German nationals who are Jews'. The attitude of the United States on the subject was different: see *U.S., Foreign Relations*, 1881, pp. 996, 1007, 1030.

[18] For a survey of these treaties see Janovsky and Fagen, *International Aspects of German Racial Policies* (1937), pp. 6-27.

members of the United Nations. Neither, as will be shown,[19] does the denial of the right of intervention reduce these provisions to no more than a political declaration. The Charter of the United Nations is a legal document; its language is the language of law, of international law. In affirming repeatedly the ' fundamental human rights ' of the individual it must of necessity be deemed to refer to legal rights—to legal rights recognised by international law and independent of the law of the State. These rights are only imperfectly enforceable, and, in so far as the availability of a remedy is the hall-mark of legal right, they are imperfect legal rights. Yet in the sphere of international law the correlation of right and remedy is not as close as within the State.[20] Moreover, irrespective of the question of enforcement, there ought to be no doubt that the provisions of the Charter in the matter of fundamental human rights impose upon the Members of the United Nations the legal duty to respect them.[21] In particular, it is clear that a Member of the United Nations who is guilty of a violation of these rights commits a breach of the Charter. There may be no international tribunal endowed with compulsory jurisdiction to ascertain the fact of such violation, but international tribunals have, as a rule, no compulsory jurisdiction in the matter of the fulfilment of international duties. This fact does not deprive them of their legal character. Moreover, in so far as the Charter forms part of the municipal law of the Members

---

[19] See below, Chapter X.

[20] See above, p. 27. The last Assembly of the League of Nations seems to have committed itself, perhaps unnecessarily, to the contrary view. It accepted a report of a Financial Sub-Committee which found that the Assembly of the League had the right, in 1939, to adopt regulations which, in effect, divested certain officials of the rights which they possessed under their contracts with the League. The Sub-Committee found that as the officials in question had no enforceable rights against the League, their claims under the contracts could not be considered as legal rights. In accordance with the report of the Sub-Committee the last Assembly decided, in April, 1946, not to give effect to a judgment of the Administrative Tribunal of the League which held that the Assembly of 1939 could not deny to the officials their legal rights grounded in the contracts. It is not clear to what extent the Assembly, in adopting the report of the Sub-Committee in 1946, acquiesced in the legal reasoning underlying that report. It would have been sufficient to lay down that, although the officials possessed legal rights under the contracts of service, those rights could be abrogated by a legislative act of the Assembly. As within the State, so also in organised international society there must reside somewhere the legal power of modifying contractual arrangements in accordance with changed conditions. For the judgment of the Tribunal see *League of Nations, Official Journal,* Special Supplement No. 194 (1946), p. 247; for the Report of the Sub-Committee see *ibid.,* pp. 261-264; for the discussion at the Assembly see *ibid.,* pp. 130-132.

[21] See below, Chapter IX.

of the United Nations it may be enforceable as such. While the law of the State is supreme so far as its courts are concerned, there is no reason why they should not resort to the Charter as a direct source of law in this respect.[22]

It would therefore appear that to the extent to which the Charter incorporates obligations to respect the fundamental human rights and freedoms it amounts to recognition of individuals as subjects of international law. These obligations and the methods of their implementation are more effective than is commonly assumed.[23] In turn, their effectiveness will depend to some extent on the final abandonment of the doctrine of the inherently inferior status of individuals in the sphere of international law.

4. CRIMES AGAINST HUMANITY AND FUNDAMENTAL HUMAN RIGHTS

Subsequent to the Second World War, the acknowledgment of fundamental human rights has taken place—indirectly, but most significantly—through the recognition of so-called crimes against humanity in Article 6 of the Charter annexed to the Four-Power Agreement of 8 August, 1945, providing for the establishment of the International Military Tribunal for the Prosecution and Punishment of the Major War Criminals of the European Axis.[24] In addition to the crimes of planning and waging wars of aggression and war crimes, the Tribunal was given jurisdiction in the matter of ' crimes against humanity '. That Article of the Charter conferred upon the Court jurisdiction with regard to ' (c) Crimes against humanity: namely, murder, extermination, enslavement, deportation, and other inhumane acts committed against any civilian population, before or during the war; or persecutions on political, racial or religious grounds in execution of or in connexion with any crime within the jurisdiction of the Tribunal, whether or not in violation of the domestic law of the country where perpetrated '. As the result of a subsequent amendment, embodied in the Berlin Protocol of 6 October, 1945, and substituting a comma for the semicolon in the section quoted above, the scope and significance of the Article were reduced from the

[22] See below, pp. 149-151.
[23] See below, Chapter IX.
[24] *Treaty Series* No. 27 (1946), Cmd. 6903.

outset inasmuch as all the crimes against humanity enumerated therein were made punishable only in so far as they were ancillary or subsidiary to other criminal acts within the jurisdiction of the Tribunal. This limitation was adopted owing to the apprehension—probably unfounded—that to give the Tribunal jurisdiction, without qualification, over crimes against humanity as defined in the Charter would be tantamount to confronting it with a multitude of charges and dangerously complicating a task in itself of unprecedented magnitude. The judgment of the Tribunal contained a further limitation which is not apparent from the terms of the Charter. The Tribunal, partly in disregard of the terms of the Charter which gave it jurisdiction in respect of crimes against humanity ' before or during the war ', in so far as they were committed in connexion with or in execution of any crime within the jurisdiction of the Tribunal, apparently declined to treat acts committed prior to the war as crimes against humanity within the meaning of the Charter.[25]

Notwithstanding these qualifications, the Charter and the judgment of the Tribunal, in so far as they recognise in principle crimes against humanity, have a direct bearing on the question of recognition, in the international sphere, of fundamental rights of the individual. Crimes against humanity are crimes regardless of whether they were committed in accordance with and in obedience to the national law of the accused. Such acts were deemed to violate the sanctity of human personality to such a degree as to make irrelevant reliance upon the law of the State which ordered them. To lay down that crimes against humanity are punishable is, therefore, to assert the existence of rights of man grounded in a law superior to the law of the State. Thus, upon analysis, the enactment of crimes against humanity in an international instrument signifies the acknowledgment of fundamental rights of the individual recognised by international law. It is possible that this result did not occur to the authors of the Charter, nor, perhaps, to the Tribunal which applied it. Yet, unless the Charter is conceived as an *ad hoc* piece of vindictive legislation enacted by the victor against the vanquished, this is its inevitable

[25] The Tribunal expressly refused to make a general declaration that such crimes were crimes against humanity. No such general declaration was required from the Tribunal. In so far as it refrained, without qualification, from treating crimes committed before the war as crimes against humanity, the judgment finds no warrant in the terms of the Charter.

and logical result. In terms of law, with the conception of crimes against humanity there must correspond the notion of fundamental human rights recognised by international law and, as a further result, of an international status of the individual whose rights have thus been recognised.[26]

The enactment, in the Charter of the International Military Tribunal, of crimes against humanity was not an isolated act. It was repeated in Article 5 of the Charter of the International Military Tribunal for the Far East established on 19 January, 1946, by a Proclamation of the Supreme Commander for the Allied Powers in the Far East. The Paris Peace Treaties of 1947 with Italy, Roumania, Hungary, Bulgaria and Finland provided for the surrender, *inter alios,* of persons accused of crimes against humanity. Above all, the Four Powers in occupation of Germany enacted legislation providing for the prosecution of crimes against humanity committed in Germany before and during the war (and probably also after the War and during the period preceding the assumption of power in Germany by the National-Socialists[27]) without stipulating for any connexion of these crimes with war crimes or crimes against the peace,[28] and expressly laying down that the criminality of such acts was independent of whether they were committed in accordance with or in violation of the domestic law of the country concerned.[29] These enactments have a

[26] For an exhaustive treatment of the question of crimes against humanity see Schwelb in *British Year Book of International Law,* 23 (1946), pp. 178-226, and *Law Reports of Trials of War Criminals* (United Nations War Crimes Commission), vol. 15 (1949), pp. 134-138.

[27] See Schwelb, *loc. cit.,* pp. 216-218.

[28] Control Council Law No. 10 of 20 December, 1945. See also the special Ordinance, passed in the British Control Zone of Germany in pursuance of Law No. 10, authorising German courts to exercise jurisdiction with regard to crimes against humanity committed by persons of German nationality against German nationals or stateless persons. Similar Ordinances were passed in other Zones.

[29] The following passage from the judgment given in 1947 in the *Justice Trial* (the *Altstötter* case) by the United States Military Tribunal at Nuremberg in answer to the plea of the accused that they acted in accordance with the provisions of their municipal law merits quotation: 'The very essence of the prosecution case is that the laws, the Hitler decrees and the Draconic, corrupt, and perverted Nazi judicial system themselves constituted the substance of war crimes and crimes against humanity and that participation in the enactment and enforcement of them amounts to complicity in crime. We have pointed out that governmental participation is a material element of the crime against humanity. Only when official organs of sovereignty participated in atrocities and persecutions did those crimes assume international proportions. It can scarcely be said that governmental participation, the proof of which is necessary for conviction, can also be a defence to the charge.' (*Law Reports of Trials of War Criminals* (United Nations War Crimes Commission), vol. 6 (1948), p. 49).

significance transcending the occasion which gave rise to them. They have become a weighty precedent binding upon all. [The principle which they enunciate is among those which the First General Assembly of the United Nations accepted, alongside the other principles of the Charter of 8 August, 1945, and the judgment of the Nuremberg Tribunal, as the basis of the codification of international law on the subject.[30]   In an indirect but compelling manner the enactment of ' crimes against humanity ' constitutes the recognition of fundamental human rights superior to the law of the sovereign State.   It may be noted that considerations of humanity, conceived as a source of legal obligations, are not limited to international criminal law.   When, in the *Corfu Channel* case, the International Court of Justice held Albania responsible for her failure to notify the existence of a minefield, it based its decision ' on certain general and well recognised principles, namely ', in the first instance, ' elementary considerations of humanity, even more exacting in peace than in war '.[31]

5.   The Individual as a Subject of International Duties.   So-called Offences against the Law of Nations

As in the case of international rights so also in the matter of international duties the accurate approach to ascertaining the legal position is to rely not on preconceived notions as to the capacity of individuals to be subjects of international law but, primarily, on the practice of States in both the international and the municipal spheres.   In the first instance, there must be considered the cases in which international law imposes directly, *i.e.,* without recourse to State legislation, duties upon individuals when not acting as organs or on behalf of States.   The rules relating to piracy can be interpreted to this effect—though, as pointed out above,[32] they may be explained as a mutual concession of jurisdiction by States over their subjects.   On the other hand, the operation of rules of warfare is, as suggested,[33] a clear example

[30] See Resolution of the General Assembly of 11 December, 1946, in which it ' affirms the principles of international law recognised by the Charter of the Nuremberg Tribunal and the judgment of the Tribunal ': *Journal of the General Assembly,* No. 75, p. 945.
[31] *Reports of Judgments, Advisory Opinions, and Orders,* 1949, p. 22.
[32] See p. 9.
[33] See above, p. 10.   There is perhaps no warrant for the suggestion advanced by Professor Kelsen that national tribunals, military and other, in applying Hague Convention No. IV for the punishment of war criminals, administer their own municipal law, into which the Hague Convention has been trans-

of the direct effect of rules of international law upon individuals. A soldier who, for the satisfaction of private gain or lust, is guilty of murder or plunder in occupied territory or, generally, in the theatre of operations, is guilty of a war crime *jure gentium*. In so far as according to the law of many States international law is part of the law of the land, the obligations of international law are directly binding upon individuals. In *Respublica* v. *De Longchamps*,[34] McKean, Chief Justice of Pennsylvania, in sentencing the accused for an assault upon the Consul-General of France, said:

> '. . . The first crime in the indictment is an infraction of the law of nations. This law, in its full extent, is part of the law of this State. . . . The person of a public minister is sacred and inviolable. Whoever offers any violence to him, not only affronts the sovereign he represents, but also hurts the common safety and well-being of nations—he is guilty of a crime against the whole world. . . . You then have been guilty of an atrocious violation of the law of nations.'

The criminal and, generally, the municipal law of various countries contains direct references to offences against the law of nations. The Constitution of the United States gives Congress the right to define and punish, *inter alia*, ' offences against the law of nations '.[35] It has been often maintained that notwithstanding

---

formed, as distinguished from international law: *International Law Quarterly,* 1 (1947), p. 160. Any such contention amounts to an assertion, which cannot be accepted, that municipal tribunals do not administer international law. A contention of that nature is expressive, at best, of the purely dialectical proposition that rules of international law incorporated into municipal law cease to be rules of international law. See *Transactions of the Grotius Society,* 25 (1939), p. 85. Professor Kelsen seems to have abandoned the view which he advanced, correctly, in 1944 (*Peace through Law,* p. 77). He then said: ' The military court, by punishing the acts, executes international law even if it applies at the same time norms of its own military law. The legal basis of the trial is international law, which establishes the individual responsibility of the person committing the act of illegitimate warfare.' The innovation, such as it was, introduced by the Charter of the International Military Tribunal of 1945, was not the declaration of individual responsibility for criminal violations of international law, but its application to the crime of aggressive war—an innovation which is not surprising seeing that before the developments culminating in the Kellogg-Briand Pact aggressive war was not a criminal act under international law as it then existed.

[34] (1784) 1 Dallas' Report 111.

[35] Article 1, section 8, clause 10. For an interesting case applying that clause to counterfeiting within the United States of notes and securities of other States see *United States* v. *Arjona,* 120 U.S. 479. For numerous other examples of municipal legislation on the same lines see Triepel, *Völkerrecht und Landesrecht* (1889), Chapter 3, § 13(1). He disapproves of that terminology: ' If, as we have demonstrated above, the individual can only be the object and not the subject of international law, then it is inconceivable that a " norm " of international law should be violated by an individual '.

the terminology used, individuals are in such cases subject to the obligations of their own municipal law as distinguished from the law of nations. There is a distinct element of artificiality in that distinction.

6. INDIVIDUALS AS ORGANS OF THE STATE. CONTRACTUAL AND TORTIOUS LIABILITY

What is much more important from the point of view of both principle and practice is the question as to who is the subject of international duties—who is the subject of international law—in the case of individuals acting not in their private capacity but on behalf of and as organs of the State. The view has been gaining ground that even in this sphere of action the subject of duty and responsibility is in every case the individual human being. It is probable that this aspect of the question has influenced the doctrines of Duguit,[36] Krabbe[37] and, more recently, Professor Scelle,[38] who have urged not that individuals can also be subjects of international law, but that they are the only subjects of the law of nations. These opinions cannot be lightly brushed aside as assertions of pure theory. The State is composed of individual human beings. Its rulers and those responsible for its actions are individual human beings. Moreover, there is cogency in the view that unless responsibility is imputed and attached to persons of flesh and blood, it rests with no one. There is finally the consideration, which has far-reaching consequences, that unless the subject of international duties is thought of as identical with the individual human being as distinguished from the mystical entity of the State, we open the door wide to that dualism of moral standards which, under the guise of ' reason of State ', has proved a disintegrating and destructive factor in the sphere of international morality and peace.

On the other hand, it must be borne in mind that the State is a corporation, a juristic person, and that reasons of convenience and justice require that, in the normal course of affairs, the collective entity of the State should be the subject of responsibility. In that sense international law is primarily a law between States. This applies, for instance, to the duties of the State with regard to

---

[36] *Traité de droit constitutionnel* (3rd ed., 1927), vol. I, pp. 713 *et seq.*
[37] *Die moderne Staatsidee* (1919), p. 273.
[38] *Précis de droit des gens*, vol. I (1932), pp. 42-44.

the fulfilment of normal obligations of treaties or of customary international law in matters of commerce, finance, or international administration. While it is true that such duties are ultimately the duties of the human agencies, it is just and proper that, in law, responsibility should be imputed to the State as a whole and that the State should appear exclusively as the subject of international law for the purpose. Independent political societies function in the form of the corporate entity of the State, and it is appropriate that the general principles of law applicable to juridical personality and to the corporate capacity for action should apply also in the case of States. The legal structure of a limited liability company is as necessary in the relations of States as in private life. It is clear that for the purposes of redress, in terms of economic compensation, for violation of treaties and of customary international law, the State as a whole is as a rule, from the practical point of view, the proper situs of attribution of responsibility.

The position is similar, though not identical, with regard to what may be called tortious responsibility, for instance, in relation to the question of responsibility for denial of justice to aliens. As a rule such tortious liability implies—and may be satisfied by— financial compensation. In practice, the subject of international liability in the matter of tort has been the State—which liability has on occasions assumed the form of penal damages.[39] But, intrinsically, there is nothing—save the traditional doctrine on the question of the subjects of international law—to prevent the tortious responsibility of the State from being combined, in the international sphere, with the responsibility of the organs directly liable for the act or omission in question. It is proper and desirable that an official who is responsible for causing serious injury to an alien by way of denial of justice or otherwise should not personally escape reprobation at the hands of an international tribunal. This, clearly, is not the existing position in international law. But there is room for envisaging an improvement of the law in the matter. The law, when thus improved, will provide that the subject of the duty to treat aliens in accordance with the minimum standard of civilisation (and, generally, in accordance with international law) is not only the

---

[39] See *e.g.*, the *Janes* case, decided by the United States-Mexican Claims Commission in 1926, reported in *Annual Digest*, 1925-1926, Case No. 158.

corporate entity of the State, but also the individual organ acting on its behalf. There would appear to be no reason why the person or persons responsible should not be made jointly liable with the State. Moreover, it may well be in such cases that what —so far as the State is concerned—is a mere tortious responsibility, may in the person of the organ concerned assume the complexion of an international criminal liability. A corrupt or criminally minded judge who has inflicted upon an alien, through a deliberate or negligent miscarriage of justice, an unjust sentence of death or imprisonment; an official who has permitted the murderer of an alien to escape; a military officer who when called in to shield an alien from the fury of a mob joins in the murderous attack [40]—all these persons could, consistently with principle, be held to have transgressed not only the law of their country but also a rule of international law directly binding upon them. Systems of municipal law which recognise a clear distinction between contractual and tortious responsibility admit in appropriate cases the liability in tort of persons acting on behalf of the corporate entity—in addition to the tortious liability of the corporation as a whole. [41] Any such development would be in accordance with what must be regarded as a well-established feature of the law of State responsibility, namely, that liability is not absolute, but depends upon the existence of fault in the person or persons of the State organs responsible for the act or omission in question. If liability is conditioned by the *mens rea* of the individual responsible, then it is proper that the penal consequences of the act or omission should attach to the human agency acting on behalf of the State or, even when not so acting, rendered capable of committing the injurious act by reason of his normally acting as agent or servant of the State.

7. CRIMINAL RESPONSIBILITY

Similar considerations apply to the question of the subjects of criminal responsibility under international law. In the field of

[40] As in *Thomas Y. Youmans* case, decided in 1926 by the United States-Mexican General Claims Commission: *Annual Digest,* 1925-1926, Case No. 162.

[41] See, as to English law, Salmond, *The Law of Torts* (7th ed. by Stallybrass, 1928): 'But it is undoubted law that the servants or agents by whom a corporation commits a tort are themselves personally liable in the same case and to the same extent as any other servants or agents who commit torts in the service or on behalf of their principals or employers' (at p. 79).

contract and, to some extent, of tort, the requirements of justice
and of international peace can be met by making the corporate
entity of the State mainly, if not exclusively, the subject of responsibility. This is not so in the sphere of criminal acts performed
by the State, *i.e.*, by persons acting on behalf of the State and
under the colour of the authority of the State. In this sphere
the analogy of municipal law must fully apply. The primary
subject of the international duty is the human agency which puts
in motion the criminal act; the criminal responsibility of the State
is of a subsidiary character. Thus it is futile to maintain that if a
cabinet minister, fully endowed with governmental authority,
orders the massacre of the nationals of a foreign State, the subject
of international responsibility is his State only, and not he himself.
The futility of that attitude has often been emphasised by the
parallel doctrine that States, because of their sovereignty, cannot
be subject to criminal responsibility. Both these views must now
be regarded as exploded. The question of the criminal responsibility of States is outside the present discussion.[42] Here we are
concerned with the view that individuals cannot be subjects of
criminal responsibility in the international sphere for the reason
that they are not subjects of international law. That view, it has
been shown here,[43] is not in accordance with the law. When the
Charter annexed to the Agreement of 8 August, 1945, setting up
the International Military Tribunal laid down that there shall be
individual liability of the defendants for criminal acts which they
committed as organs and on behalf of the German State, the only
innovation which it introduced was to give the formal imprimatur
of a general international treaty—for it was a treaty signed or
adhered to by the vast majority of the nations of the world and
subsequently endorsed by the First General Assembly of the
United Nations—to the abandonment of a doctrine which had
loomed large in the writings of publicists but which had no
foundation in the principles and necessities of international law.
That doctrine was that individuals, not being subjects of international law, cannot be subjects of international duties in the

[42] See Oppenheim's *International Law*, vol. I (7th ed. by Lauterpacht, 1948),
§ 156*b*.
[43] See above, p. 6. See also to the same effect Glaser in *Revue Pénale Suisse*,
64 (1949), pp. 283-314, and Levy in *American Political Science Review*, 37
(1943), pp. 1052 *et seq.*

criminal or any other sphere. The judgment of the Nuremberg
Tribunal treated the provision of the Charter laying down the
individual responsibility of the accused for acts committed on
behalf of the State as a self-evident rule of international law, as
a matter both of principle and of the effectiveness of the law of
nations.[44]

It is not likely that the express rejection of the view that
individuals cannot be directly subject to international duties will
remain an isolated event in international practice. The greater
the heinousness of the act and the graver the danger to international peace, the more difficult it is to accept the artificial
divorce between the State and the individuals acting on its behalf.
In the Resolution of the First General Assembly of the United
Nations of 13 December, 1946, concerning the condemnation and
prohibition of genocide, the Assembly affirmed that genocide is a
crime under international law which the civilised world condemns
and for the commission of which principals and accomplices—
whether private individuals, public officials, or statesmen, and
whether the crime is committed on religious, racial, political or
any other grounds—are punishable.[45] The Convention on the
Prevention and Punishment of the Crime of Genocide approved
by the General Assembly in 1948 lays down that genocide,
whether committed in time of peace or war, is a crime under
international law which the Parties undertake to prevent and to
punish and that the persons responsible for that crime shall be
punished ' whether they are constitutionally responsible rulers,
public officials or private individuals '.[46] The Convention thus
subjected individuals to the direct obligation and sanction of international law. The international regulation and control of atomic
energy as a potential weapon of war has also raised the question of

---

[44] See above, p. 6. In view of this it is not easy to follow Professor Kelsen
when he says that ' what really impairs the authority of the judgment is that
the principle of individual criminal responsibility for the violation of rules of
international law prohibiting war has not been established as a general
principle of law, but as a rule applicable only to vanquished States by the
victors ': *International Law Quarterly*, 1 (1947), p. 170. The language of the
judgment on the subject is studiously general.

[45] *Journal of the General Assembly*, No. 58, Supp. A-A/P.V. 55.

[46] Articles 1 and 4. For an analysis of the Convention see Stillschweig in
Friedenswarte, 49 (1949), pp. 93-104. See also Kuhn in *American Journal of
International Law*, 43 (1949), pp. 498-501.

the necessity of attaching criminal responsibility to individuals.[47]
Unless not only the State as such but also its organs are made
personally responsible for complying with the measures laid down
by the international authority, the effectiveness of the international
regulation of this vital problem will be considerably impaired.
The magnitude of the interests involved requires that that liability
should be of a criminal character.

8. The Significance of the Recognition of the Individual as a Subject of International Duties

The evolution of an international law in which the individual is
the subject of duties imposed by it is, in some respects, a corollary
of the attribution to him of rights grounded in international law.
It is difficult to urge and justify the existence of the former without admitting the validity of the latter.   The second relevant
consideration in this connexion is that, in the sphere of criminal
responsibility, the recognition of the individual as a subject of
international duties tends to diminish the necessity for and the
scope of collective punishment of States.   Such necessity cannot
always be avoided: neither is it inherently unjust, especially if
it can be effected without the indiscriminate infliction of physical
harm upon the individuals of the guilty State.   Moreover, even
if individuals may be innocent of a particular criminal act
attributable to the organs of the State, they may have had a share
in endowing that organ with power or in tolerating its rule.   If
the criminal act is successful they may all reap the fruits of trans-
gression.   However, collective responsibility is, at best, a rough
instrument of justice, and there are compelling reasons for

[47] In the First Report of the Atomic Energy Commission to the Security
Council of 31 December, 1946, the Commission suggested that the proposed
convention should include provisions ' setting forth such violations [of the
convention] as shall constitute international crimes, and establishing the
nature of the measures of enforcement and punishment to be imposed upon
persons and upon nations guilty of violating the terms of the treaty or convention' (*United Nations Atomic Energy Commission*, Special Supplement,
Report to the Security Council, p. 19).   In the Russian proposal of 19 June,
1946, the violation of the provisions of the Convention was declared to be
' a most serious international crime against humanity' (Atomic Energy Commission, *Official Records*, No. 2, p. 27).   At the meeting of the Atomic Energy
Commission of 14 June, 1946, the representative of the United States proposed a system of control under which ' the United Nations can prescribe
individual responsibility and punishment on the principle applied at
Nuremberg . . . a formula certain to benefit the world's future' (*ibid.*, No. 1,
p. 5).

reducing the scope of its operation.[48]   It can be so reduced by
the effective recognition of the individual as a subject of
international duties.   This is essentially the position in the
constitutional theory of the federal State where federal execution
against the member States as such is in the nature of an exception.
A violation of the national constitution by a member State is, as
a rule, treated as a violation of the federal law by the individuals
responsible.   They, and not the corporate entity of the member
State, are the subjects of responsibility.   It is not likely that the
gradual integration of international society in the direction of a
supra-national Federation of the World—a development which
must be regarded as the ultimate rational postulate of the political
organisation of man—will be achieved by sudden and drastic
changes in the legal organisation of mankind.   But it may be
brought nearer to realisation by the gradual adoption of the fundamental principles of federal government.   Of these, the direct
subordination of the individual to federal law, in his capacity as
a subject of the law of the Federation, is a vital link.   Here lies
the deeper significance of the affirmation of the principle that the
individual is a subject of international law in the domain both
of rights and of duties.

Finally, the full and effective acceptance of the principle that
individuals are subjects of international duties has a direct bearing
on the evolution of international morality.   The tendency to
affirm and tolerate a double standard of morality in international
relations—a tendency to assert that the individual acting as the

[48] This aspect of the matter is clearly—though perhaps with some exaggeration
—brought out in the judgment of the Military Tribunal of the United States in
Nuremberg in the *I.G. Farben* case in connection with the responsibility of
the accused for crimes against the peace. The Tribunal said: ' The defendants
now before us were neither high public officials in the civil government nor
high military officers. Their participation was that of followers and not
leaders. If we lower the standard of participation to include them, it is difficult to find a logical place to draw the line between the guilty and the innocent
among the great mass of the German people. It is, of course, unthinkable
that the majority of Germans should be condemned as guilty of committing
crimes against peace. This would amount to a determination of collective
guilt to which the corollary of mass punishment is the logical result, for
which there is no precedent in international law and no justification in human
relations. We cannot say that a private citizen should be placed in the position of being compelled to determine in the heat of war whether his government is right or wrong, or, if it starts right, when it turns wrong ' (*Law
Reports of Trials of War Criminals* (The United Nations War Crimes Commission), vol. X (1949), p. 39). Collective responsibility, in so far as it is
not individually aimed at the members of the community concerned, is not
invariably inimical to justice.

organ of the State is not bound by the universal code of ethics which obtains in the relations of individuals—has in the past received nourishment from the notion that the obligations of international law do not rest upon the individual members of the State, but upon ' the State '.[49] The unavoidable outcome must be the impairment of that moral factor which is the backbone of all law. It is not necessary to expatiate upon the consequences of the resulting position in relation to the effectiveness of international law. The two questions are interconnected.[50]

[49] This phenomenon must be distinguished—though the distinction may appear to be a subtle one—from the operation of the doctrine of ' reason of State '. The latter does not necessarily rule out the individual as a subject of legal and moral obligation. It asserts different standards of obligation.

[50] When in 1928 the German *Reichsgericht* upheld the conviction of a German national sentenced for publishing certain plans of the Reichswehr, it rejected the plea of the accused that he had acted in order to uphold the disarmament provisions of the Treaty of Versailles, which was part of German law. The Court said: ' The Reichsgericht must reject the view that the conviction of the accused would violate the rule of international law which lays down that treaties must be fulfilled in good faith. For this rule binds only the contracting parties, not individuals ': *High Treason (Treaty of Versailles) in Germany* case, *Annual Digest*, 1927-1928, Case No. 5.

CHAPTER 3

INTERNATIONAL PROCEDURAL CAPACITY OF INDIVIDUALS

1. ACCESS OF INDIVIDUALS TO INTERNATIONAL TRIBUNALS

THE traditional doctrine in the matter of subjects of international law has derived much support from the rule that only States have a *locus standi* before international tribunals. That rule has found terse expression in Article 34 of the Statute of the International Court of Justice, which lays down that ' Only States may be parties in cases before the Court '. However, the importance of this provision of the Statute, in relation to the question under discussion, ought not to be exaggerated. It is a provision defining the competence of the Court. It is not intended to be declaratory of any general principle of international law. No such principle prevents States, if they so wish, from securing to individuals and international public bodies access to international courts and tribunals. The Committee of Jurists who in 1920 drafted the Statute of the Court in its present formulation excluding individuals from appearing as parties before the Court noted in their Report that the solution adopted was ' without prejudice to any subsequent development ' of the Court.[1] Undoubtedly the excessive concentration on the question of access of individuals to international tribunals has, in some respects, tended to obscure the more general significance of the position of the individual in international law. For, as is submitted later in this Chapter, the quality of individuals as subjects of international law does not depend upon the full recognition of their procedural capacity.[2] On the other hand, the meaning and extent of the existing limitations in this sphere have lent themselves to a measure of exaggeration and generalisation which has affected the discussion of the wider problem. While some have pointed to the existing limitations of the procedural capacity of individuals as showing that they are not subjects of international law, others have relied on the doctrine that individuals are not subjects of international

---

[1] *Minutes*, p. 723.   [2] See below, p. 54.

law as a reason for denying to them any *locus standi* before international tribunals. In this, as in other matters, *dolus latet in generalibus*. International arbitral law on the question of the procedural capacity of individuals and bodies other than States has not been static. Some arbitration conventions, while in fact permitting individuals to put forward claims before the commission or tribunal, have left to the national agents of the States concerned full discretion as to the presentation of the claim and the conduct of the case. These conventions included, for example, that of 8 September, 1923, between the United States of America and Mexico providing for the setting up of a General Claims Commission.[3] In this and similar Conventions[4] the State retained full control of the claim which it espoused.[5] Agents and counsel were appointed by the Governments. It was expressly laid down that all claims must be filed by Governments or their agents and that no statements, documents, or evidence were to be received unless presented by agents. Even in these cases there was an incipient recognition of some measure of independent status of the individual claimant, in particular with regard to the duty of the State to hand over to the claimant the amount awarded in respect of the claim made on his behalf.[6]

---

[3] For the text of the Convention see Feller, *The Mexican Claims Commission* (1935), pp. 321 *et seq.* And see *ibid.*, pp. 83-90, for a lucid exposition of the position of the individual claimants before the Commission.

[4] See, *e.g.*, the British-Mexican Claims Commission established by the Convention of 19 November, 1926: *League of Nations Treaty Series*, vol. 85, p. 51.

[5] For a clear and somewhat emphatic affirmation of full State control over claims adjudicated upon by an international tribunal see the decision given in 1940 by the Court of Appeals for the District of Columbia in *Z. & F. Assets Realization Corporation et Al.* v. *Hull, Secretary of State, et Al.; Annual Digest,* 1941-1942, Case No. 134.

[6] See *American-Mexican Claims Bureau, Inc.,* v. *Morgenthau, Secretary of the Treasury,* decided in 1939 by the United States District Court for the District of Columbia: *Annual Digest,* 1938-1940, Case No. 106. See also Administrative Decision No. V by Parker, Umpire, United States-German Mixed Claims Commission (*Consolidated Edition of Opinions.* p. 190), to the effect that when an award is made on a specific claim 'the fund so paid is not a national fund in the sense that the title vests in the nation receiving it entirely free from any obligation to account to the private claimant.' And see Parker, Umpire, in Administrative Decision No. I in the Tripartite Claims Commission, 1927: 'While the nation's absolute right to control a private claim espoused by it is necessarily exclusive, because of the national interest that may be or become involved, nevertheless the private nature of such claim continues to inhere in it and the claim only in a very restricted sense becomes a national claim' (*Annual Digest,* 1927-1928, Case No. 172). See also, to the same effect, the Opinions of Van Vollenhoven, Umpire, United States and Mexico General Claims Commission, in the *William A. Parker* case (*ibid.,* 1925-1926, Case No. 178) and in the *North American Dredging Company of Texas* case (*ibid.,* Case No. 179).

In other cases the independent *locus standi* of individuals
before international tribunals has been more clearly recognised.
This was the position under the provisions of Articles 297 and
304(b)(2) of the Treaty of Versailles and of the corresponding
provisions of the other Peace Treaties. In particular, the former
Article gave the nationals of the Allied Powers the right to put
forward claims for compensation, in their own name, against the
German State. Some writers have attempted to qualify the
significance of these provisions by suggesting that the Mixed
Arbitral Tribunals were in fact joint national courts of the States
concerned entrusted with the task of applying their respective
municipal law which incorporated the relevant Articles of the
Treaty.[7] These explanations cannot be accepted as expressing
the correct legal position. Although the claimants could
avail themselves of the assistance of the agents appointed by
their Governments, there was nothing to prevent them from
pursuing their claims unaided.[8] Neither were the provisions of these treaties unprecedented. In the Statute of
the proposed international prize court as adopted in Convention
XII at the Second Hague Peace Conference, it was laid down that
individual claimants shall have a right of appeal to the court
against judgments of national prize courts. In the Treaty of 1907
between the five Central American Republics establishing the
Central American Court of Justice individuals were given direct
access to the Court.[9]

Developments have gone beyond securing to individuals direct
access to international tribunals in actions against a foreign State.
In the Upper Silesian Convention of May, 1922, between
Germany and Poland, the contracting parties provided for a
tribunal which, in effect, was given jurisdiction to entertain actions
brought by nationals of either party against their own State. The
innovation was so revolutionary that in the case of *Steiner and
Gross* v. *Polish State*—an action brought against Poland by one
of her nationals—the Polish agent contended that the Convention

[7] See, *e.g.*, Anzilotti, *Cours de droit international* (translated from the Italian,
1929), p. 136.
[8] A course apparently not always conducive to the efficient working of the
tribunals: see Blühdorn in *Hague Recueil*, 41 (1932) (iii), pp. 174-176.
[9] For an account of *Diaz* v. *Guatemala* (1908), an action for false arrest,
imprisonment and expulsion, see Hudson, *op. cit.* below (in n. 11), p. 54.

could not mean, in this respect, what on the face of it it said. The Tribunal rejected that contention.[10]

It would thus appear that there is nothing inherent in the structure of international law which prevents individuals and, generally, persons other than States from being parties to proceedings before international tribunals. The matter is one of machinery and of the determination of governments in any given case. For this reason it is probable that Article 34 of the Statute of the International Court of Justice, far from declaring an immutable rule of international law, has gone to an excessive length in giving countenance, in a rigid way, to what was assumed to be one of the consequences of the view that States only can be subjects of international law. It would have been proper and practicable for the Statute to provide that the Court shall have jurisdiction only in cases in which at least one party is a State. A provision of that nature would not have given individuals any *right* to bring a State before the Court—unless in pursuance of a previous agreement.[11] At the same time it would have made the machinery of the Court available for the solution of major controversies between States and private individuals and corporations —as well as between States and public international bodies— wherever States, in pursuance of a general or an *ad hoc* agreement, deem it convenient and desirable to acquiesce in such a course. The availability of such machinery would have been specially appropriate in a period in which the economic activities of States tend to increase. Provision could have been made for cases of that description—in particular, disputes arising out of contracts with or injuries to aliens—to be adjudicated upon by a special chamber or chambers of the Court. For this reason it has been considered proper to include in this Chapter proposals

[10] *Annual Digest,* 1927-1928, Case No. 188. The Tribunal said: 'The Convention conferred in unequivocal terms jurisdiction upon the Tribunal irrespective of the nationality of the claimants, and, the terms of the Convention being clear, it was unnecessary to add to it a limitation which did not appear from its wording' (*ibid.*).

[11] See below, p. 56. This answers, to some extent, the view put forward by Professor Hudson that 'States would probably be reluctant to confer jurisdiction upon any international tribunal which could permit them to be sued by individuals' (*The Permanent Court of International Justice, 1920-1942* (1943), p. 396). The learned author does not develop in detail the view that 'a practical approach to the problem reveals no imperative need for a permanent international tribunal to which individuals may bring their claims against States' (*ibid.*). Some of the reasons militating in the direction of some such development are stated below, pp. 52, 59.

for a modification of the present rigid formulation of Article 34 of the Statute in the direction of a less uncompromising and more practical definition of the jurisdiction of the Court.[12]

2.   OBLIGATORY JURISDICTION OF INTERNATIONAL TRIBUNALS IN CLAIMS BY PRIVATE PERSONS

There is no sufficient reason for confusing the question of the status of individuals as subjects of international law with the question of their access to international courts whenever they deem their rights under international law to have been violated by a foreign State.   Undoubtedly, a consummation of that nature would have obvious advantages.   These have been repeatedly stated.[13]   It would provide a remedy in cases in which the private individual's own State is unable or unwilling to take up the claim; in which no remedy is available for the reason that there does not exist an instrument conferring compulsory jurisdiction upon the Court; and in which the claimant is a stateless person or otherwise debarred from assistance by a State by reason of the operation of the rule as to nationality of claims.   In all these cases the provision of a remedy by way of the automatic jurisdiction of the Court would promote justice and divest the foreign State of the character—some will say, of the stigma—of an arbitrary instrumentality of power.   Moreover, it would remove a source of international friction inasmuch as it would direct private claims into the normal channels of the ordinary judicial process.   At present the espousal of a claim by the State tends to impart to the complaint the complexion of political controversy and unfriendly action.

However, to state the advantages of any such general access of individuals to international tribunals is not to present the case in its entirety.   For to confer upon individuals the general right to invoke the jurisdiction of international tribunals whenever they feel themselves aggrieved by a foreign State would be to introduce, in a wide field of international relations, the principle of obligatory

---

[12] See below, p. 58.
[13] See Hurst in *British Year Book of International Law,* 6 (1925), pp. 61-67. And see generally for the extensive literature on the question Oppenheim, *International Law,* vol. I (7th ed., 1948), p. 581, n. 4, and vol. II (6th revised ed., 1944), p. 51, n. 2.

arbitral and judicial settlement which States have so far refused to accept and which, in so far as they have accepted it, they have often circumscribed by comprehensive reservations, especially those relating to matters which are exclusively within the domestic jurisdiction of the State. Questions which may be the subject of an appeal by an individual to an international tribunal are as a rule those which normally fall within the description of matters of domestic jurisdiction. A survey of the activity of international tribunals, in particular of that of the Permanent Court of International Justice, would disclose that the majority of cases which have come before them have been cases involving private interests of aliens. There are probably decisive reasons in favour of the acceptance of the general principle of the obligatory jurisdiction of international courts in disputes between States, but so long as that principle has not been adopted it is impracticable to expect that States will adopt it indirectly without reservations and without any assurance that the right thus granted to individuals would be exercised with a restraint and a sense of responsibility which governments customarily exhibit in this sphere. For the espousal of a private claim by a government is usually preceded by a thorough examination, on the part of the department concerned, of the legal merits, and of the propriety from other points of view, of the claim in question.

Secondly, if we accept the rule that individuals can, without any limitations, hail a foreign State before an international tribunal in order to assert their rights under international law, it is not easy to see why that faculty should be confined to aliens—unless we assert with finality the view that individuals can never possess as against their own State rights under international law enforceable, at their own instance, before international tribunals. There is no warrant for any such view. The contrary of that assertion will become the case if and when fundamental human rights and freedoms acquire the undoubted character of international rights proper by virtue of an International Bill of Human Rights made enforceable before international judicial agencies.[14] In the meantime it may be premature and one-sided to urge full procedural capacity for aliens only.

[14] See below, pp. 374-377, 447-456.

3. PROCEDURAL CAPACITY AND THE QUALITY OF A SUBJECT OF LAW

Important as is the question of the procedural capacity of individuals before international tribunals, there is no reason to exaggerate its bearing on the problem of the subjects of international law. The two questions are not synonymous. The existence of a right and the power to assert it by judicial process are not identical. In the municipal sphere there are persons, such as minors and lunatics, who though endowed with rights are unable to assert them by their own action. If States were to declare, solemnly and without equivocation, that they recognise certain inalienable rights of the individual—as they have done to some extent in the Charter of the United Nations—that declaration would amount to constituting individuals subjects of international law even if it were not accompanied by the concession to them of the faculty of independent action to enforce these rights. There is a clear distinction between procedural capacity and the quality of a subject of law.

Moreover, the denial of full procedural capacity may be accompanied by the creation and recognition of remedies falling short of a right of independent action. In the Minorities Treaties concluded after the First World War certain linguistic, racial and religious minorities were made beneficiaries of rights guaranteed by the Treaties. How far did these Treaties constitute the minorities in question subjects of international law? In strict law and according to the accepted doctrine, they created rights and duties as between the contracting parties only. The practice of the Council of the League of Nations, under whose guarantee the treaties were placed, denied the minorities any formal independent right of enforcing the benefits grounded in the Treaties.[15] That restrictive interpretation of their provisions hung on the slender thread of the accepted doctrine according to which individuals are not subjects of international law and do not benefit directly from international treaties. Both these assumptions are controversial. In practice some procedural status was accorded to the minorities.[16] This was also, to a much larger extent, the position in relation to the inhabitants of mandated territories.[17]

[15] See below, p. 245.
[16] See below, pp. 245, 248.
[17] See below, pp. 244, 245.

The procedural capacity of inhabitants of territories under the trusteeship system, although falling short of judicial remedies, is fully recognised.[18]

Moreover, as the relevant instruments have shown, it is not necessary that the espousal of interests created by treaty in favour of individuals should be limited to the State of which they are nationals.[19] Such benefits can be made the subject of proceedings by any State which is a party to the treaty in question. The rule as to nationality of claims—a rule according to which an international tribunal has no jurisdiction to entertain a claim unless the person or corporation concerned was a national of the claimant State at the time of the alleged injury up to the presentation of the claim—does not necessarily apply in such cases. Nationality is no longer the only link between the individual and international law. The State invoking the provisions of a treaty in favour of an individual who is not its national no longer acts on behalf of its own particular interest; it acts on behalf of the international interest in the welfare of the individual 'or groups of individuals concerned and of its own general interest in the maintenance of respect for these treaties and for treaties generally. The same applies to treaties which regulate the condition of stateless persons. Here, once more, the parties entitled to invoke the treaty are States which, by definition, are not the home States of the persons concerned. For these have no home State. In all these treaties the right to espouse a claim is not dependent upon the nationality of the persons concerned. This relaxation of the rule of nationality of claims—a rule which in some of its aspects is an anachronism [20]—signifies a landmark in the assertion of the

18 See below, pp. 242-244.
19 Thus the Minorities Treaties of 1919 provided that any of the Allied and Associated Powers or any other Power a member of the Council of the League of Nations shall be entitled to bring, as being a dispute of an international character, before the Permanent Court of International Justice any difference of opinion as to questions of law or fact arising out of the Articles of the Treaty (Art. 12 of the Treaty with Poland). The various mandates provided for submission to the Court of any dispute between a mandatory and any other member of the League relating to the application or interpretation of the provisions of the mandate (see *e.g.*, Art. 26 of the Mandate for Palestine). The rule as to ' nationality of claims ' could not be invoked in relation to any of these provisions.
20 In general, it is probable that the rule of nationality of claims is open, in its present rigid formulation, to legitimate criticism on grounds other than that it no longer accords with international practice in all respects or with the increasing stature of the individual in the international sphere   There is no cogent reason why a State should not be able to espouse a claim of its national for the mere reason that at the time of the injury that person

international personality of the individual.   The international enforcement of his claim has ceased to be dependent invariably upon his membership of a particular State.

4. OBLIGATORY JURISDICTION OF INTERNATIONAL TRIBUNALS IN RESPECT OF PRIVATE CLAIMS

While there are, at present, weighty objections to the recognition of the right of individuals to bring States before international tribunals independently of their consent, there would appear to be no decisive reason why individuals should not be able to exercise a right of this nature within the framework of such obligations of compulsory arbitral and judicial settlement as may be undertaken by States.   Thus, when States subscribe to the obligations of the Optional Clause of the Statute of the International Court of Justice there is no intrinsic reason, save that of the traditional doctrine in the matter, why the reciprocal undertaking in question should not enure to the benefit of the nationals of the States concerned by conferring upon them a right of action in respect of the four categories of ' legal ' disputes enumerated in Article 36.   That traditional doctrine, as has been shown, is nothing but a technical rule grounded in the dogma that individuals can have no rights under international law.   If they have no such rights, then, clearly, there is nothing which they can assert

did not possess the nationality of that State—unless it be the reason that a person by deliberately assuming, *in fraudem legis* as it were, the nationality of a powerful State might be able to secure more effective protection than if he had remained the national of a weak State.   It is difficult to see the relevance of any such consideration in relation to the jurisdiction of an impartial international tribunal.   It is not permissible to assume that the latter would be inclined to afford more favourable treatment to the nationals of a powerful State.   The rule of nationality of claims, in its current formulation, is open to the objection that it complicates and makes more rigid a procedural requirement clearly controversial in itself.   It does not, of course, meet the case of persons who were stateless at the time of injury and who subsequently acquire a nationality.   Similarly—as pointed out in the Dissenting Opinion of Judge van Eysinga in the *Panevezys-Saldutiskis Railway* case decided by the Permanent Court of international Justice in 1939—one of the consequences of the rule as to nationality of claims is that in case of transfer of territory the acquiring State is unable to espouse the claim of its new nationals (Series A/B, No. 76, p. 35).   In its Advisory Opinion, given in 1949, on the *Reparation for Injuries suffered in the service of the United Nations,* the International Court of Justice pointed to the ' important exceptions ' to the rule of nationality of claims inasmuch as ' there are cases in which protection may be exercised by a State on behalf of persons not having its nationality ' (*Reports of the International Court of Justice, 1949,* p. 181).

in their own name before international tribunals. Once the cobwebs of that antiquated theory have been swept aside, the procedural incapacity of individuals is deprived of its logical foundation. In particular there disappears the reason why, in the case of two States bound by the obligations of compulsory judicial settlement, the competence of the Court should not be concurrent in the sense that it should be open either to the States concerned or to their nationals to invoke the jurisdiction of the Court within the framework of the commitment of judicial settlement. In substance the States in question would not, as the result, undertake a wider obligation. They would merely make it possible for the same claim to be put forward either by the private party aggrieved or by its State (or, in special circumstances, by both). It is true that, in theory, the result would be an increase in the number of potential claims inasmuch as private individuals might not exercise the same degree of restraint which States have on occasions shown in this connexion. It is also possible that at times the new procedural right conferred upon individuals might be abused in order to cause embarrassment or to gain notoriety. Such contingencies are remote. On the other hand, the heavy cost of international litigation would act as an effective deterrent against rash or malicious recourse to the machinery put at the disposal of private persons.

It may thus be found that the recognition of the right of access of individuals to international tribunals, in cases covered by a general commitment of obligatory settlement, would not cause a cumbersome addition to the work of the Court. The difficulties of any appreciable increase in its activity could be met by the creation of special chambers of the International Court of Justice combining the advantages of an authoritative decision and the preservation of the continuity of the law with the requirements of expeditious disposal of claims. The practical advantages of any such reform of the law have already been alluded to.[21] There is no doubt that it would be a powerful contributory factor in fostering appreciation of the place of justice in international relations and in defeating the suspicion that private persons and corporations are being denied their legal rights because of transient considerations of governmental policy. Above all, it

[21] See above, p. 51.

would administer the *coup de grâce* to the obsolete and inaccurate notion, of which it is both the cause and the effect, that individuals can have no procedural or substantive rights under international law. To make that consummation feasible the Statute of the International Court of Justice must, as suggested, be freed from the shackles of the present wording of Article 34 so as to make it possible for States to agree, either *ad hoc* or by virtue of under-takings of a general nature, to appear as defendants at the instance of private individuals or corporations of foreign nationality in all cases in which, under international law, their State possesses the right to espouse their claim. Article 34 would then run as follows: —

> The Court shall have jurisdiction:
>
> (1) in disputes between States;
>
> (2) in disputes between States and private and public bodies or private individuals in cases in which States have con-sented, in advance or by special agreement, to appear as defendants before the Court.

It is not improbable that some States would make use of that innovation, in the same way as they have availed themselves of the possibility of a simple and unqualified signature, subject to reciprocity, of the Optional Clause.[22] A significant departure in the substantive and procedural law would thus take place with-out affecting any vital interest of States. A change of that character would be in keeping with the pronouncement of the International Court of Justice in the Advisory Opinion given in 1949 in which it laid down that the United Nations is entitled to bring an international claim against a State with the view to obtaining reparation for damage caused to the United Nations or its agent in the event of an injury suffered by him in the performance of his duties.[23] For the practical effect of that pronouncement must be severely impaired by the circumstance that the United Nations cannot, according to the present wording of the Statute, be a direct party to disputes before the Court.

In the meantime, Article 34 of the Statute of the Court must, in its present formulation, be regarded as out of keeping with the

---

[22] See, for the texts of the declarations made in 1946 by China, Norway and Denmark, *American Journal of International Law*, 41 (1947), p. 13.

[23] See above, p. 22.

needs and tendencies of international law. The discussions in the Committee of Jurists who drafted the Statute of the Court in 1920 showed how strongly the adoption of Article 34 was influenced by the dogma that States only can be subjects of international law.[24] The developments of the three decades which followed might have suggested a reconsideration of that article when the Statute was revised in 1945. As it is, its adaptation to a more modern conception of international law and of international society must be kept in the forefront of any future attempts to amend the Statute of the Court. There is no justification for its retention in the present wording.[25] The question of the access of individuals to international tribunals—including the International Court of Justice—is no longer a matter to be determined by reference to an abstract, dogmatic and—upon analysis —inaccurate rule such as that individuals are not subjects of the law of nations and that it would be contrary to the very structure of international law to confer upon them a procedural capacity

---

[24] See below, p. 67, n. 13.

[25] The exercise of jurisdiction in disputes between States and private persons and bodies other than States would not be inconsistent with the limitation of the Court's function to the administration of international law in accordance with Article 38 of its Statute. For it is not suggested that the Court should adjudicate on all disputes between a State and private individuals or corporations. The suggestion is rather that the extended jurisdiction of the Court should embrace, in the first instance, such claims by private persons and organisations as constitute an element in the international obligations of the State. This applies, in particular, to claims arising out of the interpretation of treaties involving private rights and to allegations of denial of justice constituting a violation of international law. Expressed in different terms, the proposed change would mean that private individuals and organisations should be able to appear before the Court in all cases in which, under the existing law, they can invoke an international remedy only when their State takes up their case. Under existing law the Court is not precluded from deciding the merits of a private claim against a foreign State when that claim has become the subject of an international controversy as the result of being sponsored by a State. The private law element—whether tortious or contractual—is incidental to the wider international law aspect of the case. Thus a claim brought by an individual against a State for an alleged violation of the obligations of an International Bill of Rights to which that State is a party would be a claim in respect of an alleged violation of an international obligation, *i.e.*, of international law; the same applies to a claim in respect of denial of justice as understood by international law. For a lucid survey of the wide range of cases in which the Permanent Court of International Justice had to decide questions of municipal law incidental to the questions brought before it see Jenks in *British Year Book of International Law*, 19 (1938), pp. 67-103. Neither is there any good reason for excluding permanently from the jurisdiction of the International Court the wide range of relationships between the various public international organisations (including the United Nations) and their personnel. These relationships, while of a contractual character, are not as a rule governed by the private law of any particular country. The question whether they are relations of international law is one of terminology. See above, p. 34, n. 20.

in that sphere.   The matter is one of convenience, of the necessities of international peace and justice, and of the development
of international institutions as determined by agreement of
States.[26]

Any developments on the lines suggested may constitute a
stage in a change even more far-reaching.   That would consist
in conceding a right of appeal before the highest international
authority to all persons within the jurisdiction of the State
against any violations of their rights under international law—
including their rights recognised in and guaranteed by an effective
international bill of human rights.   The recognition by the international society of fundamental human rights and freedoms is
already, in essence, part of the existing law as expressed in the
Charter of the United Nations.   It is as yet an imperfect law
deliberately shorn of means of enforcement at the instance of the
individual.   But the Charter is only the first step in the inaugura-
tion of a new period in the mutual relations of the State, the
individual and the international society.   An international bill of
the rights of man may go a step further in translating the
provisions of the Charter into a more directly effective rule of
international law.[27]

[26] See above, p. 17, on the participation of private international organisations
in the proceedings connected with the advisory jurisdiction of the Court.
[27] See below, pp. 378-388.

CHAPTER 4

THE SUBJECTS OF THE LAW OF NATIONS, THE FUNCTION OF INTERNATIONAL LAW, AND THE RIGHTS OF MAN

1. The Subjects of International Law and its Development

THE results of the three preceding Chapters permit us to summarise the position with regard to the status of the individual as a subject of international law, *i.e.*, as a subject both of rights granted and of duties imposed by international law. There is no rule of international law which precludes individuals—and, generally, bodies other than States—from acquiring directly rights under customary or conventional international law and, to that extent, becoming subjects of the law of nations. The question is largely one of ascertaining what is the intention of States—and, generally, the practice of States—in each particular case. The conferment of such rights may cover either particular rights or the so-called fundamental rights of the individual in general. With regard to the latter there is room for the view that having regard to the inherent purposes of international law, of which the individual is the ultimate unit, he is in that capacity a subject of international law. Apart from the controversial doctrine of humanitarian intervention, international practice did not, until recently, accept the implications of that view. There has now taken place a decisive change also in this respect. The Charter of the United Nations, in recognising the fundamental human rights and freedoms, has to that extent constituted individuals subjects of the law of nations. The significance of that change is not impaired by the fact that it is not accompanied by the concession of independent procedural capacity. The absence of such capacity reduces the status of the individual as a subject of international law; it does not negative it. International law as a whole provides a persuasive illustration of the fact that the conception of law is not a rigid notion admitting of no gradation. The same applies to the conception of subjects of international law. Finally, the express enactment of crimes against humanity must be regarded as an indirect recognition of fundamental rights of human personality independent of the law of the State and enforceable by international law.

Similar considerations apply to the question of subjects of duties imposed by international law. In that sphere also no emphatic support for the traditional doctrine can be found in the practice of States, both international and municipal. The provisions of recent treaties—in particular in connexion with war crimes—are to a large extent declaratory of previous practice. While in the sphere of tortious responsibility the liability of the individual must continue to be predominantly subsidiary, his primary responsibility for crimes against international law is becoming increasingly recognised.

What have been the reasons which have prompted the changes in the matter of subjects of international law, with regard both to international rights and to international duties? These causes have been numerous and manifold. They have included, with reference to the recognition of the individual as a subject of international rights, the acknowledgment of the worth of human personality as the ultimate unit of all law; the realisation of the dangers besetting international peace as the result of the denial of fundamental human rights; and the increased attention paid to those already substantial developments in international law in which, notwithstanding the traditional dogma, the individual is in fact treated as a subject of international rights. Similarly, in the sphere of international duties there has been an enhanced realisation of the fact that the direct subjection of the individual to the rule of international law is an essential condition of the strengthening of the ethical basis of international law and of its effectiveness in a period of history in which the destructive potentialities of science and the power of the machinery of the State threaten the very existence of civilised life.

Above all, with regard to both international rights and international duties the decisive factor has been the change in the character and the function of modern international law. The international law of the past was to a large extent of a formal character. It was concerned mainly with the delimitation of the jurisdiction of States. Substantial portions of it were devoted to immunities of States, their diplomatic representatives, and their property. In so far as it was concerned with substantive law, it was mainly concerned with the law of war. There is not much difference in this respect between the treatises of the early publicists and those of modern writers. In traditional international law the individual played an inconspicuous part because the international interests of the individual and his contacts across the frontier were rudimentary. This is no longer the case. The interdependence of States which requires regulation is the interdependence of the individuals who compose them. An international law which disregards that fact is bound to be artificial. There is a growing tendency to take that fact into account. Of this the tripartite character of the constitution of the International Labour Organisation provides an instructive example. The provisions of the Charter of the United Nations empowering the Economic and Social Council to make arrangements for consultation with non-governmental organisations which are concerned with matters within its competence have already been noted.[1] The Committee of the Council which framed the rules governing the attribution of consultative status was careful to emphasise that the non-governmental organisations thus admitted should not be given the same rights as States which are not members of the United Nations or as governmental specialised agencies, but the innovation is significant.[2] At the same time the Constitutions of a number of governmental specialised agencies[3] made provision for consultation with and advice by private organisations. Of these arrangements those made by the International Civil Aviation Organisation[4] are particularly instructive.

[1] See pp. 23-26.

[2] Given the disposition to descend from the purely governmental plane, there are possibilities, even within the existing Charter, for the closer association of non-governmental agencies with the work of the Economic and Social Council. Thus it has been suggested that a selected number of non-governmental agencies should be given the right to have their communications distributed directly to the members of the Council without waiting for a request from them, that there should be a standing committee of the Council for consultation with such organisations accessible to them throughout the session of the Council, and that consultants should be called in at the recommendation of the Standing Committee whenever required. See *Journal of the Economic and Social Council,* First Year, No. 27, 15 June, 1946 (proposals of Mr. Winant), pp. 414-418. And see *Resolutions adopted at the Fourth Session* (February-March, 1947), pp. 46-50.

[3] See above, p. 26.

[4] Art. 79 of the Chicago Convention of 1945 provides: ' A State may participate in joint operating organisations or in pooling arrangements, either through its government or through an airline company or companies designated by the government. The companies may, at the sole discretion of the State concerned, be state-owned or partly state-owned or privately

In a different sphere, international co-operation has provided interesting instances of the relinquishment of the idea that only sovereign States may constitute the membership of international governmental organisations. Thus the authors of the Constitution of the World Health Organisation provided for associate membership of the Organisation on the part of territories or groups of territories, such as protectorates, colonies, and trust territories, which are not responsible for the conduct of their international relations.[5] The Charter of the International Trade Organisation, accepted in 1947, lays down that, in addition to the membership of fully sovereign States, full voting rights and the consequent status of a member of the Organisation may be accorded to separate customs territories invited by the United Nations Conference on Trade and Employment or proposed by the Member having responsibility for the conduct of its diplomatic relations.[6] The Convention of the Universal Postal Union signed at Paris on 5 July, 1947, provides for the membership as ' countries of the Union ' or ' administrations of the Union ' on

owned.' It has been the practice to invite unofficial organisations to send representatives to the regional Air Navigation meetings organised by the Provisional International Civil Aviation Organisation. Thus the South American meeting held at Lima in June, 1947, was attended by representatives of the States concerned and of the *Fédération aéronautique internationale* (F.A.I.), the International Air Transport Association (I.A.T.A.), and (as an observer) the Pan-American Institute of Geography and History. The South Atlantic regional meeting, held in July, 1947, included representatives of the I.A.T.A., the F.A.I., and the International Meteorological Organisation (I.M.O.). The Meteorological Division of the I.C.A.O. includes representatives of the I.A.T.A. and the I.M.O. See *Monthly Bulletin* of the I.C.A.O. (Section on Relations with other Organisations). On 11 October, 1947, the Conference of Directors of the International Meteorological Organisation—the Directors being plenipotentiaries of the various Governments—adopted a Convention for the constitution of a World Meteorological Organisation as one of the specialised agencies of the United Nations. After prolonged discussion the Conference decided in favour of separate membership of territories not in possession of sovereignty under international law. The Conference refused to accede to the view that only sovereign States could become parties to an international convention and members of an international organisation set up by it. It was decided, subject to certain conditions, to include as members of the Organisation enumerated territories or groups of territories whose mother countries were represented at the Conference and territories not specifically enumerated but maintaining meteorological services on behalf of which the Convention is applied by the State having responsibility for their international relations and approved by two-thirds of the members. The voting power of the territories thus admitted to membership was made subject to restrictions in regard to certain matters. See Cates in *Bulletin of the State Department,* 18 (1948), pp. 43-46.

[5] Art. 8. Application for such membership must be made by the member of the Organisation or other authority entrusted with the conduct of international relations.

[6] Art. 5 (3) and (4). Provision is made for the extension of rights and obligations of membership to Trust Territories and to the Free Territory of Trieste.

the part of specifically enumerated postal territories the status
of which is that of a colony or protectorate.[7] This, in fact, had
been the practice of the Universal Postal Union and the International Telecommunications Union for some time. In all these
international agencies the non-sovereign units are for most
practical purposes contracting parties and full members of the
organisation. The sovereign State is thus no longer the exclusive
person of organised international intercourse based on treaty.[8]
Administrative convenience and economic efficiency rather than
the priniciple of ' sovereign equality ' provide the test of membership. The preamble to the Charter of the United Nations opens
with the words ' We the peoples ' of the United Nations—a
significant form of words which, after some discussion, received
general approval at San Francisco ' although no other treaty
among nations had thus thought to speak for the peoples of the
world instead of merely for their governments '.[9] These developments are only indirectly germane to the question of the position
of individuals as subjects of international law, but they show, in
conjunction with the other changes outlined above, how
antiquated is the conception of international law confined to
sovereign States and their purely governmental agencies.[10] How

---

[7] Arts. 3 and 8.

[8] See the illuminating observations of Fawcett in *British Year Book of
International Law*, 24 (1947), pp. 379-381, in a note on the International
Trade Organisation, and Jessup in *American Journal of International Law*,
41 (1947), pp. 380-385. And see Scelle, *Manuel élémentaire du droit international* (1943), p. 411, who points out that ' l'obligation des gouvernements
de laisser leurs ressortissants participer au commerce international con-
stitue une des normes essentielles du droit des gens '.

[9] The Charter of the United Nations. Report of the Secretary of State to the
President of the United States, *Hearings before the Senate Committee on
Foreign Relations*, p. 51. However, it will be noted that the concluding
paragraph of the preamble refers to Governments as agreeing to the Charter.

[10] How out of date, in comparison with the recent developments and trends
of international law, appear, for instance, the dogmatic statements made
in 1904 by Anzilotti, an international lawyer of distinction, that ' it is inconceivable that there should exist subjects of international rights and duties
other than States ' (*Il diritto internazionale nei giudizi interni* (1905), p. 44),
and again in 1912 that ' it follows from the very notion of international law as
the body of rules established by the collective will of States for the regulation of their mutual relations that the subjects of that law are States and
States only (*Corso di diritto internazionale*, vol. I (1912), p. 69). But in
1929 the same author warns the student against the mistake of affirming that
States only can be subjects of international law. He suggests that, instead,
we ought to direct our attention to showing that in fact only States are
subjects of international law (*ibid.*, revised edition, translated by Gidel
(1929), p. 123). No such proof is possible consistently with the facts. But the
learned author still believes it possible to adhere to the traditional view
by suggesting that when we say that States only are subjects of international
law we refer to ' States ' not as understood in other disciplines and in

obsolete, in comparison with that almost torrential stream of changes, appear the arguments—such as those based on the status of the International Danube Commission or the provisions of the (unratified) Convention on the International Prize Court— adduced at the beginning of the twentieth century as a challenge to the doctrine that only States are subjects of international law.

It is probable that in order to comprehend fully the meaning and the potentialities of these changes it may be necessary not only to revise the traditional conception of the subjects of international law. We may have to become more conscious than we are now of the justification and the practical beneficence of proceeding on the basis of a conception of international law as being the law not of the society of States [11] but of international society in all the diversity of its manifestations requiring and admitting of legal regulation by rules other than the municipal law of States.

The issue has the appearance of a purely theoretical question, and impatience is occasionally expressed at what is believed to be the disproportionate amount of argumentative effort expended upon it.[12] The appearance is deceptive. Witness, for example,

municipal public law, but to organisms which are States in the contemplation of international law—the fact that they are States in this sense being proved by the circumstance that international law treats them as subjects of rights and duties (*ibid.*, p. 125). This reasoning amounts, it is believed, to an abandonment of the original position. With regard to individuals as subjects of fundamental rights recognised by international law Anzilotti still maintains the traditional doctrine on the ground that there does not exist a juridical system of humanity as such and that there are no fundamental rights of the individual generally recognised (*ibid.*, pp. 122-123). That view, too, must be regarded as antiquated. Note, for instance, the enactment of crimes against humanity (see above, p. 35), the recognition of fundamental human rights and freedoms in the Charter of the United Nations, and the proposed definition of human rights in an International Bill of the Rights of Man.

[11] A definition given by Westlake, *International Law*, vol. I (2nd ed., 1910), p. 1.

[12] See, *e.g.*, Briggs, *The Progressive Development of International Law* (lectures delivered at the Faculty of Law of Istanbul University in 1947), p. 29, who points out that the question whether the individual is a subject or an object of international law is immaterial so long as he actually receives the benefits stipulated on his behalf by international law. The answer is that the traditional doctrine, by emphasising the procedural limitations and otherwise, has often served as a factor impeding the full utilisation of the benefits thus conferred upon the individual. It has also frequently obstructed the development of international law in that direction. Another recent Italian writer—Ziccardi, *La costituzione dell'ordinamento internazionale* (1943), p. 364—maintains that no isolated developments constituting the individual a subject of international rights and duties justify the abandonment of the traditional doctrine. This can be done, he says, only following upon ' una congrua modificazione di tutta la struttura organizzativa dell' ordinamento '.

the rigid and decisive reliance on the doctrine of the exclusiveness of States as subjects of international law in the discussions preceding the present formulation of Article 34 of the Statute of the International Court of Justice; [13] in the determination of the question of the legal personality of international governmental agencies, including the United Nations itself; [14] in the approach to the problem of the legal personality of private international organisations; [15] in the restrictive interpretation of the procedural remedies for the implementation of the fundamental human rights and freedoms under the Charter of the United Nations; [16] in the denial of individual responsibility for criminal violations of international law; [17] and in matters of limited compass such as the nature of the contractual relation between public international organisations and their officials. [18] The other direct practical implications of the problem have already been indicated. [19] In all these the repetitive statements to the effect that ' individuals are only objects but not subjects of international law ' and that ' sovereign States only are subjects of international law ', have played a part.

2. THE SUBJECTS OF INTERNATIONAL LAW AND THE DOCTRINE OF SOVEREIGNTY

For it is in relation to State sovereignty that the question of subjects of international law has assumed a special significance. Critics of the traditional theory have treated it as an emanation

[13] See, for instance, the observations of M. Ricci Busatti and M. Fernandez adducing the orthodox doctrine in support of the opposition to conferring upon individuals the faculty of appearing as parties before the Court (*Procès-Verbaux of the Committee of Jurists,* pp. 208 and 311 respectively). See also Hudson, *The Permanent Court of International Justice, 1920-1942* (1943). pp. 186, 187. When the High Court of Australia decided, in 1945, to apply a statute which compelled aliens to serve in Australia's armed forces and which, in the view of the Court, was indisputably contrary to international law, one of the reasons adduced by the Court for its decision was that ' international law or the law of nations is a law for the intercourse of States with one another and not a law for individuals ' (*per* Starke, J., in *Polites* v. *The Commonwealth of Australia,* [1945] 70 C.L.R. 60; *Annual Digest and Reports of Public International Law Cases,* 1943-1945, Case No. 61, at p. 215).
[14] See above, p. 15.
[15] See on this subject the illuminating report by Politis to the Institute of International Law: *Annuaire,* 30 (1923), pp. 120-156.
[16] See below, pp. 234-250.
[17] See above, pp. 39, 43.
[18] See above, p. 34, n. 20.
[19] See above, pp. 46, 47.

of the doctrine of sovereignty. In their view it is State sovereignty —absolute, petty, and overbearing—which rejects, as incompatible with the dignity of States, the idea of individuals as units of that international order which they have monopolised and thwarted in its growth. It is the sovereign State, with its claim to exclusive allegiance and its pretensions to exclusive usefulness, that interposes itself as an impenetrable barrier between the individual and the greater society of all humanity. This charge, which cannot be regarded as altogether unfounded, explains much of the acerbity of the criticism. For human dignity and considerations of utility alike rebel against the idea of the State as the sole guardian of the interests of man. The purpose of the State is to safeguard the interests of the individual human being and to render possible the fulfilment, through freedom, of his wider duty to man and society. Some of these interests can be effectively safeguarded by the State in the international sphere. But it is inadmissible that the State should claim, in the conditions of the modern world, that it is the best instrument for protecting all these interests and that it is entitled to exclude from this legal sphere individuals and non-governmental bodies which may be created for that purpose. As within the State, so also in the international sphere the paramount danger arises when, in the words of John Stuart Mill in an eloquent concluding passage of his essay on Liberty, the State ' instead of calling forth the activity and the powers of individuals and bodies, . . . substitutes its own activities for theirs '. The administrative convenience resulting from the exclusive competence of the organs of the State in the international arena—in matters calling for and rendering possible the participation of private interests organised on an international basis—may be bought at the high price of stifling the individual allegiance to the international order and of sealing the fountainsprings of that private co-operative effort which is most likely to give effective expression to the interdependence of the modern world. As within the State, so also in the international sphere the dwarfing of the stature of man cannot be attempted with impunity.

It would seem, therefore, that the claim of States to the exclusive representation and management of internationally relevant interests—a claim which is an accompaniment of the current pretensions of sovereignty—lacks justification and is a lègitimate cause of resentment. But there is an even deeper connexion between the two doctrines: as shown in a widely accepted view of recognition as being in the gift of existing States, State sovereignty, the incarnation of the supreme will of the State as the exclusive source of the law, must disdain the idea of persons owing their quality as subjects of the law to a source independent of the will of States.[20] That source is the fact that, in relation to both rights and duties, the individual is the final subject of all law. To that extent the practice of States, in so far as it expressly confers rights and imposes duties upon the individual, must— important as it is in showing the artificiality and inaccuracy of the established doctrine in the matter—be regarded as essentially declaratory. This view, too, is incompatible with the notion of sovereignty as ordinarily conceived. It does not follow that it is a view which is not beneficent in practice and which is not in accordance with the true purpose of international law.

3. The Rights of Man, the Subjects of International Law, and the Future of the Law of Nations

While statements such as that individuals are only objects and not subjects of international law have been shown here to be devoid of substance, they reveal clearly the intimate connexion between the question of the subjects of international law and the notion of ' human rights and fundamental freedoms '. That notion, which has now become part of positive law and the practical application of which is the main concern of this book, demonstrates the central place which the question of the subjects of the law occupies in the system of the law of nations. The claim of the State to unqualified exclusiveness in the field of international relations was tolerable at a time when the actuality and the interdependence of the interests of the individual cutting across national frontiers were less obvious than they are today. It is this latter fact which explains why the constant expansion of the

---

[20] ' C'est le développement de la notion de la souveraineté absolue et incontrôlable qui a conduit la doctrine à ne voir dans les rapports internationaux que les Etats. Soumis à leur omnipotence, les individus en furent totalement éclipsés ': Politis, *Les nouvelles tendances du droit international* (1927), p. 58. And see the same, *La morale internationale* (1943), p. 84, where reference is made to the adherents of the rigid positivist doctrine, in this respect, as having ' atrophié et finalement faussé le droit international, en ne voyant plus en lui que le droit des Etats, alors que l'Etat n'est au fond qu'une fiction: la seule réalité qui compte est l'homme '.

periphery of individual rights—an enduring feature of legal
development—cannot stop short of the limits of the State. What
is much more important, the recognition of the individual, by
dint of the acknowledgment of his fundamental rights and freedoms, as the ultimate subject of international law, is a challenge
to the doctrine which in reserving that quality exclusively to the
State tends to a personification of the State as a being distinct
from the individuals who compose it, with all that such personification implies. That recognition brings to mind the fact that,
in the international as in the municipal sphere, the collective good
is conditioned by the good of the individual human beings who
comprise the collectivity. It denies, by cogent implication, that
the corporate entity of the State is of a higher order than its component parts. It challenges the absolute moral superiority of
groups, and in particular of the collective agency of the State
which when thus artificially personified is prone to and certainly
capable of disregard of all moral restraints.

In so far as the denial of the fundamental rights of man has
been associated with the nation-State asserting the claim to
ultimate reality and utterly subordinating the individual to a
mystic and absolute personality of its own, the recognition of these
rights is a brake upon exclusive and aggressive nationalism which
is the obstacle, both conscious and involuntary, to the idea of a
world community under the rule of law. Expressed in positive
terms, such recognition, inasmuch as it amounts to a tangible
international guarantee of the rights of man, is destined to become
a powerful source, based on mutuality of interest, of international
allegiance. An international legal system which aims at effectively safeguarding human freedom in all its aspects is no longer
an abstraction. It is as real as man's interest in the guarantee and
the preservation of his inalienable rights as a rational and moral
being. International law, which has excelled in punctilious insistence on the respect owed by one sovereign State to another,
henceforth acknowledges the sovereignty of man. For fundamental human rights are rights superior to the law of the
sovereign State. The hope, expressed by Emerson, that ' man
shall treat with man as a sovereign state with a sovereign state '[21]
may be brought nearer to fruition by sovereign States recognising
the duty to treat man with the respect which traditional law

[21] *Nature. Addresses and Lectures* (1883), p. 112.

exacted from them in relation to other States.[22] To that vital extent the recognition of inalienable human rights and the recognition of the individual as a subject of international law are synonymous. To that vital extent they both signify the recognition of a higher, fundamental law not only on the part of States but also, through international law, on the part of the organised international community itself. That fundamental law, as expressed in the acknowledgment of the ultimate reality and the independent status of the individual, constitutes both the moral limit and the justification of the international legal order. Through them, it implies the promise that the organised international society will not, in turn, degenerate into a tyrannical accumulation of power.[23] It is that danger which has been for

[22] On that plane the orthodox doctrine of equality of States, composed as they are of human beings, assumes a new and significant meaning. The fundamental rights of States are not ascertained by counting and adding the heads of the individuals who compose them. Each of these individuals is a moral finality in himself. As such they are entitled, irrespective of the size and importance of the political unit in which they are grouped, to equal respect. The happiness and well-being of one human soul are of the same absolute value when conceived in relation to an isolated individual as when weighed against the happiness and well-being of millions, including the millions organised in the body corporate of the State. The meaning here attached to the absolute value of the individual may be gauged by a juxtaposition of the views expressed by two philosophers of distinction. The first is expressed in the following passage of William James's *The Will to Believe* (1897): ' If the hypothesis were offered us of a world in which Messrs. Fournier's and Bellamy's and Morris's utopias should all be outdone, and millions kept permanently happy on the simple condition that a certain lost soul on the far-off edge of things should lead a life of lonely torture, what except a specified and independent sort of emotion can it be which would make us immediately feel, even though an impulse arose within us to clutch at the happiness so offered, how hideous a thing would be its enjoyment when deliberately accepted as the fruit of such a bargain? ' (at p. 188). Earl Russell, writing in 1946, says: ' If the theology of former times was entirely correct, it was worth while burning a number of people at the stake in order that the survivors might go to heaven, but if it was doubtful whether heretics would go to hell, the argument for persecution was not valid. . . . If it were certain that without Jews the world would be a paradise, there could be no valid objection to Auschwitz; but if it is much more probable that the world resulting from such methods would be a hell, we can allow free play to our natural humanitarian revulsion against cruelty' (*Philosophy and Politics*, A Lecture, p. 25). The answer to this philosophical view is that for the fanatic perpetrating such cruelties both the full justification of his motives and the intended results of his action are a certainty. The condemnation of such action cannot be based on a utilitarian weighing of probabilities. It can only be based on the irrefutable argument of the absolute sanctity of human personality. Coulton, *Inquisition and Liberty* (1938), p. 316, quotes a Jesuit priest as stating in 1853 that the inquisition was ' a sublime spectacle of social perfection '.

[23] For a fervent exposition of some relevant aspects of international organisation see Schindler, ' Gedanken zum Wiederaufbau des Völkerrechts ', in *Festschrift für Max Huber* (1944), pp. 99-150. See also on the close connexion between the effective recognition of human rights and a sound and improved international order the Report presented in 1947 by Judge Charles De

many the reason of the determined opposition to the idea of an organised commonwealth of nations embracing all humanity. In that perspective the acknowledgment of human rights and fundamental freedoms on the part of the Members of the United Nations assumes an added significance of its own. The consequent recognition of the individual human being as a subject of international law lends to the law obtaining between sovereign States the beneficent complexion of a law of nations conceived as the universal law of mankind.

Visscher to the Institute of International Law: *Annuaire,* 1947, pp. 4-8. The Declaration on the ' Fundamental Rights of Man as the Basis of Restoration of International Law' adopted in that year by the Institute gives expression to the same line of thought. Articles I and III of the Declaration may properly be quoted in this connexion:
' I.   La reconnaissance et le respect des droits inhérents à la personne humaine, que doit servir et non asservir l'Etat, sont intimement liés au progrès du Droit des Gens.'
' III.   Un ordre juridique efficace entre Etats est inséparable du respect de la personne humaine dans l'ordre interne de chaque Etat.
' Dans l'ordre international, la conception fonctionnelle et modératrice du Pouvoir reste obscurcie par l'emprise d'une tradition qui voit dans l'Etat souverain, organisme de sécurité et instrument de puissance, la forme la plus haute de l'ordre juridique ' (*ibid.,* p. 259).

*THE LAW OF NATURE AND THE RIGHTS
OF MAN*

CHAPTER 5

THE IDEA OF NATURAL RIGHTS IN LEGAL
AND POLITICAL THOUGHT

1. INTRODUCTORY: THE DOCTRINE OF NATURAL RIGHTS

THE object of the present Section of this book is to examine
the main foundations, legal and other, of the international
recognition and protection of fundamental human rights and
freedoms. Its purpose is to enquire into the relation between, on
the one hand, the conceptions of the law of nature and the natural
rights of man, and, on the other hand, the effective acknowledgment of these rights by international law in general and an
International Bill of Human Rights in particular. The practical
—and doctrinal—value and justification of such an investigation
are, on the face of it, open to question. For the international
recognition and protection of the rights of man is, in strict
juridical logic, independent of any doctrine of natural law and
natural rights. In fact, it is arguable that the main reason for
such international protection and for an International Bill of the
Rights of Man is the realisation of the inadequacy of the notion
of natural rights as a means for protecting effectively the rights of
man. The need, it would appear, is not for a controversial theory,
but for specific legal obligations and remedies. One, though by
no means complete, explanation of the scorn and vitupera-
tion which Bentham and others poured upon the Declaration
of 1789 was the belief that it might prove an instrument in the
hands of those anxious to find in a high-sounding phrase an easy
and nominal substitute for positive measures of remedial legislation. Accordingly, it would seem that the protagonists of the

international recognition of human rights and of an International Bill of the Rights of Man would do well to steer clear of the elusive and double-edged conceptions of the law of nature and natural rights.

To adopt that course would, it is believed, amount to misjudging alike historical experience and the essential requisites of a durable and effective protection of human rights. The law of nature and natural rights can never be a true substitute for the positive enactments of the law of the society of States. When so treated they are inefficacious, deceptive and, in the long run, a brake upon progress. However, while they are bound to be mischievous when conceived as an alternative to changes in the law, they are of abiding potency and beneficence as the foundation of its ultimate validity and as a standard of its approximation to justice. Inasmuch as, upon final analysis, they are an expression of moral claims, they are a powerful lever of legal reform. The moral claims of today are often the legal rights of tomorrow. The law of nature, even when conceived as an expression of mere ethical postulates, is an inarticulate but powerful element in the interpretation of existing law. Even after human rights and freedoms have become part of the positive fundamental law of mankind, the ideas of natural law and natural rights which underlie them will constitute that higher law which must forever remain the ultimate standard of fitness of all positive law, whether national or international.[1] For these reasons to discard, in this context, the idea of the law of nature is to deprive ourselves of that inspiration which lies in the continuity of legal and political thought on the subject and without which we cannot hope to overcome the difficulties which confront the international protection of human rights and, in particular, any effective scheme for an International Bill of the Rights of Man. Finally, to eliminate the ideas of natural law and natural rights from the consideration of the protection of the rights of man is to renounce the faculty of understanding their growth in the course of history

---

[1] Professor Huber, a former President of the Permanent Court of International Justice, says in an article entitled 'Wesen und Würde der Jurisprudenz': 'The very idea of law is weakened if it becomes detached from its ultimate transcendental relationships and if it is grounded solely in the positive legal order and thus, in the long run, in mere opportunism and power' (*Gesellschaft und Humanität. Gesammelte Aufsätze von Max Huber*, 1948, p. 38).

and their association with that law of nations which is now to become their physical sanction.

The Constitution of Virginia of 1776, the American Declaration of Independence, and the French Declaration of the Rights of Man and of the Citizen were the first constitutional instruments of modern times to proclaim that the natural rights of man must, as such, form part of the fundamental law of the State and that their protection was the reason of its existence. Since then, the theory of natural law, which had always been the main inspiration, if not the conscious instrument, of the doctrine of the rights of man, has suffered an eclipse in a century dominated by the historical and analytical trends of jurisprudence. The doctrine of the rights of man was itself assaulted from highly diverse quarters. It was attacked by those who were frightened by and hated the great revolutionary movements which proclaimed the rights of man. It was assailed, for similar reasons, by authoritarians who detected in the supposed materialism of the doctrine of natural rights a threat to religious and spiritual authority. Taine spoke of fundamental rights as being daggers pointed at human society. The doctrine of natural rights drew upon itself the condemnation, in terms of finality congenial to philosophers of the idealistic school of philosophy, in Germany and elsewhere, who saw in the State the highest end and the ultimate value.[2] It came in for castigation at the hands of those

---

[2] 'This question [the rights of individuals] is one which called for a discussion a century ago, but at the present time it can be considered a question no longer. The rights of the individual are, in short, today not worth serious criticism. . . . The welfare of the community is the end and is the ultimate standard. And over its members the right of the moral organism is absolute. Its duty and its right is to dispose of these members as seems to it best. Its right and duty is, in brief, to be a Providence to itself': Bradley, 'Some Remarks on Punishment', in *International Journal of Ethics,* April, 1894 (reprinted in *Collected Essays,* vol. I (1935), p. 158). William Wallace, the Hegelian, spoke of the State as the ultimate creator, guardian and guarantee of all rights in the world. Bosanquet wrote in a similar vein. There is in this matter an interesting similarity between the idealist schools in philosophy and in political science. With rare exceptions—notably that of T. H. Green— both are represented by the same writers. For the idealist philosopher the objective world is merely the experience thereof; the object perceived and the consciousness of it are identical. The former does not exist without the latter; things exist only because they are known. For the idealist writers in the sphere of political philosophy human rights—the ultimate substance of political association—exist only in so far as they are perceived and recognised by the State. The parallelism is well illustrated in the writings of Green. He says: 'rights are made by recognition. There is no right " but thinking makes it so " ' (*Lectures on the Principles of Political Obligation,* delivered in 1879, posthumous edition, p. 446). However, his considered view on the subject is well summarised in the sentence in which he admits

who, not without reason, discerned in the advocates of natural rights determined opponents of social progress in so far as it could be achieved by the regulative action of the State.[3] Herbert Spencer was not alone in invoking natural rights against what he called meddling legislation and against the right of the State to tax the citizen for social services.[4] In fact, there was repeated in the nineteenth century the perplexing spectacle, which had been witnessed before, of natural rights and natural law being invoked on behalf of both progress and reaction, on the side of both stability and change. But these vicissitudes of the theory of natural rights did not prevent the incorporation of what hitherto had been merely natural rights of man as part of the constitutions of practically all States of the world.[5]

There were tangible indications, expressed in a manner more eloquent than theoretical controversy, that the coming period was to be one of the triumphant assertion of the rights of man. But this was not to be. For the rights of man were given a foundation no more solid or secure than the revocable law of the sovereign State. They were denied the protection of that legal order which, by virtue of its universality and of its supremacy over the State, was alone capable of safeguarding them against the tyranny of absolutism and the arbitrariness of majority rule. The sovereign

the existence of ' rights which remain rights though any particular state or all states refuse to recognise them ' (p. 351). What is perhaps the most powerful criticism of the political implications of this aspect of the idealist philosophy will be found in Hobhouse, *The Metaphysical Theory of the State* (1918), Lecture V, and Perry, *The Present Conflict of Ideas* (1918), pp. 251-280. The political philosophy of totalitarian régimes was, not unnaturally, highly critical of the emphasis upon rights at the expense of duties. Writers who were tempted to see in these régimes more than a passing wave of retrogression were inclined to the same view. See Carr, *Conditions of Peace* (1942), p. 122. However, see Lindsay, *The Modern Democratic State,* vol. I (1943), pp. 88, 89, for a persuasive corrective of this view.

[3] See below, pp. 103-111.

[4] It is probable that the somewhat violent and ultra-individualistic character of Spencer's championship of natural rights considerably impaired its influence and was, in turn, responsible for the intemperate criticism of Spencer's views as leading to anarchy. He argued, in *Man versus the State,* that members of an incorporated body are bound to submit to the will of the majority in all matters concerning the fulfilment of the objects for which they are incorporated, but in no others; and that this applied to an incorporated nation as much as to an incorporated company (pp. 87 *et seq.*). ' Here then ', he said, ' we reach the ultimate verdict against meddling legislation. Reduced to its lowest terms, every proposal to interfere with citizens' activities further than by enforcing their mutual limitations, is a proposal to improve life by breaking through the fundamental conditions of life.' He says elsewhere: ' The great political superstition of the past was the divine right of kings. The great political superstition of the present is the divine right of parliaments ' (*ibid.*).

[5] See below, pp. 89, 90.

State, in an unprecedented ascendancy of power, became the insurmountable barrier between man and the law of mankind. The human being became, in the offensive but widely current terminology of the experts, a mere object of international law.[6] But even that was an overstatement of the existing position. In fact, the individual became only to an imperfect degree the object of protection by the law of nations. Treaties of a humanitarian character were concluded for protecting the individual in some specified spheres in relation to particular States. But the fundamental claims of human personality to equality, liberty and freedom against the arbitrary will of the State remained outside the orbit of international law save for the precarious and controversial principle of humanitarian intervention.

The results of this self-imposed limitation of the law of nations are well known. They are expressed, by most compelling implication, in one of the three solemnly proclaimed purposes of the first and second World Wars. These objects were not only the repelling of aggressive will for world domination and the building of an international system of security. The third major object of the First World War was—in the words of one who, like few statesmen of modern times, possessed the gift of expressing the enduring ends of humanity—'to make the world safe for democracy',[7] that is, we may say, to render it a secure habitation for the fundamental right of man to be governed by rulers chosen by and accountable to him. The third major object of the Second World War was essentially the same. It was given repeated expression not only by private individuals and organisations,[8] but

---

[6] See above, pp. 6-9.

[7] President Wilson referred to that phrase in insisting that its principle should be incorporated in the Covenant—as in fact it was in Article 1, paragraph 2 (see below, p. 78). He said: ' We have said that this war was carried on for a vindication of democracy. The statement did ,not create the impulse but it brought it to consciousness. So soon as it was stated that the war was being waged to make the world safe for democracy, a new spirit came into the world. People began to look at the substance rather than at the form. They knew that governments derived their just powers from consent of the governed. I should like to point out that nowhere else in the draft is there any recognition of the principle of democracy. If we are ready to fight for this, we should be ready to write it into the Covenant.' (See Hunter Miller, *The Drafting of the Covenant*, vol. I (1928), p. 165.)

[8] See, *e.g.*, the Declaration of the Rights of Man proposed by H. G. Wells in *The New World Order* (1940), pp. 139-143; Quincy Wright, *Human Rights and World Order*, Third Report of the Commission to Study the Organisation of Peace, February, 1943. At the same time the American Law Institute embarked upon the carefully planned task of preparing an international bill of human rights.

also in solemn pronouncements of the leaders of the United Nations such as the formulation of the 'four freedoms' by President Roosevelt in his Annual Message to Congress of 6 January, 1941,[9] or their (incomplete and, in a material sense, self-contradictory) reiteration in the Atlantic Charter of 14 August, 1941. The major purpose was, in the words of Mr. Churchill, to ensure that the war ended 'with the enthronement of human rights'.[10]

In the course of the First World War the call to make the world safe for democracy was more than a convenient slogan of war propaganda. It was the outcome of the realisation of two basic facts. The first was that the securing, on the part of international society, of inalienable human freedoms, through democracy, is an indispensable condition of the peace of the world. Long before that, Immanuel Kant expressed the same idea by postulating the republican form of government—one compatible with monarchy, but based on the essential safeguard of separation of powers—as one of the prerequisites of perpetual peace.[11] It was in that line of thought that the League of Nations was originally conceived as an association of democratic States.[12] The second fundamental factor which underlay the association of democracy with the idea of a world secure under the reign of law is that no legal order, international or other, is true to its essential function if it fails to protect effectively the ultimate unit

[9] *Peace and War. United States Foreign Policy, 1931-1941* (1943), p. 608. In his Special Message to Congress of 20 June, 1941, the President said: 'Our Government believes that freedom from cruelty and inhuman treatment is a natural right. It is not a grace to be given or withheld at will by those temporarily in a position to exert force over a defenceless people.'

[10] *The Times* newspaper, 30 October, 1942. It is of interest to note the use of the same form of phrase by Gladstone. He said: 'The greatest triumph of our time will be the enthronement of the idea of public right as the governing idea of European politics' (as quoted in *Speeches of the Earl of Oxford and Asquith* (1927), p. 218.

[11] See Friedrich, *The Inevitable Peace* (1948).

[12] This seems to have been the original interpretation, according to the makers of the Covenant, of Article 1, paragraph 2, which provided for the admission as new members of 'any fully self-governing State'. The French text expressed that intention more clearly: 'Tout Etat . . . qui se gouverne librement'. President Wilson's understanding of the term 'self-governing' appears clearly from his view expressed at the meetings of the Commission on the League of Nations. He said: '. . . No one would have looked at the German government before the war and said that the nation was self-governing. We know that, in point of fact, the Reichstag was controlled by the Chancellor, that it was an absolute monarchy': (Hunter Miller, *The Drafting of the Covenant*, vol. I (1928), p. 165). For an identical interpretation of the term see the views of Larnaude and Orlando, *op. cit.*, vol. II, p. 473.

of all law—the individual human being. The two decades which followed the First World War lent weight, with ominous emphasis, to these now self-evident propositions. They resulted, in the Second World War, in the widespread conviction that the effective international protection of fundamental human rights, including some form of an International Bill of the Rights of Man, was a major purpose of the war inasmuch as it is an essential condition of international peace and progress. Many believed that without such expansion of international law the fabric of international society would be built on precarious foundations.[13] Alongside that main stream of thought, the idea of a universal guarantee of the rights of man received the support of some European States bound by the obligations of the so-called Minorities Treaties. These States favoured a solution which by virtue of the generality of its application would remove from them what they conceived to be a stigma of inferiority and which would also do away with the danger of the minorities forming a State within a State and looking for protection to foreign Powers of the same race or language.[14]

Whatever may have been the sources from which originated the movement for the universal and effective protection of human rights on the part of international society, that movement became unavoidably associated with attempts to find for it some justification even more compelling than the experience of the immediate past.[15] For the question of the relation of the individual to the State—and his protection against the State—has been the perennial problem of law and politics. That problem has con-

---

[13] See above, p. 77, n. 8.

[14] For an emphatic expression of that view see the articles by President Benes in *Foreign Affairs*, 1941, and in the *Czechoslovak Year Book of International Law* (1942), pp. 1-6.

[15] It may perhaps be of interest to quote here the concluding passage of a public lecture delivered in 1943 in the University of Cambridge by the author of this book when expounding his draft of an international bill of the rights of man: ' The habitation of the rights of man within the exclusive precincts of the sovereign State has proved insecure. There are signs that, in the view of many, the time is ripe for an advance and that the rights of man ought to be anchored where they properly belong, to wit, in a universal law of organised mankind, in the law of nations. From generation to generation, in stirring times of crisis when the futility of suffering unredeemed by faith in progress threatens to stifle action and the moral fibre of peoples there springs forth the call summoning an advance in things of enduring import. That call may be drowned by the din of Armageddon and by the lassitude of its aftermath. With these discouraging possibilities we are not concerned here. But, within the precincts of this University, it is our legitimate business to enquire . . . what succour we may find in this matter in that majestic stream of the law of nature and in that law of nations whose abiding validity is now being vindicated on the field of battle.'

sisted in the reconciliation of two apparently conflicting factors. The first is that the State, however widely its object may be construed, has no justification and no valid claim to obedience except as an instrument for securing the welfare of the individual human being. The second is that the State—though not necessarily the existing sovereign State—has come to be recognised as the absolute condition of the civilised existence of man and of his progression towards the full realisation of his faculties. It is a matter of absorbing interest to note how, in the history of political and legal thought and action, the conflict between these two factors has been bridged by the notion, variously disguised, of the fundamental, natural, inherent or inalienable rights of man. These are the bounds which, it has been asserted, the Leviathan of the State must not transgress. That assertion has not been limited to those who, in Gierke's scathing comment, reduced the State to the level of an insurance society for securing the liberty and the property of the individual.[16] The idea of the inherent rights of man, ultimately superior to the State itself, is the continuous thread in the historical pattern of legal and political thought.

2. GREEK PHILOSOPHY AND THE GREEK STATE

While the ideas of the law of nature date back to antiquity, the notion and the doctrine of natural, inalienable rights of man pre-existent to and higher than the positive law of the State seem to be of more recent usage. Yet, as will be suggested here, the law of nature itself, unconsciously or by design, was often a cloak concealing the desire to vindicate the rights of man. However, quite apart from that fact, in order to judge the antiquity of the idea of the natural rights of man we must look to their substance rather than to their designation. Their substance has been the denial of the absoluteness of the State and of its unconditional claim to obedience; the assertion of the value and of the freedom of the individual as against the State; the view that the power of the State and of its rulers is derived ultimately from the assent

---

[16] Gierke, *Das deutsche Genossenschaftsrecht*, vol. IV (1913), *Die Staats-und Korporationslehre der Neuzeit*, p. 407—a paraphrase of Vico's reference to Spinoza. 'Spinoza', says Vico, 'speaks of the state as if it were a trading partnership' (as quoted by Carritt, *Morals and Politics* (1935), p. 46). **And** see above, p. 76, n. 4, for Spencer's comparison of the State with an incorporated company.

of those who compose the political community; and the insistence that there are limits to the power of the State to interfere with man's right to do what he conceives to be his duty.

These ideas are not of recent origin. They date back to Greek and Roman political philosophy. It has become almost a commonplace to maintain that any such notions were foreign to the Greek conception of the State, which, it is said, looked to expediency where we look to legitimacy, and which confounded politics and morals. We find a German writer[17] of authoritarian tendencies contrasting the conception of fundamental rights of man in the liberal bourgeois State with the austerity of the Greek City State: ' The antique State knew of no rights of freedom. A private sphere with an independent right against the political community seemed to it inconceivable. The idea of individual freedom independent of the political freedom of people and State was regarded as absurd, immoral, and unworthy of a free man. It is possible that some German writers in the nineteenth and twentieth centuries adapted their interpretation of Greek political philosophy to the urge to find an impressive precedent for their authoritarian conception of the State. That interpretation found acceptance on the part of some writers in England and the United States. Lord Acton's essay on ' Freedom in Antiquity '[18] or Ritchie's description of the Greek idea of the law of nature[19] are typical of this assessment of the position. But it is probable that that view, so widely held, needs revision.

It was no mere national complacency which made Herodotus point to the Greek *isonomia*,[20] equality before the law, as contrasted with arbitrary Persian rule, to Greek *isotimia*, conceived as equal respect for all, and to Greek *isogoria*,[21] conceived as equal freedom of speech. There may be a logical distinction between all these and the idea of inherent rights in the modern sense, but it is a distinction without substantial difference. The same applies to the references to equality of opportunity in

[17] Schmitt, *Verfassungslehre* (1928), p. 158.

[18] In *The History of Freedom and Other Essays* (edited by Figgis and Laurence, 1907), pp. 1-29.

[19] *Natural Rights* (1894), pp. 20-33. Professor Zimmern's account of the politics of fifth-century Athens gives, it is believed, a more adequate picture: *The Greek Commonwealth* (5th ed., 1931), pp. 125-197.

[20] See Herodotus, *History* (Cary's translation, 1882), Book III, p. 80.

[21] *Ibid.*, p. 53.

Pericles' funeral speech. Nor is it without importance that
the Greek *nomos* signified primarily not a legislative enactment
by the State but custom grown out of the consciousness and free
life of the community. The supremacy of custom is not consistent with the picture of an omnipotent State riding rough-shod
over the rights of the individual. There is an intimate connexion
between the Greek ideas of an orderly universe and of
political freedom under rational laws. The constitution of
the Greek State knew of some kind of distinction between
fundamental and ordinary laws inasmuch as an action was permitted against proposers of laws in derogation of the basic
constitution of the State. When, in the *Crito,* Socrates, awaiting
execution and refusing the help of friends who provided means for
his escape, gives reasons for his duty of obedience to the unjust
sentence of the State, he bases that obligation not on the absolute
claim of the State to obedience, but on an implicit contract—a
contract which, in turn, presupposes the duty of the State to allow
freedom of speech and the right to emigrate. Only so can we
explain what would otherwise be a disturbing contradiction: that
of the individualist philosopher who insisted on the right and duty
of the independence of human judgment and who died in
obedience to what he believed to be the wrong verdict of the
State. Although Plato distrusted democratic rule, in the *Prota-
goras* he made the Sophist pronounce a most striking defence of
democracy: while men differ in their aptitude for arts and professions, they have all been assigned a share of justice and fairness
which are necessary for the art of government. The anguished
defence which Sophocles put in the mouth of Antigone has often,
and justly, been quoted in this connexion: she may have transgressed Creon's decree, but she did not overstep the law of Zeus
nor the eternal precepts of justice. This, in essence, is the
assertion of the claim of the individual to be governed by a rule
of conduct superior to the arbitrary decrees of the earthly
authority. Neither, finally, is it irrelevant to point to the Stoic
philosophy in which the equality of man was extended beyond
the confines of the State and made the principal manifestation
of the universal dominion of reason and law, higher in authority
than the collective will of man acting through the laws of any
single State.[22] It was that immutable law, that inward voice of

[22] See below, p. 83.

God, in the eyes of whom all men are free and who knows of no distinction between rich and poor, or Greek and barbarians, before which all outward authority must, in the view of the Stoics, find its ultimate justification.

It is true that the precepts of philosophers were more advanced than the practice of the Greek State. But we are concerned here with the growth and influence of ideas. Moreover, that practice, though it did not protect the freedom of human personality against the intolerance of democratic majorities, gave to the individual that paramount share in the creation of the common will which made him identify himself with the State even when it contrived to compass his destruction. The martyrdom of Socrates was, in its tragic climax, a self-imposed ordinance. The tyranny of Athenian democracy was in some essential respects in the same category as the doctrine of the absolute supremacy of the legislature—which is the constitutional doctrine of many a modern State.

3. THE STOICS AND ROMAN THOUGHT

The Stoic philosophy was largely responsible for the continuation of the tradition of freedom and equality in Roman political and legal philosophy. We find it in the writings of Cicero, who left upon ancient and medieval thought a deep and beneficent impress out of all proportion to his originality as a thinker. He followed the Stoics closely in stressing the fundamental resemblance and equality of men given by the fact of their common possession of reason and of the capacity to develop and to attain virtue notwithstanding differences in learning and ability.[23] We see Seneca insisting that virtue can be attained both by the slave and by the free, and that slavery affects the body only while the mind is of necessity the slave's own and cannot be given into bondage.[24] We find the same line of thought in the work of many Roman jurists at the full height of absolutist imperial rule. We note Ulpian explaining the absolutist doctrine of *quod principi placuit, legis habet vigorem* by the qualifying statement that this is so only because the people had conferred legislative authority upon the ruler.[25] For he, like Cicero, thought that no man is free

[23] *De Legibus,* 1.10.12.
[24] *De Beneficiis,* iii, 19, 20, 28.
[25] *Digest,* I, 4.1.

unless he has a share in political authority. It was Ulpian who, in company with other Roman lawyers of the Empire, taught that whatever may be the position of the slave in civil law, this is not so by natural law, for by it all men are equal.[26] The exact meaning of these and similar passages has been disputed, but there ought to be no doubt that they served a purpose in affirming the ideas of the freedom and the equality of man. They explain the humanitarian decrees of the Emperors for the protection of slaves in a way amounting to a measure of incipient recognition of the personality, in the accepted sense, of the slave in Roman law.[27]

4.   THE MIDDLE AGES

There is a striking continuity of thought between the Stoics and the most representative political literature of the Middle Ages in the affirmation of the principle of the higher law—which is the law of nature—as the source of the rights of freedom and of government by consent. It was that feature of medieval political thought which led Gierke to assert, without undue exaggeration, that it was filled with the thought of the inborn and indestructible rights of the individual.[28]   St. Thomas Aquinas defined natural law as ' the participation in the eternal law of the mind of a rational creature '.[29]   He was reproducing the central idea of the Stoics, the idea of a law superior to the external authority of the State. The State, according to St. Thomas Aquinas, is subject to that higher law which determines the relation of the individual to the State.   The justification of the State is in its service to the individual; a king who is unfaithful to his duty forfeits his claim to obedience. It is not rebellion to depose him, for he is himself a rebel; all political authority is derived from the people, and laws must be made by the people or their representatives. Marsilius of Padua used almost identical language.   In fact, the view that the ruler is under the supremacy of the law is the principal feature of the political theory of the Middle Ages. By the end of the

[26] *Digest*, I, 17.3.2. See, *e.g.*, the decrees of Antoninus providing that an owner who kills his slave without just cause is accountable to the law, and that the master who treats his slave with cruelty may be compelled to sell him: Gaius. *Institutes*, I. 53. See also *ibid.*, I, 62, for the edict of Claudius to the effect that if a slave has been deserted by his master in grave illness, he should be set free.

[27] *De Legibus*, 1.10.12.

[28] *Op. cit.*, p. 81.

[29] *Summa*, 1a, 2ae, qu. 91, art 2.

Middle Ages the substance of what proved to be the doctrine of the natural rights of man was well established. They flowed from the conception of the law of nature realised as a higher law superior to the State. They included the right to government by consent, the right to freedom from taxation without representation, and the right to freedom from arbitrary physical constraint. The principle of the Habeas Corpus Acts latent in the 39th Clause of Magna Carta was acknowledged already in 1188 by Alfonso IX at the Cortes of Leon. The Golden Bull issued in 1222 by King Andrew II of Hungary is couched in language strikingly reminiscent of that used in Magna Carta.[30] So is the law of General Privileges granted in 1283 by Peter III of Aragon.[31] The struggle of the Parliament of Paris against arbitrary royal ordinances provided opportunities, fully used, for invoking the principles of the higher law.[32] Custom, and not the fiat of the State, was regarded as the typical manifestation of the law binding upon the individual. This was a doctrine propounded not only by leading continental jurists like Beaumanoir and Gratian. We find it in St. Germain's Dialogue *de Fundamentis Legum Angliæ*[33]; in Bracton's famous dictum that the king has two superiors, God and law[34]; in Hooker's affirmation that ' laws they are not which public affirmation hath not made so '[35]; and in the solemn language of Fortescue: ' For we have taught that all the decrees of the royal law, when they are in error, ought

---

[30] For the text see *Constitutional Provisions Governing Social and Economic Policy* (published by the International Labour Office, 1944), p. 77.

[31] See Hallam, *The State of Europe during the Middle Ages* (1828), II, p. 46.

[32] See McIlwain, *Constitutionalism and the Changing World* (1939), p. 278, who points in this connexion to the fallacy of the belief that judicial review is an American invention.

[33] IV. 8.

[34] And see Bracton's *De Legibus* (Woodbine's edn.), vol. II, pp. 29 and 30:

Quid sit libertas. Est autem libertas naturalis facultas eius, quod cuique facere libet, nisi quod iure aut vi prohibetur. Sed secundum hoc videtur quod servi sint liberi, nam et ipsi liberam habent facultatem nisi vi aut iure prohibeantur. . . . Et in hac parte ius civile vel gentium detrahit iuri naturali.

Quid sit servitus. Est quidem servitus constitutio iuris gentium qua quis dominio alieno contra naturam subicitur.

He wrote in the same work that the king ' ought not to be subject to men, but subject to God and to the law ' for ' the law makes the king '. It follows that the king must ' attribute to the law what the law attributes to him, namely, dominion and power, for there is no king where the will and not the law has dominion ' (as in Twiss's ed., 1854), f. 5b.

[35] *The Law of Ecclesiastical Polity* (Everyman's Library edn., 1925). For a lucid account of Hooker's contribution by reference to the idea of natural rights see Perry, *Puritanism and Democracy* (1944), pp. 160-165.

to be corrected by the rules of the law of nature. Thus we have also found that the rules of the political law, and the sanctions of customs and constitutions ought to be made null and void, so often as they depart from the institutes of nature's law, which we have . . . defined as the mother and mistress of all laws.' [36] We find the same doctrines, even more emphatically and in almost modern terminology, in the writings of Suarez,[37] who gave true expression to the sentiment of his time when he wrote: ' *Lex injusta non est lex.*'

5. THE REFORMATION AND THE SOCIAL CONTRACT

After the temporary wave of retrogression which in the sixteenth century was the twin and not unnatural result of the vogue of the teaching of Machiavelli and of the absolutism of the nascent national State, two factors combined to revive and strengthen the idea of the natural rights of man. The first was the direct outcome of the Reformation and of the religious struggle which followed it. Religious intolerance and persecution brought forth the insistence, with a fervour not inferior to the religious impulse itself, on the natural right of freedom of conscience and religious belief. Erasmus gave that movement an impetus which left an indelible impress on the European tradition of tolerance.[38] The Puritans and the Levellers in England inscribed it in the tenets of their political faith as the foremost inalienable right. Matters of religion were the first subject with regard to which the Revolutionary Army of 1648 set a definite limit to the sovereignty of Parliament: ' We do not empower our Representatives to continue in force, or make, any laws, oaths, covenants, whereby to compel by penalties or otherwise any person to anything in or about matters of faith, religion, or God's worship.' [39] Twelve years prior

[36] *De Natura Legis Angliæ*, I, ch. 29. And see Van Baumer, *The Early Tudor Theory of Kingship* (1940), p. 130, who points out that ' natural law may be regarded as the dominant idiom in terms of which the men of the early English Reformation cast their political ideas '.

[37] *De Legibus, ac Deo Legislatore* (1612): ' Human law cannot derogate from natural law, since if it did so, it would destroy its own foundations and consequently itself ', Book II, ch. XIV, 8. And see *ibid.*, ch. VI, 20-22 and ch. XV. 2, for a clear anticipation of the emancipation, finally effected by Grotius, of natural law from theology (see Lauterpacht in *British Year Book of International Law*, 23 (1946), p. 53, n. 1 (*in fine*)).

[38] See Lord Acton, *History of Freedom* (1907), p. 50, and *Lectures on Modern History* (1906), p. 154.

[39] From the Second Agreement of the People, 1648: *Puritanism and Liberty; being the Army Debates (1647-49) from the Clarke Manuscripts* (ed. by Woodhouse, 1938), p. 361.

to the Agreement of the People, the Puritan colonists who, under the inspiration of Roger Williams, founded Rhode Island, adopted in their compact a Declaration, truly revolutionary in character, which excluded matters of religion from the purview of the legislature.

The second factor that helped to keep alive and to instil fresh vigour into the idea of natural rights was the theory of the social contract, which took its rise in the Middle Ages and remained predominant up to the commencement of the eighteenth century. The very notion of the social contract implies, it will be noted, the existence of rights which the individual possesses before entering organised society. Most of the propounders of the doctrine of the social contract taught that there were insurmountable limits to the power of the State not only on account of the terms of the contract, but also for the simple reason that some rights, because of the nature of man, are inalienable. This, indeed, was not the invariable teaching of the school of the social contract. The appeal of the blessings of peace and the terrors of anarchy consequent upon resistance were such that some construed the social contract as an instrument of unconditional, total and irrevocable subjection. Even Grotius was not, subject to considerable exceptions,[40] far removed from that way of thinking. He argued that if according to Roman and Hebraic law a man could sell himself irrevocably as a slave, there was no reason why a people as a whole should not be able to do so.[41] The dialectical quibble by which Hobbes arrived at the same result, without any exceptions, is well known. The social contract was in his view a compact only between subject and subject, and not between the community and the ruler. The latter received all the power, but contracted no obligation. Yet this was not the typical application of the theory of the social contract.[42] This took place under the

---

[40] See below, p. 117.

[41] See below, p. 116.

[42] Hobbes' very concessions to freedom were pitfalls. Thus, for instance, he admitted that in fact the Government could not control religious belief: ' But what . . . if a King, or a Senate, or other Soveraign Person forbid us to beleeve in Christ. To this I answer, that such forbidding is of no effect; because Beleef, and Unbeleef never follow men's Commands. Faith is a gift of God, which Man can neither give, nor take away by promise of rewards, or menaces of torture' (*Leviathan*, Chapter XLII, 387). But he argues from this that since the Government cannot control religious faith it is of no importance that it can prescribe articles of belief and forms of public worship which all must accept outwardly.

influence of Locke, who excluded the inalienable rights from the scope of rights relinquished in the social contract. It was Locke's conception of the social contract which struck the deepest note in contemporary thought and which exercised a powerful influence on the early American Declarations of Rights and on the French Declarations of 1789 and 1791 in which, more emphatically than anywhere else, the principle was proclaimed that society is set up for the defence of certain inalienable rights.

The claim to religious toleration and the theory of the social contract were not the only sources of the renewed vitality of the notion of the natural rights of man. Witness Milton's appeal to the natural freedom of man as the basis of his claim to be ruled by law and not by the arbitrary whim of man; or the insistence, in the course of the Puritan revolution, on natural rights in support of political freedom, social equality and universal suffrage; or the place which Blackstone in his exposition of the laws of England assigned to the natural rights of man—an exposition which, at least in its influence, was not impaired by the seemingly unqualified acknowledgment of the supremacy of Parliament.

The Virginian Declaration of Rights of 1776; the similar constitutional enactments, in the same year, of Pennsylvania, Maryland, Delaware, New Jersey and North and South Carolina; the constitutions of New York and of New Georgia of 1777; and that of Massachusetts of 1780; the Declaration of Independence of 1776 and the Bill of Rights in the form of the first ten Amendments to the Constitution; the Declaration of the Rights of Man and of the Citizen adopted in 1789 by the French National Assembly and prefixed to the Constitution of 1791; and the Declarations prefixed to the French Constitutions of 1793 and 1795—all these mark the express acknowledgment of the inherent rights of man in the constitutional law of modern States. This was not, as is widely believed,[43] a case of a shift from natural law to natural rights. For that process, as has been pointed out, is coeval with political and philosophical thought dating back to antiquity and the Middle Ages. The notion of human nature as a source and standard of political rights is older than the end of the eighteenth century. What was new was the formal incorporation of these rights as part of the constitutional law of States and the possibility of their consequent protection not only against the

[43] See, *e.g.*, Dewey, *Freedom and Culture* (1940), p. 103.

tyranny of kings but also against the intolerance of democratic majorities.   What was new was the rejection by positive enactment—for the idea itself went back to the Middle Ages and to Bodin[44]—of the idea of the uncontrolled sovereignty of the sovereign people itself.[45]   The sovereign was subjected to the higher law, henceforth enthroned as the guarantor of the inalienable rights of man.   That subjection did not always find expression in tangible restrictions; it subjected the people not to the higher law of justice but to the higher law of the constitution which, in the last resort, could be changed by the sovereign people.   But these ' higher law ' bases of the constitution were destined to acquire a degree of sanctity which made them impervious to the vicissitudes of arbitrary change.

6.   FUNDAMENTAL RIGHTS IN MODERN CONSTITUTIONS

In the nineteenth and twentieth centuries the recognition of the fundamental rights of man in the constitutions of States became, in a paraphrase of Article 38 of the Statute of the Permanent Court of International Justice, a general principle of the constitutional law of civilised States.[46]   It became part of the law of nearly all European States.   Sweden adopted it in 1809; Spain in 1812; Norway in 1814; Belgium in 1831; the Kingdom of Sardinia in 1848; Denmark in 1849; Prussia in 1850[47]; Switzerland in 1874.   The Constitution of Liberia of 1847 opened with a Bill of Rights the first Article of which contained the statement that ' all men are born equally free and independent, and have certain

[44] See below, p. 96.

[45] It will be noted that, in No. 84 of *The Federalist,* Hamilton objected to a Bill of Rights on the ground that the people is sovereign, that it cannot be limited, and that, accordingly, the sovereign authority cannot be limited. That view did not prevail.   When in 1778 Theophilus Parson objected to the proposed Constitution of Massachusetts on the ground that it contained no Bill of Rights, he considered as firmly established the principle that ' the supreme power is limited and cannot controul the unalienable rights of mankind '. See McIlwain, *Constitutionalism and the Changing World* (1939), p. 66. In 1768 in the *Massachusetts Circular Letter* Samuel Adams, while still referring to the sovereign as supreme, spoke of man's right to retain what is his own as ' an essential, unalienable right, in nature, engrafted into the British constitution as a fundamental law, and ever held sacred and irrevocable by the subjects within the realm ' (*ibid.,* p. 72).

[46] See Barker, ' Declarations of Rights and their Bearing on Criminal Science ', in *Canadian Bar Review,* 20 (1942), pp. 510-515.

[47] The Bismarck Constitution of 1871 did not contain a list of fundamental rights, but these were included in the Constitutions of the States members of the Bund.

natural, inherent and inalienable rights'. The French Constitution of 1848 recognised 'rights and duties anterior and superior to positive laws'. After the First World War it was adopted by Germany and most of the new European States. The All-Russia Congress proclaimed in January, 1918, a 'declaration of the rights of the toiling and the exploited peoples' which was incorporated as Part I of the Constitution of 5 July, 1918. That declaration was considerably extended in the Constitution of 1936. Other States which subsequently succumbed to the wave of totalitarianism did not dispense in their revised constitutions— like those of Poland of 1935 and Roumania of 1938—with a list of fundamental rights. The Latin-American States followed in the nineteenth and twentieth centuries the general trend practically without exception. They amplified the scope of fundamental rights by enlarging on the duties of the State in the social and economic spheres and by adding considerably to the guarantees of their enforcement. States on the Asiatic continent followed suit. Thus, for instance, within a period of two years we see the adoption of chapters on the Rights and Duties of the People in the Provisional Constitution of China of 12 May, 1931, on the Rights and Duties of the Siamese in the Constitution of the Kingdom of Siam of 10 December, 1932, and on the Rights of Afghan Subjects in the Fundamental Principles of the Government of Afghanistan of 31 October, 1931. The Turkish Constitution of 1928 did not refrain from similar terminology vividly reminiscent of the Declaration of 1789: 'Every Turk is born and lives free. . . . The limits, for every one, of freedom, which is a natural right, are the limits of the freedom of others.' France herself, in the Preamble to the Constitution of 1946, solemnly reaffirmed 'the rights and freedoms of man and of the citizen consecrated by the Declaration of Rights of 1789 and the fundamental principles recognised by the laws of the Republic', and proclaimed once more that 'every human being without distinction of race, religion or belief, possesses inalienable and sacred rights'. The Constitution of Japan of 3 November, 1946, laid down, in Article 11, 'that the people shall not be prevented from enjoying any of the fundamental rights' and that 'these fundamental rights guaranteed to the people by the constitution shall be conferred upon the people of this and future generations as eternal and inviolate rights'. In the Fundamental Principles of the Italian Constitution of 23 December, 1947, ' the Republic recognises and guarantees the inviolable rights of man ' (Article 2). It states, significantly, that while ' sovereignty belongs to the people ', the latter must exercise it ' within the limits of the constitution ' (Article 2).

7. The Sanction of the Constitutions

This progress of the idea and the practice of inherent rights of man in the nineteenth and twentieth centuries has been achieved in face of constant and trenchant criticism. They have been described as fanciful, elusive, and double-edged. They have been assailed as individualistic and anti-social. An attempt to answer some of these strictures will be made elsewhere in this book.[48] But there is one objection to the notion of natural rights which, far from invalidating the essential idea of natural rights, is nevertheless in a sense unanswerable. It is a criticism which reveals a close and, indeed, inescapable connexion between the idea of fundamental rights on the one hand and the law of nature and the law of nations on the other. That criticism is to the effect that, in the last resort, such rights are subject to the will of the State; that they may—and must—be regulated, modified, and if need be taken away by legislation and, possibly, by judicial interpretation; that, therefore, these rights are in essence a revocable part of the positive law of a sanctity and permanence no higher than the constitution of the State either as enacted or as interpreted by courts and by subsequent legislation. This objection was, indeed, present to the minds of the authors of the Declaration, of 4 August, 1789, of the Rights of Man and of the Citizen. For the Assembly decreed that the Constitution should be *preceded* by the Declaration. The intention, apparently, was to endow the latter with an authority superior even to that of the Constitution. In the words of Thouret, the *rapporteur,* when a new Constitution was being framed in 1791, the Declaration was left intact on the ground that it ' had acquired, in a sense, a sacred and religious character '. Or, as Dupont de Nemours put it, it was in the minds of its authors ' the fundamental law of the laws of our own and of other nations which ought to last as long as time itself '. For this reason Duguit and other French constitutional writers have

[48] See below, pp. 98-103.

deemed it fitting to proclaim a significant hierarchy of obligations. The legislator, in this view, is bound by the Constitution, but the authors of the Constitution and of its future changes are bound by the most fundamental instrument—the Declaration of Rights. He does not state what is the legal basis and the legal sanction of that supreme Declaration of Rights—unless it be the right of revolution.[49]   A somewhat pathetic intimation of the same problem appears in the concluding passage of the Statute of Virginia for Religious Freedom of 1786.   In that passage it is conceded that it is not possible for the Assembly to secure the Bill for all time by declaring it irrevocable.   ' Yet we are free to declare, and do declare, that the rights hereby asserted are of the natural rights of mankind, and that if any act should be hereafter passed to repeal the present act or to narrow its operation such act will be an infringement of a natural right '.   Jefferson, the author of the Statute, spoke in a similar vein in his First Inaugural Address when he exhorted the nation to ' bear in mind the sacred principle that tho' the will of the Majority is in all cases to prevail, that will, to be rightful, must be reasonable: that the Minority possess their equal rights, which equal laws must protect, and *to violate would be oppression* '.[50]   The ultimate sanction of the violation of the rights of minorities is a moral one; the transgressor will have made himself guilty of oppression.   It is not surprising that the right to and the belief in the beneficence of revolution occupy a prominent place in Jefferson's writings.[51]

[49] *Droit constitutionnel* (2nd ed., 1923), vol. III, pp. 562-567.   Similarly, with regard to the German Weimar Constitution of 1919, Professor Carl Schmitt, a not altogether sympathetic commentator on that document, denied that fundamental rights—for instance, those of personal freedom—were of the same degree as the other provisions of the Constitution, and that they could be altered by the regular procedure provided for changes of the Constitution: *Verfassungslehre* (1928), p. 161.   He says: ' No German law must be interpreted or applied in derogation of it [the Weimar Constitution].   No German law must destroy a real fundamental right.   These basic principles cannot be abolished either by ordinary law or by a law changing the constitution as provided in Article 76, but only by a new fundamental constitutional law of the German people.'   See also Thoma in *Festgabe für preussisches Oberwaltungsrecht* (1925), p. 187, who speaks of fundamental rights as stations in the eternal ebb and flow of the contest between man and State.

[50] 4 March, 1801: *Writings*, vol. VIII, p. 2.

[51] ' God forbid we should ever be 20 years without a rebellion. . . . What country can preserve its liberties if their rulers are not warned from time to time that their people preserve the spirit of resistance? Let them take arms. . . . The tree of liberty must be refreshed from time to time with the blood of patriots and tyrants. It is its natural manure.' *Ibid.*, vol. X, p. 23; vol. IV, p. 467.)   Yet it is significant that, at the same time, Jefferson continued to attach importance to a Bill of Rights in the Federal Constitution.   Thus, in writing to James Madison concerning the proposed Constitution, he said:

This difficulty reveals the Achilles heel of the notion of natural rights of man so long as they depend for their validity and their practical recognition upon the uncontrolled will of the sovereign State, and so long as the ultimate sanction of their being is grounded exclusively in the law of the State. Where else can that ultimate sanction be found? It must rest in a legal source superior to that of the State. That superiority may be of two kinds. It may be that of the law of nature conceived as a limitation inherent in the nature of all rational law and as a standard of justice and fitness disregard of which must reduce law to a mere form of arbitrary power. That law of nature is not without its sanctions. For it is a factor whose operation shapes that habitual obedience which is at the basis of all positive law. It moulds the minds of rulers and legislators by instilling into them that degree of reasonableness and restraint which constitutes the barrier between obedience and rebellion. No law or legal theory can exclude it from the province of judicial interpretation of the positive law. The other legal source which is above the supreme authority of the State and in which lie the ultimate safeguards of the rights of man is the law of nations or, as it is more often called, international law. It is, predominantly, the body of rules which are voluntarily accepted or imposed by the existence of international society and which govern the conduct of States and are subject to enforcement by external sanction. The rights of man cannot, in the long run, be effectively secured except by the twin operation of the latent forces of the law of nature and of the compelling force of the law of nations—both conceived as a power superior to the supreme power of the State.

' I will now add what I do not like. First the omission of a bill of rights providing clearly, and without the aid of sophisms, for freedom of religion, freedom of the Press, protection against standing armies, restriction against monopolies, the eternal and unremitting force of the habeas corpus laws, and trials by jury in all matters of fact triable by the laws of the land and not by the law of nations ' (*ibid.*, vol. IV, p. 476).

CHAPTER 6

THE FUNCTION OF NATURAL LAW
AND THE RIGHTS OF MAN

1. HUMAN RIGHTS AND THE LAW OF NATURE IN ANTIQUITY

IT has been explained in the preceding Chapter that the recognition, by the State, of fundamental human rights must remain precarious and incomplete, in fact and in law, unless such recognition is supported by the twin sanction of the law of nature and the law of nations. This being so, it is more than of purely historical interest to trace the interaction and inward connection of these two forces and the notion of the rights of man. That connexion goes back to antiquity. Indeed, it was only within the wide confines of the cosmopolis of the City of God, in which the law of reason, being the law of nature, reigns supreme, that the Stoics envisaged the common law of humanity based on the most fundamental of all human rights, the principle of equality. They perceived the equality of man as imperfect unless apprehended as part of an œcumenical international order. It is in this sense that Seneca insisted that all men are akin by nature, which has formed them of the same elements and placed them in the world for the same end. Marcus Aurelius elaborated on the same theme: ' The common possession of reason is synonymous with the necessity of a common law. . . . That common law makes fellow-citizens of all men. If this is so, we are members of some political community in the sense that the world is in a manner a State.' There is, in fact, an intimate connection between the idea of the law of nature as the true source of legal justice and the notion of all humanity as a community of citizens equal in the eyes of nature. It is only within the structure of a wider system, in which the State has ceased to be an absolute law and purpose unto itself, that the inviolate character of inherent human rights can receive adequate legal expression and that the sanctity of the individual human being as the ultimate subject of all law asserts itself in full vigour.

The Stoics marked only the beginning of that perception of

the inevitable association between inherent human rights, the law of nations as the expression of a universal order, and the law of nature. For, as already intimated,[1] in the development of the idea of the fundamental rights of man the notion of the law of nature played the paramount and principal part. With the Stoics, Greek and Roman, with Cicero and, subsequently, with the Christian Fathers, it was natural law, as lying behind and above all positive law, which was the transcending authority delimiting the earthly power of the State in relation to the individual. From the very beginning the law of nature was brought into being for judging the legitimacy of the acts of the rulers—which meant their conformity with human rights. From man's essential nature, which is reason and which he shares with God, Cicero deduced not only a common law, but also a common share in justice.[2] He and Roman lawyers—Ulpian in particular—appealed to the law of nature as the supreme and final authority for the proposition that the slave and the free man were equal, any positive law notwithstanding. So did the Greek Stoics before him, and Seneca, the Roman Stoic, after him. So did Philip the Fair of France in 1311, who, when proposing to liberate the serfs, insisted that ' every human creature formed in the image of our Lord ought by natural law to be free '. Four years later Louis X of France in an ordinance exhorted the serfs to purchase their freedom ' comme selon le droit de nature chacun doit naistre franc '. The extent to which the issue of slavery prompted the assertion of a law of nature even by those who, like Aristotle, denied any inconsistency between the two, is not without instruction for the question of the influence of the claims of freedom upon both the rise and the growth of the theories of the law of nature.

2. THE ' HIGHER LAW ' IN THE MIDDLE AGES

The idea of the law of nature underlay most of the political and legal speculation of the Middle Ages inasmuch as it laid emphasis on the subordination of the ruler to the rule of law, which

---

[1] See above, pp. 80-89.

[2] *De Legibus* (Loeb's edition), p. 323. See also T. H. Green, *Works*, vol. II, pp. 350, 462-465, for interesting observations on the influence of Roman law, Stoic doctrine and the Christian conception of universal brotherhood as instrumental in the recognition of the rights of the individual independent of citizenship.

emphasis was its predominant theme. For when, at that time, the law of nature came to be identified with the law of God, it did not become a bulwark of established authority. It continued to be invoked as the authority for the subjection of rulers to principles of justice, for the respect for the sanctity of human personality, and for the right of the individual to defend himself against the abuses of absolutism by rebellion and by tyrannicide if need be. Thus, at a later date, the law of nature played a prominent part in the writings of the monarchomachs. In the *Vindiciae Contra Tyrannos* we find the author asserting that 'the law of nature teaches and commands us to maintain and to defend our lives and liberties, without which life is scant worth the enjoying, against all injury and violence'. Even Bodin, who laid the foundations of the modern theory of indivisible and absolute sovereignty as the essential characteristic of the State, illogically but significantly subjected that supreme sovereignty to the law of nature.[3] The theory of natural law—'radical to the very core', as Gierke put it—accompanied the birth of the modern State. It supplied the material by means of which Locke, strongly influenced by the natural law doctrines of Grotius, propounded his views on the inalienable rights of man. It had previously been invoked by Sir Matthew Hale and other English lawyers, who asserted the rule of law against the arbitrariness of the Executive.[4] Hale described as wild and 'against all natural justice' the proposition that the king may make, repeal or alter laws as he pleases. The doctrine of the law of nature was appealed to by the Puritans,

---

[3] In addition to the law of God and the fundamental laws of the Kingdom like the 'Salic' law (*De Republica*, I. 8). He was not unduly concerned with the objection, which had clearly occurred to Althusius, that an authority subject to the law of nature and the law of God cannot properly be called supreme (*Politica methodice digesta* (1603), ed. 9, No. 20). That aspect of the problem is discussed by Loyseau in his *Traité des Seigneuries*, ch. ii, p. 8 (*Les Oeuvres de Maistre Charles Loyseau* (1678)), with a clarity which warrants quotation:

'Et comme la couronne ne peut estre si son circle n'est entier, eussi la Souveraineté n'est, point, si quelque chose y defaut.

'Toutefois, comme il n'y a que Dieu qui soit toutpuissant, & que la puissance des homme ne peut estre absoluë tout a fait: il y a trois sortes des loix qui bornent la puissance du Souverain, sans interesser la Souveraineté. A sçavoir les loix de Dieux; pour ce que le Prince n'est pas moins souverain pour estre sujet a Dieu; les regles de Justice naturelle & non positives, pour a qu'il a esté dit cy-devant, que c'est le propre de la Seigneurie publique, d'estre exercée par Justice, & non pas à discretion: Et finalement les loix fondamentales de l'Estat, pource que la Prince doit user de sa Souveraineté selon la propre nature & en la forme aux & conditions qu'elle est establie.'

[4] See below, p. 135.

the Levellers and the leaders of the Revolutionary Army; it was invoked by Milton; it was relied upon by Blackstone. It was that armoury of natural law which, in Bryce's telling phrase, ' had been for nearly two thousand years a harmless maxim, almost a commonplace of morality ', and which ' became in the end of the eighteenth century a mass of dynamite, which shattered an ancient monarchy and shook the European Continent '.[5] As we have seen, it was not perhaps quite so harmless a maxim in the centuries which preceded the American and French Revolutions. It merely gathered strength. The doctrine of inherent rights as expressed in the American Declaration of Independence, in the first American Constitutions, and in the French Declaration of the Rights of Man was not an original invention. It put to revolutionary use the accumulated power of what had been for a long time the backbone of the doctrine of the law of nature on which James Otis, Samuel Adams, Jefferson and the other Fathers of the Revolution leaned so heavily. For, as has been shown, in the realm of thought—in the realm of political and legal theory—the association of the law of nature and of the natural rights of man goes back to antiquity.

In the nineteenth century that particular function of natural law was rendered both less urgent and less feasible for the reason that, apart from the defensive position in which the doctrines of natural law found themselves, that century was assimilating and putting into practice the accomplishments of the law of nature as expressed in the great American and French constitutional pronouncements. When in the twentieth century that achievement was put in jeopardy, the law of nature resumed, as we shall see, its historic function as the champion of the rights of man.

3.   NATURAL LAW AS BASED ON EXPERIENCE

What was, and is, that law of nature which, throughout the ages, proved to be the principal bearer of the idea of the indefeasible rights of man? There is in the theories of the law of nature, from Greek philosophy until modern times, a firm core both of method and of substance which bears directly, though partly in a some-

---

[5] *Studies in Law and Jurisprudence* (1901), vol. II, p. 163.

what negative fashion, upon the issue before us. In particular, we cannot hope to understand adequately the law of nature unless we disabuse our minds of the idea that it has been exclusively, or predominantly, speculative, deductive and fanciful; that it has been divorced from experience; and that its exponents have attempted to engraft upon the living body politic the products of abstract *a priori* speculation. Nothing could be farther from the truth.

From the very inception the theories of natural law were generalisations from actual experience. They were attempts to put in the form of general law the fact of a uniformity as ascertained by observation and study of evidence—although it was not always the kind of evidence that would satisfy the modern mind. Their authors endeavoured to form laws of conduct by reference to the nature of man, to his physical and mental constitution as they saw it, and to his station and purpose in the scheme of creation as they perceived it from the contemplation of the world around them. No doubt all this was speculation, but this is unavoidable whenever the human mind is at pains to forge a link of orderliness, cause and purpose between disconnected phenomena. Witness, for instance, the way in which Aristotle arrived at the conception of natural law. For him[6] it was synonymous with the legal experience of all or most peoples as contrasted with the law of one country. He distinguished between law which is in accordance with nature for the reason that it is recognised by all, and the peculiar law of individual peoples. The laws and customs followed by the generality of mankind must, in his view, be regarded as a manifestation of a common moral and mental constitution exhibiting a uniformity and regularity which nature shows in other realms of existence.

The Stoic conception—both Greek and Roman—of the law of nature was on the face of it more abstract. Actually, it was grounded on what the Stoics believed to be the fundamental fact of the common origin of man and of his common possession of and subjection to reason conceived as the central and ruling power of the world. In that sense human relations are governed by a law coeval with man, in its essence unalterable, anterior to the State, and of necessity incorporated in the law of any State

[6] In addition to his conception of nature as implying a rational design in the universe, manifested, though never fully realised, in the material world.

worthy of the name. In the Epicurean philosophy we find a conception of the law of nature which is almost utilitarian in character. Inasmuch as natural justice prescribes what is good for the greatest number, the law of nature was identified with the common good. Some of the imperialist jurists of the Middle Ages followed the same line of utilitarian reasoning when they taught that as God wills the happiness of those whom he has created, utility is the best standard of the right conduct as being in conformity with the law of nature and the law of God.

Cicero's conception of natural law was, in the same sense, inductive: ' Universal consent is the voice of nature.' [7] ' In every matter the consent of nations is to be considered as the law of nature.' [8] His influence on later Roman jurists is undeniable in this matter as in others. For the *jus naturale* of the Roman jurists was not a mere abstraction. It was the right law, the law appropriate to the individual and social nature of man, deduced not from a speculative void but from the general condition of mankind at large. The *jus gentium,* with a fair admixture of equity, was positive law. But it was often described as that part of natural law which had been accepted and acted upon by the civilised communities of the Mediterranean world. The actual difference between *jus gentium* and *jus naturale* was not considerable. They often merged one into the other. The institution of slavery, which must be alien to any law of nature that is not an abuse of language (though Aristotle and others tried to justify it by reference to natural law), prevented any such identification. But *jus gentium* and *jus naturale* came sufficiently close together to act as a reminder that the notion of the law of nature was not pure speculation.

The position was essentially the same in the Middle Ages and in the period which followed it. When the upholders of the law of nature propounded that it was established by the reason of the thing, they did not refer to the reason of the thing as conceived by their own speculation and their own individual opinion. Evidence of constant and immemorial usage was required—though opinions differed as to the kind of evidence needed. There is not much

[7] ' Omnium consensus naturæ vox est ' (Tusc. i.XV.35).
[8] ' Omni autem in re consensio omnium gentium lex naturæ putanda est ' (*ibid.*, i.XIII.30).

difference between founding the law of nature on the animal and social nature of man, as Grotius did, and basing it on social solidarity, as does Duguit.

4.   THE ALLEGED ARBITRARINESS OF NATURAL LAW

There is nothing inevitably arbitrary about the law of nature. On the contrary, it has been a constant challenge to arbitrariness in the name of what is in the long run universal—because generally accepted—and commendable to reason and to the nature of man, including his sense of justice.   Its essence is not, as some have thought, the opposition of the ideal law to the law as actually in operation.   Actual law is often the full embodiment of natural law or it is an approximation to it (which is merely another way of saying that law is the realisation of the maximum of socially obtainable justice).   It is only when the positive law of any given time and place departs from what reason, the sentiment of right and the general legal experience of mankind make to constitute the law of nature that the latter assumes the character of a challenge and a protest.   In this sense the law of nature is both an expression of reality and a standard of fitness.   This is the true meaning of the view of St. Thomas Aquinas, that God Himself is subject to the law of nature, or of the view of Grotius that natural law ' would have a degree of validity even if we should concede that which cannot be conceded without the utmost wickedness, that there is no God, or that the affairs of man are of no concern to Him '.[9]

The law of nature has incurred the charge of being fanciful and speculative.   Undoubtedly, it is not capable of exact demonstration in the same way as a clear rule of positive law (although we often find that a rule of positive law is less clear than at first appears and that it leaves room, or calls for, interpretation by reference to that indefinite law of nature).   It is certainly less precise and amenable to proof than laws in the domain of physics or mathematics.   This is so for the reason that it applies to the more complicated sphere of human nature and the social relations of

---

[9] *Proleg.* 11.   Elsewhere—in Book I, I, x, 5—he says: ' The law of nature, again, is unchangeable—even in the sense that it cannot be changed by God. Measureless as is the power of God, nevertheless it can be said that there are certain things over which His power does not extend.'   And see *British Year Book of International Law,* 23 (1946), p. 53, n. 1, *in fine,* for the writer's references to the continuity of mediæval thought on the subject.

man. Thus Locke was of the opinion that the natural constitution of man—of man in the state of nature—was one of equal and peaceful individuals who submitted themselves to the rule of the State because of the inconvenience which would result from the fact that in the state of nature every person preserves the right of judgment in disputes with others.[10] Hobbes, on the other hand, was of the view that the natural constitution of man was one of aggressive and vicious enmity towards others and that consequently any form of tyranny was preferable to the state of natural anarchy. But these differences do not affect the reality of the law of nature; they do not reduce it to a mere postulate or presumption. The social nature of man; the generic traits of his physical and mental constitution; his sentiment of justice and moral obligation; his instinct for individual and collective self-preservation; his desire for happiness; his sense of human dignity; his consciousness of man's station and purpose in life—all these are not products of fancy but objective factors in the realm of existence. As such, they are productive of laws which may be flouted by arbitrariness, ignorance, or force, but which are in conformity with the more enduring reality of reason and the nature of man. The authors of the Declaration of Independence referred to its principles as expressive of self-evident truths. There is, in that confident application of the Euclidian principle of self-evident truths to the notion of natural rights of man, an assertion, which is far from being arbitrary, of a direct relation between natural rights and scientific laws.[11] It was in that sense that

[10] An inconvenience not so great, however, as to justify submission to a tyrannical rule. This would mean 'to think, that men are so foolish that they take care to avoid what mischief may be done them by pole-cats, or foxes, but are content, nay, think it safety, to be devoured by lions' (*First Essay on Government*, VII, 93).

[11] James Otis wrote in 1766 in the same sense (*The Rights of British Colonies Asserted and Proved*): 'Nor do the rights of British colonies rest on a charter from the Crown. . . . Old Magna Carta was not at the beginning of all things. . . . A time may come when Parliament may declare every American charter void, but the natural, inherent, and inseparable rights of the colonists as men and as citizens would remain, and, whatever become of charters, can never be abolished till the general conflagration'. Hamilton used similar language: 'The sacred rights of mankind are not to be rummaged for among old parchments or musty records. They are written, as with a sunbeam, in the whole volume of human nature, by the hand of Divinity itself, and can never be obscured by mortal power' (as quoted by Lord Acton, *History of Freedom and Other Essays* (1907), p. 587). Judge Jerome Frank, who disapproves of the terminology of natural law, asserts that the term 'natural law' is 'peculiarly afflicted with warring definitions', that it 'has lent its protection to an unusually large number of vicious

Jefferson—perhaps the most consistent and influential modern exponent of the doctrine of natural rights—found their source in the universal law of nature. He did not consider natural rights as constituting primarily a moral claim. They were ' in the very nature of things '. In saying that ' the God who gave us life gave us liberty at the same time ',[12] he was not enunciating a doctrine of theology or ethics. He was giving expression to what he conceived to be an underlying objective reality—obscured and violated, for a time, by social institutions and positive law—but none the less a reality. This was essentially the meaning of the rousing slogan which he adopted as his family motto: ' Rebellion to tyrants is obedience to God '—in the revolt against the injustice of laws and governments denying the inalienable rights of man there lies true submission to fundamental and more enduring facts of existence.

The very conception of natural rights conceived as the means to the supreme end of enabling man to fulfil his duty follows from the realisation that, as a matter of scientific fact, man is distinguished from other living beings by being a rational and moral person who must shape his life in accordance with moral and rational purposes.[13] The question to what extent and in what

causes ', and that ' the same cannot be said of the word " justice ".' (*Interpretations of Modern Legal Philosophies*: Essays in Honor of Roscoe Pound (1947), p. 259, n. 332). But it is questionable whether the term ' justice' is less elastic and less liable to be abused than the notion of natural law —just as it is questionable whether the guiding tenets of utilitarianism are fundamentally different from the ideology of natural law which it opposed. Compare, for instance, John Stuart Mill's *Dissertations and Discussions*, III, p. 243, and his *Political Economy*, V, XI, s. 2. In the former he suggests that the doctrine of natural law has exhausted what good influence it ever had. In the second he insists that ' there is a circle around every individual human being which no government ought to be permitted to overstep '. On the way in which the ' devil of natural law had most of the disciples of the Historical School in his grip, although they did not realise it ' see Rümelin in *The Jurisprudence of Interests* (ed. by Magdalena Schoch (1948), p. 8).

[12] *Works* (Ford's edition, 1892-1899), vol. I, p. 447. And see Malone, *Jefferson the Virginian* (1948), pp. 176, 177. There is perhaps no better and clearer affirmation of the positive character of natural law, thus conceived, than the famous passage in the Third Book of Cicero's *Republic*: ' . . . Neither the Senate nor the people can absolve us from our obligation to obey this law. . . . It will not lay down one rule at Rome and another at Athens, nor will it be one rule today and another tomorrow. But there will be one law, eternal and unchangeable, binding at all times, upon all peoples. . . . The man who will not obey it will abandon his better self, and, in denying the true nature of a man, will thereby suffer the severest of penalties, though he has escaped all the other consequences which men call punishments ' (translation by Sabine and Smith).

[13] See Maritain, *Le droit de l'homme et la loi naturelle* (1942), pp. 84, 85, on the correlation of moral obligation and natural rights.

sense man's inalienable rights are natural rights—rights grounded in nature—must remain a matter of emphasis. It may well be that nature is indifferent to his life, freedom, and happiness, that it favours the strong and assails the weak, and that freedom and happiness, far from being the gift and right of nature, are the product of conscious effort. But it is indisputable that man's claim to recognition of inalienable rights is part of his moral constitution as a rational being endowed with conscience. To that extent they are manifestly part of nature. There is nothing fanciful in Kant's affirmative comparison of the absolute reality of man's sense of duty with the awful magnificence of the starry heavens above. Inasmuch as that sense of duty expresses itself in the recognition of the absolute of value of man and in the prohibition of treating him otherwise than as an end in himself— and this is one of the central aspects of Kant's ethics—it amounts to an affirmation, in a different sphere, of the natural rights of man. For these reasons it would be better if there were less complacency in comparing the fanciful law of nature, which—it is said—is a matter of bare and arbitrary assertion, with positive law said to be clear and undisputed. For positive law is not always clear and undisputed. If it were, the function of judges would be purely automatic. For a similar reason there is less substance than is generally assumed in the assertion that natural law is incapable of proof. In the fields of philosophy, law and ethics, there are few propositions, if any, which are capable of exact proof.

5. THE LAW OF NATURE AS A LEVER OF PROGRESS AND AS AN INSTRUMENT OF REACTION

It is true—and here we approach the second and no less persistent source of criticism—that that law of nature has often acted in the opposite direction. Aristotle justified slavery as a natural institution on the ground that some men are by nature free and capable of guiding their lives towards a rational end, while others are by nature slaves capable of just enough reason to comprehend it in others. The barbarians were by nature slaves. The slave has by nature no sense of freedom and no understanding of the higher art of existence in political society. His purpose and destiny is to serve others. Only the Greeks had by nature the physical and mental qualities required for political existence.[14]

This appeal to the law of nature as a justification of legal and, subsequently, economic slavery is a frequent occurrence. In 1785 we find the Rev. Joseph Townsend in his *Dissertation on the Poor Laws*[15] voicing the same view: ' It seems to be the law of nature that the poor should be to a certain degree improvident, that there may always be some to fulfil the most servile, the most sordid, and the most ignoble offices in the community. The stock of human happiness is thereby much increased.' He was not unmindful of the lot of the poor: ' As for the lowest poor . . . the desire of obtaining bread will quietly dispose the mind to undergo the greatest hardships, and will sweeten the severest labours. The peasant with a sickle in his hand is happier than the prince upon his throne.'

The opposition to female suffrage—in fact the opposition to the removal of most of the degrading aspects of inequality of women—has often been supported by reference to the law of nature. That opposition included Rousseau for whom

[14] *Politics*, I.1.5. He says: ' Inferior kinds of men are by nature slaves, and it is better for them, as for all inferiors, to be under the rule of a master. For that man is by nature a slave who can be, and therefore is, the property of someone else, and has sufficient intelligence to understand, but not to reason. The lower animals, however, do not even understand; they merely obey their instincts. As a matter of fact, the use of slaves and of domestic animals does not differ much: from the physical labour of both are obtained the services necessary for life.' Aristotle deplored the fact that there was no certain distinguishing mark to serve as an infallible index of the slave, although he thought that in general this might be observed in the cringing manner of the inferior. Equality, says Aristotle, can apply only to those equal by birth and power. ' Equality is regarded and is just not for all, but for equals. Similarly inequality is regarded, and is so by nature as just, but not for all, but only for those who are not equal ' (*ibid.*, III.5.8). Neither was he at a loss to answer the embarrassing question as to the noblest families being made prisoners of war and sold as slaves. His answer was: ' Victory is always owing to some superior advantage: so that it seems that violence does not prevail without ability.' Nearly two thousand years later Sir Thomas Smith in *The Commonwealth of England* (published first as *De Republica Anglorum* (1567) and reprinted in 1589 under the English title), wrote in a similar vein: ' A bondman or a slave is as it were (saving life and humane reason) but the instrument of his Lord, as the axe, the sawe, the chessyll and gowge is of the charpenter.' Between the master and his slave ' there is no mutuall societie or portion, no law or pleading betweene thone and thother . . . there is no right, law nor commonwealth compact, but only the will of the Lord and segnior ' (ed. of 1906 by Alston. p. 20).

[15] Quoted in Sidney and Beatrice Webb, *English Poor Law History*, Part II, vol. I (1929), p. 8.

the exercise of political power by man was a natural and inalienable right, the clearest emanation of the law of nature.[16]

At various periods upholders of economic stability appealed to natural law as the basis of the sanctity of contracts and property; the critics of the prohibition of usury found in it a useful argument. So did the opponents of State interference in the economic sphere. In 1604 a Committee of the House of Commons asserted that as merchandise was the principal trade of the country it was ' against the natural right and liberty of the subjects of England to restrain it into the hands of some few '.[17] Adam Smith availed himself of it in advocating ' the obvious and simple system of natural liberty '.[18]

The reliance upon natural law on the part of vested interests inimical to the economic freedom of man was destined to prove a persistent feature of the nineteenth century. It was especially in the United States, in the second half of the nineteenth century, that the ideas of the law of nature and of natural rights were resorted to in an attempt to curb State interference with rights of private property and freedom of contract. The Fourteenth Amendment to the Constitution adopted in 1868 provided that ' no State shall deprive any person of life, liberty, or property without due process of law; nor deny to any person within its jurisdiction the equal protection of the laws '. The expression ' due process of law ' became henceforth the pivotal constitutional

---

[16] He argued strongly that the wife should have no religion except that of her husband. 'Even if that religion is false, the docility with which wife and daughter submit to the order of nature effaces in the sight of God the sin of error. Being incapable of judging themselves, they ought to accept the decision of their fathers and their husbands like that of the Church': *Emile, Livre* V. In view of this it is perhaps not surprising to see Lecky, *Democracy and Liberty,* vol. II (1896), p. 453, condemning the appeal to natural law on both sides: 'The inalienable right which, according to the school of Rousseau, every man possesses to a share of political power, and the irreversible law of nature which pronounces women to be dependents of men, and unfit for any share in the ruling power, are equally baseless.'

[17] Quoted by Tawney, *Religion and the Rise of Capitalism* (1926), p. 179. Some of Bentham's criticism of the Declaration of Rights drawn by Sieyès is couched in similar language. The Declaration provided that ' every citizen who is unable to provide for his own wants, has a right to assistance '. If this, Bentham said, is a right against individuals, then it overturns the idea of property. If it is a right against the community, then it is vague, and it may not be possible to satisfy it as in the case of scarcity. The Declaration, in Bentham's view, changed what is a duty of benevolence into an absolute right, which would give the indigent class a false and most dangerous idea. It would mean the destruction of gratitude on the part of the poor to their benefactors, and arm them against all owners of property.

[18] Burke, in *Thoughts and Details on Scarcity* (1795), spoke of the ' laws of commerce' as ' the laws of nature and consequently the laws of God': *Works* (ed. of 1852), vol. V, pp. 203, 204.

problem of the United States. The Amendment was passed largely for the protection of the Negro population. But the Supreme Court soon held that the safeguards of the Amendment extended only to such rights, and those were few, as Negroes enjoyed by virtue of their general citizenship of the United States; it did not protect them against State legislation in other spheres, including the civil liberties of the first eight amendments to the Bill of Rights.[19] While, thus, the main purpose of the Amendment suffered a restriction which defeated its apparent purpose, the Amendment became, by an unexpected turn of judicial interpretation, to a considerable extent an instrument for the protection of vested interests and economic stability against social legislation and economic change. At the end of the century the Supreme Court interpreted the concept ' due process of law ' not as a restriction of a procedural character, but as a substantive limitation intended to secure respect for the inalienable, natural rights —of which that of private property was foremost—and for the fundamental unwritten principles of the constitution and of government as determined by the inherent rights of the individual expounded in the Declaration of Independence. The ideas of natural law and natural rights were revived and endowed with fresh vigour for that purpose. By reference to the natural rights of man courts in the United States often declared to be unconstitutional legislation for securing humane conditions of work, for protecting the employment of women and children, for safeguarding the interests of consumers, and for controlling the powers of trusts and corporations. This, to be sure, was not the end of the development. At the beginning of the twentieth century the Supreme Court held in what is still the governing decision that the fourteenth amendment did not afford protection in all matters covered by the eight amendments to the Constitution, but, in effect, only when so required by what at any particular time constitutes ' civilised decency ' and ' fundamental conceptions of justice '—a version of ' natural law '.[20] This has been interpreted, more recently, as meaning not only that the fourteenth amendment

---

[19] In the well-known *Slaughter House Cases* ((1873) 16 Wallace 36) the Supreme Court declined, out of respect for the sovereignty of the States, to apply the doctrine of natural rights to the protection of the interests of the Louisiana butchers threatened by a State monopoly. But the powerful dissenting Opinion of Mr. Justice Field, based on the inalienable right of man to property, was not without influence.

[20] *Twining* v. *New Jersey* (1908) 211 U.S. 78.

did not protect all the rights of the eight amendments, but that it could protect rights other than and additional to those safeguarded by these amendments—a most potent source of application of natural law.[21]   There is no compelling reason for assuming that the notion of natural law will be used, as in the past, for safeguarding entrenched interests and for retarding the cause of human freedom.   The indications are to the contrary.[22]   But past history explains why natural rights have been regarded in some quarters in the United States with suspicion and bitterness, and why writers affirming the supremacy of a higher law over the legislature have nevertheless spoken with impatience of the *damnosa hæreditas* of natural rights.[23]

It was not only in the economic sphere that natural law was found convenient as a fertile source of reasoning.   In the Middle Ages it was relied upon by the supporters both of the Empire and of the Papacy—both sides claiming the right and the capacity to give a more correct interpretation of the law of nature.   It was identified with the law of God; as such it was a weapon for establishing the supremacy of the Church.   Catholic writers invoked it as supporting the view that the Scriptures cannot be taken literally, as claimed by the reformers, but must be interpreted in the light of reason and of the law of nature.   In general, it was grossly exploited for a variety of causes.   Sir John Fortescue, in a learned and highly laboured argument in his *De Natura Legis Naturæ*, availed himself of it as a plea for the Lancastrian title to the Crown of England.   It has been invoked by enemies of political freedom and champions of absolutism. While Bossuet for that purpose derived all political authority from God, Filmer relied on natural law.   Paternal authority was to him the only inalienable natural right; it was preserved in every State with a monarchical form of government.   ' There is ', he said, ' a natural right of a supreme father over every multitude, although many at first do most unjustly obtain the exercise of

[21] *Adamson* v. *California* (1947) 332 U.S. 46.   See below, p. 156.   As Mr. Justice Frankfurter put it in *Louisiana ex rel. Francis* v. *Resweber* ((1947) 67 Sup. Ct. 974): ' In an impressive body of decisions this Court has decided that the Due Process Clause of the Fourteenth Amendment expresses a demand for civilised standards which are not defined by the specifically enumerated guarantees of the Bill of Rights.   They neither contain the particularities of the first eight amendments nor are they confined to them . . .'

[22] See below, pp. 157, 361.

[23] See below, pp. 108, 109.

it.'[24]   More recently, it has been invoked as justifying interference with personal liberty on eugenic grounds, for the reason that
the unborn have their natural rights as much as the living.[25]   The
theories of some of the most outspoken advocates of war and
imperialism have been based on the idea of the law of nature.
In justifying and extolling war as an institution Treitschke
appealed ' to the laws of human thought and of human nature '
which ' forbid any alternative '.[26]   Much of Mahan's doctrine
was based on the same notions.   To him the Monroe Doctrine
was ' a moral question, based upon considerations substantially
just, one of natural right, of policy, not of legal right . . . it is the
reflex, as against distant outsiders, of the instinctive impulse
toward self-preservation, and as such represents natural right—
which is moral right—as opposed to legal '.[27]   In the same way
in the eighteenth and nineteenth centuries natural law was
invoked in support of an intransigent brand of *laisser faire,*
and, through Darwinism, it was used as a justification of war and
of excesses of competition alien and hostile to elementary conceptions of social justice.   Supposed laws of cause and effect were
elevated to the dignity of principles of ethics.

The abuse of the idea of natural law in the defence
of causes both paltry and iniquitous has caused many to
reject it with impatience.   This is perhaps the principal reason
why a practical reformer like Jeremy Bentham, a great judge
like Mr. Justice Holmes,[28] and a legal philosopher like Hans

[24] *Patriarcha: or, The Natural Power of Kings* (1680), Chapter I, 10.
[25] Dean Inge, *Liberty and Natural Rights* (a lecture, 1938), p. 33.   For a
denial, on eugenic grounds, of what many consider to be the natural right to
marry, see Jethro Brown, *The Underlying Principles of Modern Legislation*
(1912), pp. 262-271.   On the natural rights of animals see *A Tract on the
Rights of the Brute Creation,* quoted in *Annual Register,* 1776, Misc. Essays,
p. 176.
[26] *Politics,* vol. I, p. 65.
[27] *Works. Armaments and Arbitration,* I (1912), p. 82.
[28] ' There is no mystic over-law to which even the United States must bow ':
The Western Maid (1922) 257 U.S. 419, 432.   See also the following passage
from Holmes's classical article: ' For my own part, I often doubt whether
it would not be a gain if every work of moral significance could be banished
from the law altogether, and other words adopted which should convey legal
ideas uncolored by anything outside the law ': *Harvard Law Review,* 10
(1896-1897), p. 464.   In general, Holmes's attitude towards natural rights was
influenced by the fact that, on the whole, he was disposed to favour what he
considered to be the social interest in preference to individual rights.   See
Lowry, ' Mr. Justice Holmes: The Community *vs.* The Individual ', in *California Law Review,* 36 (1948), pp. 390-404.   For a different approach to the
question see the Opinions of some of the Justices of the Supreme Court in the
recent case of *Adamson* v. *California* (1947), 332 U.S. 46.   In that case the
Supreme Court, by a majority, declined to accede to the view that the Four-

Kelsen [29]—all believers in social progress—have treated the law of nature with little respect. However, the rejection of an actually or potentially beneficent notion for the reason that it may be and has been abused savours of a kind of realism which has often led mankind to defeat. It may be doubted whether, in our impatience with the ' *damnosa hœreditas* ' of natural rights, we really advance matters by asserting that the sovereign power is

teenth Amendment incorporated all the original eight articles of the Bill of Rights and made it, as the result, the object of federal protection. (The Court held that although comment upon testimony in a federal court would violate the Fifth Amendment, such comment in a State court was not sufficiently violative of conceptions of decency in civilised society as to be prohibited by the Federal Constitution.) Apparently the Court, in the language of the dissenting Opinion of Mr. Justice Black, held that it was for the Court, and not for the rigid clauses of the Bill of Rights, to decide what constitutes ' civilised decency ' and ' fundamental liberty and justice '. In the words of Mr. Justice Frankfurter: ' In the history of thought " natural law " has a much longer and much better founded meaning and justification than such subjective selection of the first eight Amendments for incorporation in the Fourteenth.' For comment on this case see Coudert in *American Bar Association Journal,* 34 (1948), p. 19.

[29] See Kelsen, *Die philosophischen Grundlagen der Naturrechtslehre und des Rechtspositivismus* (1928; Philosophische Vorträge, Kant-Gesellschaft No. 31), pp. 37-41. Professor Kelsen considers the typical function of the natural law school to have been the defence of established authority and institutions—of established governments, of private property, of slavery, of marriage. But there is probably a distinct element of exaggeration in his suggestion that reliance on natural law for the purpose of challenging the established order was in the nature of an exception and that all authoritative adherents of the natural law doctrine belong to the conservative school. This, he suggests, is shown by the fact that the classical period of the natural law school coincided with that of the most arbitrary absolutism. Does not that fact support a view contrary to that advanced by Professor Kelsen? Nor is it easy to accept his suggestion, which is an ingenious one, that the alleged revolutionary character of the natural law doctrine was a deliberate invention of the historical school anxious to fasten upon their opponents that unpopular label. See also Jerome Frank in *Interpretations of Modern Legal Philosophies.* Essays in Honor of Roscoe Pound (1947). p. 223, who advances the view that throughout its long history the notion of natural law ' has as often been the shield of arch-conservatism as the sword of radicalism '. And see the same author's *Fate and Freedom* (1945), Chapter XII. Dean Pound, in referring to the phrase that the natural rights of man became as tyrranical as the divine right of Kings, submits that of that saying American constitutional law gave ' ample proof ' in the last quarter of the nineteenth century: *The Task of Law* (1944), p. 28. On the other hand, a qualified American writer, while fully noting the dangers of abuse and of a tendency to conservatism, says: ' No one should fail to acknowledge the noble rôle that the theory of natural rights has played in the historic process of human liberation ': Morris R. Cohen, *Law and the Social Order* (1937), p. 155. See also, to the same effect, Chroust in *Interpretations of Modern Legal Philosophies, op. cit.* above, p. 80; Pollock, *Essays in the Law* (1900), p. 31. Pollock says: ' Their variety [applications of the term " law of nature "] have tended to obscure the central idea which underlies them all, that of an ultimate principle of fitness with regard to the nature of man as a rational and social being, which is, or ought to be, the justification of every form of positive law.' And see Vinogradoff, *Collected Papers,* vol. II (1928), p. 377, and Whitehead, *Adventures of Ideas* (1933), p. 22: ' Great ideas often enter into reality with evil associates and with disgusting alliances.'

limited not by any higher law of the natural rights of man but by the nature of law itself and its inherent limitations. For this is a circumlocution. There is no such thing as the nature of law as distinguished from the nature of man, to whom it is addressed and whose interests it serves. Moreover, it is not only the law of nature which has been exposed to the gross exploitation of special pleading. In every field of thought and in every discipline, including that of logic, the same notions have supplied arguments for divergent and conflicting propositions. In the realm of ideas there is no formal tribunal to which appeal can be made against the ingenuity of partisanship.[30] In a sense the very misuse of the notion of natural rights has been a tribute to the vitality and inner worth of the law of nature. Witness the embarrassed abundance of argument by dint of which Aristotle attempted to prove that slavery was consistent with the law of nature—an argument invoked as self-evident, in defence of slavery, by some of the descendants of the fathers of the American revolution for whom the doctrine of the equality of man was a no less self-evident truth.[31] Above all, those impatient with the misuse of the

[30] Bentham's irritation at the vagueness and inconclusiveness of the appeal to the abstract principles of the law of nature was most emphatic. Such appeal. he said, is ' but womanish scolding and childish altercation, which is sure to irritate and which never can persuade,—*I* say that the legislature *cannot* do this—*I* say it *can*. *I* say that to do this, exceeds the bounds of its authority—*I* say, it does *not*. It is evident that a pair of disputants setting out in this manner may go on perplexing and irritating one another for everlasting, without the smallest chance of ever coming to an agreement. It is no more than announcing, and that in an obscure and at the same time, a peremptory and captious manner, their opposite persuasions, or rather affections, on a question of which neither of them sets himself to discuss the grounds ': *A Fragment on Government: Works*, vol. I (ed. by Bowring, 1843), p. 29. In comparison, Bentham thought, somewhat naïvely, that no disagreement is possible so long as the argument proceeds from the principle of utility.

[31] Abraham Lincoln castigated in a bitter passage that perversion of argument: ' When we were the political slaves of King George, and wanted to be free, we called the maxim that " all men are created equal " a self-evident truth; but now when we have grown fat, and have lost all dread of being slaves ourselves, we have become so greedy to be masters that we call the same maxim " a self-evident lie " ' (*Complete Works*, vol. I, p. 215). Yet, and this reveals the complexities of the problem, Lincoln set practical limits to what he considered the proclamation of the self-evident truth in the matter of equality. He said: ' I think that the authors of that notable instrument [the Declaration of Independence] intended to include all men, but that they did not intend to declare all men equal in all respects. They did not mean to say that all were equal in color, size, intellect, moral development, or social capacity. They defined with tolerable distinctness in what respects they did consider all men created equal—equal in certain inalienable rights, among which are life, liberty, and the pursuit of happiness. This they said and this they meant. They did not mean to assert the obvious untruth, that all men were then actually enjoying that equality, nor yet that they were about to confer it upon them. In fact, they had no power to confer

notion of the law of nature fail to realise that this has not been the typical service which it has been called upon to perform. The typical, predominant and, in point of time, anterior use to which it has been put was that of the assertion and defence of the imprescriptible rights of the liberty and the equality of man.[32]

6.   The Law of Nature as the Expression of Inalienable Rights of Man

This fact reveals a further significant link in the chain of political and legal thought.   The doctrine of the law of nature was, as we have seen, the bulwark and the lever of the idea of the natural rights of man.   But it was the latter which, in a most substantial sense, called the doctrine of the law of nature into being.   Legal and political theories are not, as a rule, leisurely speculations of philosophers unrelated to human needs and aspirations; nor are they in the same category as the calm and detached generalisations through which the scientist masters the phenomena of the physical world.   They are pragmatic and teleological; they serve a purpose.[33]   That purpose of the theory of the law of nature, to which it owed its origin to a large extent, its sustenance throughout the centuries, and its periodic revivification, has been the vindication

such a boon. They meant simply to declare the right, so that the enforcement of it might follow as fast as circumstances should permit. They meant to set up a standard maxim for free society which should be familiar to all and revered by all—constantly looked to, constantly labored for, and even though never perfectly attained, constantly approximated; and thereby constantly spreading and deepening its influence and augmenting the happiness and value of life to all people, of all colors, everywhere.' (As quoted by Holcombe, *Human Rights in the Modern World* (1948), p. 27.) It is not surprising that when the American representative on the Human Rights Commission advocated in 1948 the adoption of a somewhat nominal Declaration which would not be legally binding, she quoted from Lincoln's speech referred to above. (E/CN. 4/SR.48, p. 6.)'

[32] While doctrines of natural law have been invoked in defence of private property, they have also been adduced as a powerful argument against it. Witness, for example, the way in which Henry George explained the failure of ancient civilisations by reference to their denial, through private property in land of the most fundamental of all natural laws, namely, man's freedom 'to use the earth as he breathes the air': *Progress and Poverty* (1889), pp. 239, 264-266, 354-357.

[33] See Leslie Stephen, *History of English Thought in the Eighteenth Century,* vol. II (1902), p. 131, who points out that a political philosophy is usually ' the offspring of a recent, or the symptom of an approaching, revolution '. Locke's *Treatises* were written, in the words of their author, in order ' to establish the throne of our great restorer, our present King William; to make good his title, in the consent of the people . . . and to justify to the world the people of England, whose love of their just and natural rights, with their resolution to preserve them, served the nation when it was on the very brink of slavery and ruin ': *Works*, vol. V (1802), p. 209. And see Perry, *Puritanism and Democracy* (1944), pp. 124, 127.

of the rights of man. Historically, the doctrine of natural law is rooted deep in the claims of freedom against the tyranny of the State and the injustice of its institutions.

The doctrine of natural law thus called into being and periodically resuscitated by its parent, progeny and ally—the rights of man—in due course fulfilled functions other than buttressing the claims of the indestructible human rights. But the original connexion never disappeared. The doctrine of the fundamental rights of the individual owed as much to the idea of natural law as the latter owed to the former. The interaction was constant and mutually beneficial. That drama in the realm of thought was re-enacted, under the impact of the same dynamic cause, at the beginning of the twentieth century during and after the First World War and in the course of the rise of totalitarianism in the decade preceding the Second World War. The renaissance of the law of nature at the beginning of the twentieth century was not yet another theory of the judicial function. It was the un- mistakable result of the urge to find a spiritual counterpart to the growing power of the modern State. In so far as that power increasingly assumed the menacing shape of unbridled sovereignty of the State in the international sphere, it became the promoter of international anarchy and threatened, through the spectre of modern war, both the rights of man and the heritage of his civilisation. The movement towards the revival of natural law after the First World War was a manifestation of the resulting wide-spread sense of danger. When in the following decade pagan absolutism as perfected in the German State threatened to engulf man, in countries opposed to that ideology the tradition of the law of nature became once more a vital element in the affirmation of the sanctity of the individual and in the craving to find a basis of the law more enduring than the enforceable will of the sovereign. In so far as totalitarianism and its denial of funda- mental human freedoms drew their mystical inspiration from the philosophical revolt against reason—one of the most characteristic manifestations of the German National-Socialist and Italian Fascist doctrines—it was inevitable that the desire to vindicate human rights should, once more, ally itself with the rationalist foundations, truly laid by Locke, Newton and Jefferson, of the philosophy of natural law. Only so can we explain the fervour and intensity of the periodic resurgence of the idea of natural law in the twentieth century. Only so can we explain why, at the very time when the international recognition of human rights has become to a substantial extent part of positive law and when attempts are made, through an International Bill of Human Rights and otherwise, to make that recognition more effective, there is no inclination to jettison the appeal to the natural rights of man and to the law of nature conceived as the justification and the measure of all man-made law.

CHAPTER 7

THE LAW OF NATIONS AND THE INALIENABLE RIGHTS OF MAN

1. INTERNATIONAL LAW AND THE LAW OF NATURE

IT has been shown in the preceding Chapter that the intimate relation between the law of nature and the notion of the inherent rights of man has not been a one-way movement of ideas, and that the doctrines of natural law owed as much, in their rise and in their growth, to the ideas of the inalienable rights of man as the latter owed to the former. We can trace the same mutuality of influence in the relations of international law and the law of nature.

The modern law of nations as it came into being after the Reformation and as it was formulated by Grotius and his immediate predecessors, originated in the historic necessity of regulating the relations of the new sovereign States which arose on the ruins of the temporal unity of Christendom. But the manner, the speed and, to a high degree, the substance of the transformation of that historic necessity into a working body of rules were determined to a large extent by the doctrine of the law of nature as modernised and secularised by Grotius. He availed himself of the law of nature, to which he gave fresh vitality and authority, as one of the foundations of modern international law. But much of the new vigour and dignity which he imparted to the law of nature came from the fact that it was made the basis for the so much needed law governing the relations of sovereign States. International law, by thus endowing the law of nature with a great historic function, gave it a new lease of life and a new significance.

But here again, in a different sphere and to a different degree, there was repeated the phenomenon which we observed in the relation of the law of nature and the ideas of the rights of man. One of the factors which in the seventeenth and eighteenth centuries gave new vitality to the law of nature was the need for a law of nations. Subsequently, the law of nature gave as much as

114

it had received—and much more. In fact, it is difficult to exaggerate the part which the law of nature played in the creation and development of the law of nations. It did so not only *eo nomine*, but also through the constant influence of Roman law, the written reason, the *ratio scripta*. When, in 1758, Vattel was calling his treatise *Le Droit des Gens, ou Principes de la Loi Naturelle, appliqués à la conduite et aux affaires des Nations et des Souverains*, he was giving expression to one of the salient features of modern international law. In this respect—the recourse to natural law—there was only a difference of emphasis between so-called naturalists, Grotians, and positivists. The rigid distinction between these three schools of thought was an afterthought of the positivist period in the twentieth century—a period which was but of short duration. With the Statute of the Permanent Court of International Justice, which declared ' general principles of law as recognised by civilised States '— in some ways a modern version of the law of nature—to be one of the primary sources of international law, what was of the essence of the law of nature, namely, its conformity with the actual legal experience of mankind,[1] came once more into its own. It was elevated not to the dignity—for it had an abundance of that in its own right—but to the formal status of a source of the law of nations. We may now recall that the law of nature which thus acted through the ages as the principal vehicle of the development of international law owed much of its appeal, of its *raison d'être* and of its very origin to its connexion with the affirmation of the rights of man. International law is thus indirectly under an obligation to the notion of inherent human rights.

2. THE FOUNDERS OF INTERNATIONAL LAW AND THE NATURAL RIGHTS OF MAN. GROTIUS

The relation, as outlined above, between international law and fundamental human rights is more substantial than one of indebtedness. For international law has in this matter given more than it has taken. In the first instance, the founders of modern international law were instrumental, in various and often circuitous ways, in stressing the value and importance of the

[1] See above, p. 100.

natural rights of man. The issue presented itself in a clear-cut form to Francisco de Vitoria, perhaps the greatest of the scholastic writers who preceded Grotius in the sixteenth century. In his work *De Indis Noviter Inventis,* composed in 1532, he propounded the view that the primitive peoples of America were entitled to the protection of the rules of law and justice applicable to all the peoples of the world. Even after Christianity had been proposed to them with simple proof and they refused to accept it, this would not make it lawful to wage war upon them and to deprive them of their possessions.

Grotius, it is true, appeared in one vital respect to have adopted an attitude inconsistent with the recognition of the inherent rights of man. For he seemed to deny the right of resistance—a right which, in the absence of effective protection by the society of States, is the supreme assertion of the inalienable rights of man. That right of resistance, he taught, although following from the natural right to ward off injury, is limited within the State in the interest of public peace and order. It would seem that, to his mind, most evils were preferable to civil strife. He adduced some specious arguments based on the contention that by Hebraic and Roman law a person could sell himself irrevocably as a slave. But it would be misleading to judge the attitude of Grotius to the ideas of political freedom by his views on the right of resistance. This is so not only because of the personal circumstances in which he found himself when writing *De Jure Belli ac Pacis.* He was at that time in France—a fugitive from a temporary eruption of Calvinistic intolerance in Holland. He lived under the protection of Louis XIII, the powerful monarch to whom he dedicated his work. It is understandable, if not pardonable, that he made a point of denying to peoples the right to punish and coerce kings. But there is more to it than an explanation in terms of personal circumstance. For while Grotius denied the right of active rebellion, he was emphatic that there was no duty to carry out orders which were contrary to the law of nature or to the commandments of God.[2] Secondly, even with regard to active resistance, Grotius admitted of exceptions which to a large extent nullified his principal thesis, such as in the case of ' rulers who are responsible to the people, whether such power was conferred at

[2] *De Jure Belli ac Pacis,* Book I, Ch. IV, i.3. And see the writer's article entitled ' The Grotian Tradition in International Law ', in *British Year Book of International Law,* 23 (1946), pp. 43-46.

the beginning or under a later arrangement, as at Sparta '.[3] ' If such rulers transgress against the laws and the state, not only can they be resisted by force, but in case of necessity, they can be punished with death.' The passage is obscure; it is entitled ' that the right to make war may be conceded against him who has the chief authority among a free people '.[4] If the passage means anything at all, it largely nullifies his sweeping denial of the right of resistance. It would mean that that right is excluded only with regard to absolute monarchies in which the people surrendered unconditionally all their rights.

Grotius also admits of other weighty exceptions to the principle of non-resistance. These include the wide and elastic case of resistance against extreme oppression; for this, he says, is a case of self-defence: ' I should hardly dare indiscriminately to condemn either individuals, or a minority which at length availed itself of the last resource of necessity.' [5] Thirdly, we must remember that on a wider view it is not the principle of non-resistance, explained to some extent by the personal circumstances of the great jurist and attenuated by the elastic exceptions, which is the proper measure of his attitude. That measure is the fact that the human being is the centre of the Grotian system both in the internal and in the international sphere. He identifies the law of nature with the nature of man conceived both in abstract isolation and as a social being. ' For the very nature of man, which even if we had no lack of anything would lead us into the mutual relations of society, is the mother of the law of nature.' [6] And it will be noted that one of the main features of his teaching is the insistence that the standards of justice applicable to individuals are valid in relation to States.[7] These, he maintains, in relation to mankind at large occupy the position which individuals occupy within the State.[8] Finally, in assessing the place of Grotius in the matter of the fundamental rights of man we must not forget that it is from him that originates the idea of international humanitarian intervention for the protection of

[3] *Ibid.*, Book I, Ch. IV, viii.
[4] *Jus belli dari posse in principem populi liberi*, Book I, Ch. IV, viii.4.
[5] Book I, Ch. IV, VII.4.
[6] *Proleg.*, 16.
[7] *Ibid.*, 21.
[8] *Populi respectu totius generis humani privatorum locum obtinent* (*Mare liberum*, Ch. V).

those rights. He claimed for rulers the right to demand punishment
' not only on account of injuries committed against themselves or
their subjects, but also on account of injuries which do not directly
affect them but excessively violate the law of nature or of nations
in regard to any persons whatsoever '.[9] And he lays it down
elsewhere that when a tyrant practises against his subjects
atrocities which no just man can approve, ' the exercise of the
right vested in human society is not precluded '.[10] It was this
conception of the law of nature, with man and his welfare
occupying the centre of the system—a direct link with the
Thomist view of natural law—which passed from Grotius to
Locke and, through him, to the wide scene of the revolutionary
declarations of 1776 and 1789.

3.   THE SAME.   VATTEL.   WOLFF.   PUFENDORF

Vattel, second only to Grotius in authority and influence, went
beyond the founder of modern international law in defending the
fundamental rights of man.   He insisted that obedience ought not
to be absolute or blind, and that no agreement can bind or even
authorise subjects to violate the natural law.   It is convenient to
quote his words in full [11]:

> ' It is taken for granted that every citizen impliedly agrees to
> this diminution of his rights, because without it society could not
> exist.   But when it is a case of clear and glaring wrongs, when a
> prince for no apparent reason attempts to take away our life, or
> deprive us of things without which life would be miserable, who
> will question the right to resist him?   The care of our existence
> is not only a matter of natural right but of natural obligation as
> well; no man may give it up entirely and absolutely; and even
> though he could give it up, is it to be thought that he has done
> so by the compact of civil society when he entered into it for the
> sole purpose of obtaining greater security for his personal safety?
> The welfare of society does not indeed demand such a sacrifice.
> As Barbeyrac has well said in his notes on Grotius, " if it is in
> the interest of the public that those who obey should put up with
> some inconveniences, it is none the less for the public interest that
> those in authority should fear to test their patience too severely ".'

[9] *De Jure Belli ac Pacis,* Book II, Ch. XX, xl.1.
[10] Book II, Ch. XXV, viii.2.
[11] Book I, Ch. IV, § 54 (as translated by Fenwick in the Carnegie Endowment
edition of 1916).

Neither is Vattel's insistence on the freedom of philosophical discussion without interest; [12] nor his distinction between ordinary laws and the fundamental laws of the constitution which, he says, even the nation as a whole ought not to change lightly; [13] nor his denial that the Prince can change, or be absolved from obedience to, fundamental laws even if he is generally invested with legislative power. [14]   The person of the Prince is sacred and inviolable, but only for so long as he does not transgress the fundamental law: ' The moment he attacks the Constitution of the State the Prince breaks the contract which bound the people to him; and the people become free by the act of the sovereign and henceforth they regard him as an usurper seeking to oppress them.' [15]   In elaborating this right of resistance Vattel uses language substantially reminiscent of that of Locke.   He goes considerably beyond Grotius in admitting the right of resistance regardless of whether the Prince is an absolute ruler or not, for even if the people have surrendered their rights without express reservation, there is always the implied reservation of the supreme right of resistance.   Moreover, he says, when the ruler gives his subjects a lawful cause for resisting him, any foreign power may rightfully assist the oppressed people. [16]   Here, once more, we have the recognition—especially significant in the case of Vattel, whose respect for the sovereignty of States otherwise knows few limits— of the right of international intervention to safeguard the fundamental rights of the individual.   It is not surprising that Vattel became a popular source of quotation by the theorists of the American Revolution.

The contribution of the writers on international law to the stock of ideas on the rights of man came also by way of elaboration of the doctrine of equality of States.   The analogy of the equality of individuals proved a fertile source of argument, and there was no hesitation in relying on it on a liberal scale.   ' Just as the tallest man ', says Wolff, ' is no more a man than the dwarf, so also a nation, however small, is no less a nation than the greatest nation.   Therefore, since the moral equality of men has no relation to the size of their bodies, the moral equality of nations

[12] Book I, Ch. XI. § 114.
[13] Book I, Ch. III, § 35.
[14] Book I, Ch. IV, §§ 46, 47.
[15] Book I, Ch. IV, § 51.
[16] Book II, Ch. IV, § 56.

also has no relation to the number of men of which they are composed.' [17]   And it was not without an eye on the question of equality of States that Pufendorf wrote his well-known chapter on the natural equality of men.[18]   However, Pufendorf's more direct contribution lay in his affirmation of the subjection of the legislator to the higher law of human nature and of reason.[19]

Was it a mere coincidence that the three greatest figures in the literature of international law in the seventeenth and eighteenth centuries were the three principal writers who exercised a powerful influence upon the growth and acceptance of the ideology of the inalienable rights of man?   One explanation, as already suggested, is that the law of nature, which was one of the starting points of that ideology, itself acquired fresh vigour by having become the basis of the system of international law.   By dint of that renewed vitality, purged by Grotius and others of its clericalism, it was enabled to continue with increased power its age-old function of supplying the foundation and the stimulus for transforming, at the end of the eighteenth century, the idea of natural rights into a dynamic political principle.   Another explanation is that the law of nations, in itself conceivable only as being above the legal order of sovereign States—in the same way as the higher law of nature is superior to them—is not only a law governing their mutual relations but is also, upon final analysis, the universal law of humanity in which the individual human being as the ultimate unit of all law rises sovereign over the limited province of the State.

4. The Doctrine of Humanitarian Intervention.
The Fundamental Rights of Aliens and Nationals

International law has contributed in a more direct way to the maintenance of the rights of man and the protection of his welfare by the significant, though hesitating and infrequent, practice of humanitarian intervention such as that on behalf of the Greek people in 1827 and, subsequently, of the oppressed Armenians— and Christians generally—in Turkey; by the practice, which began in the middle of the seventeenth century, of safeguarding through treaties the right of religious freedom; by the long series

[17] *Jus gentium methodo scientifica pertractatum* (1764), Proleg. § 16.
[18] *De Jure Naturæ et Gentium* (1688), Book III, Ch. 2.
[19] *Ibid.*, Book VIII, Ch. I, §§ 2, 6.

of treaties of a humanitarian character ranging from slavery conventions to the imposing structure of conventions concluded under the aegis of the International Labour Organisation; by the Minorities Treaties entered into after the First World War; and by the systems of mandates and trusteeship set up, respectively, after the two World Wars. In fact, we can trace two strains in modern international law. One has been concerned with the relations between States as such: with the law of treaties, with the jurisdictional immunities of diplomatic representatives and of foreign States generally, with acquisition of territory, and with the rules governing the conduct of war. The other has used international law for promoting and protecting, through international co-operation and international institutions, the interests and welfare of the individual. The great and increasing volume of what is conveniently described as international legislation has been largely devoted to that latter aspect. Those developments have been traced in some detail in Part I of this book.

Although international law does not at present recognise, apart from treaty, any fundamental rights of the individual protected by international society as against the State of which he is a national, it does acknowledge some of the principal fundamental rights of the individual in one particular sphere, namely, in respect of aliens. These are entitled to treatment conforming to a minimum standard of civilisation regardless of how the State where they reside treats its own nationals. That minimum standard of civilisation comprises, in particular, the right of personal liberty and, generally, the right to equality before the law. International tribunals have repeatedly declared it to be a rule of international law. The result, which is somewhat paradoxical, is that the individual in his capacity as an alien enjoys a larger measure of protection by international law than in his character as the citizen of his own State. In current theory and terminology these are not the rights of the alien; they are the rights of his State to insist that its nationals should be treated in accordance with certain principles. But this is not necessarily an accurate generalisation of the procedural incapacity of individuals in existing international law—an incapacity which has already been lifted in many spheres. Moreover, under the practice of the systems of protection of minorities and, even more so, of mandatory government, the procedural capacity of the individual received incipient recognition by the admission of petitions which, while conferring no legal *locus standi* upon the individual, set in motion the appropriate international procedure. Under the trusteeship system these developments have received added emphasis.[20] International practice has recognised a measure of direct access of individuals to international tribunals, as well as their capacity to acquire rights directly under treaties.[21]

Finally, the fundamental rights of the individual have been recognised—directly and indirectly—as part of international law in two basic international instruments: directly, in the repeated clauses of the Charter of the United Nations relating to human rights and fundamental freedoms[22]; indirectly, in the provisions of the Charters of the International Military Tribunals of Nuremberg and the Far East relating to crimes against humanity.[23]

5. The Interaction of International Law, the Law of Nature and the Doctrine of Natural Rights

This, then, is the past contribution of the law of nations to the idea and the actual protection of the rights of man. It has expressed itself in the work and in the influence of the leading publicists, in the practice of safeguarding the rights of man through humanitarian intervention and through a variety of treaties, and in a measure of recognition of the rights of aliens and of the individual generally. In order to realise fully the significance, past and future, of the contribution of international law in that sphere we must have before our mind's eye the intricate picture, which it has been attempted to sketch in this Chapter, of the inward relation and mutual influence of the law of nature, the law of nations and the rights of man. We have seen how the notion of the rights of man derived its strength and sustenance from the law of nature. We have ascertained how the law of nature owed much of its vitality and growth to its association with the notion of the rights of man. We have followed the part which the law of nature played in the creation of modern international law and the accession of strength which it in turn received

[20] See below, pp. 242-244.
[21] See above, pp. 29, 30, 49, 50.
[22] See above, pp. 33-35, and below, pp. 145-154.
[23] See above, pp. 35-38.

from the law of nations. We have traced the benefits which international law obtained—indirectly, through the law of nature —from the notion of the rights of man, and what it has contributed to it. Each of the three has been in relation to the two others the recipient and the benefactor, the master and the tool, the originator and the product.

This picture of the most intimate connexion between the rights of man, the law of nature and the law of nations may appear to some to be dialectical to the point of ingenuity. Nevertheless, it is this picture which probably represents a true account of the history of political and legal thought on this central issue. Moreover, it is believed to be expressive of a deeper unity. In the theories of the law of nature the starting point and the irreducible element has been the individual human being. The law of nations, and, we may say, the law of nature, by denying, as they needs must do, the absolute sovereignty of States, give their imprimatur to the indestructible sovereignty of man. It is probably the natural law of humanity to develop its capacities to all attainable perfection. This is also an essential part of man's moral duty. That duty man has a natural right to fulfil—through freedom. Inasmuch as freedom means the fullest development of the possibilities of human personality it is not a means of the highest order, but an end in itself. The State is to ensure that freedom. The law of nations, conceived in the fulness of its proper function, exists for the double purpose of accomplishing that object by making man's freedom secure from the State and by rendering the State secure from external danger. It is not enough to say that the law of the State is circumscribed by its purpose and by the external nature of its power. Democracy, although an essential condition of freedom, is not an absolute safeguard of it. That safeguard must lie outside and above the State.

6. THE INTERNATIONAL ORDER AND THE INALIENABLE RIGHTS OF MAN

In that scheme of things the sovereign national State, whether or not it be the permanent form of the political organisation of man, is not an end unto itself but the trustee of the welfare and of the final purpose of man. In that scheme of things it is for international society to ensure the fulfilment of that trust through a fundamental enactment—an International Bill of the Rights of Man—conceived not as a declaration of principles but as part of positive law, *i.e.,* as part of the constitutional law both of States and of the society of States at large. In relation to the national declarations of rights, a true International Bill of the Rights of Man would constitute an advance commensurate with that which the Declarations of 1776 and 1789 marked upon the law of the eighteenth century. These Declarations drew upon themselves a volume of criticism hardly surpassed in passionate condemnation and in the ingenuity of its dialectics. Yet in retrospect the strictures of Burke,[25] of Bentham[26] and of

[25] Burke, who described the Declaration of 1789 as a ' digest of anarchy ', was more temperate in his criticism than Bentham. He did not deny ' the real rights of man '; he did not even deny that they can be discerned. But he challenged the wisdom of defining them: ' If civil society be made for the advantage of man, all the advantages for which it is made become his right (*Reflections on the French Revolution* (Dent's ed., 1910), p. 56). Previously, although he had attacked the theorists of the French Declaration, he invoked, in his great speech on the American rebellion, ' the natural rights of mankind '. These, he said, ' are indeed sacred things, and if any public measure is proved mischievously to affect them, the objection ought to be fatal to that measure, even if no charter at all could be set against it. Only a sovereign reason, paramount to all forms of legislation and administration, should dictate '. This language is not far removed from that of The French Revolution.

[26] In 1795 Bentham collected his critical observations on the subject in some essays entitled ' *Anarchical Fallacies: being an examination of the Declarations of Rights issued during the French Revolution': Works* (Bowring's edition, 1843), II, pp. 491 ff.). One line of Bentham's criticism was that if the purpose of the Declaration was to limit the power of the representative bodies elected by the people, that object was not possible of achievement. For the legislature was elected by the people, and the people could not bind itself—a view set forth by Hamilton in his opposition to the Bill of Rights (*The Federalist,* No. 84). Bentham's main argument (lucidly summarised by Halevy, *The Growth of Philosophic Radicalism* (English translation, 1928), pp. 175 *et seq.*) was that the Declaration amounted to saying that ' every law, or other order, divesting a man of the enjoyment of life or liberty is void ', and that consequently all penal laws are void. There was no law which, in his view, could not be met by the unanswerable argument that it had abrogated the Declaration of Rights. Some of Bentham's criticism is due to an ultra-positivist view of the law of the clear Austinian brand: ' Right is the child of law; from real laws come real rights, but from imaginary law, from laws of nature, come imaginary rights, a bastard brood of monsters. . . . Natural rights is simple nonsense; natural and imprescriptible rights (an American phrase), rhetorical nonsense, nonsense upon stilts.' Elsewhere he says: ' Unbounded resistance to oppression; that is, unbounded exercise of the faculty of guarding himself against whatever unpleasant circumstance may present itself to his imagination or his passions under that name. Nature, say some of the interpreters of the pretended law of nature—nature gave to each man a right to everything; which is, in effect, but another way of saying—nature has given no such right to anybody; for in regard to most rights, it is as true that what is every man's right is no man's right, as that what is every man's business is no man's business.' (*Anarchical Fallacies, op. cit.,* vol. II, p. 502.) Much of

von Gentz [27]—as well as of modern critics such as Ritchie [28]—appear petty and petulant.   The cautious faith of Jefferson [29] and of Sir James Mackintosh [30] stands out in comparison as a more

Bentham's opposition is explained by the sincere apprehension of the practical reformer lest mere talk about natural rights be regarded by some as a sufficient substitute for legislation.   Moreover, although J. S. Mill referred, somewhat sweepingly, to Bentham's system as dealing almost entirely with the business relations of life, the following statement of Bentham's is significant: 'The happiness of the worst man of the species is as much an integrant of the whole mass of human happiness as is that of the best man.'   In fact, notwithstanding the vigour with which Bentham rejected the idea of the law of nature, his statement of the utilitarian principle may be regarded, without undue ingenuity, as a variant of the doctrine of natural law. Similarly, the cogency of his formal criticism of the French Declaration is somewhat impaired by the suggestion of an alternative put forward by his disciple Dumont: 'Instead of a Declaration of the Rights of Man there should have been prefixed to the constitution a few *social maxims*, founded upon general utility, and pointing out precisely the " object of society, and the duties of government".   These maxims would never have pretended to the honour of forming the *credo* of a political religion.' (*Groenvelt Letters*, p. 228.) The difference between 'a few social maxims' prefixed to the Constitution and a Declaration of Rights preceding the Constitution is one of form.   A certain measure of inconsistency in this respect is also common to some modern critics of natural rights.   Thus an emphatic opponent of individualism spoke of the duties of the State to prevent unemployment as constituting, in a specific sense, a right to work: see Jethro Brown, *The Underlying Principles of Modern Legislation* (1912), p. 285.

[27] *Ueber die Deklaration der Rechte* (1792), republished in Friedrich von Gentz, *Ausgewählte Schriften* (1837).   But it is indicative of the temper of the period that Gentz fully accepted the doctrine of natural rights and the theory of the social contract.   He says: 'That man, when he enters the world, brings with him rights of which nothing but his own free will may deprive him even to the smallest extent—of this nowadays no person doubts who has devoted some passing thought to man conceived as a moral entity and properly described as a human being' (p. 64).   But after describing the Declaration as 'one of the most important documents in the history of this century ', he subjected it to destructive criticism on the lines of Burke and Bentham.   His conclusion was that 'the system of the French rights of man combines all errors which can possibly underlie a constitution, in particular a systematic constitution.   It is inaccurate in itself; it is inapplicable; it is destructive of its own purposes.   Even the greatest admirer of the highest good of humanity, even the warmest friend of the people, can hardly suppress a smile on beholding the caricature drawn up by the French legislature under the title of rights of man '. (*Ibid.*, p. 108.)

[28] *Natural Rights* (1894).   See also Jethro Brown, *op. cit.*, pp. 235-297.

[29] In a letter to Madison written in 1789 he said: 'The declaration of rights is like all other human blessings, alloyed with some inconveniences, and not accomplishing fully its object.   But the good, in this instance, vastly over-weighs the evil.'   In another letter to Madison, written in the same year, he said: 'Experience proves the inefficacy of a bill of rights!   True. But though it is not absolutely efficacious under all circumstances, it is of great potency always, and rarely inefficacious. . . . There is a remarkable difference between the character of the inconveniences which attend a declaration of rights, and those which attend the want of it.   The inconveniences of the declaration are that it may cramp government in its useful exertions.   But the evil of it is short-lived, moderate and reparable.   The inconveniences of the want of a declaration are permanent, afflicting, and irreparable.' (*Democracy*, by Jefferson, selected by Padover, 1939, pp. 76, 77.)

[30] *Vindiciæ Gallicæ* (1791), Section IV.   For a sound assessment of the value of the Declaration of Rights see Dicey, *Law and Public Opinion in England during the Nineteenth Century* (1905), p. 171.   See also Laski, *Liberty in the Modern State* (1930), p. 52; Gooch, in *The Evolution of World-Peace* (2nd ed. by Marvin, 1933), pp. 98-104.

accurate expression of the enduring strivings and accomplishments of humanity and justifies Lord Acton's judgment that the single confused page of the Declaration of 1789 outweighs libraries and is stronger than all the armies of Napoleon. At the same time, the lesson of the century and a half which have followed these Declarations shows that the rights of man are beset by mortal dangers and must largely remain in the realm of theory unless they are made secure in the firm anchorage of the international legal order. Only so can we resolve the contradiction, which has always been a favourite theme of the opponents of declarations of rights of man, between the supremacy of the law within the State and the notion of fundamental human rights.

Any such consummation, in which the rights of man will form part of the positive law of the society of States, will not mean that the law of nature has played its part in the matter and must henceforth be consigned to the province of historical research. The law of nature must supply, as it has done in the past, much of the spiritual basis and much of the political inspiration of that elevation of the rights of man to a legal plane superior to the will of sovereign States. Nothing short of that spiritual basis will be of sufficient authority to lend permanent support to an innovation so significant and so far-reaching. The view that the rights of man are grounded in positive law only is mischievous not only when related to the positive law of the State; it is equally objectionable in relation to the positive law of international society. The law of nature is in no sense a substitute for positive law; it cannot by itself supply the solution of the problem of the rights of man. Whenever that happens the doctrine of natural rights degenerates into a doctrine of vested rights. Whenever the law of nature is treated as an alternative to changes in existing law it ceases, on balance, to be a beneficent force and becomes a check upon progress. If the enthronement of the rights of man is to become a reality, then they must become part of the positive law of nations suitably guaranteed and enforced. That consummation cannot be achieved—it is liable to be retarded—by solemn incantations in the form of declarations of principle.[31]

---

[31] See below, pp. 394-428, on the Universal Declaration of Human Rights adopted in 1948 by the General Assembly of the United Nations.

CHAPTER 8

THE ENGLISH SOURCES OF THE DOCTRINE
OF FUNDAMENTAL RIGHTS

GREAT BRITAIN has remained outside the orbit of the general trend to safeguard the basic rights of the individual in a comprehensive fundamental enactment covering the totality of civil liberties. This is not for the reason that Great Britain does not possess a written constitution. For much of her constitutional law in the sphere of human rights has in fact been reduced to written form. The reason is that Great Britain is a country with a flexible as distinguished from a rigid constitution. The provisions of the Habeas Corpus Act, or of the Bill of Rights of 1689 or, indeed, any other part of statutory or common law relating to the liberties of the subject can be changed overnight by the ordinary process of legislation, *i.e.,* by a simple majority of both Houses of Parliament assented to by the King. It is also true that, with weighty exceptions, the doctrine of natural rights—a potent source of constitutional enactments bearing upon human freedom —found no favour with English political and legal thinkers throughout the nineteenth century. However, this is only one half of the story. For it is not the formal structure of the English constitution, nor the impatient refutations of the Declarations of Rights by Burke and Bentham, nor the negative and complacent attitude of the analytical school which, in this matter, have become the common heritage of the world. The latter has been the result of the long list of English constitutional charters of liberty; the works of Milton, of Sidney, of Halifax, and, above all, of Locke; of the doctrines of the Puritans and of the Cromwellian revolution; and of the veneration of fundamental rights of freedom by great lawyers from Bracton through Coke to Blackstone, whose chapter on the ' Absolute Rights of the Individual ', although lending itself to conflicting interpretations,[1] was not inferior in its beneficent influence to the impressive solemnity of the language in which he extolled them.

[1] See below, pp. 136, 137.

The English contribution to political thought and practice in this sphere may best be gauged by its influence on the successive constitutions of American States prior to the Bill of Rights. These pronouncements—and they were the principal source of the French Declarations[2] and, with them, of the constitutional practice of most States—owe their origin in varying degrees of importance to a variety of causes and influences of which the English sources were the most prominent and most easily discernible. There was, first, the English constitutional practice of safeguarding the rights of the subject by way of statutory enactment, beginning with Magna Carta and its successive confirmations, continuing through the Habeas Corpus Act and the Petition of Right, and ending with the Bill of Rights and the Act of Settlement—a practice which, contrary to the current view, was not altogether alien to English political doctrine.[3] The second was the influence of the English political and legal doctrines of freedom and toleration, especially those of the Puritan revolution and of the writings of Milton, Sidney, Locke and Blackstone.[4] In the period immediately preceding the American revolution, at a time of the ascendancy of a corrupt Parliament guided by a venal Government and a self-willed monarch, the people of England successfully asserted, in effect against Parliament itself, the essence of their traditional rights and freedoms and gave a powerful stimulus to American

[2] Of this Condorcet's writings bear convincing testimony. In his work *On the Influence of the American Revolution in Europe,* published in 1786, he set out a list of the rights of man which included the security of the person, the security and free enjoyment of property, and participation, directly or through representatives, in legislation. In his " Instruction by the Provinces to their Representatives at the States General of 1789 " the list was enlarged to include the right to be tried by judges appointed according to law, and to control of taxes and expenditure. The Bill of Rights of Virginia of 1776 was referred to by Lafayette in his speech to the Constituent Assembly of France: *Mémoires et Correspondance de Lafayette* (1838), vol. II, p. 305 (cited from Vinogradoff, *Collected Papers,* vol. II (1928), p. 375).

[3] Thus Cromwell gave lucid expression to the idea of a fundamental organic law: ' In every Government there must be Somewhat Fundamental, Somewhat like a Magna Charta, which should be standing, be unalterable. . . . That Parliaments should not make themselves perpetual is a Fundamental. Of what assurance is a *Law* to prevent so great an evil, if it lie in the same Legislature to *unlaw* it again?' (Carlyle, *Oliver Cromwell's Letters and Speeches,* Part VIII, Speech III). See also John Wildman, *Truth's Triumph* (1647), p. 11: ' I believe that the freedoms of this Nation will never be secure, untill the extent of the power and trust of the people's reservations to themselves be clearly declared.'

[4] See below, pp. 136, 137.

resistance and to the American doctrines of the higher law.[5] The Bill of Rights Society, the repeated elections of Wilkes, the triumphant vindication of the right of petition—these were portents and events watched and applauded on the other side of the ocean.[6] The third powerful influence in bringing about the American Declarations of Rights lay in the precedents of the early history of the American colonies, with their own Puritan tradition of toleration and the first political compacts which they set up as the basis of their political life. The fourth was the influence of continental thought in the domain of political theory, in particular of Montesquieu. The fifth was the desire of the authors of the American Bill of Rights to safeguard freedom not only against the encroachments of the Executive but also against the tyranny of the Legislature and its majorities. Finally, at the time of the rise of American independence the doctrine of natural rights was, as it had always been, the handmaid of political

[5] There is in the ' Declarations and Resolves of the First Continental Congress ' of 1774 an interesting mixture of these two elements. In that document the inhabitants of the English colonies in North America asserted their various rights by reference to ' the immutable laws of nature, the principles of the English constitution, and the several charters or compacts ': *Documents Illustrative of the Formation of the Union of the American States* (selected by Col. Tansill, 1927, 69th Congress, 1st Session, House Document No. 398). And see John Adams' insistence at that time that the colonies should ' recur to the law of nature, as well as to the British constitution, and our American charters and grants ': *Works of John Adams,* 10 vols. (1850-1856), vol. X, p. 172. We find the same combination of the two elements in Otis's *The Rights of the British Colonies Asserted and Proved* (1764). The colonists, he said, are ' by the law of God and nature, by the common law, and by Act of Parliament . . . entitled to all the natural, essential, inherent and inseparable rights of our fellow subjects in Great Britain ' (p. 35). In 1765 the Massachusetts Assembly declared that ' there are certain essential rights of the British Constitution of government, which are founded in the law of God and nature, and are the common rights of mankind ' (as quoted by Wright, *American Interpretations of Natural Law* (1931), p. 72). With others the claim to freedom was based on the law of nature pure and simple. The language of John Dickinson of Pennsylvania, in his *Address to the Committee of Correspondence in Barbados,* is unequivocal: ' King or parliaments could not *give* the *rights* essential to happiness, as you confess those invaded by the Stamp Act to be. We claim them from a higher source, from the King of Kings and Lord of all the earth. They are created in us by the decree of Providence, which establish the laws of nature. They are born with us, and cannot be taken from us by any human power, without taking our lives. In short, they are founded on the immutable maxims of reason and justice ' (*Writings,* Forde's edition, vol. 14, p. 262). Jefferson, of course, was in the same group. Above all, Hamilton gave weighty and eloquent expression to this trend of revolutionary thought. (See above, p. 101.) See also Jellinek, *La déclaration des droits de l'homme et du citoyen* (French transl., 1902); Becker, *The Declaration of Independence: A Study in the History of Political Ideas* (1922); McIlwain, *The American Revolution: A Constitutional Interpretation* (1923).

[6] See Chapters IV and V of G. O. Trevelyan's *The Early History of Charles James Fox* (1880).

9

necessities and aspirations. It was the appointed weapon of a nation in revolt[7]—the main reason for its unpopularity in the country of its origin.[8]

Closer investigation of these sources of the American Declarations of Rights cannot be attempted here. They have been summarised in order to throw into relief the part played by British legal and political thought. For of all the factors mentioned, the English contribution was the most direct and most readily acknowledged. This is not generally admitted. Many have doubted whether there is any material connexion between the English charters of liberty and the doctrine of fundamental rights as adopted in the American and French Declarations. They have pointed to the now generally adopted view that the first historic document of the liberty of the subject, Magna Carta, was never what tradition and popular understanding believed it to be, namely, a vindication of the liberties of the people as a whole. It is now commonly accepted that the crucial Clause 39 of the Charter was a partisan instrument extorted from the King for the benefit of the feudal claims and privileges ' inimical alike to the Crown and to the growth of really popular liberties '.[9] It excluded the jurisdiction of the King's justices and stipulated for the trial of the feudal barons by their equals. This is now the recognised interpretation of Clause 39, which provided that no free man can be taken or imprisoned, or, generally, his person interfered with, except by the lawful judgment of his peers or of the law of the land. When, in *Darnel's Case*,[9a] John Selden argued that since Magna Carta no freeman ought to be imprisoned except according to the law of the land, and not by special command of

---

[7] See above, p. 111. And see, in particular, Chapter VIII, entitled ' The Making of the American Mind,' in Perry, *Puritanism and Democracy* (1944).

[8] See Miller, *Origins of the American Revolution* (1943), p. 173: ' Natural law was the first line of colonial liberty.' And see *ibid.*, pp. 215, 216, for interesting examples of English impatience with the use of the ' laws of nature ' as a starting point of revolutionary propaganda in the rebellious colonies: 'Americans stoutly insisted upon the right of interpreting natural law, which, Britons remarked, was submitting the laws of the empire not to God or Nature, but to a " jury of Bostonians " ' (*ibid.*).

[9] McKechnie, *Magna Carta* (1905), p. 449. See also Pollock and Maitland, *History of English Law* (2nd ed., 1923), vol. I, p. 173: ' Even in the most famous words of the Charter we may detect a feudal claim which will only cease to be dangerous when in the course of time men have distorted their meaning:—a man is entitled to the judgment of his peers; the King's justices are no peers for earls or barons . . .' See also McIlwain, *Constitutionalism and the Changing World* (1939), p. 87.

[9a] (1627) 3 St. Tr. 1.

the King, he pointed out that this right was limited to freemen; villeins—he contended—were bound to the land under feudal law, and had no remedy against arbitrary imprisonment.[10]

Yet the fact remains that in the history of fundamental rights no event ranks higher than that charter of concessions which the nobles wrested from King John. This is not a mere case of *communis error facit jus.*[11] For the essential feature of that event is the limitation of the power of the supreme authority; and the exclusion of the arbitrary power of man over man is the essence of freedom. The jurisdictional privilege which the barons secured, not without the support of other classes of the people, was not an exemption from the ordinary and regular processes of the law. It was a security against the arbitrary proceedings of the King's justices, against a tyrannical *droit administratif*. In this respect the meaning of Magna Carta is today essentially what it was in 1215. It is of no decisive significance that, in the main, only one class of the people benefited directly from that limitation of the royal power; what matters is the fact of the limitation. For it is this aspect of Magna Carta which became part and parcel of general consciousness. The vindication of human liberties does not begin with their complete and triumphant assertion at the very outset. It commences with their recognition in *some* matters, to *some* extent, for *some* people, against *some* organ of the State. Milton's defence of freedom is a landmark in the history of the rights of man; but the limitations which he put on that freedom are utterly unacceptable to its modern conception. He excluded from toleration ' popery and open superstitution which, as it extirpates all religious and civil supremacies, so itself should be extirpate, provided that all charitable and compassionate means be used to win and regain the weak and misled '.[12] For ' that

[10] The critical interpretation of Magna Carta is not of recent date. In 1645 we find Walwyn saying: ' Magna Charta hath been more precious in your esteem than it deserves; for it may be made good to the people and yet in many particulars they may remain under intolerable oppression ' (*England's Lamentable Slavery* (1645), p. 5). At the same time Overton referred to it as ' being but a beggarly thing, containing many marks of intolerable bondage ' (*A Remonstrance of Many Thousand Citizens* (1646), p.15).

[11] As McKechnie puts it, the greatness of *Magna Carta* ' lies not so much in what it was to its framers in 1215, as in what it afterwards became to political leaders, to the judges and lawyers, and to the entire mass of the men in England in later years': *Magna Carta* (2nd ed., 1914), p. 134. For Voltaire's reference to Magna Carta as the ' charter of liberty' see his *Lettres sur les Anglais*, pp. 64, 65.

[12] *Areopagitica (in fine).*

also which is impious or evil absolutely either against faith or manners no law can possibly permit that intends not to unlaw itself '. The Puritans who founded some of the American colonies were the champions of religious tolerance and democratic rule; but they were not unduly particular in setting a limit to either. According to many of the emigrants in the *Mayflower,* the ' good and religious man had a right to rule the evil and irreligious '. Neither were they too liberal in conceding the attributes of a ' good and religious man '. In 1656 some of the colonies decided on the exclusion of all ' Quakers, Ranters, and notorious heretics '. John Cotton limited religious toleration to ' circumstantials as distinguished from fundamentals '.[13] In his opinion and that of many other Puritans ' freedom was the prerogative of righteousness; the well-being of society required that the sinner should remain subject to the saint '.[14] Locke excluded from the principle of toleration opinions contrary to human society or to the moral precepts which are necessary to the preservation of civil society: ' those who attribute unto the faithful, religious, and orthodox, that is in plain language to themselves, any peculiar privilege or power above other mortals, in civil concernments; or, who upon pretence of religion, do challenge any manner of authority over such as are not associated with them in their ecclesiastical communion '; and ' those who deny the being of God for the taking away of God though but even in thought, dissolves all society '.[15] The authors of the French Declaration of the Rights of Man did

---

[13] A limitation which was refuted by Roger Williams in *The Bloudy Tenents of Persecution, for cause of Conscience, in a Conference between Truth and Peace* (1644). The Fundamental Articles of New Haven and the Massachusetts Body of Liberties of 1641 came near to setting up theocracies pure and simple. The privileges of the latter were enjoyed mainly by the freemen and members of the church who comprised only one-fifth of the total population. ' Democracy ', wrote John Cotton, ' I do not conceive that even God did ordain as a fit government, either for church or commonwealth ' (Hutchison. *The History of the Colony of Massachusetts Bay* (1765), p. 497). Jefferson's Bill of Religious Freedom suffered many a vicissitude before it became law. A sufficient number of the members of the legislature regarded it as a ' diabolical measure ' to prevent its passage when first introduced (see Jefferson's *Works,* Ford's ed., vol. II, p. 237).

[14] Perrington, *Main Currents of American Thought,* vol. I (1927), 'The Colonial Mind, 1620-1850 ', p. 33.

[15] *A Letter Concerning Toleration* (first letter): *Works,* vol. VI, p. 46. As he puts it in the same place, he excluded ' Papists for having the intent of exalting an authoritarian church above the state ' (*ibid.*). At the end of his Fourth Letter on Toleration Locke discusses the contention of his correspondent that ' every magistrate is by the law of nature under an obligation to use force to bring man to the true religion '. For some interesting observations on the limits of toleration from this point of view see Perry, *Puritanism and Democracy* (1944), pp. 545 *et seq.*

not consider freedom of association to be a necessary consequence of individual liberty.

These examples, which could be multiplied, show that the historic value of any single pronouncement affirming the rights of man as against authority is not dependent upon the degree of its completeness. Of that truth Magna Carta, even as rediscovered in its limited objective, is a paramount illustration. Its repeated confirmation, the Petition of Right, the Habeas Corpus Act, the Bill of Rights, and the Act of Settlement, drew their strength and continuity from the original document. What was of decisive and, ultimately, of permanent significance was that for the first time, in a basic constitutional document, a restraint was put upon the supreme power. It was this idea, not its temporary limitation to the charmed circle of the barons, that became a power in history. For that circle was destined to expand. In the course of time the original limitation became a dim memory which nothing but the industry of modern scholars would have resuscitated. The Bill of Rights of 1689 suffered, in a different sphere, from similar limitations. It was described by Burke and Macaulay as conservative. It was the work of Churchmen and of the rich Whig gentry who perpetuated their hold on the country to the exclusion of the masses of the people. It contained no reference to the liberties of the subject. And yet, by submitting the Crown to the supremacy of Parliament and by enthroning the right of resistance—which Locke, the theorist of the Whig revolution, considered to be valid against Parliament itself—as part of a fundamental constitutional document, it accomplished, in the perennial struggle for freedom, what Lord Acton described as ' the greatest thing done by the English nation '.[16]

Nor is the importance of the English contribution seriously influenced by the fact that the rights secured by the successive charters of liberty were not treated as inherent rights belonging to the Englishman as a person. They were claimed as based on statute, on grant, on long practice; they invoked prior laws, customs, and established liberties. The appeal was to the native rights of the Englishman, not to the natural rights of man. This, of course, was not invariably so. The language of the Levellers

[16] *Lectures on Modern History* (edited by Figgis and Laurence, 1906), p. 231.

and the Puritans, and the names of Milton,[17] Sidney,[18] Locke, [19] and Blackstone[20] forbid any such generalisation. But on the whole it is true that appeals to the law of nature in support of the freedom of the individual were less frequent in the eighteenth century in England than elsewhere. This was so for the very good reason that once the claims of freedom assumed the complexion of statutory enactment and of the tradition of the common law, it was easier and more plausible to invoke those rather than the precepts of the law of nature and the principle of inalienable rights.

Finally, we cannot hope to gain a proper understanding of the English contribution to the common stock of the constitutional doctrine of the rights of man without a critical examination of a view which, if accepted, would substantially reduce the significance of that contribution. It has been maintained that the very conception of inalienable and fundamental rights superior to the State was unknown to English legal and political tradition for the reason that the rights of the Englishman were secured only against the Executive, and not against the Legislature; that the successive crises and revolutions made little difference in this respect; and that what happened in 1689 was

[17] *The Tenure of Kings and Magistrates* (1649; *Works*, Bohn's ed., vol. II, p. 8): ' No man who knows aught, can be so stupid as to deny; that all men were born free . . . It being thus manifest, that the power of kings and magistrates is nothing but what is only derivative, transferred, and committed to them in trust from the people, to the common good of them all, in whom the power yet remains fundamentally, and cannot be taken from them, without a violation of their natural birthright.'

[18] *Discourse concerning Government* (1698), Ch. 1, § 2: ' that man is naturally free, that he cannot be justly deprived of his liberty without cause, and that he does not resign it nor any part of it, unless it be in consideration of a greater good which he proposes to himself.' God had implanted the principle of liberty in the breast of man, and the rights of the people proceed from nature. He says elsewhere: ' That which is not just is not law; and that which is not law ought not to be obeyed ' (*ibid.*).

[19] ' To understand political power aright, and derive it from its original, we must consider what estate all men are naturally in, and that is, a state of perfect freedom to order their actions within the bounds of the law of Nature, without asking leave or depending upon the will of any other man. A state also of equality, wherein all the power and jurisdiction is reciprocal, no one having more than another, there being nothing more evident than that creatures of the same species and rank, promiscuously born to all the same advantages of Nature, and the use of the same faculties, should also be equal one amongst another, without subordination or subjection ' (*Second Treatise on Government, II*, 4). ' Men, being, as has been said, by nature all free, equal and independent, no one can be put out of this estate, and subjected to the political power of another without his own consent, which is done by agreeing with other men, to join and unite into a community . . .' (*ibid.*, VIII). And see below, pp. 137, 138.

[20] See below, p. 136.

merely that the absolutism of the Whig Parliament replaced the absolutism of the King. Neither, it has been said, knew or recognised the indefeasible rights of man. This view is only partly true; and that part is not wholly relevant to the issue. In the first instance, the doctrine of the absolute supremacy of Parliament, unrestricted by a higher law, is of comparatively recent origin. It is not a doctrine which Bracton, or Coke, or Hooker, or Sir John Holt would accept.[21] Secondly, that assertion of the supremacy of Parliament must be treated in its historical context. In its primary sense it was a vindication of the right of the subject to be governed not by the arbitrary power of the king, but by the people through its freely elected representatives; it was one stage in the long process of asserting the right of man to freedom. What, from the point of view of the historian in the twentieth century, may have been the replacement of one kind of arbitrariness by another was an essential stage in a historical process—quite apart from the fact that the arbitrariness of Parliament is preferable to the arbitrariness of a king or a dictator.

Moreover, it is of interest to note how, even in the seventeenth and eighteenth centuries, when the doctrine of the supremacy of Parliament was asserted apparently without reservation, it was often accompanied in the writings of the foremost lawyers and political thinkers by the qualification of the overriding authority of a higher law. Coke laid down in clear terms the doctrine of the supremacy of Parliament: ' Of the power and jurisdiction of the parliament, for making of laws in proceeding by bill, it is so transcendent and absolute, as it cannot be confined either for causes or persons within any bounds.' [22] But in *Doctor Bonham's Case*,[23] and elsewhere,[24] he qualified the supremacy of Parliament

---

[21] ' The omnipotence of Parliament was not the orthodox theory of English law, if orthodox at all, even in Holt's time. It was formally adopted, and then not without lip-service to natural law, in Blackstone's *Commentaries* ': Sir Frederick Pollock in *Law Quarterly Review*, XXXIX (1923), p. 165.

[22] *Institutes*, edition of 1671, Part IV, Chapter I.

[23] (1610) 8, Co. Rep. 114a, 118a.

[24] In *Calvin's Case* (1608), 7, Co. Rep. 1, at 4b, he puts the same proposition in the following way: ' 1. That ligeance or obedience of the subject to the Sovereign is due by the law of nature; 2. that this law of nature is part of the laws of England; 3. that the law of nature was before any judicial or municipal law in the world; 4. that the law of nature is immutable and cannot be changed.' His answer to the suggestion of a Member of Parliament that sovereign power had no bounds was that ' sovereign power was

by making the interpretation of statutes subject to an overriding law of nature. There has been controversy as to whether the precedents on which Coke relied in *Doctor Bonham's Case* justified his conclusion. Some have doubted whether the relevant passage in the judgment of the great lawyer was in fact intended to deny the absolute supremacy of Parliament. But the very controversy is significant.[25]

It is even more so in the case of Blackstone. Was his homily on the law of nature which rendered void an Act of Parliament inconsistent therewith merely lip-service, seeing that no lawyer before him had affirmed so emphatically that ' the power of Parliament is absolute and without control? ' [26] Parliament, according to Blackstone, can do ' everything that is not naturally impossible '. But he thought that to refer to that power as ' the omnipotence of Parliament ' was ' a figure rather too bold '. And, possibly, his reference to Parliament as being empowered to ' do everything that is not naturally impossible ' ought to be interpreted in the light of his statement in the preceding chapter that ' the principal aim of society is to protect individuals in the enjoyment of those absolute rights which were vested in them by the immutable laws of nature '. Is it ' naturally possible ' for Parliament to divest the subject of rights vested in him by the ' immutable laws of nature '? It may not be profitable to engage in a textual interpretation of Blackstone. His insistence on the absolute supremacy of Parliament was probably due to the realisation, with which no lawyer can lightly dispense, of the necessity of a supreme power ' which must in all government reside somewhere '. Blackstone's glorification of the supremacy of Parliament may have been invoked by those in England who sought for legal arguments to support the claim to impose the will of the Parliament at Westminster upon the rebellious

no parliamentary word ' and that ' Magna Charta is such a fellow that he will have no sovereign '. From a speech by Sir Edw. Coke on the Petition of Right, 1628, quoted in Rushworth, *Historical Collections of Private Passages of State, Weighty Matters of Law, Remarkable Proceedings in Five Parliaments*, vol. I (1659), p. 562.

[25] See Plucknett in *Harvard Law Review*, 40 (1926), pp. 30-70; Thorne in *Law Quarterly Review*, 54 (1938), pp. 543-552; and Holdsworth, *History of English Law*, vol. V (1924), p. 475. And see Gardiner, *The Constitutional Documents of the Puritan Revolution* (1906), pp. 65-66 on the bill which Coke proposed to the House of Commons ' for the better securing of every freeman touching the propriety of his goods and liberty of his person '.

[26] *Commentaries*, Book I, Ch. 2, iii.

American colonies in matters of taxation and otherwise. But those rebellious colonies relied repeatedly upon Blackstone in asserting those inalienable and absolute rights of man which, in his words, ' the first and primary end of human laws is to maintain and regulate '. These rights are the right of personal security, the right of personal liberty, and the right of property. With regard to the last-mentioned, the colonies were specially interested in the principle that ' no subject of England can be constrained to pay any aids or taxes, even for the defence of the realm or the support of government, but such as are imposed by his own consent, or that of his representatives in parliament '.[27] The great constitutional charters of liberty, from Magna Carta to the Act of Settlement, Blackstone described as a ' declaration of our rights and liberties '—which, in fact, is the phraseology of the Bill of Rights.[28] There ought to be no doubt that, notwithstanding the strictures of Bentham and some modern critics,[29] the influence of the great lawyer was, on balance, a powerful factor in the cause of freedom and of the inalienable rights of man.

Unlike in the case of Blackstone, there was no ambiguity about the position of Locke, to whom the American and other declarations of rights are more indebted than to any other writer. His is not merely a defence of freedom against the arbitrariness of the Executive.[30] It is a vindication of the rights of man against the Legislature; it is a denial of the ultimate legal sovereignty of the State; it is an assertion of the legal right of rebellion against the State encroaching upon the natural rights of man. These views he does not put forward lightly and without having faced the necessity of a supreme centre of authority within the State.[31] He advances them with a clarity which discourages any attempt at paraphrasing his exposition. He says in his *Second Treatise of Civil Government*:

[27] *Commentaries*, Book I, Ch. I, iii.
[28] 'An Act declaring the Rights and Liberties of the Subject, and settling the Succession of the Crown.'
[29] See, *e.g.*, the interesting essay by Judge Jerome Frank, entitled ' A Sketch of an Influence', in *Interpretations of Modern Legal Philosophies. Essays in Honor of Roscoe Pound* (1947), pp. 189-261.
[30] He had previously been dismissed from Oxford University by Charles II.
[31] That necessity was vividly present before the minds of the political thinkers prior to the Revolution of 1688, as may be seen from the emphatic observation of Halifax: ' I lay down then as fundamental, first that in every constitution there is some power which neither will nor ought to be bounded': *Political and Miscellaneous Thoughts and Reflections, Works*, pp. 213, 214.

'Though the legislative, whether placed in one or more, whether it be always in being, or only by intervals, though it be the supreme power in every commonwealth; yet, first, it is not, nor can possibly be absolutely arbitrary over the lives and fortunes of the people. For it being but the joint power of every member of the society given up to that person, or assembly, which is legislator, it can be no more than those persons had in a state of Nature before they entered into society and gave it up to the community: for nobody can transfer to another more power than he has in himself; and nobody has an absolute arbitrary power over himself, or over any other, to destroy his own life, or take away the life or property of another. A man, as has been proved, cannot subject himself to the arbitrary power of another; and having in the state of nature, no arbitrary power over the life, liberty, or possession of another, but only so much as the law of nature gave him for the preservation of himself, and the rest of mankind: this is all he doth, or can give up to the commonwealth, and by it to the legislative power, so that the legislative can have no more than this.' [32]

And he says again, in the same work:

'Though in a constituted commonwealth, standing upon its own basis, and acting according to its own nature, that is, acting for the preservation of the community, there can be but one supreme power, which is the legislative, to which all the rest are and must be subordinate, yet the legislative being only a fiduciary power to act for certain ends, there remains still in the people a supreme power to remove or alter the legislative, when they find the legislative act contrary to the trust reposed in them: . . . And thus the community perpetually retains a supreme power of saving themselves from the attempts and designs of anybody, even of their legislators, whenever they shall be so foolish, or so wicked, as to lay and carry on designs against the liberties and properties of the subject. . . . And thus the community may be said in this respect to be always the supreme power. . . .' [33]

Paine's disquisition on the Rights of Man is in its essential aspects little more than a repetition or elaboration of the teaching

---

[32] xi., § 135.

[33] xiii., § 149. There is no contradiction between Locke's rejection of innate ideas and his insistence on the natural rights of man. He opposed equally the arbitrariness of authority and of 'first principles'—an attitude which, in his view, was alone consistent with the development of human freedom. For lucid observations on this aspect of Locke's teaching see *General Education in Free Society. Report of the Harvard Committee* (1946), p. 50.

of Locke.[34]   However, Paine's contribution lies outside the survey of the English influence upon the American formulations of the rights of man in the early constitutions of the States and in the Federal Bill of Rights. Of these American instruments it may be said, without fear of exaggeration, that their philosophy was decisively influenced by the English exponents of natural rights and that there are, few passages in them, especially in the Bill of Rights, which are not either strikingly reminiscent or a practically literal reproduction of some of the English constitutional charters of liberty.[35]

The above observations on one aspect of the English share in the development of the doctrine of the rights of man tend to show that the degree of the English influence was not determined by such factors as the absence of an express legal doctrine of natural rights, or the paucity of reliance upon natural law, or the absence of a written constitution, or the eventual acceptance of the doctrine of the supremacy of Parliament. It was determined by causes more fundamental and more enduring. These were: a powerful political tradition of freedom conceived, in the words of the Act of Settlement, as ' the birthright of the English people ' ;. the enunciation of the principle of natural rights of man by leaders of the Puritan revolution and by writers of the calibre of Milton, Locke, and Blackstone; and, above all, a succession of statutory charters of personal freedom which, any constitutional doctrine notwithstanding, acquired the character of fundamental

---

[34] He says: ' Men are all of one degree and consequently all men are born equal, and with equal Natural Rights. . . . Natural Rights are those which appertain to man in right of his existence. Of this kind are all the intellectual rights, or rights of the mind, and all those rights of acting as an individual for his own comfort and happiness, which are not injurious to the natural rights of others.' (*Rights of Man, Works* (edition of 1894), II, p. 304.) He goes on to say: ' From these premises two or three certain conclusions will follow: First, that every civil right grows out of a natural right; or, in other words, is a natural right exchanged. Secondly, that civil power properly considered as such is made up of the aggregate of that class of the natural rights of man which becomes defective in the individual in point of power, and answers not his purpose, but, when collected to a focus, becomes competent to the purpose of every one. Thirdly, that the power produced from the aggregate of natural rights, imperfect in power in the individual, cannot be applied to invade the natural rights which are retained in the individual, and in which the power to execute is as perfect as the right itself ' (*ibid.,* p. 307).

[35] The provision as to the independence of judges derived from the Act of Settlement of 1701, which laid down that judges' commissions shall for the future be made *quam diu se bene gesserint* and not *durante beneplacito*.

laws of the kingdom and which enabled Blackstone to say that ' the absolute rights of every Englishman (which, taken in a political and extensive sense, are usually called their liberties) as they are founded on nature and reason, so they are coeval with our form of government '.[36] They made it possible to secure in practice the rights of man at a time when, at the height of the Cromwellian dictatorship, the acquittal of Lilburne made Cromwell remark that he regarded the outcome of the trial as a severer blow than a lost battle.

It is permissible to hope that these fundamental aspects of English constitutional doctrine may in the long run prove decisive in determining the attitude of Great Britain to an International Bill of the Rights of Man, and not the supposed or actual difficulties such as the critical attitude, in the nineteenth century, to the idea of natural rights,[37] the absence of a written constitution, or the doctrine of the absolute supremacy of Parliament. The absence of a written constitution is hardly relevant. For the question of codifying the entirety of constitutional law in the form of a written document does not arise. Parts of it may be and have occasionally been reduced to writing not only in the sphere of the liberties of the subject, but also with regard to the highest matters of the legislative power proper, as in the Parliament Act of 1911 or the Statute of Westminster of 1931. Undoubtedly the supremacy of Parliament and the absence of judicial review of legislation from the point of view of its conformity with the constitution or with the international obligations of Great Britain are factors to be considered in connexion with the proposal for an International Bill of the Rights of Man forming an integral part of the law of States. But there is no reason why the implementation of the Bill of Rights within each State should not, if necessary, take place in accordance with the.

[36] *Commentaries,* Book I, Ch. I.
[37] Some of the typical English opposition to the idea of a Bill of Rights was expressed in connexion with the proposal to introduce into the Irish Home Rule Bill of 1912 a clause on life, liberty, property, and due process of law (a clause introduced by Gladstone in the Irish Home Rule Bill of 1893). Mr. Asquith, in objecting in 1906 to the proposed clause, pointed out that it was ' full of ambiguity, abounding in pitfalls and certainly provocative of every kind of frivolous litigation '. Phrases such as ' equal protection of the laws ' and ' just compensation ' were, in his view, ' matters of opinion, bias, or inclination and judgment, which cannot be acted on under anything like settled rules of law ': *Parl. Deb.,* House of Commons, vol. 42 (1912), col. 629. When in 1911 a ' Right to Work Bill ' was introduced in the House of Commons, it was supported by many by an appeal to natural rights: see Jethro Brown, *op. cit.,* p. 273.

constitutional forms and traditions of the country concerned.[38] Moreover, it is not inconceivable that the supremacy of Parliament may be deliberately made to yield to an International Bill of Rights. For the notion of natural and inalienable human rights, to which that Bill would give expression, is in fact a denial of the absolute supremacy of any earthly legislative power. It is true that Parliament cannot bind its successors. Yet, by agreeing to the conclusion of a fundamental treaty, Parliament in fact limits its own freedom of action and that of its successors in the international sphere. The Draft of an International Bill of Human Rights, presented in 1947 to the Commission on Human Rights by the Government of the United Kingdom—the first complete and reasoned draft of a Bill of Rights presented on behalf of a Government—is of considerable interest in this connexion.[39] But there is no such mystic virtue and no such immutability surrounding the formal principle of the supremacy of Parliament as to exclude altogether the possibility of reasonable adaptations to vital requirements of international society. Essentially, the difficulty is more apparent than real. Treaties, suitably agreed to by Parliament, are part of the law of the land. So long as they are in force they are binding upon the judicial and other authorities of the State. The question whether they are binding as part of a rigid constitution or as part of the ordinary law is largely theoretical. So is the possibility that Parliament may deliberately violate the obligations of a fundamental international enactment.

---

[38] See below, pp. 356-359.

[39] The Draft provided that 'every State is, by international law, under an obligation to ensure' the effective protection of the freedoms as laid down in the Bill. At the same time the authors of the Draft discouraged the idea of embodying the provisions of the Bill in the constitutional law of States. 'Some countries, like the United Kingdom, have no rigid constitution and, as a matter of internal law, it is not possible to surround any provision with any special constitutional guarantee. No enactment can be given a greater authority than an Act of Parliament, and one Act of Parliament can repeal any other Act of Parliament. Therefore, the legal provisions which safeguard human rights can only have as their special safeguard the solemn international obligations undertaken in the Bill, together with the firm foundation which these principles have in the deepest convictions of Parliament and the people' (Comment to Article 2, Part I).

PART TWO

HUMAN RIGHTS UNDER THE CHARTER OF THE UNITED NATIONS

CHAPTER 9

THE LEGAL EFFECT OF THE PROVISIONS
OF THE CHARTER

1. THE LEGAL NATURE OF THE OBLIGATIONS OF THE CHARTER IN THE MATTER OF HUMAN RIGHTS AND FUNDAMENTAL FREEDOMS

THE purpose of the first Part of this book was to show that the significant provisions of the Charter of the United Nations in the matter of human rights and fundamental freedoms are not an artificial innovation which is out of keeping with the essential purpose of international law, with the modern tendencies of its development, and with the sources from which it has drawn its vigour and its dignity. This applies both to the question of the subjects of the law of nations and, above all, to the place which the recognition and protection of human rights occupies in the scheme of international law conceived as the universal law of mankind and based on the enduring foundations of the law of nature. Such innovation as there is consists in the fact that that recognition and protection have now assumed the complexion of legal rights of individuals and of legal obligations of States and of the United Nations as a whole. Admittedly, the legal nature of these rights and obligations is controversial. For at first sight it would appear to be an exaggeration to describe the recognition and protection of human rights in the Charter as implying legal rights and duties. In so far as such protection signifies the safeguarding of human rights and fundamental freedoms through a legally authorised and effective machinery of compulsion, it would seem that the authors of the Charter rejected the idea of a guarantee thus conceived. When at the Conference at San Francisco it was proposed that the Charter should ensure not

145

10

only ' the promotion ' but also ' the protection ' of human rights and fundamental freedoms, the suggestion was discarded on the ground that the proposal, if accepted, might be interpreted as giving the United Nations the right to impose actively upon the Members the observance of human rights and freedoms and that it would thus raise hopes going beyond what the United Nations could successfully accomplish.[1] It is not necessary to comment here in detail upon the persuasiveness of these and similar arguments—except, perhaps, to the extent of suggesting that the willingness of the Members of the United Nations to undertake fully effective binding commitments would have influenced decisively the capacity of the Organisation to accomplish the great purpose proclaimed in its Charter.

Neither, it would seem, is there to be found in the corresponding provisions of the Charter an unequivocal indication of the intention to ensure the compulsive protection, amounting to intervention, of human rights. The Preamble, in its first substantive passage, proclaims the reaffirmation of faith in fundamental human rights and the dignity and worth of the human person. The statement of the Purposes of the United Nations includes international co-operation in promoting and encouraging respect for human rights and fundamental freedoms.[2] The enumeration of the functions of the General Assembly comprises the initiation of studies and making of recommendations for the purpose ' of assisting in the realisation ' of these rights and freedoms.[3] The promotion of universal respect for, and observance of, human rights and freedoms figure in the statement of the objects of the Organisation in the field of economic and

---

[1] See, on the proposal of the Delegate of Panama on these lines and its rejection by the Committee, *Conference Doc.* 756, I/1/25, 2 June, 1945. France urged that it should be declared as one of the Purposes of the Organisation ' to see to it that the essential liberties of all are respected without distinction of race, language, or creed ': *Doc.* 215, I/1/10, p. 13. Brazil, the Dominican Republic and Mexico proposed, among the Purposes, ' to ensure respect for human rights and fundamental freedoms ': *ibid.,* p. 7. And see Robinson, *Human Rights and Fundamental Freedoms in the Charter of the United Nations* (1946), pp. 36-38. See also *Doc.* 723, I/1/A/19 (1 June, 1945), p. 10. See also Webster, ' The Making of the Charter of the United Nations ' (offprint from *History,* March, 1947, vol. 33, No. 115, p. 35), who points out that the initiative for the insertion in the Charter of the provisions relating to human rights was largely due to Soviet Russia.

[2] Art. 1, para 3.

[3] Art. 13.

social co-operation[4] and of the system of trusteeship.[5] The Economic and Social Council is authorised to make recommendations for the purpose of promoting respect for, and observance of, human rights and fundamental freedoms.[6] The restraint exhibited by these provisions, studiously falling short of conferment of direct executive authority, is impressive in its consistency. This caution is made more conspicuous by the choice of the agencies entrusted with the implementation, such as it is, of the provisions of the Charter. These agencies are the General Assembly and the Economic and Social Council. By the terms of the Charter both these organs are deprived of executive and legislative powers of binding decision. The only organ of the United Nations which is endowed with that power to a high degree, namely, the Security Council, has no ordinary jurisdiction in the matter of human rights—except, it will be submitted, when the degree and scope of their violation are such as to constitute a threat to international peace and security.[7]

From the above exposition of the limitations of the protection which the Charter affords to human rights and freedoms there may be drawn the easy—and inaccurate—conclusion that its provisions on the subject are a mere declaration of principle devoid of any element of legal obligation. Any such conclusion is no more than a facile generalisation. For the provisions of the Charter on the subject figure prominently in the statement of the Purposes of the United Nations. Members of the United Nations are under a legal obligation to act in accordance with these Purposes. It is their legal duty to respect and observe fundamental human rights and freedoms. These provisions are no mere embellishment of a historic document; they were not the result of an afterthought or an accident of drafting. They were adopted, with deliberation and after prolonged discussion before and during the San Francisco Conference, as part of the philosophy of the new international system and as a most compelling lesson of the experience of the inadequacies and dangers of the old. Nothing but most explicit terms of the Charter would justify the conclusion that these Articles were contemplated as being devoid of any effect from the point of view of either the legal obligation resting upon

[4] Art. 55.
[5] Art. 76.
[6] Art. 62.
[7] See below, p. 185.

the Members or the duty incumbent upon the United Nations as a whole. There is a mandatory obligation implied in the provision of Article 55 that the United Nations ' shall promote respect for, and observance of, human rights and fundamental freedoms ' ; or, in the terms of Article 13, that the Assembly shall make recommendations for the purpose of assisting in the realisation of human rights and freedoms. There is a distinct element of legal duty in the undertaking expressed in Article 56 in which ' All Members pledge themselves to take joint and separate action in co-operation with the Organisation for the achievement of the purposes set forth in Article 55 '.[8] The cumulative legal result of all these pronouncements cannot be ignored. The legal character of these obligations of the Charter would remain even if the Charter were to contain no provisions of any kind for their implementation. For the Charter fails to provide for the enforcement of its other numerous obligations the legal character of which is undoubted.

Neither is the legal nature of the obligations of the Charter in the matter of human rights and fundamental freedoms decisively influenced by the fact that the Charter does not define the human rights and freedoms which the Members of the United Nations are bound to observe. Undoubtedly, that circumstance impairs the juridical character of these obligations inasmuch as a certain amount of clarity and precision is an important requisite of the law. This has been the reason for the importance justly attached to the framing of an International Bill of Human Rights—although, as submitted below, even in that instrument detailed definition is neither essential nor desirable.[9] There is a difference between urging that the legal character of a rule is

---

[8] It has been suggested that neither Article 56 nor any other Article of the Charter contains an express legal obligation to respect human rights and freedoms. See Brunet, *op. cit.* below, p. 164, who gives an interesting account of the history of that Article at the Conference at San Francisco. It is difficult to accede to that view. The terms of Article 56 point to a clear legal undertaking. This also seems to have been the view of the Rapporteur of the Committee: see *Documents of the Conference*, vol. X, pp. 350, 385, 402. The fact that the obligation refers to its fulfilment in co-operation with the Organization does not detract from its juridical nature. The question, to which Professor Brunet seems to attach importance, whether the exception of domestic jurisdiction applies to Articles 55 and 56 is probably irrelevant. The circumstance that an obligation cannot be enforced by means of intervention has no bearing upon the question of its legal nature. And see below, p. 166.

[9] See below, pp. 327-333.

destroyed and admitting that its effectiveness is diminished as the result of the absence of a full measure of definition.

Any construction of the Charter according to which Members of the United Nations are, in law, entitled to disregard—and to violate—human rights and fundamental freedoms is destructive of both the legal and the moral authority of the Charter as a whole. It runs counter to a cardinal principle of construction according to which treaties must be interpreted in good faith.[10] The interpretation, here urged, of Article 2 (7) in relation

[10] But see, for an emphatic expression of a different view, Hudson in *American Journal of International Law*, 42 (1948), pp. 105-108, who suggests that an interpretation construing the relevant provisions of the Charter as imposing upon the Members of the United Nations the legal obligation to respect human rights and freedoms may act in the direction of disintegrating the Charter. It is difficult to accede to that view. It is more probable that the requirement of good faith in the interpretation of treaties and an enlightened conception of the purposes of the Charter and of the intention of its authors support the view put forward in the text above. In a letter to the Attorney-General of the United States, addressed on 4 November, 1947, in connection with the cases of *McGhee* v. *Sipes* and *Shelley* v. *Kraemer* (see below, p. 150) then pending before the Supreme Court, the Legal Adviser to the State Department advanced the following assertion with regard to Articles 55 and 56 of the Charter: ' The Articles of the Charter referred to in your letter are not interpreted by the Department of State as imposing a legal obligation to guarantee observance of specific human rights and fundamental freedoms without distinction as to race, sex, language or religion. The Articles do appear to place member States under the obligation to co-operate with the United Nations in the carrying out of its function, which is stated here and elsewhere in the Charter as being the promotion of universal respect for and observance of human rights and fundamental freedoms. . . .' In so far as the language of the Opinion implies that there is no obligation upon Members of the United Nations to respect human rights and freedoms —the Opinion refers to a ' legal obligation to guarantee observance of specific human rights and fundamental freedoms '—it is not believed to advance a sound, or defensible, legal proposition.

See also *Sipes* v. *McGhee* (1947), 316 Mich. 614, where the Supreme Court of Michigan, partly with reference to the contention that one of the results of the provisions of the Charter in the matter of human rights and fundamental freedoms was to render unenforceable in the United States restrictive covenants on account of race and colour, said: ' We do not understand it to be a principle of law that a treaty between sovereign nations is applicable to the contractual rights between citizens of the United States when a determination of these rights is sought in State courts. So far as the instant case is concerned, these pronouncements are merely indicative of a desirable social trend and an objective devoutly to be desired by all well-thinking people. These arguments are predicated upon a plea for justice rather than the application of the settled principles of established law.' It may be difficult to follow the statement quoted above, coming as it does from a court of a country in which treaties are the supreme law of the land. Similarly, the interpretation of the provisions of the Charter in the matter of human rights and fundamental freedoms as ' merely indicative of a desirable social trend and an objective devoutly to be desired by all well-thinking people ' is open to question. In the same year the New York Supreme Court in *Kemp* v. *Rubin* (69 N.Y.S. (2d) 680) upheld the validity of a restrictive covenant of a similar nature. The Court said, with reference to the defendant's contention referring to the provisions of the Charter on the subject: ' These treaties have nothing to do with domestic matters nor with agreements between citizens of the United States.'

to the provisions of the Charter in the matter of human rights does not purport to be based on the principle of effectiveness as a governing rule of construction. Undoubtedly, notwithstanding the respect which they have occasionally expressed for the principle of restrictive interpretation of obligations limiting the sovereignty of States, the Permanent Court of International Justice and its successor have acted in fact upon the rival and opposite rule of interpreting treaties so as to make them effective rather than ineffective. But the principle of effectiveness, when applied to the exclusion of others, is not free of doubt. It disregards the circumstance that the parties often intend the treaty to be less effective rather than more effective. The intention of the parties must remain the governing consideration. But that intention must, in turn, be interpreted in accordance with the requirements of good faith and of decency. It would be contrary both to these requirements and to the principle of effectiveness if the repeated and solemn provisions of the Charter in the matter of human rights and fundamental freedoms, coupled with the clear legal obligation to promote respect for them by joint and separate action, were interpreted as devoid of the obligation to respect them.

Admittedly, there is in the Charter no express provision in which the Members of the United Nations agree, *eis verbis,* to respect human rights and fundamental freedoms. But it would

To make this statement even more debatable, the Court added: 'In fact, Article 2, Section 7, of the United Nations Charter . . . expressly so provides'—an admission that, but for the (questionable) applicability of Article 2, Section 7, of the Charter, the 'treaties' in question would not have been altogether irrelevant to the issue. The Supreme Court of the United States reversed the decisions of the Michigan Supreme Court in the case referred to above on the ground that it would be contrary to the Constitution to enforce restrictive covenants of that nature (68 Sup. Ct. 836). The Court made no direct reference to the Charter, but the following passage from the Opinion of Vinson, C.J., in *Hurd* v. *Hodge,* a case *in pari materia,* is of interest: 'The power of the federal courts to enforce the terms of private agreements is at all times exercised subject to the restrictions and limitations of the public policy of the United States as manifested in the Constitution, treaties, federal statutes and applicable legal precedents. Where the enforcement of private agreements would be violative of that policy, it is the obligation of courts to refrain from such exertions of judicial power' (*ibid.,* p. 853). In its 'Brief for the United States' as *amicus curiæ* in this case, as well as in *Shelley* v. *Kraemer,* the Department of Justice cited the Resolution of the General Assembly of 1947 condemning religious and racial persecutions and discrimination. It relied, *inter alia,* on that Resolution in support of the proposition that the 'enforcement of racial restrictive covenants is contrary to the public policy of the United States' (pp. 98-100). And see below, p. 156, n. 23, concerning *Re Drummond Wren,* where the decision of the Court relied on the provisions of the Charter as an ingredient of public policy.

be out of keeping with the spirit of the Charter and, probably, with the accepted canons of interpretation of treaties, to attach decisive importance to that omission. It would have been otiose to the point of pedantry for the draftsmen of the Charter to incorporate an explicit provision of this nature in a document in which the principle of respect for and observance of human rights and fundamental freedoms is one of the main pillars of the structure of the Organisation created by the Charter. The repeated reference to that principle is not the vague expression of a trend or a pious hope.[11] This is a matter in which, perhaps more than in others, care must be taken not to permit the task of interpretation to degenerate into an attempt at deriving the maximum advantage from the economy of expression of a basic international instrument. It is not without significance that in some judicial pronouncements, including those of Justices of the Supreme Court of the United States, these provisions of the Charter have been treated as a source of self-executory legal obligations affecting private rights.[12]

[11] In connexion with the discussion, before the Sixth Committee of the Third General Assembly in 1948, of the legality of the action of Soviet Russia in preventing Russian wives married to foreigners from leaving Russian territory (see below, p. 204), Professor Spiropoulos, the representative of Greece, assumed that ' as the obligation to respect human rights was placed upon Member States by the Charter, it followed that any violation of human rights was a violation of the provisions of the Charter' (A/C.6/SR.138, p. 8). On the other hand, it appears that in the view of the representative of the United Kingdom, expressed in connexion with the discussion on this subject, a violation of fundamental human rights on the part of a Member of the United Nations does not necessarily involve a breach of a legal obligation. He suggested that even if the International Court of Justice were to find the Russian action to be in accordance with international law, such action would still be in violation of fundamental human rights—a view which seems to imply that the observance of fundamental human rights by a Member of the United Nations does not constitute a legal obligation.

[12] In the Concurring Opinions of four Justices of the Supreme Court in *Oyama* v. *California* (1948), 332 U.S. 633, the provisions of the Charter in the matter of human rights were relied upon as a source of legal obligations. In his Concurring Opinion Mr. Justice Murphy, joined by Mr. Justice Rutledge, said: ' Moreover, this nation has recently pledged itself through the United Nations Charter to promote respect for, and observance of, human rights and fundamental freedoms for all without distinction as to race, sex, language or religion. The Alien Land Law stands as a barrier to the fulfilment of that national pledge. Its inconsistency with the Charter, which has been duly ratified and adopted by the United States, is but one more reason why the Statute must be condemned.' In his Concurring Opinion Mr. Justice Black, joined by Mr. Justice Douglas, said: ' There are additional reasons now why that law stands as an obstacle to the free accomplishment of our policy in the international field. One of these reasons is that we have recently pledged ourselves to co-operate with the United Nations to " promote . . . universal respect for, and observance of, human rights and fundamental freedoms for

Members of the United Nations seem to recognise that, in the words of the representative of the United States at the Third General Assembly in 1949, ' we have all committed ourselves to promote respect for and observance of human rights and fundamental freedoms '.[13] That Assembly, when adopting a Resolution recommending the Government of Soviet Russia to withdraw the measures taken with regard to wives of citizens of foreign nationality,[14] interpreted Article I, paragraph 3, of the Charter as binding all Members to encourage ' respect for human rights and fundamental freedoms ' and Article 55(c) as being one in which Members undertook to promote ' universal respect for, and observance of, human rights and fundamental freedoms '. The Resolution relied, *inter alia,* on what it considered the binding obligations of the Charter in the matter of human rights and fundamental freedoms.[15] It has been maintained that Members of the United Nations committed themselves to promote respect for and observance of human rights, but that they did not undertake the obligation to respect and observe them.[16] However, the legal duty to promote respect for human rights includes the legal duty to respect them. It comprises, in addition, the obligation to further the adoption of means and establishment of agencies for the effective international enforcement of these rights. The Charter does not provide for such enforcement; it provides for the obligation—which is an express legal obligation—to promote it.

The terms of the various trusteeship agreements, which in the matter of fundamental human rights refer to the obligations of the Charter, leave no doubt that the broad language of the

all without distinction as to race, sex, language, and religion ". How can this nation be faithful to this international pledge if state laws which bar land ownership and occupancy by aliens on account of race are permitted to be enforced? ' See also above, p. 150, for an indirect recognition of the legal effect of that Charter by reference to the public policy of the United States as manifested, *inter alia,* in treaties. And see in particular *Re Drummond Wren,* below, p. 156.

[13] Statement made by Mr. Cohen on 28 April, 1949 (*Department of State Bulletin,* XX (1949), p. 613).

[14] Doc. A/842.

[15] 25 April, 1949: Doc. A/842. The Resolution of the General Assembly unanimously adopted on 19 November 1946, in the matter of non-discrimination called on governments to conform both to the letter and the spirit of the Charter.

[16] See, *e.g.,* the observations of Professor Hudson in the course of the discussion in the International Law Commission in 1949: A/CN.4/SR.23, p. 10.

Charter in the matter of human rights does not deprive it of the character of a legal obligation.[17]

It may be said that States when signing or adhering to the Charter clearly did not intend to assume an absolute, literal and immediate legal duty to give effect to the most comprehensive obligation to respect human rights and fundamental freedoms without discrimination as to race, sex, language, or religion. It may be urged, for instance, that they did not assume a rigid obligation of this nature in respect of discrimination on account of sex—a subject which is admittedly of great complexity.[18] However, like all provisions of international treaties so also the wide obligations of the Charter in this matter—covering as they do most comprehensively the relation of man and State—must be interpreted in a reasonable way. The obligation exists and it must be given effect in good faith, having regard to the circumstances and conditions of each State. Thus, although a reasonable interpretation of the Charter does not require that Members of the United Nations should henceforth with one stroke grant full equality to women in all respects, a State would no doubt act contrary to its obligations under the Charter if, under the impact of an anti-feminist régime, it were drastically to curtail the existing rights of women. A State would act contrary to its clear legal obligations under the Charter if it were to impose fresh discrimination on a religious, ethnical or racial group. And there would be no doubt a flagrant breach of its legal obligations if it were to embark upon active persecution of persons under its jurisdiction on account of their race, language or religion.

When it is maintained, therefore, that a construction of the Charter which interprets its provisions as imposing a legal duty upon the Members of the United Nations derogates from the integrity of international instruments,[19] the term 'integrity' is used in a specific sense divorced from its ordinary connotation. For the same reason it is unnecessary—and to some extent objectionable—to deduce the obligation to respect human rights and fundamental freedoms not from the provisions of the Charter bearing directly on the subject, but from the purposes and

[17] See below, p. 160.
[18] See below, pp. 338-340.
[19] See Hudson, cited above, at p. 149.

principles of the Charter in which the Members undertake to act in a manner consistent with and calculated to promote international peace and security.[20] Undoubtedly, international peace and security must be threatened whenever there takes place a violation of human rights on a scale so large and in a manner so brutal as to shock the conscience of mankind. But the obligations of the Charter are not confined to the duty to avoid flagrant breaches of human rights *en masse* in a way endangering international peace. Experience has shown that governments may see a danger to peace not in these acts violative of the rights of man, but in attempts to prevent and to remove them by collective action.

2. EXTENT OF THE LEGAL OBLIGATIONS OF THE MEMBERS OF THE UNITED NATIONS

The obligations of the Members of the United Nations probably

---

[20] See the observations of Professor Brierly in the International Law Commission in 1949: A/CN.4/SR.23, p. 11, and of Professor Hudson (above, p. 152, n. 14).

At the first session of the International Law Commission in 1949 Professor Hudson, Chairman of the Commission, reiterated that view. He pointed out that the Charter did not 'expressly' make it a duty of States to respect human rights and fundamental freedoms. He submitted, however, that inasmuch as the Charter required them to maintain international peace and security, the duty of a State to 'treat its own population with respect for human rights and fundamental freedoms for all' could be implied if the object was to cause to prevail upon its territory conditions which did not menace international peace and security (A/CN.4/SR.20, p. 15). At a subsequent meeting of the International Law Commission the Chairman, after quoting the provisions of Article 13(1), 55(c), 76(c), and 62(2) of the Charter, felt justified in drawing the conclusion that 'Member States had not, by signing the Charter, assumed a legal obligation to treat persons under their jurisdiction with respect for human rights and fundamental freedoms without distinction as to race, sex, language, or religion. They had merely agreed to promote international co-operation to that end' (A/CN.4/SR.23, p. 10). Professor Brierly, after stating that he agreed with the Chairman and that the proposed Article of the Declaration of Rights and Duties of States laying down that they were under a duty to respect human rights and fundamental freedoms 'would mark a revolutionary change in international law, since it brought into the domain of international law a matter which hitherto had been one of purely domestic jurisdiction —the treatment by a State of its own nationals', proceeded to qualify his statement in a way which probably amounts to a disagreement with the Chairman. He said: 'There was some reason for saying that that change had in fact taken place. There were the Nürnberg principles, and there was the implication in the Charter that respect for human rights within a State was an important element in securing peaceful and friendly relations with other States. It could well be argued that international law to-day did impose a duty on States to respect the human rights of their nationals' (*ibid.*, p. 11). Previously Professor Brierly had expressed the view that in proclaiming that duty the Declaration did not go beyond the principles of the Charter, 'although it did to some extent go beyond the obligations set forth therein' (A/CN.4/SR.20, p. 15). Professor Scelle disagreed with the Chairman. He 'felt that recognition of fundamental human rights constituted a true legal obligation under positive law' (p. 14).

include the duty to promote and to ensure the respect of human
rights and fundamental freedoms not only in relation to legislative
and administrative action by the authorities of the State conceived
as an international person, but also, in certain cases, in relation
to the local autonomous subdivisions of the State and even
private bodies and individuals. Discrimination and segregation,
in denial of elementary human rights, by reason of race, creed,
colour or national origin, may occur not only as the result of
acts or omissions of the central authority of the State.
In the economic and social sphere the denial of or attack
upon human rights may take place through actions of
autonomous subordinate bodies, of private organisations and
institutions, and even of private persons. Historically, Bills
of Rights were enacted as a measure of protection against
the arbitrariness or injustice of governments.[21] In modern
times, this is not the only source of oppression or of denial
of human rights. When large bodies of citizens are segregated
in crowded and unhealthy areas, when they are refused admission
to non-governmental educational institutions enjoying a
virtual monopoly of status such as schools and universities benefiting from direct or indirect governmental support,[22] or when,
through a policy of segregation, they are refused the advantages
of public services, amenities, and means of transportation—in all
these cases there takes place a denial of human rights and fundamental freedoms. There are persuasive reasons for asserting that
the duty of a Member of the United Nations to protect the rights
of man against acts other than those perpetrated directly by its
own authorities follows from the obligations of the Charter of
the United Nations in all cases in which the assistance of the State
or of its resources is being sought or used for purposes inimical
to those fundamental objects of the Charter. In refusing to
enforce restrictive covenants based on racial origin, the High
Court of Ontario relied to a large extent upon the indirect effect
of the provisions of the Charter of the United Nations, to which

---

[21] See below, p. 343, n. 40.
[22] But see the decision of an American Federal Court in *Norris* v. *Mayor and
City Council of Baltimore* (1948), 78 F. Supp. 451, to the effect that the
Fourteenth Amendment was not applicable with respect to a private school
which, although receiving substantial public assistance, discriminated against
Negroes. For an adverse criticism of the decision see *Harvard Law Review*,
62 (1948), p. 126.

Canada is a party, in the matter of human rights and fundamental freedoms.[23]

In these and similar matters the denial of human rights is not the result of mere private malice. In the words of a Dissenting Opinion in a case involving restrictive covenants which came before the United States Court of Appeals for the District of Columbia: ' The question in these cases is not whether the law should punish racial discrimination, or even whether the law shall try to prevent racial discrimination, or whether the law should interfere with it in any way. The question is whether the law should affirmatively support and enforce racial discrimination '.[24] Recent significant decisions of the Supreme Court of the United States in the same matter are based on that view.[25] The decisions are significant, for although restrictive covenants by reference to race, colour and religion were not by any means a novelty, it was for the first time that the Supreme Court denied the right of judicial agencies to enforce covenants of this nature. No direct reference to the Charter was made in these decisions of the Court, but it is probable that, apart from other factors, the inarticulate impact of the Charter was instrumental in prompting these revolutionary decisions.[26] For although they referred to international treaties generally as one of the various elements determining public policy in the United States, it is clear that particular importance was attached to the Charter of the United

[23] *In re Drummond Wren* (1945), 4 Ontario Reports, pp. 778, 781; *Annual Digest and Reports of Public International Law Cases,* 1943-1945, Case No. 50. The Court, in declaring the restrictive covenants in question to be void and without effect, invoked, *inter alia,* relevant passages of the Preamble and of Articles 1 and 55 of the Charter as well as the Atlantic Charter, not as direct sources of legal obligation in the municipal sphere but as ingredients of public policy upon which the validity of the covenants depended. The learned Judge said: ' The common law courts have, by their actions over the years, obviated the need for rigid constitutional guarantees in our policy by their wise use of the doctrine of public policy as an active agent in the promotion of the public weal.'

[24] As quoted in the *Report of the President's Committee on Civil Rights* (1947), p. 70.

[25] See *Shelley* v. *Kraemer, McGhee* v. *Sipes,* and *Hurd* v. *Hodge,* referred to above, p. 149, n. 10.

[26] *Shelley* v. *Kraemer* (above, p. 149). In 1926 the Court held that the enforcement of such private agreements did not violate the 5th, 13th or 14th Amendments: *Corrigan* v. *Buckley,* 271 U.S. 323. See also Sayre, ' Shelley v. Kraemer and United Nations Law ' in *Iowa Law Review* 34 (1948), pp. 1-11, and Ming, ' Racial Restrictions and the Fourteenth Amendment: The Restrictive Covenant Cases ' in *The University of Chicago Law Review,* 16 (1949), pp. 203-238.

Nations. That was the only new factor in the situation; the others had existed before.[27]

Neither do these decisions mark the limit of the possible legal emanations of the Charter. For there is room for the view that, because of the Charter of the United Nations, the State may be under a legal duty to prevent the denial of human rights through private action taken on such a scale as to assume the complexion of a public mischief. Various States of the United States, such as New York, New Jersey, Indiana, Wisconsin, and Massachusetts, and various local authorities, such as the municipalities of Chicago and Minneapolis, have enacted and enforced legislation making it an offence to deny employment by way of discrimination on account of race, creed, or national origin. These and similar measures were taken without direct reference to the Charter of the United Nations.

The question whether the provisions of the Charter of the United Nations impose upon its Members the implied obligation to protect human rights and fundamental freedoms against action emanating from quarters other than the State authority directly accountable under international law is of particular importance in relation to federal States. It was on the Charter of the United Nations, in particular on Article 55, that, in this respect, reliance was placed by the Committee appointed by the President of the United States in December, 1946, to enquire into civil liberties. The Committee suggested in its Report—one of the most outspoken and impressive documents of all time bearing

[27] It was only by way of exception that, prior to the Charter of the United Nations, the courts of the United States regarded restrictive covenants on account of race as being contrary to the Fifth and Fourteenth Amendments of the Constitution inasmuch as judicial enforcement of such covenants involves discriminatory public action. For a survey of these decisions see ' Race and Discrimination in Housing' by Groner and Helfeld in *Yale Law Journal*, 57 (1948), pp. 426-458. On occasions courts have denied that enforcement of restrictive covenants is discriminatory seeing that, in law, any group regardless of race or colour is entitled to invoke such restrictive provisions. The spirit of such dialectical reasoning may be gauged from the argument relied upon in a case involving a restrictive covenant against Negroes. The Court said, in pointing to the fact that restrictive covenants against prostitutes may be enforced: ' Yet even prostitutes are a class of our citizenry. If one class may by contract be denied the privilege of use and occupancy, why not another? White may exclude black. Black may exclude white': *Perkins* v. *Trustees of Monroe Ave. Church* (1946), 79 Ohio App. 457, 70 N.E. 2nd 487, 491. On the other hand, see the Dissenting Opinion of Edgerton J. in *Hurd* v. *Hodge* (1947), 162 F. 2d at p. 239, in which it was pointed out that the formal argument of the equality of available remedies ' amounts to saying that if Negroes are excluded from decent housing they may retaliate by excluding whites from slums '. And see below, pp. 340-342.

upon human rights—that the decision given in 1920 by the Supreme Court of the United States in *Missouri* v. *Holland*[28] could be made the starting point for the enforcement of the Charter by Congressional action binding upon all the States of the Union. In that case the Supreme Court affirmed the right of Congress to enact legislation intended to give effect to treaty obligations in cases in which, in the absence of a treaty, Congress had no power to pass statutes encroaching upon the jurisdiction of the States as guaranteed by the Constitution. In the view of the Committee the decision in *Missouri* v. *Holland* was of ' obvious importance ' as a possible basis for legislation by Congress in the matter of civil rights, notwithstanding existing constitutional limitations.[29] (This, in fact, is the alternative—and, it is believed, the preferable— method to that proposed by the representatives of the United States in connection with the drafting of the Covenant of Human Rights. On that occasion the United States attempted to solve the difficulty by, in effect, exempting federal States from the obligations of the most important provisions of the Covenant.[30]) Apart from the problem raised by the federal structure of States it is probable that no recourse to a particular constitutional precedent is necessary in order to enable States to fulfil their obligation under the Charter to protect human rights against violations from any quarter whatsoever. In many countries the Charter of the United Nations has indisputably become part of the law of the land. Thus according to the French Constitution of 1946 treaties ratified by the State derogate from any contrary municipal law without any further act of the national legislature other than that necessary for the ratification of the treaty.[31] This applies also to the Charter of the United Nations. Admittedly, its provisions are directly applicable in the realm of municipal law only to the extent to which they constitute legal obligations of the State. This is an additional reason why the question of the nature of the provisions of the Charter in the matter of human rights is of paramount importance. Once their legal nature is placed outside the realm of controversy, it is probably legitimate to assert that the duty of

[28] (1920), 252 U.S. 416. See also, for the same suggestion, Carr, *Federal Protection of Civil Rights* (1947), p. 205, n. 9.
[29] At p. 110.
[30] See below, p. 359.
[31] Articles 26 and 27. See the decision of the Court of Appeal of Paris of 10 November, 1947, in *Chonchol* v. *Dame Vita* for a striking application of that provision of the Constitution: Sirey. 1948. II. p. 83.

the State to promote the observance of and respect for human rights extends to the obligation to withhold the direct or indirect assistance of its law in support of the denial, from whomsoever emanating, of human rights and fundamental freedoms.

The provisions of the Charter on the subject impose legal obligations not only upon the Members of the United Nations. They imply a comprehensive legal obligation upon the United Nations as a whole. They not only authorise the various organs of the United Nations to take steps for encouraging and promoting the realisation of that crucial purpose of the Charter. They lay down that the United Nations *shall* promote ' universal respect for, and observance of, human rights and fundamental freedoms ' (Article 55(c)). It is true that the phraseology—' the United Nations shall promote '—applies also to the other objects of the Economic and Social Council such as the promotion of higher standards of living, full employment, conditions of economic and social progress and development, solution of international economic and social problems, and international cultural and educational co-operation. But the degree of legal obligation is particularly high with regard to a subject matter which, as in the case of human rights and freedoms, is a constant and fundamental theme of the Charter. There is laid down here a clear duty of collective action. Moreover, that duty exists irrespective of any explicit pronouncement of the Charter to that effect. It is an inescapable principle of interpretation that whenever an international instrument defines, in its constitution, the purposes of its being, the right and obligation to give effect to those purposes are inherent in it and nothing short of an express derogation from that implicit authority can legitimately restrict the powers and obligations in question.

Finally, one of the results of the provisions of the Charter in the matter of human rights and fundamental freedoms is to effect a far-reaching change in the position of the individual in international law. If these provisions of the Charter constitute legal rights and obligations, then they signify the recognition, in an international treaty of wide generality, of rights of the individual as such. They transfer the inalienable and natural rights of the individual from the venerable but controversial orbit of the law of nature to the province of positive law, of international law. They thus mark a significant step towards the recognition of the individual as a subject of the law of nations. They are not accompanied by the full conferment of international procedural capacity upon the individual to enable him to enforce, in his own right and in the judicial sphere, the legal benefits of the status thus acquired. But their silence on the subject does not imply a denial of any capacity whatsoever to vindicate his rights before international organs. On the contrary, such capacity will be determined not by any preconceived notions on the question whether the individual can under international law derive rights under treaties and enforce them in his own name, but by the degree to which the United Nations and its organs will assume the function of translating into reality the provisions of the Charter. In proportion as they do that, the procedural capacity of the individual to petition the United Nations will be joined to his new status in international law. In turn, the full realisation of the significance of his new status, brought about by the recognition of his fundamental rights and freedoms, as a subject of international law, will enable him to assert them more effectively in the international sphere. In particular, there is henceforth no excuse for curtailing or keeping in check his right of effective petition by reliance upon the obsolete doctrine that he is not a subject of the law of nations.[31a]

3. HUMAN RIGHTS AND FUNDAMENTAL FREEDOMS UNDER THE TRUSTEESHIP SYSTEM

In relation to the Trusteeship System the legal character of the obligations of the Charter on the subject seems to have been generally recognised. Article 76 of the Charter provides that 'The basic objectives of the trusteeship system, in accordance with the Purposes of the United Nations laid down in Article 1 of the present Charter, shall be: . . . (c) to encourage respect for human rights and for fundamental freedoms for all without distinction as to race, sex, language, or religion, . . .'. In the various trusteeship agreements these provisions have been translated into clear legal obligations. Thus Article 7 of the Trusteeship Agreement for the former Japanese Mandated Islands provides as follows: ' In discharging its obligations under Article 76 (c) of the Charter, the administering authority shall

[31a] See above, pp. 25-47, and below, pp. 240-251.

guarantee to the inhabitants of the trust territory freedom of conscience, and, subject only to the requirements of public order and
security, freedom of speech, of the Press, and of assembly;
freedom of worship, and of religious teaching; and freedom of
migration and movement '.[32] It will be noted that that Article
refers to the ' obligations ' of Article 76 (c) of the Charter.
Similar provisions, without direct reference to the obligations of
Article 76, have been incorporated in other trusteeship agreements. Thus, for instance, Article 14 of the Trusteeship
Agreement for the Territory of Togoland under British administration provides that ' subject only to the requirements of public
order, the Administering Authority shall guarantee to the
inhabitants of the Territory freedom of speech, of the Press, of
assembly, and of petition '.[33] The legal character of these provisions is reinforced by the right of petition, which is fully
recognised and effectively regulated in detail,[34] to the Trusteeship
Council and by the machinery of supervision, including visits to
trust territories.[35] The result, somewhat paradoxical, is that there
is a wider and more explicit measure of international enforcement
of—some—human rights and fundamental freedoms of inhabitants of trust territories than in other parts of the world.

4. HUMAN RIGHTS IN THE PEACE TREATIES

The Peace Treaties concluded at Paris in 1947 between the Allied
Powers on the one hand and Italy, Roumania, Bulgaria, Hungary
and Finland on the other, provided that these five States ' shall
take all measures necessary to secure to all persons under [their]
jurisdiction, without distinction as to race, sex, language or
religion, the enjoyment of human rights and fundamental free-

[32] 124th Meeting of the Security Council, Doc. S/318.
[33] First General Assembly, Doc. T/8. See also Article 13 of the Agreement
relating to the Cameroons, and Article 13 of the Agreement relating to
Tanganyika. Article 8 (e) of the Agreement relating to the Territory of New
Guinea under Australian administration guarantees ' to the inhabitants of the
Territory, subject to the requirements of public order, freedom of speech, of
the Press, of assembly and of petition, freedom of conscience and worship
and freedom of religious teaching '. Other trusteeship agreements include
identical or similar provisions.
[34] See below, p. 244.
[35] On April 25, 1947, the Trusteeship Council approved the text of a provisional
questionnaire to form the basis for the annual reports to be submitted by the
administering authorities (Doc. T/44). The questionnaire included numerous
items relating to the observance of human rights and fundamental freedoms.
On the treatment of petitions by the Trusteeship Council see below,
pp. 242-244.

doms, including freedom of expression, of Press and publication, of religious worship, of political opinion and of public meeting '.[36] While the legal nature of the corresponding provisions of the Charter may be a matter of controversy,[37] the mandatory provisions of these Peace Treaties leave no room for doubt on the subject. The binding force of these obligations is not affected by the circumstance that, on the face of it, they do not seem to be immediately self-executory. The fact that the Treaties lay down that the States concerned ' shall take all measures necessary to secure ' human rights and fundamental freedoms does not mean that until such legislative and other measures have been taken the international obligation is not fully effective in the international sphere.[38]

In one respect the legal nature of the obligations of these Treaties in the matter of human rights is more pronounced inasmuch as they provide for machinery for settling, so long as the general provisions of the Charter in the matter are not given their full and proper effect, disputes concerning the interpretation and application of the Treaties. The machinery provided is complicated and unorthodox,[39] but so long as the States bound

[36] Article 15 of the Treaty with Italy; Article 3 of the Treaty with Roumania; Article 3 of the Treaty with Bulgaria; Article 2 of the Treaty with Hungary; Article 6 (1) of the Treaty with Finland. Similar provisions were inserted in the Treaty with Italy concerning territories ceded by Italy (Art. 19 (4)) and in the Permanent Statute for the Territory of Trieste (Art. 4). The explicit language of the Peace Treaties would seem to suggest that their provisions in the matter of human rights partake of a more pronounced legal quality than that inherent in the corresponding provisions of the Charter. This is so only if it is assumed that the Charter does not impose a legal obligation to respect human rights and fundamental freedoms— an assumption which has been shown to be incorrect (see above, pp. 148-152). There is thus no warrant for the view that in this matter the victors—representing as they claimed to do the cause of human freedom threatened by the defeated States—imposed upon the latter binding obligations which they themselves had been unwilling to assume. This is so notwithstanding the possible argument that some of the defeated countries had allied themselves with a régime contemptuous of human rights and freedoms and that therefore special assurances might have been considered necessary on their part.

[37] See above, p. 148.

[38] So far as the letter of the obligation is concerned the five States put on their statute book constitutional enactments embodying fundamental human rights, e.g., the Italian Constitution of 22 December, 1947; the Finnish Form of Government Act of 17 July, 1949; the Roumanian Constitution of 13 April, 1948.

[39] Thus, for instance, with respect to Roumania, Bulgaria and Hungary the Treaties provide that any dispute concerning the interpretation or execution of their provisions, if not settled by direct diplomatic negotiations, shall be referred to the Heads of the Diplomatic Missions of the Soviet Union, the United Kingdom and the United States in the capitals of the respective countries. Any such dispute, if not solved within two months by agreement between the Heads of Mission, shall be referred, unless the parties agree to a different mode of settlement, at the request of either party to the dispute,

by the obligations of these Treaties and the States concerned with their enforcement are determined to act in accordance with them, that machinery is adequate for the purpose of initiating an international procedure with a view to enforcing the clauses relating to human rights. Since the ratification of the Treaties frequent occasion has arisen for setting that machinery in motion. Originally the only way in which some of the principal signatories deemed it feasible to draw attention to a violation of these Treaties and to insist on the observance of their provisions was to refuse to vote for the admission of Roumania, Hungary and Bulgaria to the United Nations on the ground that in view of the persistent violations of human rights by those States they could not be deemed to fulfil one of the conditions of admission, namely, ability to carry out international obligations.[40] Subsequently the United States, Great Britain and other signatories of these Treaties invoked the machinery provided therein for settling disputes arising out of the interpretation and application of their provisions. The effective resort to that machinery was frustrated by the refusal of the Governments of Soviet Russia and of Hungary, Roumania and Bulgaria to abide by a clear provision of the Treaties and to participate in the procedure laid down in them. [41] In 1949, at the Second Session of the

to a commission composed of one representative of *each* [*sic*] party and a third [*sic*] member selected by mutual agreement of the two parties from nationals of a third party or, failing such agreement, by the Secretary-General of the United Nations. The decision of the majority of the Commission shall be binding upon the parties.

[40] See, in respect of the applications of Roumania, Bulgaria and Hungary, *Minutes* of the 204th, 205th and 206th Meetings of the Security Council.

[41] In April and May, 1949, the Governments of Great Britain and the United States informed Soviet Russia that a dispute had arisen between them and the Governments of Bulgaria, Hungary and Roumania concerning the interpretation of the human rights clauses of the Peace Treaties and asked that a conference of the Heads of the Diplomatic Missions of Soviet Russia, the United States and Great Britain in these countries be convened for the purpose of examining the dispute. The Soviet Government declined to accede to the request on the ground that the action taken by Bulgaria, Roumania and Hungary ' far from constituting a violation of the Peace Treaties, pursues the aims provided for in those articles of the Peace Treaties . . . which made it incumbent upon the Governments of Bulgaria, Hungary, and Roumania to pursue measures for the dissolution of organisations of a Fascist type to prevent in the future the existence of activity of organisations of such a type hostile to the democratic rights of the peoples ' (Russian Note of 19 July, 1949). For the British and American Notes see *Bulletin of State Department*, 20 (1949), p. 755, and 21 (1949), p. 29. For the Resolution of the Third General Assembly of 30 April, 1949, referring to the accusations against the Governments of Bulgaria and Hungary see Doc. A/842; *Bulletin of State Department*, 20 (1949), p. 612. In a previous Note of 11 June, 1949) the Russian Government asserted that the measures complained of were carried out in order to fulfil the articles of the Peace Treaties and were ' fully within the domestic juris-

Third General Assembly, Bolivia and Australia brought before the United Nations, by reference to the provisions of the Charter and of the Paris Peace Treaties, the question of the observance by Bulgaria and Hungary of human rights and fundamental freedoms, including questions of religious and civil liberties.[42]

The Paris Conference of 1946 rejected the proposal, put forward by Australia, for establishing a European Court of Human Rights charged with the enforcement of the relevant clauses of these Treaties on the ground that the implementation of obligations concerning human rights falls within the province of the organs of the United Nations; that ' as long as no fundamental understanding has been arrived at on the principles involved, it is impossible in the present state of international law to compel a State to accept the decisions of an international legal body in this matter '[43] ; and that, in any case, the implementation of provisions concerning human rights would be covered by the machinery laid down in the Treaty for settling disputes arising out of the interpretation and application of the Treaty.   The first of the reasons would be valid if the Economic and Social Council and the Commission on Human Rights had effectively claimed the right to ensure the observance of human rights—a view which

diction of these countries as sovereign States '.   There is no doubt that the Russian Government in arrogating to itself a power of decision which the Treaties left to a conference of ambassadors or to an independent commission committed a breach of the Treaties in question.   The three countries directly concerned adopted a similar attitude.   In a Note of 19 September, 1949, presented to the Governments of these States, Great Britain accurately described their refusal to join in establishing a commission provided for in the Peace Treaties as a deliberate breach of their obligations.   The Note said : ' His Majesty's Government do not recognise any right in the Bulgarian Government to arrogate to itself the sole interpretation of the treaty of peace, to which it is itself only one party.   Article 36 would be meaningless if the Bulgarian Government were to be the sole arbiter of the execution of its obligations under the peace treaty.   As to the suggestion that the action of his Majesty's Government in invoking the peace treaty constitutes an unwarranted intervention in Bulgarian internal affairs it is obvious that the sovereignty of Bulgaria is in fact limited by the international obligations of the Bulgarian Government.   The claim that the Bulgarian Government has complied with Article 4 [relating to the prevention of activities hostile to democratic rights] of the treaty does not excuse breaches of other Articles.   Article 4 was not intended to be used as a cloak for the denial of the fundamental freedoms specified in Article 2 nor as a pretext for the suppression of all opposition to the rule of a majority.'   The United States delivered similar Notes.   At the Fourth General Assembly the United States proposed that the question of the obligation of the States concerned to participate in the machinery provided by the Treaties for the settlement of disputes should be submitted for an Advisory Opinion of the International Court of Justice.   The proposal was adopted.

[42] See below, p. 205.

[43] As quoted in the Report of Dr. Martin, cited below, p. 165.

had not at that time commended itself to these bodies[44]—and if a legal basis could be found for their acting in that capacity apart from the provisions of the Charter and in relation to States which are not Members of the United Nations. There must be serious objection to the second reason given, namely, that so long as there is no 'fundamental understanding' concerning the meaning of human rights and freedoms, the enforcement of these rights by a judicial agency—national or international—is impossible. The Treaties refer expressly to some—the most important—of these rights and freedoms, such as freedom of expression, of Press and publication, of religious worship, of political opinion and of public meeting. Judicial tribunals in various countries have experienced no undue difficulty in interpreting these freedoms, however generally formulated, in the light of varying circumstances. [44a] The objections to the idea of an international court as the normal agency of first instance to enforce respect for human rights are stated elsewhere in this book. They are not of the kind advanced by the Paris Peace Conference.[45] The eventual admission of the States concerned as Members of the United Nations need not necessarily affect the continuation of the special régime of enforcement of the provisions relating to human rights. There is no principle of law which prevents any Member of the United Nations from undertaking, in this respect, obligations of a character more stringent than those applicable to other Members of the Organisation. On the other hand there is objection to a situation in which, in a matter as basic as human rights and fundamental freedoms, different procedures of supervision and enforcement—unless voluntarily accepted—rest upon different Members of the United Nations. Once an effective International Bill of Human Rights has been accepted by most Members of the United Nations, including the States bound by the special provisions of the Peace Treaties imposed upon them, the reason will have disappeared for any differentiation of treatment and obligations in this respect.

[44] See below, pp. 225, 226.
[44a] See below, pp. 327-333.
[45] For an interesting suggestion linking the enforcement of the relevant provisions of the Paris Peace Treaties with Articles 55 and 56 of the Charter and with the Human Rights Commission see the Report of Dr. Andrew Martin presented to the International Law Association at Brussels in 1948.

CHAPTER 10

EFFECT OF THE CLAUSE OF DOMESTIC JURISDICTION
(*Article 2 (7) of the Charter*)

1. THE RELEVANCE OF THE EXCLUSION OF MATTERS OF DOMESTIC JURISDICTION. THE MEANING OF ' INTERVENTION '

THE extent to which the purpose of the Charter in the matter of the protection of human rights is affected by Article 2, paragraph 7—the clause of 'domestic jurisdiction'—has justly been regarded as of crucial significance. That provision—so far the most frequently invoked—of the Charter lays down as follows:

> Nothing contained in the present Charter shall authorize the United Nations to intervene in matters which are essentially within the domestic jurisdiction of any state or shall require the Members to submit such matters to settlement under the present Charter; but this principle shall not prejudice the application of enforcement measures under Chapter VII.

The view has been widely expressed that the effect of that clause is to reduce to a minimum or to render altogether nugatory the protection of human rights in pursuance of the Charter.[1] Whatever truth there may be in that assertion, the question must be distinguished from that of the legal obligation of the Members of the United Nations to respect human rights and fundamental freedoms. Even if the United Nations had no power at all to enforce it, directly or indirectly, the legal duty itself would still

[1] See below, p. 173. And see, for instance, Professor Rappard's suggestion that ' as almost all, if not all, measures violating the fundamental rights of the individual, however defined, are held to be such matters [of domestic jurisdiction], one cannot escape the conclusion that the United Nations have denied themselves the possibility of protecting such rights by international legal action ' (*The Annals of the American Academy of Political and Social Science*, January, 1946, p. 119). The accuracy of that suggestion probably depends on what is meant by ' international legal action '.

remain in full vigour.[1a] Any Member disregarding that obligation would be acting contrary to one of the fundamental purposes of the Charter.[2]

The answer to this question as to the extent to which the 'domestic jurisdiction' clause of Article 2, paragraph 7, affects the protection of human rights by the United Nations depends upon the interpretation of the two principal terms of that paragraph: 'intervene' and 'matters which are essentially within the domestic jurisdiction of any state'.

Paragraph 7 of Article 2 refers only to such action on the part of the United Nations as amounts to intervention; it does not rule out measures falling short of intervention. Intervention is a technical term of, on the whole, unequivocal connotation. It signifies dictatorial interference in the sense of action amounting to a denial of the independence of the State. It implies a peremptory demand for positive conduct or abstention—a demand which, if not complied with, involves a threat of or recourse to compulsion, though not necessarily physical compulsion, in some form. This has been the current interpretation of the term 'intervention'. In the words of Professor Brierly, in order that we may speak of intervention in its scientific as distinguished from its popular connotation, 'the interference must take an imperative form; it must either be forcible or backed by the

---

[1a] See above, p. 148.

[2] Thus it is by reference largely to the clause of domestic jurisdiction that Brunet (*op. cit.*, p. 177) arrives at the conclusion that 'pour le moment, on ne peut pas dire que, sauf dans les cas où un Etat commettrait une violation grossière des droits de l'homme, ou des attentats graves et répétés aux libertés fondamentales des individus, il impose réellement aux Etats l'obligation juridique de respecter les droits et les libertés de leurs ressortissants'. It is not clear why the fact of systematic and gross violations should make a difference to the question of the legal nature of the obligation unless it is assumed that they amount to a threat to international peace (see below, p. 186), and as such justify intervention. The obligations in the matter of human rights are, it is submitted, legal obligations regardless of the manner of interpretation of Article 2, para. 7. The learned author, while denying the legal nature of the relevant provisions of the Charter, considers unilateral declarations such as the Atlantic Charter of 14 August, 1941, or the Declaration of the United Nations of 1 January, 1942, to be 'des engagements solennels liant des signataires les uns vis-à-vis des autres' (p. 199). The difficulty is increased by the fact that in Professor Brunet's view the question of human rights is altogether outside Article 2, para. 7, so that apparently intervention is possible in any case. Yet it is hardly possible to speak of the legal right of intervention in the absence of a legal duty which such intervention is intended to enforce. The writer has been informed that Professor Brunet is now of the view that the Charter does impose legal obligations upon the Members of the United Nations in the matter of human rights and fundamental freedoms.

threat of force '.[3] Oppenheim described intervention as ' dictatorial interference by a State in the affairs of another State ', and
emphasised that ' intervention proper is always *dictatorial* interference, not interference pure and simple '.[4] Professor Verdross
speaks of intervention as taking place when a State threatens
another with an evil if the latter refuses to yield in a matter which
international law leaves to its exclusive jurisdiction.[5] Professor
Stowell, in the leading monograph on intervention, refers to it
throughout as action aiming at enforcement.[6] There are few
topics of international law in which the uniformity of definition is
so impressive and instructive. In order to justify the use of the term
' intervention ' in its accepted scientific connotation there must
be an attempt to ' impose the will '[7] of one or more States upon
another State in an ' imperative form '.[8]

Intervention is thus a peremptory demand or an attempt at
interference accompanied by enforcement or threat of enforcement in case of non-compliance. Enforcement, in this connexion,
may mean either direct measures of compulsion or such indirect
pressure as is associated with non-compliance with a legal obligation or with a pronouncement of an international authority
having binding legal effect.[9] That interpretation of the term

---

[3] *The Law of Nations* (4th ed., 1949), p. 284. Lawrence (*International Law*
(3rd ed., revised, 1905)) uses almost identical terms: ' The essence of intervention is force, or the threat of force, in case the dictates of the intervening
power are disregarded ' (p. 116).

[4] *International Law*, vol. I (2nd ed., 1912), § 134.

[5] *Völkerrecht* (1937), p. 203.

[6] *Intervention in International Law* (1921).

[7] See Spiropoulos, *Traité théorique et pratique de droit international public*
(1933), p. 131; Accioly, *Traité de droit international public*, vol. I (translated
from the Portuguese, 1940), p. 279.

[8] Strupp in *Hague Recueil*, 47 (1934) (i), p. 513.

[9] The writer has expressed this view in the following manner in his seventh
edition of volume I of Oppenheim's *International Law* (1948, p. 378): ' In so
far as a " recommendation ", although not implying a legal obligation to
accept it, is calculated to exercise direct pressure, likely to be followed by
measures of enforcement, upon a State in a matter which is essentially
within its domestic jurisdiction, it is probable that it would come within
the terms of Article 2 (7). Other recommendations, even if addressed to
individual States, are not excluded by the terms of that provision. The
same applies to recommendations which are general in character.' This
statement of the legal position was relied upon by the representative of
India in answer to the repeated contention of South Africa, in September,
1948, that the General Assembly of the United Nations had no jurisdiction
to entertain the Indian complaint concerning the treatment of Indians in
South Africa. He said: ' . . . . the term " intervention " has a well-known
technical meaning in international law; it means dictatorial interference.
Let us suppose that this General Assembly discusses this subject, studies it,
ascertains the facts and makes certain suggestions which may help the
Governments concerned to arrive at a settlement of the problem. None
of these processes involve intervention in the sense which that term has in

' intervention ' supplies an answer to the question of the limits of the action of the organs of the United Nations undertaken in order to encourage and promote the observance of human rights and freedoms. Thus it would follow that the General Assembly, or the Economic and Social Council, or any other competent organ of the United Nations, are authorised to discuss a situation arising from any alleged non-observance by a State or a number of States of their obligation to respect human rights and freedoms. The object of such discussion may be the initiation of a study of the problem under the ægis of the United Nations; it may be a recommendation of a general nature addressed to the Members at large and covering in broad terms the subject of the complaint; or it may even be a recommendation of a specific nature [10] addressed to the State directly concerned and drawing its attention to the propriety of bringing about a situation in conformity with the obligations of the Charter.[11] None of these steps can be considered as amounting to intervention. None of them constitutes peremptory, dictatorial, interference. None of them subjects to coercive action, or to a threat thereof, the unwilling determination of a State. They may mould its attitude, but this is a matter different from compulsion. There is no legal obligation to accept a recommendation or to take into account the general sense of a discussion or to act upon the findings of an enquiry. Admittedly, pressure of the public opinion of the world as expressed through

international law, and therefore none of these processes are barred by the language of Article 2, paragraph 7, of the Charter' (A/PV. 146, p. 21). See also for an expression of the same view by the Indian representative at the Third General Assembly (2nd Part): A/PV. 212, pp. 102-105, 106 (14 May, 1949).

[10] See below, p. 172, on the difficulty of distinguishing between general and specific recommendations.

[11] See below, p. 204. It is suggested by Goodrich and Hambro, in relation to Article 2 (7), that 'while discussion does not amount to intervention, the creation of a commission of inquiry, the making of a recommendation of a procedural or substantive nature, or the taking of a binding decision constitutes intervention under the terms of this paragraph': *Charter of the United Nations* (2nd ed., 1949), p. 120. It is doubtful whether this is an accurate statement of the legal position. In the discussion concerning the complaint of the World Federation of Trade Unions in the matter of the violation of Trade Union rights, the Argentinian representative urged before the Economic and Social Council, in March, 1949, that as under Article 2 (7) the United Nations was not competent to intervene in matters which were essentially within the domestic jurisdiction of any State, that principle applied *a fortiori* to non-governmental organisations. Yet he did not deny that the Economic and Social Council had the right, in the economic and social field, 'to recommend that Member States should adopt certain measures'. He insisted that such recommendations were not 'mandatory'; *Economic and Social Council, Official Records, Fourth Year, Eighth Session,* February-March, 1949, p. 47.

these channels may be made to bear upon the recalcitrant State. That kind of persuasion no provision of the Charter would have been able to prevent. Undoubtedly, when a ' recommendation ' is in fact in the nature of a decision the disregard of which may in certain eventualities involve coercion, it is arguable—we cannot put it higher than that—that it may fall within the terms of Article 2, paragraph 7. This might be the case with regard to recommendations of the Security Council acting, at an advanced stage of the dispute, under Chapter VI of the Charter, *i.e.,* in connexion with disputes likely to constitute a threat to peace— although in such cases, because the dispute has assumed an international character and is no longer essentially within the domestic jurisdiction of the State, the applicability of Article 2, paragraph 7, may become altogether doubtful.

One of the reasons for the comprehensive formulation of Article 2, paragraph 7, as finally adopted, was the desire to exclude the possibility of the Economic and Social Council making a specific recommendation, addressed to the parties to the dispute, in a matter which is primarily within their domestic jurisdiction. This does not mean that Article 2, paragraph 7, excludes recommendations, either general or specific, with regard to other spheres of the activities of the United Nations.[12] In these

[12] For a suggestion that the Economic and Social Council in considering questions which arise out of tariffs or commercial policies may make recommendations to Governments generally rather than to specific Governments, see the testimony of Dr. Pasvolsky, representing the State Department, before the United States Senate Foreign Relations Committee in the course of the Hearings on the Charter of the United Nations (Revised Edition, p. 310). The tenuous nature of the distinction between general and specific recommendations may be gauged from the fact that he admitted that the reports and recommendations, though general, might refer to specific conditions. He pointed out, in answer to questions, that such reports and recommendations might be the result of investigations specially made in particular countries— such investigations, in turn, following from the right of the various agencies of the United Nations to initiate studies and reports; that the United Nations would wish to concern itself with such matters as currency policies and subsidies to the merchant marine and to make recommendations on them as in other matters affecting international economic relations; that such recommendations would have ' considerable effect '; that although persistent disregard of such recommendations might cause ill-will and difficulties, a similar result would follow from a mere discussion arising out of a complaint; and that ' as complaints can be made at any time and in any way ' it was useful to provide machinery for adjusting them. He admitted that ' as the Organisation takes over the function of making studies and recommendations on human rights, it may wish to make studies in those fields and make pronouncements ' (*ibid.,* pp. 310-311). The Chairman of the Committee and Senator Vandenberg—both of whom took an active part in the drafting of the Charter—expressed no doubt as to the power to make recommendations, but recalled that the latter were not binding.

other spheres a recommendation, even if specifically addressed to a State, not being in the nature of a binding decision the disregard of which may entail legal consequences, does not constitute intervention. Neither would an enquiry amount to intervention, so long as it does not take place in the territory of the State concerned against its will. The wide limitation of Article 2, paragraph 7, was inserted at San Francisco—in contrast with the limitation of the Dumbarton Oaks Proposals, which excluded intervention only in connexion with the settlement of disputes—for the reason that, as in the meantime the United Nations and, especially, its Economic and Social Council were granted broader powers and authority, it was necessary expressly to exclude the possibility of their ' interfering directly in the domestic economy, social structure, or cultural or educational arrangements of the Member States '.[13] The intention was to rule out direct legislative intervention by the United Nations in matters normally reserved to the legislature of the State. The problem was, as one of the Delegates of the United States put it at the San Francisco Conference: ' Shall the organisation itself intervene in the domestic life of the Member States or shall it deal with it through national governments? '[14] Or, as stated in the American Official Commentary in relation to the powers of the Economic and Social Council: ' Unlike the Security Council, the Economic and Social Council was not to have any coercive powers . . . it could not interfere with the powers and functions of sovereign States. It could not command performance by individual member nations; it should not reach into domestic affairs of Members. Its tools and procedure are those of study, discussion, report and recommendation. These are the voluntary means of a free and voluntary association of nations.'[15] Direct legislative interference by the United Nations—*i.e.,* an attempt to impose upon States rules of conduct as a matter of legal right—would clearly come within the orbit of intervention.[16]

[13] *Official American Commentary* (as cited above), p. 58.
[14] As quoted by Robinson, *op. cit.,* p. 44.
[15] *Official American Commentary,* p. 103.
[16] The question whether the Economic and Social Council is entitled to make recommendations addressed to individual Members of the United Nations was raised in 1948 in connexion with the dispute between Yugoslavia and the United States concerning the retention by the United States of the Yugoslav gold reserves. These reserves were deposited in the United States by Yugoslavia during the Second World War. They were subsequently retained by the United States as security in respect of

It may be argued that, inasmuch as Article 2, paragraph 7, excludes from the exception of domestic jurisdiction enforcement action under Chapter VII, the interpretation here adopted

certain claims of the United States. Yugoslavia then brought the matter before the Economic and Social Council on the ground, *inter alia,* that the action of the United States in retaining the gold deposits had effects detrimental not only to Yugoslavia but also to world economy in general. The United States challenged the jurisdiction of the Council, one of the reasons being that it had no competence to deal with the matter as it had no power to make recommendations to individual Members of the United Nations. In fact, the Economic Committee, in reporting to the Council on 4 March, 1948, in the sense that the latter had no jurisdiction in the matter raised by Yugoslavia, formally expressed the view that 'Article 62 of the Charter does not empower it [the Council] to make recommendations to individual members of the United Nations ' (E/743. 4 March, 1948). That view, however, did not secure general acceptance. In particular, the representative of Australia doubted its accuracy (see E/AC.6/23). Similarly, in the legal opinion prepared by the Secretary-General the view was expressed: ' (b) That the Council has jurisdiction to deal with the item in question and any other international economic matter from the economic aspect. (c) That the Council has also jurisdiction to deal with the item in question and any other international economic matter from the dispute aspect, provided it considers such dispute to be related to an international economic problem and to be of a nature such as would primarily be the concern of the Council ' (E/AC.6/25, p. 6). On the other hand, the representative of the United States, in a detailed memorandum, produced evidence purporting to prove, largely by reference to the preparatory work of the Conference, that no recommendations by the Economic and Social Council to individual States were admissible under the Charter. Eventually, the Council adopted a Resolution declining jurisdiction on grounds other than that principally relied upon by the United States (E/764, 9 March, 1948). The main reason adduced for the decision was that the Council had no jurisdiction to take cognisance of the juridical issues involved in the dispute. It appeared that before Commission II (and its Committee II/3) of the Conference at San Francisco the Australian proposal in connexion with the present Article 62 (1) was as follows: ' The Economic and Social Council shall have power . . . to make on its own initiative, recommendations to the General Assembly *or to individual members of the United Nations* with respect to international economic, social, cultural and other like matters, for the advancement of human welfare.' The unpublished records of the United States Delegation contain the following summary of the records of the relevant sub-committee of 18 and 19 May, 1945: ' (3) Paragraph (b) was unanimously approved with the additions of the words " studies, reports and " before " recommendations ".   (4) In the course of discussion on the preceding item, the Australian proposal that the Economic and Social Council might make reports to individual member governments was voted down.'   Meeting of 19 May: ' At the request of the United States, the Committee reconsidered its action of 18 May and agreed, Australia dissenting, to language which would restrict recommendations to individual members' (United States Mission to the United Nations, Press Release 396, 2 March, 1948). Apart from the character of the preparatory task involved, it is doubtful whether the evidence cogently supports the argument contended for. It is possible that the elimination of the reference to recommendations to individual States was merely intended to exclude a phrasing under which recommendations could be addressed to the General Assembly only, as distinguished from the members of the United Nations. While recourse to preparatory work in the interpretation of treaties is generally admitted, there has been, for good reasons, no tendency to question the soundness of the ruling of the Permanent Court of International Justice in the Advisory Opinion on the *European Commission of the Danube* (Series B, No. 14, p. 32) to the effect that recourse to preparatory work is not permissible with regard to confidential records known only to some of the parties.

is open to question. For, it may be said, if enforcement measures under Chapter VII are expressly taken out from the limitation of Article 2, paragraph 7, then it is clear that that provision contemplates—and excludes from the competence of the United Nations—such acts of intervention as do not amount to enforcement. The answer to this is that there exist degrees and measures of enforcement and intervention which are less drastic and far-reaching than those falling within the terms of enforcement action under Chapter VII. Thus, for instance, a peremptory recommendation by the Security Council, accompanied by a distinct intimation of action against the non-complying State, would be covered by the limitation imposed by Article 2, paragraph 7—assuming always that the question is one ' essentially within the domestic jurisdiction ' of the State concerned.

2. The Meaning of the Term ' Essentially Within the Domestic Jurisdiction of any State '

In interpreting the terms of Article 2, paragraph 7, commentators have concentrated their attention on the meaning of the phrase ' matters which are essentially within the domestic jurisdiction of any state '. They have taken it for granted that the term ' intervention ' is synonymous with interference and any other kind of active concern with matters falling within that sphere— an assumption which, as has been shown, is unwarranted [17].

[17] See, *e.g.*, Robinson, *op. cit.*, pp. 41-46, 70, 74-76, 79, who treats the terms intervention and interference as synonymous and who regards as intervention recommendations addressed by the General Assembly or the Economic and Social Council to particular States. He is of the view (see p. 78) that as the recommendations of the General Assembly could be construed as pressure by the public opinion of the world ' and consequently on a strict interpretation as " intervention ", they fall within the prohibition of Article 2, paragraph 7. The learned writer assumes that because of the prohibition of intervention the Assembly is not authorised to make recommendations, under Articles 10 and 13, in relation to matters of domestic jurisdiction (*op. cit.*, pp. 74, 78). It is submitted that on a strict, as distinguished from a popular, interpretation of the term, such kind of pressure cannot be regarded as intervention. See also Kelsen in *Yale Law Journal*, 55 (1946) pp. 997-1007, who, without discussing the meaning of the term ' intervention ', attributes a devastating effect to Article 2, paragraph 7, of the Charter. He considers that it is hardly possible for the Economic and Social Council to fulfil effectively its functions of study, report and recommendation under Article 62 without intervening in matters of domestic jurisdiction (p. 1007). The same applies, in his view, to the obligation of co-operation, under Article 56, for the purpose of promoting, *inter alia*, respect and observance of human rights and freedoms in conformity with Article 55. There is no warrant in the terms of the Charter for these pessimistic conclusions.

However, quite independently of the interpretation of the term ' intervention ', there is no justification for the view that Article 2, paragraph 7, in so far as it refers to matters which are essentially within the domestic jurisdiction of States, reduces most of the provisions of the Charter, including those relating to human rights and freedoms, to a mere form of words. Undoubtedly, the limitation expressed in Article 2, paragraph 7, is, because of its generality, one of the governing rules of the Charter. But that governing effect does not reach beyond its ascertainable terms. The degree of its clarity and rigidity is determined both by its natural meaning and by other provisions of the Charter. If, for instance, the Charter were to contain a definite ruling that certain categories of questions are ' international ' as distinguished from ' domestic ', Article 2, paragraph 7, would not apply to such matters. The result must be the same, or similar, in relation to matters which are manifestly international either as the result of their repercussions or because the Charter or some other treaty has made them the subject of international obligations. Whether they are so is a matter of careful examination of any particular situation and of a conscientious interpretation of that most difficult Article of the Charter—an interpretation aiming at the effectiveness of the repeatedly stated purposes of the Charter as a whole and reducing to its true proportions any excessive prominence claimed for seemingly categorical limitations. The construction of Article 2, paragraph 7, is not a legitimate occasion for a pessimistic exercise in frustration such as is expressed in assertions that that clause reduces most of the obligations of the Charter to a euphemistic declaration; that it leaves to every Member of the United Nations the right to determine whether a matter is or is not within its domestic jurisdiction; and even that with regard to such matters there is no room for the obligations of the Charter prohibiting recourse to force.[18]

There has been an inclination to assume that the change of phraseology in the Charter, as compared with the corresponding Article of the Covenant of the League of Nations, implies a restriction of the competence of the United Nations more drastic than that contemplated in the Covenant. The latter, without ruling out altogether the competence of the League, laid down,

[18] See below, p. 181, n. 34.

in Article 15 (8), that the Council should make no recommendation with respect to matters which were claimed and found by the Council to be, *according to international law,* within the exclusive domestic jurisdiction of the State. It may be argued that under the Covenant such questions as conferment of nationality, admission of aliens, or regulation of tariffs, though ' essentially within the domestic jurisdiction of the State ', ceased to be matters which ' according to international law ' are ' exclusively within the domestic jurisdiction of the State ' as soon as they became the subject of regulation by customary or conventional international law[19]; while under the Charter these matters, though regulated by international law, would still be matters which are ' essentially ' within the domestic jurisdiction of the State. There is little persuasive force in this somewhat verbal argument. For it may be said, with equal justification, that a matter is essentially within the domestic jurisdiction of the State only if it is not regulated by international law or if it is not capable of regulation by international law. There are few such matters, if any. It is arguable that a matter is essentially one of domestic concern if it is incapable by its nature of assuming an international complexion, *i.e.,* if it cannot have international repercussions. It may be difficult to adduce examples of such matters. There is no technical—or immutable—sense attaching to the term ' essentially '.[20] In the modern age of economic and political interdependence most questions which, on the face of it, appear to be essentially domestic are, in fact, essentially international.

---

[19] A principle clearly affirmed by the Permanent Court of International Justice in the Advisory Opinion concerning the *Tunis and Morocco Nationality Decrees:* Series B, No. 4, pp. 23-24.

[20] As is shown by the attempt, in the official *American Commentary,* to explain the substitution of the term ' essentially ' for ' solely ' as used in the Dumbarton Oaks Proposals: ' It seemed ineffectual to use " solely " as a test in view of the fact that under modern conditions what one nation does domestically almost always has at least some external repercussions. It seemed more appropriate to look to what was the essence, the heart, of the matter rather than to be compelled to determine that a certain matter was " solely " domestic in character ' (p. 58). It is not easy to follow the meaning of the explanation. The ' essence, the heart, of the matter ' seems to be that in modern conditions the domestic and international aspects are closely interwoven. See, for instance, the emphatic affirmative answer given by the representative of the State Department in the course of the Hearings before the Senate Foreign Relations Committee to the question of Senator Barkley: ' Is it not true that almost every problem that concerns international relations must originate somewhere, and that somewhere usually is within the domestic boundaries of one nation and may leap over into another nation and create an international situation?' (p. 312).

In the practice of the United Nations the terms ' exclusively ' and ' essentially ' have been treated as synonymous.[21]

In the light of the above interpretation the restriction upon the competence of the United Nations would seem to go less far than that imposed upon the competence of the League of Nations. For a matter may be according to international law as it stands at present within the exclusive domestic jurisdiction of the State, while at the same time, because of its international implications and the growing interdependence of States, it may be essentially an international matter as distinguished from a matter of domestic jurisdiction. In particular, it is not essentially a matter of domestic jurisdiction if it has become the subject of international obligations undertaken by the State. It has been submitted that—independently of the question of their enforceability—the respect and observance of human rights have become a subject of international obligations in the legal sense of the term. The fact that these obligations constitute, in various ways, a persistent theme of the Charter and one of its principal features, adds emphasis to that submission. Finally, as has been suggested and as will be shown in more detail later,[22] a dispute or situation ceases to be essentially within the domestic jurisdiction of a State if its nature or repercussions are such as to constitute a direct or potential threat to international peace and security. This applies not only to recommendations of the General Assembly under Article 14 [23]—a power which the General Assembly possesses in any case for the reason that recommendations are not affected by the prohibition of intervention—but also to the jurisdiction of the Security Council.[24]

It also appears from the official commentary submitted to the President of the United States, a country which played

---

[21] See below, p. 208.

[22] See below, p. 184.

[23] According to which the General Assembly may recommend measures for the peaceful adjustment of any situation, regardless of origin, which it deems likely to impair the general welfare or friendly relations among nations.

[24] See below, p. 185. Dr. Robinson (*op. cit.*, pp. 80-81), in somewhat pessimistic apprehension of the restraints of Article 2, paragraph 7, regards it as an open question whether the General Assembly may act, under Article 11, paras. 2 and 3, in questions relating to international peace and security if they arise out of matters of domestic jurisdiction. He suggests that even the fact of calling the attention of the Security Council to a situation likely to endanger international peace and security (Article 11, para. 3) ' might well be regarded as intervention in domestic affairs '. There seems to be no warrant for that interpretation.

a prominent part in the formulation of Article 2 (7) that the change in the wording of the clause, inasmuch as it omits any reference to international law, cannot be interpreted as constituting a further intentional limitation upon the activities of the United Nations as compared with those of the League of Nations. The reason given for the omission of the reference to international law was that ' international law on the subject was indefinite and inadequate ' and that ' to the extent that the matter is dealt with by international practice and textbook writers, the conceptions are antiquated and not of a character which ought to be frozen into the new organisation '.[25] It is not easy to follow the meaning of that explanation. For, clearly, an international tribunal, in conformity with the weighty pronouncement of the Permanent Court of International Justice in the Advisory Opinion concerning the *Tunis and Morocco Nationality Decrees,*[25a] would interpret the term ' international law ' by reference to the developing content of customary and conventional international law, and not to any rigid conception obtaining at the time of the adoption of the Charter. The more accurate explanation of the change is probably that it is merely verbal and devoid of legal consequences.[26] The Charter contains a number of such inconsequential changes as compared with the Covenant of the League of Nations.

It follows from what has been said above that in interpreting Article 2, paragraph 7, of the Charter the Members and organs of the United Nations ought to act on the view that in adopting Article 2, paragraph 7, the authors of the Charter did not, either inadvertently or by design, introduce a disintegrating element into the Charter; that in excluding matters which are essentially within the domestic jurisdiction of States they did not include within that exception matters which are the subject of international obligations (for these are not essentially within the domestic jurisdiction of States); that these international obligations include the observance of and respect for human rights and freedoms—one of the fundamental principles of the Charter; and that, as the practice of the United Nations has shown, a matter is no longer essentially within the domestic jurisdiction of a State if it has become a matter of international concern to the extent of becom-

[25] Robinson, *op. cit.,* p. 58.
[25a] See above, p. 175, n. 19.
[26] See Llewelyn Davies in *Transactions of the Grotius Society,* 32 (1946), p. 64.

ing an actual or potential danger to the peace of the world. That interpretation of the Charter has much more to commend it than one which reduces it to an absurdity. The provisions of the Charter—its solemn and repeated provisions—in the matter of human rights would be rendered meaningless if Article 2, paragraph 7, were interpreted as excluding, for instance, the right of investigation and recommendation. What, in that case, would be the meaning of Article 62, paragraph 2, which lays down that the Economic and Social Council ' may make recommendations for the purpose of promoting respect for, and observance of, human rights and fundamental freedoms for all '? Article 2, paragraph 7, retains a sense and a purpose even if we consider it as not excluding recommendations; Article 62, paragraph 2, retains no sense and purpose if, by reference to Article 2, paragraph 7, we exclude the right of recommendation.

The interpretation which is here submitted as the accurate interpretation of the Charter does not, in turn, reduce the categorical provision of Article 2, paragraph 7, to a mere form of words. For although—on that construction—human rights and freedoms, having become the subject of a solemn international obligation and of one of the fundamental purposes of the Charter, are no longer a matter which is essentially within the domestic jurisdiction of the Members of the United Nations, there still remain important questions which may remain within that category for the reason that they have not been made, as yet, the subject of international obligations. These, in particular, are questions which, as a matter of history, have prompted the reservation of matters of domestic jurisdiction, namely, those relating to admission of aliens and to commercial policies, especially the regulation of tariffs. In the Covenant of the League of Nations and in the Charter of the United Nations these questions determined the insistence of the United States and Australia upon the reservation of matters of domestic jurisdiction. They are questions which are typical of—according to some, largely identical with—' matters of domestic jurisdiction '. They are so to such a degree that, in relation to them, particularly exacting proof would be required that a dispute or situation connected with them has become a matter of international concern because of considerations of international peace. For in relation to them the exclusiveness of domestic jurisdiction has been traditionally a rule of international law. Viewed in that historical perspective, Article 2, paragraph 7, would still retain a tangible meaning and purpose even if—as the terms of the Charter bid us—we decline to regard human rights and freedoms as falling within the realm of matters which are exclusively within the domestic jurisdiction of States.[27] It is in the light of these considerations that we may view the subsequent attitude of Australia—the State largely responsible for the present text of Article 2, paragraph 7— in relation to human rights and freedoms. At the Paris Peace Conference in 1946 and before the Commission on Human Rights[28] the Australian representatives were most prominent in sponsoring the case for an International Court of Human Rights—a proposal in relation to which the notion of human rights as being essentially and exclusively a matter of domestic jurisdiction appears archaic. Even more symptomatic was the attitude, in the course of the discussion before the Security Council and the General Assembly in the matter of the situation in Spain, of the Australian delegate who in 1945 was instrumental in bringing about the present rigid formulation of Article 2, paragraph 7 [29].

The two lines of approach suggested here with regard to the interpretation of Article 2, paragraph 7, of the Charter appear to be to some extent mutually exclusive. If ' human rights and freedoms ' are not comprised within the category of matters essentially within the domestic jurisdiction of the State, then it would appear that the competence of the United Nations in respect of them is wholly unrestricted; that it covers both intervention conceived as imperative acts of dictation and persuasive measures of interference such as recommendations and investigation; and that in that case the distinction, as set out above at some length,

---

[27] Thus viewed, the expression ' matters essentially within the domestic jurisdiction of any state ' is a generalisation of some specific matters which created apprehension among the States responsible for the clause. This is a phenomenon not unusual in the practice of States in connexion with the exercise of the treaty-making power. Witness, for instance, the use, in the reservations to the Optional Clause of Article 36 of the Statute of the International Court of Justice, of the phrase ' past disputes '. The intention is to remove from the jurisdiction of the Court some definite categories of disputes present to the minds of Governments, such as certain territorial claims or disputes arising out of the conduct of hostilities. Yet the expressions used for that purpose are of a generality transcending the immediate occasion which gave rise to them and undermining the effectiveness of the undertaking as a whole.

[28] *Minutes of the Commission*, 5 and 6 February, 1947, Doc. E/CN/4/SR.15 and 16.

[29] See below, p. 189.

between coercive intervention and acts falling short of it, is irrelevant.   The answer to this criticism is a twofold one:

In the first instance, the language of Article 2, paragraph 7, of the Charter as related to human rights and freedoms partakes, because of its comprehensiveness, of a degree of elasticity which precludes any rigid construction in the direction of either of the two extremes of interpretation, namely, prohibition of all interference (including investigation and recommendation) or authorisation of intervention of any kind on the ground that human rights and freedoms do not fall within matters essentially within the domestic jurisdiction of States.   The correct interpretation must, for the reasons given, be in the nature of a compromise. That compromise means that the question of human rights and freedoms, although it has become an international matter by virtue of the terms of the Charter and is as such outside the prohibition of intervention, must nevertheless, except in extreme cases involving the peace of the world, be deemed to admit only of such measures of protection and implementation as fall short of coercive intervention.[30]   Secondly, that conclusion finds support in the language of the Charter inasmuch as—with the exception of allowing intervention in connexion with enforcement action under Chapter VII—the Charter does not go beyond the authorisation of study, investigation, and recommendation.   All those do not amount to intervention in its technical sense.   This does not mean that they are doomed to utter ineffectiveness.[31]

3.   The Determination Whether a Matter is Essentially Within the Domestic Jurisdiction of the State

The issue involved in the interpretation of the clause of domestic jurisdiction is one pertaining not only to human rights and freedoms—a no mean issue in itself.   The question is one of the effectiveness and authority of the Charter as a whole.   It has been submitted above that even if we assume that in the matter of

---

[30] Except, it must be noted, in relation to the wide and coercive powers of the Security Council, as to which see below, p. 185.

[31] To put these conclusions in different words: The interpretation here suggested of Article 2, para. 7, would be entitled to serious consideration even if it resulted in the admissibility of intervention in its accepted technical meaning. It receives a weighty accession of persuasiveness if, in refraining from pressing the argument to its full logical conclusion, we assert that ' intervention '—*i.e.,* interference—extends merely to action falling short of intervention understood as a measure of interference accompanied by a legal claim to dictate the conduct of the State concerned.

human rights the United Nations has divested itself of coercive powers, *i.e.*, of the right of legal compulsion through intervention, this does not mean that it has deprived itself of the power of influencing the conduct of its members by means short of intervention thus conceived. There is no reason why the process of interpretation should transform the imperfections of the Charter into manifest absurdities. Within that category there must be included the suggestion that every Member of the United Nations retains the power to determine with finality whether a matter is or is not one of essentially domestic jurisdiction or that the effect of Article 2, paragraph 7, is to permit Members to have recourse to force notwithstanding its solemn renunciation in the Charter.[32] This latter view need not be examined here as it is not germane to the subject under consideration. But it is necessary to comment, as being directly relevant, on the suggestion that it is within the competence of each Member of the United Nations to decide, with an effect finally determining the legal position, whether a matter is within its domestic jurisdiction. There is no warrant for any such view.[33]

Undoubtedly, the Charter contains no provision conferring authority upon any of the organs of the United Nations to decide that preliminary question. But this is not an omission peculiar to the question of domestic jurisdiction. It applies to most of the provisions of the Charter. The authority to decide upon disputed questions of interpretation of the Charter belongs, in principle, to the organ charged with its application.[34] For that

[32] Both these contentions are put forward with his usual lucidity by Professor Kelsen in *Yale Law Review*, 55 (1946), pp. 998-1002.

[33] That view is expressly rejected in the official *American Commentary*, p. 58. Professor Kelsen suggests that if a dispute is concerned with a ' domestic' matter. it is not ' international', and that, therefore, it is not covered by the principle obliging the members of the United Nations not to use force ' in their international relations' (*loc. cit.,* p. 1001). The argument is an example of the somewhat pessimistic inclination to extract a conspicuous element of absurdity from an admittedly imperfect document. It is clear that matters which are indisputably and exclusively domestic can—for that very reason—become the subject matter of international relations and international friction. There is an obvious difference between the freedom not to submit a dispute to settlement and the right to settle it by force.

[34] Professor Kelsen points out that if a Member refuses to settle a dispute under Article 33, para. 1, on the ground that it concerns a matter essentially within its domestic jurisdiction, the Security Council can act only if it assumes the power to decide whether the matter is within the domestic jurisdiction. He suggests that the assumption of such a power would be in disregard of the terms of the Charter (*loc. cit.,* p. 1006). There is probably no sufficient ground for that view, and it is unlikely that any Member of the United Nations would put forward a suggestion of this kind.

reason there is no force in the suggestion that, seeing that at the Conference at San Francisco the proposal to confer upon the International Court of Justice jurisdiction in the matter was expressly rejected,[35] Members of the United Nations have retained the power of the ultimate determination of the issue. The fact that the Charter does not confer that competence upon the International Court does not mean that, as a result, that power has been retained by the individual Members of the United Nations.[36] On the contrary, as is clearly shown by the deliberations of the relevant Committee at San Francisco,[37] the position is the same as with regard to any other disputed interpretation of the Charter, namely, that the power of interpretation, at least in relation to any given situation, belongs to the organ concerned, *i.e.,* the General Assembly or the Economic and Social Council. The decisions of these organs on the subject do not amount to a general interpretation of the Charter. But it is their duty, with regard to any individual case, to interpret the legal provisions of the Charter in accordance with good faith and not by reference to arbitrary considerations of political interest. With regard to any question involving fundamental human rights and freedoms their decision as to the jurisdiction of the United Nations cannot properly disregard the principle that such questions are, by virtue of the primary purpose of the Charter and its frequent provisions, an international and not a domestic matter. In the practice of

[35] A proposal made by the Greek delegation: see *Documents of the Conference,* vol. VI, p. 433. Similar proposals were made by Brazil, Czechoslovakia, Ecuador, Mexico, Peru, Turkey, and Venezuela: see vol. XII, pp. 190-192 (Report of Sub-Committee III/2/A). See also *San Francisco, Doc.,* vol. VI, pp. 494-499, 507-513). Before the ' Interim Committee (the ' Little Assembly ') set up by the General Assembly in 1948 the representative of Ecuador proposed a recommendation by the General Assembly to the effect that if a party to a dispute invokes Article 2, para. 7, as a reason for refusing to employ the methods of pacific settlement as envisaged by Article 33 of the Charter, the International Court of Justice shall determine the issue. (See U.N. Doc. A/AC/18/63; A/AC/18/SC.2(3): reprinted in *International Conciliation,* October, 1948, No. 444, p. 572.)

[36] Thus Professor Brunet seems to assume that because of the omission in Article 2, para. 7, of any reference to international law, the power of decision whether a matter is within the domestic jurisdiction of a State is left to the discretionary will of the State or States concerned (*La garantie internationale des droits de l'homme* (1947), p. 162). Yet he suggests, simultaneously, that because of the rejection of the proposal to confer the power of decision upon the International Court, that Article, like other Articles of the Charter, will be interpreted ' by the organs and [sic] by the Members themselves ' (*ibid.*). See also Kelsen, *loc. cit.*

[37] See *San Francisco, Doc.,* vol. VI, p. 509; vol. XIII, pp. 703-712. It appears, in fact, from the discussion in Committee I/1 on 14 June, 1945—*Doc.,* vol. VI, No. 1019-I/1/42—that no member of the Committee entertained any doubt on the question.

the United Nations the plea of domestic jurisdiction has been invoked with great frequency. But it is significant that, with isolated exceptions,[38] it has not been asserted by any State that it is within the competence of the State invoking Article 2, paragraph 7, to determine whether it is applicable in any given situation. The United States, who, in the matter of the compulsory jurisdiction of the International Court of Justice under Article 36 of the Statute, expressly reserved that right, has deprecated any such attempt in relation to Article 2, paragraph 7, of the Charter.[39] When Great Britain, in a matter connected with Non-Self-Governing Territories under Article 73 of the Charter, objected, by reference to Article 2, paragraph 7, to a proposed recommendation by the General Assembly, her representative merely insisted that the recommendation required a two-thirds majority.[40]

4. THE POWERS OF THE SECURITY COUNCIL AND MATTERS
OF DOMESTIC JURISDICTION

It must be borne in mind that the Charter itself limits the reservation of matters of domestic jurisdiction through the exception of ' the application of enforcement measures under Chapter VII '. Under Article 39 in that Chapter ' the Security Council shall determine the existence of any threat to the peace . . . and shall make recommendations, or decide what measures shall be taken in accordance with Articles 41 and 42, to maintain or restore international peace and security '. The formula referring to ' the application of enforcement measures under Chapter VII ' was adopted at San Francisco after considerable discussion. The clause as originally suggested by the Great Powers referred generally to action under Chapter VII. The Australian delegation successfully objected to the proposed formula on the ground that under Chapter VII the Security Council is authorised to take two types of measures: (1) recommendations calling for action or abstention on the part of the State or States concerned to remove a ' threat to the peace, breach of the peace or act of aggression ' ; or (2) actual decisions decreeing enforcement. It was urged that the formula as originally proposed would give to the Security Council the power to make

[38] See the Czechoslovak case, below, pp. 200, 201.
[39] See below, p. 201.
[40] See below. p. 202.

substantive recommendations for the settlement of disputes involving matters which are essentially within the domestic jurisdiction of States—a power which Australia was reluctant to concede. As the result, the Conference adopted a more rigid limitation of the exception to the reservation of Article 2, paragraph 7.

The formula as finally accepted provides an instructive illustration of the very limited usefulness of attempts at seemingly absolute safeguards of this nature. If a situation has become ripe for enforcement action under Chapter VII, then, clearly, it has ceased to bear on a matter which is essentially within the domestic jurisdiction of States. In that case the reservation of Article 2, paragraph 7, ceases to apply, and any saving reference to matters of domestic jurisdiction becomes totally ineffectual. The discussions in the Security Council in 1946 in connexion with the Spanish question revealed practically general agreement that a matter which has become manifestly one of international concern by constituting an actual or potential threat to international peace ceases to be a matter essentially within the domestic jurisdiction of States.[41] The Australian delegate who at San Francisco was responsible for the rigid formulation of Article 2, paragraph 7, elaborated in detail and with much force the view that that provision no longer applies in contingencies of this nature.[42] It ceases to be operative not only in respect of the powers of the Council under Chapter VII, but also in relation to its competence under Chapter VI, which gives it wide powers of investigation and recommendation with regard to any disputes and situations which might lead to international friction or endanger the maintenance of international peace and security (Articles 33-37). In fact, although the Security Council's Sub-Committee on the Spanish Question found unanimously that the Security Council itself had no jurisdiction to deal with the question under Chapter VII (relating to enforcement)—not because the matter was one of domestic jurisdiction, but because it did not constitute an actual threat to peace—it held that it could do so under Chapter VI (relating to peaceful settlement of disputes). It is hardly open to question that no reservation of domestic jurisdiction prevents the Security Council from investigating whether a dispute or situation falls within its

[41] See below, p. 190.
[42] See below. p. 189.

powers either under Chapter VI or under Chapter VII; that such investigation, as a rule, necessarily includes an enquiry upon the merits; and that, once it has been found that a situation or dispute has an international character in the sense of the relevant Articles of the Charter, the exception of domestic jurisdiction no longer applies. This is so irrespective of the question whether a recommendation by the Security Council, not being legally binding, can constitute intervention; or whether investigation by that body has that effect. The matter is admittedly of considerable difficulty. For although a recommendation of the Security Council is not legally binding,[43] its rejection may constitute a political link in the chain of events leading to enforcement action. As such it may be regarded as ' dictatorial interference '. However, the question is largely theoretical for, as pointed out above, the operation of Article 2, paragraph 7, is excluded in such cases for the reason that the matter is no longer one essentially within the domestic jurisdiction of the State concerned.

What is the significance of the legal position thus ascertained in relation to the protection of human rights and freedoms? The Security Council is not the normal instrument of the United Nations in that sphere. It cannot, as a rule, be concerned with isolated violations of human rights. It is not within its province to frame general policies for implementing that objective of the Charter. But, as shown, it constitutes an unlimited reservoir of power—a power not confined to recommendations and not impeded by the reservation of domestic jurisdiction—for the protection of human rights and freedoms when their violation results[44] in situations or disputes which might lead to international friction or endanger the maintenance of international peace and security or constitute a threat to peace. Situations or disputes of

---

[43] For this reason it is difficult to follow the view put forward by Dr. Kopelmanas, in an able analysis of the subject, that the function of the Security Council—as well as that of the General Assembly—as an agency for settling disputes comes within the limitation of Article 2, para. 7: *L'organisation des Nations Unies,* vol. I (1947), p. 236. Neither is it easy to assent to the view that ' dès la première enquête sur la nature du différend jusqu'à la recommandation sur le fond, tous les actes du Conseil n'ont qu'un but, ils visent à imposer à l'Etat une conduite déterminée à propos de questions qui font l'objet de la procédure de règlement ' (*ibid.*). There is, apart from enforcement action, no question of the Security Council having, in law, the right to *impose* a definite line of conduct upon the parties.

[44] And, for the purposes of investigation, when it is alleged to result or have resulted in such situations or disputes.

this nature may arise in relation to States which by reason of a systematic and flagrant denial of human rights become a source of international friction and of an actual or potential danger to peace; or they may originate in isolated outrages of such magnitude or cruelty as to shock the conscience of civilised mankind and impose an intolerable strain upon peaceful relations. Such perversions of the power of the State as those evidenced in the racial, religious and political persecutions in Germany before the Second World War would be a proper subject of action by the Security Council, under both Chapter VI and Chapter VII of the Charter, inasmuch as they caused international friction and difficulties through forced emigration and otherwise and inasmuch as they were a link in the vast ramifications of the design against the peace of the world.[45]   But no special circumstances such as these are required in order to bring contemptuous disregard of human rights within the orbit of the peace-preserving function of the Security Council.   The correlation between peace and observance of fundamental human rights is now a generally recognised fact.   The circumstance that the legal duty to respect fundamental human rights has become part and parcel of the new international system upon which peace depends, adds emphasis to that intimate connexion.   While during the discussions at San Francisco no sufficient support was found for the proposal that the Organisation should normally ' assure ' or ' protect ' the fundamental rights and freedoms,[46] as distinguished from ' promoting and encouraging respect ' for them, there was no dissent from the statement of the Rapporteur of the relevant Committee that if

[45] The British Prime Minister, in introducing the Charter of the United Nations, emphasised repeatedly in the House of Commons that, notwithstanding the clause of domestic jurisdiction, events such as the racial persecution in Germany before the War would not constitute a bar to action by the United Nations: House of Commons, *Debates,* vol. 413, pp. 663, 671.   See also *Documents of the San Francisco Conference* on the similar attitude of the French Government: vol. IV, Doc. 2-G/7 (o) and Doc. 976-1/1/40, p. 5. In its Report to the Economic and Social Council of 24 May, 1946, the Commission on Human Rights pointed to the possibility of the Commission assisting the Security Council in the task entrusted to it by Article 39 of the Charter by drawing its attention to cases where violations of human rights may constitute a threat to peace (*Journal of the Economic and Social Council,* First Year, No. 14, p. 162).   There is probably no decisive reason for confining the interest of the Security Council in the matter to the situation covered by Article 39.   Article 34, in Chapter VI, is equally applicable.   It will be noted that under Article 65 the Economic and Social Council is authorised to furnish information to the Security Council.

[46] See above, p. 146.

' such rights and freedoms were grievously outraged so as to create conditions which threaten peace, then they cease to be the sole concern of each State '.[47] (From this point of view there are considerable potentialities in Article 99 of the Charter, which authorises the Secretary-General to bring to the attention of the Security Council any matter which in his opinion may threaten the maintenance of international peace and security. The clause of domestic jurisdiction of Article 2, paragraph 7, presents no impediment in the way of the exercise of this particular function of the Secretary-General. The matters referred to in Article 99 are not, by definition, essentially within the domestic jurisdiction of any State.)

Neither, finally, is the clause of domestic jurisdiction relevant to the negative and somewhat ineffectual method of securing the observance of human rights by means of expulsion,[48] under Article 6 of the Charter, of Members who persistently violate its Principles—a matter which may be conveniently referred to in this connexion seeing that expulsion takes place on the recommendation of the Security Council. Expulsion cannot be regarded as intervention in matters which are essentially within the domestic jurisdiction of the State. It is a—somewhat symbolic—act of disapproval which has become necessary because effective intervention has not been found feasible. There is no sufficient reason for doubting that Article 6 is applicable as a sanction for persistent violation of the obligations of the Charter in the matter of human rights and freedoms. That Article refers to persistent violations of ' the Principles contained in the present Charter '. Does the term ' Principles ' refer to the ' Principles ' of Article 2 or, generally, to the principles of the Charter? The ' Principles ' of Article 2 contain no specific reference to human rights and freedoms. It is probable that if the draftsmen of the Charter had had in mind the particular terms of Article 2, they would have said so; they would not have used the more general term ' the Principles contained in the present Charter '. There is no doubt that respect for and observance of fundamental human rights is among the principles of the Charter. It is also indirectly among the Principles of Article 2, which lays down that ' 2. All Members . . .

[47] Doc. 723, I/1/A/19, p. 10.
[48] See below, p. 293.

shall fulfil in good faith the obligations assumed by them in accordance with the present Charter '.[49]

5. THE CASE OF SPAIN BEFORE THE SECURITY COUNCIL
AND THE GENERAL ASSEMBLY

The first two cases which came before the United Nations and which bear directly upon the interpretation of Article 2, paragraph 7, tend to show that the construction here suggested is in accordance with what is becoming the accepted interpretation of this crucial provision of the Charter.   In view of the importance of these cases it may be useful to comment upon them in so far as they are relevant to the question here discussed.

The Spanish case arose out of the reference by Poland to the Security Council, in April, 1946, of the question of the internal régime in Spain and its effects upon international peace and security.   The Polish representative moved a resolution requesting the Security Council to declare that the Franco régime in Spain ' led to international friction and endangered international peace and security ' and to call upon all Members of the United Nations to sever diplomatic relations with Spain.   The history of the prolonged and eventually inconclusive debate before the Security Council need not be recounted here.[50]   Its important feature, in connexion with Article 2, paragraph 7, is that although the members of the Security Council opposing the Polish resolution— as well as a Sub-Committee appointed by the Council [51]—came to the conclusion that the question did not fall within the orbit of enforcement action under Chapter VII (the only express exception to the prohibition of ' intervention ' under Article 2, paragraph 7), no member of the Security Council challenged its right to take cognizance of what was on the face of it a typical question falling essentially within the domestic jurisdiction of a State.   There was general agreement that expressions of disapproval could be voiced and measures of moral pressure could be taken against the Franco régime—though there was disagreement as to the nature

---

[49] The main element of doubt on this question springs from the fact that Article 6 refers to Principles, with a capital ' P ', and thus creates the impression that the intention is to refer only to the Principles of Article 2.   The capital ' P ' is probably an oversight.   In the Russian text the word is printed with a small ' p '.   In the corresponding Article of the Dumbarton Oaks Proposals the word ' principles ' was spelt with a small ' p '.

[50] See *Journal of the Security Council,* First Year, Nos. 31, 32, 38, 40-42.

[51] See *Report of the Sub-Committee on the Spanish Question.*

of the measures to be adopted. It thus became clear at an early stage: (a) that certain measures of interference did not constitute ' intervention ' ; and (b) that matters within the domestic jurisdiction of a State were not 'essentially' so if they had international repercussions, notwithstanding the fact that they did not constitute an existing threat to peace under Article 39.

It was with regard to this latter issue, directly relevant to the present discussion, that the proceedings of the Security Council elicited significant expressions of opinion. Dr. Evatt, the representative of Australia, who had a substantial share in the drafting of Article 2, paragraph 7, dissociated himself repeatedly and emphatically from the view that the question before the Security Council was one essentially within the domestic jurisdiction of Spain. He quoted the following passage from the memorandum presented by the Australian delegation to the relevant Committee of the San Francisco Conference: ' Once a matter is recognised as one of legitimate international concern, no exception to the general rule is needed to bring it within the powers of the Organisation. The general rule itself ceases to apply as soon as a matter ceases to be one of domestic jurisdiction.' [52] The decisive fact, in his opinion, was that there existed a situation, resulting from the internal régime in Spain, which was likely to endanger international peace and security, and that the object of the action proposed was to remove a danger to international peace and a cause of international friction. He said: ' The only things we are forbidden to intervene in are matters essentially within the domestic jurisdiction of any State. If they are not essentially of that character and if they do bear upon international security, then the United Nations is not entitled, but bound, to act in appropriate cases.' [53] He said previously: ' When you look at the internal affairs of a country you start with the postulate that it is no business of any other nation to concern itself how the people of that country govern themselves. That is, prima facie, primarily a matter of domestic concern, but if the facts indicate that that régime by its nature, by its conduct, by its operations is likely to interfere in international peace and likely to be a menace to its neighbours, then the existence of that régime is no longer a matter of essentially domestic concern.' [54] The only complication

[52] *Journal of the Security Council,* First Year, No. 37, 12 June, 1946, p. 728.
[53] *Journal of the Security Council,* First Year, No. 39, 22 June, 1946, p. 767.
[54] *Ibid.*

introduced by the learned delegate was that, after having shown that intervention was permissible for the reason that the matter was not one essentially within the domestic jurisdiction of Spain, he proceeded to suggest that the proposed action—*i.e.,* severance of diplomatic relations—was not one of intervention in the domestic affairs of Spain seeing that the object of the action was international in its purpose and method. It was true, he admitted, that that international objective ' may be served by a withdrawal of the Franco régime ', but, he explained with some ingenuity, ' how that action is to be brought about is a matter entirely for the Spanish Government and people '.[55] The Russian[56] and French[57] representatives were firmly of the opinion that the matter was not one essentially within the domestic jurisdiction of Spain. The representative of the United States dissociated himself from the view that the Security Council was precluded by the terms of Article 2, paragraph 7, from adopting the proposal recommending to the General Assembly the passing of a resolution recommending to its Members the severance of diplomatic relations with Spain.[58] The United Kingdom was the only permanent member of the Security Council firmly—though not to the extent of casting an adverse vote—adhering to the view that Article 2, paragraph 7, was applicable to the case at issue.[59]

[55] *Ibid.,* No. 37, p. 729. At a previous meeting the Australian representative, after affirming the importance of Article 2, para. 7, and after stating that the matter before the Security Council was *prima facie* one of domestic jurisdiction, proceeded to emphasise that ' the line between what is of international concern and what is of domestic concern is not fixed '; that ' it is mutable ' and that ' it seems reasonably clear that a government of fascist origin may by its actions, by its policy, both at home and abroad, in conjunction with reactionary groups of other countries, seriously threaten international peace ': *ibid.,* No. 29, 25 April, 1946, p. 578.

[56] He said: ' It is clear from the Charter that the intervention of the Organisation in the internal affairs of a State must not take place in normal conditions, that is, when the internal situation of any country does not constitute a threat to international peace and security. The Charter permits and provides for the necessity of applying certain measures in respect of States whose internal conditions constitute a threat to international peace and security. Article 2 of the Charter likewise clearly refers to this ': *Journal of the Security Council,* First Year, No. 29, 25 April, 1946, p. 570.

[57] *Ibid.,* No. 39, 22 June, 1946, p. 772.

[58] *Ibid.,* No. 40, 25 June, 1946, p. 782.

[59] *Ibid.,* No. 39, 22 June, 1946, p. 760. There was in the course of the discussion of the Spanish case general agreement that the Security Council was competent to entertain the Polish proposal under Chapter VI, in particular by reference to Article 35, if it found that the situation in Spain led to international friction and endangered international peace and security. It was also agreed that an investigation was permissible with a view to ascertaining whether such a situation had arisen. This was clearly expressed in the Australian Resolution adopted by ten out of the eleven members of the Security Council: *Journal of the Security Council,* First Year, No. 32, p. 628.

The position was not essentially dissimilar before the General Assembly, which, after a prolonged discussion, expressed the view that the ' Franco Fascist Government of Spain . . . does not represent the Spanish people ', and recommended that it ' be debarred from membership in international agencies established by or brought into relationship with the United Nations, and from participation in conferences or other activities which may be arranged by the United Nations or by these agencies, until a new and acceptable government is formed in Spain ' ; that ' if, within a reasonable time, there is not established a government which derives its authority from the consent of the governed, committed to respect freedom of speech, religion and assembly and to the prompt holding of an election in which the Spanish people, free from force and intimidation and regardless of party, may express their will, the Security Council consider the adequate measures to be taken in order to remedy the situation ' ; and that ' all Members of the United Nations immediately recall from Madrid their Ambassadors and Ministers plenipotentiary accredited there '.[60] These recommendations received the assent of countries, such as the United States and Great Britain, which opposed the more drastic proposal for severance of diplomatic relations with Spain. It can thus be said that the recommendations as finally adopted secured the agreement of practically all the Members of the United Nations. They were acquiesced in by States which, even before the General Assembly, adhered to the opinion that the matter was one of domestic jurisdiction. Yet it is clear that, in its Resolution, the General Assembly interfered in the most typically exclusive matter of domestic jurisdiction, namely, the internal government of a State; that it threatened further action in case the demand should not be complied with; and that it embarked upon a measure of coercive action by recommending the recall of ambassadors.

The Governments which voted for the Resolution might have been able to maintain that the measures recommended in it were not sufficiently compulsive to amount to intervention in the strict sense of the word. This would be to assert—and the assertion is not an inaccurate one—that measures of pressure and interference short of direct physical compulsion do not amount to interven-

[60] *General Assembly, Journal,* No. 75, pp. 825, 826.

tion.[61]   Or it may be said that Article 2, paragraph 7, did not apply for the reason that the matter had ceased to be one within the domestic jurisdiction of Spain.   This, as we have seen, was the view of some States.[62]

6.   THE INDIAN-SOUTH AFRICAN DISPUTE

The dispute between India and South Africa which came before the General Assembly in November, 1946, shed equally instructive light on the question at issue.   India brought before the General Assembly a complaint on the ground that, as the result of certain discriminatory land tenure and other laws directed against Indians, South Africa violated agreements concluded in

[61] The representative of the United States, while opposing the measures proposed against Spain on the ground that they would run counter to the principle of non-intervention laid down in Article 2, para. 7, thought it consistent with the Charter ' to remind the Spanish people of the reasons why they were not eligible for membership in the United Nations and to suggest to them the conditions they should create to regain their place among the Society of Nations ' (*Journal of the United Nations*, No. 59, Suppl. No. 1 (5 December, 1946), p. 240).   He voted for the recommendation set out above. providing, *inter alia,* for the recall of ambassadors and ministers plenipotentiary.   This was also the attitude of the United Kingdom (see the speech of Sir Hartley Shawcross, *ibid.,* p. 249, who, while maintaining the view of his Government that the Spanish question was a matter of domestic jurisdiction, did not oppose the measures included in the recommendation of the General Assembly as adopted).

[62] See above, p. 190.   Important qualifications of the term ' intervention ' came from some Latin-American States.   These qualifications are of particular significance as coming from States which, as a matter of national tradition, have exhibited emphatic disapproval of intervention.   The representative of Panama, in supporting the proposed measures against Spain, emphasised that the term ' intervention' had an established connotation; that it had been used in the past in relation to the unilateral action of the Great Powers such as military occupation or punitive expeditions for the purpose of securing control in certain countries; that while the principle of non-intervention was firmly embedded in the doctrine and practice of the Western hemisphere, it ' did not prevent the system of collective action built up in San Francisco from working in the interest of peace and human rights ' (*Journal of the United Nations,* No. 59, Suppl. No. 1 (5 December, 1946), p. 240); that Article 2, para. 7, did not in general prevent collective action for enforcing the principles of the Charter; and that severance of diplomatic relations did not in any case constitute an act of intervention ' since it was a well-known principle of international law that the independence of States did not depend on their being recognised by other countries ' (*ibid.,* p. 241).   The Cuban delegate equally emphasised that collective action of the United Nations as a whole did not constitute intervention in the sense of Article 2, para. 7 (*ibid.,* p. 242).   This was also the view of Costa Rica (*ibid.,* p. 254), and of Chile and Mexico (*ibid.,* pp. 254, 256, respectively).   A similar view expressed by the French representative merits quotation.   He said: ' The resolution which we have before us does not imply that the decision taken by the General Assembly of the United Nations is in any way compulsory.   It is a recommendation to each of the Member governments, and they remain free to act upon that recommendation.   I cannot see any intervention on the part of the United Nations.   I can only see a reaffirmation of an act of national sovereignty.'

1927 and 1932 between India and herself. It was also alleged that, apart from any international agreements, the discriminatory legislation violated the provisions of the Charter in the matter of human rights and freedoms. South Africa denied the existence of any international agreements bearing on the question and maintained that, as the alleged discriminatory legislation affected Indians who were nationals of South Africa, the matter was one essentially within her domestic jurisdiction and as such covered by the terms of Article 2, paragraph 7, of the Charter. South Africa demanded that the preliminary question as to the competence of the United Nations should be submitted for an Advisory Opinion of the International Court of Justice. That request, sponsored by a Resolution put forward by Great Britain, the United States, and Sweden, was not acted upon.[63] Instead, the General Assembly adopted, by a majority, a Resolution put forward by France and Mexico, which in fact claimed for the General Assembly the right to assume jurisdiction over the dispute. Its terms are of sufficient importance to merit quotation in full:

> The General Assembly,
> Taking note of the application made by the Government of India regarding the treatment of Indians in the Union of South Africa, and having considered the matter:
>
> 1. *States* that, because of that treatment, friendly relations between the two Member States have been impaired and, unless a satisfactory settlement is reached, these relations are likely to be further impaired ;
>
> 2. Is of the opinion that the treatment of Indians in the Union should be in conformity with the international obligations under the agreements concluded between the two Governments and the relevant provisions of the Charter ;
>
> 3. *Therefore requests* the two Governments to report at the next session of the General Assembly the measures adopted to this effect.[64]

What is the effect of that Resolution upon the interpretation of Article 2, paragraph 7? In the first instance, the proceedings before the General Assembly failed to substantiate the view that a State is entitled to decide unilaterally whether a matter is or is not covered by the exception of Article 2, paragraph 7. South Africa

---

[63] See below, p. 197, n. 77.
[64] General Assembly, *Journal*, No. 75, p. 831.

urged, in a pressing and persuasive manner, the propriety of submitting the preliminary question to the International Court of Justice.[65] She did not claim to be entitled to pronounce on the matter herself with an effect decisive for the course of the dispute before the General Assembly. Neither was any such suggestion made by any State supporting the South African request.

However, the Resolution of the General Assembly had a significance going beyond that preliminary issue. It amounted to a clear rejection, by two-thirds of the United Nations, of the devastating possibilities conjured up by commentators of Article 2, paragraph 7. It was in accordance with the construction, suggested above, of the meaning of the principal terms of that Article. That Resolution is a recommendation; it is not an imperative act imposing a legal obligation. Such recommendations, however great their persuasive force may be, do not constitute ' intervention '. This view was stressed with particular emphasis by a number of Latin-American States.[66] Secondly, the Resolution of the General Assembly is based on the view, which, it has here been suggested, is in accordance with the Charter, that

[65] The following extract from General Smuts' speech may usefully be quoted:
' The only question at issue was . . . whether there are international obligations arising under Agreements between the two Governments or from the provisions of the Charter which have been broken by South Africa. The complaint of India could only be based on legal obligations which South Africa has failed to observe, and these obligations must therefore be ascertained and reported on by the tribunal which has been expressly created for such purposes. South Africa's right to go to this Court cannot be denied her. The right of free access to the courts is one of the fundamental freedoms which are not denied the individual citizen or subject of a State; still less should it be denied a sovereign State Member of this august Organisation ' (*Journal of the General Assembly*, No. 54, Suppl. A (9 December, 1946), p. 349).

[66] Thus the Mexican representative said: ' It is sufficient to peruse Articles 10 and 14 of the Charter in order to be persuaded that the General Assembly has full and complete power to make recommendations to the Members of the United Nations on whatever matters and questions fall within the framework of the Charter save for what is provided in Article 12.
' We have raised to the category of an inter-American axiom the principle of non-intervention. It is an active principle of incalculable value to the relations of the States with each other, whose sovereignty and juridical equality is consecrated by the Charter in Article 2, paragraph 1. . . . It would be a sophism and a dangerous play of words to speak of intervention when one has merely a fully justified collective action on the part of the General Assembly, an action expressed by means of a moderate, courteous, conciliatory recommendation strictly in conformity with the Charter and that does not contain even implicitly any obligation that would be in violation with Article 2, paragraph 7.
' Let us honestly [*correctement*] apply the word intervention to an arbitrary action of one or several States which might tend to interfere in the internal or external affairs of another State. Such an action we condemn energetically ' (*Journal of the General Assembly*, No. 54, Suppl. A.PV/51, 9 December, 1946).

questions relating to human rights and freedoms are matters which by reason of their solemnly proclaimed international character are not essentially within the domestic jurisdiction of States in the full sense of Article 2, paragraph 7. That view was given clear expression by some States in the course of the debate.[67] Others, including Soviet Russia, voiced the opinion that the matter was no longer one essentially within the domestic jurisdiction of South Africa seeing that it was governed by a particular international agreement.[68]

It is significant that when the question came before the General Assembly in 1947 South Africa did not, with the same emphasis, invoke Article 2, paragraph 7. She contended that the discriminatory action which formed the subject matter of the Indian complaint was not prohibited by the Charter. Thus South Africa maintained that the purpose of the Charter ' is not to deal with every conceivable right, whatever the political, social, economic, racial or religious structure within which it exists may be, but only with such rights as may be regarded as fundamental, as so essential for ' the dignity and worth of the human person ' as to demand recognition in all countries at all times in regard to

[67] The Chinese representative, in supporting the Resolution, urged, *inter alia,* that the matter was not one of domestic jurisdiction on the ground not only that it was covered by the Cape Town Agreement of 1926 but also because it fell under the provision of Article 1, para. 3, of the Charter which lays down as one of the Purposes of the United Nations ' co-operation . . . in promoting and encouraging respect for human rights and for fundamental freedoms ' (*Journal of the General Assembly,* No. 54, Suppl. A (9 December, 1946), p. 362). The representative of Panama said: ' Are human rights essentially within the domestic jurisdiction of the State? My answer is no, and a hundred times no. I submit that by the San Francisco Charter human rights have been taken out of the province of domestic jurisdiction and have been placed within the realm of international law ' (*ibid.,* No. 54, Suppl. A-PV/51, p. 368. 9 December, 1946).

[68] The Russian representative declared that as the matter was governed by agreements between South Africa and India it was an international question and ceased to be one of domestic jurisdiction. He also added the somewhat unexpected argument that Article 2, para. 7, merely provided that the Charter shall not *require* a Member to submit a dispute to the United Nations; it did not *prohibit* it from doing so (*ibid.,* No. 55, Suppl. A-PV/52, 10 December, 1946). It would also appear from the remarks of the representative of the United States that, in his view, a matter was not essentially within the domestic jurisdiction if it was governed by an international agreement. He said: ' The Union contends in good faith that it has entered into no international agreement with India with respect to this particular subject. It also contends, as a corollary, that the matter is essentially within the domestic jurisdiction of the Union. This latter contention, if correct, would remove the problem entirely from the scope of the General Assembly's power of intervention because of Chapter I, Article 2, para. 7, of the Charter ' (*ibid.,* No. 54, Suppl. A (9 December, 1946), p. 351).

all human beings '.[69] She also contended that the Charter does not impose any immediate ban upon discrimination even when the latter affects fundamental human rights, and that ' until fundamental human rights have been defined and have received recognition in a binding form, the provisions of the Charter cannot be said to extend to human rights other than those which are today in international law accepted as being so fundamental that they are not merely of domestic importance but the concern of the society of nations '.[70]   South Africa insisted that discrimination is not necessarily evidence of oppression, of cruelty or of inhumanity; that it may be designed to ensure peaceful development towards the preservation of the racial and cultural identities of various groups by differentiation and by separation into different areas and different groups; and that ' the truly fundamental human rights of all races cannot be safeguarded in the Union without distinctions in regard to non-fundamental rights '.[71] These propositions may have been controversial, but the absence of reliance on the reservation of domestic jurisdiction is not without interest.   On that occasion India did not succeed in mustering the two-thirds majority of the General Assembly, necessary for the reaffirmation of the Resolution adopted in 1946.[72]   Most of the States which voted against the reaffirmation of the Resolution did so on the ground that it would impair the prospect of successful negotiations between the parties.[73]

In 1948 South Africa once more reverted to the assertion that the General Assembly was not competent to proceed with the discussion of the question.   In opposing its inclusion in the agenda the representative of South Africa maintained that as the matter was one of purely domestic jurisdiction ' a discussion [*sic*] of it would be a violation of Article 2, paragraph 7, of the Charter '; that that paragraph, designed to protect States from interference in their domestic affairs, expressed one of the most fundamental

[69] *Treatment of Indians in the Union of South Africa.   Union Government's Statement to the United Nations General Assembly,* 15 September, 1947.
[70] *Ibid.*
[71] *Ibid.*
[72] Thirty-one States voted for the Resolution and nineteen against it.
[73] This, for instance, was the view of the United States.   The representative of El Salvador objected to the Resolution on the ground that it would not be proper to single out one country in which the protection of basic human rights was alleged to be inadequate.   It was well known, he said, that such rights were unevenly safeguarded in various countries.   (*Journal of the General Assembly,* Second Session, No. 58, p. 5.)

principles of the Charter; that ' without it there could have been no United Nations ' ; and that without it ' certainly the Union of South Africa would never have signed the Charter '.[74] The General Committee, without an opposing vote, decided to include the matter in the agenda. Similarly unsuccessful was the South African plea before the General Assembly. She appealed to the General Assembly to recognise its error on the two previous occasions.[75] She invoked, in particular, the assistance of the smaller nations for whom, it was asserted, ' the just and strict interpretation of Article 2, paragraph 7 of the Charter ' is the only safeguard against encroachments upon their sovereignty—a safeguard which the Great Powers, in view of their right of veto, could afford to treat with equanimity.[76] No support was forthcoming for the South African plea.[77] In the course of the Second

[74] A/BUR/SR.43.

[75] A/PV.146, p. 11. The South African representative said: ' By now discarding a jurisdiction which was wrongfully assumed, in our opinion to the serious detriment of racial relations in South Africa, the Assembly would be enhancing rather than diminishing the prestige of the United Nations.'

[76] A/PV.146, p. 12.

[77] It may be useful to consider the implications of the refusal of the majority of the Members of the United Nations to agree, in connexion with the Indian-South African dispute, to a submission of the preliminary jurisdictional question for an Advisory Opinion of the International Court of Justice. (Also, in the course of the discussion concerning Spain the suggestion was made by the British delegate that the interpretation of Article 2, para. 7, be submitted to the International Court of Justice for an Advisory Opinion (*Journal of the Security Council*, First Year, No. 39, p. 763)). Are there sufficient grounds for sharing the regret that a question of law of the greatest significance was not submitted for an authoritative decision by the judicial organ of the United Nations? There were reasons, seemingly of a compelling nature, militating in favour of the course urged by South Africa. The issue touched the interpretation of a fundamental provision of the Charter—a legal issue *par excellence*. The right to have a disputed question of law determined by an impartial judicial tribunal was justly claimed to be one of those fundamental human rights the promotion of which is one of the principal objects of the Charter. Weighty considerations of statesmanship counselled the lifting of a highly political and emotional issue above the hazards of partisanship and alignments of voting. Recourse to a judicial decision was particularly indicated at a time when an opportunity presented itself of asserting, at the very outset of its existence, the usefulness and authority of the International Court of Justice. The persuasive force of all these considerations was emphasised by the inadequacy of the argument by reference to which some States resisted submission to the Court.

On the other hand, there is room for the view that the judicial determination, at the inception of the work of the United Nations, of the meaning of a crucial clause of the Charter of this character would not have been in the best interests either of the United Nations or, perhaps, of the Court itself. For the possibility must be considered that although on a proper interpretation of the terms ' intervention ' and ' matters essentially within the domestic jurisdiction of any State ' there is no contradiction between Article 2, para. 7, and a distinct measure of effectiveness of the action of the General Assembly and other organs of the United Nations in the promotion of human rights and freedoms and in other spheres, a judicial decision may not be the proper

Part of that Session the General Assembly adopted a instrument for finally removing what at first sight creates the impression of a substantial and disquieting contradiction. It is possible that the authors of the Charter, in so far as they stipulated both for the unqualified exclusion of matters of domestic jurisdiction from the competence of the United Nations and for the fulfilment of the purpose of the Charter in relation to fundamental human rights and freedoms, used language which on the face of it implies a contradiction. That apparent inconsistency could have been resolved by the Court by way of interpretation, on the lines here suggested, of the technical terms which the authors of the Charter used in Article 2, para. 7. It is highly probable that, on that interpretation, the Court would have found that the competence of the United Nations to entertain the Indian request depended upon the object of the request and that if its purpose was merely to obtain an expression of opinion of the General Assembly by way of recommendation or in some other similar way, Article 2, para. 7, would not apply for the reason that there was, in that case, no question of ' intervention '. Probably the Court would have added that as the General Assembly has, in any case, no power of decision, it must be assumed that no question of intervention was involved in the Indian application. Or the Court might have found that, for the reasons outlined above, the matter was not one essentially within the domestic jurisdiction of South Africa and that on that ground the General Assembly was free to entertain the Indian request. Or the Court might have combined the two reasons. But it is clear that, however well-founded its Opinion, based on these premises, would have been, it would have given rise to the criticism that in adopting the method of a somewhat technical interpretation—which would have come as a surprise to some of the authors of the Charter—the Court had in fact resorted to judicial legislation in respect of a highly political and dynamic provision of the Charter.

Alternatively, the Court might have resolved the apparent or real contradiction in favour of the Indian request by what might have been regarded as a piece of judicial legislation in conformity with the wider purpose of the Charter. For the possibility of a contradiction in the terms of Article 2, para. 7, and of the Charter in general—a contradiction created by the resolve, or the necessity, to couch in general language the desire to meet what were probably limited contingencies—cannot be excluded. The Governments responsible for the present formulation of Article 2, para. 7, may have been conscious of some such inconsistency and they may have been content—or must be deemed to have been content—to leave it to time and circumstances to remove it. A Court confronted with a concrete situation and precluded from admitting a patent contradiction in a basic international instrument might, with perfect propriety, have availed itself of the elastic wording of Article 2, para. 7, in order to render effective the wider purposes of the Charter. But if the interpretation adopted by the Court were to create the appearance of judicial legislation, the question would arise whether that result could not more properly have been achieved by the political organ of the United Nations, namely, the General Assembly. The decisions and recommendations of the General Assembly, by their very nature, partake of a degree of adaptability which takes account of the element of growth and change in the development of the United Nations and which may be absent in a clear-cut judicial decision answering in a brief affirmative or negative the question put before the Court. When that question pertains to a problem of crucial importance for the life of the United Nations, the necessity for pragmatic solutions from case to case and from incident to incident becomes particularly apparent. From that point of view there would appear to exist some reason for caution in instilling, through the imprimatur of the highest judicial organ of the United Nations, an element of rigidity into one of the fundamental provisions of the Charter at a time when, owing to the prevalent state of political uncertainty and the weakness of the United Nations in the initial stages of its activity, there might have been a leaning towards a restrictive interpretation of its Charter. For these reasons the failure of the First General Assembly to submit for an Advisory Opinion of the International Court of Justice the interpretation of Article 2, para. 7, though disquieting from

Resolution[78] inviting the Governments of India, Pakistan and South Africa to enter into discussions on the subject at a round-table conference 'taking into consideration the purposes and principles of the Charter of the United Nations and the Declaration of Human Rights'.[78a]

7. OTHER CASES OF APPEAL TO ARTICLE 2, PARAGRAPH 7

Of the two cases analysed above, that relating to the dispute between India and South Africa is probably the more significant. In that case the recommendation of the General Assembly was addressed directly to the parties to the dispute—both Members of the United Nations. Undoubtedly, it is impossible to divorce it, in relation to some of the States which voted for the Resolution, from the political considerations which moved them. Thus, for instance, the Chinese representative was not uninfluenced by the belief that the policy of South Africa was directed not only against Indians but against Asiatics generally. Yet the course of the discussion before the General Assembly and an analysis of the voting, especially on the part of the Latin-American States, suggest that the guiding motive of the attitude of the majority was deep concern for the moral authority and effectiveness of the United Nations as determined by its Charter.

However, the South African-Indian controversy and the issue of Spain, although most instructive, have not been the only cases

many points of view and objectionable in principle, was to some extent less open to criticism than may appear at first sight. But only to some extent. For it is not improbable that the Opinion of the Court would have been confined to the immediate issue before it without attempting a comprehensive and final interpretation of Article 2, para. 7, in a manner suggested by the representatives of some States. In view of the persistence with which Article 2, para. 7, has been and is likely to be invoked as a stereotyped plea often appealed to by the same States with little regard to or apparent intention of consistency, the balance of argument would be that it is desirable for the United Nations to avail itself of the services and the authority of its highest judicial organ for removing a disturbing source of confusion and uncertainty which is derogatory to the dignity of the United Nations and to its efficacy as an instrument of settling disputes and of international administration and co-operation. Thus Sir Hartley Shawcross, speaking on behalf of the United Kingdom, said: 'Until the measure of the domestic jurisdiction clause in Article 2, paragraph 7, of our Charter has been authoritatively defined, this doubt, this difficulty as to what we are entitled to deal with and what is excluded from our jurisdiction must always bedevil the relations between our member States and endanger our Organisation': *Journal of the General Assembly*, No. 54, 9 December, 1947, p. 378.

[78] By 47 votes to 1, with 10 abstentions.

[78a] *Official Records of the Third Session of the General Assembly, Part II, Resolutions*, p. 6.

which have illustrated the essential insignificance and ineffectiveness of the clause of domestic jurisdiction as formulated in the
Charter.   When in July, 1947, Australia and India brought
before the Security Council the situation resulting from the out-
break of hostilities between Holland and Indonesian forces, the
former objected to the jurisdiction of the Security Council on
the ground of Article 2, paragraph 7.   The Council, without
expressly resolving this aspect of the question, did in fact assume
jurisdiction.   The situation was complicated by the circumstance
that Holland had previously concluded agreements with the
authorities of what purported to be the Indonesian Republic and
that some Members of the United Nations had recognised it at
least *de facto*[79]—a consideration which on the face of it seemed
to take the question out of the sphere of domestic jurisdiction.
However, independently of that aspect of the matter some
members of the Security Council expressed doubts whether the
question was governed by the exception of Article 2, paragraph 7.[80]   When, in December, 1948, Dutch troops proceeded
to offensive action against the forces of the Indonesian Republic,
the Security Council, in disregard of the emphatic protests of the
Dutch representative, peremptorily ordered a cessation of
hostilities.

In March, 1948, Chile brought before the Security Council the
situation resulting from the change of régime in Czechoslovakia—
a change which, it was alleged, was due to the interference by and

[79] See Delson in *Columbia Law Review*, 49 (1949), pp. 344-361.
[80] Thus the representative of Colombia said: 'Can armed conflicts between
any of the Western Powers and their colonies, such as the conflict we have
under consideration, be considered strictly domestic affairs over which neither
the United Nations nor any of its organs has jurisdiction? ' (22 August, 1947:
S/PV.192, p. 82).   Previously, in connexion with the Ukrainian request,
submitted in January, 1946, for an investigation of the situation arising out
of the presence of British troops in Indonesia, Great Britain and Holland
objected to the request by reference, *inter alia,* to Article 2, para. 7.   On that
occasion the Soviet representative said: 'There are matters, however, which,
though formally comprised in the domestic jurisdiction of a given State,
border upon external political relations, or even encroach directly upon
external political relations, threatening the peace and security of the peoples.
Such matters cannot be left to be settled by the State itself, notwithstanding
the principle of sovereignty.   Does not the Charter represent certain limitations of the sovereignty of sovereign States?' (*Journal of the Security Council,*
First Year, No. 11, p. 20).   For the British view see *ibid.,* p. 197.   Mr. Bevin,
referring to Article 2, para. 7, said: 'When internal troubles arise, are we
always going to be sending commissions to investigate and deal with the
problems arising within a sovereign Power?   I cannot agree to it as a matter
of principle.'   The Australian representative saw, in principle, no objection
to investigation (*ibid.,* No. 13, p. 231).   The Council rejected the Ukrainian
resolution for reasons, apparently, not connected with Article 2, para. 7.

the pressure from Soviet Russia. The Czechoslovak representative refused the invitation to take part in the deliberations of the Council on the ground that ' the discussion of internal matters before the Security Council is in contradiction to the provisions of the Charter '.[81] Soviet Russia, on that occasion, relied strongly on Article 2, paragraph 7. The Security Council, by an overwhelming majority, asserted its jurisdiction. But it is of interest to note that the Argentinian and other representatives insisted on the full application of Article 2, paragraph 7, as giving jurisdiction to the Council on the ground that the complaint arose out of the interference by Soviet Russia, in violation of Article 2, paragraph 7, in the domestic affairs of Czechoslovakia.[82] The representative of the United States emphasised that because of its international character the question, covered as it was by international agreements, was no longer essentially within the domestic jurisdiction of Czechoslovakia.[83] Even more significant was the view, coming as it did from the representative of the United States, that it was for the Security Council, and not for Czechoslovakia or any other member of the Council, to determine whether the matter was essentially within the domestic jurisdiction of Czechoslovakia.[84]

Article 2, paragraph 7, was invoked in opposition to the proposal, put forward in connexion with Chapter XI of the

[81] *U.N. Bulletin,* IV (1948), May 1, 1948, p. 383.

[82] *Security Council, Official Records,* Third Year, No. 53, p. 3.

[83] He said: ' It has been argued that these charges cannot be considered by the Security Council because of the provision contained in Article 2, para. 7, of the Charter providing that the United Nations cannot intervene in matters which are essentially within the domestic jurisdiction of a State. However, the charges are based on the allegation of an illegal intervention by one State in the internal affairs of another State, leading to the impairment of its political independence. Moreover, the restoration and maintenance of democratic institutions in liberated Europe, including Czechoslovakia, was the subject of an international Agreement concluded at Yalta by Marshal Stalin, Prime Minister Churchill and President Roosevelt in February, 1945. Consequently, if the charges are true, Article 2, para. 7, clearly could not be a bar to Security Council jurisdiction over this question': *Security Council, Official Records,* Third Year, 1948, No. 56, p. 26.

[84] He said: ' This invitation has now been rejected. Why? The rejection is based on the thesis that this case comes under Article 2, para. 7. This, as I have pointed out, is a matter for determination by the Security Council. The new Czechoslovak régime and the U.S.S.R. are attempting to decide that question for the Security Council, and to dictate a unilateral and prejudiced opinion on this point to the Security Council. This is a high-handed and arbitrary way of behaving which would be surprising had it not come from these régimes': *Security Council, Official Records,* Third Year, 1948, No. 56, p. 32.

Charter relating to Non-Self-Governing Territories, for the creation of a committee to examine information received under Article 73 (e) of the Charter. The First Assembly, at its second Session, adopted the proposal[85]—though it rejected, apparently as being contrary to Article 2, paragraph 7, another proposal asking the countries concerned for information on participation by the native population in local government, receipt of petitions by the organs of the United Nations, and periodic missions to those territories. At the same time the Assembly accepted a resolution recommending Members having responsibilities for the administration of non-self-governing territories to convene conferences of representatives of non-self-governing peoples ' chosen or preferably elected in such a way that the representation of the people will be ensured to the extent that the particular conditions of the territory concerned permit, in order that the letter and spirit of Chapter XI of the Charter may be observed and the wishes and aspirations of the non-self-governing peoples may be observed '.[86] The proposal that the Economic and Social Council, ' together with the Administering Authorities concerned ' should convene such conferences was not accepted after a number of delegates had objected to it by reference to Article 2, paragraph 7.[87] The difference between the two proposals was not as wide as might appear at first sight. On the broad—and inaccurate —interpretation of the term ' intervention ' the recommendation as accepted was inconsistent with Article 2, paragraph 7. It contemplated a course of action lying in the sphere of what was essentially within the domestic jurisdiction of the States concerned. The recommendation which was rejected did not confer any authority upon the Economic and Social Council which could be exercised without the concurrence of the Administering States.

[85] *Resolutions of the Assembly,* p. 1242 (*Plenary Meetings,* pp. 1357-1369).

[86] *Plenary Meetings,* First Assembly, Second Part, p. 1356.

[87] See, *e.g.,* p. 1336 for the observations of the British representative. He said: ' This resolution, as now drafted, is an infringement of Article 2, para. 7, of the Charter because it places the Economic and Social Council alongside the governments of the metropolitan territories as responsible for calling conferences in territories administered by sovereign governments. This is a serious matter, and we must be careful how we deal with the Charter. We must adhere to it in the spirit and in the letter.' The French representative expressed a similar view (p. 1562). But see *ibid.,* pp. 1337-1342, for the observations of the representative of India to the contrary effect. See also the Preface to the United Nations publication (1948, VI B. 1) entitled ' Non-Self-Governing Territories. Summaries and Analyses of Information Transmitted to the Secretary-General during 1947.'

Similarly, although the Greek Commission of Investigation established in pursuance of the Resolution of the Security Council of 19 December, 1946, considered itself precluded by the terms of Article 2, paragraph 7, from making ' any suggestions in matters which are essentially within the domestic jurisdiction of the countries concerned ', it added the following observation: ' In the event the Greek Government decides to grant a new amnesty for political prisoners and guerillas, the Commission suggests that the Security Council make known to the Greek Government its willingness, if that Government so requests, to lend its good offices in order to secure by all possible means the realisation of this measure.' [88] It is extremely doubtful whether the internal conditions of Greece, after they had become—directly or indirectly— the subject of international enquiry, remained a matter essentially within the domestic jurisdiction of Greece. It is equally doubtful whether the suggestion of the Commission, notwithstanding the guarded language in which it was couched, did not in fact amount to a recommendation relating to a matter within the domestic sphere of Greece.

An emphatic rejection of the view that the question of observance of human rights was within the scope of Article 2, paragraph 7, came from the General Assembly in 1948 in connexion with the proposal, put forward by Chile and accepted by the Assembly, to address a specific recommendation to Soviet Russia to permit the wives of Russian origin married to foreign diplomats to leave Russian territory. The Chilean representative elaborated in detail the view that the action of Soviet Russia in not permitting her nationals married to foreigners to leave the country was a violation of human rights and fundamental freedoms; that the latter were not within the sphere of matters reserved exclusively to the domestic jurisdiction of States; and that as the result of international agreements, including that embodied in the Charter, the question of the observance of human rights did not fall within the terms of Article 2, paragraph 7, of the Charter.[89] His views received wide support, including that of the representative of the United States who considered that the provisions of

[88] *Year Book of the United Nations,* 1946-1947, p. 371.
[89] A/C.6/SR.134, pp. 11-14. See also A/C.6/SR.138, p. 8, for a similar view of the Greek representative.

Article 2, paragraph 7, did not prevent the United Nations from considering the case of Russian wives prohibited from leaving the Union of Soviet Socialist Republics.[90] Subsequently the Assembly adopted a Resolution[91] which recalled the Preamble and Articles 1 and 55 of the Charter as well as the relevant provision of the Universal Declaration of Human Rights and the Resolution of the Economic and Social Council of 1948 deploring legislative or administrative provisions which deny to a woman the right to leave her country of origin and to reside with her husband in any other country. The Assembly declared, in the Resolution, that such action by Members of the United Nations was not in conformity with the Charter and recommended that Soviet Russia should withdraw the measures adopted by her in the matter. The discussion and recommendation of the Economic and Social Council, in the same year, in the matter of forced labour and trade union rights are noted elsewhere.[92] With regard to both

---

[90] A/C.6/SR.135, p. 15. This was also substantially the view of the representative of Great Britain. In addition, while admitting that legally the Soviet Government was entitled to prevent its nationals from leaving the country. the British representative apparently regarded as relevant the question of ' the extent of that right and the manner in which it was exercised '. He suggested that when the practice of refusing permission to nationals to leave the country was carried to the length of preventing wives from accompanying their husbands abroad ' the abuse of that right constituted . . . a flagrant violation of the fundamental liberties of the human being '. It is not clear from the record whether such abuse of the right in question constituted, in the British view, a valid reason for making inapplicable the exception of Article 2, para. 7: A/C.6/SR.135, p. 9. He was of the view that even if the action of Soviet Russia were justified in law, ' the Soviet authorities would still be in the position of having violated fundamental human rights ' (A/C.6/SR.137, p. 7)—a view which can only be based on the assumption that there is no legal obligation to respect fundamental human rights (see above, p. 151, and below, p. 401). Before that Session of the Assembly Soviet Russia invoked once more Article 2, paragraph 7 (A/SR.196, p. 18). The representative of Chile, in replying to the Russian argument, pointed to the draft of a resolution submitted in the same year by Soviet Russia to the Economic and Social Council in connexion with the charges brought by the World Federation of Trade Unions against certain countries, including Chile, on account of illegal violations of trade union rights. He reminded the Assembly that Soviet Russia did not regard that matter as falling within the domestic jurisdiction of States, that she considered these measures to be contrary to the Charter, and requested action by the Economic and Social Council (*ibid.,* p. 6).

[91] On 25 April, 1949; by 39 votes to 6, with 11 abstentions: Doc. A/PV.197.

[92] See above, p. 25. With regard to the latter, the Economic and Social Council adopted in March, 1949, a Resolution drawing the attention of all Member States to the importance of ensuring within their respective territories the full exercise of trade union rights and in particular to the principles contained in the Freedom of Association and the Protection of the Right to Organise Convention, 1948, adopted by the International Labour Organisation (E/1236). As to the former, see below, p. 216, n. 20.

questions the various States concerned raised, unsuccessfully, the plea of domestic jurisdiction.

8. THE CLAUSE OF DOMESTIC JURISDICTION AND NON-MEMBER STATES. THE CASE OF BULGARIA AND HUNGARY

The case of the observance by Bulgaria and Hungary of their obligations under the Peace Treaties of Paris and of the principles of the Charter in the matter of human rights requires separate treatment inasmuch as it provides an instance of action by the General Assembly, in connexion with Article 2, paragraph 7, in relation to States not Members of the United Nations. The case is of importance not only because of the attempt to apply the principles of the Charter in the matter of human rights and fundamental freedoms to States which were not Members of the United Nations. The main reason for its significance lies in its contribution to a clarification of the position with regard to the interpretation of the clause of domestic jurisdiction. Accordingly, it is desirable to give here a detailed account of the attitude adopted by the members of the General Assembly.

The matter was brought before the Third Session of the General Assembly in April, 1949, by Bolivia and Australia on account of the action of Bulgaria and Hungary, alleged to be contrary to the principles of the Charter and to the Peace Treaties signed by those countries, in the matter of human rights and fundamental freedoms.[93] Although the charges referred especially to the trials of church leaders[94] in those States and the denial of elementary judicial safeguards to the accused, they covered, in effect, the wider background of the violation of personal and political rights in those countries. While the Bolivian proposal was largely limited to a discussion and study by the General Assembly of the immediate issues connected with the trials, Australia was of the view that, given a prima facie case of violation of human rights, the duty of the General Assembly was to investigate the facts and to appoint a committee to study the situation and to advance conclusions and recommendations.

[93] See above, pp. 161-163.
[94] The item of the agenda proposed by Bolivia was: 'Study of the Legal Proceedings against Cardinal Mindszenty of Hungary in relation to Article 1, paragraph 3, and Article 55, paragraph c, of the Charter.' The Australian proposal referred to the ' Observance of fundamental freedoms and Human Rights in Bulgaria and Hungary, including the question of religious and civil liberty, in special relation to recent trials of church leaders '.

The debate before the General Assembly, and its General and *ad hoc* Committees, was significant for the reason that, notwithstanding the political implications of the case, the discussion was conducted by reference to the wider principle of the interpretation of the Charter as a whole. In particular, apart from the attitude of the Slav countries, which, with some interesting and unexpected qualifications,[95] invoked Article 2, paragraph 7, of the Charter as precluding any discussion of the subject by the General Assembly, the attitude of the overwhelming majority of the Members of the United Nations exhibited a remarkable uniformity of opinion with regard to the two principal aspects of the problem. Some States stressed the fact that no prohibition of intervention precluded the General Assembly from acting in a manner falling short of intervention, *i.e.*, by way of discussion and recommendation. Others laid emphasis on the fact that as the matter was not one essentially within the domestic jurisdiction of the States concerned, the limitation of Article 2, paragraph 7, did not apply at all. Some members of the General Assembly invoked both these factors. Finally, there was a consensus of opinion that the circumstance that the State or States concerned were not Members of the United Nations did not absolve the latter of the duty—or divest it of the right—to promote respect for and observance of human rights and fundamental freedoms.

The view of the United States—a country which had a substantial share of responsibility for the formulation of Article 2, para-

---

[95] Thus the Polish delegate admitted that, notwithstanding paragraph 7 of Article 2, the United Nations was entitled to intervene whenever, in law or in fact, a State Member denied the exercise of human rights to its whole population—as, in his view, was the case with regard to the treatment of Indians in South Africa—but that there was no right of intervention in case of individual violations of human rights (A/BUR/SR.58). The distinction cannot claim the merit either of clarity or of logic, but the admission was significant as suggesting a departure from rigid reliance on the alleged absolute character of paragraph 7. The same delegate insisted that it would be contrary to Article 2, paragraph 7, to discuss the matter seeing that the judgments in question were still subject to review on appeal (*ibid.*)—a suggestion that, but for the fact that the local remedies had not been exhausted, the complaint would properly fall within the jurisdiction of the General Assembly. The Czechoslovak representative (A/SR.189, p. 8) admitted that on some previous occasions, as in the case of Indonesia, Czechoslovakia supported the jurisdiction of the General Assembly notwithstanding Article 2 (7), but that that was ' a case of gross violation of rights ' by a not unimportant member of the international community (Holland). According to him, the test of application of Article 2 (7) was whether the issue represented a threat to international peace and security—an exception which, in the matter of human rights, is of considerable elasticity and wide potentialities. For it was on that ground that reliance was placed by some States affirming the jurisdiction of the General Assembly in the present case. See below, p. 207.

graph 7—regarding the legal position was stated, after some initial hesitation,[96] with considerable clarity. The representative of the United States affirmed the jurisdiction of the General Assembly for the twin reason that the action contemplated in the motion did not amount to intervention, and that the question before the General Assembly, arising as it did out of international treaties, was no longer one essentially within the domestic jurisdiction of the States concerned. As to the first aspect, he expressed the emphatic view that having regard to Articles 55 and 56 of the Charter the General Assembly was entitled, in the matter of human rights, to exercise the powers of discussion and recommendation conferred upon it in Articles 10 and 14. He said: 'Article 2, paragraph 7, of the Charter, regarding non-intervention in matters of essentially domestic jurisdiction, was not intended to preclude discussion in the Assembly on the defence of human rights and fundamental freedoms, should the need arise. Moreover, there was nothing to prevent the Assembly from expressing an opinion or making a recommendation when a particular country constantly and deliberately refused to recognise those human rights.'[97] He added, accurately, that ' generally speaking ... no organ of the United Nations could impose corrective action in such matters if there had been no breach of the peace or threat to international peace and if there was no treaty providing foi such action '. Previously the United States based the competence of the General Assembly on the independent ground that the matter had ceased to be essentially within the domestic jurisdiction of the countries concerned seeing that their conduct in the matter of human rights created a situation prejudicial to international peace.[98] This was also the view of Canada.[99]

[96] The representative of the United States originally objected to the form of a submission referring to the obligations of the Charter. He favoured a formula limiting the question to the observance of the Peace Treaties concluded by these countries (A/BUR/SR.58, p. 4). That attitude was subsequently abandoned.

[97] A/AC.24/SR.35, p. 20. He previously gave expression to the same view before the General Assembly (A/SR.189, p. 12).

[98] Thus before the General Committee the representative of the United States considered that notwithstanding Article 2, para. 7, the General Assembly was ' authorized to examine such matters when violations of great moral principles prejudicial to friendly relations between nations were involved '. He relied on Articles 1 (3), 10, 14, and 35 (1) of the Charter. At the same time he expressed the opinion that human rights were not essentially within the domestic jurisdiction of a State when they are covered by treaty obligations (A/BUR/SR.59, p. 15).
A/BUR/SR.58, p. 21.

The representative of the United Kingdom was of the opinion that as Bulgaria and Hungary had undertaken in the Peace Treaties definite obligations with regard to human rights, the matter was obviously outside the scope of Article 2, paragraph 7.[1] In support of this view he adduced the Advisory Opinion of the Permanent Court of International Justice in the matter of the *Tunis and Morocco Nationality Decrees,* where the Court laid down that once a question—such as that of nationality—becomes the subject matter of a definite international obligation it ceases to be within the exclusive domestic jurisdiction of a State. He apparently attached no importance to the fact that, unlike the Covenant, the Charter refers to matters which are ' essentially ' (not ' exclusively ') within the domestic jurisdiction of a State. China expressed a similar view.[2] The French representative had no doubt that the United Nations was competent seeing that no action amounting to intervention was called for: ' all that was required was a discussion of the subject, to be followed if necessary by an investigation '.[3]

Dr. Evatt, the representative of Australia and Chairman of the General Committee, gave a ruling, framed with careful deliberation, that the jurisdiction of the General Assembly was clearly established as the cumulative result of Article 10 of the Charter which gave it the right to ' discuss any question or any matters within the scope ' of the Charter and of Article 55 which imposed upon the United Nations the duty to promote universal respect for, and observance of, human rights and fundamental freedoms. He said: ' The right of discussion provided for in Article 10 of the Charter was one of its most important provisions. There was not a single question or matter coming within the scope of the Charter, relating to its aims, its principles, or any of its provisions, which could not be discussed by the General Assembly. If any question was covered by an Article of the Charter, that question would no longer be a matter essentially within the domestic jurisdiction of a State. Whether a State in which human rights had been violated was or was not a Member of the United Nations had, in his view, no bearing on the question.'[4]

[1] *Ibid.,* p. 17.
[2] A/AC.24/SR.38, p. 9.
[3] A/BUR/SR.58, p. 21.
[4] A/BUR/SR.58, p. 13. The delegate of New Zealand similarly submitted, in the first instance, that in view of the central position which human rights

The attitude of the Latin-American States was of particular interest in view of their traditional attachment to the principle of non-intervention. With isolated exceptions[5] they asserted the jurisdiction of the General Assembly for the reason that the contemplated action did not amount to intervention, or that the prohibition of intervention could not be allowed to nullify the major and more fundamental purpose of the United Nations in the matter of human rights, or that the only type of intervention which was obnoxious was that by individual States as distinguished from the United Nations as a whole. According to the representative of Brazil, 'to maintain that fundamental human rights were matters falling exclusively within the domestic jurisdiction of States, was nothing less than a denial of the various provisions of the Charter connected with such matters'.[6] The representative of Chile, in stressing that the abuse of Article 2 (7) of the Charter might paralyse the United Nations, claimed that the jurisdiction of the General Assembly included not only discussion but also recommendation. He drew attention to Article 14 of the Charter, which provided that 'the General Assembly may recommend

and fundamental freedoms occupied in the scheme of the Charter any ambiguity in Article 2 (7) must be interpreted so as to exclude human rights from its operation—though he was prepared to admit that 'certain less fundamental rights' remained within the orbit of that paragraph. In any case he was emphatic that with regard to any infringement of the fundamental right of fair trial: 'the General Assembly was fully qualified to discuss it, enquire into it, make recommendations upon it, implore the Governments responsible for redress, and, if it deemed necessary, condemn them on the basis of available evidence' (A/AC.24/SR.36, pp. 7, 8).

[5] The representative of Argentina considered that Article 2 (7) was applicable: 'Paragraph 7 was a solemn undertaking. Moreover, it had been a *sine qua non* for the adherence of various States to the multilateral treaty that the United Nations Charter was.' In his view it was also clear from paragraph 6 of Article 2 that the Charter could not be binding upon third parties (A/AC.24/SR.41, p. 7).

[6] A/AC.24/SR.37. According to the representative of El Salvador, to accept any such contention would render the provisions of the Charter ' no more than the expression of a juridical and political romanticism, unworthy of the times and of the serious intentions implicit in all the acts and documents in which the United Nations had expressed its principles and purposes in connexion with human rights' (A/SR.203, p. 3). The Bolivian representative repudiated the contradictory thesis that the authors of the Charter, while recognising that human rights were a basic element in the philosophy of the Charter, regarded Article 2 (7) as a barrier against the fulfilment of that object of the Charter. In any case, he said, what was proposed was not any coercive action against Hungary but merely that the United Nations should discuss a question which had given rise to grave concern to peoples throughout the world (A/SR.189, p. 18). Subsequently he said: 'Respect for human rights was a condition of peace, and peace was indivisible. The United Nations, as the guardian of peace, was qualified to intervene whenever those rights were threatened. To invoke Article 2, paragraph 7, in order to sidestep that responsibility would lead to ludicrous results and in effect make many other provisions of the Charter inapplicable' (A/SR.201, p. 17; see also A/BUR/SR.58, p. 19).

measures for the peaceful adjustment of any situation, . . . including situations resulting from a violation of the provisions of the . . . Charter '. The Preamble and various Articles of the Charter proclaimed respect for human rights and fundamental freedoms for all. Accordingly, ' the United Nations was competent to deal with these questions and to make any recommendations it might deem useful in this connexion. Although such recommendations could not be binding on Hungary and Bulgaria, nothing would prevent the General Assembly from making them '.[7] The repudiation, on the part of Peru, of the plea of domestic jurisdiction was even more general in character: ' The question of domestic jurisdiction did not deprive the Organisation of its rights. Domestic jurisdiction was the jurisdiction conferred on a State by international law; that concept, worthy as it was of respect, and directly related to the concept of national sovereignty, must not, however, come into conflict with another principle which must also play a major part in international life, the protection of human rights. . . . Whatever the rights of domestic jurisdiction—and he was among the foremost in recognising them—they must of necessity be limited when it was a question of human rights.' [8]

Of special interest were the broad pronouncements of some Latin-American States in the matter of intervention. The delegate of Panama insisted that the limitation of paragraph 7 of Article 2 was subordinated to the obligation to fulfil the Purposes and Principles of the Charter as stated in Articles 1 and 2. ' It was inconceivable that human rights could be systematically violated in a given country, whether it was a Member or not of the United Nations, without the intervention of the latter.' [9] The representative of Uruguay expressed the emphatic view that as respect for human rights was an incontestable obligation under the Charter, Article 2, paragraph 7, could not prevent the intervention of the

---

[7] A/BUR/SR.58, p. 116. Similarly, the delegate of Ecuador repudiated the idea that Article 2 (7) should be construed so as to deprive the United Nations of all means of action in the matter of human rights. ' The word " intervention " implied some kind of violent action the aim of which was to impose someone else's will or the acceptance of requests or demands which corresponded, in fact, to coercive measures by one State in regard to another State. It was obvious that the word " intervention " could not apply to recommendations by the United Nations. Such recommendations were not compulsive: they might be addressed in a general way to all States, or more particularly, to certain States only ' (A/SR.203, p. 16).

[8] A/SR.190, pp. 12, 13.

[9] A/BUR/SR.58, p. 19.

United Nations in a case involving human rights.[10] Cuba based her attitude squarely on the distinction between collective and individual intervention: ' Cuba did not wish to grant any State the right to intervene in the domestic affairs of other States, but the principle of non-intervention should not imply that the United Nations, acting on behalf of world public opinion and in accordance with the Charter, should refuse all collective intervention.' [11]

In accepting jurisdiction in the matter the General Assembly declined to act on the view that it had no legal power to impose obligations upon or to influence the conduct of non-member States.[12] Eventually the General Assembly adopted a Resolution in which, after noting that the Governments of Bulgaria and Hungary had been accused of acts contrary to the purposes of the United Nations and to their obligations under the Peace Treaties to ensure to all persons within their respective jurisdictions the enjoyment of human rights and fundamental freedoms, it expressed its deep concern at the grave accusations made against these countries regarding the suppression of human rights and fundamental freedoms within their territories. It noted with satisfaction that steps had been taken by several States signatories to the Peace Treaties with Bulgaria and Hungary regarding these accusations, and expressed the hope that measures would be diligently applied, in accordance with the Treaties, in order to ensure respect for human rights and fundamental freedoms. It ' most urgently' drew ' the attention of the Governments of

[10] A/SR.190, pp. 7-9. The fact that the States directly concerned were not signatories of the Charter was, in his view, irrelevant.

[11] A/AC.24/SR.37, p. 14; also SR.35, p. 6. Moreover, the Cuban delegate pointed out that there was no question here of intervention contrary to the Charter; the matter was not ' essentially' within the domestic jurisdiction; it was one of international interest. Also, in any case the General Assembly had full rights of discussion and recommendation under Articles 10 and 13 (A/AC.24/SR.35, p. 6).

[12] The representative of Chile was particularly insistent that the fact that Hungary and Bulgaria were not Members of the United Nations was not a valid reason for denying the competence of the General Assembly under Article 10. There could be no doubt that universal respect for human rights was one of the fundamental objectives of the United Nations: ' The argument that the jurisdiction of the United Nations was limited to Member States only created the dangerous premise that by withdrawing from the Organisation a State could act in open violation of the most elementary principles of the Charter' (A/AC.24/SR.38, p. 9). The Polish representative attempted to establish a distinction, in this connexion, between Article 17 of the Covenant of the League of Nations and Article 2, paragraph 6, of the Charter.

Bulgaria and Hungary to their obligations under the Peace
Treaties, including the obligation to co-operate in the settlement
of all these questions '. It also decided to retain the question on
the agenda for the next Session of the General Assembly.[13]

In view of the detailed manner in which numerous Members
of the United Nations defined their attitude in the matter, the case
of Bulgaria and Hungary is of particular importance for the
interpretation of Article 2, para. 7, of the Charter.   While the
General Assembly is competent to interpret the Charter, the
construction which Members of the United Nations have put on
this—and other—Articles of the Charter has not always been
consistent and has often been dictated by political considerations.
Yet when, as in the case of Hungary and Bulgaria, that attitude
is given expression by an overwhelming majority of the Members
of the United Nations[14] and, after a full discussion, by reference
to wider principle, it must be regarded as a positive contribution
to the interpretation of the Charter.   In conformity with an
established principle of interpretation it would probably be so
treated by the International Court of Justice.[15]   For this reason,
notwithstanding any views to the contrary expressed elsewhere
in this Chapter,[16] the discussion and the vote of the General
Assembly in that case are in themselves a weighty argument in

---

[13] A/851. The draft Resolution was adopted by 34 votes to 6, with 9 abstentions.

[14] Apart from the Slav States, the only European State which expressed doubts
as to the competence of the General Assembly was Belgium.   Before the
ad hoc Political Committee the Belgian representative, in a somewhat dis-
cursive statement, maintained that owing to Article 2 (7) the United
Nations was not entitled to intervene in the matter and that the enforcement
of the Treaties in question was left to the machinery provided therein.
However, he added that ' the fact that the matter fell essentially within the
domestic jurisdiction of States did not mean that the Assembly was necessarily powerless ' but that ' its action must not go as far as intervention,
which was forbidden by the Charter ' (A/AC.24/SR.35).   The Scandinavian
States originally opposed the Resolution on the—tenuous—ground that the
Peace Treaties provided for an effective procedure (A/AC.24/SR.39, pp. 17,
18; A/SR.189, p. 4).   They voted for the Resolution.

[15] See, e.g., the pronouncements of the Permanent Court of International Justice with regard to *contemporanea expositio* in the Advisory Opinions on
the *Competence of the International Labour Organisation* (Series B, No. 2,
p. 39) and the *Jurisdiction of the Courts of Danzig* (Series B, No. 15, p. 18).
The representative of Lebanon rightly pointed out that if the term ' intervene '
were to be interpreted in the widest sense, it would have to be assumed that
all Members of the United Nations, including even those who were now
invoking paragraph 7 of Article 2, were constantly violating the Charter
(A/AC.24/SR.39. p. 4).   It would be difficult for the Court to interpret the
Charter on the basis of any such assumption.

[16] See above, p. 198, n. 77.

favour of a clarification of this important aspect of the Charter
by an authoritative pronouncement of the highest judicial organ
of the United Nations.

9. THE CLAUSE OF DOMESTIC JURISDICTION IN THE SCHEME OF THE CHARTER

The question of the meaning of paragraph 7 of Article 2 of the
Charter is of decisive importance for the international protection
of human rights under the Charter. For that reason it has been
considered proper to discuss here at some length the question of
its interpretation. It has been shown that the terms of Article 2,
paragraph 7, construed in accordance with accepted canons of
interpretation, the history of its adoption, and its actual application in practice, forbid us to yield to the facile conclusion that the
result of that clause is to nullify the legal purpose of the provisions
of the Charter in the matter of human rights and freedoms and
to reduce them to a political declaration and a statement of
a ' social trend '. These provisions were intended to be and
remain a legal obligation of vast potentialities. The extent to
which those possibilities will materialise must depend, among
other factors, upon the strength and the authority of the United
Nations—in the same way as the latter will depend, to a large
extent, upon the implementation of its fundamental purpose in
the matter of promoting respect for and observance of human
rights and freedoms. Commentators can, in a small measure,
contribute to that end by resisting the tendency to a juristic
pessimism which finds no warrant in the seventh paragraph of
Article 2.

The interpretation, here attempted, of Article 2, paragraph 7,
seems to justify the following conclusions: (a) Article 2, paragraph 7, while denying the right of intervention, does not exclude
measures falling short of intervention as understood in international law; (b) Article 2, paragraph 7, while laying down that
intervention is not authorised by the terms of the Charter, does not
prevent Members of the United Nations from extending their
obligations in this respect in any subsequent instruments to which
they may choose to become parties[17] ; (c) matters essentially

---

[17] Article 2 (7) of the Charter has been repeatedly invoked by representatives
of Governments in opposition to various proposed clauses of the International Bill or Declaration of Human Rights. Yet reliance on Article 2 (7)

within the domestic jurisdiction of a State do not comprise questions which have become a subject of international obligations by custom or treaty or which have become of international concern by virtue of constituting an actual or potential threat to international peace and security; (d) inasmuch as the question of the observance of fundamental human rights and freedoms is a basic legal obligation of the Members of the United Nations and, particularly, inasmuch as it may become a matter of international concern in the sense indicated, it is outside the reservation of Article 2, paragraph 7; (e) in any case the terms of Article 2, paragraph 7, do not exclude, on the part of the organs of the United Nations, the procedures of investigation, study, report, and recommendation, seeing that these do not amount to intervention in the accepted legal connotation; (f) there may be room for a more rigid interpretation (subject to (c) above), in favour of the jurisdictional freedom of States, of the reservation of Article 2, paragraph 7, with regard to subjects such as the admission of aliens or regulation of tariffs, which, as a matter of history, have become closely associated with the conception of matters essentially within the domestic jurisdiction of States.

These conclusions may usefully be read in the light of the following considerations on the place and usefulness of Article 2, paragraph 7, in the scheme of the Charter: In the Dumbarton Oaks Proposals the clause of domestic jurisdiction was inserted as a qualification of the obligations of the Members and of the competence of the Organisation in the matter of peaceful settlement of disputes. In the course of the Conference at San Francisco that clause was given a place in the statement of Principles for the seemingly unobjectionable reason that, as the result of the enlargement in the Charter, as compared with the Dumbarton Oaks Proposals, of the functions of the United Nations, it was deemed necessary to safeguard the independence of the Members by prohibiting, as a general principle, intervention

of the Charter is, in this connexion, clearly irrelevant. There is nothing in the Charter to prevent members of the United Nations from agreeing to restrictions of their sovereignty beyond those imposed by the Charter. An International Bill of Rights will be binding only upon States which accept its obligations. Any 'intervention' resulting from the Bill of Rights thus accepted will be due not to any authorisation of the Charter, but to the free will of the States concerned. It was equally—or more—inaccurate to invoke the limitations of Article 2 (7) in relation to the so-called Declaration on Human Rights—a document which is not intended to impose any obligations at all.

in the internal affairs of States.[18] That precaution was unnecessary. There is nothing in the competence of the Economic and
Social Council, of the General Assembly, or, except in relation to
Chapter VII of the Charter, of the Security Council which renders
intervention possible. These organs of the United Nations are
not, as a rule, competent to render any decisions binding upon
the United Nations. They can study, discuss, and recommend.
Subject to the exception of Chapter VII, they cannot, in law,
impose their will upon the Members.

On the other hand, no provision of the Charter could, in fact
or in law, prevent these organs from studying, investigating or
discussing any question placed before them, at least to the extent
of deciding whether a matter is or is not essentially within the
domestic jurisdiction of the State concerned—which preliminary
decision is often to a large extent a decision on the merits.
Neither does there exist any legal obstacle to their power of
recommendation. Moreover, if a dispute or situation arising out
of what one State claims to be exclusively a matter of domestic
jurisdiction has reached the stage when another State considers
it to constitute or likely to constitute a threat to peace or
to the maintenance of international security and brings it as such
before the United Nations, that fact in itself shows, as a rule, that
the question is no longer a matter essentially within the domestic
jurisdiction of a State. The true protection of the independence
of States within the framework of international organisation lies
not in any formal reservation of domestic jurisdiction to the
exclusion of collective intervention. It lies in the fact that international law recognises definite spheres within which the
jurisdiction of States—unless limited by international custom or
obligations of treaties—is supreme. The reservation of domestic
jurisdiction cannot accomplish the impossible and combine the
acceptance of obligations with freedom from obligation. Any
attempt made, in the atmosphere of rapid decisions and deficient
scientific preparation characteristic of international conferences,
to achieve that contradictory result is bound to produce formulas
which, while of sweeping comprehensiveness, are of limited usefulness and applicability. Of this, the fate, to a large extent at the

---

[18] See *Documents of the Conference,* vol. VI, pp. 441, *et seq.* And see the lucid
exposition by Brunet, *La garantie internationale des droits de l'homme* (1947),
pp. 158-162.

hands of those who were most conspicuous in drafting it, of the seventh paragraph of Article 2 of the Charter provides an interesting and instructive example.

Quite apart from the question of complaints and disputes concerning violations of human rights or otherwise, it is clear that to attach a popular meaning, as distinguished from its scientific connotation, to the term ' intervention ' in Article 2, paragraph 7, would mean to deprive the organs of the United Nations—in particular the Economic and Social Council—of the possibility of performing their functions as laid down in the Charter and as generally understood. The overwhelming majority of questions which have come before the Economic and Social Council have been concerned with matters which fall essentially within the domestic jurisdiction of States. This is so for the simple reason that one of the main objects of the United Nations is to promote co-operation in and advancement, through international action, of matters of this nature. So long as such action falls short of coercive, dictatorial, legislative interference—so long as it falls short of intervention—it is consistent with and dictated by the purposes of the Charter. This explains why even States, such as Soviet Russia, which as a rule have opposed action by the United Nations as contrary to Article 2, paragraph 7,[19] have often proposed recommendations of specific action in the internal sphere.[20]

[19] See below, p. 217, n. 2.

[20] Thus in connexion with the question of equal pay for women, brought in 1948 before the Economic and Social Council by the World Federation of Trade Unions, the Russian representative on the Council proposed, in 1949, a Resolution recommending ' all States Members of the United Nations to establish by legislation in the shortest possible time equal pay for equal work for men and women, irrespective of nationality, race and religion, and to extend similar measures to non-self-governing territories ' (E/SR.236). In the same year the Russian representative proposed a Resolution noting that certain specified countries violated the principles laid down by the General Assembly and the Economic and Social Council concerning trade union rights recommending that those countries should ' take effective measures at the earliest possible date to implement the principles governing trade union rights proclaimed by the organs of the United Nations and recommending that they should submit a report on the measures taken by them in the fulfilment of the Resolution ' (E/1224). Similarly, in the same year, in connexion with the question of forced labour brought by the American Federation of Labour before the Economic and Social Council, the Russian representative proposed the setting up of an international commission consisting of representatives of the manual and intellectual workers united in all existing trade unions for the purpose of ' a comprehensive and objective investigation of the real working conditions of workers and employees in the countries where private capitalist ownership prevails, and also in the U.S.S.R. and in the People's Democracies ' (E/1194). South Africa was perhaps the only country which, because of her understanding of the meaning of Article 2, paragraph 7,

The circumstance that the effects of Article 2, paragraph 7, are not as devastating as is occasionally assumed does not mean that it is a satisfactory feature of the Charter. Although it falls short of the consequences which some commentators attribute to it, namely, of reducing to an absurdity substantial parts of the Charter, it constitutes a source of uncertainty and of a limitation of its usefulness and authority. The potentialities of Article 2, paragraph 7, for mischief, abuse and confusion are still considerable, notwithstanding the chastening experience of its application in the course of the first five years of the existence of the United Nations.[21] For that negative reason—but for no other—it will continue to be one of the most important Articles of the Charter until it has either been formally removed by way of an express amendment of the Charter or until it has become even more generally discredited than is the case at present. In the meantime it will continue to be invoked, with little regard for consistency, as a convenient starting point for delay and obstruction, both in the matter of disputes and of development of international organisation generally,[22] in the same way as the argument of restrictive interpretation of treaties limiting the sovereignty of States has been relied upon before international tribunals.

The fact that it is for the organ concerned—and not for the interested Member of the United Nations—to decide whether a matter is covered by the limitation of Article 2, paragraph 7, helps to draw attention to its artificiality as a safeguard of the sovereignty of the Members of the United Nations. That fact

refused to collaborate in these matters. Thus she declined to give information concerning the violation of trade union rights on the ground that that provision ' which is overriding of anything else contained in the Charter . . . precludes any organ of the United Nations from intervening in the domestic affairs of member nations ' (March, 1949; E/1225).

[21] It is stated by Goodrich and Hambro (*op. cit.*, above, p. 120) that ' the practice of the United Nations makes it clear, as indeed does the phraseology of Article 2 (7), that the word " intervention " as used in the paragraph is not to be given a narrow technical interpretation.' It is not believed that the practice of the United Nations substantiates that statement.

[22] See, *e.g.*, the attitude of Soviet Russia with regard to the proposed international control of atomic energy (*Security Council, Official Records,* Second Year, p. 452) or in the matter of a proposed resolution concerning stateless persons (U.N. Doc. E/SR., p. 159). As to the International Bill of Human Rights see below, p. 299. In his Dissenting Opinion on the question of admission of a State to membership of the United Nations (Art. 4 of the Charter), Judge Krylov invoked Article 2, para. 7, as a reason for holding that ' a Member of the United Nations is not justified in basing his opposition to the admission of a particular State on arguments which relate to matters falling essentially within the domestic jurisdiction of the applicant State ': Advisory Opinion of 28 May, 1948, p. 113.

also raises the question whether Article 2, paragraph 7, is a workable provision at all from the point of view of procedure. When a dispute or situation is brought before the Security Council, an affirmative vote of that body is necessary to sustain the objection to the jurisdiction of the Security Council. This means that, as the matter is one of substance, a single vote of a permanent member of the Security Council (unless it is a party to the dispute) may defeat the appeal to Article 2, paragraph 7.[23] The result is that the vote of one permanent member may invest the Council with jurisdiction. On the other hand, if the matter is put before the Security Council in the form of the question whether it has jurisdiction, a vote of one permanent member (or, if the question is regarded as one of procedure, of a majority of the members of the Council) may prevent it from assuming jurisdiction. Thirdly, in practice it might be difficult to prevent the Security Council from discussing what, in effect, would be the substance of the matter as a preliminary to its decision whether it has jurisdiction or whether the matter is covered by the provision of Article 2, paragraph 7. The same object may be achieved by the device of the Security Council placing a matter provisionally on its agenda without formally resolving the question of its jurisdiction. The application of Hyderabad in connexion with the invasion of that State by India in 1948 was considered by the Security Council at great length in that manner.[24] With regard to matters submitted to the General Assembly or the Economic and Social Council the procedure of voting in these bodies is different and the result, with regard to the subject under discussion, would correspondingly vary. Thus, for instance, it is probable that, having regard to Article 18 of the Charter, the decision to the effect that a matter is covered by Article 2, paragraph 7, of the Charter, and therefore outside the jurisdiction of the General Assembly, would require a two-thirds majority of that body. A decision of the Economic and Social Council on the matter can in every case be effected by an ordinary majority. As a result, in view of the peculiarity of the

[23] It has been suggested (see Fincham, *op. cit.*, p. 167) that the concurrence of any seven members of the Security Council is sufficient for upholding a resolution to the effect that it has jurisdiction in a dispute placed before it. This is so, it is urged, for the reason—which is controversial—that the decision does not affect the substance of the dispute.

[24] See the statement of the President of the Security Council on that occasion that 'the adoption of the agenda does not decide or affect in any way the question of the Security Council's competence': S/P.V.37, p. 40.

voting procedure, a situation may arise in which the Security Council may consider a matter to be outside its jurisdiction while, with regard to the same matter, the General Assembly or the Economic and Social Council may arrive at a different conclusion.[25]

As embodied in the Charter, the reservation of domestic jurisdiction, far from constituting a safeguard for what has been traditionally regarded as the province of domestic jurisdiction of States, leaves the door wide open for active concern by the United Nations with matters which affect the internal sovereignty of States but which at the same time are covered by the various provisions of the Charter. The evaluation put forward in this Chapter of the legal effectiveness and usefulness of Article 2, paragraph 7, is not the result of an ingenious interpretation of the Charter calculated to ensnare the Members of the United Nations in the meshes of a technical expression which they may have used inadvertently and which has a result directly opposed to what they intended.[26] It is a result of the fact that the legal and technical interpretation of the Charter—as here suggested—is believed to be in accordance with the spirit and purpose of the Charter as a whole. Any other construction would reduce some of the most significant of its provisions to a mere form of words. This applies in particular to the provisions of the Charter relating to human rights and freedoms. Undoubtedly, there is an element

[25] See on this aspect of the matter Kopelmanas, *op. cit.*, p. 236, and Fincham, *op. cit.*, pp. 166-169. Neither are the vagaries of Article 2, para. 7, limited to accidents of voting. Thus, assuming—an assumption not easily realisable in practice—that the Security Council has no jurisdiction, because of Article 2, para. 7, in a dispute before it under Chapter VI, a State so minded may, by forcing the pace of the dispute, contrive to bring the controversy within the orbit of the enforcement measures of Chapter VII where the exception of domestic jurisdiction cannot be invoked. The problem of voting in the Security Council with regard to matters of domestic jurisdiction under Article 2, para. 7, was discussed by the Interim Committee of the General Assembly. No recommendation was made on the subject. A number of States suggested that in cases of disagreement on the question of applicability of Article 2, para. 7, the Security Council, without voting on the matter, should request an Advisory Opinion of the International Court of Justice. See Liang in *American Journal of International Law*, 42 (1948), p. 890.

[26] It is probable that the inadvertence, if any, was due to the inescapable realities of the subject matter rather than to any oversight of the draftsmen of the Charter. For this, it appears, was also the experience of the corresponding clauses of the Covenant. Thus Dr. Kopelmanas says, rightly, with regard to Art. 15 (8) of that instrument: 'Conçue en vue de renforcer l'autonomie de l'ordre interne, l'exception de l'article 15 alinéa 8 aboutit en fait, en raison des difficultés procédurales de son application et de la fluidité de son contenu, à élargir le domaine dans lequel l'ordre international peut imposer sa supériorité aux ordres internes': *op. cit.*, vol. I. p. 214.

of tautology in this point of view. For it may be argued that all these provisions are qualified by the overriding exception of Article 2, paragraph 7.[27] However, it has been shown here that the terms of that Article, interpreted in accordance with the accepted terminology of international law, the history of its drafting, and the practice of the United Nations, do not imply a decisive—or even substantial—restriction of the competence of the United Nations in the matter of human rights and fundamental freedoms.

[27] This is the view ably propounded by Fincham, *op. cit.,* p. 176, who, however, in substance arrives at conclusions identical with those propounded in the text above. See also the able study of the subject by Berthoud in *Annuaire Suisse de droit international,* 4 (1947), pp. 17-104.

CHAPTER 11

THE COMMISSION ON HUMAN RIGHTS AND THE EFFECTIVE RIGHT OF PETITION

1. HUMAN RIGHTS AND THE ORGANS OF THE UNITED NATIONS

THE question, discussed in the preceding Section of this book, whether the provisions of the Charter in the matter of human rights and fundamental freedoms constitute legal rights and obligations is not one of mere legal theory. For decisive practical consequences follow from the answer to that question. If, as there submitted,[1] these provisions involve legal rights and obligations, then they imply a legal duty not only of the Members of the United Nations but also of the United Nations as a whole to implement the purpose of the Charter. It is with that latter question that we are concerned in this Chapter. By virtue of the Charter the organs of the United Nations are not only empowered, within the limits of the Charter, to adopt measures and create machinery for realising its objects in the matter of human rights and fundamental freedoms. The Charter imposes upon them a legal duty to act in that way.

The principal organs of the United Nations competent to implement the provisions of the Charter in the matter of human rights are the General Assembly and the Economic and Social Council acting either by itself or through the Commission on Human Rights. The functions of the General Assembly on the subject, while of great importance, are of a residuary character. Article 10 gives the General Assembly the widest powers of discussion. According to Article 13 of the Charter the General Assembly

---

[1] See above, pp. 145-154.

is competent to initiate studies and make recommendations concerning the promotion and observance of human rights. This clearly includes the power of discussion of any complaint concerning human rights brought before it by a Member State. That power of discussion and recommendation has been exercised on a number of occasions, as with regard to the treatment of Indians in South Africa,[2] the question of Russian-born wives married to foreign nationals,[3] and even the conduct of non-member States as in the case of alleged breaches of the clauses of the Peace Treaties by Hungary, Roumania and Bulgaria.[4] Article 13 provides that the ' further responsibilities, functions, and powers ' of the General Assembly with respect to these and cognate matters shall be exercised in conformity with the provisions of Chapter IX relating to International Economic and Social Co-operation and Chapter X which defines the functions of the Economic and Social Council.

The Economic and Social Council and, in particular, the Commission on Human Rights, which is its organ, are the main instruments of the Charter for giving effect to its principles and obligations in the matter of human rights. The responsibility of the Economic and Social Council is of a general character. It co-ordinates, it supervises, it provides the requisite authority. But the promotion of human rights and fundamental freedoms does not constitute the exclusive domain of its jurisdiction.[5] The Council has established a number of commissions covering a wide range of matters of economic and social interest. These include commissions on employment and economic questions generally, transport and communications, statistics, social questions, status of women,[6] narcotic drugs, fiscal matters, and population. There are also regional economic commissions for Europe and for Asia and the Far East. The object of these Commissions has so far been almost exclusively advisory and deliberative. Thus, for instance, the Economic and Employment Commission advises the Council on economic questions in order to promote higher

[2] See above, pp. 192-198.
[3] See above, pp. 203, 204.
[4] See above, pp. 205-212.
[5] A survey of its activities, as set forth in its annual reports to the General Assembly, illustrates the variety and multiplicity of its functions. See below, p. 250.
[6] See below, p. 262.

standards of living and on the prevention of wide fluctuations in economic activity and the promotion of full employment by co-ordination of national employment policies and by international action.

However, there is nothing in the terms of the Charter or in the constitution of the Economic and Social Council which confines its part—or that of its commissions—to the purely deliberative function of advice, study, and initiation of policy through drafting conventions and otherwise. Thus, for example, in the field of international control of drugs the Council and the Commission on Narcotic Drugs have assumed supervisory and, in part, executive functions previously exercised, under the ægis of the League of Nations, by the Permanent Central Opium Board and the Supervisory Body. Similarly, it will be shown that the legitimate function, properly conceived, of the United Nations and its principal organ in the sphere of human rights is one of active assistance in the fulfilment of the purposes of the Charter. With regard to the Commission on Human Rights, ample authority for such assistance is to be found, in the first instance, in its original terms of reference as laid down by the Economic and Social Council.[7]

2. THE COMMISSION ON HUMAN RIGHTS AND THE IMPLEMENTATION OF THE CHARTER

The significance of the Commission on Human Rights is to some extent indicated by the fact that it is the only Commission specifically referred to in the Charter. Article 68 of the Charter provides that the Economic and Social Council ' shall set up commissions in economic and social fields and for the promotion of human rights, and such other commissions as may be required for the performance of its functions '. The early establishment of the Commission on Human Rights was expressly recommended by the Committee charged with the preparation of the First General Assembly.[8] These proposals were approved by the General Assembly. In February, 1946, the Economic and Social Council decided to establish a Commission on Human Rights

[7] *Journal of the Economic and Social Council*, First Year, No. 29 (13 July, 1946), p. 520. And see below, p. 229.
[8] It figured as the first on the list of the six Commissions recommended.

charged with submitting proposals, recommendations and reports to the Council concerning: (a) an international bill of rights; (b) international declarations or conventions on civil liberties, the status of women, freedom of information, and similar matters; (c) the protection of minorities; (d) the prevention of discrimination on grounds of race, sex, language or religion.[9] By the terms of the same Resolution the Commission—the ' nuclear ' Commission —was to consist of nine members appointed in their individual capacity. On 21 June, 1946, the Council decided to set up a full Commission on Human Rights composed of one representative from each of eighteen Members of the United Nations selected by the Council.[10] The terms of reference of the Commission as outlined above were confirmed subject to the addition of an important new sub-paragraph as follows: ' (e) any other matter concerning human rights not covered by items (a), (b), (c) and (d) '.[11]

The conclusions, as outlined above,[11a] which follow from the letter and the spirit of the Charter with regard to the functions of the United Nations in the matter of human rights were accepted by the Commission on Human Rights at an early stage of its activity. In May, 1946, the Commission adopted a Report to the Economic and Social Council in which it put on record its views on the vital question of the implementation of the Charter. It stressed ' the need for an international agency of implementation entrusted with the task of watching over the general observance of human rights '.[12] It recommended that ' it shall be considered that the purpose of the United Nations with regard to the promotion and observance of human rights, as defined in the Charter of the United Nations, could only be fulfilled if provisions were made for the implementation of the observance of human rights and of an international bill of rights '.[13] Finally, it proposed that ' pending the eventual establishment of an agency of implementation the Commission on Human Rights might be recognised as qualified to aid the appropriate organs of the United Nations in

[9] Resolution of 16 February, 1946 (Doc. E/20).
[10] See below, p. 256.
[11] *Journal of the Economic and Social Council,* First Year, No. 29 (13 July, 1946), p. 520.
[11a] See above, p. 220.
[12] *Journal of the Economic and Social Council,* First Year, No. 14 (24 May, 1946), p. 164.
[13] *Ibid.*

the task defined for the General Assembly and the Economic and Social Council in Articles 13, 15 and 62 of the Charter concerning the promotion and observance of human rights and fundamental freedoms for all, and to aid the Security Council in the task entrusted to it by Article 39 of the Charter, by pointing to cases where violation of human rights committed in one country may, by its gravity, its frequency, or its systematic nature, constitute a threat to peace'.[14] The Economic and Social Council, without going to the length of identifying itself with all the recommendations of the Commission, adopted the substance of its proposals. In a Resolution adopted on 21 June, 1946, it laid down as follows: —

> 'Considering that the purpose of the United Nations with regard to the promotion and observance of human rights, as defined in the Charter of the United Nations, can only be fulfilled if provisions are made for the implementation of human rights and an international bill of rights, the Council requests the Commission on Human Rights to submit at an early date suggestions regarding the ways and means for the effective implementation of human rights and freedoms, with a view to assisting the Economic and Social Council in working out arrangements for such implementation with other appropriate organs of the United Nations.'[15]

Subsequently these two bodies did not find it possible to adhere to the view, as formulated above, as to the nature of their functions. In February, 1947, the Commission on Human Rights adopted a Report on the subject of implementation which, in essence, amounted to a reversal of its previous attitude. It laid down a general rule to the effect that 'the Commission recognises that it has no power to take any action in regard to any complaints concerning human rights'. It also recommended regulations governing the procedure concerning petitions brought before it in the matter of violation of human rights.[16] It will be submitted[17] that the procedure thus adopted amounts to a denial of the effective

[14] *Ibid.*

[15] *Journal of the Economic and Social Council*, First Year, No. 29 (13 July, 1946), p. 522.

[16] Economic and Social Council, Doc. E/259.

[17] See below, p. 241.

right of petition and to an abdication of the crucial function of the United Nations in this respect. In the same year, the Economic and Social Council approved both the general principle adopted by the Commission in the matter of its right to take action upon the petitions brought before it and the procedure recommended by it for dealing with petitions. It is convenient to set forth the relevant portion of the Resolution adopted by the Council :

' The Economic and Social Council . . .

' Approves the statement that " the Commission recognises that it has no power to take any action in regard to any complaints concerning human rights."

' Requests the Secretary-General :

(a) to compile a confidential list of communications received concerning human rights before each session of the Commission, with a brief indication of the substance of each;

(b) to furnish this confidential list to the Commission, in private meeting, without divulging the identity of the authors of the communications;

(c) to enable the members of the Commission, upon request, to consult the originals of communications dealing with the principles involved in the promotion of universal respect for and observance of human rights;

(d) to inform the writers of all communications concerning human rights, however addressed, that their communications have been received and duly noted for consideration in accordance with the procedure laid down by the United Nations. Where necessary, the Secretary-General should indicate that the Commission has no power to take any action in regard to any complaint concerning human rights;

(e) to furnish each member State not represented on the Commission with a brief indication of the substance of any communication concerning human rights which refers explicitly to that State or to territories under its jurisdiction without divulging the identity of the author;

' Suggests to the Commission on Human Rights that it should at each session appoint an *ad hoc* committee to meet shortly before the next session of the Commission for the purpose of reviewing the confidential list of communications prepared by the Secretary-General under paragraph (a) above and of recommending which of these communications, in original, should, in accordance with paragraph (c) above, be made available to members of the Commission on request.'[18]

That Resolution was subsequently amended by the addition, at the end of paragraph (b), of the words ' except in those cases where the authors state that they have already divulged or intend to divulge their names or that they have no objection to their names being divulged '. Paragraph (e) was correspondingly altered by the addition of the words ' except as provided in paragraph (b) above '.[19]

3. THE DELIBERATIVE AND IMPLEMENTING FUNCTIONS OF THE ORGANS OF THE UNITED NATIONS

In the Resolution cited above, the Economic and Social Council answered what would appear to be the fundamental problem of the main organ of the United Nations for the protection of human rights under the Charter, namely, the Commission on Human Rights. That problem can be put in simple words: Is the Com-

[18] Resolution No. 75 (V), Doc. E/505.
With regard to petitions relating to human rights and fundamental freedoms in trust territories, a joint committee of the Economic and Social Council and Trusteeship Council made a recommendation, subsequently approved, to the effect that such petitions should be examined, primarily, by the Trusteeship Council without prejudice to the competence of the Human Rights Commission and the Commission on the Status of Women to evidence an active interest in the subject-matter of the petitions. The terms of the recommendation were as follows:
' It is recommended, as a matter of principle, that all petitions to Organs of the United Nations (such as petitions on Human Rights or on the Status of Women) which emanate from, or relate to conditions in, any Trust Territory should be dealt with by the Trusteeship Council in accordance with paragraph (b) of Article 87 of the Charter.
' In order that such petitions may be proceeded with with the minimum delay, they should be communicated immediately to that part of the Secretariat of the United Nations assigned to the Trusteeship Council.
' It is recommended that the Trusteeship Council should then communicate to the appropriate Commissions, for such assistance as the Council may desire under Article 91 of the Charter, those parts of such petitions as relate to matters which are the Commissions' special concern. It is recommended also that the Trusteeship Council should communicate to the appropriate Commissions those petitions which it may receive direct and which may contain matters of concern to them.
' It is further recommended that, when the Trusteeship Council comes to consider petitions concerning Human Rights or the Status of Women which may be referred to it in accordance with the procedure recommended above, the Trusteeship Council should give consideration to the extent to which the procedure for dealing with such petitions prescribed by the Economic and Social Council in its resolution of 5 August, 1947, can be followed.
' The right of the Commissions concerned to take cognisance of petitions in accordance with the above-mentioned resolutions is recognised, and their comments thereon should be welcomed ': E. & T/C.1/2, Rev. 1. See also E/CN.4/27; E/PV.119.
[19] Resolution 116 A (VI).

mission on Human Rights—according to the Charter, the powers
of the Economic and Social Council of which it is the organ, and
its own terms of reference—a deliberative body for study,
initiative, and recommendation, or is it an instrument for ensuring
the protection, within the limits of the Charter, of human rights
and fundamental freedoms? In particular, to what extent, if any,
is the Commission on Human Rights the proper instrument for
redressing violations of human rights and freedoms? The
question bears directly upon the effectiveness of the Charter in
relation to a fundamental purpose of the United Nations.

It may be assumed[20] that the Charter rejected the idea of
intervention, conceived in its accepted legal usage, for the purpose
of effectively guaranteeing human rights through compulsory legal
acts—except, probably, in cases in which such violation, because
of its international repercussions, constitutes a danger to peace.
But did the United Nations deprive itself of all faculty to influence, by means short of intervention, the situation brought about
by a violation of human rights? There is no warrant for answering this question with a clear affirmative. In the words, already
quoted, of Article 62,[21] the Economic and Social Council ' may
make recommendations for the purpose of promoting respect for,
and observance of, human rights and freedoms '. This function
of the Council is referred to specifically in addition to the wide
terms of the first paragraph of Article 62 which lays down that
' the Economic and Social Council may make or initiate studies
and reports with respect to international economic, social,
cultural, educational, health, and related matters, and may make
recommendations with respect to any such matters to the General
Assembly, to the Members of the United Nations, and to the
specialised agencies concerned '.[22] It will be noted that while with
regard to the economic and other matters enumerated in paragraph 1 it is stated that these questions must be ' international ',
no such qualification appears in paragraph 2. All these methods

---

[20] As to the controversial nature of this assumption see above, pp. 173-180.

[21] See above, p. 147.

[22] These terms of reference are as wide as those relating to the functions of the
General Assembly under Article 13. In a limited sense they are wider inasmuch
as, in paragraph 3, the Council is authorised to draft conventions for submission to the General Assembly. No such express power was granted to
the General Assembly—though that power is clearly implied and has in fact
been exercised. It is clear that the authority, under paragraph 1 of Article 62,
to prepare studies and reports extends also to recommendations under
paragraph 2.

are also within the sphere of the organ of the Council specially delegated for that purpose, namely, the Commission on Human Rights. The function of the Commission is to submit proposals, recommendations, and reports to the Economic and Social Council on specific matters and, generally, on any matter relating to human rights. There is nothing in the terms of its reference or in the Charter to prevent the Commission, when confronted with a complaint, from discussing it, investigating it, and making a recommendation or report on the subject—either in general terms or with specific reference to the State concerned—to the Economic and Social Council.[23] In the Resolution, referred to above, of June, 1946, the Council instructed the Commission 'to make studies and recommendations and provide information and other services at the request of the Economic and Social Council '.[24] There is nothing to prevent the Commission from setting up effective machinery for that purpose. A Commission on Human Rights which by a self-denying ordinance is precluded from taking other than purely nominal action with regard to complaints of violations of human rights would not be fulfilling the object which according to the letter and the spirit of the Charter it is in a position to fulfil. The implementation, with the active participation of the organs of the United Nations, of the legal obligations in the matter of human rights is one of the major purposes of the Charter. For these are legal obligations. They are no longer a mere postulate of the law of nature and of the inalienable rights of man. The Charter does not provide for implementation in the full sense of the term. It does not authorise enforcement through intervention conceived as dictatorial and direct interference. This fact does not deprive the organs of the United Nations of the right—nor release them from the duty—to make their contribution towards the implementation of its provisions by other means of considerable potency.

4. VIOLATIONS OF HUMAN RIGHTS AND ACTION OF THE ORGANS OF THE UNITED NATIONS

The crucial aspect of the Report, referred to above, of the Commission—a Report confirmed by the Economic and Social Council —was the statement that it has no power to take any action in

[23] See below, p. 230.
[24] See above, p. 224.

the matter of violations of human rights brought before it. There is no legal justification for that statement. These bodies, and, in particular, the Commission on Human Rights, are not only entitled to take such action. By the terms of the Charter they are bound to do so. While the purely deliberative and advisory character of the various Commissions of the Economic and Social Council may be in accordance with the character of the task which they have been called upon to perform, this is not the case in relation to the Commission on Human Rights. The purpose of the United Nations demands that full effect be given, within the limits of the Charter, to its provisions requiring the United Nations to ' promote human rights ' and to make recommendations for that purpose. The organs of the United Nations are entitled and bound by the Charter to take cognizance of violations of human rights and to initiate such action upon them as is not expressly excluded by the Charter. They are under a duty to receive petitions alleging violations of human rights, to examine them, and, on the basis of such examination, to take all requisite action short of intervention. The United Nations will fail in a crucial—perhaps *the* crucial—aspect of its purpose unless it becomes axiomatic that it must take an active interest in any violation of human rights with a view to remedying situations the continuation of which is contrary to the Charter. Admittedly, neither the Commission on Human Rights nor the Economic and Social Council, nor any other organ of the United Nations (subject to the express exceptions laid down in Article 2, paragraph 7), have the right of intervention in its legal technical sense. But the Commission is entitled—and bound—to take any other action short of intervention in its accepted sense, such action including, in successive stages, examination, enquiry, investigation, report (including publication thereof), and recommendation.[25] In the

---

[25] It was assumed by the Chairman of the Commission, in January, 1947, that it had no power to conduct an enquiry but that it had the right to submit recommendations to the Economic and Social Council and to forward to the latter any complaint which it considered justified (*Minutes of the Commission*, E/CN.4/SR.4). There seems to be no legal authority for the suggestion that the Commission has no power to conduct enquiries. Moreover, it is difficult to see how the Commission can consider a complaint to be justified if it has no possibility of enquiring into it. The Australian representative went to the length of denying that the Commission was entitled to study communications received by it (*ibid.,* p. 7). The public, he added, must not be allowed to assume that the Commission is a tribunal. There is clearly no warrant for the view that the Commission is not entitled to study the communications received. Such study is essential to the proper fulfilment by the Commission of its terms of reference.

same way that the promotion of respect for human rights constitutes a fundamental purpose of the Charter, so action, thus conceived, in the matter of violations of human rights represents a fundamental aspect of that function of the United Nations. This is believed to be the accurate legal position with regard to this crucial aspect of the Charter. Yet the Working Group on Implementation, which was composed of some members of the Commission on Human Rights deliberating in the course of its session at the end of 1947 and which adopted an able and comprehensive report, considered that the purported absence of a right on the part of the Commission to take action in the matter of petitions followed from an ' elementary yet imperative judicial concept '.[26] The States assembled at the Peace Conference in Paris in 1946 did not take that negative view of the powers of these organs of the United Nations. The Legal and Drafting Commission of the Conference, in rejecting the proposal put forward by Australia for the establishment of a special European Court for Human Rights, expressed the view that ' the implementation of human rights is a task of universal import which under the Charter of the United Nations is entrusted to the Economic and Social Council which has set up a Commission of Human Rights ' and that ' these two bodies have power both to formulate the principles and to decide on the steps to be taken to ensure that they are respected '.[27]

The issue raised by the above-mentioned Report of the Commission and the Resolution of the Economic and Social Council is of decisive importance for the cause of human rights and for the United Nations. The effective right of petition must be deemed to be an irreducible right of the individual not only in relation to his own nation but also in relation to the United Nations. There is no effective right of petition if the petitioned authority has ' no power to take any action ' on the subject-matter of the complaint.

In the matter of communications relating to violations of human rights the problem before the Commission is similar to that which confronted the organs of the League of Nations in the

---

[26] Economic and Social Council, Doc. E/600 (17 December, 1947), p. 52. And see below, pp. 308, 386.

[27] *Minutes of the Drafting and Legal Commission* (as cited in Dr. Martin's Report, ' Human Rights in the Paris Peace Treaties,' submitted to the International Law Association at Brussels in 1948), p. 10.

matter of protection of minorities. The substantial difference is that, with regard to the protection of human rights and the United Nations, the scope of the problem is very considerably wider. It comprises all Members of the United Nations and not only a limited number of States bound by Minorities Treaties; it embraces, potentially, all human beings. Yet the difficulties are in many respects similar: the apprehension of an unwieldy mass of petitions; the possibility of their being abused for the purpose of malevolent propaganda or self-seeking advertisement; and the fact that a considerable number of petitions may, on their own showing, be without foundation. However, while bearing in mind all these difficulties, we may not find it easy to appreciate the reasons which could, in law, justify the ruling that ' the Commission recognises that it has no power to take any action in regard to the complaints concerning human rights '. If ' action ' refers to ' intervention ' in its legal sense, then the ruling is not open to objection—except in contingencies amounting to a threat to international peace—other than the charge of laxity of language. But if by ' action ' we mean measures other than intervention in its technical sense, then the Resolution of the Commission gives rise to legitimate criticism. Like the Economic and Social Council in general, so also the Commission on Human Rights ' may make recommendations for the purpose of promoting respect for, and observance of, human rights and fundamental freedoms for all '.[28] The language is explicit. So are the terms of reference of the Commission.[29] Nothing in the Charter excludes either a general recommendation arising out of an individual complaint or a series of analogous complaints; or a specific recommendation addressed to a named State; or a request for information or comments on the subject of petitions received; or, with the consent of the State concerned, an investigation undertaken in its territory and with its co-operation; or, without the consent of the State in question, an investigation conducted outside its territory and not requiring its co-operation; or the initiation of a study, in fact indistinguishable from investigation, of the conditions underlying the complaint either in relation to the State concerned or to the general problem involved in the

[28] Article 62 (2).
[29] See above, p. 224.

complaint; or the publication of the results of the investigation; or discussion of the specific and general aspects of the complaint.

These and similar measures constitute action, short of intervention, on the communications received by the Commission. The effectiveness of such action falls short of a judicial or semi-judicial pronouncement accompanied, if need be, by executive enforcement, but it seems pessimistic and unwarranted to consider it as totally ineffectual. There is nothing in the Charter which calls for—or, indeed, permits—the exclusion of such measures. To rule them out in advance is fully out of keeping with the purpose of the Commission on Human Rights. Admittedly the difficulties involved in the method of treatment of a multifarious mass of petitions and communications are such as to tax heavily the resources and resourcefulness of the organ concerned.[30] But it is doubtful whether the issue can properly be avoided by a clear *non possumus*. Instead, safeguards and remedies must be sought and applied which would make it practicable for the Commission to fulfil what is an imperative task. The methods of the Minorities Section of the League of Nations, of the Mandates Commission, and of the Trusteeship Council afford much guidance in this respect.[31] Additional methods must be devised for coping with the danger of the task of the Commission being hampered by frivolous and unfounded communications— although experience (including the experience of the Trusteeship Council[32]) has shown that the dangers of abuse of the right of petition may be exaggerated and that ignorant, frivolous or malicious complaints can be disposed of without difficulty and without doing violence to the requirement of a fair hearing. The necessary safeguards may have to include the rule that a communication from the Government of a State should be regarded as meriting *prima facie* both consideration and a requisite measure of publicity. A similar principle may be made to apply to communications emanating from or supported by public—though not necessarily official—bodies, institutions or societies of recognised standing and devoted to the protection of human rights in general or to the interests of particular groups and minorities in so far as they come within the scope of human rights and freedoms as

[30] See below, p. 240.
[31] See below, pp. 244, 245.
[32] See below, p. 242.

envisaged by the Charter.   Above all, as suggested below, the
Commission on Human Rights must be provided with a
machinery—fully adequate in numbers, ability, and impartiality
—to examine, in the first instance, the petitions received.   That
task cannot satisfactorily or consistently with the general
efficiency of the Commission be performed by its members.

5.   THE PROCEDURE OF PETITIONS AND THE COMMISSION ON HUMAN RIGHTS

The procedure adopted by the Commission on Human Rights in
the matter of the treatment of complaints concerning human
rights must be considered in the light of the legal position as outlined above.   That procedure, as we have seen, is characterised
by a refusal to admit that there is vested in the Commission the
power to take any action in the matter of complaints concerning
human rights.   Apparently the expression ' any action ' inaccur-
ately expresses the intention of the Commission and of the
Council, for the procedure adopted contemplates *some* action.
That action consists in the first instance in the compilation by
the Secretariat, *i.e.,* by the Division of Human Rights, of a confidential list of communications received and in furnishing that
list, at a private meeting, to the members of the Commission.
There is, further, a provision enabling members of the
Commission, if they so desire, to consult the originals of the
communications.   However, that provision refers, apparently,
only to ' communications dealing with the principles involved in
the promotion of universal respect for and observance of human
rights '.   The authors of the communications are to be informed
that the latter will be dealt with in accordance with the normal
procedure outlined above and that in any case the Commission
has no power to take any action in regard to any complaint concerning human rights.   In view of this it is difficult to see what
is the purpose of the decision that an *ad hoc* committee of the
Commission should meet *shortly* before each session to review the
confidential list of communications prepared by the Secretariat and to recommend which should be made available.
That suggestion, it has been noted, is qualified by the clause
which limits these communications to those ' dealing with the

principles involved in the promotion ' of human rights and which makes such availability dependent upon the request of the members of the Commission.

The procedure adopted by the States represented on the Economic and Social Council and by the Commission on Human Rights for dealing with communications alleging or concerning violations of human rights and fundamental freedoms amounts to a renunciation by these bodies of a power and an obligation grounded in the Charter. It constitutes a denial of the effective right of petition inherent in the Charter. In view of this it is not necessary to indicate here in detail the drawbacks of such rudimentary procedure as has been adopted. These defects include not only the stringent prescriptions of secrecy. The objections to the principle of secrecy are obvious, unless it is imperatively required for the protection of the authors of petitions—though even in this respect the efforts of the United Nations must be directed towards devising means of protection other than secrecy.[33]

[33] At its meeting in December, 1947, the Commission envisaged a slight modification of the principle of secrecy by suggesting to the Economic and Social Council that the list of communications which the Secretary-General (*i.e.,* the Division of Human Rights) is to be instructed to prepare for the members of the Commission shall be divided into two parts: (a) a non-confidential list of communications the authors of which have divulged their names or state that they have no objection to their names being divulged; and (b) a confidential list of other communications (Doc. E/600, p. 8). No action was taken upon these suggestions. In 1949, in a Memorandum submitted to the Commission (E/CN.4/165), the Secretary-General proposed a different classification of communications. He suggested that there should be two lists of communications: (a) a confidential list containing complaints of violations of human rights and requests for action on the part of the Commission; and (b) a non-confidential list containing communications dealing with principles involved in the promotion of respect for and observance of human rights. No radical change was implied in these suggestions. For according to the principal Resolution—75 (V)—members of the Commission can consult, at their request, the originals of the latter group. The suggested change meant merely that the list of such communications bearing on questions of principle —but not the communications themselves—should no longer be confidential. Possibly the suggestion meant also that the names of the authors of the communications should no longer be confidential. The resulting difference is a trifling one—although it was urged by the Secretary-General that the standing of the organisation from which the communication originates or the authority wielded by the individual author of the communication might give particular weight to it. In fact the nature of the proposed changes illustrates vividly the lack of reality of that aspect of the work of the Commission. The same applies to the suggestion made by the Secretary-General in the same Memorandum that. while the list of communications relating to complaints should continue to be confidential, it was not necessary that, subject to certain safeguards, the identity of their authors should not be divulged. Commenting on the practice of publicity followed by the Mandates Commission and the Council of the League of Nations in the matter of examination of petitions, Lord Hailey, a distinguished authority on the subject, said: 'Only those who have had experience in the internal working of an official administration, in

Experience has shown that, apart from isolated exceptions, complaints come from persons resident outside the territory of the State against whom a charge of violation of human rights has been brought. As stated in a Memorandum of the Secretary-General,[34] ' the negligible number of possible cases where secrecy may be required does not justify the maintenance of rules under which the whole procedure is veiled by anonymity and the members of the Commission on Human Rights are prevented from arriving at an opinion on the seriousness or otherwise of a certain allegation '.[35]

The involved language of the Resolution of the Economic and Social Council of 5 August, 1947, which confirmed the recommendations made by the Commission on Human Rights, fails to convey the extraordinary degree of the abdication, on the part of the United Nations, of its function in the sphere of encouragement and promotion of fundamental human rights and freedoms. As a result of that Resolution members of the Human Rights Commission are not entitled to consult the originals of communications received by the Secretariat in the matter of violations of human rights except, upon their request, those ' dealing with the principles involved in the promotion of universal respect for and observance of human rights '. They are not entitled to read the actual complaints of violations of human rights. What they are entitled to is to receive a list of these complaints compiled by the Secretariat. Thus the basic source of information, with regard to what, on any reasonable interpretation of the Charter, would appear to be the principal function of the Commission,

circumstances where there is no organisation of public opinion, can appreciate the strength of the influence which can be exerted by publicity of the nature of that involved in the proceedings of the Commission and Council ' (as quoted by Duncan Hall, *op. cit.,* p. 212). In March, 1948, the Economic and Social Council, following upon a recommendation of the Commission, relaxed the injunction of secrecy by prescribing that the confidential list of communications submitted to the Commission before each session may divulge the identity of the authors of communications in cases where the latter state that they have already divulged or intend to divulge their names or that they have no objection to their names being divulged (Resolution 116 A of 1 March, 1948). On one occasion the Russian representative objected to the consideration of anonymous communications for the reason that the United Nations ' should not deal with unsubstantiated or unreliable communications, presented without due consideration by irresponsible people to spread hatred among the nations for political or other purposes ' (Meeting of the Commission of 20 February, 1948: E/AC.7/SR.32, p. 4).
[34] See above, p. 235, n. 35.
[35] E/CN.4/165, p. 11.

is consigned to the files of an official in the Division of Human Rights whose business it is ' to inform the writers of all communications concerning human rights . . . that their communications have been received and duly noted for consideration in accordance with the procedure laid down by the United Nations '. It would appear that in respect of petitions the Commission on Human Rights has placed itself in a position inferior to that of the members of the Security Council, who are entitled to receive, on request, copies of all communications from private individuals and non-governmental bodies relating to matters of which the Security Council is seised.[36] In view of this there is a distinct—and disturbing—element of artificiality in the resolution, specially passed by the Economic and Social Council,[37] giving the members of the Sub-Commission on the Prevention of Discrimination and the Protection of Minorities, with respect to communications bearing on discrimination and minorities, the same facilities as are enjoyed by members of the Commission on Human Rights. For these facilities are rudimentary to the point of being nominal.

The undoubted difficulties inherent in the operation of the system of protection of human rights cannot be solved by verbal devices which create an impression of evasiveness that is out of keeping with the character of the task entrusted to the Commission. After having adopted a system under which it is left to the initiative of its members to make themselves acquainted with the details of the communications, otherwise shrouded in secrecy, the principal Resolution referred to above[38] requests the

---

[36] Annex to the Provisional Rules of Procedure of the Security Council (Doc. S/96/Rev. 3).

[37] Resolution 116 A (VI). A report, of 24 May, 1948, of the *ad hoc* Committee instructed to consider communications received states that after taking note, in the course of two meetings, of the confidential list prepared by the Secretary-General, the Committee decided that there was no occasion for bringing any of the communications on the list to the special notice of the Commission with a view to consulting the originals (E/CN. 4/96). The passage apparently refers to communications dealing with ' principles,' for with regard to communications alleging actual violations of human rights the Commission seems to have effectually precluded itself from examining the originals of petitions received. With regard to communications relating to ' principles ' it is not easy to see how, from a summary list prepared by an official of the Secretariat, the Committee can form an adequate opinion as to the nature of the communication. In general, the number of complaints and communications received has been small—a circumstance which may be the result of the view adopted by the Commission as to the nature of its functions.

[38] See p. 226.

Secretary-General to inform the writers of all communications concerning human rights that their communications would be brought to the attention of the Commission on Human Rights. Yet, under the system adopted, there is no guarantee that they will be brought to the attention of the Commission as a whole.[39] By December, 1947, the Sub-Commission on Non-Discrimination came to the conclusion that the system, which was of the Commission's own making, of dealing with complaints and petitions was out of keeping with its function as envisaged by the Charter and by public opinion. In a recommendation adopted in December, 1947, the Sub-Commission found that ' the present system of transmitting communications and petitions was by no means satisfactory for the members of the Commission themselves ' for the reason—which seems to be in the nature of a *non sequitur*—that ' the Commission *in corpore* has no powers to take any action in regard to complaints relating to human rights '. It is not clear to what extent the expression ' *in corpore* ' was intended to convey the suggestion that some action might be possible at the instance of the individual Governments represented on the Commission. The Committee then proceeded to express the hope that the Economic and Social Council might soon find means for reversing the trend initiated by the Commission. It said :

> ' The Committee assumes that as the Commission's work will soon have reached a more advanced stage, the Economic and Social Council will take a decision on the recommendations which it asked the Commission to make to it, regarding " the ways and means for the effective implementation of human rights and fundamental freedoms ". When that has been done, a basis will have been provided for settling the method of communicating and examining petitions, without there being too great an inequality between those concerning trust territories and all the others.' [40]

No action was taken by the Commission on this general expression of hope. But the Commission accepted, and the Economic and Social Council subsequently approved, the recommendation that the principle of secrecy in the list of communications prepared by the Secretariat need not apply to cases where the

---

[39] See above, pp. 234, 236.
[40] E/CN.4/64, p. 2. And see above, p. 225.

authors of the communications do not attach importance to secrecy being preserved.[41]

[41] See above, p. 236, and below, p. 286. The confused and inconclusive discussion of the Commission at the beginning of 1947 of the question of petitions is of interest. At one stage the representative of the Philippine Republic proposed the setting up of a sub-committee of the members charged with the duty to study communications addressed to the Secretary-General, the Economic and Social Council, or the Commission, and to make recommendations. He pointed out that although the proposal did not imply that the Commission was to be a court of appeal, public opinion would regard it as such; it represented the conscience of the world (E/CN.4/SR.4, p. 5). The proposal was adopted by the votes of India, Lebanon, the Philippine Republic, the United States and Uruguay. Australia, Soviet Russia and the United Kingdom voted against. China, Egypt and Iran abstained. As was rightly pointed out by the Australian representative, the Philippine proposal was obscure inasmuch as, on the face of it, the purpose of the sub-committee which was to be set up was merely to study the use to be made of communications. In that case it would be deceiving the authors of communications, who expected effective action (*ibid.,* p. 7). On the other hand, he said, if as the result of a misunderstanding the idea were to spread that the sub-committee was entitled to study the actual communications, the Commission would be flooded with them. ‘The public must not be allowed to think that the Commission was a tribunal.’

While some members of the Commission stressed the importance of public opinion, the Belgian representative expressed the view that the Commission should not be subjected to the pressure of public opinion as reflected in communications received from organisations not possessing consultative status. He was therefore opposed to the setting up of a sub-committee to study them (E/CN.4/SR.3, p. 6). The Chairman suggested that the Commission had no power to conduct an enquiry, or to put its decisions into force, but that it had the right to submit recommendations to the Economic and Social Council and ‘to forward to it any complaint which it considered justified’ (E/CN.4/SR.4, p. 3). It was not explained how, in the absence of the right to make investigations, the right to make recommendations could be effectively exercised. The Chinese representative insisted that the chief function of the Commission was to draft the International Bill of Rights and that therefore all communications on that subject should be brought to the Commission’s notice immediately. ‘As regards all other communications the Commission should therefore refrain from raising false hopes’ (*Discussion of the Report of the Sub-Committee on Handling of Communications*: E/CN.4/SR.16 (6 February, 1947). The question was discussed in some detail whether a sub-commission should be created for the purpose of receiving and examining petitions. The view prevailed that the creation of such a sub-commission would be dangerous inasmuch as it would tend to create the impression that the Commission ‘was seized of the communications and was prepared to take action upon them’ (Representative of Belgium, *ibid.,* p. 10). While thus the majority of the Commission deprecated the idea of an effective right of petition, the representative of Uruguay drew attention to the statement of M. Laugier, Assistant Secretary-General, to the effect that the task of the Economic and Social Council and of the Commission was to create machinery for the examination of all communications concerning the violation of human rights (E/CN.4/SR.4). The representative of India went far in the direction of urging adequate machinery for the examination of complaints—although the force of her proposals was somewhat weakened by the fact that they were intended, in the first instance, to provide a remedy for the situation confronting ‘four million Indians who had been transplanted to various parts of the world under the ægis of the colonial governments concerned’ (E/CN.4/SR.2, p. 3).

At the meeting of the Commission in July, 1948, the Soviet representative stated in clear terms the opposition of his country to measures of implementation. He urged that proposals to grant to a committee the right to make recommendations to member Governments constituted inadmissible interference in the domestic affairs of a State and an infringement of

Undoubtedly, under a system of effective petition the United Nations and its organs may be burdened and embarrassed by communications which are malevolent, clearly unfounded, uninformed, or, while well-founded in law, petty and insignificant. Many of the petitions may imply an unjust affront to the dignity and good name of States. Yet it must become axiomatic that the sanctity of human rights and an effective system of petitions on their behalf are entitled to no less consideration than the dignity of sovereign States. A reconciliation of these two opposing considerations—assuming that there exists an inherent opposition between them—cannot be effected by a renunciation of the function of the United Nations in relation to a vital aspect of its purpose. The difficulties cannot be met by a self-imposed limitation on the part of the Commission on Human Rights. They can be solved only by the adoption of the twin principle that: (a) all communications and petitions, with the exception of those of an obviously frivolous character, must automatically— either in full or in a summary—reach all members of the Commission, and (b) that a procedure, semi-judicial and semi-administrative in character, must be devised for selecting such communications and petitions as call for full discussion and, generally, for further action by the Commission. Such procedure, to be authoritative and effective, must be entrusted to a standing body of a mixed character composed of members of the Commission on Human Rights and, mainly, of a trained staff of experts of high quality and impartiality.

The deliberations of the Commission on Human Rights and of the Economic and Social Council have abounded in allusions to the necessity of not creating vain hopes among the authors of petitions. But these are not hopes of persons ignorant of their rights and placing their faith in a non-existent law. These hopes are grounded in the fundamental charter of the international

national sovereignty; the right to make such recommendations belonged to the General Assembly alone. He also suggested that as, according to the proposals for implementation, international investigations could be conducted only on the basis of individual cases, they were likely to increase the causes of friction among nations (E/CN.4/SR.81, p. 14). This was also the view of the Byelorussian representative (*ibid.*, p. 19). But the Soviet representative had no hesitation, at the meeting of the sub-commission on the prevention of discrimination and the protection of minorities in December, 1947, in urging immediate consideration by the sub-commission of the question of the Negro problem in the United States and of the question of discrimination against women (E/CN.4/Sub.2/SR.13, p. 2. For the formal proposal see E/CN.4/Sub.2/SR.24).

community and in the resulting changes in the status of the individual in the international sphere. The fact that the Charter of the United Nations has gone a long way towards recognising the status of the individual as a subject of international law cannot be altogether without influence upon his procedural capacity. Such hopes will not be in vain if the United Nations and its organs adhere to the spirit of the Charter with regard to the promotion of respect for and observance of human rights and fundamental freedoms. Five years after its establishment the United Nations not only had not achieved any approximation to providing itself with adequate instruments for fulfilling its purpose in that most significant sphere.[42] It was out of keeping with the paramount importance of the principle of effective petition in the scheme of the international protection of human rights that the task of examining petitions should be entrusted to a small body of men, an *ad hoc* committee of the Commission on Human Rights, meeting hurriedly ' shortly before the next session ' for the purpose of reviewing a confidential list of petitions—not the petitions themselves—with a view to recommending what petitions should, provided that they are concerned with principles involved in the promotion of human rights, be communicated to those members of the Commission who desire to receive them—such communication apparently bringing to an end the function of the Commission on the subject.[43]

---

[42] When, in December, 1947, the Australian representative proposed, in the sub-commission on the prevention of discrimination and the protection of minorities, that the Economic and Social Council be asked to extend its resolution of 5 August, 1947 (paragraph (e), see above, p. 226), concerning communications so as to include the words ' that the Secretary-General tactfully requests, by official letter, the Governments affected to give any comment or information they desire on the petitions ', the proposal secured only two votes. There were eight abstentions and one vote against the proposal (E/CN.4/Sub.2/SR.16, p. 9). Actually—and the fact is an indication of the true potentialities of the Commission as distinguished from its own estimate of them—a number of States have availed themselves of the possibility indirectly offered by the above-mentioned paragraph (e) of the Resolution and have sent to the Secretary-General comments on the facts alleged in the communications. Subsequently—in Resolution 192 (VIII)—the Economic and Social Council requested the Secretary-General to ask Governments sending their replies whether they wished them to be presented to the Commission in summary form or in full. The replies sent in are distributed among members of the Commission as confidential documents.

[43] The nature of the functions of the Commission as then interpreted may be gauged from the fact that, in the course of the meeting at Geneva in December, 1947, the *ad hoc* Committee held one meeting. The practical result of the work of the *ad hoc* Committee was the decision: (a) to transmit to the members of the Commission an analysis, prepared by the Secretariat, of communications received and bearing upon general principles,

The work of the Trusteeship Council is instructive as showing that the danger of an international agency of this character being swamped by petitions may to a large extent be imaginary. Strange and extraordinary petitions there may be which, however well-meaning, neither deserve nor require prolonged consideration even if treated with the respect and deliberation which are due, in the first instance, to every petition. Thus at its session in 1947 the Council, after some discussion, decided to treat as admissible, at least to the extent of informing the petitioner of the receipt thereof, a petition signed by a certain Raja Mahendra Pratap, containing a proposal for the establishment of a Jewish State in Tanganyika.[44] It considered in some detail a somewhat theoretical enquiry by a person from Tanganyika as to whether the Trusteeship Council could institute an enquiry into his complaints against the Government of Tanganyika.[45] It discussed the admissibility of a number of petitions requesting international control and administration of the polar regions by the Trusteeship Council,[46] and although it had no difficulty in finding that they were outside the proper competence of the Council it agreed that the reply should not be purely formal and negative but that it should be drafted in such a form as to draw the attention of the petitioners to the proper body within the United Nations which might be competent to consider the matter. Similarly, courteous consideration was given to the petition from the International Service Seminar, Indian Mountain School, Lakeville, Connecticut, asking that strategic areas, both on land and at sea, should be placed under international control and protected by the United Nations.[47] There were a number of petitions relating to alleged discrimination on account of sex in the matter of the application of International Labour Conventions to some trust territories [48]; a request for international control of production and distribution

and (b) to recommend that the communications referred to in that analytical statement be made available to the members of the Commission at their request (Doc. E/600, pp. 7-8). The members of the Commission also received a list, prepared by the Secretariat, of communications not involving, on the face of it, questions of principle. These are petitions proper. Each petition—their number has run into hundreds—is summarised in three or four lines in the list prepared by the Secretariat. The purely nominal character of the information thus received is apparent.

[44] T/PV.31, p. 15.
[45] *Ibid.*, pp. 42 *et seq.*
[46] *Ibid.*, pp. 62 *et seq.*
[47] *Ibid.*, pp. 71 *et seq.*
[48] *Ibid.*, pp. 58 *et seq.*

of strategic raw materials in non-self-governing territories or trust areas [49]; a petition asking for the placing of the former Italian colonies under an Italian trusteeship [50]; and, once more from the indefatigable International Service Seminar of the Indian Mountain School, Lakeville, a petition concerning modifications of Articles 73 and 87 of the Charter.[51]

The Council declined to act on the warnings of the Belgian representative pointing to the dangers of receiving petitions too easily. He said: 'We might be swamped by petitions. If you were to see the list which the Secretary-General publishes of communications received, you would see that this list is interminable. If each of these petitions has to be examined by an organ of the United Nations, then the agencies of the United Nations will never finish their work.'[52] He was answered by the Mexican representative—an answer which seems to have represented the sense of the Council and which merits quotation:

> 'I consider that the more active the United Nations is and the more interest it arouses among peoples, the more vital and the more important will it then become. We shall be very satisfied if, at each session, we are given the work of examining two or three hundred letters, because these two or three hundred letters will mean that people have faith in the Organisation and see in it a means of solving personal, national or international problems. I consider that it is the duty of the Council to examine all petitions even though some of them might seem to be or might prove to be futile.' [53]

[49] *Ibid.*, p. 72.
[50] *Ibid.*
[51] *Ibid.*, p. 76. Among the terms of reference, laid down in 1949 by the Trusteeship Council, for the United Nations Visiting Mission to Trust Territories in West Africa was the directive to the mission 'to accept or receive petitions and . . . to investigate on the spot, after consultation with the local representative of the Administering Authority concerned, such petitions dealing with the conditions of the indigenous inhabitants as are, in its opinion, sufficiently important to warrant special investigation': Doc. T/348.
[52] T/PV.31, p. 64. See also *ibid.*, pp. 104-106, for an elaboration of this view.
[53] *Ibid.*, p. 67. See also *ibid.*, pp. 115 *et seq.* And see pp. 126 and 131 for observations of the Chinese and French representatives in support of the Mexican view. The former said: 'It seems to me that at this stage of the development of the Trusteeship System it is more important to safeguard the integrity of the right of petition, the right of direct access for a petitioner, however humble, to the highest international organ which has the primary duty of supervising the functioning of the system. It seems to me that the contents of these petitions are of secondary importance.' In this connexion there may be noted the negative attitude of the Mexican representative before the Third Committee of the General Assembly in 1948 in connexion with the proposed incorporation of the right of petition as part of the Declaration of Human Rights.

At its Third Session in 1948 the Trusteeship Council, which considered in detail thirteen petitions, declined to commit itself to a ruling, urged by Great Britain and Belgium, that only a resident of a trust territory and a spokesman of its inhabitants should be entitled to appear in person before it. It decided that each case of this nature must be considered on its merits.[54]

6. THE NATURAL RIGHT OF PETITION

There is no prospect of the fulfilment of the purpose of the Charter in the matter of human rights and freedoms unless an effective right of petition is accepted as being of the essence of the system established by the Charter. The Charter does not refer to the right of petition as a safeguard of human rights and fundamental freedoms. Yet this is a right which must be held to be implied in the Charter as the very minimum of the means of its implementation. There was no mention of the right of petition in the system of mandates established after the First World War. That omission was not accidental, for proposals to that effect were submitted by Great Britain and the United States and considered by the Peace Conference.[55] However, subsequent to the establishment of the Mandates Commission the right of petition was regarded as a natural concomitant of the system established by the Covenant. No substantial opposition was encountered when, in July, 1922, the British Government submitted detailed proposals on the subject[56]—although care was taken to spare the susceptibilities and to ensure the full co-operation of the Mandatory Power.[57] The receipt and

[54] U.N. Doc. T/Pet. 2/40; 40/Add. 1. This was a petition submitted by a citizen of the United States of America who had lived for many years in Tanganyika and who requested that the Council send a mission to that territory in order to investigate practices of the administering authority said to be contrary to the interests of the native population. For a list of 27 petitions dealt with by Resolutions of the Trusteeship Council at its Fourth Session from 24 January to 25 March, 1949, see U.S. *Bulletin of State Department*, XX (1949), pp. 614-615.

[55] See *U.S. For. Rel.*, Paris Peace Conference, 1919, vol. III, p. 719. And see, for a detailed account, Duncan Hall, *Mandates, Dependencies and Trusteeships* (1948), p. 199.

[56] League of Nations, Doc. C.485, 1922, VI, C.P.M. XII, 1 August, 1922.

[57] Thus, for instance, the Third Assembly decided in 1923 that petitions emanating from inhabitants of mandated territories must be sent to the Mandates Commission through the intermediary of the local administration and the Mandatory Power, and that no petition emanating from a source other than the inhabitants of mandated territories should be considered by the Commission before the Mandatory Power had had full opportunity to express its views: *Records of the Third Assembly*, Plenary Meetings (1922), I, p. 166.

examination of petitions became subsequently one of the main features of the system of mandates. In fact, the rules of procedure, ultimately adopted, concerning petitions did not differ substantially from those adopted in 1947 by the Trusteeship Council in pursuance of Article 87 (b) of the Charter of the United Nations, which expressly envisaged the acceptance and examination of petitions in consultation with the administering authority.[58]

Similarly, although under the system of protection of minorities within the framework of the League of Nations there was no provision in the various Minorities Treaties for the recognition of the full legal right of effective petition, that fact did not prevent the evolution of a procedure of petitions regulated in minute detail. Admittedly, the Council of the League adhered throughout to the view that petitions were primarily in the nature of a source of information enabling the members of the Council to fulfil their duties and that the procedure adopted did not confer legal rights upon the petitioners themselves. But, after a time, the procedure evolved by the Minorities Section of the Secretariat and the Minorities Committee of the Council provided for a full examination of the receivability of the petitions and of the petitions themselves. The ultimate fate of petitions depended upon the action of the members of the Council, and this fact constituted the decisive weakness of the entire system.[59] But the detail and the elaboration of the system actually in operation invite comparison with the rudimentary—in fact, nominal—procedure for the examination of and action upon petitions adopted by the Commission on Human Rights. Yet it is significant that while disclaiming the right ' to take any action ' upon petitions

---

[58] See *Summary of the Procedure to be followed in the Matter of Petitions Concerning Mandated Territories* (as codified in 1927): Permanent Mandates Commission, *Minutes,* XII, pp. 176-178; Doc. C.P.M. 558 (1). And see, in particular, Duncan Hall, *op. cit.,* pp. 315-318. This applies, primarily, to petitions concerning proceedings pending before courts or with regard to which courts have jurisdiction. See *Minutes of the Sixth Session of the Permanent Mandates Commission,* pp. 168, 169 (Doc. C.386, M.132, 1925); and see Rule 81 of the Provisional Rules of Procedure adopted in 1947 by the Trusteeship Council: ' Normally petitions shall be considered inadmissible if they are directed against judgments of competent courts of the Administering Authority or if they lay before the Council a dispute with which the courts have competence to deal. This rule shall not be interpreted so as to prevent consideration by the Trusteeship Council of petitions against legislation on the grounds of its incompatibility with the provisions of the Charter of the United Nations or of the Trusteeship agreement, irrespective of whether decisions on cases arising under such legislation have previously been given by the courts of the Administering Authority.'

[59] See below, p. 375.

received by it, the Commission has not disclaimed the right to receive petitions, to acknowledge their receipt and to examine them. There is no express authority in the Charter either for such initial procedure or for 'taking action' upon petitions received. There is ample—and imperative—authority for both in the purpose of the Charter and in the obligation of the organs of the United Nations to give effect to it. This—and not the denial of it—is an 'elementary judicial concept'[60] which provides adequate authority for making effective the object of the Charter even prior to the acceptance of an enforceable International Bill of Human Rights.

The result of the attitude of the Commission on Human Rights in the matter of petitions has been that what would otherwise have been considered a clear right of the individual has acquired the character of a controversial privilege not lightly to be conceded. When the Third General Assembly of the United Nations discussed the right of petition, to national authorities or to the United Nations, as part of the proposed Universal Declaration of Human Rights,[61] no majority could be secured for including the right of petition in an instrument which in any case was not considered legally binding.[62] The proposal to that effect was opposed not only by Soviet Russia— on the ground that 'it would show disrespect of national sovereignty to permit individuals to petition the United Nations'.[63]

[60] See above, p. 231.

[61] The Commission on Human Rights considered the following Article, without, however, proposing that it should become part of the Declaration: 'Everyone has the right, either individually or in association with others, to petition or to communicate with the public authorities of the State of which he is a national or in which he resides, or with the United Nations.' At the General Assembly France proposed the incorporation of the following Article: 'Everyone has the right, either individually or in association with others, to petition or to communicate with the public authorities of the State of which he is a national or in which he resides. He also has the right to petition or to communicate with the competent organs of the United Nations in matters relating to human rights.'

[62] The Belgian representative expressed doubts 'as to the legal correctness of including the problem of petitions in a declaration which would not legally bind its signatories' (A/C.3/SR.160, p. 2).

[63] A/C.3/SR.160, p. 5. This was in addition to the argument that it was premature to include in the Declaration an Article based on the assumption that the rights contained in it would be violated. See also *ibid.*, p. 8, for the further contention of the Soviet representative that the proposal would be contrary to Article 2 (7) of the Charter. He replied in detail to the argument that inhabitants of metropolitan territories should have at least the same rights as inhabitants of trust territories, who enjoyed the right to present petitions to the United Nations. For, in his view, the United Nations examined petitions from trust territories for the precise reason

Many other States questioned the propriety of its inclusion in the Declaration. They were successful in their opposition. One of the reasons for the opposition was the circumstance (irrelevant in an instrument which is not legally binding) that there did not exist at that time an international machinery for entertaining petitions—a reminder that the Commission on Human Rights had been successful in its self-effacing abdication of the right to take action on petitions submitted to it. Instead, the General Assembly adopted a Resolution, put forward by France and Cuba, requesting the Economic and Social Council to ask the Commission on Human Rights to continue the examination of the problem of petitions in connexion with the study of the draft Covenant on Human Rights and measures of implementation. The Resolution was preceded by a Preamble laying down that ' the right of petition is an essential human right as is recognised in the constitution of a great number of countries '.[64] The minority of States which, in the Third Committee, opposed the Preamble included Soviet Russia (and her allies), Sweden, China, the United Kingdom, and the United States of America—a significant combination.[65]

The General Assembly, it is believed, was not given to exaggeration when it described the right of petition as an essential human right. This is so although within the State the rise of modern democratic institutions and of representative government has rendered the traditional right of petition obsolete to a large extent. Prior to these developments the right of petition, occasionally abused for factional purposes and, for that reason, curtailed by the legislature, asserted itself triumphantly in most countries. In England, by the beginning of the eighteenth century, the right of petition, after many vicissitudes, was fully

that these territories were not governed in accordance with the sovereign will of their inhabitants (A/C.3/SR.159, p. 10). This was also the view of the Argentinian representative who, relying on Article 2 (7) of the Charter, stated in this connexion that 'the world situation was not sufficiently advanced to permit of the abolition of the principle of national sovereignty, which the Charter recognised' (*ibid.*, p. 2). On the other hand, the representative of Australia, a country which had played a prominent part in the adoption of Article 2 (7), was fully in favour of the international right of petition. He pointed out that there was nothing irrevocable about the sphere of domestic jurisdiction; that the transfer of the latter to international jurisdiction would constitute not a violation but an exercise of national sovereignty; and that a country could always demand guarantees against irresponsible petitions (*ibid.*, p. 4).

[64] *Records of the General Assembly*, A/PV.185, p. 167.
[65] And see below, p. 287.

recognised. It had previously been challenged and occasionally suppressed by Parliament on the ground that it was abused or exercised in a tumultuous manner prejudicial to public order.[66] One of the first acts of the Restoration Parliament was to pass a statute regulating disorderly petitions and providing that no petition shall be presented by more than twenty persons except with the consent of three or more justices of the peace.[67] But soon after, Parliament formally resolved that ' it is and ever has been the undoubted right of the subjects of England to petition the King for the calling and sitting of Parliaments and the redressing of grievances '.[68] The two Resolutions of the House of Commons of 1669 are to the same effect.[69] The Bill of Rights of 1688 asserted that ' it is the right of subjects to petition the King ' and that ' all commitments and prosecutions for such petitioning are illegal '. In the eighteenth century, during a period when the corruption of Parliament by a venal Executive reduced to vanishing point the principle of constitutional government, the right of petition proved a potent weapon of popular criticism. George the Third, seated on his throne, listened patiently and with apparent courtesy to the rebellious remonstrance presented in 1770 in the form of a petition by the Lord Mayor and the Sheriffs attended by an immense multitude. ' We owe to Your Majesty ', the petitioners said, ' an obedience under the restriction of the laws; and Your Majesty owes to us that our representation, free from the force of arms or corruption, should be preserved to us in Parliament.' [70] In the debate in Parliament, upon a motion condemning the petition, Burke and Wedderburn vindicated the right of petition in the matter of summoning and dissolving Parliament in language which has resounded through generations and whose force is not yet spent. During the discussion on the Seditious Meetings Bill in 1795 Pitt affirmed ' the right of the people to express their opinions on political men and measures, and to discuss their right of petitioning all branches

[66] For references see Emden, *The People and the Constitution* (1933), p. 73, n. 1.
[67] 13 Chas. II, c. 5.
[68] 4 *Parl. History*, p. 1774.
[69] ' That it is the inherent right of every commoner in England to prepare and present petitions to the House of Commons in case of grievance, and of the House of Commons to receive the same.
    ' That it is an undoubted right and privilege of the Commons to judge and determine, touching the nature and matter of such petitions, how far they are fit and unfit to be received.'
[70] G. O. Trevelyan, *The Early History of Charles James Fox* (1880), Chapter VI (p. 239).

of the legislature '.[71]   The middle of the nineteenth century signified the high-water mark of petition as an instrument for influencing Parliament.   This was so even after the failure of the Chartist petitions.   In 1848 Disraeli affirmed the right of petition as being a vital element of the liberties of the subject.   He said:

> ' There is an idea that the presentation of a petition is an empty form—that it is ordered to lie on the table, and is never heard of again.   Now it is as well that our constituents should know that every petition laid on the table is scrutinised by a select committee of the most experienced and influential members of this House—that every petition which, from the importance of its subject or the ability of its statements appears to merit particular notice, is printed at the public cost, and afterwards circulated among members; and I believe that at this moment the right of petition . . . is a more important and efficient right than has ever been enjoyed at any time by the people of England in this respect.' [72]

But petitions are not an end in themselves.   They lose their urgency and vitality in proportion as more effective measures are found for the protection of the rights of the subject.   As has been rightly pointed out, in proportion as the franchise has been extended and the representation of the people adequately provided for, the *raison d'être* of petitions has to that extent disappeared.[73].   Moreover, at a time when the government of the country is, in effect, no longer directly in the hands of Parliament but in the hands of the Ministries concerned, it is natural that petitions should be directed to the persons with whom the decision actually lies rather than to Parliament.   The Anti-Slavery petitions in 1833, the petitions of the Anti-Corn Law League in 1840, and the petitions in 1841 and 1886 for a legal limitation of working hours were all addressed, in the form of deputations, to the Minister concerned.   But direct petitions to Parliament are by no means a matter of the past..   In the Fourteenth Edition of Sir Erskine May's *Parliamentary Practice,* published in 1946, it is stated that ' the right of petitioning the Crown and Parliament for redress of grievances is acknowledged as a fundamental principle of the constitution '.[74]   As late as the Session of 1942-3

---

[71] 21 *Parl. History,* p. 367.
[72] 101 *Parl. Deb.,* 3 s., 673.
[73] Emden, *op. cit.*
[74] By Sir Gilbert Campion, p. 794, where on pp. 794-805 the law relating to public petitions is set out in full.

the House of Commons agreed, as a measure of economy, to allow signatures on the back of the petition sheet and the sheets attached thereto to be counted whether or not the prayer was repeated at the top of the page.[75]

The position is essentially the same in France, where the right of petition has been traditionally regarded as a fundamental right in a twofold sense—as a manifestation of freedom of expression and as a consequence of individual liberty and security inasmuch as everyone is entitled to bring a complaint against arbitrary acts of authority. The rights of freedom of expression and personal security figure prominently in the Declaration of 1789 and, as suggested by Duguit,[76] this is probably the reason why the right of petition is not mentioned in the Declaration. However the Constitutions of 1791 and 1793 refer to it expressly. The latter lays down, in Article 32, that ' the right to present petitions to the holders of public authority must in no case be prohibited, suspended, or limited '. In French legal literature a distinction has occasionally been made between petitions aiming at remedying an individual grievance (the right of such petitions being one which the legislature might regulate but which it must not limit or suppress) and petitions presented by an individual or group of individuals in the general interest. But the Assembly of 1791 rejected the suggestion that the latter might be limited; by an overwhelming majority it endorsed the view that the right of petition is ' an imprescriptible right of all men living in society . . . a right of every thinking creature '.[77] It is now generally accepted in France that there is no legally relevant distinction between the two kinds of petition. Both, says Duguit, ' are an expression of a natural right and may be presented by all persons, including those who do not enjoy political rights and foreigners '.[78] A series of enactments, in particular those of 1852 and 1879, have regulated the right of petition—largely with a view to preventing their abuse for purposes of political propaganda and of disturbing public order. The regulations of the Chamber and of the Senate contain detailed provisions on the subject.[79] In the former petitions are sent, as a rule, to one of the relevant Standing Com-

---

[75] *H.C. Deb.*, 1942-3, vol. 390, col. 1113.
[76] *Traité de droit constitutionnel*, 2nd ed., vol. V (1925), p. 440.
[77] Duguit, *op. cit.*, p. 443.
[78] *Op. cit.*, p. 444.
[79] See Pierre, *Traité de droit politique*, Supplement (1919), pp. 786 *et seq.*

mittees, which decides whether to forward them to the Minister concerned or to the full Chamber or merely to register them. The petitioners are informed of the decision of the Committee. As in England, so also in France it is recognised that petitions may have become obsolete at a time when parliamentary institutions and courts provide more rapid and effective ways of redress. But, as in many other countries,[80] the institution of petition as such remains both part of the existing statutory law and of the heritage of the imprescriptible rights of the individual.

This somewhat detailed survey of the development of the right of petition within the State explains its place in the scheme of protection of human rights. It has been treated throughout as a fundamental right. Its urgency varies with the development of political institutions and available judicial and other remedies. In relation to the United Nations and the human rights and fundamental freedoms which constitute a crucial aspect of its Charter, the right of petition is as urgent and the necessity for its full recognition as imperative as it was at the initial stage of development within the State. So long as, in the absence of an extension of the obligations of the Charter through an effective Bill of Rights or otherwise, the judicial or political remedies against the violation of its provisions remain in a rudimentary stage, the full right of petition, followed by investigation and recommendation, must be considered as inherent in the Charter and as following imperatively from the obligation to interpret it in good faith.

[80] See Leclerc, *Le droit de pétition* (1913). When in 1948 and 1949 attempts were made in the United States to restrict the opportunities for organised pressure of professional lobbyists in both Houses of Congress, the attempts were resisted for the reason, *inter alia,* that they were calculated to interfere with the right of petition as guaranteed in the Constitution.

CHAPTER 12

THE ORGANISATION AND COMPOSITION OF THE COMMISSION ON HUMAN RIGHTS

1. THE FUNCTION OF THE COMMISSION AND ITS RESOURCES.

A SUBSTANTIAL part of the explanation of the studied restraint exhibited by the Commission on Human Rights in the interpretation of the scope of its functions is the circumstance that its composition and the machinery at its disposal have not been such as to enable it to fulfil the task of effective action, within the limits of the Charter, upon petitions alleging violation of human rights. The same applies to the Economic and Social Council. The latter is a body meeting for brief periods for the purpose of creating, co-ordinating the activities of, and receiving reports from various organs and laying down lines of policy on subjects covering practically the whole range of international administration and government.[1] It cannot be expected that the Economic

[1] The agenda of the Ninth Session of the Economic and Social Council in 1949 comprised fifty-two items, including the following: Report of the Ad Hoc Committee on the Factors bearing upon the Establishment of an Economic Commission for the Middle East; Report of the Transport and Communications Commission; International Facilities for the Promotion of Training in Public Administration; Report of the Secretary-General on Housing and Town and Country Planning; Study of Statelessness; Report of the Economic and Employment Commission; Economic Development of Under-Developed Countries ; Measures to increase Availability of Food ; Availability of D.D.T. Insecticides; Report of the Fiscal Commission; Report of the Statistical Commission; Report of the Commissions for Europe and for Asia and the Far East; Report of the Population Commission; Report of the Social Commission; World Social and Cultural Situation; Social Problems of the Aboriginal Populations and other Under-Developed Groups of the American Continent; Report of the Commission on Human Rights; Survey of Forced Labor and Measures for its Abolition; The Problem of Slavery; Trade Union Rights; Report of the Committee on Declaration of Death of Missing Persons; Report of the Commission on the Status of Women; Report of the Sub-Commission on Freedom of Information and of the Press; Freedom of Information: Resolutions from the Final Act of the United Nations Conference on Freedom of Information; Report of the Commission on Narcotic Drugs; Report of the United Nations International Children's Emergency Fund; Report of the Secretary-General on the United Nations Appeal for Children; Implementation of Recommendations on Economic and Social Matters; Relations with and Co-ordination of Specialised Agencies; Report of the International Labour Organisation; Report of the Food and Agriculture Organisation; Report of the United Nations Educational,

and Social Council will be in the position to devote more than formal attention either to the question of petitions or, generally, to the complex problems confronting the Commission on Human Rights. For that reason it is easy to understand the grounds which prompted the proposal advanced by a group of members of the Commission to the effect that the Economic and Social Council should delegate to the Commission the right to make recommendations in the matter of human rights.[2] However, the proposal, which does not seem to appreciate the powers already enjoyed by the Commission,[3] still leaves open the question whether the Commission itself, as at present constituted, is capable of sustaining that burden and whether, in the absence of recognition of the right of the Commission to take action, in the form of appropriate investigation and report, upon petitions presented to it, the power to make recommendations is not devoid of substance.

The Commission on Human Rights meets, as a rule, twice a year for periods of four to six weeks. The Division of Human Rights is a relatively small department of the Secretariat devoted largely to research and to the preparation of meetings and memoranda. The task of coping adequately with a mass of petitions coming from many parts of the world would require a body of persons of the highest qualifications and impartiality aided by a competent subordinate staff. It would necessitate a

Scientific, and Cultural Organisation; Report of the World Health Organisation; Report of the International Civil Aviation Organisation; Report of the International Telecommunication Union; Report of the Universal Postal Union; Report of the International Refugee Organisation; Relations with Inter-Governmental Organisations; Reports of the Council Committee on Non-Governmental Organisations; Co-Ordination of Cartographic Services of Specialised Agencies and International Organisations; Use of the Central Library at Geneva by the United Nations and the Specialised Agencies.

[2] Report of the Working Group on Implementation set up by the Commission on Human Rights in the course of its Session in December 1947 (Doc. E/600, p. 48). The Report says: ' The Economic and Social Council is known to be overburdened with functions; so overburdened, indeed, that it cannot always carry out with desirable efficiency the many and varied tasks imposed upon it. In contrast, the Commission on Human Rights is a specialised organ with clear-cut purposes. Hence it would appear to be better qualified than the Council to deal with human rights and, in particular, to discharge the function, always a delicate one, of elaborating recommendations.'

[3] The Commission is already, by its terms of reference (see above, p. 224), empowered to make recommendations. The proposal would therefore seem to imply the suggestion that the Council should relinquish that right. This, however, would not appear to have been the intention of the Report, for it suggests that the Council should retain ' the whole of its prerogatives ' (*ibid.*).

Commission on Human Rights sitting in almost permanent session and exclusively devoted to reaching decisions on the information collected and on findings arrived at by the expert bodies. It would also require a subdivision of the Economic and Social Council, or a similar body, devoted exclusively to formulating conclusions on a higher level of policy. There is no such machinery in existence. It can be created—or developed—within the framework of the Charter without a formal amendment thereof.

The existence or otherwise of the requisite machinery is a function of the will of Governments and not of any inherent limitations of the Charter. If the States composing the Economic and Social Council and the Commission on Human Rights act on the view that these bodies ' have no power to take any action ' upon petitions alleging violations of human rights, then there will be no inducement to create machinery commensurate with the purposes of the Charter. It is probable that, apart from the possibilities afforded by the adoption of an effective International Bill of Rights, the United Nations will not be in a position to fulfil adequately its function in the matter of human rights and freedoms until what is now the Commission on Human Rights has undergone fundamental changes.[4] These include not only the transformation of the Commission into a body with a status analogous to that of the Economic and Social Council or the Trusteeship Council. They also comprise the equipment of that body with a staff able to cope adequately with the task of receiving and examining petitions and, by initiating any further requisite action, able to assume the executive responsibility for the fulfilment of an essential purpose of the Charter. The devotion and competence of the Division of Human Rights as constituted in the first years of the existence of the United Nations are not in question. But it seems futile to expect it, with its present resources and status, to be more than a permanent secretariat of one of the numerous Commissions of the Economic and Social Council.

2.   THE COMPOSITION OF THE COMMISSION ON HUMAN RIGHTS

In any consideration of the functions of the Commission on Human Rights the question which requires special attention is that

---

[4] See below, p. 257.

of the proper basis of the composition of the Commission. The Nuclear Commission[5] recommended, by a majority,[6] that all members of the full Commission on Human Rights should serve as non-governmental representatives appointed by the Economic and Social Council from a list of nominees submitted by the Member States of the United Nations.[7] In making that recommendation the Commission expressed the view that as the Economic and Social Council consisted of representatives of governments it was desirable that the composition of the Commission should be on a different basis. The Council overruled that recommendation. In its Resolution of 21 June, 1946, it laid down that the Commission on Human Rights shall consist of one representative of each of eighteen Members of the United Nations selected by the Council.[8] The Resolution of the Council was in accordance with the principle applied by it to the composition of the other Commissions responsible to it. It was prompted by the view, freely expressed in the course of the deliberations of the Council, that unless the members of the Commission on Human Rights and of other Commissions are representatives of governments, their work would tend to become academic and unreal.[9] Whatever force there may be in that contention in relation to the Commissions of the Council in general— a view which apparently was not shared by the Preparatory

[5] See above, p. 224.
[6] The representative of the Soviet Union disagreed with this recommendation. He expressed the view that all members of the Commission and its sub-commissions should be appointed as government representatives in the same way as the members of the Economic and Social Council.
[7] *Journal of the Economic and Social Council*, First Year, No. 14, p. 161.
[8] *Journal of the Economic and Social Council*, First Year, No. 29, p. 520. It was also laid down that in order to secure a balanced representation in the various fields covered by the Commission, the Secretary-General should consult with the Governments so selected before the representatives were finally nominated by these Governments and confirmed by the Council. The Resolution provides that the term of office shall be for three years. The continuity of the work of the Commission is to be secured by a device according to which for the initial period one-third of the members shall serve for two years, one-third for three years, and one-third for four years, the term of each member to be determined by lot.
[9] It has been pointed out to the writer that the decision of the Council, which had the support of the United States, was in the nature of a compromise between the original view of the United States that all members of the Commission should be independent experts and the view that the members of the Commission should be representatives of governments. The compromise is said to consist in the requirement that the Governments in question should consult with the Secretary-General before appointing their representatives. It is doubtful whether such consultation is more than a formality and whether it affects to any appreciable extent the independence of the Commission.

Commission of the First General Assembly[10]—there ought to be no doubt that the Commission on Human Rights is in this respect in a category of its own. To apply, in this connexion, to the Commission on Human Rights the same principles as, for instance, apply to the Statistical Commission or the Transport and Communications Commission, is to introduce into the treatment of this subject a distinct element of incongruity.[11] The provisions of the Charter in the matter of the protection and promotion of human rights by the United Nations mark a new chapter in the history of the vindication of the rights of man against the State. That task is henceforth to be brought nearer solution under the ægis and with the co-operation of the organised community of States. But the essential elements of the problem remain the same. They are not comparable with those of other Commissions, the principal object of which is to introduce a measure of co-ordination and co-operation into the activities of governments.

In view of this, the mechanical application to the Commission on Human Rights of the principle of purely governmental representation is open to objection.[12] This is so even if, as the

---

[10] That Commission recommended that commissions should in most cases contain a majority of government officials or other governmental representatives. It seems that the Preparatory Commission envisaged cases in which the governmental representatives would be in a minority.

[11] The Minutes of the Commission reveal that the voting records the attitude of the countries represented on the Commission and not of the individuals casting the vote. On occasions members of the Commission make formal declarations as to the attitude of their Governments.

[12] Because of the exclusively governmental nature of the composition of the Human Rights Commission some questions tend to assume a political character which they would not otherwise possess. Thus in the matter of the *Year Book on Human Rights* the Commission decided, in June, 1948, that decisions of national courts bearing on human rights should not be recorded in the *Year Book*. Yet that is the kind of information, otherwise not easily accessible, for which the reader would naturally look in the *Year Book*. One of the underlying reasons for that decision was that the publication of such decisions might, on occasions, create an unfavourable impression as to the position of human rights in the State concerned. At a subsequent session of the Commission the decision previously taken was reversed, and the Secretary-General was requested to include in the future important decisions of courts bearing on human rights. In 1949 the question came before the Economic and Social Council, which postponed the matter to a further session and requested the Secretary-General to prepare sample studies for the Commission on Human Rights (Resolution 192 (VIII) B; Doc. E/1163/Rev.1). For a memorandum of the Secretary-General on the objects of the *Year Book* in the matter of reports of decisions of courts, see Doc. E/CN.4/169, which contains examples of various types of cases and of methods of their reporting. It would seem that reports of judicial decisions are of general interest only if they refer to cases in which the decision of the court is based on or contains observations on either: (a) the international obligations of the State bearing on human rights such as the Charter of the United Nations or other international treaties referring to human rights; or (b) human rights included in national bills of rights or constitutions.

deliberations of the Commission have often shown, the individuals representing governments are imbued with a devotion and fervour indicative of the transcending importance of the task entrusted to them.   Highest considerations of statesmanship and of the successful accomplishment of the purpose of the United Nations require that the constitutional question of the composition of the Commission should become the subject of discussion and eventual revision of the method adopted by the Economic and Social Council in 1946.   Such revision need not discard altogether representation of governments.   But it is probable that the Commission on Human Rights will not attain the full stature of moral authority and practical effectiveness until it includes, in addition to persons appointed by governments, private individuals of distinction, full independence and experience, chosen irrespective of nationality by a selective process which in itself would be a guarantee of the impartiality and high quality of its members. In its present composition the Commission on Human Rights, like other Commissions of the Economic and Social Council, is no more than a conference of representatives of States.   Any criticism of its activities or of its interpretation of the Charter is therefore not a criticism directed against an abstract body or its individual members, but against the attitude of the States represented on the Commission.   Unless there is a clear realisation of that fact we run the danger of attributing to a collective body, called 'the Commission on Human Rights', the responsibility which rests upon the Governments concerned.   It is upon those Governments—and not upon an abstract entity styled 'the Commission on Human Rights'—that rests the responsibility for the fate which befell the protection of human rights under the Charter in the initial period of the existence of the United Nations. Thus the decision that the Commission had no power to take any action upon complaints of violations of human rights did not follow inescapably from a clear provision of the Charter; it was fully—and more accurately—open to the Commission to adopt a contrary conclusion.   The interpretation adopted by the Commission was a political decision of Governments which recoiled from the implications of one of the most fundamental purposes of the Charter.   In its present composition the Commission on Human Rights has no reality except as an assembly of representatives of governments.   The tendency must be resisted to use it as a screen for concealing an attitude of Governments which is out of keeping with the purposes of the Charter. On occasions, individual members of the Commission, yielding to their personal inclination and appreciation of the significance of the task entrusted to them, have succeeded in influencing the attitude of their Governments. But this has not been—and, in the nature of things, could not be—the typical case. Moreover, while the members of the Commission are representatives of governments bound to act and normally acting on their instructions, the Governments represented on the Commission have not invariably considered themselves bound by the declarations of their representatives.

Secondly, any consideration of the necessary reorganisation of the Commission on Human Rights—or of the body which may take its place—must take into account not only the impartiality but also the efficiency of its work. If the business of the Commission is, in addition to an intricate and involved task of draftsmanship, to promote actively the observance of human rights, on the basis of an effective right of petition, through supervision, enquiry and recommendation, then the proper fulfilment of that function requires that its members should be able to devote all their time to the accomplishment of their task. Their active membership of the Commission cannot be in the nature of brief interludes between the periods in which they pursue their ordinary avocations. Any failure to appreciate that administrative aspect of the functions of the Commission must result in an inclination, on the part of the Commission, to interpret the legal scope of its activities by reference to the time available for their performance. A purely physical factor may thus be elevated to the status of a legal construction of the provisions of the Charter.

Finally, at least as long as the Commission is composed exclusively of representatives of governments, it would seem appropriate that the competent organs of the Secretariat—acting under the Secretary-General—should be able to avail themselves freely of that measure of independence and of the formal right of initiative which, in a different sphere, is enjoyed and often exercised by the Secretary-General of the United Nations. Under Article 99 of the Charter the Secretary-General may bring to the attention of the Security Council any matter which in his opinion may threaten the maintenance of international peace and security. But the responsibilities of the Secretary-General, as the highest official of the organised international community endowed with a personality distinct from that of its individual members, go beyond that specific authorisation. These responsibilities have often been exercised to the point of open or implied criticism of the actions of Members of the United Nations. There are compelling reasons why, in the sphere of human rights, the permanent civil service of the United Nations should make its distinctive and independent contribution to the promotion of the purposes of the Charter. In fact, in 1949 the Secretary-General in a Report on the ' Present Situation with regard to Communications Concerning Human Rights ', summarising the experience of the first phase of the activities of the Commission on Human Rights, took an important step in that direction. In particular, the Report— though hesitating, controversial in its interpretation of the powers of the Commission, and confined, in its practical proposals, to matters of minor detail—drew attention to the necessity of revising the ruling that the Commission has no power to take any action with regard to any complaints concerning human rights. While absolving the Commission of responsibility for that ruling, it urged, with greater justification, that the ruling ' is bound to lower the prestige and the authority not only of the Commission on Human Rights, but of the United Nations in the opinion of the general public '.[13]

---

[13] E/CN.4/165, p. 5. Actually, the ruling in question emanated from the Commission itself (see p. 225 above). The Economic and Social Council confined itself to approving the ruling almost as a matter of routine. The Secretary-General assumed that the ruling was technically correct so far as the jurisdiction of the Commission was concerned—as distinguished from the jurisdiction of the Economic and Social Council, the General Assembly and the Trusteeship Council. As pointed out elsewhere in this book (see above, pp. 227-234), that view is probably inaccurate. The Secretary-General stated that ' in the light of Resolution 75 (V) it is clear that the Council, while charging the Commission with the task of giving advice and assistance to the Council to enable it to discharge its responsibility of promoting universal respect for and observance of human rights and submitting proposals, recommendations and reports to the Council regarding " any other matter concerning human rights" [see above, p. 224], did *not* delegate to the Commission the right to take any action in regard to any complaint concerning human rights '. It is difficult to follow that statement. The power and the duty to submit to the Council ' proposals, recommendations and reports ' with regard to ' any other matter concerning human rights ' includes the power and the duty to investigate complaints with the view to enabling the Commission to submit proposals, recommendations and reports. However that may be, the question transcends the interpretation of any particular

3. THE FIRST PHASE OF THE ACTIVITIES OF THE COMMISSION ON HUMAN RIGHTS

The first period of the activity of the United Nations, and especially of its principal organs created for the promotion of the observance of human rights and fundamental freedoms, marked a recession from the high purposes of the Charter in that field. Various causes combined to produce that effect. In the first instance, at the time when, at the end of the Second World War, the idea of human rights was being incorporated in the Charter, circumstances were not favourable to a universal and unqualified observance of human rights and freedoms in accordance with the letter and the spirit of the Charter. In a number of countries the turmoil of war and the aftermath of invasion by the enemy resulted in forms of government out of keeping with the generally accepted conception of democratic freedom. In some of the defeated States which had been responsible for the gravest crimes ever committed against man, the régime of military occupation and supervision ruled out, for the time being, any substantive adherence to rigid standards of human rights and freedoms. The same applied to the treatment of former nationals of—or those ethnically connected with—those States in the territories detached from them and, in some cases, in the territories previously belonging to Members of the United Nations. These anomalies, to some extent unavoidable and in many cases not inconsistent with justice, were of a transient character. Attempts, during that period

resolution of the Economic and Social Council or of the Commission on Human Rights. The question is one of the fulfilment in good faith of a fundamental purpose of the Charter. That issue must necessarily become obscured by concentration on matters of minor compass. Thus, for instance, the Memorandum of the Secretary-General, referred to above, was devoted largely to the question of secrecy with regard to communications submitted to the Commission in the matter of human rights. It was suggested that the rule of secrecy should continue to apply to lists of communications— though not necessarily to the names of their authors (see above, p. 238)— containing complaints and requests for action but not to the relatively unimportant communications dealing with general principles involved in the promotion of respect for and observance of human rights. It was also proposed that, once the rule as to the anonymity of the authors of complaints has been relaxed, there would be no reason for the continuation of the rule preventing members of the Commission from consulting the originals of communications containing complaints (see above, p. 236). Finally, the proposal was made for putting States represented on the Commission on the same footing with other States which, according to paragraph (e) of Resolution 75 (V), are entitled to receive, before the meeting of the Commission, a brief indication of the substance of communications referring explicitly to them or to the territories under their jurisdiction so as to enable them to comment on such communications (see above, p. 226).

of transition, to define in detail the competence of the United Nations in the matter of human rights were likely to be influenced by the tendency to take account of the anomalous conditions of the post-war period in terms of general limitations upon the work of the United Nations. There was significance in the fact that by the end of 1949 the position in the matter of petitions fell short of the powers and duties of implementation outlined in the Resolution of the Economic and Social Council adopted in 1946. That circumstance reveals the dangers of a premature crystallization of the functions of the organs of the United Nations in the matter of human rights during what is essentially a period of transition. In the meantime, it will be in accordance with the purposes of the Charter if the activities of the organs of the United Nations devoted to the cause of human rights are exercised in such a manner as to leave room for developments in the direction of enhancing the effectiveness of the protective function of the United Nations. Any attempts in the opposite direction are contrary to the enduring tendencies of mankind. The law on the subject is sufficiently elastic to leave room for growth. It is also sufficiently elastic to leave full scope for enlightened public opinion to exert its beneficent influence.

The second explanation of the negative results of the first stage of the activities of the Human Rights Commission is that its energies were devoted almost exclusively to the drafting of an International Bill of Human Rights. As is shown elsewhere, the labours of the Commission in this respect have resulted in the production of a Declaration which is not and is not intended to be a legally binding document and which cannot be regarded as constituting progress in the direction of the effective protection of human rights under the ægis of the United Nations.[14] The possibility—we cannot put it higher than that—of the adoption by the majority of the Members of the United Nations of a true Bill of Rights conceived as an enforceable part of international law ought not to provide a cause or be used as a justification for the abandonment or neglect of that substantial measure of legal protection of human rights which already forms part of the Charter. Yet that is what happened in the first period of the activities of the Economic and Social Council and of the Commission on Human Rights. A break with the past, in this

[14] See below, pp. 394-428.

vital respect, is imperative if violence is not to be done to the letter
and spirit of the Charter and to an essential purpose of the United
Nations.

4.   THE COMMISSION ON THE STATUS OF WOMEN

For the sake of completeness an account may be given in the
present Chapter of the Commission on the Status of Women and
of the Sub-Commissions on Prevention of Discrimination and
Protection of Minorities and on Freedom of Information and of
the Press.

In 1946 the Economic and Social Council established a Commission on the Status of Women—previously functioning as a
Sub-Commission—charged with the function of preparing recommendations and reports to the Economic and Social Council on
promoting the rights of women in political, economic, social and
educational fields and also with submitting recommendations to
the Council on urgent problems requiring immediate attention in
the field of the rights of women.   The latter task was subsequently
made specific by being coupled with that of the implementation
of the principle that men and women have equal rights.   In 1947
the Commission formulated the Principles and Aims of its work.
With regard to the former, it laid down that as freedom and
equality are essential to human development and that ' since
woman is as much a human being as man, she is entitled to share
these attributes with him '.   In order to achieve that goal, the
Commission intended ' to raise the status of women, irrespective
of nationality, race, language, or religion, to equality with men in
all fields of human enterprise, and to eliminate all discrimination
against women in the provisions of statutory law, in legal maxims
or rules, or in interpretations of customary law '.[15]   The Commission then formulated its aims which are of a somewhat broad
nature and which have not yet secured confirmation on the part of
the Economic and Social Council.[16]

---

[15] Economic and Social Council, *Official Records,* Second Year, Fourth Session,
Suppl. No. 2.   This is the principal document bearing on the functions of the
Commission on the Status of Women.

[16] The aims formulated by the Commission cannot be easily summarised, and
it is convenient to reproduce the relevant part of the statement in full:
A. Political
Equal participation of women in government and the possibility of
exercising all the rights of citizenship, irrespective of race, language, or
religion, and of assuming all the duties of a citizen, which comprise: (1)

On the recommendation of the Commission the Council invited Member States to give replies to a questionnaire on the legal status and treatment of women, especially in the field of public law and the franchise.[17] The Trusteeship Council was

universal adult suffrage; (2) equal right to vote; (3) equal right to be elected; (4) equal right to hold public office.

B. Civil

Full equality for women to exercise all civil rights, irrespective of nationality, race, language, or religion, including among others:

1. *Marriage.* Freedom of choice, dignity of the wife, monogamy, equal right to dissolution of marriage.
2. *Guardianship.* Equal right to guardianship of her own and other children.
3. *Nationality.* Right to retain her own nationality, and, for her children, the right to choose the nationality of the mother upon attaining their majority.
4. *Legal capacity.* Equal right to enter into contracts and to acquire, dispose of and inherit property.
5. *Domicile.* A married woman to have the same right to establish her domicile as a man or a single woman.

C. Social and Economic

Full opportunity for women to take equal part in social life, which implies full opportunity of fulfilling their duties towards society.

1. To prevent discrimination against women in social and economic status and customs, irrespective of nationality, race, language or religion. Women should be given equal rights with men with respect to labour, wages, holidays, and other economic and social rights.
2. To abolish prostitution.
3. Not only should no limitation be applied to women because of their sex, in regard to the enjoyment of full equality in the exercise of social rights and the assumption of labour duties, but consideration on grounds of health should be given equally to men and women, and special consideration to women on grounds of motherhood. With that aim in view, the Commission shall try to obtain, among other benefits, State protection of the interests of the mother and child by providing holidays with pay for the mother before and after childbirth; by arranging leave of absence during working hours for nursing mothers, without deductions for such time from wages; by the establishment of special rooms for nursing the children; and by the organisation of a wide network of nursing homes and medical consultation centres, *crèches* and kindergartens, and other facilities.
4. There should be an effective system of health and social insurance legislation providing equal preventive and remedial opportunities for women and including special provisions for maternal and child welfare.

D. Education

Equal opportunity for compulsory, free and full education, equal opportunity in all specialised fields and the right to enjoy scientific discoveries applied to human growth and development.

(Economic and Social Council, *Official Records,* Second Year, Fourth Session, Supplement No. 2, *Report of the Commission on the Status of Women,* 1947, pp. 10-11.)

[17] Previously the General Assembly adopted on 11 December, 1946, the following Resolution (No. 56 (1)):

' Whereas in the Preamble of the Charter the peoples of the United Nations have reaffirmed faith in the equal rights of men and women, and in Article 1 it is stated that the purposes of the United Nations are, among others, to achieve international co-operation in promoting and encouraging respect for human rights and for fundamental freedoms for all without distinction as to sex, and to be a centre for harmonising the actions of nations in the attainment of these common ends;

invited to pay special attention to the inclusion of these matters in its own questionnaires. At a subsequent meeting, in January 1948, the Commission examined the existing legal and customary disabilities of women and considered the means of abolishing political inequality; of removing discrimination against women resulting from conflicts between national laws relating to nationality, domicile, marriage, and divorce; of affording women equal educational rights; of ensuring equal rights for women with men with respect to employment and remuneration therefor; and of removing restrictions on married women with regard to the control of their property and earnings.[18] On the recommendation of the Commission or on its own initiative the Economic and Social Council adopted a number of Resolutions bearing on the status of women. Thus it noted that some States had reported limitations on the use of the franchise and eligibility for public office, and requested Member States, where women do not yet possess the same political rights as men, to grant them such rights in the various spheres of national life.[19] It deplored all legislative measures forbidding mixed marriages between persons differing as to colour, race, nationality, citizenship or religion or other restrictions upon the freedom to choose a spouse[20] or denying to a woman the right to leave her country of origin and reside with her husband in any other country.[21] It affirmed the principle of equal rights of men and women laid down in the Preamble of the Charter of the United Nations and approved the principle of equal remuneration for work of equal value for men and women workers and called upon Member States to implement that principle.[22]

As in the case of the Commission on Human Rights, the com-

' Whereas certain Member States have not yet granted to women political rights equal to those granted to men, [the Assembly]

Therefore (a) recommends that all Member States, which have not already done so, adopt measures necessary to fulfil the purposes and aims of the Charter in this respect by granting to women the same political rights as to men;

(b) invites the Secretary-General to communicate this recommendation to the Governments of all Member States.'

See also below, pp. 338-340.

[18] A useful survey of the work of the Commission will be found in the yearly *Report of the Economic and Social Council to the General Assembly.*

[19] Resolution 154 (VIII).

[20] With the exception of restrictions based on family relationships, age, or similar grounds.

[21] Resolution 154 (VIII).

[22] Resolution 121 (VI).

position of the Commission on the Status of Women is purely governmental.[23] Similarly, with regard to communications and petitions, the Economic and Social Council adopted for the Commission on the Status of Women the same principles as those adopted for the Commission on Human Rights.[24]

5. THE SUB-COMMISSIONS OF THE COMMISSION ON HUMAN RIGHTS

(1) The Sub-Commission on Prevention of Discrimination and Protection of Minorities.—That body was set up by the Commission on Human Rights in 1946. In February, 1947, the Economic and Social Council defined the task of the Sub-Commission as being: ' (a) In the first instance, to examine what provisions should be adopted in the definition of the principles

---

[23] See above, p. 255.

[24] See Report of the Sub-Committee on Communications to the Commission on the Status of Women of 14 February, 1947 (E/CN.6/19). One of the communications sent to the Commission and listed in the above Report was a protest against the formulation of any international law condemning a whole nation, since women should not be held responsible where they do not enjoy equal rights with men. And see Report of the Social Committee to the Economic and Social Council, 4 August, 1947 (E/521). The Sub-Committee on Communications recommended as follows: ' (a) The Secretary-General should be requested to compile a confidential list of communications received concerning the Status of Women, before each session of the Commission. (b) This confidential list and the contents thereof, together with the names of any organisations sending such communications, should be communicated to the members of the Commission at least fourteen days before the opening of each session. (c) The members of the Commission should have the right, upon request, to consult the originals of these communications. (d) The Secretary-General should be requested to inform the writers of all such communications that these will be brought to the attention of the Commission on the Status of Women.' Through a somewhat pathetic report of 12 January, 1948, of the *ad hoc* Committee on Communications, the Commission on the Status of Women recognised that its functions were limited to recommending which communications bearing upon the principles relating to the promotion of the rights of women in political, economic, civil, social and educational fields should be made available in original to members of the Commission on request. Thereupon the Committee requested the Secretariat to produce the originals of the communications in question and, after having considered them, decided that certain of them should be made available to the members of the Commission on request. The list appended to the recommendation was not such as to stimulate the curiosity or interest of the members of the Commission (E/CN.6/66: 12 January, 1948). In August, 1947, a joint committee of the Economic and Social Council and the Trusteeship Council adopted, with regard to petitions relating to women, the same procedure as that applicable to petitions referring to human rights generally (E. & T/C.1/SR.2). It was decided that the Trusteeship Council should communicate to the appropriate Commissions those petitions which it received directly and which contained matters of concern to the Commissions, and should, under Article 91 of the Charter, avail itself, when appropriate, of the assistance of the Commissions in respect of such petitions (*ibid.*, p. 4).

which are to be applied in the field of the prevention of discrimination on grounds of race, sex, language, or religion, and in the field of the protection of minorities, and to make recommendations to the Commission on urgent problems in these fields; (b) to perform any other functions which may be entrusted to it by the Economic and Social Council or the Commission on Human Rights.' Previously, the General Assembly adopted, in November, 1946, a unanimous Resolution[25] declaring that ' it is in the highest interests of humanity to put an immediate end to religious and so-called racial persecutions and discrimination ', and calling ' on the governments and responsible authorities to conform both to the letter and to the spirit of the Charter of the United Nations, and to take the most prompt and energetic steps to that end '.

The Sub-Commission is composed of twelve members appointed by the Economic and Social Council subject to the consent of their Governments. In effect, though not in form, the members of the Sub-Commission are representatives of governments—a solution which was criticised, somewhat unexpectedly, by the representatives of Soviet Russia and Czechoslovakia. The work of the Sub-Commission, in conformity with its limited terms of reference, has been advisory and, to a large extent, somewhat theoretical.[26] Thus the main efforts of the Sub-Commission during its first Session in December 1947 were concentrated on considering and proposing amendments to the articles of the Declaration of Human Rights prepared by the Drafting Committee of the Commission on Human Rights.[27] However, the Sub-Commission has tended, not altogether without success, to assert a measure of independence with regard to the implementation of the provisions of any Bill of Rights to be adopted and the examination of complaints of violations of human rights. It succeeded in

[25] No. 103 (1).

[26] In March 1948 the Economic and Social Council requested the Secretary-General to organise studies and prepare analyses designed to assist the Sub-Commission in determining the main types of discrimination in so far as they affect human rights and fundamental freedoms. In the same Resolution the Council advised UNESCO of the interest of the United Nations in effective educational programmes in the field of prevention of discrimination and protection of minorities and suggested co-operation, for that purpose, between the United Nations and UNESCO (Doc. E/749). The Council also requested the Secretary-General to study the question whether and to what extent the treaties relating to international obligations undertaken to combat discrimination and to protect minorities—the so-called Minorities Treaties—should be. regarded as being still in force.

[27] See Doc. E/CM.4/21, Annex F, Articles 6, 13, 15. 28 and 36.

obtaining a decision of the Economic and Social Council, of 1 March, 1948, which gave to the members of the Sub-Commission, with respect to communications bearing on discrimination and minorities, the same facilities as are enjoyed by the members of the Commission.   These facilities, as has been noted above,[28] are of a rudimentary character.   But the innovation is significant. Moreover, the Sub-Commission has considered in detail schemes for the implementation of a Bill of Rights, in particular with regard to non-discrimination and the protection of minorities.[29] Proposals for the investigation of complaints have been discussed by the Sub-Commission.   In December 1947 the Soviet representative on the Sub-Commission proposed, *inter alia,* the consideration of ' the petition presented to the United Nations twice since 1946 by fifteen million Negroes residing in the United States of America, who are subjected to discrimination on racial grounds '.[30]   The proposal was not in harmony with the consistent attitude of Soviet Russia, and the States associated with her, in rejecting any developments said to endanger the sovereignty of States and the exclusiveness of their domestic jurisdiction.[31]   But it revealed the potentialities of the Commission and of its Sub-Commissions in this matter.

(2) The Sub-Commission on Freedom of Information and of the Press was set up at the first Session of the Commission on Human Rights in 1946.   The members of the Sub-Commission were appointed by the Economic and Social Council in the same way as the members of the Sub-Commission on Prevention of Discrimination and the Protection of Minorities.[32] The Council formulated the terms of reference of the Sub-Commission as follows: (a) In the first instance, to examine what rights, obligations and practices should be included in the concept of freedom of information and to report to the Commission on

[28] See pp. 235-237.
[29] See, in particular, the proposal put forward on behalf of India providing for the examination by the organs of the United Nations of complaints of violations of the Bill of Rights and for the creation of a special chamber of the International Court of Justice for these matters (E/CN.4/Sub.2/27). The proposal put forward by the United States was of a somewhat nominal character. It provided for the examination of such complaints only as were made by a Member of the United Nations, or by any of its principal organs, or by a Specialised Agency (E/CN.4/Sub.2/12).
[30] E/CN.4/Sub.2/24.
[31] See below, pp. 298-300.
[32] See above, p. 266.

Human Rights on any issue that may arise from such an examination; (b) to perform any other functions which may be entrusted to it by the Economic and Social Council or by the Commission on Human Rights. The first aspect of the task allocated to the Sub-Commission was clearly of an advisory and deliberative nature. Thus it examined and submitted to the Commission recommendations on the relevant articles of the Declaration of Human Rights and of the draft Covenant on Human Rights.[33] These recommendations, in turn, formed the basis of the recommendations made on this subject by the United Nations Conference on Freedom of Information which took place in 1948.[34] The Sub-Commission also submitted an interim report on the rights, obligations, and practices which should be included in the concept of ' freedom of information '.

The more substantial task of the Sub-Commission consisted in its participation in the preparatory work of the United Nations Conference on Freedom of Information which, in pursuance of a Resolution of the General Assembly of 1947,[35] took place at Geneva from 23 March to 21 April, 1948. The Conference prepared three draft conventions: (1) Draft Convention on the Gathering and International Transmission of News; (2) Draft Convention concerning the Institution of an International Right of Correction; and (3) Draft Convention on Freedom of Information. As a result, the Third General Assembly adopted, in May 1949, the text of a Convention on the International Transmission of News and the Right of Correction. The Convention is of limited compass. The Parties to the Convention agree to

---

[33] Article 18. For the Report of the Sub-Commission see Doc. E/CN.4/80.

[34] Doc. E/CN.4/80. And see below, n. 35.

[35] Resolution 59 (1). The Resolution was as follows: The General Assembly, whereas

Freedom of information is a fundamental human right and is the touchstone of all the freedoms to which the United Nations is consecrated;

Freedom of information implies the right to gather, transmit and publish news anywhere and everywhere without fetters. As such it is an essential factor in any serious effort to promote the peace and progress of the world;

Freedom of information requires as an indispensable element the willingness and capacity to employ its privileges without abuse. It requires as a basic discipline the moral obligation to seek the facts without prejudice and to spread knowledge without malicious intent;

Understanding and co-operation among nations are impossible without an alert and sound world opinion which, in turn, is wholly dependent upon freedom of information:

Resolves therefore, in the spirit of paragraphs 3 and 4 of Article 1 of the Charter, to authorise the holding of a conference of all Members of the United Nations on freedom of information.

expedite, in a manner consistent with their national laws and regulations, the procedure for entry, residence and travel of foreign correspondents nationals of the Contracting Parties; they undertake not to expel foreign correspondents on account of any lawful exercise of their activities; and they agree not to censor outgoing despatches in peace-time except on the ground of national defence. Finally, the Convention provides for an international right of correction ' in cases where a Contracting State contends that a news despatch capable of injuring its relations with other States or its national prestige or dignity transmitted from one country to another by correspondents or information agencies of a Contracting or non-Contracting State and published or disseminated abroad is false or distorted ' (Article 9).

PART THREE

THE INTERNATIONAL BILL OF THE RIGHTS OF MAN

THE PROBLEMS OF THE BILL OF RIGHTS

CHAPTER 13

THE SUBSTANCE AND THE ENFORCEMENT OF THE BILL OF RIGHTS

1. THE PROGRESS OF THE BILL OF RIGHTS WITHIN THE UNITED NATIONS

ALTHOUGH an International Bill of the Rights of Man is not specifically referred to in the Charter, it has been treated as inherent in it. In fact, the proposal for an International Bill of Rights was put forward already in the course of the drafting of the Charter. The proposal was not proceeded with for the reason that it was deemed to require consideration more detailed than was possible during a conference convened for the purpose of drafting the basic instrument of the United Nations.[1] But the Preparatory Commission charged with arranging the programme of the First General Assembly and with setting in motion the work of the United Nations envisaged the preparation of a Bill of Rights as one of the first tasks of the Commission on Human Rights. The first General Assembly endorsed that view. In 1946 the Economic and Social Council put on record the view that 'the purpose of the United Nations with regard to the promotion and the observance of human rights, as defined in the Charter of the United Nations, can only be fulfilled if provisions are made for the implementation of human rights and of an international bill of rights'.[2] In the course of the Second Part of that Assembly general agreement was expressed as to the

[1] See Report of Committee I of Commission I, of 13 June, 1945, I/1/34(1).
[2] *Journal of the Economic and Social Council,* First Year, No. 29, p. 521.

273

importance of proceeding with the drafting of a Bill of Rights.[3]
The General Assembly referred to the Economic and Social
Council, for study by the Commission on Human Rights, a draft
declaration, submitted by the Panamanian delegate,[4] on fundamental human rights and freedoms. With marked restraint the
General Assembly, without fixing any final date, expressed the
hope that the question would be referred back to it in order that
it might be included in the agenda of the next Session.[5]

The Commission on Human Rights itself has treated the
preparation of the Bill of Rights as its principal task in the initial
phase of its activity. After discussing, in January, 1947, the
general features of the Bill, it appointed a committee of its
members charged with the task of preparing a draft of the Bill.
The Drafting Committee met in the same year. It took as the
basis of its discussions a Draft Outline of the Bill prepared by
the Secretariat[6] and a more complete Draft submitted by the
representative of Great Britain. It was unable to produce an
agreed draft, largely owing to differences of opinion on the question whether the Bill ought to be in the nature of a declaration of
principles or a binding and effective international instrument.
It was at that juncture that the notion began to take shape of
solving the difficulties surrounding the adoption of an international Bill of Rights by the device of adopting, in the first
instance, a Declaration the acceptance of which would be secured
by the fact that its provisions were not to be of a binding

---

[3] For the discussion on the subject see *Journal of the General Assembly*. No. 53,
8 December, 1946, pp. 284-289. The following passage from the statement
of M. Pezel, the French representative, is of interest: ' When a modern people
became conscious of its personality and organised its society, it established
the standards of its new life. The United Nations had taken the first step
towards a new life which embraced the whole world. Therefore, the United
Nations had to declare to the knowledge of all men what would be the
standards of their future civic, social and economic life. . . . There was
another compelling reason for the United Nations to take action in this
matter. The human person and human rights had been the first victims of
the fascist régimes. The triumph over Nazi totalitarianism would not be
complete without a declaration that fundamental human rights would be
codified and carried into effect, first under the moral protection of the United
Nations and, at a later stage of their evolution, under their effective guarantee '
(*ibid.*, p. 287).

[4] Doc. A/234.

[5] *Journal of the General Assembly*, No. 75, 15 January, 1947, p. 830.

[6] In its work the Secretariat was assisted by a number of private drafts—in
particular that proposed under the auspices of the American Law Institute.
Use was also made of the draft submitted in the present author's *International Bill of the Rights of Man* (1945).

character.[7] In pursuance of that idea the Committee prepared for the consideration of the full Commission a draft of a Declaration of that nature.

The Report[8] and the Drafts of the Committee were considered in detail by the Commission in the course of December 1947. Its deliberations resulted, in effect, in the final abandonment of the task originally entrusted to it, namely, the drafting of a single International Bill of Human Rights. Instead, it was definitely decided to prepare separate drafts of a Declaration—an instrument not intended to be binding—covering comprehensively a wide range of rights and a so-called Covenant limited in scope and containing only rudimentary provisions of international supervision and enforcement. In addition, a small Committee of the Commission sitting at the same time—the Working Group on Implementation—prepared a detailed report on Implementation, *i.e.*, on the methods of giving effect to the international guarantees of the observance of the Bill of Rights.[9] The Commission, after detailed discussion, provisionally adopted drafts of a Declaration and a Covenant for submission to

[7] Suggestions were also made—and appropriately discarded—for solving the difficult problems of the contents and the enforcement of the Bill of Rights by adopting a Declaration—not binding as such and not enforceable—to be followed, if agreement could be reached, by separate conventions embodying the various rights recognised in the Declaration. The drawback of that method is that it would result in the unedifying spectacle of the fundamental rights of man being made the object of isolated treaties concluded by a limited number of States and subject to termination and the other vicissitudes to which treaties are liable, and ratified, hesitatingly and spasmodically, by an even smaller number—an undignified anti-climax to the solemn proclamation of human rights and to what ought to have been a decisive landmark in the history of freedom. The analogy, apparently relied upon by the adherents of this proposal, with the multifarious conventions concluded under the auspices of the International Labour Organisation is inappropriate. The natural rights and freedoms of man are not in the same category as his interest, great as that is, in the conclusion of the Convention on the Maintenance of Migrants' Pensions Rights, 1935, or on Reduction of Hours of Work in Glass Bottle Works, 1935, or on Recruiting of Indigenous Workers, 1936, and other even more important conventions respecting the conditions of work. It will also be observed that the ratification of these Conventions has been far from general. With insignificant exceptions they have not been ratified by the majority of States. The average number of ratifications of the thirty International Labour Conventions between 1930 and 1940 does not exceed eight. There is little persuasive force in the suggestion that the moral attraction of conventions on international human rights will be so irresistible as to make their general ratification probable.

[8] For the Report of the Drafting Committee see Doc. E/CN.4/21.

[9] The report of the Commission containing Draft Articles for an International Declaration on Human Rights, Draft Articles for an International Covenant on Human Rights and the Report of the Working Group on Implementation are contained in Doc. E/800 and in *Economic and Social Council, Official Records, Third Year, Sixth Session*, Suppl. No. 1 (1948).

Governments with the view to obtaining their comments.   It decided merely to take note of the more drastic report of the Working Group on Implementation [10] and reserved the matter for further discussion.   In June 1948 the Commission, after receiving the report of the Drafting Committee on the Declaration, finally adopted a Draft of the Declaration for submission to the Economic and Social Council.   It also decided to forward to the Council the draft of the Covenant adopted in 1947 and to continue the study of the question of implementation.   The Council found no time to examine either the Declaration or the Covenant, but decided that the Draft of the Declaration be submitted to the next Session of the General Assembly, which met in Paris in September.   The Third Committee of the Assembly devoted practically all its time to an examination of the draft and submitted it to the General Assembly, which adopted it, without dissent, by forty-eight votes (with nine States abstaining). The character and the significance of the Declaration are discussed elsewhere in this book, where it is submitted that the Declaration is an instrument which does not possess—and does not purport to possess—legal force or authority and that its moral significance is controversial.[11]

During its session in May and June, 1949, the Commission completed the Draft of most of the articles of the proposed Covenant on Human Rights, and decided to submit it to Governments for observations.[12]   It also prepared, for the same purpose, a questionnaire on implementation accompanied by proposals submitted in the matter by various Governments represented on the Commission.   The Commission decided that, after having received the answers and comments of Governments, it would present the complete Covenant to the Economic and Social Council in time for submission to the General Assembly in 1950.

2.   THE ' COVENANT ' OF HUMAN RIGHTS.

The various proposals for a ' Covenant ' of Human Rights, the Covenant itself when adopted, the Universal Declaration on Human Rights, and similar drafts and instruments must be

[10] See below, p. 386.
[11] See below, pp. 394-428.
[12] For the report of the Commission see Doc. E/1371; E/CN.4/350.

regarded as stages in the adoption of an International Bill of Human Rights conceived as an effective part of the law of nations commensurate with the ideals of the Charter, the enduring aspirations of mankind and the requirements of international peace. In the meantime, it is convenient, in order to gain a picture of the problems besetting the International Bill of Human Rights and of the position reached in the initial period of the effort to achieve it, to give an account of the main features of the proposed Covenant in the form in which, in 1949, it was submitted for consideration by Governments.[12a]   In the introductory Part of the Draft provision was made for the incorporation of the obligations of the Covenant as part of municipal law, and tentative articles were drafted for a rudimentary measure of enforcement.[13]   The substantive part of the Draft included Articles on the right to life, prohibition of torture and cruel punishment, prohibition of physical mutilation or compulsory 'medical or scientific experimentation' (an article which the Commission decided to refer to the World Health Organisation for an 'Advisory Opinion'), prohibition of slavery and forced labour, freedom from arbitrary arrest (an article not voted upon in view of the absence of agreement on the previous article, relating to the suppression of constitutional guarantees, which, in turn, was deemed to be connected with the question of enforcement the consideration of which was postponed), prohibition of imprisonment for non-compliance with contractual obligations, the right of free movement within the State and the right to leave it and return to it, expulsion of aliens, certain safeguards in criminal trials, including the prohibition of retroactive operation of criminal laws, the right 'to recognition as a person before the law', freedom of religion, freedom of speech, assembly and association, and equality before the law and freedom from discrimination.   The principal Article in the concluding Part of the Draft limited the obligations of Federal States to matters subject to federal jurisdiction.[14]   The Draft Covenant did not contain articles bearing either on the political

[12a] For a lucid analysis of some of the provisions of the proposed Covenant see Fawcett in *Law and Contemporary Problems* (Duke University Law School. 14 (1949, No. 3)). See also *ibid.*, Hyman on the constitutional aspects of the Covenant.

[13] See below, pp. 359-361.

[14] See below, p. 359.

right to government by consent [15] or on social and economic rights. With regard to the latter, the Commission adopted a somewhat contradictory Resolution recognising the necessity of including these rights in the Covenant and requesting the Economic and Social Council to request the Security Council to prepare a survey of the activities of various specialised agencies in the field in order to enable the Commission to determine whether these subjects shall be included in the Covenant or in later conventions.[16]

The Commission also approved a lengthy questionnaire on the international supervision and guarantees of the observance of the Covenant by way of complaints of Governments and petitions of individuals and private groups and organisations; on the setting up of an international court of human rights; and on the powers of the various organs of the United Nations in this respect. It postponed the consideration of an Article adopted in a previous report and containing a guarantee of a highly rudimentary nature. That Article provided: ' On receipt of a request to this effect from the Secretary-General of the United Nations made under the authority of a resolution of the General Assembly, the Government of any party to this Covenant shall supply an explanation as to the manner in which the law of that State gives effect to any provisions of this Covenant.' [17] It also adopted provisionally [18] an Article laying down that in time of war or other public emergency a State may take measures derogating from its obligations under the Covenant to an extent strictly limited by the exigencies of the situation; that no derogation from some, as yet unspecified, articles of the Covenant shall be permissible; and that a State availing itself of the right of derogation shall inform fully the Secretary-General of the measures taken, the reasons thereof, and the cessation of these measures. In addition, various States or groups of States submitted their own proposals for implementation.   These included a proposal by Australia— studiously elaborate in detail but incomplete and contradictory in its crucial aspect—for the setting up of an International Court

[15] Significantly, a proposal to that effect came from Soviet Russia. See below, p. 283.
[16] E/CN.4/350, pp. 14, 15.
[17] Article 3.
[18] ' Pending the completion of its work on Part II (the substantive articles) of the Covenant.' In turn, some of the Articles of Part II were adopted provisionally ' until a final vote had been taken on Article 4 '.

of Human Rights[19]; a proposal by India for the establishment
of a Committee of independent persons empowered, *inter alia*, to
receive and investigate petitions from individuals and to report to
the Commission on Human Rights cases in which its efforts to
settle the grievance by negotiation with the Governments
concerned had not been successful (it will be noted that the
Commission, according to its ruling which was still in force at
that time, had no power to take action on petitions)[20]; a much
wider proposal submitted by France for a Special Commission
having jurisdiction to hear petitions by both States and private
individuals and organisations and empowered to make recommendations to the Contracting Parties;[21] and by the United States
and the United Kingdom for the setting up of a committee
appointed by States for receiving complaints of States and
reporting to the Secretary-General on the results of its findings.[22]
The measure of disagreement on the crucial question of implementation was shown by the fact that on the question of
admissibility of petitions by private individuals the Commission
was equally divided.[23]

What is the explanation of the fact that the only result, in
the period under review, of a considerable effort centring round
an International Bill of Human Rights was a Declaration, without
legal force and of controversial moral authority, and the incomplete project of a Bill of Rights limited in scope, defective in
formulation, and lacking in any measure of agreement with
regard to some of the essential aspects of enforcement? One
explanation of that negative result was the failure to realise
the magnitude and unprecedented difficulty of the problem—a
lack of appreciation combined with the determination to show a
semblance of results after years of considerable effort on a matter
which international public opinion associated with the fulfilment
of the highest hopes of a new era. That determination was not

[19] See below, p. 308.
[20] See below, p. 307.
[21] See below, p. 307.
[22] See below, p. 289.
[23] The States voting in favour of a resolution laying down that the right of
petition by individuals, groups, and organisations should be recognised forth-
with in the Covenant were: Australia, Denmark, France, Guatemala, India,
Lebanon, the Philippines and Uruguay. Those voting against were: China,
Egypt, Iran, the Ukraine, the Union of Soviet Socialist Republics, the United
Kingdom, the United States and Yugoslavia—a significant alignment of
opinion.

always wholly divorced from considerations of domestic policy in some States. It was stimulated by the ease with which the language of international pronouncements lends itself to the enunciation of results and agreements which are more apparent than real. There was also insistence on the view, which is entitled to respect, that progress, however modest and nominal, is preferable to no progress at all. That view is open to the retort that purely nominal measures which create an unwarranted appearance of success are inimical both to progress and to international morality. Above all, such apparent solutions have the unavoidable effect of concealing the true difficulties of the problems involved. These difficulties must be faced with regard both to the contents of the Bill of Rights and to its enforcement.

3. The Contents of the Bill of Rights.

In assessing the difficulties connected with the question of the scope of rights to be protected by an International Bill of Human Rights there must be borne in mind the cardinal fact that these are not confined to the personal rights of freedom traditionally associated with Bills of Rights. There are three categories of rights, all of which are the legitimate—and imperative—object of international recognition and protection.

There are, in the first instance, what may be described as personal rights. These have traditionally formed part of bills of rights within the State. Most of them are accepted by civilised States. They are non-controversial so long as no attempt is made to regulate them in exhaustive detail in a manner providing for all contingencies [24] or aiming at solving general problems of social and political philosophy.[25] They include the right to life and

[24] See below, pp. 329-333.
[25] The Commission on Human Rights was confronted, at the very outset of its task of drafting the Bill of Human Rights, with attempts of this nature. Thus the representative of Uruguay demanded that the right of citizenship should be extended so as to grant to human beings a certain degree of world citizenship and ' to offer the individual the possibility of participating personally in the international organisation of the Community of Nations ' (5 February, 1947, E/CN.4/SR/14, p. 2). The Lebanese representative urged the adoption of the following principles: 1, The human being is more important than the racial, national, or other group to which he may belong; 2, The human person's most sacred and inviolable possessions are his mind and his conscience, enabling him to perceive the truth, to choose freely, and to exist; 3, Any social pressure on the part of the State, religion or race, involving the automatic consent of the human person is reprehensible; 4, The social group to which the individual belongs may, like the human person himself, be wrong or right: the person alone is the judge (*ibid.*, p. 3). The British representative, a distinguished Trade Union leader, remarked, with reference

inviolability of the person; freedom of speech, opinion, religion, association and assembly; sanctity of the home and secrecy of correspondence; freedom from arbitrary arrest; proper safeguards in criminal trials; equality before the law; and freedom from discrimination on account of religion, race, ethnical origin and political opinion. Other personal rights such as the right to a nationality, to asylum, and to emigration have been controversial. Yet it is doubtful whether they can be omitted from an international bill of rights without detracting from its essential purpose. But the feature common to all these rights is that they are, in general, capable of judicial enforcement in the national and international spheres. If an international Bill of Rights could be confined to the sphere of personal rights, the problem would be substantially simplified. The question is whether it is possible, consistently with the true purpose and the dignity of the Bill, to simplify it in that manner.

In particular—and this brings us to the second category of rights—can a Bill of Rights disregard the political rights of freedom, *i.e.,* the fundamental right of man to government by consent—the right to be governed by persons freely chosen by him, accountable to him and replaceable by him in free, periodic and secret elections, which means in effect the right to government based on democracy in the accepted sense? Without an effective guarantee of these political rights of freedom, personal freedom and equality before the law must be, at best, precarious; at worst they may be meaningless. Unless a Bill of Rights provides safeguards against dictatorship and tyranny, it must to a large extent fail in its purpose. The insistence on an International Bill of

to the suggestion of the Lebanese representative, that in organised society it was not possible to prevent groups from exercising a certain pressure upon individuals and suggested that this was the price to be paid for freedom of association (*ibid.,* p. 4). The Commission discussed at some length the question whether the Bill of Rights should include a statement of the duties of the individual. The Russian representative reminded the Commission of Article 12 of the Soviet Constitution which lays down that work is ' a duty and honour for every able-bodied citizen, in accordance with the principle: no work, no food '. He asked that the Bill should include the obligation of the individual to work for the community ' by which he meant his country as well as the United Nations ' (*ibid.,* p. 3). The French representative proceeded to draw from this the conclusion that parallel with a list of the rights of the individual the Declaration ought to draw up a list of the rights of the community (*ibid.,* p. 5). Similarly detailed consideration was given to the necessity of affirming the right to existence. While the French representative thought it fundamental to affirm that right expressly, the Australian representative regarded it as unnecessary seeing that it is a right recognised by the law of all States (4 February, 1947, E/CN.4/SR/13).

Rights and the proclamation of the enthronement of the rights of man as a major purpose of the Second World War were prompted by the experience of dictatorships the essence of which was the denial of the political right of freedom. The contempt for personal rights of freedom was, in those countries, a corollary of the major evil of tyranny. In so far as political freedom expresses itself in freedom of criticism, of opinion, of speech, of assembly and association and in freedom from discrimination on account of political views, it falls within the first category of rights described above and as such is capable of enforcement by judicial and similar means.

There is no intrinsic reason why the right to free, secret and periodic elections should not be similarly recognised by law and declared enforceable. The Bill of Rights enacted in 1947 by the Canadian Province of Saskatchewan provides that 'every qualified voter resident in Saskatchewan shall enjoy the right to exercise freely his franchise in all elections and shall possess the right to require that no legislative assembly shall continue for a period in excess of five years'.[26] The Bill enacts penalties for and remedies against the violation of that, as well as of its other provisions. In most countries the law provides for judicial and other safeguards of the exercise of the right of suffrage and of integrity of elections;[27] it also regulates the duration of the life of the legislature. Numerous recent constitutions contain provisions to a similar effect.[28]

While there is thus no warrant for assuming that no judicial

[26] Article 7. For the text of the Bill see *United Nations Year Book on Human Rights*, 1947, p. 73.

[27] See, for instance, in Great Britain the Representation of the People Acts of 1918 and 1928 and the judicial safeguards of the right to be put on the election register, with the right of appeal from a decision of the registration officer to the County Court and, on point of law, with a further right of appeal to the Court of Appeal. And see the early case of *Ashby* v. *White* (1703), 2 Lord Raymond, 938; K. & L. 72, where it was decided that the unjustifiable refusal to accept the vote of a person who is on the register is an infringement of the right of property. In France 'le contentieux de l'opération électorale', described by a competent authority as ' simple, rapide, sans frais', abounds in judicial safeguards culminating in a well defined jurisdiction of the Court of Cassation. See Duez, *Traité élémentaire de droit constitutionnel* (1926), pp. 383-391. As to the United States see in particular the well known case of *Nixon* v. *Condon*, 286 U.S. 73; 52 Sup. Ct. 484, where the Supreme Court applied the provisions of the Fourteenth Amendment in order to prevent the disfranchisement of Negroes as the result of the machinery of primary elections. And see below, p. 361, n. 11.

[28] See, for instance, Article 132 of the Constitution of the Republic of China of 1 January, 1947, which lays down that suits arising out of elections shall be tried by a court of law.

remedies are possible for the enforcement of the right to government by consent and that at least some of these remedies are not capable of judicial application in the international sphere, it is clear that the international guarantee of that right cannot be primarily of a judicial character. The international guarantee of the democratic form of government—it would be nothing else than that—would operate primarily through organs which are non-judicial in character. For in no other sphere is it possible for a régime so minded to disregard the purpose and spirit of the law while paying homage to its letter. It is of interest to note that while the draft of the so-called Covenant put forward by the Commission on Human Rights contained no reference to government by consent, the Government of Soviet Russia proposed the addition of the following article: 'Every citizen, irrespective of race, colour, language, religion or sex, shall be guaranteed by the State an opportunity to take part in the government of the State, to elect and to be elected to all organs of authority on the basis of universal, equal and direct suffrage with secret ballot, and to occupy any State or public office. Property, educational or other qualifications restricting the participation of citizens in voting at elections to representative organs shall be abolished.'[29] The nature of the international non-political organ primarily entrusted with the task of securing the observance of the Bill of Rights is discussed below.[30] In fact, the fulfilment of some such function as the supervision of the clauses of the Bill relating to government by consent is one of the principal motives of the proposal, put forward in this book, for an organ of that character as distinguished from a purely judicial agency.[31]

The factor which in the past has led many, including the author of the present book, to urge an alternative protection,[32] by way of international guarantees, of the political rights of

---

[29] Doc. E/CN.4/350, p. 47. In this, as in other matters, the insistence by the Soviet Government on the detailed directives to be given to the State in the Bill of Rights was accompanied by a determined refusal to acquiesce in any measure of international guarantee or supervision to ensure the fulfilment of these directives. And see below, pp. 288-300.

[30] See below, pp. 373-381.

[31] See below, p. 377.

[32] This was the approach adopted in my book entitled *International Bill of the Rights of Man* (1945), where the relevant article of the draft there proposed provided in a somewhat dialectical fashion for the ' effective right of citizens to choose their governments and legislators on a footing of equality, *in accordance with the law of the State*, in free, secret, and periodic elections '.

freedom—as well as the reasons which have led others to ignore that right altogether—has been the belief that in that way it may be possible to secure adherence to a universal bill of rights on the part of States possessing a totalitarian form of government diametrically opposed to prevalent conceptions of democracy. That hope is probably unlikely to materialise. Moreover, it must remain a matter of controversy whether considerations of this nature are such as can legitimately be taken into account. However that may be, the difficulty cannot be solved by way of recognising the right to government by consent in a Declaration which is not legally binding and ignoring it in an instrument which purports to impose binding obligations. Yet this is the solution which has been attempted. In the Universal Declaration of Human Rights adopted in 1948,[33] it is laid down in Article 21: 'The will of the people shall be the basis of the authority of government; this will shall be expressed in periodic and genuine elections which shall be by universal and equal suffrage and shall be held by secret vote or by equivalent free voting procedures.' No reference is made to the subject in the various drafts of the so-called Covenant on Human Rights.

Similar considerations apply to the third category of rights, which for the sake of convenience may be referred to as social and economic rights. They include the right to social security, the right to work under fair and just conditions, the right to equality of educational opportunity, and the like. These claims did not figure prominently in the traditional bills of rights. They are enumerated at considerable length and with much elaboration in modern constitutions. In some constitutions—as, for instance, that adopted by France in 1946—they are the subject of an express guarantee by the nation.[34] There has been a wide and growing acceptance of the view that personal and political freedom is impaired—if not rendered purely nominal—unless its enjoyment is made practicable by a reasonable guarantee of social and economic freedom. According to that view, which is fully

[33] See below, p. 394.
[34] The Preamble to the Constitution provides: ' . . . The nation ensures to the individual and the family the conditions necessary to their development. It guarantees to all, and notably to the child, the mother and the aged worker, protection of health, material security, rest and leisure. Every human being who, because of his age, his physical or mental condition, or because of the economic situation, finds himself unable to work, has the right to obtain from the community the means to lead a decent existence.'

entitled to respect, the precious rights of personal liberty and political freedom may become a hollow mockery for those whom the existing social and economic order leaves starving, insecure in their livelihood, illiterate, and deprived of their just share in the progress and well-being of the society as a whole. An International Bill of Rights which leaves these human claims out of account is incomplete to a degree which, in the view of many, is fatal to the authority and dignity of the enactment as a whole.

At the same time it is difficult to deny that social and economic rights cannot be made part of the enforceable law in the same way as other rights. They are not so, as a rule,[35] within the State. Undoubtedly States have enacted legislation on such matters as security of employment, the minimum wage, paid holidays, and the safeguarding, in various fields, of decent conditions of work for men and women. Legislation has occasionally been enacted depriving the employer of the right of arbitrary dismissal. But these benefits are seldom due to enforceable general clauses of t e Constitution. They are due to specific legislation. In

[35] But only as a rule. The Saskatchewan Bill of Rights of 1947 provides, in Article 19 (1), that ' every person and every class of persons shall enjoy the right to education in any school, college, university or other institution or p.ace of learning, vocational training or apprenticeship without discrimination because of the race, creed, religion, colour or ethnic or national origin of such person or class of persons '. Article 16 provides for a remedy in the Court of King's Bench, brought by any person against the persons responsible for the deprivation, abridgment or other restriction of the rights guaranteed by the Bill.

In general, in that sphere, Bills of Rights within the State have been a solemn declaration of purpose and an enunciation of the legal and political basis of the life of the community without being accompanied by any provision for enforcement. Of these, the French Declaration of 1789 is the typical example. It has remained part of the French constitution without visibly occupying a prominent place in the daily administration of justice. It has not been invoked as a check upon legislation or a direct source of legal rights and remedies enforceable by courts. But it has underlain much of the development of French law since the Revolution. The *Code Civil* and the mass of legislation engrafted upon it have been in many respects a conscious attempt to translate into practice the principles of the Declaration. (See for a graphic account of this process Ripert, *Le régime démocratique et le droit civil moderne* (1936), pp. 69-130.) The elaborate provisions of Part II of the German Constitution of 1919 bearing upon the Fundamental Rights and Duties of Germans are in the same category. Maxims such as that ' the organisation of economic life must correspond to the principles of justice and be designed to ensure for all a life worthy of human beings ' (Article 151) were not intended to, and could not in the nature of things, be the subject of enforcement by courts. The same applies to the detailed social and economic provisions in numerous recent constitutions. (See the valuable volume published in 1944 by the International Labour Office and entitled ' Constitutional Provisions concerning Social and Economic Policy '.)

general, even within the State social and economic rights in their totality cannot be expressed in the Constitution in such a way as to provide remedies directly enforceable by courts. The same applies to an International Bill of Rights. Moreover, in that particular sphere the international judicial enforcement of an international enactment, in relation to States of differing economic structure, standards of life and cultural tradition, is probably impracticable. That does not mean that the recognition of these rights in an international instrument must be reduced to a mere declaration which is not legally binding upon States or that it must be ignored altogether. The difficulty surrounding this problem can be solved by giving to social and economic claims a place in an enforceable bill of rights without making such enforcement primarily judicial in character.[36] The obligations of the Bill of Rights in this respect can be made real inasmuch as they will constitute a legal obligation of the State—an obligation subject to international interest, to discussion and recommendation by international agencies and, in case of grave and persistent violations and neglect, to appropriate international action. The very fact that within the State constitutional provisions and clauses of Bills of Rights in the matter of social and economic rights must be predominantly in the nature of a declaration of principle renders international guarantees and remedies—not necessarily judicial—proper and imperative.

4. ENFORCEMENT OF THE INTERNATIONAL BILL OF RIGHTS. THE RIGHT OF PETITION

The preceding consideration of the contents of the Bill of Rights—especially in relation to rights of political freedom and to social and economic rights—brings into prominence the second crucial question of the Bill of Rights, namely, the question of enforcement. Unless it is realised that, in addition to any judicial organ that may be created, the Bill of Rights must provide for an agency—a Commission or Council—of a different character, these problems of the contents of the Bill of Rights will be insoluble. That subject is discussed in the following Section of this book, which contains a draft of a pro-

[36] For an elaboration of this point see below, pp. 355, 377.

posed Bill of Rights and comment thereon.[37]   In that Section, too, there will be found a discussion of national measures of enforcement, for—as pointed out there [38]—preoccupation with international guarantees ought not to obscure the fact that the main agency for enforcing the Bill of Rights must be the State and its organs.   In the present context we are concerned with what appears to be the most controversial aspect of enforcement in the international sphere, namely, the question whether individuals and private bodies and organisations should be granted the right to bring petitions and institute proceedings before international organs entrusted with jurisdiction in the matter of human rights.   The degree of divergence of views in the matter is illustrated by the fact that the Commission on Human Rights was equally divided on the subject.[39]   The importance of the right of petition by individuals and its place in relation to the powers and duties of the Commission on Human Rights have been surveyed in the preceding Part of this book,[40] and much that is said there applies also to the Bill of Rights.

Unless an effective right of petition—which means a right of petition coupled with the right to have it investigated with the view to such action being taken upon it as is necessary—is granted to individuals concerned or to bodies acting on their behalf, any international remedy that may be provided will be deficient in its vital aspect.   The denial, to individuals affected, of the right of direct access to international agencies is tantamount to a withdrawal, to a large extent, of the principal benefit conferred by the Bill.   It wholly disregards the enhanced stature of the individual which follows naturally from an enactment of that kind.   It is rooted in the rigid notion of the individual conceived as a mere object of international law.[41] Moreover, in so far as the object of that limitation is to safeguard the sovereignty and dignity of the States concerned, it is unlikely to achieve that object.

If the right of bringing complaints on account of the violation of the Bill of Rights is limited to States parties to the Bill of

[37] See below, p. 373.
[38] See below, p. 356.
[39] See above, p. 279.
[40] See above, pp. 244-251.
[41] See above, p. 7.

Rights,[42] the individual will have no redress unless he petitions a foreign State and enlists its active support to the point of bringing a complaint against the offending State. In what ways and by what devious methods of persuasion shall he attempt to obtain the assistance of that foreign State or States? Are we entitled to exclude the possibility that their attention will be effectively solicited only when their interests are at stake—it being either some direct interest or the indirect interest of embarrassing a foreign Government?[43] Or is it the underlying assumption of any such scheme that the interest of the foreign friendly State or States ought to be enlisted only if the violations of the rights of the individual are on such a scale and of such enormity as to warrant the action of foreign States, and that single violations of individual rights, however outrageous, are of no consequence? If that is so, what becomes of the sanctity of the rights of the individual which the Covenant is supposed to uphold? Are we to renounce the principle that a fundamental right of a single individual is as absolute and as sacrosanct as aggregates of rights of aggregates of persons?

Neither is it easy to see how the sovereignty and dignity of the signatories of the Bill can be better safeguarded by the elimination of the petition by the individual and the substitution for it of a procedure initiated by a State. In the case of a petition by an individual the complaint remains as a rule within the orbit of a grievance which can be redressed by appropriate judicial or administrative remedies. When the same case is taken up by a State, the complaint assumes immediately a political complexion. The original nature of the issue becomes obliterated

[42] See below, p. 290.
[43] The following extract included in a report submitted in 1926 by Sr. de Mello Franco, the Brazilian representative, to the Council of the League of Nations is relevant: ' Owing to the fact that the members of the Council are delegates of the Governments of States represented on the Council of the League of Nations, and that these members for this reason look at matters from a political point of view, each decision to intervene in a minorities question will necessarily by its nature have the character of a political act influenced by factors hostile to another State. . . . The members of the Council will, for this reason, endeavour as far as possible to put on one side complaints which are addressed to them ' (*Official Journal*, 1926, p. 138). When the Minorities Treaties were being drafted in 1919 some delegates, in particular Lord Robert Cecil, urged that individuals and groups of individuals whose rights under the treaties had been violated should be given the status of a party before the Permanent Court of International Justice. See Robinson and others, *Were the Minorities Treaties a Failure?* (1943), p. 137.

by considerations and stratagems of international politics. Is it more conducive to the preservation of the sovereignty and dignity of a State if a complaint concerning the treatment of an individual or of a group of individuals is brought by a foreign State rather than by the person or persons concerned? It may be argued that foreign States will refrain from pressing unduly numerous individual cases. That argument is controversial. Or is it to become a test of the friendliness of a Signatory State whether it refrains from taking up charges of violation of the Covenant? It is an illusion to assume that petty, ill-founded, or malevolent petitions can come only from individuals and not from Governments. Governments, if they are so minded, can press unfounded complaints with a frequency and persistency commensurate with the vastness of the resources available to a State. It would thus appear that the elimination of private petitions will not necessarily achieve the purpose of preventing complaints which are unfounded or malicious. On the other hand, in so far as it will accomplish the object of stifling—as the result of the connivance, complicity, servility or indifference of foreign Governments—such petitions as merit attention and examination, it will stultify the principle of implementation. The insistence on the right of the individual to lodge petitions is due to factors more real than any supposedly purely academic emphasis on the status of the individual as a subject of international law. It is due to a practical assessment of the merits of the procedure initiated by individuals as compared with that of governmental authorities. The organisation of such a procedure raises issues of great complexity. They are capable of a solution more reasonable, more just and in the long run more practicable than reliance upon the restrained attitude of friendly Governments.

These objections to the exclusion of the right of individuals to initiate proceedings before international organs apply even more strongly in relation to the proposals in which the international organ in question is not a court or another body of persons independent of Governments, but the Governments themselves. This was the proposal put forward in 1949 jointly by Great Britain and the United States in connection with the so-called Covenant.[44] It was proposed there that if a State Party

---

[44] E/CN.4/350, p. 80.

to the Covenant considers that another Party is not giving effect to its provisions it may bring the matter to the attention of that State, and if the matter ' is not adjusted between them ' within six months either State may bring it before a Human Rights Committee. Thus a breach—or alleged breach—of the Covenant was to become the subject-matter of a dispute between States. The institution of proceedings, their conduct and their continuation before the Committee were left to the discretion of Governments. The proposed Committee was to be set up from a panel of persons designated by States Parties to the Covenant to serve in their personal capacity.[45] It was proposed that each Committee shall establish its own procedure; that, apparently, only the States concerned shall have the right to make submissions to it orally or in writing; that its hearings and other meetings shall be in closed session; that the State concerned shall supply the Committee with information on the subject of the dispute; and that the Committee shall within six months report its findings to the States concerned and to the Secretary-General of the United Nations for publication.[46]

Considerations connected with the dignity of sovereign States and the traditional conception of the inferior status of the individual have not been the only reason which has prompted the negative attitude of Governments to the question of the right of petition by individuals.   The other—and perhaps equally important—reason has been the apprehension that the international organ concerned, whether it be a court or other agency, would be flooded by a mass of petitions, some of them paltry, uninformed or malicious, with the result that its work would be made impracticable. These fears are largely hypothetical, exaggerated and probably unfounded.[47]   It has been shown in

----

[45] Each Party to the Covenant was to nominate to the panel, for a period of five years, two of its nationals ' of high moral character and of suitable ability and qualifications '. It was proposed that ' upon notice being given to the Secretary-General, a Human Rights Committee shall be established of five members selected from the panel, one member by the State or States referring the matter, one member by the other States and three by agreement between them ' and that ' if any place on the Committee has not been filled within three months, the Secretary-General shall select a person from the panel to fill it '.

[46] It was also proposed that the Committee may ask the United Nations Commission on Human Rights to request the International Court of Justice for an advisory opinion on legal questions.

[47] See below, p. 375.

another Section of this book, in connexion with the discussion of the competence of the Commission on Human Rights, that the question of petitions by individuals is essentially a matter of machinery.[48] The work of the Trusteeship Council has shown that there is no difficulty in relieving the international organ concerned, at an early stage and without any technical embarrassment, of any accumulation of petitions which do not merit detailed examination.[49] The creation of adequate machinery doubtless constitutes a problem which is serious and intricate in many respects, but we are not at liberty to permit the fundamental right of petition to founder on the rock of that difficulty. The provision of a non-judicial organ as the normal instrument for acting on petitions in the first instance will be a substantial factor in solving a problem the dimensions of which can easily be exaggerated. A Bill of Human Rights from the international enforcement of which the individual human being—its exclusive beneficiary—has been eliminated, will be lacking, from the very outset, both in effectiveness and in moral authority.

5. The Enforcement of the International Bill of Rights. The International Judicial Determination of Human Rights

Similar considerations apply to the question of recourse of individuals to international courts for the protection of their rights under the Bill of Rights. In the matter of the fundamental rights of man the remedy is not complete—it is defective—unless in the last resort a judicial remedy is available. Limitations— of the kind discussed elsewhere in this book [50]—of resort to judicial protection may be necessary in the initial stages of the international supervision of the observance of human rights, but the reasons and the degree of such limitations require exacting proof. Their principal justification must be mainly their temporary character and the desirability of protecting international judicial agencies themselves. But that task, in turn, must be fulfilled by an organ which, although not judicial, is not a committee sitting behind closed doors and which is inaccessible to the individual. That organ must itself be of such authority as to

[48] See above, pp. 229-241.
[49] See above, pp. 242-244.
[50] See below, pp. 373-378, 381-387.

inspire confidence. Neither must it be given the power to deny
the right to a judicial remedy except in cases so compelling as
to enable it to reach a decision to that effect by a substantial
majority of its members. Moreover, the difficulties militating
against the jurisdiction of an international court of a universal
character do not, as will be shown,[51] apply with equal force to a
regional court or a tribunal to which only a limited number
of States are parties. The paramount factor in the situation
is the fundamental character of the right to a judicial determination of the fundamental rights of man.

6. THE ENFORCEMENT OF THE INTERNATIONAL BILL OF RIGHTS.
   THE NATURE OF INTERNATIONAL SANCTIONS.

The purpose of international sanctions in the matter of human
rights must be primarily remedial. It is only in the last resort
and in extreme cases that they need to be thought of as punitive.
The fact that they must be principally of a remedial nature
signifies that the term 'enforcement', although accurate, need
not be understood as implying, normally, the employment of
physical force or other drastic method of compulsion. Enforcement in this connexion means international action aiming at
securing the observance of the obligations of the Bill of Rights.
Such action includes, in the first instance, investigation of complaints, whether brought by States or individuals, of violations of
the Bill of Rights. It must comprise, secondly, general supervision—independent of petitions and under the responsibility of
the international agency concerned acting on its own information
—of the observance of the clauses of the Bill. Thirdly, it must
include efforts at remedying by conciliation and persuasion such
violations of the Bill of Rights as investigation may reveal to
have taken place. It comprises, fourthly, either the judgment
of a court or the finding and recommendation of a non-judicial
body which is legally binding upon the signatories of the Bill
of Rights. A finding which, if amounting to an ascertainment
of a breach of the Bill of Rights, is not accompanied by a legally
binding recommendation of appropriate action on the part of
the State concerned, is a deficient method of enforcing the Bill
of Rights. It leaves open to the State in question the plausible

[51] See below, pp. 453-456. And see pp. 381-387.

faculty of putting its own interpretation on the results of the investigation or adducing its own excuses for avoiding requisite action. A State which flouts public opinion by action found contrary to the Bill of Rights will have no hesitation in persevering in its attitude by dint of specious and righteous appeals to a variety of arguments. There is for that reason a decisive disadvantage in any proposals—such as those put forward in 1949 by the United States and Great Britain as well as by other States [52]— which limit the part of the international organs concerned to a mere ascertainment of facts or which fail to provide for the binding character of recommendations made by them. It is illogical—as it is inconsistent with the authority of the Bill of Rights—to adopt the Bill as a legal obligation and to decline, at the same time, to accept the legal duty to act upon the finding of the bodies whose function is to assist in giving effect to them. Admittedly, it is arguable that even with regard to findings and recommendations which are legally binding the main sanction continues to lie with public opinion, but there is an essential difference in the effectiveness, even in relation to public opinion, of a pronouncement which is legally binding and one which is not—just as there is a difference in the refusal to abide by a judgment of the International Court of Justice and the failure to act upon an Advisory Opinion given by it. Moreover, a legally binding pronouncement can, when disregarded, be made the starting point for more compelling measures of coercion.

In this connexion reference must be made to the sanction of expulsion from the United Nations such as has been occasionally proposed in connexion with the Bill of Rights. The narrow limits of the effectiveness of that sanction are determined by the fact that a State which has violated the obligations of the Bill on a scale so vast as to bring upon itself the penalty of expulsion will pay little attention to public disapproval and condemnation implied in that sanction. It does not offer a remedy for particular violations, however serious and repulsive, of human rights. The penalty

---

[52] According to the British-American proposal the Committee shall within six months of its first meeting report ' its findings of fact ' to the States concerned and to the Secretary-General for publication. Apparently, unlike in the French proposal, the Committee was to have no power of recommendation. It was confined to ' fact finding '—a limitation which it is not easy to understand seeing that the facts relating to alleged breaches of the Bill will not as a rule be in dispute. The question will be whether the action of the State is in accordance with the Bill of Rights.

of expulsion will apply, as a rule, to cumulative violations of human rights on a large scale.[53] But no true progress is likely in the effective protection of human rights until it becomes axiomatic that there must be a remedy for grave violations of the rights and the dignity of man, of the individual man—and not only for outrages *en masse*. Moreover, expulsion is not a remedy for a wrong; it is a sanction, of dubious effectiveness, which may perpetuate the wrong. Upon analysis, expulsion from the United Nations as a penalty for the violation of obligations in the matter of human rights means release from these obligations. Assuming that the Bill of Rights is permitted to operate within the United Nations, the more effective remedy would be to expel the offending State from membership of the specialised agencies, such as the International Postal Union, and other organisations operating under the ægis of the United Nations. Formal penalties are out of place in relation to persistent and grave breaches of the obligations bearing upon one of the fundamental objects of the United Nations.[54]

The latter consideration brings clearly to mind the fact that whatever may be the ordinary machinery for giving effect to the international guarantees of the Bill of Rights, that guarantee must, in the last resort, be of a political and coercive nature. There is no necessity to specify its details in the Bill—so long as the effect of its provisions is to make it clear, in a general way, that public opinion, however potent its influence and disapproval may be, is not the only and final guarantee of the observance of its obligations. The essence of an International Bill of Rights

[53] Article 7 of the Draft of the Bill of Rights submitted in 1947 by the United Kingdom provided as follows: ' The parties hereto agree that any one of them which is found by a Resolution of the General Assembly adopted by a two-thirds majority persistently to have violated the provisions of this Bill of Rights should be deemed to have violated the principles of the Charter of the United Nations and therefore be liable to expulsion from the Organisation under Article 6 of the Charter '. It will be noted that the provision, in itself, could have had little effect. The parties to the Bill could not, in this matter, bind either the General Assembly or the Security Council, which alone have jurisdiction in the matter of expulsion.

[54] In this respect a Bill of Rights operating within the United Nations would enjoy a distinct advantage over one functioning within a regional or *ad hoc* organisation. But even with regard to these, in so far as its members are also members of the United Nations, such breaches of the Bill of Rights as would constitute serious violations of the provisions of the Charter in the matter of human rights and fundamental freedoms in a manner affecting international peace and security might come within the orbit of the drastic powers of the Security Council. See above, pp. 183-188.

is neither the recognition nor the definition of human rights, but their effective protection by international law. Their definition, within reasonable limits,[55] is useful and desirable. It is not essential. A general formulation of human rights and fundamental freedoms might be a workable basis for their international protection. Their detailed and minute definition—assuming that it is possible and desirable—would, if unaccompanied by the effective guarantee of the international community, constitute a nominal and deceptive solution of the problem.

---

[55] See below, pp. 327-333.

CHAPTER 14

THE BILL OF RIGHTS WITHIN AND OUTSIDE THE UNITED NATIONS

1. THE OBSTACLES TO A BILL OF RIGHTS WITHIN THE UNITED NATIONS

THE general considerations of the preceding Chapter and the experience of the first phase of the drafting of the Bill of Rights make it possible to assess the place, within the United Nations, of a universal Bill of Human Rights and the alternatives thereto. In the initial stages of the existence of the United Nations no substantial progress was achieved in the direction of a Bill of Rights constituting an enforceable part of the law of nations. The difficulties surrounding the consummation of that object were met by provisional and largely nominal solutions such as the adoption of the Universal Declaration of Human Rights which was not intended to be legally binding. In the proposals, which have achieved a certain degree of crystallisation, for a Bill of Rights intended as a binding legal obligation, some of the essential aspects of a Bill of Rights, such as political rights of freedom and social and economic rights, were disregarded; the right of the individual, the sole beneficiary of the Bill, to seek redress in his own name was refused recognition; the notion of an international judicial organ as one of the means for the redress of grievances found little response; and the question of the eventual enforcement of the Bill through collective coercive action was avoided. The causes which led, in the initial stage of the existence of the United Nations, to the emasculation of the idea of a true Bill of Rights among Members of the United Nations are not necessarily permanent. The ideological and political cleavage between the leading Members of the United Nations supplies a partial explanation of that result. The achievement of a binding International Bill of Human Rights of a universal character is dependent upon a community of outlook and of basic political ideas in the matter of the relation between man and State which was at that time absent within the United Nations. The absence of these factors is not necessarily incompatible with the normal functioning of the United Nations in other respects and with the peaceful development of international relations. But their absence must influence powerfully the attitude of States to the crucial clauses of the Bill of Rights. Neither can it be altogether without effect upon those aspects of the Bill which, although essentially non-controversial, become the subject of controversy on account of the atmosphere of political cleavage and tension between the leading Members of the United Nations.

However, to reduce the reasons of the slow progress—amounting in many respects to recession—of the cause of the Bill of Rights within the United Nations to the general factor of ideological and political differences among its members is to simplify a complex issue. These causes and the conditions of future progress can only be understood by examining the attitude of the leading—and other—Members of the United Nations, especially those represented in the Commission on Human Rights. This applies particularly to the position of Soviet Russia and the United States.

The answer to the question as to whether the basic economic and political system of Soviet Russia is such as to permit her at any future date to participate in an enforceable Bill of Rights must remain a matter of speculation and controversy. For this reason no attempt will be made here to answer the question whether a communist and corporative system is intrinsically compatible with the principles of democracy, as generally conceived, and the recognition of personal rights of freedom as generally interpreted. But a study of the history of the first period of the efforts to achieve a Bill of Rights shows that Soviet Russia was unwilling to become a party to an enforceable Bill of Rights. That fact was only partly obscured by the circumstance that that State—and those associated with it—used language implying the absence of fundamental disagreement on principle. There was no opposition on the part of Soviet Russia to the unqualified recognition of personal rights of freedom or even of the political right to government by consent.[1] On the contrary, she advanced proposals in this respect going beyond those put forward by other

[1] See above, p. 283.

States.   But it was clear that her representatives used language which, in that sphere of human rights, had a distinctly specific connotation.[2]

The same applied, even more conspicuously, to the question of enforcement—of ' implementation ':   Soviet Russia repeatedly and emphatically urged the widest recognition of the principle of implementation.   The main reason for her refusal to associate herself with the Universal Declaration of Human Rights was the fact that that document contained no provision for implementation.   However, in using that term the representatives of Soviet Russia were referring to implementation *by the State*.   They insisted that the international instruments in question should contain not only a mandatory duty, binding upon States, to enforce them but also detailed indications, in particular in the sphere of economic and social rights, of the manner in which these obligations shall be given effect.   At the same time, the representatives of Russia— and those associated with her—rejected, without qualification, what in this connexion is generally regarded as implementation, namely, supervision, investigation and enforcement by international agencies.[3]   This they considered as utterly contrary

[2] For illuminating comment on this aspect of the question see Holcombe, *Human Rights in the Modern World* (1948), pp. 76-112.   At the first meeting of the Drafting Committee in 1947 the Russian representative used picturesque language in relation to the proposed Declaration.   It was, he said, to sound a bugle call to mankind; it should state principles for which men would be ready to stake their lives and which should recall the fighting spirit of the two historic pronouncements of freedom, the American Declaration of Independence and the French Declaration of the Rights of Man: *Minutes*, Sixth Meeting, p. 4.   For a different Russian view of the value of the Declaration of 1789 see the first Communist Manifesto of 1917 drafted by Sverdlov and proclaiming the necessity of a Soviet Declaration of Rights as distinguished from that of 1789 which was 'a declaration of the rights of the bourgeoisie, the right freely to exploit the people'.   It is of interest in this connexion to note the critical view of Magna Carta expressed by the English revolutionary leaders during the Civil War.   See above, p. 131, n. 10.

[3] In connexion with the drafting of the 'Covenant' in 1949 the Russian representative insisted repeatedly on 'provisions for implementation'.   He considered as a fundamental defect in the draft the fact of the 'absence of any provision obliging States to take effective steps and to create the necessary conditions in order to ensure the enjoyment of all the freedoms affirmed'.   Thus, he pointed out, it was useless to affirm the right of the freedom of the Press unless 'the people's representative organisations were given the means of enjoying that freedom, *i.e.,* access to the printing presses and the necessary materials' (E/CN.4/S.R.89, p. 14).   At the same time he emphatically and repeatedly gave expression to the view of Soviet Russia that it was for the Governments to take the necessary measures of implementation. He 'could not support the position of some delegations that measures of implementation might imply the use of international organs such as the International Court of Justice or international commissions in order to coerce Governments, as that would mean interference in matters within the

to national sovereignty, as a veiled attempt at domination by other States, and as inconsistent with the provisions of Article 2, paragraph 7, of the Charter. That attitude found repeated expression in formal and emphatic declarations.[4] Notwithstanding occa-

domestic jurisdiction of States and would therefore be contrary to the Charter' (E/CN.4/SR.90, p. 6). He used identical language in opposing emphatically the right of petition to international organs (E/CN.4/SR.105, p. 10; E/CN.4/SR.111, p. 10). In summing up the results of the efforts of the Commission to draft the 'Covenant', the Russian representative said in 1949: 'The innumerable suggestions for implementation discussed in the Commission showed that the primary aim of some members and their Governments was not to draft a satisfactory Covenant and effectively to guarantee human rights and freedoms, but to provide grounds and excuses which would enable them to interfere in the domestic affairs of other States and to spread international friction and conflict': E/CN.4/SR.135, p. 21. Previously he submitted that 'it would be physically impossible for the United Nations to make the necessary administrative arrangements to ensure the consideration of individual petitions which the two and a half thousand million inhabitants of the globe might put forward' (*ibid.*, SR.133, p. 4). In the course of the discussion before the Commission in 1949 the Ukrainian representative suggested that the Covenant should not use the term 'arbitrary'. He said: 'Democratic States could not pass arbitrary laws; if they did so they would become undemocratic. Who was going to pass judgment on whether a law was arbitrary or unreasonable? Such an attitude reflected a constant tendency to intervene in the sovereign rights of certain States': E/CN.4/SR.119, p. 17.

In view of the confusion caused by that ambivalent use of the term 'implementation' it is convenient to quote in full the statement made in 1948 on this subject by the Russian representative before the Commission on Human Rights:

'The Soviet delegation has studied the drafts and implementation proposals presented to the Commission on Human Rights, in particular, those submitted by the United States, China, France, Australia and the Working Committee set up by the Commission at its second session. It notes that all these drafts and proposals interpret implementation to mean not a system of measures for ensuring that human rights are implemented and guaranteed in every country by the State and society, but, rather, a system of international methods of pressure to be exercised through special organs established for this purpose (*e.g.*, an international court, international committee or a United Nations public prosecutor, etc.), and intended to force individual States to take particular steps connected with the execution of the Convention on Human Rights. It is clear, therefore, that such "implementation" may become a means of interfering in the internal affairs of a State party to the Convention, and of undermining the sovereignty and independence of particular States.

'The implementation plan entails the establishment of various international instances in which communications and complaints with regard to the violation of human rights, from both States and Governments and private individuals or associations of such individuals, would be considered. This conflicts with the whole system of international public law regulating the relations between States. In addition, the plan, if it is adopted, will have the effect of transforming a dispute between a private individual or group of individuals and their State or Government into an international dispute, thereby substantially enlarging the area of international differences, frictions and incidents, unnecessarily burdening and aggravating international relations and undermining the foundations of peace.

'Furthermore, the transference to a special committee, special international court or even, as contemplated in some implementation plans, to the Commission on Human Rights of the prerogative conferred upon the General Assembly and the Economic and Social Council of making recommendations to States on questions of human rights would upset the powers

sional departures—in relation to domestic affairs of other States[5] —from the principle denying any right of international supervision and implementation, the attitude of Soviet Russia on the subject became so clear and well defined as to justify the view that in the foreseeable future no Russian participation in an enforceable international bill of rights could be expected.[6]

This was so although the opposition of that country to an effective Bill of Rights represented only one aspect of a more complex picture, and although it gave no conclusive answer to the potentialities of the Russian contribution to the Bill of Rights in the future. These potentialities cannot be lightly dismissed. While some States have stressed the libertarian aspect of the Bill of Rights, Soviet Russia has insisted on its purposes in relation

as established by the Charter and the distribution of those powers as between the main and auxiliary organs of the United Nations, and would further encourage interference in the internal affairs of Members of the United Nations which is contrary to the Charter. Since what is required is an international document calculated to serve the purpose of maintaining and strengthening international peace and developing good neighbourly relations between nations, the Soviet delegation disapproves of all the drafts and proposals on implementation presented to the Commission and considers them unsatisfactory.' (Doc. E/CN.4/350, pp. 78, 79.) In a reply, sent in December 1949, to the questionnaire prepared by the Secretary-General in connexion with proposals for implementing the provisions of the 'Covenant', the Government of Soviet Russia stated as follows: ' Regarding the proposals on measures for implementing the Declaration of Human Rights and the covenant, the Government of the Union of Soviet Socialist Republics considers that the implementation of the Declaration of Human Rights and the covenant is a matter which solely concerns the domestic jurisdiction of the State, and accordingly sees no need for any international agreements on the subject ' (E/CN.4/353). And see above, p. 213.

[5] See above, pp. 190, 195, 204, 216, 267.

[6] The Russian attitude was already clearly revealed at the meeting of the Drafting Committee in 1947, when the Russian representative deprecated the inclusion in the Bill of too detailed provisions on the ground that they would interfere with the jurisdiction of national governments and would show a lack of confidence in the legislatures of other countries (*Minutes of the 3rd Meeting of the Drafting Committee*, p. 2). On a subsequent occasion he urged, perhaps somewhat inconsistently, that while the Bill of Rights must ' prevent the rebirth of fascist systems and fascist ideology', it ' must not be of such a nature as to interfere in the internal system of various governments' (*ibid., 5th Meeting,* p. 5). He objected to the proposal to set up an International Court of Human Rights on the ground that the creation of an outside organism which would take upon itself the function of regulating the relations between the governments and their citizens would ' inevitably lead to the destruction of governments' and ' would violate the provisions of international law' (*ibid.,* p. 9). On the other hand, he apparently set no limits to the enforcement of the prohibition of discrimination which, he said, must be regarded as ' an international political fact' and ' must be destroyed wherever it still exists' (*ibid.,* p. 7). At a later stage he stated expressly: ' It is not sufficient simply to proclaim the principle of equality or of non-discrimination; that idea must be implemented . . . an acceptable and effective means of implementation would have to be devised (*ibid., 6th Meeting,* p. 13). And see above, n. 5.

to the principles of equality and social welfare. Russian legislation has been prominent not only in the abolition of discrimination on racial, religious, and national grounds, but also in the prohibition of such discrimination and of incitement to it by quarters other than the State itself. So pronounced is the attitude of Soviet Russia with regard to this aspect of human rights that in the statements of her representatives on the Commission on Human Rights there is to be found an occasional advocacy of the international implementation of the principle of non-discrimination.[7] In the field of the full and unqualified provision of equality of cultural opportunity for the national and ethnic minorities Soviet Russian practice has opened a new and significant chapter. The contribution of the Russian Constitution of 1936 and of Russian practice generally to the recognition of the right of the individual to work, to social security, to medical care, to adequate leisure, and to education constitutes a lasting and beneficent influence. This vindication of the dignity of man through the full acknowledgment of his rights in those spheres has not been accompanied by a parallel recognition of his personal and political freedoms. But there is probably no compelling necessity for assuming any absolute permanency of this feature of the Soviet Russian State. It is possible that the fundamental ideas of a comprehensive Bill of Rights—to which Russian doctrine and practice have made a contribution—may yet prove a bridge to wider international co-operation. In the meantime, although the refusal of Soviet Russia to consent to the principle of international enforcement of a Bill of Rights may for the time being render impossible her participation in it, such abstention need not be considered as synonymous with a permanently negative attitude to the adoption, under the ægis of the United Nations, of international machinery for the implementation of an International Bill of Rights.

The second factor of importance which determined the fate of the Bill of Rights within the United Nations during the period under review was the attitude of the United States. Although combined with full and active co-operation at the various stages of the elaboration of the Bill, the attitude of the United States— a distinguished representative of which was Chairman of the

[7] See above, n. 5.

Commission on Human Rights—approached, in many material
aspects, that assumed by Soviet Russia. The United States was
to a large extent responsible both for the adoption and the speedy
realisation of the idea of a Declaration which was to be neither
binding nor enforceable and which was to be followed by a
binding Covenant of limited compass. The United States was
opposed to what must be regarded as an indispensable condition
of effective protection of human rights, namely, the recognition
of the effective right of petition by private individuals and groups.
Moreover, in its proposals for a ' Covenant ' of Human Rights the
United States insisted on inserting a qualifying provision to the
effect that those parties to the Covenant who are Federal States
shall assume binding obligations with regard to such matters only
as the Federal Government regards as appropriate under its
constitutional system for federal action, and that with regard to
other articles the obligations of the party to the Covenant shall be
limited to bringing its provisions, with a favourable recommendation, to the notice of the States or provinces. As in the United
States the bulk of the provisions of an International Bill of Rights
fall, according to the Constitution, within the province of the
States, the effect of that clause would be to render the obligations
of the United States largely nominal. It is significant that, when
the International Law Commission accepted in 1949 the draft of
a Declaration of the Rights and Duties of States, the only two
dissenting votes were those cast by nationals of the United States
and Russia—the former voting against the draft on the ground of
his opposition to the article which provided that ' every State has
the duty to treat all persons under its jurisdiction with respect
for human rights and fundamental freedoms, without distinction
as to race, sex, language or religion '.[8]

It is beyond the scope of this book to enquire in detail into the
reasons for that attitude of the United States—a State which has
been the cradle of modern bills of rights and which has an
incomparable tradition of idealism and individualism. These

---

[8] It is probably true to say that, for the reasons set out in the text, opinion
in the United States generally was not at that time favourable to an effective
Bill of Rights binding upon the United States. See, for instance, Holcombe,
Human Rights in the Modern World (1948), in which the author considers
even a non-binding Declaration covering the personal rights of freedom to
be too ambitious. He proposes instead a Bill of Rights limited to the somewhat obscure suggestions of Immanuel Kant put forward in his *Eternal ace*
and restricted to the rights of man as citizen of the world as expressed in
' conditions of universal hospitality' (pp. 134-140). And see below, pp. 359-364.

reasons can be indicated in general outline. The first is the traditional reluctance of the United States to submit to obligations involving the possibility of international interference in the sphere of its domestic jurisdiction and a consequent impairment of the sovereignty of one or both branches of its supreme legislative organ. It is sufficient to mention the part played by the United States in the inclusion of the clause of domestic jurisdiction in Article 15 (8) of the Covenant of the League of Nations and in Article 2 (7) of the Charter of the United Nations, as well as the form of the acceptance—which is, as the result, largely nominal— by the United States of the obligations of the Optional Clause of Article 36 of the Statute of the International Court of Justice.[9] With regard to the latter the action of the United States was in keeping both with past reluctance to assume binding obligations in the field of compulsory judicial settlement and with its traditional attachment to the cause of judicial settlement of international disputes—a duality of purpose which was repeated, in a different manner, in relation to the international protection of human rights. The second explanation of the attitude of the United States lies in the difficulty arising out of the constitutional division of powers between the Union and the component States—a matter discussed in detail elsewhere in this book.[9a] There is, thirdly, the intricate problem created by the condition and the treatment of the Negro population in some of the States of the United States. In the period under review the dominant tendency was to adjust the level of the International Bill of Human Rights—a basic international instrument—to the urgent domestic requirements of the United States. There was as yet no attempt to rely on the alternative method of invoking the vital needs of the international community, identified in this case with the cause of a Bill of Rights, as a reason and the method of international treaties as an instrument for overcoming an internal problem of baffling complexity and ethical urgency. Detailed suggestions to that effect were made in the momentous and statesmanlike report of the Committee on Civil Liberties appointed by the President of the United States in 1946.[10]

It would be improper to offer outside advice on what is a

[9] See below, p. 362, n. 17.
[9a] See below, pp. 359-364.
[10] See above, p. 157.

problem of extreme domestic complexity. The factors recounted above have been merely noticed as an explanation of the attitude taken by the United States and as a basis for the assessment of the future prospects of an enforceable Bill of Rights. Moreover, there are powerful forces at work in the United States which may set a limit, by means other than constitutional amendment, to the exclusive jurisdiction of member States in matters affecting the fundamental rights of man. This is yet another reason why it is permissible to cherish the hope that various factors bound up with the tradition of that country as well as the potent, even if inarticulate, impact of the existing obligations of the Charter may assert themselves to a greater degree than has been the case in the past. The historic part which the United States, since the Declaration of Independence and its own Bill of Rights, has played in promoting human freedoms, as well as its rapidly increasing part in international co-operation and in ensuring international peace—of which latter task the securing of the rights of man is an integral part—permit the expectation that that country may yet make a decisive contribution to the international protection of human rights. In the meantime it may be preferable to leave to the forces of democracy in the United States the opportunity to vindicate fully through the slower processes of education and persuasion the idealistic and libertarian tradition of its people in relation to human rights.[11]

2. THE BILL OF RIGHTS AND SURRENDER OF SOVEREIGNTY

While in the case of Soviet Russia and the United States the reasons for the opposition to an effective Bill of Rights could be explained in terms of problems peculiar to these States, the negative attitude of some other countries was due largely to doubts as to the practicability of a Bill of that

[11] The advance in the attitude of the United States in the direction of recognition of the principle of international supervision of the observance of the Bill of Rights may be seen from a comparison of the proposals put forward by the United States jointly with China in 1948 and those formulated in 1949 jointly with Great Britain. In the former the proposed Committee was to be a ' Committee of the Covenanting States ' which was to ' consider a complaint referred to it and, in view of all the circumstances, make a recommendation addressed to the State or States concerned, looking to an amicable solution ' (Doc. E/CN.4/145). The cause of the protection of human rights, solemnly acknowledged in a binding legal instrument, was committed to a diplomatic Committee empowered to make recommendations ' looking to an amicable solution '. The proposals made in 1949 were more in keeping with the professed purposes of the Covenant.

character and partly to a reluctance to acquiesce in the limitations of sovereignty implicit in it. Thus, for instance, the attitude of Great Britain—who associated herself with the United States in the proposals put forward in 1949 [12]—was mainly based on the view that international organs would not be in the position to cope with what might prove an unwieldy mass of private petitions. That view is probably untenable,[13] but it must be taken into account in assessing the difficulties of a Bill of Rights. It arose to a large extent from the conviction that the functioning of schemes of implementation based on private petitions depends on the availability of an international staff of the highest quality and from doubts as to the prospects of a satisfactory solution of that aspect of the problem. There was as yet no appreciation of the fact that that difficulty cannot properly be solved by rejecting an indispensable condition of the effective protection of human rights.[14]

Neither was it as yet sufficiently realised that if the Bill of Rights is not to be a mere gesture, it cannot be brought about without the signatory States sacrificing some attributes, both substantive and formal, of their sovereignty. A Bill of Rights worthy of the name is not a consummation which can be achieved without some States giving up practices and constitutional principles in a way necessary to ensure an irreducible minimum standard of respect for fundamental human rights and of the requisite international guarantees. In current terminology, that consummation cannot be accomplished without some sacrifices of sovereignty not only in respect of the substance of the Bill but also of its enforcement. The essence of a Bill of the Rights of Man is that it implies a limitation upon the existing and the future powers of the State. There is no country so advanced or entitled to such absolute

---

[12] See above, pp. 289, 290.

[13] See above, p 290.

[14] See above, p. 291. In its comments submitted in 1948 on the question of the right of petition in connexion with the proposed Covenant the Government of the United Kingdom drew attention to the dangers of an unconditional right of petition to the United Nations. It was pointed out that such petitions might become the means of transmitting ' the most secret information contrary to national security', 'enticement to commit offences', and matters which are ' libellous ' or otherwise transcending the limits laid down in the Covenant on the freedom of expression' (Doc. E/CN.4/82/Add. 9, p. 7). It is submitted that these dangers are probably exaggerated. To the extent to which they are real they can be met, without undue difficulty and without receiving any publicity, by the machinery suggested below (see p. 375).

conviction of the excellence of its law and its institutions as not to be able to make a contribution to the common stock of a Bill of Rights by consenting to some change in its legal and constitutional system. The attitude of caution in the matter was not limited to Great Britain. It was shared, largely on account of the federal structure of her constitution, by Canada.[15] Some—though not all —States of Latin America found it difficult to divorce their attitude to the question of the implementation of the Bill of Rights from their traditional suspicion of external interference in their domestic affairs.[16]

These obstacles in the way of an international Bill of Rights are not necessarily of a permanent character. Thus, for instance,

[15] See below, p. 362, n. 15.

[16] See, for instance, the attitude of the representatives of Mexico and Argentina with regard to the right of petition discussed in the Third Committee of the General Assembly in 1948 in connexion with the Declaration of Human Rights. The former objected to the recognition of the right of petition to the United Nations. He said: 'In the present stage of the international community its inclusion might not yet be opportune, particularly because it might appear to set a form of international jurisdiction above the sovereign jurisdiction of States. . . . The creation of a supernational body would become necessary; but that was contrary to Article 2 of the Charter. The whole conception, indeed, was not in accordance with the Charter which referred only to the promotion of respect for human rights, but nowhere made their protection obligatory. In present circumstances that protection could only be a matter of national legislation.' A/C.3/SR.158, p. 9. The Argentinian representative used almost identical language: A/C.3/SR.159, p. 3.

The Draft Declaration of the International Rights and Duties of Man adopted in December 1945 by the Inter-American Juridical Committee lays down that 'the provisions of this Declaration shall be a part of the law of each individual State, to be respected and enforced by the administrative and judicial authorities in the same manner as all other laws of the State' and that 'the provisions of the Declaration shall not be abrogated or modified except in accordance with the terms of an inter-American agreement or an agreement of the United Nations binding upon the American States' (*American Journal of International Law*, 40 (1946), Suppl., p. 99). In the Report accompanying the Draft Declaration the question of international enforcement was discussed in substantial detail, and a proposal was made for the creation of a Consultative Commission on the Rights of Man —a body the function of which would be to serve as a central agency for the study of the practical problems involved in the protection of the rights of man and the submission of recommendations to the American Governments as a body (but not to particular Governments) through the Economic and Social Council. The Report provided expressly that no recommendation shall be made in connexion with a specific case to a particular Government except with the consent of the Council. It was admitted that the Juridical Committee 'has not found it desirable to enter into the question of the measures to be taken to assure the fulfilment by each State of the obligations contained in the Declaration' (*ibid.,* p. 113). The Report conceded the possibility that systematic and serious violations of human rights, although outside the competence of the proposed Commission, might create a situation involving a threat to peace and calling for the adoption of the procedure envisaged for such cases among the American nations. As to the Resolution on the Inter-American Court to Protect the Rights of Man adopted by the Ninth International Conference of American States in 1948, see below, p. 387.

there are no compelling reasons for assuming that Great Britain will not resume the position of leadership to which she is entitled by virtue of her historic contribution to the ideas and the practice of the rights of man.[17]   Moreover, there is a considerable number of States which are prepared to agree to a substantial measure of surrender of sovereignty implied in the acceptance of international supervision by way of an international court of human rights and similar agencies.   Thus, among the States represented on the Commission on Human Rights, France put forward in 1948 a detailed scheme embodying a well-defined procedure of non-judicial character.   The French representative declared that ' in questions concerning human rights it is morally impossible to declare petitions *a priori* inadmissible unless they are sponsored by a State '.[18]   The authors of the scheme admitted that it involved a limitation of sovereignty.   They recalled in this connexion the Preamble to the French Constitution of 1946 in which that country declared herself ready ' on condition of reciprocity to accept the limitations of sovereignty necessary to the organisation of peace '—a clear acknowledgment that the protection of the inalienable rights of man is of the essence of the defence of peace.   The proposal, which showed a distinct continuity with the ideas of the Declaration of 1789, was outspoken in matters of substance.   Similarly, in the same year the representative of India put on record the view that the proposal then submitted by the United States and China ' leaves aside the more momentous question of implementing human rights and fundamental freedoms at the instance of aggrieved humanity '.[19] She urged that the right of petition should not be denied to individuals and that although some petitions may prove frivolous or malicious means must and can be found for dealing with any such abuse of the right of petition.[20]

[17] See above, pp. 127-141.   It was Great Britain which was the first country to submit to the Commission on Human Rights a full and reasoned draft of a Bill of Rights.   That draft contemplated some measures of implementation. It was not cast in the frame of a semi-diplomatic procedure by a Committee of Governments.   The draft envisaged some action by the General Assembly, including the expulsion of a State violating the provisions of the Bill.

[18] Doc. E/CN.4/147, p. 5, and E/CN.4/82/Add.10.   See also the Report of the Commission on Human Rights of 1949, E/CN.4/350, pp. 70-74.

[19] E/CN.4/153.

[20] In 1949 India proposed, as the principal organ of implementation, a Standing Committee of not less than five independent persons set up by the Economic and Social Council from lists submitted by States parties to the Covenant.

Australia has identified herself, more emphatically than any other State, with the proposal for an International Court of Human Rights open alike to States and individuals and private organisations.[21]   According to that proposal the Statute of the Court is to form an integral part of the Covenant the signatories to which undertake to comply with the decision of the Court. Provision is made, in case of non-compliance, for a recommendation of the General Assembly with the view to giving effect to the judgment of the Court.   These proposals of Australia are significant, coming as they do from a country which had a major share of responsibility for the insertion of the clause of domestic jurisdiction in Article 2(7) of the Charter.   Of the other countries represented on the Commission of Human Rights Lebanon and Belgium have been foremost in the advocacy of an effective Bill of Rights.[22]

3.   THE ALTERNATIVES TO A BILL OF RIGHTS WITHIN THE UNITED NATIONS

While, as has been shown, the obstacles in the way of an effective universal Bill of Human Rights within the United Nations need not necessarily be of a permanent nature, it is desirable to consider the alternatives to a universal Bill from the point of view of its operation within the orbit of the United Nations.   A Bill of Rights could become part of the law of the United Nations to the extent of making the machinery and the agencies of the United Nations available for its operation only if it could secure the support of at least two-thirds of the Members of the United

The function of the Committee, which was to act either on its own information or on receipt of petitions from individuals, groups, associations or States, was to 'remedy through negotiations any violations of the Convention or Conventions on Human Rights and to report to the Commission on Human Rights those cases of violation which it is unable to remove by its own exertions': E/CN.4/350, p. 77. The unsatisfactory feature of the proposal was that the report of the Committee, which was to sit in private session, was to be made public only if the Commission deemed it desirable.

[21] See E/CN.4/AC.1/27 and E/CN.4/350. The apparent inconsistency between Articles 17 and 19 of the Draft Statute of the proposed Court was probably due to an oversight in drafting.   While according to the former the parties in cases before the Court shall be States, individuals, groups of individuals and national and international associations, the latter laid down that the jurisdiction of the Court shall comprise cases submitted to it by parties to the Covenant or the Commission on Human Rights.

[22] In 1949 Denmark, Guatemala and Uruguay, as members of the Commission on Human Rights, voted in favour of the recognition of the right of petition by individuals.

Nations in a way making possible a recommendation of the General Assembly instituting special organs for that purpose or making available the existing organs. In so far as the continued operation of these organs in that sphere would require periodic recommendations of the General Assembly, for instance, in the field of the budget of the United Nations, the number of States supporting the Bill would have to be considerably larger so as to ensure its unimpeded operation from year to year. Support by a two-thirds majority of the Members of the United Nations would be required whether the Bill is framed in accordance with the principles outlined in the present book or whether it is a Bill on the lines of the proposals for the ' Covenant ' advanced by the Commission on Human Rights. Whatever may be the character of the Bill thus adopted it will not automatically affect the obligations which rest upon its signatories by virtue of the Charter or the competence of the existing agencies of the United Nations in the matter of human rights, such as the General Assembly, the Economic and Social Council, or the Commission on Human Rights. However, as the General Assembly is competent to create new organs of the United Nations and to prescribe the activities of the existing organs, it would be possible, by a Resolution of the General Assembly, to make provision for avoiding a multiplicity of organs or functions in relation to States Members of the United Nations bound by the more stringent obligations of a Bill of Rights to which they have subscribed.

At the same time, there must be envisaged the position with regard to an International Bill of Rights in case it should prove impossible to secure for its support a two-thirds majority of the Members of the United Nations. Probably, it would have been improper for the Commission on Human Rights—an organ of the United Nations—to consider that contingency. However, unless the view is to prevail that a Bill of Rights within the United Nations must be achieved at all costs—even at the cost of reducing its contents and instruments of enforcement to the lowest common denominator—that contingency must be contemplated and alternative solutions sought and examined. There is nothing to prevent Members of the United Nations, however limited in number, from concluding *inter se* agreements for the achievement of ends to which they attach importance. This, for instance, might be the case in relation to a regional organisation of States, such as those grouped in the Council of Europe—a matter which is discussed in another Chapter of this book in connexion with the proposed European Court of Human Rights.[23]   It might be possible for other States to adhere to the regional association. But there is no reason why an international organisation—an international Union—created specially for that purpose should not be set up on another than a purely regional basis.   Thus an International Bill of Rights may come into being, in the first instance, outside the orbit of the United Nations by way of a decision of a limited number of States willing, by their example, to provide the nucleus of attraction for the future expansion of the Bill.   There is danger in the attempt to adopt, in a deceptive pursuit of immediate universality, a Bill of Rights which is defective in its essential aspects.   If, in determined disregard of the temptations of rapid success, that peril is successfully overcome, a Bill of Rights may evolve which will be both an achievement and a promise of a further transformation of the law of nations from a law of States to a law of international society with the individual human being at the very centre of its constitu-tional structure.   Thus conceived the Bill of Rights might become the turning-point in the history of the United Nations and of the world.   It might not only provide a direct contribution to international peace which history has shown to be connected in intimate ways with the rights of man.   It might also, by making the individual a subject of the international commonwealth, prove to be the first decisive step in the constitution of the Federation of the World which must, till accomplished, be regarded as the primary political goal of humanity.

As has been shown, that object cannot be attained without a determined resolve on the part of Governments—and peoples—to acquiesce in a substantial limitation of their national sovereignty. In one sense that surrender of sovereignty is more theoretical than real.   This applies in particular to the contents of the Bill of Rights.   Its provisions, as stated in the proposed Covenant or in the draft outlined in this book, are largely declaratory of the human rights and fundamental freedoms founded on the general principles of law recognised by civilised States.   Very little of the substantive law of England would require to be changed as the

[23] See below, pp. 435-456.

result of the adoption of the Bill. The same applies to most—though not all—other countries. In the field of enforcement the competence of international organs to scrutinise and, if need be, to pass judgment upon the conformity of the conduct of the organs of the State with its international obligations in the matter would constitute a serious encroachment upon the freedom of the State only on the assumption that its conduct will be contrary to its international obligations or that the international authorities will fail in the proper exercise of the powers conferred upon them.

Yet, in another sense, the limitation of sovereignty implied in a Bill of Rights is far from being nominal. For in an effective Bill of Rights the State would surrender its freedom of action and its legislative supremacy with regard to matters relating to the most essential aspect of its law and constitution. The sovereignty of its legislature and the finality of the judgments of its highest courts would become subject to the limitations of the treaty and to discussion and review on the part of international organs.[24] The reality of that impairment of sovereignty cannot be concealed by dint of verbal devices. A ' Covenant ' which, while purporting to constitute a legally binding obligation, fails to provide effective means of international guarantee and supervision does not differ substantially from a ' Declaration '. The same must be said of a ' Covenant ' which, while purporting to provide for ' implementation ', in fact fails to endow the organs of the international community with authority to examine, at the instance of the true beneficiaries of the Covenant, and to pass binding judgment, whether by a court or otherwise, upon the conduct of States.

4. THE OBLIGATIONS OF THE CHARTER AS INDEPENDENT OF THE BILL OF RIGHTS

What will be the effect upon the protection of human rights within the United Nations if no International Bill of Rights conceived as an enforceable legal instrument is adopted by a sufficiently large number of Members of the United Nations to make it part of the law of the United Nations? While any such result would disappoint the hopes which many have attached to that particular aspect of the progress of human rights, it would

[24] See below. pp. 357, 453-456.

leave intact the legal obligations resting upon Members of the United Nations by virtue of the Charter and the legal powers which it confers upon the organs of the United Nations. Undoubtedly, the fulfilment of these obligations by the Members of the United Nations and by its organs would be facilitated[25] if human rights and fundamental freedoms were to be defined by means of a Bill of Rights adopted as a binding legal instrument. The cause of human rights would be advanced if, in a Bill of Rights, the powers of discussion and recommendation which the United Nations and its organs already possess with regard to human rights were enlarged by an independent right of investigation and enforcement—of ' intervention '—in case of violation of the rights and freedoms recognised and safeguarded by the Charter. A Bill of Rights would put the right of petition on a firm and uncontroversial basis and would direct it into the secure channels of judicial protection. Without a Bill of Rights—properly so-called—these developments will not come to speedy fruition. But the obligations of the Charter and the powers and duties of the organs of the United Nations will remain. It has been shown elsewhere in this book that they constitute a legal reality independent of any Bill of Rights.[26]

---

[25] That they are, in essence, independent of such recognition is shown above, p. 150.

[26] This fact has been obscured by the exclusive preoccupation, on the part of the Commission on Human Rights, with the drafting of the Bill—in the same way as the crucial question of international guarantees has been obscured by an exaggerated emphasis on the definition of the rights to be protected. See above, p. 261, and below, p. 329.

THE PRINCIPLES OF AN INTERNATIONAL
BILL OF THE RIGHTS OF MAN

CHAPTER 15

THE OBLIGATIONS OF THE BILL OF RIGHTS

1. DRAFT OF THE INTERNATIONAL BILL OF THE RIGHTS OF MAN*

PREAMBLE

Whereas the enthronement of the rights of man was proclaimed to be a major purpose of the struggle out of which the United Nations was born:

Whereas the Charter of the United Nations has solemnly recognised the fundamental rights and freedoms of man;

Whereas the promotion of human rights and fundamental freedoms is among the primary purposes of the United Nations;

Whereas its Members have pledged themselves to joint and collective action for the fulfilment of these purposes;

Whereas the denial of human rights and fundamental freedoms is and has proved to be a danger to the peace of the world;

Whereas the right of man to freedom comprises the right of self-government through persons chosen by and accountable to him;

Whereas, for that reason, the observance of the principles of democracy must, irrespective of the form of government and of the economic system, be placed under the protection and the guarantee of international society;

Whereas the principle of equality of man demands an equal opportunity of self-government and cultural development;

Whereas the dignity of man, the dictates of justice, and the principles of social solidarity in modern society require that no person shall suffer undeserved want and that the State shall safeguard

* For the history of this Draft see below, p. 321.

313

effectively the right to work under proper conditions of employment, the right to education, to social security, and to a just share in social progress;

Whereas the sanctity of human personality and its right to develop to all attainable perfection and to fulfil, in freedom, its duty to man and society require effective provision for its protection through international enactment, supervision and enforcement;

The Special General Assembly of the United Nations now approves this International Bill of the Rights of Man.

PART 1

CHAPTER 1

Article 1

The life and liberty of the person shall be inviolate within the limits of the law.

No person shall be deprived of liberty save by a judgment of a court of law or pending trial in accordance with the law. Detention by purely executive order shall be unlawful in time of peace. There shall be protection from arbitrary and unauthorised arrest and detention.

The law shall provide safeguards against prolonged detention preceding trial, against excessive bail or unreasonable refusal thereof, against denial of just guarantees in respect of evidence and procedure in criminal cases, against the refusal of protection in the nature of the writ of habeas corpus, against the retroactive operation of criminal laws and against punishment which is cruel, inhuman, or offensive to the dignity of man.

Article 2

No State shall permit slavery or legal relations substantially identical therewith, or traffic in slaves, or compulsory labour in any form other than public service, equally incumbent upon all, or as part of punishment pronounced by a court of law.

Article 3

There shall be full freedom of religious belief and practice.

Article 4

The freedom of speech, of expression of opinion, and of imparting and receiving information in writing and by other means shall not be denied or impaired.

Article 5

There shall be full freedom of association and assembly.

Article 6

The sanctity of the home and the secrecy of correspondence shall be respected.

Article 7

There shall be full freedom of petition to the national authorities and to the United Nations.

Article 8

All nationals of the State shall enjoy full equality before the law and equal treatment in all respects by the authorities of the State. In particular, there shall be no discrimination on account of religion, race, sex, colour, language, national origin, or political creed. No State shall lend the assistance of its judicial and other organs and resources for the purpose of enforcing or practising discrimination, from whatever source it may originate, contrary to the objects of this Bill of Rights.

Article 9

Aliens and stateless persons shall not be denied the full and equal protection of the Articles of this Chapter of the Bill of Rights and of other rights granted to them by the law of the State in which they reside. No alien or stateless person legally admitted and permanently residing within the State may be expelled except in pursuance of a judicial decision or recommendation as a punishment for serious offences laid down by law as warranting expulsion.

Article 10

Within the limits of public security and economic capacity of the State, there shall be full and effective recognition of the right of asylum for political offenders and for fugitives from persecution.

Article 11

Every person shall be entitled to the nationality of the State where he is born unless and until on attaining majority he declares for the nationality open to him by virtue of descent.

No person shall be deprived of his nationality by way of punishment or be deemed to have lost his nationality except concurrently with the acquisition of a new nationality.

The right of emigration and expatriation shall not be denied.

Article 12

No State shall deprive its citizens of the effective right to choose their governments and legislators on a footing of equality according to universal suffrage, in free, secret, and periodic elections. The freedom of the elections shall not be limited to lists proposed or in effect determined by the Government.

Article 13

Whenever the political condition or the stage of development of communities which have not yet attained full political independence or which constitute a colony or a trust territory require the application of the principle of trusteeship or of political tutelage, such modification of the right of self-government shall be subject, in accordance with the Charter of the United Nations, to the effective recognition of the principle of the eventual independence of these communities in accordance with their development and the wishes of their populations.

Article 14

In States inhabited by a substantial number of persons of a race, language or religion other than those of the majority of the population, persons belonging to such ethnic, linguistic or religious minorities shall have the right to establish and maintain, out of an equitable proportion of the available public funds, their schools and cultural and religious institutions and to use their own language before the courts and other authorities and organs of the State.

CHAPTER 2

Article 15

States shall, within the limits of their economic capacity and development, make provision for securing effectively the right to work, to education, and to public assistance in case of unemployment, old age, sickness, disablement, and other cases of undeserved want.

Article 16

States shall, through national legislation and international co-operation, endeavour to secure just and humane conditions of work.

PART 2

CHAPTER 1

Article 17

Every State shall, by appropriate constitutional means, adopt Chapter 1 of Part 1 of this International Bill of the Rights of Man as part of its domestic law. The effect of such adoption shall be an obligation to abrogate or to alter any existing statute or any other rule of law inconsistent with these Articles of the International Bill of the Rights of Man. The Parties to this Bill of Rights shall communicate to the Secretary-General the legislative and other measures taken in order to give effect to that obligation. The Bill of Rights shall not be abrogated or modified, by legislative action or otherwise, save in pursuance of international agreement or authorisation.

Nothing in the constitution of any Federal State shall relieve that State of the obligations of this Bill of Rights.

Article 18

The obligations of this Bill of Rights shall be binding upon States in relation both to their metropolitan territory and to any other territory under their control and jurisdiction.

Article 19

The enforcement of any law, including the temporary suspension of the rights guaranteed by this Bill of Rights, necessary for safeguarding the legal rights of others or providing for the safety, public order, good morals and welfare of the community or intended to secure human rights and fundamental freedoms shall not be deemed to be inconsistent with the observance of this International Bill of the Rights of Man.

The provisions of this Article shall not be used or applied in a manner contrary to the purposes of the Bill of Rights.

CHAPTER 2

Article 20

This International Bill of the Rights of Man shall be placed under the guarantee of the United Nations. Its observance shall be a matter of concern to all the United Nations.

Article 21

There shall be established a Human Rights Council which shall be responsible to the General Assembly for the promotion of the purposes of this Bill of Rights and for the supervision of the observance of its Articles.

The Human Rights Council shall be composed of nine persons possessing the highest qualifications and not representing any Government. The members of the Council shall be selected by an electoral body consisting of the Secretary-General of the United Nations, the Director of the Division of Human Rights, four representatives of States appointed by the General Assembly, two permanent members of the Security Council designated by a simple majority of its members, and four Judges of the International Court of Justice appointed by the President with the approval of the Court. The Council shall include not less than three persons of judicial experience.

The members of the Council shall devote their whole time to the fulfilment of their functions. They shall not engage in any other profession or occupation. They shall receive salaries commensurate with the importance and the dignity of their office.

They shall hold office for a period of six years, subject to the first election taking place in such a manner as to ensure a substantial measure of continuity in the composition of the Council.

The Council shall present an annual report to the General Assembly.

Article 22

The Council shall set up Commissions and other organs to assist it in the fulfilment of its functions.

The Council shall formulate, for approval by the General Assembly, Rules of Procedure for the investigation of petitions. These Rules shall be based on the recognition of the right of petition of any State, organisation, body, or individual.

Article 23

The Council shall, through appropriate organs, collect information and receive and investigate petitions and representations bearing on the observance of this Bill of Rights. It shall, in proper cases, communicate such petitions to the State concerned and receive its observations thereon. It shall, on the initiative of any of its members or of the Secretary-General of the United Nations, take cognizance of or appropriate action on any alleged violations of the provisions of this Bill of Rights. The Council shall not act on its own initiative nor proceed with any petition or representation brought before it unless it is established that the remedies reasonably available in the State concerned have been exhausted. The Council shall, by a concurring vote of any seven of its members, be entitled to conduct an enquiry within the territory of the State concerned which shall afford full facilities necessary for the efficient conduct of the investigation.

Article 24

At any stage of the procedure the Council, acting on its own initiative or on the request of the State the action of which is the subject of an investigation, shall be entitled to ask the International Court of Justice for an Advisory Opinion on any legal issue involved in the interpretation or the application of this Bill of Rights. The present Article shall be considered, for this purpose, as implying the authorisation by the General Assembly as provided for in Article 96 of the Charter of the United Nations.

The General Assembly may at any time entrust to an International Court of Human Rights the functions to be exercised under this Bill of Rights by the International Court of Justice.

Unless otherwise decided by the concurring vote of any seven of its members, the Council shall publish the results of its investigation. The State concerned shall be entitled to appeal to the International Court of Justice or any subdivision thereof, or, when established, to the International Court of Human Rights, on any question of law or fact on which the finding of the Council is based. The same right of appeal to the International Court of Human Rights, when established, shall be open, by leave of the Council, to any individual or private body in respect of a petition brought by it. No such leave of appeal shall be refused except by a two-thirds majority of the members of the Council.

Article 25

In all cases in which the results of the investigation disclose an infraction of this Bill of Rights the Council shall make appropriate recommendations to the State concerned. If the State concerned fails to comply with the recommendations of the Council, the latter may bring the matter before the General Assembly which, after any further investigation and after calling upon the State concerned to comply with the recommendations, shall, in the case of continued non-compliance, take such action as may be appropriate in the circumstances. The Parties to this Bill of Rights agree that the recommendations of the General Assembly shall be legally binding upon them. Where the infraction of this Bill of Rights is such as to constitute a threat to international peace and security, the General Assembly shall transmit the case to the Security Council for such further political, economic, or military action as may be deemed necessary to ensure compliance with the Bill of Rights.

Article 26

Nothing in this Bill of Rights shall be deemed to impair the powers and functions of the General Assembly, the Security Council, the Trusteeship Council, the Economic and Social Council or its Commissions, as set out in the Charter of the United Nations.

PART 3

Article 27

The International Bill of the Rights of Man shall enter into force, as an instrument operating within the framework of and guaranteed by the United Nations as soon as it has received the assent of two-thirds of the Members of the United Nations. It shall become binding, without any necessity for ratification, upon Members of the United Nations whose duly accredited and authorised representatives present at this Special General Assembly cast their vote in favour of the Bill or who at any future Session of the General Assembly make a declaration accepting its Articles as binding upon their State. Any State which is not a member of the United Nations may accede to this Bill of Rights by a declaration deposited with the Secretary-General.

Article 28

The Articles of this Bill of Rights may be amended by a vote of the General Assembly provided that such vote receives the concurrence of two-thirds of the Members of the United Nations bound by the Bill of Rights. States which do not concur in the amendment shall remain bound by the Bill as hitherto. They may at any time accept the obligations of all or some amendments by a declaration deposited with the Secretary-General of the United Nations.

Article 29

Any State which is a Party to this Bill of Rights may withdraw from its obligations by notice given to the Secretary-General of the United Nations. The notice shall not become operative until one year after it has reached the Secretary-General. It shall be without effect upon the progress of petitions and complaints brought prior to that date.

2. THE CONTENTS OF THE BILL OF RIGHTS AND THE PROBLEM OF UNIVERSALITY

The principles of an International Bill of Human Rights can be set out either in the abstract or by reference to a concrete scheme embodying definite obligations binding upon States. It is the latter method which I propose to follow in this Section. The Draft of an International Bill of the Rights of Man, which appears at the beginning of this Chapter, follows in general outline the draft published in 1945 in my book of the same title and of the draft submitted by me to the Brussels Conference of the International Law Association in 1948. The principal aspects of these proposals have been retained in the present Draft. These comprise the inclusion in the Bill not only of personal rights of freedom, but also of political and social and economic rights; the full recognition of the right of petition by individuals; the principle of international supervision and enforcement applying, in different ways, to various categories of rights; and the establishment of a non-judicial organ endowed with substantial powers of investigation and recommendation as a preliminary stage to any judicial proceedings.

However, while the main features of these drafts have remained substantially unaltered, the experience of the first phase of the fulfilment of the obligations of the Charter in the sphere of human rights and freedoms and of the drafting of the Bill by the Commission on Human Rights has led to some far-reaching changes and modifications. In particular, there have been abandoned those attempts at compromise solutions which were dictated by the desire—or hope—of achieving universality. Thus, for instance, with regard to the rights of political freedom, *i.e.,* the right to government by consent, Article 11 of the draft provided previously as follows: ' No State shall deprive its citizens of the effective right to choose their governments and legislators on a footing of equality, *in accordance with the law of the State,* in free, secret, and periodic elections.' The important though somewhat ingenious qualification implied in the words ' in accordance with the law of the State ' was inserted, not without considerable hesitation, in order to meet the case of States in which the form of government is in fact totalitarian and in which the equality, freedom, and secrecy of the periodic right of franchise is to a large extent nominal. That, admittedly strained, relaxation of principle was open to—and met with—criticism. There is no longer sufficient justification, assuming that it existed at the outset, for such attempts at compromise once the achievement of universality proves, for the foreseeable future, to be impracticable. Experience has shown that attempts at universality have the effect of interfering decisively with the consistency and the moral authority and purpose of an international enactment such as the Bill of Rights without eliciting a corresponding spirit of concession or securing the desired universal character of the instrument as eventually adopted. It is not permissible to disregard that lesson of experience. I have also been unable to resist the force of the objection that it is difficult to justify the attempt to adapt, in this respect, the Bill of Rights to the conditions of electoral franchise obtaining in some parts of the United States or in South Africa— for the desire to meet the difficulties presented by the position in those countries was, too, one of the reasons for the form in which that crucial Article of the Bill of Rights had been drafted. Consequently, with regard to Article 12 of the present draft, the important qualification as expressed in the phrase in question has now been omitted.

Similarly, I have modified somewhat my previous views in so far as, because of considerations of universality, I tended to give prominence to the difficulties inherent in the international judicial protection of human rights through the International Court of Justice or a separate International Court of Human Rights. The main objection to an extension of the jurisdiction of international courts to cover complaints of violations of human rights is that, because of the universal character of the Bill and the resulting wide diversity of legal and political systems, the variety of national tradition, and the geographical vastness of the area covered by the Bill of Rights, it may not be practicable to entrust to an international judicial tribunal the normal jurisdiction in the matter. These objections do not apply with the same force to a Bill of Rights which is not universal. However, the present draft is still based on the view that the jurisdiction of an international court must be of a residuary nature and additional to the functioning of a commission or council of a non-judicial character.

The draft here submitted is cast in the form of legal obligations binding upon States. The rights of individuals follow from these obligations. The draft does not lay down that ' everyone ' ' everywhere ' has the right to inviolability of his person or to freedom of religion. It imposes upon the State the legal duty to respect these rights. The draft deliberately refrains from following the phraseology of instruments such as the Universal Declaration of Human Rights in which the intended absence of legal obligation is emphasised by the scrupulous avoidance of language implying a legal obligation binding upon the State to respect the individual rights recognised therein.

In contradistinction to the procedure adopted by the Commission on Human Rights, the present Draft is intended as a single Bill of Rights without the distinction, which is believed to be artificial, between a ' Declaration ', a ' Covenant ' and ' Provisions for Implementation '. No authority for any such distinction could be derived from the original terms of reference of the Commission or from the logical requirements inherent in the task of drafting a Bill of Rights. Normally, what has been given the name of a Universal Declaration of Human Rights would constitute the Preamble to the Bill of Rights; the ' provisions for implementation ' would normally form an integral part of its executory provisions. Divorced from the Bill of Rights, they are expedients obscuring the true nature of the problem involved.

Finally, the Draft is submitted largely on the assumption that the Bill of Rights, while falling short of universality, will be adopted in the form of a recommendation having the support of at least two-thirds of the General Assembly. Article 27 of the Draft declares the Bill to be binding upon those Members of the United Nations who will have voted for its adoption. In addition, while not binding upon other Members of the United Nations, the Bill thus adopted would nevertheless become part of the law of the United Nations to the extent that it would operate as part of its machinery and within the framework of its organisation. For according to the Charter the General Assembly is authorised to create organs for furthering the purposes of the United Nations.

The promotion of human rights and fundamental freedoms, through the ' joint action ', in the language of Article 56 of the Charter, of more than two-thirds of its members who, through a Bill of Rights, have defined and extended their existing obligations under the Charter, must be regarded as promoting the purposes of the United Nations. This would be an instance of a recommendation which, although, as such, not binding upon members who have not voted for it, is nevertheless not without legal effects within the United Nations.[1]

In the relevant parts of this Chapter there is formulated an alternative text of the Articles of a Bill of Rights adopted outside the United Nations, in so far as these Articles bear upon international supervision and enforcement and in so far as the co-operation of the organs of the United Nations is required for their application. In case the Bill of Rights should not, because of the impossibility of securing the necessary support of a two-thirds majority of the Members of the United Nations, become part of the law of the United Nations, other organs of international supervision and enforcement, limited to and created by the signatory States, will become necessary. This, as has been shown,[2] is a contingency which must be taken into consideration and which is distinctly preferable to adapting the contents of the Bill of Rights to the lowest common denominator of a large number of States comprising the requisite two-thirds majority of the Members of the United Nations.

It is now proposed to comment briefly upon the various Articles of the proposed draft of the Bill of Rights. For more detailed comment on the individual Articles the reader is referred to my book, already mentioned,[3] on the International Bill of the Rights of Man. However, it is doubtful whether such reference is necessary in respect of all articles of the Bill. When the United Nations was being set up, an International Bill of Human Rights was still in the nature of a novelty and an elaboration of its proposed articles was essential. Since then the idea and the fundamental clauses of a Bill of Rights—though not as yet its

---

[1] See below, p. 413.

[2] See above, p. 309.

[3] See above, p. 321. For the sake of convenience the book will be cited here as *I.B.R.M.*

implications—have been generally accepted. It is with these implications that the present book is primarily concerned.

3. THE BASES OF THE BILL. THE PREAMBLE. THE LAW OF NATURE. THE DUTIES TO THE STATE

Preamble (see pp. 313-321)

An International Bill of the Rights of Man is not the proper occasion for formulating the controversial principal problems of the political and social philosophy in an age of transition of unprecedented complexity and intensity of experience. For this reason there will not be found either in the Preamble to the present Draft or among its substantive Articles statements such as that embodied in Article 1 of the Universal Declaration of Human Rights adopted in 1948 which lays down that ' all human beings are born free and equal in dignity and rights ' and that ' they are endowed with reason and conscience and should act towards one another in a spirit of brotherhood '. The purpose of the Bill is to secure, through positive international action, the observance of the rights which it proclaims and, in so far as it is essential for their observance, the general definition of those rights. This is also the reason why the present draft refrains from invoking the right of resistance as the ultimate sanction of its observance—a warning for which there may possibly be found some logical justification in a municipal constitutional enactment clearly implying the sovereignty of the national legislature but which is out of place in an international instrument providing for an international guarantee, as against the sovereign State, of the fundamental rights of man.[4]

---

[4] See above, p. 92, as to the Virginian Bill on Religious Freedom. It is probable that the attitude of political philosophers to the right of resistance has been determined less by the premises of their teaching than by the more accidental factors of the historical circumstances of their time and of their own craving for peace. The latter factor explains the attitude of Grotius (see above, p. 116) and of Kant, who repudiated expressly the right of resistance against the supreme legislative power of the State. Luther's views on the right of resistance belong to the same category: ' It is in no wise proper for anyone who would be a Christian to set himself up against his government, whether it acts justly or unjustly. . . . There are no better works than to obey and serve all those who are set over us as superiors. For this reason also disobedience is a greater sin than murder, unchastity, theft and dishonesty': ' On Good Works ', *Works* (transl. by Lambert, vol. VI, p. 256). Rousseau's doctrine of despotic democracy repudiated it by obvious implication. He deprecated, for the same reason, constitutional guarantees of fundamental rights. ' As the sovereign

Neither is reference made in the Preamble to the law of nature as the ultimate source of the rights and freedoms recognised and protected by the Bill of Rights. Any such reference—which is believed to be expressive of an enduring verity—is not essential in an international enactment the purpose of which is to give the natural rights of man the tangible guarantee of the positive law. This does not mean that the law of nature conceived as the true foundation of the positive law thus enacted will henceforth lose its significance and vitality. It will remain forever as the irreducible source, the corrective and the final and inescapable sanction, when all others have failed, of the rights of man. This is the reason why prominence is given in the first Part of this book to the law of nature and its relation to human rights and international law.[5]

It is only in one respect that it has been thought proper to introduce in the Preamble an affirmation of a wider political and jurisprudential principle, namely, the right of human personality to ' fulfil, in freedom, its duty to man and society '. The Bill of Rights is not the proper occasion for affirming the obligations of the individual to the State. This is so not because it is based on any distinctly individualistic philosophy. The reason why a Bill of Rights need not concern itself with the duties of man to society is that its object is limited to the protection of his rights as against the State. History has shown that there is a need for such protection. There is no imperative necessity to safeguard the

power is formed wholly of the individuals who compose it, it neither has nor can have any interest contrary to theirs; and consequently the sovereign power need give no guarantee to its subjects, because it is impossible for the body to wish to hurt all its members'; *Contrat Social* (1762; Cole's translation), Book I, Chapter 7. With Locke who, in the last Chapter of the *Two Treatises of Civil Government*, has provided the best discussion of the right of revolution, the justification of rebellion was a justification of the revolution of 1688. The Declaration of 1789 proclaimed the natural and inalienable right of resistance alongside of the rights of liberty, property and security. Article 33 of the Declaration of Rights of 1793 laid down expressly that ' resistance to oppression is the consequence of all other rights of man'. While subsequent French constitutional enactments did not refer *expressis verbis* to the right of resistance, it is arguable that they recognised it inasmuch as they confirmed the principles of the Declaration of 1789. The same applies to the Constitution of 1946. See also below, p. 330, n. 11.

The Ninth International Conference of American States adopted in 1948 a Resolution forwarding for study by the Inter-American Juridical Committee a proposal by Cuba laying down that ' the right of resistance is recognised in case of manifest acts of oppression or tyranny '. (*Annals of the Organisation of American States*, vol. I (1949), p. 136.)

[5] See above, pp. 73-126.

State against man. Too much has been heard of his duty to the State and too much has been done to give effect to it. But it is consonant with the dignity and the proper understanding of the Bill of Rights to emphasise that the rights to be protected are conceived as a means to enable man to do his duty, in freedom, to man and society. We need not pause to answer the question whether freedom thus conceived is an end in itself or a means to a higher aim.

4. RIGHTS OF PERSONAL FREEDOM. THE LIMITS OF ELABORATION IN THE BILL OF RIGHTS

Article 1

The life and liberty of the person shall be inviolate within the limits of the law.

No person shall be deprived of liberty save by a judgment of a court of law or pending trial in accordance with the law. Detention by purely executive order shall be unlawful in time of peace.

There shall be protection from and compensation for arbitrary and unauthorised arrest and detention.

The law shall provide safeguards against prolonged detention preceding trial, against excessive bail or unreasonable refusal thereof, against denial of just guarantees in respect of evidence and procedure in criminal cases, against the refusal of protection in the nature of the writ of habeas corpus, against the retroactive operation of criminal laws and against punishment which is cruel, inhuman, or offensive to the dignity of man.

The provisions of this Article refer to the primary and, historically, the first and most fundamental aspect of human freedom— the security of life and limb against direct violence on the part of authority, or indirect violence in the form of arbitrary arrest or of denial of necessary safeguards in criminal trials. In keeping with the scheme adopted in this present Draft, the Article avoids detailed elaboration of the safeguards provided therein. Such elaboration must, at best, be incomplete. At worst it may be misleading, liable to abuse, incompatible with the wide acceptance of the Bill and hampering the work of judicial and other enforcing agencies in the international sphere. Thus no attempt has been made here to define cases in which arrest is permissible[6] or to

[6] In connexion with Article 5 of the proposed 'Covenant' on Human Rights the representatives of Australia, Denmark, France, Lebanon and the United Kingdom voiced doubts whether their Governments would be able to accede to a Covenant imposing, in this respect, obligations as elastic as those expressed in paragraphs 1 and 2 of Article 4 which laid down as follows: ' 1. No one shall be subjected to arbitrary arrest or detention; 2. No one shall be deprived of his liberty except on such grounds and in accordance with such procedure as may be established by law.' That provision, especially the use of the term ' arbitrary ', the representatives of those States regarded as lending itself to a variety of meanings. They considered it uncertain whether paragraph 2 repeated, expanded, or limited paragraph 1 and whether the words ' as may be established by law ' would effectively fulfil the intended purpose. They pointed out that ' any dictator would be prepared to accept such an article '. Instead of paragraph 1 these States proposed the following article, defining cases in which arrest and detention are lawful: —

' (a) the lawful detention of a person after a conviction or as a security measure involving deprivation of liberty;

' (b) the lawful arrest and detention of a person for non-compliance with the lawful order or injunction of a court;

' (c) the arrest of a person effected for the purpose of bringing him before the competent legal authority on a reasonable suspicion of having committed an offence or which is reasonably considered to be necessary to prevent his committing a crime or fleeing after having done so;

' (d) the lawful detention of persons of unsound mind or of minors, by lawful order, for the purpose of educational surveillance;

' (e) the lawful arrest or detention of a person to prevent his effecting an unauthorised entry into the country or of a person against whom deportation or extradition proceedings are pending.'

They expressed the view that the clauses thus suggested were both ' brief and comprehensive ' (E/CN.4/350). It may well be doubted whether this is so. ' Lawful detention . . . as a security measure involving deprivation of liberty ' may meet all the requirements of a dictator. The same applies to the proposed paragraph 3. There is no escape from the fact that while in this respect—as in many others—a Bill of Rights ought not to be so vague as to be meaningless, any elaboration of detail is impracticable and tends to defeat its object. Allowance must also be made for the peculiarities of the law of some countries which, although open to criticism, are not necessarily such as to offend against the fundamental purposes of the Bill. Thus, in 1948, some countries (including the United Kingdom) proposed that arrest and detention of persons suffering from serious contagious disease should be lawful (E/800, p. 21). Other suggestions included the arrest and detention of alcoholics, arrest for the purpose of removal from one province to another, arrest for breach of military discipline, arrest as a means of satisfaction of a judgment in civil cases involving wrongdoing or by way of punishment in such cases, detention of enemy aliens, or—as suggested by the Chinese representative— ' arrest of persons who trespass on prohibited property or areas; arrest of persons for disturbing public order such as shouting "fire" in a theatre when there is no fire; arrest of persons for speeding while driving through a crowded street in the city, and arrest of persons who attempt to commit suicide.' (E/800, pp. 22, 23). It is clear that these and similar attempts at completeness must tend to defeat the object of the principal provision. If persisted in they would require numerous amendments in the law of various countries and delay or render impracticable the acceptance of the Bill. It will be noted that in Great Britain Parliament and the courts possess the right of arbitrary arrest for contempt of these bodies. For some illuminating statements on the question of freedom of speech in relation to imprisonment for contempt of court see *Craig* v. *Harney* (1947), 67 Sup. Ct. 1249, where the Supreme Court of the United States reversed the conviction of the accused who described the judge's ruling as arbitrary and a ' travesty of justice ': ' But the law of contempt is not made for the protection of judges who may

consider the exceptions to the prohibition of the retroactive operation of laws. With regard to the latter, Article 19 of the present
Draft provides for the exceptions necessary to secure human
rights and fundamental freedoms.[7] That exception is sufficiently
wide to permit retroactive effect to be given to crimes against
humanity.

An example of the drawbacks of excessive elaboration of
detail was provided by an article of the proposed Covenant which
laid down that ' everyone who has undergone punishment as a
result of an erroneous conviction for crime shall have an enforceable right to compensation ' and that ' this right shall accrue to
the heirs of a person executed by virtue of an erroneous
sentence '.[8] The right to compensation on account of unlawful
arrest and detention or of erroneous conviction—or even for a
conviction resulting from a culpable miscarriage or denial of
justice—is not generally conceded even by the law of the most
advanced States.[9] It is difficult to see why, if the right to compensation is included in the Bill, it should not apply to the
violation of provisions such as the prohibition of torture,
inhuman punishment, arbitrary expulsion of aliens or denial of
justice on account of discrimination of various types. Neither is
there any logical—or other convincing—reason why the right
to compensation should accrue only to the heirs of a person
executed by virtue of an *erroneous* sentence and not to the heirs of
persons executed by virtue of a deliberately unjust sentence or
of a person who died as the result and in the course of unjust
imprisonment. The provision of an enforceable right to

---

be sensitive to the trends of public opinion. Judges are supposed to be men
of fortitude, able to thrive in a hardy climate' (*per* Mr. Justice Douglas).
'The liberties guaranteed by the First Amendment . . . are too highly
prized to be subjected to the hazards of summary contempt procedure ' (*per*
Mr. Justice Murphy).

[7] See below, p. 365.

[8] Article 13.

[9] The United States expressly asked for the deletion of that provision. The
right of compensation is not recognised in every one of the countries which
associated themselves with the proposal. While pointing out that French
law provided for compensation only in cases of unlawful administrative
arrest, the French representative agreed to the more general clause ' as evidence
of good will and in the conviction that the article was a step forward'
(E/CN.4/S.R.96, p. 4). However, he subsequently urged that the text should
not provide ' indiscriminately' for a right to compensation and that the
Covenant should proclaim the principle of compensation while leaving to the
signatories the option to adapt their legislation to the principle thus proclaimed
(E/CN.4/S.R.102, p. 7).

compensation does not in itself constitute a safeguard. For such compensation, if the authorities of the State concerned are so minded, may be inadequate or purely nominal, and an appeal to the international jurisdiction would be necessary to make that right truly effective. On the other hand, no express provision of the Bill of Rights would seem to be necessary in order to give an international court or commission the power to recommend compensation in case of culpable miscarriage or denial of justice. Similarly, unless an appeal, with a suspending effect, is allowed to an international authority, it is difficult to visualise the working of the provision to the effect that sentence of death may be imposed ' only as a penalty for the most serious crimes ' and that no one may be executed ' save in virtue of the sentence of a competent court . . . and not contrary to the principles expressed in the Universal Declaration of Human Rights '.[10]

These and similar proposals provide an instructive illustration of the dangers and of the unwisdom of an excessively detailed elaboration of the Bill of Rights. Such details may go beyond the generally accepted practice and for that reason hamper the adoption of the Bill. In other cases they may set a standard which either is below the general practice or which crystallizes practices capable of or calling for improvement.[11] Above all, if

[10] Provisional text, as proposed by the Commission on Human Rights, of Article 5 of the Covenant.

[11] The proposals put forward in 1949 by the representatives of Australia, Denmark, France, Lebanon, and the United Kingdom for an Article of the ' Covenant ' relating to the right to life illustrates that aspect of the question. The proposed Article was as follows: —
' 1. No one shall be deprived of his life intentionally.
' 2. There shall be no exception to this rule save where the death results
 ' (a) in those States where capital punishment is lawful, from the execution of such penalty in accordance with the sentence of a Court;
 ' (b) from the use of force which is no more than absolutely necessary
  ' (i) in defence of any person from unlawful violence;
  ' (ii) in order to effect a lawful arrest or to prevent an escape from lawful custody;
   or
  ' (iii) in action lawfully taken for the purpose of quelling a riot or insurrection, or for prohibiting entry to a clearly defined place to which access is forbidden on grounds of national security.'
The Russian representative criticised the paragraph which authorised the use of force to quell a rebellion without specifying the nature of the rebellion. He urged that there were cases in which rebellion would be lawful, in particular in cases of denial of essential rights and fundamental freedoms (E/CN.4/SR.91, p. 4). The Chairman of the Commission, who made an impressive plea against loading the principal provision with detailed exceptions, cited as an example the law of the United States where in cases of shipwreck, where an excessive number of survivors threatens to sink a lifeboat,

accepted, they would impose an additional strain upon the international agencies—judicial and other—charged with the implementation of the Bill of Rights. It is arguable that the absence of definition would involve a corresponding enlargement of the powers of the international agencies concerned, but there is probably little substance in that argument. A general prohibition of arbitrary arrest would not give these agencies discretionary powers wider than those implicit in a detailed regulation.

These difficulties illustrate the dangers—and the futility—of attempts at an excessive definition of the rights protected by the Bill of Rights. It is probable that persistence in that tendency would make a Bill of Rights impracticable, if not impossible. The insistence on ' no enforcement without previous definition ' may easily—and plausibly—become a weapon of obstruction. Undoubtedly, it is true that human rights and fundamental freedoms must be defined in order to be enforceable. But it is equally true to say that these rights and freedoms, even if not defined in detail, are capable of judicial and non-judicial enforcement by reference to general principles of law. National courts have found no difficulty in enforcing the general provisions of Bills of Rights of their countries. The only occasion on which an international court was called upon to interpret ' fundamental rights ' of the individual supplies an instructive illustration of the same fact. In its Advisory Opinion, given in 1935, on the Consistency of Certain Danzig Legislative Decrees with the Constitution of the Free City of Danzig[12] the Permanent Court of International Justice found that certain decrees which, in effect,

it is not a crime to draw lots and throw the necessary number overboard (*ibid.*, pp. 5, 6). The representative of the United Kingdom urged, somewhat optimistically, that the list was fully complete: ' No one had yet referred to a case which that list did not cover ' (E/CN.4/SR.98).

With regard to (b) (i) of these proposals it is clear that unlawful violence done to a person may be such as not to justify the taking of the life of the offender even if it is absolutely necessary to prevent such violence, for instance, in cases of unlawful imprisonment. As to (b) (ii) there are many States which do not permit the taking of life for the purpose of effecting a lawful arrest. The law of some American States denies the right to use force dangerous to human life except in respect of arrest for felonies committed with violence. See Warner, ' Modern Trends in the American Law of Arrest ' (*English Studies in Criminal Science, Pamphlet Series,* 1943), p. 18. Referring to the detailed list of exceptions, the Russian representative on the Human Rights Commission pointed out in 1949, perhaps not without some reason, that, in that respect, the Covenant as contemplated would be a covenant on the rights of police rather than on human rights (E/CN.4/S.R.98).

[12] P.C.I.J. Series A/B, No. 65.

gave Danzig courts the right to inflict punishment for acts which
were not criminal at the time when they were committed were
contrary to the Danzig Constitution.   In making that pronouncement the Court did not rely on any express prohibition of
retroactive punishment.   No such prohibition formed explicitly
part of the Danzig Constitution.   The Court relied on the fact
that the various provisions of the Danzig Constitution referring
to ' fundamental rights and freedoms ', such as those relating to
the liberty of the person and the freedom of opinion and association, made the Free City a State under the rule of law and that
retroactive punishment was contrary to the principles of a constitution embodying fundamental rights and duties.   Moreover,
there is a *via media* between the elastic formula of the Charter
which refers generally to human rights and fundamental freedoms
and a meticulously detailed definition which in many ways
approaches a legislative codification going beyond generally
accepted practice.[13]   The inelegant and undignified learning

---

[13] On the disadvantages of excessive elaboration, in particular with regard to
the general clause limiting the operation of the Covenant, see the useful
comments submitted by the Government of the United States in 1947 in
connexion with the proposed Covenant.   It may be useful to reproduce the
relevant passage in full:
  'An essential difficulty with the expression of specific limitations is that,
by common rules of construction, such expression implies the exclusion of
others.   It would thus be open to argument that any other limitations imposed
by law are contrary to the treaty.   To give a hypothetical example, it might
be necessary, for the protection of the public welfare, to enact new Legislation
restricting obnoxious medical advertising transmitted by television.   Action
of this sort would be perfectly proper, but it would not be appropriate at this
time to cover the specific point in a broad general instrument affecting fundamental rights only, in many countries, a substantial proportion of which are
not concerned today with television. Other technological developments, whose
nature cannot be forecast in any way, are bound to arise.   To require formal,
solemn amendments of the Covenant to cover each of these developments
would be clearly impractical. . . . The only type of document on which
general agreement can possibly be secured is one of a general nature.
  ' Detailed specific provisions purporting to set forth all possible limitations would be particularly unfortunate in countries like the United States
where the basic constitutional document describes treaties, together with
the Constitution and laws, as the supreme law of the land.   Treaty provisions
which, while not intended to change the existing law, are capable of creating
confusion and raising multifarious controversies are obviously to be avoided.
For this reason alone there might be considerable doubt as to the ability of
the United States to accept a Covenant containing such specific limitations.
  ' The foregoing argument presents one detailed reason why, in attempting
to draft a treaty on the extremely broad and complex subject of human rights,
the best and perhaps the only practicable approach is to have a clear and
simple document.   It is quite possible that a Covenant which attempts to go
into too great detail, even if it could be ratified, would be so complex and
confused as to be unworkable in practice.' (Doc. E/CN.4/82, p. 11.)
  The fact that in the course of the drafting of the Covenant the United
States proposed somewhat detailed clauses does not detract from the cogency
of these considerations.

which has accompanied attempts to define the traditional rights of freedom from arbitrary arrest[14] or freedom of expression of opinion[15] or the prohibition of cruel punishment[16] shows the dangers and the inconvenience of that method of an exhaustive codification of large sections of what would be in effect the criminal law of the world. It is possible that the Bill of Rights may provide the starting point for efforts of this nature.[17] But these are tasks to be performed by bodies of qualified and independent experts working over prolonged periods of time and able and free to produce such partial codifications of constitutional and criminal law by methods other than those of rapid discussion and voting by what are essentially political assemblies.

5. SLAVERY AND FORCED LABOUR

Article 2

No State shall permit slavery or legal relations substantially identical therewith, or traffic in slaves, or compulsory labour in

[14] See above, p. 328.

[15] See below, p. 336. And see below, p. 335, as to forced labour.

[16] See, for instance, the Draft Code, prepared by Professor Glaser, of Minimum Rules for the Treatment of Persons Suspected or Accused of Crimes (*The Journal of Criminal Science*, ed. by Radzinowicz and Turner, 1948, pp. 157-164).

[17] Before the Human Rights Commission the Russian representative urged in 1949 that it was essential that the 'Covenant' should contain an article prohibiting corporal punishment (E/CN.4/SR.92). It is not believed that corporal punishment, whatever may be its defects, comes within the prohibition of the Article as formulated. No foresight of draftsmanship can rule out or comprise all contingencies. Nor is there a ready answer, easily secured by definition, to such contingencies. Thus, for instance, it would be futile to enumerate examples of or exceptions to the prohibition of 'cruel and unusual punishment' as provided in the Eighth Amendment to the Constitution of the United States. In *Louisiana ex rel. Francis* v. *Resweber*, 67 Sup. Ct. 374 (1947), the Supreme Court was confronted with a case of a Negro who had been sentenced to death by electrocution. The first attempt at execution had failed because of a mechanical defect. He claimed that a second attempt to execute him would amount to an imposition of 'cruel and unusual' punishment. The Court was almost equally divided on the question. Four Justices (including the Chief Justice) held that the Constitution gave protection against cruelty inherent in the method of punishment and did not cover a situation where there was no intent to inflict pain. Mr. Justice Frankfurter, concurring with the majority, said: 'Were I to hold that Louisiana would transgress the Due Process Clause if the State were allowed, in the precise circumstances before us, to carry out the death sentence, I would be enforcing my private view rather than that consensus of society's opinion which, for purposes of due process, is the standard enjoined by the Constitution.' But the following passage from the Opinion of the dissenting Justices merits quotation: 'How many deliberate and intentional re-applications of electric current does it take to produce a cruel, unusual and unconstitutional punishment? While five applications would be more cruel and unusual than one, the uniqueness of the present case demonstrates that, today, two separate applications are sufficiently "cruel and unusual" to be prohibited.'

any form other than public service, equally incumbent upon all, or as part of punishment pronounced by a court of law.

There is general agreement on this aspect of the Bill. The actual dimensions of the problem of slavery are small[18] and, to that extent, the provisions of the Bill of Rights are more in the nature of an affirmation of principle than of a remedy against a widespread and menacing evil. But the principle itself is of an importance so fundamental as to warrant its express recognition in the Bill. Moreover, with regard to slavery, nothing short of a clear international prohibition can cut decisively through the cobweb of secondary considerations, some of them of a humanitarian character, which in certain countries have prevented the full abolition of slavery. In this connexion the words ' or legal relations substantially identical therewith ', although detracting from the simplicity of the article, have been added in order to secure the purpose of the general prohibition. It is possible that the rigid prohibition of slavery, and its cognate forms, may on occasions produce hardships for persons freed of the formal bondage of slavery. Similar arguments were put forward in this connexion before the American Civil War and since then. They do not touch the core of the problem. Such cases of hardship as may be due to the abolition of slavery must— and can—be met by remedial measures of social welfare and economic policy specially designed for the purpose.[19]

With regard to compulsory labour the words ' other than public service, equally incumbent upon all ' are wide enough to include the various contingencies calling for personal performance of services. Any detailed enumeration of these

[18] See the Report by the Acting Secretary-General of the League of Nations in October, 1945. on the Work of the League during the War (League of Nations Publications, General, 1945.2., Part II, paragraph 4, pp. 109, 110) where it is stated, in the light of the work of the Advisory Committee of Experts on Slavery set up by the Assembly Resolution of 1932, that ' slavery and slave trade are on the point of disappearing completely' and that 'continuous progress was being made regarding the solution of the problems which presented themselves in certain countries in connexion with other institutions or instances resembling slavery to a greater or lesser degree'. In 1949 the General Assembly requested the Economic and Social Council to study the problem of slavery at its next session (A/783). In the same year the Council instructed the Secretary-General to appoint a committee to survey the field of slavery and other institutions or customs resembling slavery and to suggest methods of attacking the problems involved (E/1454). For the discussion before the Economic and Social Council in 1949 see E/SR.298, 300 and 301.

[19] In Jefferson's *Notes on Virginia* there will be found detailed suggestions for the solution of problems of slavery on these lines (*Writings,* Ford's edition, 1892-1899, vol. 3, pp. 243, 244).

contingencies, while appropriate in a special convention bearing on the subject, is out of keeping with the character of the Bill.[20] On the other hand, the words ' as *part* of punishment pronounced by a court of law' are explicit enough to prohibit a system in which judicial punishment is designed to provide the State with cheap labour on a large scale.[21]

6. FREEDOM OF RELIGION, OPINION AND ASSOCIATION

Articles 3, 4, 5, 6

3. There shall be full freedom of religious belief and practice.

4. The freedom of speech, of expression of opinion, and of imparting and receiving information in writing and by other means shall not be denied or impaired.

5. There shall be full freedom of association and assembly.

6. The sanctity of the home and the secrecy of correspondence shall be respected.

[20] As an example of detailed regulation which is fully appropriate in a particular convention but which is out of place in a general Bill of Rights, reference may be made to Article 2 of the Forced Labour Convention concluded in 1930 under the auspices of the International Labour Organisation. That Article provided, in part, as follows: —

' 1. For the purposes of this Convention the term " forced or compulsory labour " shall mean all work or service which is exacted from any person under the menace of any penalty and for which the said person has not offered himself voluntarily.

' 2. Nevertheless, for the purposes of this Convention, the term " forced or compulsory labour " shall not include:

' (a) Any work or service exacted in virtue of compulsory military service laws for work of a purely military character;

' (b) Any work or service which forms part of the normal civic obligations of the citizens of a fully self-governing country;

' (c) Any work or service exacted from any person as a consequence of a conviction in a court of law, provided that the said work or service is carried out under the supervision and control of a public authority and the said person is not hired to or placed at the disposal of private individuals, companies or associations;

' (d) Any work or service exacted in cases of emergency, that is to say, in the event of war or of a calamity or threatened calami.y, such as fire, flood, famine, earthquake, violent epidemic or epizootic disease, invasion by animal, insect or vegetable pests, and, in general, any circumstance that would endanger the existe.ce or the well-being of the whole or par; of the population.'

The original intention to incorporate that Article in the Bill of Rights was, properly, abandoned. And see below, p. 336, on the definition of freedom of information. For a prolonged discussion before the Commission on Human Rights on the treatment of conscientious objectors in connexion with forced labour see E/CN.4/S.R.94.

[21] In 1949 the Economic and Social Council adopted a Resolution (195(VIII)) on ' Survey of Forced Labour and Measures for its Abolition '.

It is convenient to group these four Articles together. They give expression to the rights of personal freedom traditionally associated with Bills of Rights. Their qualifications, which are common to all other rights guaranteed by the Bill, are stated in the general limiting clause of Article 19.[22] They are universally recognised[23] as an essential part of any Bill of Rights. The main factor which may impede their general acceptance is the tendency, already referred to,[24] to elaborate them and all their possible

[22] See p. 365 below.

[23] For their historic foundations and other comment thereon see the writer's *An International Bill of the Rights of Man* (1945), pp. 104-115.

[24] See above, p. 280. The same tendency is exhibited in Article 16 of the proposed 'Covenant' relating to freedom of religion. 'This right', it is there provided, 'includes freedom [of everyone] to change his religion or belief, and freedom, either alone or in community with others and in public or private, to manifest his religion or belief in teaching, practice, worship and observance.' It is clear that all these are implicit in the freedom of religion.

A forbidding example of prolixity and elaboration in regard to the simple right of freedom of speech will be found in the text of the relevant Article 17 submitted in 1949 by the United Nations Conference on Freedom of Information. The text proposed was, in part, as follows:—

'1. Every person shall have the right to freedom of thought and the right to freedom of expression without interference by governmental action; these rights shall include freedom to hold opinions, to seek, receive and impart information and ideas, regardless of frontiers, either orally, by written or printed matter, in the form of art, or by legally operated visual or auditory devices.

'2. The right to freedom of expression carries with it duties and responsibilities and may, therefore, be subject to penalties, liabilities or restrictions clearly defined by law, but only with regard to: (a) matters which must remain secret in the interest of national safety; (b) expressions which invite persons to alter by violence the system of government; (c) expressions which directly incite persons to commit criminal acts; (d) expressions which are obscene; (e) expressions injurious to the fair conduct of legal proceedings; (f) infringements of literary or artistic rights; (g) expressions about other persons natural or legal which defame their reputations or are otherwise injurious to them without benefiting the public; (h) the systematic diffusion of deliberately false or distorted reports which undermine friendly relations between peoples and States.

'A State may establish on reasonable terms a right to reply or a similar corrective remedy': *Economic and Social Council. Official Records,* 4th Year, 9th Session, Suppl. No. 10.

The Drafting Committee of the Commission on Human Rights did not consider the list sufficiently exhaustive and added a further list of possible limitations:—

'1. The disclosures of professional secrets contrary to law. 2. The disclosures arising out of marital and personal relationships. 3. Expressions which are fraudulent or part of a fraudulent scheme. 4. Expressions detrimental to public decency or morals (for example, detailed crime stories, reports on executions and suicides, sensational court reports). 5. Matters of contract. 6. Control of advertising or economic matters. 7. Proper conduct of political elections or campaigns. 8. Matters affecting the civil service. 9. Disclosures of governmental information (other than in cases involving national safety, for example, in economic and social matters, such as crop

qualifications in a manner derogatory to the purposes and the dignity of the Bill.

7. THE RIGHT OF PETITION

Article 7

There shall be full freedom of petition to the national authorities and to the United Nations.

The historic and juridical bases of the right of petition, within both the national and the international spheres, are examined in other parts of this book, namely, in relation to the powers of the organs of the United Nations under the Charter[25] and in connexion with the general question of the enforcement of the Bill of Rights.[26] It is shown there that within the State the importance of the right of petition has diminished in proportion as other means of redress, normally available in democratic society, have become available. These developments have not affected the basic character of the right of petition and no Bill of Rights can disregard it. Similarly, in the international sphere the right of petition will, in due course, be directed into the normal channels of a judicial and semi-judicial procedure. When that happens its recognition in the Bill of Rights will become to a large extent declaratory. It will be none the less essential.

reports, income tax reports, recipients of unemployment relief, and pending judicial decisions). 10. Communications with foreign governments. 11. Profanity in public places. 12. Operation of radio broadcasting and similar media without a licence. 13. Statements by corporations, partnerships or individuals, in the issue of bonds and shares of stock. 14. Unforeseeable future matters relating to development of new media of information or new social practices.'

Various States suggested further limitations too numerous to be enumerated here. Thus South Africa suggested, among others, the following: —

' The prohibition of opprobrious epithets, jeers or jibes in connexion with the fact that any person has continued or returned to work or has refused to work for any employer, or the sending of information as to any such fact to any person in order to prevent any other person from obtaining or retaining employment, etc., etc.

' The restrictions imposed upon the publications of preparatory examination and trial proceedings, where the offence charged involves any indecent act or an act in the nature of extortion, or upon the publication of information which is likely to reveal the identity of an accused person under nineteen years of age or of a child concerned in proceedings before a children's court.' Many other limitations were added by South Africa and other States.

[25] See above, pp. 248-250.

[26] See above, pp. 286-290, and below, pp. 375-377.

22

8. EQUALITY BEFORE THE LAW AND FREEDOM FROM DISCRIMINATION

Article 8

All nationals of the State shall enjoy full equality before the law and equal treatment in all respects by the authorities of the State. In particular, there shall be no discrimination on account of religion, race, sex, colour, language, national origin, or political creed. No State shall lend the assistance of its judicial and other organs and resources for the purpose of enforcing or practising discrimination, from whatever source it may originate, contrary to the objects of this Bill of Rights.

The principle of equality before the law and of prohibition of discrimination is of the essence of the rule of law and of human freedom. It is independent of the question of the natural equality of all human beings—which, notwithstanding some recurrent shallow criticism, is both an inescapable postulate of ethics and, with regard to most fundamental aspects of human existence, a fact of nature.[27] The foundations and limitations of the principle of equality have been examined elsewhere,[28] and comment is required only with regard to two questions which are likely to figure prominently in the application of the principle of equality in the future. These are the question of non-discrimination on account of sex and the question of the duty to prevent discrimination by persons and bodies other than the State.

The prohibition of discrimination on account of sex raises one of the most difficult issues connected with the substantive provisions of the Bill of Rights.[29] To include specifically non-discrimination on account of sex among the obligations of the Bill is either to jeopardize, to that extent, its binding character or to make it impossible for some States to subscribe to it consistently

---

[27] See above, Chapter V. ' Democracy, like Christianity, would be meaningless if all human beings were identical; the whole point of Christianity is that, though, in fact, men differ morally, intellectually and materially, each one is treated by God as equal and of equal cosmic value; the whole point of democracy is that, in fact, men are unequal in physical, mental and moral endowments, and should be treated by the State as of equal social and political value ': Woolf, *After the Deluge*, vol. I (1931), p. 260.

[28] See *I.B.R.M.*, pp. 115-119.

[29] It must be noted that the second sentence of Article 8 which prohibits discrimination is not intended to be exhaustive. It elaborates the general principle of equality announced in the first sentence. While it particularises some of the typical causes of discrimination, it cannot be interpreted as permitting others, for instance, discrimination on account of membership of a social class or status associated with property.

with a determination to abide by its provisions. It is a fact that in many countries of advanced civilisation the full legal equality of the sexes has not yet been achieved; that its absence is not regarded by public opinion—including in some cases a substantial minority of women—as inconsistent with the general principle of equality before the law; and that the unqualified introduction of the principle of full equality of the sexes would be difficult to achieve and would be resisted. In Switzerland women do not possess and, according to some, have not pressed for the right to vote or to be candidates in the elections to the national legislature. In many countries the disabilities of women have a religious origin and their removal is likely to encounter fanatical opposition.[30] In Belgium women voted for the first time in the general elections of 1949. The suffrage was conferred upon women in Panama in 1946, in Venezuela in 1947 and in Argentina in 1948. In many Latin-American States women are still denied the suffrage although these countries as a whole have been most prominent in urging equality of rights for women.[31] In Great Britain, after a protracted enquiry into the question of equal pay for men and women, the Government arrived in 1948 at the conclusion that it was not as yet feasible to adopt the principle of equal pay.[32] The enquiries conducted in connexion with the work of the Commission on the Status of Women[33] revealed the wide range of inequality in many respects. It may be argued with much force that the principle of equality of men and women is so com-

[30] When in 1949 the proposal was made in the Iranian Chamber to confer the right of suffrage upon women the authors of the proposal were shouted down as atheists. Similar charges were made in the same year against the protagonists of female suffrage in India and Egypt.

[31] The Ninth International Conference of American States adopted in 1948 a Convention on the Granting of Civil Rights to Women. Article 1 of the Convention provided: 'The American States agree to grant to women the same civil rights that men enjoy.' The same Conference adopted another Convention, Article 1 of which provided: 'The High Contracting Parties agree that the right to vote and to be elected to national office shall not be denied or abridged by reason of sex.' The Conference also adopted an Organic Statute of the Inter-American Commission of Women. For the text of the Conventions and of the Statute see *Annals of the Organization of American States*, vol. I, No. 1 (1949).

[32] It was stated in 1948, in a memorandum of the Secretary-General of the United Nations (E/1096), that, according to the information supplied to him, the Government of the United Kingdom 'cannot at this time apply the principle'. For a general discussion of the question of equality of pay see *Economic and Social Council, 4th Year*, 8th Session, *February-March*, 1949, pp. 92-100.

[33] See above, p. 262.

pelling and its continued denial so intolerable that, as in the case of slavery, the difficulties surrounding the subject must be regarded as of secondary nature; that the same applies to arguments based on the physical constitution of women and their claim, conceded in most countries, to special and more favourable treatment in some respects; and that participation in an international enactment of that nature may assist States in terminating what is essentially a relic of the past and a challenge to justice.   The subjection of women in the political, civil and economic spheres and the slowness of the process of their emancipation are a reflection upon modern civilisation as a whole,[34] and it seems proper that the collective effort of the international community should become available for remedying the evils of what has now become an anachronism.   On the other hand, in view of the prevailing practice in a considerable number of States, the inclusion of a clear obligation to abolish discrimination on account of sex may put the observance of the Bill of Rights under considerable strain. That contingency, as well as the fact that it is impossible to disregard the principle of non-discrimination on account of sex without weakening the moral authority of the Bill, raises the question whether in this particular matter the Bill ought to leave open the avenue, which must remain exceptional, of adding a limited reservation, in the form of a separate Declaration,[35] relating to the scope or the time of the operation of the Bill in this respect.

9.   DISCRIMINATION BY BODIES OTHER THAN THE STATE

Another aspect of the question of equality and non-discrimination which requires comment is the extent to which the obligation of non-discrimination includes acts of bodies other than the State itself.   In the first instance, it is clear that such obligation must cover cases in which, although discrimination originates in a private act—such as a contract containing a restrictive covenant on account of race or origin—the courts of a country are called

[34] See Lecky's *Democracy and Liberty,* vol. II (1896), pp. 415-461.   It is of interest to note that Mormons, notwithstanding their polygamous creed, were among the first to grant full suffrage to women.   See Lecky, *op. cit.,* vol. I, pp. 453 *et seq.*

[35] See below, p. 390.

upon to lend the assistance of the State to the enforcement of the private act in question. The view has been expressed elsewhere in this book that such enforcement by the State of acts of discrimination of private origin is contrary to its own principal obligation of non-discrimination.[36] The matter is of sufficient importance to warrant a separate clause of the Bill of Rights. The same applies to acts of discrimination by authorities, bodies and organisations which although not directly organs of the State are indirectly so inasmuch as they are in receipt of State assistance through subventions, grants, exemptions from taxation, and similar facilities. The words of the present draft— ' no State shall lend the assistance of its judicial or other organs and resources for the purpose of enforcing or practising discrimination '—are designed to give expression to this particular obligation of the State.

It may be a matter for discussion whether the State is not bound to prevent, by legislative action, discrimination by private individuals and bodies of individuals, licensed by the State, who perform a public function as in the case of innkeepers or owners of other establishments normally open to the public at large. The Bill of Rights enacted in 1947[37] by the Canadian Province of Saskatchewan lays down that ' every person and every class of persons should enjoy the right to obtain the accommodation or facilities of any standard or other hotel, victualling house, theatre or other place to which the public is customarily admitted, regardless of the race, creed, religion, colour or ethnic or national origin of such person or class of persons '. In various countries, such as Great Britain,[38] there is a statutory or common law duty of the innkeeper not to discriminate against members of the public asking for accommodation and other services. There may be substance in the view that in so far as private individuals and bodies obtain a licence for fulfilling services of a social and public character, or are granted special facilities or exemptions by the State, they are its organs. No attempt has been made in the present Draft to make the Bill of Rights sufficiently wide to

---

[36] See above, pp. 155-157, in relation to the obligations of the Charter.

[37] Article 11 (*Year Book of Human Rights,* 1947, p. 73).

[38] At common law it is an actionable wrong for an innkeeper to refuse accommodation to a person who desires it: *Lamond* v. *Richard* [1897] 1 Q.B.541. The same applies to a common carrier: *Great Western Rly. Co.* v. *Sutton* (1869), L.R. 4 H.L., p. 237.

cover discrimination by private individuals and bodies in other respects. It is clear that a State which lends the arm of the law for the enforcement of such discrimination would be failing in its duties under the Bill of Rights.[39]   There remains the no less

[39] The representative of France proposed in 1949 an Article in the Covenant according to which 'any advocacy of national, racial or religious hostility that constitutes an incitement to violence or hatred shall be prohibited by the law of the State'.   A provision of this nature probably goes beyond the normal scope of a Bill of Rights.   No such protection was accorded by the 'Covenant' proposed in 1949, which laid down that 'everyone shall be accorded equal protection against any incitement to such discrimination'— a provision which means merely that if such protection is accorded it shall be accorded equally to everyone. In fact, most States represented on the Commission declined to accept such an obligation on the ground that its enforcement would be contrary to freedom of speech.   On the other hand, while the Bill, as here drafted, does not impose upon the State the obligation to prohibit acts of that nature, the general clause of Article 19 certainly gives it the right, notwithstanding any provisions relating to freedom of speech and opinion, to prohibit incitement to discrimination and hatred on racial and other grounds. Moreover, the toleration of incitement to violence may be inconsistent with substantive obligations of the Bill relating to security of life and equality before the law.

Reference may be made here to the following 'rights' which have appeared in the various proposals for Bills of Rights but which do not figure in the present draft.

The right to legal personality.—This right figures both in the Universal Declaration of Human Rights and in the proposed Covenant of Human Rights.   The first provides, in Article 6: 'Everyone has the right to recognition everywhere as a person before the law'.   An identical provision appears in the proposed 'Covenant'.   It is difficult to visualise the meaning of the right to a legal personality, and representatives of various Governments on the Commission acquiesced in its inclusion with much hesitation. The proposal apparently had its origin in the practice of National-Socialist Germany.   It is probably undesirable to give to such essentially transient practices the dignity of express refutation in a special Article of the Bill of Rights.

The right to marry.—The same consideration applies to the prominence given to the 'right to marry'—a matter largely connected with the controversy which has centred on the question of Russian-born wives, married to foreign citizens, to whom the Soviet Government has denied the possibility to leave the country (see below, p. 401).   It is difficult to postulate an absolute right to marry and to deny to the State the faculty to limit or prohibit marriages for eugenic reasons, or on account of blood or similar relationships.   It is sufficient to recall the controversy, in England and some other countries, in the matter of the right to marry the sister of a deceased wife.   There must also be considered prohibitions on religious grounds and the attitude of most States to polygamy.   In *Cleveland* v. *United States* (67 Sup. Ct. 13 (1946)) the Supreme Court was divided on the question of the opprobrium attaching to Mormon polygamous marriages. Mr. Justice Murphy objected to the condemnatory characterization, by the majority, of polygamy. He pointed out that it was a common form of marriage in ancient times, often mentioned in the Old Testament, and that it should not be classed with prostitution or debauchery.   It may be noted that John Stuart Mill—no mean apostle of liberty—was far from conceding any absolute right to marry.   He was of the opinion that the laws in those countries which forbid marriage unless the parties can show that they have the means of supporting a family, do not exceed the legitimate powers of the State, and, though the question depends on local circumstances and feeling, are not objectionable as violations of liberty.   (*On Liberty*, Chapter IV.)

The right of property. For reasons stated in more detail elsewhere (*I.B.R.M.,*

urgent question whether, in modern conditions, the duty of the State ought not to go beyond that and whether there ought not to be a right of protection against organised oppression from whatever source it may originate.[40]

10. The Rights of Aliens. Expulsion of Aliens

Article 9

Aliens and stateless persons shall not be denied the full and equal protection of the Articles of this Chapter of the Bill of Rights and of other rights granted to them by the law of the State in which they reside. No alien or stateless person legally admitted and permanently residing within the State may be expelled except in pursuance of a judicial decision or recommendation as a punishment for serious offences laid down by law as warranting expulsion.

This Article substantially reaffirms the existing rule of international law in the matter of treatment of aliens. It is implicit in the previous Articles in which the protection of the rights laid down there is not limited to the nationals of the State. The Draft does not provide for full equality of aliens and nationals— except with regard to the personal rights of freedom enumerated in Chapter 1 of the Bill. It is, to that extent, partly declaratory of existing international law. But only partly. For although the latter secures to aliens treatment in accordance with a minimum standard of civilisation, the Bill of Rights must—as does the present draft—go beyond that. The Bill of Rights

pp. 163, 164) no provision is made in the present draft for respect for the rights of private property. In particular the draft does not include a prohibition of expropriation without compensation. However, such action by the State would be prohibited in so far as it offends against the principle of equality before the law. Neither can the provisions of the Bill of Rights affect the rule of international law according to which respect is due to the property of aliens, with the result that expropriation without compensation— which need not amount to full compensation (see the author's observations in Oppenheim, *International Law*, vol. I, 7th ed., 1948, p. 318)—is unlawful. On the omission of reference to the rights of property in the Declaration of Independence see Malone, *Jefferson the Virginian* (1948), pp. 227, 228.

[40] See President Truman's address at the Lincoln Memorial in Washington in June 1947: 'We cannot be content with a civil liberties program which emphasises only the need of protection against the possibility of tyranny by the Government. . . . The extension of civil rights today means not protection of the people against the Government, but protection of the people by the Government' (as quoted by Scott in *Canadian Bar Review*, 27 (1949), p. 536, and by Carr, *Federal Protection of Civil Rights* (1947), p. VII). See also the Bombay Harijan (Removal of Disabilities) Act, 1946 (*Year Book of Human Rights*, 1947, p. 159).

is expressive of more than a minimum standard of civilisation. In addition, the Bill guarantees to aliens the equal protection of such other rights as they are granted by the law of the State. It is not the purpose of the Bill of Rights to interfere with the rule, however unsatisfactory or petty it may be on occasions in its specific application, that legal limitations with respect to the exercise of professions, acquisition of property, and the like, may be imposed upon aliens.

In comparison the provision relating to expulsion of aliens requires amplification. It is not sufficient to lay down that ' no alien legally admitted to the territory of a State shall be expelled therefrom except on such grounds and according to such procedure and safeguards as are provided by law.'[41] The administrative and legal procedure may be fully complied with, and yet expulsion may result in hardship which is offensive both to justice and to human dignity. For this reason it is necessary in this respect to distinguish between aliens who are only temporarily present in the country and those who reside there permanently, in particular if they have established a family and a business there. The State must enjoy a greater degree of latitude with regard to an alien who has contrived to obtain admission for the purpose of an isolated political or commercial venture than in relation to a foreigner permanently established in the country. With regard to the latter the Bill of Rights would seem to be the proper occasion for reaffirming the principle— which has been crystallizing into a principle of international law —affording the alien a substantial measure of protection against arbitrary expulsion.'[42] It will be noted that the present Draft requires not only a judicial decision or recommendation as a condition of expulsion. It also requires that such a decision or recommendation should take place in respect of serious offences only.

The present Draft places stateless persons on the same footing as aliens with regard to both equality of treatment and liability to

[41] Article 12 of the Covenant as proposed in 1949 by the Commission on Human Rights.

[42] *I.B.R.M.*, pp. 124, 125. The Supreme Court of the United States observed in *Fiswick* v. *United States* (67 Sup. Ct. 224 (1946)): ' although deportation is not technically a criminal punishment, it may visit great hardship on the alien. *Bridges* v. *Wixon*, 326 U.S.135. . . . As stated by the Court, speaking through Mr. Justice Brandeis in *Ng Fung Ho* v. *White*, 259 U.S.276, 284, deportation may result in the loss " of all that makes life worth living ".'

expulsion. There is otherwise no protection for these persons except in so far as the Bill applies to all individuals within the jurisdiction of the State. If Article 11 [43] of the proposed Bill becomes law the causes of statelessness will disappear. But there will remain stateless persons both on account of past practice and because of the continued operation of the law of States not bound by the Bill of Rights.

11. THE RIGHT OF ASYLUM

Article 10

Within the limits of public security and the economic capacity of the State, there shall be full and effective recognition of the right of asylum for political offenders and for fugitives from persecution.

The question of the right of asylum is one of the intricate problems of the Bill of Rights. The right of States to grant asylum in respect of political offences notwithstanding any existing extradition treaty has been generally recognised both in extradition treaties and by virtue of what has now become a customary rule of international law. According to the predominant view the principle underlying that practice is not a legal right which the person accused of a political offence is entitled to invoke in his or her own name.[44] Neither is a State under a legal obligation to grant asylum from persecution. Yet although the difficulties which would result in this respect from the assumption of a legal obligation, conferring a direct right upon individuals, are of a most serious character, an international enactment concerned with the fundamental rights and freedoms of the individual cannot ignore that question. Nor can it, consistently with its own dignity and purpose, contrive to solve it by verbal niceties and formulas.[45] From the point of view of strict logic the provision of the right of asylum from persecution would seem unnecessary or even obnoxious. For if the Bill of Rights is adhered to there ought to be no room for persecution. It has also been argued that the existence of a right of asylum might encourage States to indulge in persecution of persons whom other

---

[43] See below, p. 347.

[44] But see *Fiscal* v. *Samper,* decided in 1934 by the Spanish Supreme Court: *Annual Digest,* 1938-40, Case No. 152.

[45] See below, p. 422, with regard to the Universal Declaration of Human Rights.

States would then be under a duty to receive.[46]   Moreover, in an international system in which the right to government by consent has become an effective part of the law, there ought not to be a justifiable cause for revolutionary activities calling, in turn, for political asylum.   These logical objections do not touch the core of the problem—quite apart from the fact that there may be revolutions and persecutions in countries not bound by the Bill of Rights.

At the same time it may seem impracticable to impose upon a State a rigid duty to receive any number, however great, of political offenders and victims of persecution.   Thus it would have been difficult for neighbouring States to receive all the victims of the racial persecution by National-Socialist Germany— though the eventual fate of those victims, whose regulated and proportional absorption by these States would not have proved altogether above their resources, is in itself a most compelling argument in favour of some such solution as that envisaged in the present Draft.   It provides for a duty of asylum, on the part of States, ' within the limits of public security and the economic capacity of the State '.   Of these limits the State must be the sole judge.   To that extent the legal obligation would be imperfect. But it would be a legal obligation, to be executed in good faith. It would be a contribution to restoring active faith in the worth and dignity of man.   For the same reason its absence would derogate from the authority of a Bill of Rights.[47]

12.   The Right to Nationality.   Emigration and Expatriation

Article 11

Every person shall be entitled to the nationality of the State where he is born unless and until on attaining majority he declares for the nationality open to him by virtue of descent.

---

[46] See below, p. 421.

[47] For recent constitutional regulation of the right of asylum see, for instance, the Italian constitution of 1947 which provides, in Article 10, that ' any alien debarred in his own country from the effective exercise of democratic liberties guaranteed by the Italian Constitution shall have the right of asylum in the territory of the Republic on conditions laid down by law ' and that ' no alien may be extradited for political offences '.   Article 26 applies the same principle to nationals.   The Preamble to the French Constitution of 1946 lays down that ' anyone persecuted because of his activities in the cause of freedom has the right of asylum within the territories of the Republic '.

No person shall be deprived of his nationality by way of punishment or deemed to have lost his nationality except concurrently with the acquisition of a new nationality.

The right of emigration and expatriation shall not be denied.

The object of the first two paragraphs of this Article is to assure to the individual the effective right to a nationality or, to put it negatively, to protect him from statelessness.[48] Nationality may not be a ' natural ' or ' inalienable ' right. Its importance is conditioned by the existence of sovereign States claiming to be the indispensable link between the individual and international law. It is that very claim which makes statelessness illogical and objectionable. The Bill of Rights is the proper occasion for laying down the principle—and the obligation—of the progressive abolition of statelessness. This is so although there are indications that the concept of nationality, as a requisite of protection, may be losing its former rigidity. Witness, for instance, the status, in Great Britain, of the citizens of the Republic of Ireland —a country which considers itself a foreign State in relation to Great Britain; or, generally, the multiplicity and interplay of nationalities within the Commonwealth; or, as shown in the Nationality Act of 1948, the abandonment of the view that naturalisation in a foreign country automatically brings British nationality to an end.[49] The undoubted relaxation of the rule as to nationality of claims has acted in the same direction.[50] Thus it is now generally agreed that, in effect, parties to an international instrument—such as a Minorities Treaty or Mandate or Trust Agreement—are entitled to act on behalf, or take up the case, of individuals who are not their nationals. The same applies to any treaty regulating statelessness or the condition of stateless persons. Moreover, as the Charter of the United Nations imposes the obligation to respect human rights and fundamental freedoms regardless of nationality and as the same applies to any proposed Bill—or Covenant—of human rights it would appear that, *pro tanto,* the importance of nationality has been diminished. Nevertheless the evils of statelessness, and especially its implication that the State can play fast and loose with what is at present

[48] See *I.B.R.M.,* pp. 126-128.

[49] See on all these aspects of the British Nationality Act, 1948, Mervyn Jones in *British Year Book of International Law,* 25 (1948), pp. 158-179.

[50] See above, p. 55.

an essential legal attribute of human personality, are such that no adequate Bill of Rights can leave that problem on one side. This circumstance explains why the recognition of the right to a nationality has figured prominently in the various proposals for Bills of Rights.

However, as with regard to the other aspects of the Bill of Rights, this is not a problem which admits of merely verbal solutions. In particular, it cannot be solved by the adoption of a formula prohibiting the State *arbitrarily* to deprive its citizens of their nationality. States do not purport to act arbitrarily in that matter. They act for what they believe or allege to be good reasons such as punishment for disloyalty or political offences generally. These reasons cannot be supported by reference to wider principles. In some countries—such as the United States and Great Britain—the objectionable character of deprivation of nationality for disloyalty is emphasised by the fact that the practice is confined to naturalised persons—as if the latter, for the mere reason that their nationality is due to a voluntary act, were bound by a more exacting duty of allegiance.[51] Nothing short of a general enactment—for which the Bill of Rights provides a proper opportunity—can do away with that practice. In other respects, such as loss of nationality upon marriage,[52] recent legislation of many States, largely following upon the Hague Convention of 1930, has clearly adopted the principle that no loss of the previous nationality ought to occur unless a new nationality is acquired. In a different sphere, the general adoption of the principle outlined in the first paragraph of the proposed Article 11 would contribute substantially to the abolition of statelessness and to the recognition of the right of the individual to a nationality. No vital—or even important—interest prevents any State from adopting the territorial principle, without

[51] According to Swiss law both naturalised and Swiss-born citizens can be deprived of their nationality for anti-national activities outside the country: (1941) 57 *Recueil Officiel*, p. 1289; *Eidgenossische Gesetzsammlung*, No. 21 (1949).

[52] International practice has in other respects tended to acknowledge the principle of equality of the sexes in the matter of nationality. Thus while, previously, in cases of cession or annexation of territory, the option of nationality on the part of the husband covered his wife, recent peace treaties lay down that the option of the husband shall not constitute option on the part of his wife. See, for instance, Article 19 of the Peace Treaty with Italy of 1947.

necessarily abandoning the principle of descent, as the basis of acquisition of nationality by birth.

The same applies to the right of expatriation, *i.e.,* the right of the individual to divest himself of his existing nationality by assuming the nationality of another State. The unqualified recognition of that right is not only desirable for the sake of avoiding international friction of the kind which during a substantial period of the 19th century marred the relations of Great Britain and the United States. It is also essential, once more, for the assertion of the dignity of man otherwise tied by irrevocable bonds to the nationality of a State which he may find inconvenient or hateful. Many States have now recognised the right of expatriation, but the only measure of international agreement that could be reached on the subject at the Hague Codification Conference in 1930 was that relating to such minor matters as the grant of expatriation permits and the like.

The right of emigration—the practical benefits of which are rigidly circumscribed by the absence of a corresponding right of immigration—is of similar significance. There seems to be no compelling reason militating against its recognition. Even the duty of military service need not stand in its way so long as the State is free to prescribe that a person thus withdrawing himself from that duty shall forfeit the right of returning to his country.[53] The refusal to allow emigration on the ground of non-fulfilment of financial obligations is no more justifiable than imprisonment for debt.[54] The abuse of the right of emigration for the purpose of avoiding family obligations of maintenance could be countered by a convention for international maintenance orders to which the signatories of the Bill of Rights would be

[53] The 'Covenant' proposed in 1949 provided, in Article 11 (2), that 'anyone is free to return to the country of which he is a national'. As the 'Covenant' left unimpaired the right of States to deprive a person of his nationality, a State might be able to avoid the obligations of that Article by the simple expedient of depriving the person in question of his nationality.

[54] In the proposal for the 'Covenant' submitted by the Commission on Human Rights in 1949 it was provided, in Article 10, that 'no one shall be imprisoned merely on the grounds of *inability* to fulfil a contractual obligation '—a provision which leaves intact the right to imprison a person for 'unwillingness' to fulfil a financial obligation. The representative of the United Kingdom suggested that 'a person who did not pay a contractual debt when he had the means of doing so committed a crime by the very fact that he did not fulfil an obligation' (E/CN.4/S.R.102, p. 9).

expected to become parties. The ' Covenant ' proposed by the Commission on Human Rights rendered the right of emigration illusory to a large extent by making it dependent upon ' any general law, adopted for specific reasons of national security, public safety, or health '.[55]

13. THE RIGHT TO GOVERNMENT BY CONSENT

Article 12

No State shall deprive its citizens of the effective right to choose their governments and legislators on a footing of equality according to universal suffrage, in free, secret, and periodic elections. The freedom of the elections shall not be limited to lists proposed or in effect determined by the Government.

The significance of the above provision of the Bill of Rights and the feasibility of its judicial enforcement in the national and international sphere are discussed elsewhere in this book.[56]   In consenting to that Article the parties to the Bill would, to some extent, provide, as does the Constitution of the United States in the matter of Republican Government, a guarantee of the democratic form of government—a step which, if accompanied by the adoption of the practice of refusing recognition to revolutionary governments declining to submit the confirmation of the revolutionary change to a popular vote, under international supervision, would go far in the direction of making the right of man to government by consent both real and enduring.[57]

The concluding sentence of the Article is intended to meet the

---

[55] Article 11.   The same Article provided, subject to the same comprehensive limitation, that ' everyone has the right to liberty of movement and is free to choose his residence within the borders of each State '—a provision which, if adopted, would probably make illegal direction of labour in accordance with enactments such as the British Control of Engagements Order—a measure repealed in 1950.   The Australian representative before the Commission pointed out that the restrictions on the freedom of movement of indigenous peoples were in their interest.   They were backward in many respects and it was not always desirable to encourage their contacts with the white population.   In urban centres they were liable to contract diseases from which the white population was more or less immune.   It was also necessary to regulate the movements of newly arrived immigrants (E/CN.4/SR.106, p. 3).

[56] See above, pp. 281-284.

[57] On the close connexion between the right to government by consent and the law of recognition of governments see the author's *Recognition in International Law* (1947), pp. 169-174.   For a useful survey of the question of free elections in Eastern Europe after the Second World War see Stone in *Bulletin of State Department,* 17 (1947), pp. 311-323

expedient adopted by some States of totalitarian complexion. Experience has shown that without some such safeguard the freedom of elections is to a large extent nominal.

14. DEPENDENT COMMUNITIES AND THE RIGHT TO GOVERNMENT BY CONSENT

Article 13

Whenever the political condition or the stage of development of communities which have not yet attained full political independence or which constitute a colony or a trust territory require the application of the principle of trusteeship or of political tutelage, such modification of the right of self-government shall be subject, in accordance with the Charter of the United Nations, to the effective recognition of the principle of the eventual independence of these communities in accordance with their development and the wishes of their populations.

While, as stated in Article 17, the obligations of the Bill of Rights are binding upon States in relation both to their metropolitan territory and to any other territory under their control and jurisdiction, the principle of government by consent cannot fully apply to territories which do not as yet enjoy full self-government. Such denial, in relation to colonial peoples and territories under trusteeship, of a fundamental human right can be justified on the sole ground that it is temporary and that it takes place in the interest of the territories and the populations concerned and not for the benefit of the administering State. The temporary nature of that deprivation of the right to government by consent is expressed both in Article 76 of the Charter (in relation to trust territories) and in Article 73 (in relation to other non-self-governing territories). The former refers to ' progressive development towards self-government or independence '; the latter speaks of ' peoples which have not yet attained a full measure of self-government '. The proposed Article 13 of the Bill of Rights gives expression to that recognition of the principle of the eventual independence of these communities. It recognises the general competence of the United Nations in the matter. The problem raises the question of the co-operation between the organs of the United Nations specially entrusted with the territories in question and the organs, such as the Economic and Social Council and the Commission on Human Rights, concerned with the implementation of human rights and fundamental freedoms. Experience has shown that that co-operation is fully practicable.[58]

15.   THE RIGHTS OF MINORITIES

Article 14

In States inhabited by a substantial number of persons of a race, language or religion other than those of the majority of the population, persons belonging to such ethnic, linguistic or religious minorities shall have the right to establish and maintain, out of an equitable proportion of the available public funds, their schools and cultural and religious institutions and to use their own language before the courts and other authorities and organs of the State.

The problem of ethnic, linguistic, or religious minorities within the national State is not only a question of preservation of international peace—with which experience has shown it to be closely connected. It is also a problem of a fundamental human right. Political minorities may be oppressed by discrimination in civil and political life. The duty of abstention from discrimination follows directly from the principle of equality. It is provided for in another part of the Bill of Rights.[59] But a minority may suffer for reasons other than denial of equality before the law. It may be oppressed as the result of deprivation of legitimate opportunities for the maintenance and development of the qualities and of the heritage of its distinct entity. These may be as precious to it as any other fundamental rights. Minorities have sacrificed their life and freedom in order to preserve them. From this point of view the claims of the ethnic, religious or linguistic minorities are no less entitled to respect than other rights guaranteed by the Bill. Inasmuch as such minorities are required to make their contribution to the national resources without receiving the opportunity—in the same or similar measure as the members of the majority—of maintaining and developing values which are dear to them, they are denied equality before the law. The cultural and linguistic unity of the national State

[58] See above, p. 227.
[59] See above, p. 338.

at the expense of its minorities is not an ideal entitled to respect so absolute as to sanction the denial of equality thus conceived. The intimate connexion between the principle of equality before the law and the assurance for minorities of ' suitable means for the preservation of their racial peculiarities, their traditions, and their national characteristics' was clearly shown by the Permanent Court of International Justice in the Advisory Opinion, given in 1935, on the *Minority Schools in Albania*. The Court said: ' These two requirements are indeed closely interlocked, for there would be no true equality between a majority and a minority if the latter were deprived of its own institutions, and were consequently compelled to renounce that which constitutes the very essence of its being as a minority.' [60] It was a sign of political and moral retrogression in international relations after the Second World War that that aspect of the protection of minorities received less attention than after the termination of the First World War. That retrogression found expression, among others, in the fact that even in the Universal Declaration of Human Rights—a document which did not impose legal duties upon any State—no room was found for the positive recognition of what must be regarded as a basic human right of the members of national minorities.[61] Yet the principles underlying this aspect of the Bill of Rights are already enshrined in the practice of many States.[62] Their urgency has been recognised in the creation, in connexion with the work of the Commission on Human Rights, of the Sub-Commission on Non-Discrimination and Protection of Minorities.[63] They are capable of legislative regulation enforced by courts. The adequacy of such legislation and the manner in which it is given effect by courts are a proper subject of appeal to and investigation by an international authority. The activity of the Permanent Court of International Justice showed that that

[60] P.C.I.J., Series A/B, No. 64, p. 17.
[61] See below, p. 424.
[62] See *I.B.R.M.*, p. 154. And see *ibid.*, pp. 151-155.
[63] See above, p. 265. In 1949 the Sub-Commission on Prevention of Discrimination and Protection of Minorities asked the Commission on Human Rights to forward to the General Assembly a draft resolution recommending that, in the interest of enabling recognised minority groups to maintain their cultural heritage, Member Governments should provide adequate facilities in districts, regions, and territories where those groups represent a considerable portion of the population for: (a) the use in judicial procedure of their own language; and (b) the teaching in State-supported schools of the language of such groups.

aspect of the protection of minorities is a suitable subject of international judicial review.[64]

16. SOCIAL AND ECONOMIC RIGHTS

Article 15

States shall, within the limits of their economic capacity and development, make provision for securing effectively the right to work, to education, and to public assistance in case of unemployment, old age, sickness, disablement, and other cases of undeserved want.

Article 16

States shall, through national legislation and international co-operation, endeavour to secure just and humane conditions of work.

These two Articles represent the social and economic provisions of the Bill of Rights. In a distinct sense they approach a mere declaration of policy in the same way in which modern constitutions, which almost invariably contain detailed declarations on the subject, give expression to what is now generally regarded as an essential purpose and justification of the State. The main difficulty connected with this category of rights is that of international supervision and enforcement. Subject to the unavoidable qualification of all rights—such as that expressed in Article 19 relating to public welfare or the legitimate rights of others[65]—there is no insuperable difficulty in assuring compliance on the part of a State with the other obligations of the Bill of Rights such as freedom from arbitrary arrest, freedom of association, the right to nationality or the right of suffrage. But there is no specific test of observance, in an individual case, of the obligation to secure just and humane conditions of work, or the right to work, or adequate opportunities of education. This is so largely for the reason that while the compliance with other obligations of the Bill of Rights may fairly be deemed dependent on the will of the State and its organs, that cannot always be said with regard to obligations in the sphere of social and economic rights.

[64] See the Advisory Opinion, referred to above (p. 353), on the *Albanian Minority Schools*. See also the Advisory Opinion, given in 1932, on the *Treatment of Polish Nationals and Other Persons of Polish Origin or Speech in the Danzig Territory*, Series A/B, No. 44. And see Feinberg, *La juridiction de la Cour Permanente de Justice Internationale dans le système de la protection internationale des minorités* (1931).
[65] See below, p. 365.

Thus the securing of the right to work, to education, and to public assistance in case of unemployment and old age, depends on the economic condition and development of each State. Moreover, while with regard to personal rights of freedom the test is, in principle, absolute and admitting of no qualifications, the social and economic rights are to a large extent related to the predominant standard of life and a variety of social and economic factors in the country concerned.

However, although in this sphere there can be no question, as a rule, of a direct judicial remedy, national or international, available to individuals, the affirmation of these rights need not be merely in the nature of a declaration divorced from any obligation of observance. Whether a State is persistently neglectful of its duties in this respect and whether it declines a reasonable measure of international co-operation, such as effective participation in conventions concluded under the auspices of the International Labour Organisation, is not a matter of purely discretionary judgment. But the method of the ascertainment of that fact must be different. It must take place through non-political international agencies[66] able and authorised to act, not only upon specific complaints but also by reference to the general conduct and attitude of a State, and to influence its actions in ways other than a formal judicial finding.[67] Even so the affirmation of social and economic rights must in some measure approach a general declaration of principle. However, reasons have been given why these rights must form an integral part of the Bill of Rights.[68]

---

[66] See above, p. 285.

[67] See above, p. 286.

[68] See above, pp. 284-286. In 1949, at the meeting of the Commission on Human Rights which proposed a provisional draft of the Covenant for submission to Governments, the Australian representative put forward detailed Articles relating to economic and social rights. These Articles, introduced in an address which merits careful reading (E/CN.4/S.R.131, pp. 2-5), dealt with the right to work, with wages and working conditions, with protection against unemployment, illness, and old age, with limitation of working hours, with the right to education, and, somewhat incongruously, with the right to nationality. The proposals contained the constructive suggestion, which is partly in accordance with the views put forward in this book, that specialised agencies shall be entrusted with the task of reporting upon the steps taken by various States for the implementation of social rights. There seems, accordingly, to have been no justification for the emphatic observation of the representative of the United Kingdom, in announcing the intention of the British delegation to vote against the inclusion of the relevant Articles in the Covenant, that it was 'necessary to combat the illusion that a gesture alone would suffice to transform the structure of States from top to bottom', and that 'the Commission must refrain from drafting Articles which would make it impossible for many countries to adhere to the Covenant' (*ibid.*, p. 5).

CHAPTER 16

THE IMPLEMENTATION AND ENFORCEMENT OF THE BILL OF RIGHTS

1. THE INCORPORATION OF THE BILL OF RIGHTS AS PART OF MUNICIPAL LAW

THE Articles, commented upon in this Chapter, of the Bill of Rights are concerned with the question of its implementation and enforcement, both national and international. The preoccupation with the enforcement of the Bill of Rights ought not to conceal the fact that the most effective way of giving reality to it is through the normal activity of national courts and other organs applying the law of the land. Only in cases of an allegation that the national legislature has deliberately violated the Bill of Rights or that the highest national courts and agencies have become guilty of an unredressed denial of justice in violation of the law of the land will there be occasion for the international procedure contemplated in Part II of the Bill of Rights. For that reason provision must be made, in the first instance, for the incorporation as part of the municipal law of the Signatory States of those provisions of the Bill of Rights which lend themselves to enforcement by means of national legislation. These are the rights which form the subject matter of Part I, Chapter I, of the Bill of Rights, namely, all rights other than those in the economic and social spheres.

Article 17

Every State shall, by appropriate constitutional means, adopt Chapter I of Part I of this International Bill of the Rights of Man as part of its domestic law. The effect of such adoption shall be an obligation to abrogate or to alter any existing statute or any other rule of law inconsistent with these Articles of the International Bill of the Rights of Man. The Parties to this Bill of Rights shall communicate to the Secretary-General the legislative and other measures taken in order to give effect to that obligation.

356

The Bill of Rights shall not be abrogated or modified, by legislative action or otherwise, save in pursuance of international agreement or authorisation.

Nothing in the constitution of any Federal State shall relieve that State of the obligations of this Bill of Rights.

It does not appear essential that the provisions of the Bill of Rights should be made part of the written constitution of the Signatory States—a difficulty which is insurmountable in States which do not possess written constitutions. The main difference between the incorporation of the Bill of Rights as part of the constitution of States bound by the Bill and its incorporation as part of the ordinary law of the land is that in countries with a written constitution, unless the first alternative is adopted, it would not be possible for courts to exercise the power of declaring national legislation unconstitutional as being contrary to the provisions of the Bill of Rights. This they would be able and bound to do if the Bill of Rights were made part of the constitution. However, the difference is not as far-reaching as may seem at first sight. For, admittedly, if the Bill is incorporated as part of ordinary municipal law, national courts would be prevented from annulling or declaring unconstitutional any subsequent national legislation inconsistent with the Bill. But unless such subsequent legislation is clearly and deliberately contrary to the Bill of Rights which is part of the international obligations of the State—a remote contingency—courts, in countries without a written constitution, will, in pursuance of an established rule of construction, go to the utmost length in interpreting subsequent legislation so as not to make it conflict with the international obligations of the State. In the exceptional cases in which the legislature were deliberately to flout the international obligations of the State the proper remedy would not be judicial review by national courts but appropriate action by international agencies.

The second apparent advantage of incorporating the Bill of Rights as part of the constitution of the State would be to make it impossible for the legislature to depart from its provisions except by way of constitutional enactment. However, the object of making the personal and political rights of freedom part of constitutional law may be achieved—and achieved more successfully—by means of the international obligation of the State not to alter its municipal law in this respect except in pursuance of international agreement or authorisation. This, as the case may be, may mean either the United Nations or, if the Bill of Rights comes into being outside it, the Signatory States themselves. The provisions of the Bill thus incorporated would be only those relating to personal and political rights of freedom. For only these rights can properly be enforced by judicial or administrative process. For the reasons stated, the same degree and kind of enforceability are not feasible with regard to social and economic rights.[1]

Finally, the question arises whether the manner of the adoption of the Bill of Rights should be based on the assumption that its obligations would become automatically part of the law of the State or whether provision should be made for such express legislative changes as may be required to bring the law of the State into conformity with the Bill of Rights. While in some States treaties become automatically the supreme law of the land, this is not so in others. Thus, for instance, in Great Britain the provisions of treaties affecting private rights do not become part of municipal law unless and until they have been made so through an enabling Act of Parliament. And even in countries, such as the United States, where treaties concluded in accordance with the Constitution become the supreme law of the land, the difference between self-executory treaties and others is not invariably clear. In view of this, the most appropriate course would seem: (a) for the Signatory States to bind themselves to make the Bill of Rights part of their national—not necessarily constitutional—law by such means as the constitution provides; (b) to lay down that the effect of the Bill shall not necessarily be the automatic abrogation or modification of such parts of municipal law as are inconsistent therewith, but the obligation to enact such alterations as may be necessary;[2] (c) for the Signatory States to accept the obligation to communicate to the United Nations the measures taken in that connexion. While, in general, it is not to be expected

---

[1] See above, p. 355.

[2] In the 'Covenant' proposed by the Commission on Human Rights in 1949, Article 2 (2) provided that 'each State party hereto undertakes to ensure that any persons whose rights or freedoms as therein defined are violated shall have an effective remedy before the competent national tribunals notwithstanding that the violation has been committed by persons acting in an official capacity'. It is difficult to see the object of that provision. It is of the essence of the rule of law that once the obligations of the Bill of Rights have been made part of the law a judicial remedy, except with regard to so-called 'acts of State', is available against persons violating these obligations.

that the Bill of Rights will necessitate far-reaching changes in the law of the States which will adopt it, a reasonable period of time ought to be allowed to each State for a comprehensive survey of its law in relation to the requirements of the Bill of Rights.

2. THE POSITION OF FEDERAL STATES

In this connexion there must be considered the question of the position of Federal States in relation to the Bill of Rights. The general aspect of that problem is discussed elsewhere in this book.[3] The conclusions reached there are incorporated in the last paragraph of the proposed Article. It is a conclusion reached with much hesitation. More than any other provision, it exposes the Draft to the charge of dogmatism and rigidity. For its practical effect may well be, though this is not inescapably so, that great and freedom-loving States may remain outside the orbit of countries voluntarily submitting to that most significant measure of international progress. Yet, in a distinct sense, this question is the touchstone of the reality of the Bill of Rights. What would be the authority of a Bill of Rights which in effect releases a number of signatories from its principal obligations? That precisely would be the result of the provision in the 'Covenant' proposed by the Commission on Human Rights in 1949 and laying down that: —

'(a) With respect to any Articles of this Covenant which the Federal Government regards as wholly or in part appropriate for federal action, the obligations of the Federal Governments shall, to this extent, be the same as those of parties which are not Federal States;

'(b) In respect of Articles which the Federal Government regards as appropriate under its constitutional system, in whole or in part, for action by the constituent States, Provinces, or Cantons, the Federal Government shall bring such provisions, with favourable recommendation, to the notice of the appropriate authorities of the States, Provinces or Cantons at the earliest possible moment.'[4]

[3] See above, p. 303.

[4] It will be noted that according to the proposal of the United States it is for the Federal Government itself—and not for any outside body—to decide whether an Article of the Bill of Rights comes within the sphere of Federal action. For a discussion of the subject see E/CN.4/S.R.129.

Undoubtedly there are weighty reasons favouring the acceptance of that drastic limitation of the obligations of Federal States. In the first instance, there are already, to take the crucial example of the United States, some rights protected by the International Bill of Rights with regard to which the jurisdiction of the United States is paramount over that of the States of the Union. While the clauses of the original Bill of Rights of the United States—the first eight Amendments to the Constitution—are a limitation upon the Congress only,[5] this does not apply to later Amendments, in particular to the Fourteenth Amendment in which the final sentence of Section 1 reads as follows:—

> ' No State shall make or enforce any law which shall abridge the privileges or immunities of citizens of the United States, nor shall any person deprive any person of life, liberty, or property, without due process of law; nor deny to any person within its jurisdiction the equal protection of the laws.'

That Amendment in itself, even in its literal interpretation, subjects to federal jurisdiction a considerable segment of the rights protected by an International Bill of Rights. But the Supreme Court has gone beyond this literal interpretation. Although originally it refused to hold that ' the privileges and immunities of citizens of the United States ' covered the civil liberties of the Bill of Rights,[6] its more recent practice has tended to affirm the authority of the Fourteenth Amendment in relation to at least some fundamental civil liberties such as the freedom of the Press [7] and, generally, ' those fundamental principles of liberty and justice which lie at the base of all our civil and political institutions '.[8] In a somewhat hesitating manner the Supreme Court has held these fundamental principles to cover freedom of religion,[9] freedom of speech,[10] and the right of assembly and

---

[5] The proposal put forward in 1789 to limit the power of the States was not accepted. Thus Congress considered—and rejected—the proposal.

[6] *The Slaughter-House Cases* (1873), 16 Wallace, 36. See also *Maxwell* v. *Dow* (1900), 176 U.S.581; *Twining* v. *New Jersey* (1908), 211 U.S.78

[7] *Near* v. *Minnesota* (1931), 283 U.S.697.

[8] *Palko* v. *Connecticut* (1937), 302 U.S.319, 328.

[9] *West Virginia State Board of Education* v. *Barnette* (1943), 319 U.S.624.

[10] *Thornhill* v. *Alabama* (1940), 310 U.S.88; *Carlson* v. *California* (1940), 310 U.S.106. But see *Colgate* v. *Harvey* (1935), 296 U.S.404; *Madden* v. *Kentucky* (1940), 309 U.S.83.

petition, but not, it appears, safeguards in criminal trials and in the matter of unreasonable search and seizure.[11]

It is thus clear that an important breach has been opened in the restrictive interpretation of the Fourteenth Amendment. More-over, there are significant indications that the latter may be extended to cover, in effect, not only direct State action, but also enforcement by the State of discrimination on the part of private individuals and bodies.[12] To these developments there must be added the distinct tendency, which has manifested itself in a variety of ways, of extending Federal jurisdiction and limiting the juris-diction of the States by reference to the twin doctrines of *Missouri* v. *Holland*[13] permitting congressional legislation in matters,

[11] *Sed quaere.* On the intimate connexion of the various freedoms guaranteed by the Constitution see the following passage in the Dissenting Opinion of Mr. Justice Frankfurter in *Harris* v. *United States* (1947), 67 Supt. Ct. 1098: ' How can there be freedom of thought or freedom of speech or freedom of religion, if the police can, without warrant, search your house and mine from garret to cellar merely because they are executing a warrant of arrest? How can men feel free if all their papers may be searched, as an incident to the arrest of someone in the house, on the chance that something may turn up, or rather, be turned up? Yesterday the justifying document was an illicit ration book, tomorrow it may be some suspect piece of literature.' And see Carr, *Federal Protection of Civil Rights* (1947), pp. 12 *et seq.* See also Konvitz, *The Constitution and Civil Rights* (1947). The ' equal protection of the laws ' clause in the Fourteenth Amendment has been used against exclusion of Negroes from juries and from primary elections. See, in particular, *Smith* v. *Allwright* (1944), 321 U.S.649, where the Court said (*per* Mr. Justice Reed): ' When primaries become a part of the machinery for choosing officials, state and national, as they have here, the same tests to determine the character of discrimination or abridgment should be applied to the primary as are applied to the general election '. On the possible far-reaching effects of the decision see *Columbia Law Review*, 47 (1947), pp. 76-98. See also *United States* v. *Saylor* (1944), 322 U.S.385, where the Court asserted the power of the Federal Court to punish election frauds. Federal protection has been extended to Negroes in the field of transportation. In 1946 the Supreme Court, basing its decision on the commerce clause of the Constitution rather than on the 14th Amendment, invalidated, apparently for the first time, a statute involving segregation of whites and Negroes in the matter of transportation: *Morgan* v. *Virginia* (1946), 328 U.S. 373. Similar developments have taken place in the field of education (see *Sipuel* v. *Board of Regents* (1948), 332 U.S.631) and Negro labour rights. See the instructive note on the subject in *Yale Law Journal*, 56 (1946-1947), pp. 1059-1067. Increased protection has been granted to Jehovah's Witnesses, an unpopular religious group. In 1943 the Supreme Court, reversing its previous decision, held that a resolution of a local school board requiring all children to salute the United States flag violated the First Amendment: *West Virginia State Board of Education* v. *Barnette* (1943), 319 U.S.624. And see generally Morroe Berger in *Columbia Law Review*, 49 (1949), pp. 201-230. On the Federal power to prosecute violence against minority groups see *Yale Law Journal*, 57 (1948), pp. 855-873.

[12] See *Shelley* v. *Kraemer*, referred to and commented on above, pp. 149, 152.

[13] (1920) 252 U.S.416. For a similar trend in Australia see *R.* v. *Burgess, ex parte Henry* (1936), 55 C.L.R. 608. On the other hand see, as to Canada, the decision of the Judicial Committee of the Privy Council in *Attorney-General for Canada* v. *Attorney-General for Ontario*, [1937] A.C. 326—as to which see *Canadian Bar Review*, 15 (1937), pp. 393-507 (a symposium).

otherwise within the jurisdiction of States, covered by a treaty and the doctrine extending Federal jurisdiction by reference to the vital necessities of the foreign intercourse of the Union.[14]

These possibilities—which, it appears, operate also, though in a different way, in Canada [15]—cannot be lightly disregarded. They might receive a powerful accession of strength from the fact of the United States becoming a party to an International Bill of Rights. To some extent, and in different spheres, similar forces might operate in this matter in other Federal States.

These are weighty considerations. Yet, for the reasons stated,[16] they cannot be regarded as decisive. In addition, the fact that important signatories of the Bill are only nominally parties to it, would undermine its general effectiveness and its moral authority. The experience of the Optional Clause of the Statute of the International Court of Justice is not without instruction in this respect.[17] Moreover, if the United States were to become, without

[14] See, *e.g., United States of America* v. *Curtiss-Wright Export Corporation* (1936), 299 U.S.304 (on the delegation of legislative powers to the Executive in matters relating to foreign relations); *United States* v. *Pink* (1942), 315 U.S.203 (in the matter of the overriding effect of international instruments in relation to the law of the States); *Hines* v. *Davidowitz* (1941), 312 U.S.52 (in the matter of the power of the States to register aliens).

[15] For a constructive and illuminating attempt at an analysis of this aspect of the question see Scott, ' Dominion Jurisdiction over Human Rights and Fundamental Freedoms ', in *Canadian Bar Review,* 27 (1949), pp. 498-536. Professor Scott surveys the various spheres of law where Federal legislation is already paramount or where Federal influence, for instance, by withholding subsidies and facilities, can be exercised to induce the Provinces to respect fundamental human rights. He maintains that freedom of religion, speech and association are, in effect, within Federal jurisdiction. He suggests —perhaps not quite convincingly—that by defining seditious conspiracies and unlawful assemblies the law—the Criminal Code—permits all associations which do not come within the prohibition (p. 520). But see, as to religious freedom, the testimony of Mr. F. P. Varcoe, Deputy Minister of Justice, before the Joint Committee referred to below in this note stating that as to freedom of religion there ' would seem to be no constitutional safeguard ' (*ibid.,* 26 (1948), p. 710). And see Glen How, ' The Case for a Canadian Bill of Rights ', *ibid.,* pp. 759-796. In 1947 a Joint Committee of the Senate and House of Commons was established to consider the need for a Bill of Rights for Canada and to determine the responsibilities of Canada under an International Bill of Rights adopted by the United Nations. For the Report of the Committee recommending against the adoption, ' without a great deal of further study ', of a Bill of Rights for Canada by Federal Statute or by amendment of the Constitution see *Proceedings,* King's Printer, Ottawa, 1947-48, p. 207. See also *Canadian Bar Review,* 26 (1948), pp. 706-714, for some of the answers received by the Committee.

[16] See above, pp. 360, 361.

[17] Thus it must remain a matter for controversy whether the signature of the Optional Clause by the United States, in the manner in which it was effected, was beneficial to the cause of obligatory judicial settlement of international disputes. There is room for the view that an undertaking which, substantially, leaves it to the free judgment of the State concerned to decide whether it is bound to comply with it, undermines the authority of the system of which that

qualifications, a party to the Bill of Rights—an event which could not materialise except with the consent of two-thirds of its Senate, but which could come about without resort to constitutional amendment—it is possible that by way, *inter alia,* of the nascent judicial doctrine already referred to, means falling short of constitutional amendment could be found for extending the jurisdiction of the United States to cover the observance of human rights by and within the States.[18] Finally, it is arguable that if an International Bill of Human Rights were to come into being, with the United States outside it because of the constitutional position with respect to the exclusive jurisdiction of the member States in most matters pertaining to human rights, that very circumstance might act as a factor in moulding public opinion and emphasising the contradiction between the humanitarian and libertarian tradition of the United States and its self-imposed exclusion from the International Bill of Rights.

These conflicting considerations explain why the solution accepted in the proposed draft is advanced with much hesitation. It is natural that, in the circumstances, the mind turns to the possibility of a compromise solution. A compromise might consist in adopting an unqualified Bill of Rights subject to the possibility of a reservation, open to Federal States, permitting them for a limited period to consider themselves, at their option, exempted from the operation of the Bill of Rights in matters which according to their constitution fall within the jurisdiction of the component States. An exemption of that nature might in itself act as a stimulus for adjusting the national constitution, within the period agreed upon, to the obligations of the Bill of Rights. A constitutional amendment of that nature, most comprehensive in its scope, could be effected through one sentence: ' Nothing in this Constitution shall be construed as preventing the Federation from giving effect to the International Bill of the Rights of Man.' In the United States the Amendment might take the form of an express provision laying down that the ' due process' clause covers the rights and freedoms of the International

undertaking is a part. In 1946 the United States adhered to the Optional Clause subject to reservations, one of which excluded from the purview of the signature ' disputes with regard to matters which are essentially within the domestic jurisdiction of the United States of America as determined by the United States of America '.

[18] See *Missouri* v. *Holland,* above, p. 361.

Bill of Human Rights.   There is nothing offensive to national dignity in the contemplation of some such amendment.   This would not be a case of tampering with the Constitution for the sake of an international treaty of limited scope such as the various conventions concluded under the auspices of the International Labour Organisation.[19]   It would be a voluntary submission and an act of homage by the sovereign State to an international enactment second in importance only to the Charter of the United Nations itself and second to none in dignity and moral appeal.

3.   THE BILL OF RIGHTS AND NON-METROPOLITAN TERRITORIES

Article 18

The obligations of this Bill of Rights shall be binding upon States in relation both to their metropolitan territory and to any other territory under their control and jurisdiction.

The fundamental nature of the rights recognised and guaranteed by the Bill of Rights requires that it should apply to all persons subject to the jurisdiction of the State, whether they live within

---

[19] Article 19 (7) of the Constitution of the International Labour Organisation runs, in part, as follows:—

' 7. In the case of a federal State, the following provisions shall apply:

'(a) in respect of Conventions and Recommendations which the federal Government regards as appropriate under its constitutional system for federal action, the obligations of the federal State shall be the same as those of Members which are not federal States;

'(b) in respect of Conventions and Recommendations which the federal Government regards as appropriate under its constitutional system, in whole or in part, for action by the constituent States, provinces, or cantons rather than for federal action, the federal Government shall—

' (i) make, in accordance with its Constitution and the Constitutions of the States, provinces or cantons concerned, effective arrangements for the reference of such Conventions and Recommendations not later than eighteen months from the closing of the session of the Conference to the appropriate federal, State, provincial or cantonal authorities for the enactment of legislation or other action;

' (ii) arrange, subject to the concurrence of the State, provincial or cantonal Governments concerned, for periodical consultations between the federal and the State, provincial or cantonal authorities with a view to promoting within the federal State co-ordinated action to give effect to the provisions of such Conventions and Recommendations; . . .

' (iv) in respect of each such Convention which it has not ratified, report to the Director-General of the International Labour Office, at appropriate intervals as requested by the Governing Body, the position of the law and practice of the federation and its constituent States, provinces or cantons in regard to the Convention, showing the extent to which effect has been given, or is proposed to be given, to any of the provisions of the Convention by legislation, administrative action, collective agreement, or otherwise.'

For the reasons stated in the text above, the analogy of the International Labour Organisation is hardly applicable to the question under discussion.

its metropolitan territory enjoying full self-government or within a colony or any other dependent territory. As to the latter, the only exception—which is of a provisional character—is explicitly laid down in Article 13 of the Bill.[20] Subject to that exception there is no justification for limiting the obligations of the Bill of Rights to the metropolitan territory of the Parties thereto. There are compelling reasons for avoiding any ambiguity in this respect.[21] With regard to Trust Territories, the Bill of Rights gives greater precision to human rights and fundamental freedoms incorporated in the Trust Agreements without necessarily affecting the machinery laid down therein for the protection and enforcement of these rights.[22]

4. LIMITS OF THE OPERATION OF THE BILL OF RIGHTS. SUSPENSION OF CONSTITUTIONAL GUARANTEES

Article 19

The enforcement of any law, including the temporary suspension of the rights guaranteed by this Bill of Rights, necessary for

---

[20] In the discussions which took place in the Human Rights Commission in 1949 no convincing reasons were adduced in support of the view that non-metropolitan territories should not be automatically included within the purview of the Bill. Thus, for instance, the French representative pointed out that the principle of equality of the sexes could not be applied immediately in all such territories in so far as family law was concerned (E/CN.4/S.R.129, p. 17). However, the same argument could be applied to some metropolitan territories. The admittedly difficult problem of equality of the sexes admits of a solution different from that of excluding certain territories from the scope of the Bill. See above, p. 339, and below, p. 390. The explanation of the representative of the United Kingdom that by virtue of the Charter itself the wishes of the populations concerned must be taken into consideration (*ibid.*, p. 22) carries little conviction. It is safe to assume that none of the provisions of the Bill of Rights is contrary to the interests of the peoples. For these reasons there is room for the view—which is probably the accurate view—that no constitutional and formal grounds ought to be allowed to stand in the way of the automatic extension to colonial territories of conventions of a universal and compelling character. For the contrary view see the observations of the representative of the United Kingdom in the Third General Assembly (Part I) in connexion with the Convention on Prevention of Genocide (*Official Records, Plenary Meetings*, p. 838).

[21] The 'Covenant' proposed by the Commission on Human Rights in 1949 contained no specific provision in this respect, but reproduced a previous draft laying down that 'a State party to this Covenant may at the time of its accession thereto or at any time thereafter by notification addressed to the Secretary-General of the United Nations declare that this Covenant shall extend to any of the territories for the international relations of which it is responsible'. In 1949 the United States proposed an identical Article. On the other hand Soviet Russia urged that the Covenant shall extend or be applicable to the metropolitan territory 'as well as to all the other territories (non-self-governing, trust, and colonial territories) which are being administered or governed by the metropolitan power in question'.

[22] See above, pp. 161, 265.

safeguarding the legal rights of others or providing for the safety, public order, good morals and welfare of the community or intended to secure human rights and fundamental freedoms shall not be deemed to be inconsistent with the observance of this International Bill of the Rights of Man.

The provisions of this Article shall not be used or applied in a manner contrary to the purposes of the Bill of Rights.

The proposed Article is concerned with two limitations which, in one way or another, apply to practically all the substantive provisions of the Bill of Rights. It is axiomatic that the natural rights of the individual find a necessary limit in the natural rights of other persons. Freedom of speech and expression of opinion are unavoidably circumscribed by the right of other members of the community not to be molested by slander, libel, incitement to violence, nuisance or undue interference with their privacy. The Declaration of 1789, while laying down that every citizen has the right to speak, write and publish freely, added, in Article 11, ' sauf à répondre de l'abus de cette liberté dans les cas déterminés par la loi '. Similarly, the fundamental rights of the individual must in certain cases yield to the vital necessities of the State, *i.e.,* as put in the present draft, to the ' safety, public order, good morals and welfare of the community '. While, ultimately, the existence of the State is justified only when conceived as a means for the advancement and the happiness of the individual human being, as a general rule *salus rei publicæ* provides a *prima jacie*—though not necessarily the final—justification of invasion of private rights, however fundamental. There is no inevitable contradiction between the essential purpose of the Bill of Rights in securing human rights and fundamental freedoms and the welfare and exigencies of the State so long as it is clearly established that these limitations must not operate in a manner contrary to the purpose of the Bill of Rights and that the State is not the final arbiter in the matter.

The qualifications as formulated are generally accepted and need no elaboration. Moreover, they not only do not require elaboration; they discourage it. Whether in any particular case the fundamental rights of the individual have been infringed, without sufficient justification, on account of the rights of other persons or of the interests of the State cannot usefully be determined by formulas and rules accepted in advance. That fact must, in case of need, be determined by an impartial and independent agency—it being understood that in the last resort that agency cannot be the State. For, ultimately, the essential meaning of the protection of the rights of man is that they must be protected against the State. From these considerations there follow some guiding principles for the formulation, in this respect, of an International Bill of Human Rights: —

(a) In the first instance, it is unnecessary and impracticable to enumerate these qualifications in connexion with every relevant article of the Bill. Such enumeration, unless it is to be repetitive, must be incomplete. The 'Covenant' proposed by the Commission on Human Rights in 1949 provided, separately, with regard to Articles on freedom of speech, assembly and association,[23] for a limitation of this nature. But these are not the only occasions when a State may be compelled to depart, even in circumstances other than 'time of war or other public emergency threatening the interests of the people',[24] from the observance of some of the obligations of the Bill of Rights. Safeguards in criminal trials, prohibition of expulsion of aliens, the right of emigration, and even freedom to manifest or practise religion, may require temporary limitation. The distribution or sale of religious tracts or bills by Jehovah's Witnesses was held by the Supreme Court of the United States to be a manifestation of religious freedom the restriction of which cannot be tolerated except for most cogent reasons. The Canadian Supreme Court has held otherwise.[25] The reasons for its decision are controversial

---

[23] Thus, with regard to the latter it lays down that 'this freedom shall be subject only to such limitations as are pursuant to law and as are necessary for the protection of national security, public order, public safety, health and morals or the fundamental rights and freedoms of others'.

[24] Article 4 of the proposed Covenant.

[25] See the much discussed case of *Saumur* v. *Recorder's Court of Quebec et al.* [1947] K.B.308; Supreme Court [1947] S.C.R. 492, where the accused, an evangelist and one of Jehovah's Witnesses, was convicted for offending against a by-law of the city of Quebec prohibiting the distribution of tracts and pamphlets in the streets without written permission of the Chief of Police. But see the following passage in Mr. Justice Douglas' judgment in *Murdock* v. *Pennsylvania* (1943), 319 U.S.105: —
'The hand distribution of religious tracts is an age-old form of missionary evangelism—as old as the history of printing presses. . . . It has the same claim to protection as the more orthodox and conventional exercises of religion. It also has the same claim as the others to the guarantees of freedom of speech and freedom of the press. . . . But the mere fact that the religious literature is " sold " by itinerant preachers rather than " donated " does not

and have—justly it is believed—been exposed to criticism. But circumstances are conceivable in which some such restriction may justifiably be regarded as necessitated by considerations of public welfare and order.

(b) Secondly, the principle must be accepted that although the fundamental rights guaranteed by the Bill of Rights must yield to considerations of public welfare and be exercised in accordance with the law of the State, that law and its application must not be such as to be contrary to the purpose and the spirit of the Bill of Rights. In the last resort the rights of man and not the State—*i.e.,* the view taken of the State by the persons who govern it at any given time—must be supreme.[26] This is of the very essence of the international protection of human rights. That principle was recognised, with a hesitation which, in effect, rendered the provision meaningless, in an Article of the ' Covenant' proposed in 1949 by the Commission on Human Rights relating to freedom of association.[27] That Article provided that ' everyone has the right to freedom of association with others' and that ' this freedom shall be subject only to such limitations as are pursuant to law and as are necessary for the protection of national security, public order, public safety, health or morals, or the fundamental rights and freedoms of others'. The words ' pursuant to law', unless qualified, would mean, in effect, that the State would be able to avoid its international obligations in the matter by enacting laws limiting the freedom of association. In an apparent attempt to obviate that possibility the last paragraph of the proposed article provided that ' national legislation shall neither prejudice, nor be applied in such a manner as to prejudice, the guarantees provided for in the International Convention on Freedom of Association and Protection of the Right to Organise, *in so far as States parties to that Convention*

transform evangelism into a commercial enterprise. If it did, then the passing of the collection plate in church would make the church service a commercial project. . . . Freedom of speech, freedom of the press, freedom of religion are available to all, not merely to those who can pay their own way. . . . It is a distortion of the facts of record to describe their activities as the occupation of selling books and pamphlets.'

[26] The fact that that overriding principle is occasionally urged in unexpected quarters does not derogate from its cogency. On the insistence of the Russian representative that suspension of the operation of the Bill would be justified only if it were in the interest of the people see E/CN.4/S.R.127, p. 7.

[27] Article 19.

are concerned '. The italicised passage is an example of preten-
tious evasiveness wholly unbecoming in a document of this
nature. For the meaning of that passage is no more than that
those parties to the Bill of Rights who are bound by the Convention on Freedom of Association shall be bound by that Convention. The latter, concluded in 1948 under the auspices of the
International Labour Organisation, is of considerable importance
for the subject here discussed. Article 8 of that Convention
provides that in exercising the rights provided for therein 'workers
and employers and their respective organisations, like other
persons or organised collectivities, shall respect the law of the
land '. At the same time that Article lays down that ' the law
of the land shall not be such as to impair, nor shall it be so
applied as to impair, the guarantees provided for in this Convention'. As by virtue of the Constitution of the International
Labour Organisation the International Court of Justice is
endowed with compulsory jurisdiction in disputes relating to the
interpretation and application of conventions concluded under
the auspices of the Organisation, and as that Constitution also
provides for machinery for dealing with complaints by organisations of workers and employers against alleged violations of the
Conventions, the principle adopted in Article 8 of the Convention
is both novel and far-reaching inasmuch as it subjects the
limitations grounded in national law to the overriding limitations
of the principal obligation undertaken in the Convention. A
principle of that nature, if adopted effectively—but not nominally,
as in the proposed Article referred to above—with respect to all
Articles of the Bill of Rights, would go a long way towards
solving a crucial problem of the Bill of Rights.[28] The ' saving '
clause or the ' general limitation ' clause [29] is both essential and

[28] For a valuable memorandum prepared by the Secretary-General in 1949 and
comparing the Convention on Freedom of Association with the provisions of
the proposed Article 19 of the Covenant see Doc. E/CN.4/164.

[29] It was because of these saving clauses that Bentham, with much impatience,
described as valueless Declarations of Rights such as the French Declaration
of 1791. They could be received, he said, ' without making any alteration
into the constitutional codes of Prussia, Denmark, Russia or Morocco':
Anarchical Fallacies (1824), *Collected Works* (1843), vol 2, p. 510. ' Nothing
can be more fallacious than a declaration which gives me with one hand,
what it authorises the taking from me with the other ' (*ibid.*, p. 534). And
see Schwarzenberger, ' Bentham's Contribution to International Law ' in
Jeremy Bentham and the Law (A Symposium, 1948, ed. by Keeton and
Schwarzenberger), pp. 178, 179.

unavoidable in a Bill of Rights. It need not nullify its major purpose.

The otherwisè perplexing difficulty of reconciling the supremacy of the law of the land with the limiting force of the Bill of Rights can and must be solved by the admission of the principle that, as in the case of action in self-preservation and self-defence under general international law,[30] the question whether the law of the State and its application are in conformity with the Bill of Rights is one which, ultimately, must be subject to the jurisdiction of the organs established by the Bill of Rights. The State must possess the power to limit the right of free speech and expression of opinion in accordance with the law of sedition which it may enact and apply. That law must be obeyed. But no such absolute obedience to it can be exacted as would deprive the citizen of the right to test its conformity with the Bill of Rights before an international authority. Subject to such ultimate control, the supremacy of the law of the State is unavoidable if the Bill of Rights is not to degenerate into an instrument of anarchy and a source of danger to the existence of the State. Without such ultimate control, the Bill of Rights is no more than an ineffectual declaration of principle.

These considerations are of assistance in solving the question, which has been a source of perplexity in relation to the Bill of Rights, of the temporary suspension of the constitution or of constitutional liberties, in time of war or otherwise. The State cannot part with that right. On the other hand, that right, if uncontrolled, can be used—and has been used—for the destruction of the fundamental constitutional rights of the citizen. In some countries—it would be invidious to enumerate them—the

---

[30] As stated by the writer in his Seventh Edition of vol. I of Oppenheim's *International Law* (1948): 'The reason of the thing . . . makes it necessary for every State to judge for itself, in the first instance, whether a case of necessity in self-defence has arisen. But, unless the notion of self-preservation is to be eliminated as a legal conception, or unless it is to be used as a cloak for concealing deliberate breaches of the law, it is obvious that the question of the legality of action taken in self-preservation is suitable for determination and must ultimately be determined by a judicial authority or by a political body . . . acting in a judicial capacity (§ 130, p. 266). The same principle is summarised by Joseph-Barthélemy and Duez as representing the Anglo-French-American doctrine in the matter of State and government action in necessity: ' Il existe une supériorité momentanée des faits sur cette grande prévision humaine qu'est la constitution, mais il n'y a pas de supériorité juridique de la nécessité sur la constitution ' (*Traité élémentaire de droit constitutionnel*, 1926, p. 238).

temporary suspension of the constitution was, or has been, a prominent feature of national life. It has transformed the constitution of a democratic State into an instrument of tyranny. The importance of this aspect of the problem has been recognised in the discussions concerning the Bill of Rights. Thus in the Draft submitted to the Commission on Human Rights by the United Kingdom in 1947 it was proposed that, in time of war or other national emergency, a State may take measures derogating from its obligations under the Bill to an extent strictly limited by the exigencies of the situation and that any State availing itself of that right shall inform the Secretary-General of the United Nations fully of the measures thus enacted and the reasons therefor as well as of the cessation of these measures. That provision was incorporated, almost literally, in the 'Covenant' proposed by the Commission in 1949. The proposal was inadequate. A power must rest with the agencies charged with the implementation of the Bill of Rights to determine, if need be, that there was originally no sufficient justification for the suspension of the constitutional guarantees of the Bill of Rights, either in their entirety or in relation to its individual provisions,[31] or that the justification for it has disappeared and that the continued suspension of all constitutional liberties or of some of them is no longer consistent with the obligations of the Bill of Rights. In political science and jurisprudence the question of State emergency and of the suspension of constitutional guarantees has been discussed in the past largely as a problem between the executive and the legislature. The Bill of Rights will transfer the problem to a higher plane. It will henceforth become a problem of reconciling the supremacy of the highest power within the State with the paramountcy of the international order safeguarding the rights of man against the State itself.

[31] So long as that power is vested in an international agency, it is not necessary—and it is impracticable—to enumerate rights and freedoms which must not in any case be suspended. No instrument or enactment can foresee in advance the extent or nature of possible emergencies. The Belgian Constitution of 1831 stipulated for some rights, such as freedom of the press, of religion, and of association, which were guaranteed absolutely, but this is exceptional. Thus, for instance, in Switzerland, although the Constitution declares freedom of religion to be inviolate, that freedom is subject to Federal and cantonal legislation when political considerations of ' public order and peace ' so require (Article 49). The same applies to the freedom of the press. See generally, in relation to control of political extremism, Loewenstein in *Columbia Law Review*, 38 (1938), pp. 591-622 and 725-774, especially pp. 768-774.

5. THE COLLECTIVE GUARANTEE OF THE UNITED NATIONS AND OF THE SIGNATORIES OF THE BILL

Article 20

This International Bill of the Rights of Man shall be placed under the guarantee of the United Nations. Its observance shall be a matter of concern to all the United Nations.

The above Article is self-explanatory. Its purpose is to lay down not only that the Bill of Rights constitutes an international legal obligation binding upon the parties to it, but also that the question of the fulfilment of its provisions has ceased to be a matter within their exclusive domestic jurisdiction. What in relation to the Charter is in the nature of an inference to be proved in the teeth of its Article 2(7),[32] is here clearly removed from the sphere of controversy. Moreover, the observance of the obligations of the Bill of Rights is made a matter of concern not only for the United Nations as a whole, but for each and every Member of the United Nations.

The Article is drafted on the assumption that the Bill of Rights, although not accepted by all the Members of the United Nations, will receive sufficient support to enable it to become part of the law of the United Nations to the extent of making possible the full participation of its organs in the international supervision and enforcement of the Bill. As pointed out above,[33] such a consummation can be achieved only if the Bill secures the support of at least two-thirds of the members of the General Assembly. But the contingency must be envisaged that no such majority of the Members of the United Nations may be forthcoming. In that case the States adhering to the Bill of Rights will have to provide organs of their own—including a supreme organ in the form of an Assembly meeting at periodic intervals. As these States would continue to be bound by the obligations of the Charter, the result would be a certain degree of duplication of jurisdiction, which would raise problems more serious than arise at present should the organs of the United Nations, in particular the Commission on Human Rights, assume the powers which they are entitled to exercise under the Charter and which,

[32] See above, Chapter IX.
[33] See pp. 308-311.

so far, they have disclaimed the right to exercise. In that case a working arrangement preventing overlapping of competencies would be both necessary and practicable. However that may be, in the contingency here envisaged Article 19 would have to be formulated as follows: 'The observance of this International Bill of the Rights of Man shall be a matter of common concern to all its Signatories and it shall be placed under their collective guarantee.' A further problem would arise if a State which is a party to a general Bill of Rights outside the United Nations were to become, in addition, a party to a regional system of protection of human rights such as is envisaged in connexion with the proposed European Court of Human Rights within the Council of Western Europe.[34]

6. THE HUMAN RIGHTS COUNCIL. THE DUAL CHARACTER OF THE IMPLEMENTATION OF THE BILL

Article 21

There shall be established a Human Rights Council which shall be responsible to the General Assembly for the promotion of the purposes of this Bill of Rights and for the supervision of the observance of its Articles.

The Human Rights Council shall be composed of nine persons possessing the highest qualifications and not representing any Government. The members of the Council shall be selected by an electoral body consisting of the Secretary-General of the United Nations, the Director of the Division of Human Rights, four representatives of States appointed by the General Assembly, two permanent members of the Security Council designated by a simple majority of its members, and four Judges of the International Court of Justice appointed by the President with the approval of the Court. The Council shall include not less than three persons of judicial experience.

The members of the Council shall devote their whole time to the fulfilment of their functions. They shall not engage in any other profession or occupation. They shall receive salaries commensurate with the importance and the dignity of their office.

They shall hold office for a period of six years, subject to the

[34] See below, pp. 435-441.

first election taking place in such a manner as to ensure a substantial measure of continuity in the composition of the Council.

The Council shall present an annual report to the General
Assembly.

The scheme here adopted for the international supervision and
enforcement of the Bill of Rights is based on two main considerations: the first is the unqualified recognition of the right of
petition by individuals and by private groups and organisations;
the second is the recognition of the dual nature of the agencies
to be entrusted with the international supervision and implementation of the Bill of Rights. It is convenient to consider this
latter aspect first.

The tendency, which is a natural one, is to follow the experience of the constitutional law of States and to consider courts to
be the proper instrumentality for vindicating the rights and
freedoms of the individual. The implication of that tendency
is to regard an International Court of Human Rights, open not
only to States but also to individuals and private bodies, as the
best method of serving the purposes of the Bill.

There are three main objections to considering an International Court as the principal and exclusive organ for securing
the observance of the Bill of Rights. Probably none of these
objections, when taken in isolation, are decisive. As will be seen,
they are all controversial. However, their cumulative effect has
led me—not without hesitation and only in relation to a general
international Bill of Rights embracing a considerable number of
States such as that equal to a two-thirds majority of the General
Assembly—to propose a system in which the judicial arm, however important, is not the primary organ of implementation of
the Bill of Rights. What are these objections?

(1) In the first instance, there is a possibility that an international court might be overwhelmed by a multitude of complaints
coming from distant parts of the world. It might not be
practicable for a strictly judicial body to devise machinery for
examining in an informal manner complaints submitted to it
with the view to eliminating cases which are frivolous, malicious,
based on obviously deficient information as to the correct legal
position, or otherwise not deserving of serious consideration. Yet
such methods are possible. They have been resorted to by non-

judicial bodies in connexion with the protection of minorities,[35] the system of mandates,[36] and the trusteeship system.[37] There seems to be no reason why an international court should not be able to devise some such preliminary procedure, for instance, by deputing some of its members to examine complaints in the first instance and, with the consent of the President, to reject those which clearly do not call for consideration. Neither is it altogether certain that the availability of the international court—or of a non-judicial agency open to individuals—will open wide the flood-gates of petitions. The enforcement of the Bill of Rights must constitute, in the initial stages of its operation, a process of trial and error. It is difficult to foresee what will be the effect of a Bill of Rights, provided with instrumentalities of international supervision, upon the functioning of the international organs in question. It is not easy to forecast whether it will result in a flood of petitions and complaints, or whether the existence of the Bill will act as a restraining influence not only upon the conduct of States, but also upon the litigious propensities of individuals. There is nothing irrevocable in any machinery that may be adopted. Moreover, the constitution of the court—or of the non-judicial agency—may leave room for necessary adaptations, such as enlargement of the number of judges (or of members of the Human Rights Council), the setting

[35] According to the Resolution of the Council of the League of Nations of 5 September, 1923 (*League of Nations, Official Journal*, 1923, p. 1293) the Secretary-General was given the power to decline to forward to the State concerned petitions which offended against one of the following conditions: (a) if the petition was not concerned with the protection of minorities in accordance with the relevant treaties; (b) if it was submitted in the form of a request for the severance of the territorial tie with the State in question; (c) if it emanated from an anonymous or unauthenticated source; (d) if it was couched in violent language. In the same Resolution a further, somewhat questionable, condition was added, namely, that the petition must not contain information or refer to facts which were recently the subject of a petition submitted to the ordinary procedure. The fact that the decision on the 'receivability' of the petition was entrusted, without any safeguards, to the Secretary-General, an administrative official, was subjected to pertinent criticism.

[36] According to the Report adopted by the Council of the League of Nations in 1923 the Chairman of the Mandates Commission was given the power to decide that a petition, being 'obviously trivial', did not deserve further attention (*League of Nations, Official Journal*, 1923, p. 200).

[37] Under Rule 85 of the procedure of the Trusteeship Council the Secretary-General is entitled—and bound—not to circulate petitions which are 'manifestly inconsequential'. He is, however, under an obligation to communicate a list of the latter, with a summary of their contents, to the members of the Trusteeship Council.

up of additional chambers, or a regional subdivision of the work involved.

(2) There is a second, and more substantial, argument against a purely judicial procedure and in favour of making a non-judicial body the main instrument of the international guarantee. The complaints and petitions on account of alleged violations of the Bill of Rights will touch upon vital aspects of national sovereignty in matters which, while of a distinctly legal character—because bearing upon the interpretation and application of an international legal instrument—exhibit at the same time an acute political complexion. This applies conspicuously to a sphere where the rights of man and the interests of the State (or, more accurately, the view which the government in power takes of these interests) conflict or appear to do so. In that sphere, more than in any other, the solution often depends upon the application of what has been described as inarticulate major premises. These are not, in essence, of a legal character. In cases such as the justification of the suspension of civil liberties in a state of emergency,[38] the importance of the individual interest involved as compared with the general interest supposedly at stake cannot always be gauged by the ready application of a legal rule.[39] This does not mean that the claim of the individual is of an inferior nature, or that it ought to be sacrificed. But it does mean that the proper procedure for resolving the conflict is not invariably

---

[38] See Lord Atkinson in *Rex* v. *Halliday* [1917] A.C. 260, 271: "However precious the personal liberty of the subject may be, there is something for which it may well be, to some extent, sacrificed by legal enactment, namely, national success in the war, or escape from national plunder or enslavement.'

[39] This aspect of the procedural safeguards to the Bill of Rights is clearly illustrated by the following passage from Dr. Kaeckenbeeck's *The International Experiment of Upper Silesia* (1942)—a book which gives an account of one of the most valuable international experiments in the field of protection of human rights: ' . . . There are cases in which . . . the reactions of a whole nation, with all their consequences, national and international, are in no way commensurate with the satisfaction which an individual receives from the strict recognition of a right; or cases in which the strict satisfaction of an individual's right may so affect State interests or national feelings that the benefit of justice is outweighed tenfold or a hundredfold by impending dangers or inconveniences. In such hard cases the only method by which the international judge can avoid both the condemnation of his conscience as a judge and the heavy responsibility of spreading discord is conciliation' (p. 503). It may not be easy to assent to the proposition of the learned author that justice may, in such cases, be outweighed, to the extent indicated, by other considerations. But the passage quoted shows the importance of a procedure of conciliation, at least at a preliminary stage, in the matter of claims of individuals on account of the violation of their rights by the State. This does not mean that a judicial or arbitral organ is the best—or even the proper—instrument of conciliation.

of a judicial character. A combination of a semi-judicial and a political procedure of conciliation and compromise would, in such cases, appear to provide, in the first instance, the appropriate remedy. A court must, as a rule, confine itself to the ascertainment of the legality or otherwise of the action complained of. *Tertium non datur.* It cannot propose a course of action which would render a formal finding unnecessary. This can properly be done by an organ which, although not disregarding the legal aspects of the complaint and although empowered to pronounce on both facts and law and to make a binding recommendation,[40] can avail itself of the more elastic procedure of conciliation and attempts at a compromise—so long as it is clear that the procedure of conciliation is one to which not only States but also individuals are parties and that compromise does not necessarily mean compromise at the expense of the fundamental rights protected by the Bill.

(3) Finally, the creation of a non-judicial organ is necessitated by the fact that social and economic rights, which form an indispensable part of the Bill, are not such as to lend themselves to enforcement by judicial process. At the same time they cannot be permitted to remain a mere declaration of principle. For that reason they seem to be the proper subject matter for a general guarantee and supervision by a body of the kind here contemplated operating through a procedure more elastic and informal than is permissible in the case of a court.

These, then, are the reasons which have prompted the scheme here propounded.[41] That scheme, while it does not exclude the

---

[40] Once more, it is useful to quote the conclusions reached, in a different sphere, by Dr. Kaeckenbeeck: ' Conciliation is facilitated by wide powers of decision, if these are wielded with discretion. Merely advisory authority, not backed by other factors, is not conducive to conciliation whenever one party has made up its mind not to listen to mere suggestions or half words. . . . It was therefore unwise . . . to entrust the protection of minorities to an organ deprived of wider powers of decision or coercion. . . . In cases in which the Arbitral Tribunal was given jurisdiction to condemn theoretically, while being expressly deprived of the power to grant redress, the result was failure of protection and endless worry ' (*op. cit.,* p. 518).

[41] It was first set out by the writer of this book in his *An International Bill of the Rights of Man* (1945), pp. 202-213, and in his Reports to the International Law Association in 1947 and 1948. In 1948 and 1949 Professor Cassin, the French representative in the Human Rights Commission, who has made perhaps the most notable contribution to its work, proposed a similar scheme based on the recognition of the right of petition by individuals and the power of the Commission to make recommendations. There is, however, no reference to the question of the binding character of the recommendations. See E/CN.4/358 (1949), pp. 70 *et seq.* The proposals put forward jointly by the United States and Great Britain are discussed above, p. 289.

jurisdiction of a court, is based primarily on the functioning of an organ which, although including persons of judicial experience, is non-judicial in character. That organ must be the pivot of the supervision of the observance of a Bill of Rights which embraces the large majority of members of the United Nations. Its importance explains the elaborate composition of the body which is to be responsible for its selection. That the members of the Council must be persons independent of Governments is obvious. For the same reasons their election cannot be entrusted to a political body and exposed to the hazards and absence of responsibility which characterise a purely political election. This also explains the proposed conditions of their tenure of office.

In case the Bill of Rights should materialise outside the United Nations, it will be necessary for the signatory States to organise themselves for that purpose. In particular, it will be necessary for them to set up a body in the nature of an Annual Conference which will bear the supreme responsibility for the supervision and the enforcement of the Bill of Rights. The Annual Conference would, in that case, perform the functions assigned to the General Assembly in the proposed Article 21. As, unlike in the case of the General Assembly of the United Nations, the business of the Bill of Rights would be the sole preoccupation of the Annual Conference, there would be no reason why it should not be entrusted with the task of selecting the members of the Human Rights Council—provided that the process of election is preceded by adequate preparation.

7. THE ORGANISATION AND JURISDICTION OF THE HUMAN RIGHTS COUNCIL

Article 22

The Council shall set up Commissions and other organs to assist it in the fulfilment of its functions.

The Council shall formulate, for approval by the General Assembly, Rules of Procedure for the investigation of petitions. These Rules shall be based on the recognition of the right of petition of any State, organisation, body, or individual.

This Article lays down, in the first instance, the principle that, in view of the complexity and comprehensiveness of the work of the Council, it shall have the duty and be empowered to set up commissions and other organs to assist it in its task. Only experience can show to what extent it will be necessary for the Council to avail itself of that authority.

The second principle, which is the most essential feature of the scheme and the reasons of which are discussed elsewhere,[42] is the recognition of the right of petition not only of States but also of individuals and private bodies or organisations.

Article 23

The Council shall, through appropriate organs, collect information and receive and investigate petitions and representations bearing on the observance of this Bill of Rights. It shall, in proper cases, communicate such petitions to the State concerned and receive its observations thereon. It shall, on the initiative of any of its members or of the Secretary-General of the United Nations, take cognizance of or such appropriate action on any alleged violations of the provisions of this Bill of Rights. The Council shall neither act on its own initiative nor proceed with any petition or representation brought before it unless it is established that the remedies reasonably available in the State concerned have been exhausted. The Council shall, by a concurring vote of any seven of its members, be entitled to conduct an enquiry within the territory of the State concerned which shall afford full facilities necessary for the efficient conduct of the investigation.

Three provisions of this Article require comment:

In the first instance, it is the right and duty of the Council to take cognisance *proprio motu, i.e.,* through one of its members or its organs, of any violations of the Bill of Rights. As a rule, allegations of breaches of the Bill of Rights will be brought before the Council by a State or a private individual or organisation. This will be the normal source of the jurisdiction of the Council. But provision must be made for cases of violations of the Bill in which for some reason or other no appeal is made to the Council. Moreover, as the responsibility of the Council for the realisation of the purposes of the Bill is of a general and comprehensive character, it is desirable that the Council should not be dependent exclusively on outside sources setting its activity

[42] See above, pp. 286-291.

in motion. In particular, it must be able to act in cases where no actual violation of the Bill has taken place, for instance, when an act of the legislature violative of the Bill of Rights has not yet been applied in a way causing individual injury. Similarly, in the sphere of economic and social rights, where no question of individual injury will as a rule arise, the Council must be empowered and enabled to act on its own initiative. On the other hand, it does not appear that, for that purpose, the office of an Attorney-General, as occasionally suggested, is desirable or proper.

The second question, which is of some difficulty, concerns the right of the Council to conduct an inquiry within the territory of States parties to the Bill. That right exists in relation to Trust Territories, and experience has vindicated its usefulness and practicability. In view of the seriousness of the decision to conduct a local inquiry, the special safeguard of a qualified majority of seven out of the nine members of the Council seems to be appropriate. Even so, the proposal is admittedly far-reaching. An alternative solution would be to make an inquiry within the territory of the State dependent upon the consent of the State concerned—subject to its obligation not to refuse such consent if the inquiry is decided upon by the unanimous vote of the members of the Council.

Thirdly, action on the part of the Council must be conditioned by the previous exhaustion of local remedies which can *reasonably* be held to be available in the State concerned. The notion of exhaustion of local remedies as a prerequisite of the international procedure of protection is well established in international law, and it is consistent with the purposes of the Bill to recognise its operation also in that sphere. The practice of international tribunals has developed means of preventing the requirement of exhaustion of legal remedies from becoming an instrument of delay and injustice. Thus it has been clearly recognised in many instances that no question of exhaustion of legal remedies arises when, owing to the circumstances of the case, there are in fact no legal remedies to exhaust [43] or when the act complained of consists in a legislative measure or in a decision of a tribunal

[43] See, *e.g.*, *Brown's Case*, decided in 1923 by the British-American Claims Arbitral Tribunal: *Annual Digest of International Law Cases*, 1923-24, Case No. 35.

or an act of government against which there is no appeal.[44] The Council, not being a strictly judicial body, will be in a position to prevent the requirement of exhaustion of legal remedies from obstructing its activities. Without that requirement the international machinery would be unworkable and liable to be abused.

8. The Judicial Enforcement of the Bill of Rights

Article 24

At any stage of the procedure the Council, acting on its own initiative or on the request of the State the action of which is the subject of an investigation, shall be entitled to ask the International Court of Justice for an Advisory Opinion on any legal issue involved in the interpretation or the application of this Bill of Rights. The present Article shall be considered, for this purpose, as implying the authorisation by the General Assembly as provided for in Article 96 of the Charter of the United Nations.

The General Assembly may at any time entrust to an International Court of Human Rights the functions to be exercised under this Bill of Rights by the International Court of Justice.

Unless otherwise decided by the concurring vote of any seven of its members, the Council shall publish the results of its investigation. The State concerned shall be entitled to appeal to the International Court of Justice or any subdivision thereof, or, when established, to the International Court of Human Rights, on any question of law or fact on which the finding of the Council is based. The same right of appeal to the International Court of Human Rights, when established, shall be open, by leave of the Council, to any individual or private body in respect of a petition brought by it. No such leave of appeal shall be refused except by a two-thirds majority of the members of the Council.

While the Council must be the primary organ for giving effect to the purposes of the Bill of Rights, it is necessary—and indeed indispensable—that the judicial arm should play its proper part in the international protection of human rights. In the first instance, such assistance may be forthcoming by way of an Advisory Opinion of the International Court of Justice given at the request of the Council. Although the Council, which will

[44] See, *e.g.*, the *Finnish Ships Case*: *ibid.*, 1933-1934, Case No. 91. And see generally and for detailed references Oppenheim, *International Law*, vol. I (7th ed. by Lauterpacht, 1948), p. 327.

contain members of judicial experience,[45] will be able and entitled to take decisions on legal questions incidental to cases brought before it, it may find it desirable, in matters of importance, to have behind its decision the authority of the principal judicial organ of the United Nations. Secondly, provision must be made for an unqualified right of appeal to the Court on the part of the State directly concerned. An adverse finding of the Council may be highly prejudicial both to its interests and to its reputation. Neither can such right of appeal be wholly denied to the individual—though in that case, at least in the initial stages of the operation of the Bill, it will be desirable to make the exercise of that right dependent upon leave by the Council. It is in keeping with the status of the individual as the sole beneficiary of the Bill of Rights that the right of appeal should not be denied to him except for compelling reasons recognised as such by a two-thirds majority of the members of the Council.

However, unless the Statute of the International Court of Justice is altered so as to enable individuals to be parties to cases before the Court, the right of appeal must be contingent upon the setting up of an International Court of Human Rights. The establishment of the latter will, in any case, be necessary if the Bill of Rights materialises outside the orbit of the United Nations. In that case it will be for that Court to render Advisory Opinions at the request of the Council. However, it is necessary to consider the problem of an International Court of Human Rights not only in relation to any particular regional association that may be set up for the purpose, but in connexion with the Bill of Rights generally. The right of eventual judicial determination of fundamental rights which are being denied or disputed is in itself a fundamental right. There is only one justification for impairing it, namely, the provision of remedies—such as the proposed Human Rights Council—which approximate as closely as possible to judicial safeguards and impartiality. Even so, a system of international protection of human rights which rules out altogether that eventual remedy is unsatisfactory and ought not to be envisaged as a permanent solution. This means that in the long run an International Court of Human Rights must be regarded as an essential part of the Bill of Rights. In view of

[45] See above p. 373.

this it is necessary to review some of the objections militating against the setting up of a Court of that nature. These objections are admittedly of a serious character. In 1945 they led me to the conclusion that an International Court of Human Rights is not practicable.[46] They can no longer be regarded as decisive.

To admit the validity of the objections raised against the establishment of a Court of Human Rights is to admit their validity also in relation to a non-judicial body such as the proposed Human Rights Council. There is probably no substance in either. In the first instance, as already pointed out,[47] there is no foundation for the apprehension that direct access of individuals to the Court may result in a flood of cases rendering its activity wholly impracticable. This is so in particular if it is borne in mind that complaints and petitions will be brought in the first instance before the non-judicial body—the Council— which will dispose of the bulk of the cases brought before it and which will eliminate complaints and petitions that clearly do not call for or deserve further investigation. The requirement, as here proposed, of a qualified majority of the Council for the refusal of leave to appeal to the Court provides a sufficient safeguard against any undue denial to the individual of the right to a judicial remedy. At the same time, the same provision coupled with the power of the Council to eliminate at an early stage petitions which deserve no consideration, will be a guarantee against the work of the Court being hampered and its authority impaired by an indiscriminate resort to its jurisdiction.

The more serious difficulty arises from the fact that the jurisdiction of the court to review executive, judicial, and legislative acts of the highest organs of the State will constitute a pronounced degree of surrender of national sovereignty and, in respect of some countries (such as Great Britain), a departure from the constitutional principle of the absolute sovereignty of the legislature and the inadmissibility of judicial review of the validity of its acts. The practical implications of such surrender of sovereignty are discussed elsewhere in this book.[48] They exceed in scope and significance the limitation of sovereignty

---

[46] *An International Bill of the Rights of Man* (1945), pp. 12-14.

[47] See above, p. 290.

[48] See below, p. 453, in connexion with the proposed European Court of Human Rights.

implied in the acceptance of the substantive safeguards of the Bill of Rights. They amount to a conferment upon the International Court of powers which are most comprehensive and, in a sense, unforeseeable. However, any discussion of the international protection of human rights must remain sterile unless it is realised that such protection cannot be achieved without limitations upon the sovereignty of States. The appreciation of that fact may be delayed by the use of language which is artificial and by the adoption of solutions which are nominal. But it cannot be so delayed for long. Once that is realised, the conferment of compulsory jurisdiction upon an international court in the matter of the Bill of Rights differs only in degree from the submission to the compulsory jurisdiction of international courts in general. It is only because of the still lingering notion of the inferiority of the individual that the jurisdiction of international courts in relation to the Bill of Rights assumes the alarming complexion usually associated with it.

Moreover, the impact of the innovation may be softened, without detracting from its reality and effectiveness, by shaping the jurisdiction of the Court in such a way as not to confer upon it the power of a formal nullification of acts of the highest judicial or legislative organs of the State. That jurisdiction may be exercised by way of declaring the incompatibility of the measures or acts in question with the obligations of the Bill of Rights and, whenever appropriate, by decreeing compensation. It would then be for the State to take requisite action in compliance with the judgment of the Court, as it would be for the international agencies entrusted with the enforcement of the Bill of Rights to draw the consequences from the failure of the State in question to act upon the finding of the Court.

Finally, the possibility could be considered of giving a measure of elasticity to the composition of the International Court by enlarging its permanent international nucleus through the addition, in individual cases, of judges who are nationals of the State concerned so as to render it, in a sense, an enlarged Court of Appeal of that State. Thus whenever a case affecting a State comes before the Court, the composition of the latter, assuming that it is composed normally of eleven judges, could be increased by three members, nationals of the State concerned and holding high judicial office in that State. These persons would have the power of decision and voting on the same footing as the permanent members of the Court. Their participation would not decisively affect the character and the continuity of the Court. On the other hand, it would ensure that decisions vitally affecting the constitution and the sovereignty of the State concerned are not given by a small majority of foreign judges. If some such arrangement is adopted, a judgment given against the State by a decision concurred in by all the judges who are nationals of that State would be fully acceptable to its public opinion, for it would indicate that there has taken place an obvious violation of the Bill of Rights. If all the nationals of that State were to vote in favour of upholding the measures taken by it, an adverse decision would be made correspondingly difficult, while an unfavourable decision given by a majority including one or more of the nationals of that State would not be open to the objection that it is a judgment of a purely foreign tribunal and would to that extent be more acceptable to public opinion. Moreover, some such modification of the composition of the Court in individual cases would go a long way towards meeting the objection that a foreign tribunal, not conversant with the laws and traditions of the State, is called upon to pronounce on matters touching the very core of national life and of national sovereignty. There may also be some wider significance in an attempt, implied in the proposal here put forward, at a combination of—and the raising of the rigid barrier between—national and international jurisdiction. However that may be, it must become clear that the question of an International Court of Human Rights accessible to individuals cannot be solved by a purely negative attitude rooted in the traditional approach to the position of the individual in international law. That that approach is refuted both by practice and principle is one of the main theses of this book.[49] The former President of the Upper Silesian Arbitral Tribunal, which admitted actions by individuals against both foreign and their own States,[50] summarises the result of a long experience in the following words:

[49] See above, pp. 48-60.
[50] See *Steiner and Gross* v. *Polish State*, decided by the Upper Silesian Arbitral Tribunal in 1928: *Annual Digest*, 1927-28, Case No. 188.

25

'That many complaints of individuals should in the end remain unsubstantiated or prove futile cannot cause any surprise. But it would be unjust to deduce from this an argument against the right of direct appeal by individuals, just as it would be fallacious to deduce from the absence of cases introduced by the Governments themselves a proof that all was for the best in the best of worlds, or an argument in favour of restricting to Governments the right of instituting proceedings before international protective organs. This might give an illusion of tranquillity, but no assurance of justice.' [51]

In the discussions concerned with international safeguards of human rights, in connexion with the Charter of the United Nations, the Bill of Rights and otherwise, the proposals for an international court of human rights have not been confined to writers.[52] Thus during the Paris Peace Conference in 1946 Australia advanced a proposal for a European Court of Human Rights entrusted with jurisdiction in respect of the clauses relating to human rights in the Peace Treaties with Hungary, Bulgaria, Finland and Italy.[53] In December 1947 the representatives of States composing the Working Group on Implementation—a committee of the Commission on Human Rights—considered another Australian proposal for setting up an International Court of Human Rights and gave it general approval.[54] The Group unanimously answered in the affirmative the question whether 'an international Court be empowered to constitute the final guarantor of human rights?' and whether the Court 'should have the right to pronounce final and binding decisions?' [55] Apparently the Group did not commit itself to an expression of view as to whether the Court should be open directly to individuals. The detailed proposal put forward by Australia in 1949 did not contain a clear answer to that question.[56] Yet that is a question which is of the very essence of any scheme for an

[51] Kaeckenbeeck, *op. cit.,* p. 482.
[52] See, *e.g., Brunet, La garantie internationale des droits de l'homme* (1947), pp. 353-354.
[53] See above, p. 205.
[54] For the Report of the Group, which was composed of representatives of Australia, Belgium, Iran, and India, see Doc. E/800 and, also, *Economic and Social Council, Official Records, Third Year, Sixth Session,* Supplement No. 1, pp. 48-53.
[55] Three members of the Group voted in favour of the establishment of a new Court while the Indian representative was of the opinion that a Chamber of the existing International Court of Justice would meet the need.
[56] See above, p. 308.

international court charged with the interpretation of the Bill of Rights. It is equally of the essence of the matter that that question should be answered in the affirmative.[57] The rights of man must be protected at the instance of man. In the Preamble to the Resolution of the Ninth International Conference of American States adopted in 1948 and recommending that the Inter-American Judicial Committee should propose a draft statute of an International Court to guarantee human rights it was stated that there can be no genuine protection of human rights unless they are safeguarded by a competent court and that ' where internationally recognised rights are concerned, juridical protection, to be effective, should emanate from an international organ '.[58]

9. THE NATURE OF THE RECOMMENDATIONS OF THE HUMAN RIGHTS COUNCIL

Article 25

In all cases in which the results of the investigation disclose an infraction of this Bill of Rights the Council shall make appropriate recommendations to the State concerned. If the State concerned fails to comply with the recommendations of the Council, the latter may bring the matter before the General Assembly which, after any further investigation and after calling upon the State concerned to comply with the recommendations, shall, in the case of continued non-compliance, make such recommendations as may be appropriate in the circumstances. The Parties to this Bill of Rights agree that the recommendations of the General Assembly shall be legally binding upon them. Where the infraction of this Bill of Rights is such as to constitute a threat to international peace and security, the General Assembly shall transmit the case to the Security Council for such further political, economic, or military action as may be deemed necessary to ensure compliance with the Bill of Rights.

The provisions of this Article are self-explanatory. They are based on the principle that while the procedure before the Human Rights Council must aim at the removal of the grievance, if any, by persuasion, conciliation, and other suitable action, the Council is bound, in case of failure of its efforts, to make

[57] As to the proposed European Court of Human Rights, see below, p. 449.
[58] *Annals of the Organisation of American States*, 1 (1949), p. 133.

definite recommendations to the State concerned. These recommendations, although of considerable moral authority, would not be legally binding. However, if not complied with, they would become the starting point of a procedure before the General Assembly ending, if circumstances so require, with a legally binding recommendation. The recommendation would be binding not only upon the State directly concerned, but also upon all parties to the Bill. For the recommendation may prescribe coercive action, in which the parties to the Bill will be legally bound to participate, in case the State concerned should persist in its refusal to abide by its obligations under the Bill of Rights. The latter is an international legal obligation; it is part of international law. Its ultimate sanction—like the sanction of international law—is not public opinion, but such measures of compulsion as are appropriate in the circumstances and as are politically available. This applies, in particular, to cases—referred to in the last sentence of the Article—in which the violation of the Bill of Rights constitutes a threat to international peace and security. In these cases the necessity would arise for action by the Security Council in accordance with its powers and obligations under the Charter.

The provisions of this Article would have to be suitably altered in case the Bill of Rights should come into being outside the United Nations. In that case the Annual Conference of the Signatories thereto would take the place of the General Assembly. Yet the jurisdiction of the Security Council would probably remain unaltered, seeing that it is open to any Member of the United Nations to bring before the Security Council any dispute or situation affecting international peace and security. It would not matter whether the case is thus brought before the Council by an individual Signatory of the Bill or collectively by all or some Signatories who are Members of the United Nations.

10. THE BILL OF RIGHTS AND THE POWERS OF THE UNITED NATIONS UNDER THE CHARTER

Article 26

Nothing in this Bill of Rights shall be deemed to impair the powers and functions of the General Assembly, the Security Council, the Trusteeship Council, the Economic and Social

Council or its Commissions, as set out in the Charter of the United Nations.

Even if the Bill of Rights enters into force as part of the law of the United Nations as the result of a decision of a requisite majority of the General Assembly, it will still be necessary to lay down the principle that it leaves unimpaired the powers and functions of the organs of the United Nations referred to in this Article. This is so not only because those powers can be altered only in consequence of a properly ratified amendment of the Charter. It is so also because those powers must continue to be exercised in relation to those Members of the United Nations which decline to subscribe to the Bill of Rights.

11. ACCEPTANCE OF THE BILL OF RIGHTS. THE PROBLEM OF RESERVATIONS

Article 27

The International Bill of the Rights of Man shall enter into force, as an instrument operating within the framework of and guaranteed by the United Nations, as soon as it has received the assent of two-thirds of the Members of the United Nations. It shall become binding, without any necessity for ratification, upon Members of the United Nations whose duly accredited and authorised representatives present at this Special General Assembly cast their vote in favour of the Bill or who at any future Session of the General Assembly make a declaration accepting its Articles as binding upon their State. Any State which is not a Member of the United Nations may accede to this Bill of Rights by a declaration deposited with the Secretary-General.

Reasons have been given in another part of this book why a Bill of Rights which will come into being under the ægis of the United Nations as part of the law of the United Nations and which will require the co-operation of its organs must receive the assent of at least two-thirds of its members.[59] The significance of the Bill of Rights, which in historic importance would be second only to the Charter itself, requires that a Special General Assembly should be dedicated to its discussion and adoption. Yet there would be no justification for excluding non-members of the United Nations from participation in the Bill.

[59] See above, p. 309.

In case it should prove impossible to secure the requisite majority of the members of the United Nations, the Bill of Rights could come into being by means of a treaty providing, in the accepted form, for ratification by the signatories and for future accession by other States by means of a declaration deposited with the Human Rights Council. No large number of States would be required to provide the necessary minimum of signatories.

In connexion with the present Article reference must be made to the question of possible reservations to the Bill of Rights. The dignity and effectiveness alike of the Bill demand that there should be no room in it for reservations of any kind or description. The Bill of Rights is a Bill of the fundamental rights of man. The idea of any reservations to them is, *prima facie,* objectionable. In view of the numerous provisions of the Bill, of the large number of signatories, and the necessity—if they are to be legally effective—of the reservations being assented to by other signatories, the procedure for making them part of the Bill would be difficult to the point of becoming unworkable. Moreover, if reservations were to be appended in large numbers they would lend substance to the charge that governments hope to contrive to become parties to a basic international enactment without undue sacrifice. Reservations would be justified and, probably, necessary if—contrary to considerations urged in this Chapter—the Bill were to contain elaborate details, distinctions, and qualifications. This in itself is a compelling argument against burdening the Bill with an excess of definition and spurious learning.[60]

[60] It was proposed by Denmark in 1949 that the final Article of the Covenant should include a general reservation in the following form: ' If the existing laws of a State regarding any of the rights and freedoms defined in this Covenant do not give full effect to the provisions of the Covenant, such State may, by an express statement made to that effect on deposit of its instrument of ratification or accession, reserve its right to maintain its customary law on the subject.' It was added that ' a State making any such reservation undertakes to examine the possibilities of modifying its legislation, within a reasonable space of time, with a view to giving full effect to the provisions of this Covenant ' (E/CN.4/350, p. 51). This unorthodox suggestion of simultaneously accepting the Bill of Rights and contracting out of some of its obligations without the specific consent of other contracting parties was apparently due to the proposal to insert in the Bill of Rights a provision against compulsory medical interference with the human body, in particular by way of compulsory sterilisation. The law of Denmark allows that procedure in certain cases. (For a discussion on the subject see E/CN.4/S.R.91, pp. 11-14.) A provision of this character would probably be outside the minimum requirements of the Bill and, therefore, unnecessary. But in case

There are two possible exceptions to the principle of excluding reservations to the Bill of Rights. The first is connected with the temporary suspension of the operation of the Bill in relation to Federal States. For the reasons stated above,[61] this is not a solution which can be lightly accepted. However, should it be adopted as an alternative preferable to the total abstention of Federal States from participation in the Bill, the best method of giving effect to it would be by way not of a technical reservation, but of a special Declaration or Protocol attached to the Bill of Rights and assented to by the other Parties.

The same procedure could be adopted with regard to the difficult question of non-discrimination on account of sex. While the principle in question must form an integral part of the Bill of Rights, there are compelling considerations for enabling the Signatories, while bound by the principal obligation, to postpone its full operation in some respects.[61a]

12. AMENDMENT OF THE BILL OF RIGHTS

Article 28

The Articles of this Bill of Rights may be amended by a vote of the General Assembly provided that such vote receives the con-

it should be generally regarded as an indispensable part of the Bill, the proper course would be for States attaching importance to becoming a party to the Bill to change their law in that respect. There is little authority in a Bill of Rights which can be accepted by every State without any change in its law. It was suggested by the Danish representative in 1949 (E/CN.4/S.R.88, p. 14) that if States were permitted to make reservations this would make it unnecessary to reduce the 'general limitation clause' to the lowest common denominator and that, accordingly, the general level of obligations assumed by States under the Covenant would be correspondingly higher. The argument seems deceptive. It received the 'whole-hearted support' of the Belgian delegation on the ground that it would make possible the ratification of the Covenant by a large number of States (*ibid.*, S.R.89, p. 18). The fate of the Universal Declaration on Human Rights provides an instructive example of the fact that universality is expressive neither of the effectiveness nor of the legal or moral authority of an international instrument. Similar and stronger objections apply to the suggestion, put forward in connexion with the question of implementation, that a single instrument, on the analogy of the General Act for the Pacific Settlement of International Disputes of 1928, should embody various degrees of obligation, and that the parties to the Bill should have the option of adhering to one or more parts of it (E/CN.4/S.R.114, p. 5). The probable result would be a general adherence to the purely nominal provisions of the instrument. See also E/CN.4/S.R.95, p. 9, for a similar suggestion of the Danish representative in connexion with the Article relating to deprivation of liberty. While urging the necessity of a detailed list of exceptions, he insisted at the same time on the right of States to contract out of these exceptions by way of reservations.

[61] See above, p. 363.
[61a] See above, pp. 339, 340.

currence of two-thirds of the United Nations bound by the Bill of Rights. States which do not concur in the amendment shall remain bound by the Bill as hitherto. They may at any time accept the obligations of all or some amendments by a declaration deposited with the Secretary-General of the United Nations.

The above Article, which is concerned with the amendment of the Bill of Rights, needs no elaboration. In case the Bill of Rights should be adopted by means of a treaty concluded outside the United Nations the power of amendment would necessarily rest with the Signatories of the Bill—or a two-thirds majority of them—assembled at the Annual Conference. The States not accepting the amendments would continue to be bound by the original Bill of Rights.

13. WITHDRAWAL FROM THE BILL OF RIGHTS

Article 29

Any State which is a Party to this Bill of Rights may withdraw from its obligations by notice being given to the Secretary-General of the United Nations. The notice shall not become operative until one year after it has reached the Secretary-General. It shall be without effect upon the progress of petitions and complaints brought prior to that date.

The Bill of Rights will be a Treaty the parties to which will undertake obligations of a most far-reaching character. They will limit their sovereignty and surrender their freedom of action with regard to matters which, save for the obligations of the Charter, are exclusively within their domestic jurisdiction. They will, in effect, confer upon external agencies—judicial and non-judicial— the power to review decisions of their highest courts and decrees and statutes passed by their sovereign parliaments. In the same way as in the Charter of the United Nations the Members have limited their external sovereignty in relation to the right of war, they will, in the Bill of Rights, part with a substantial portion of their internal sovereignty. They will have embarked upon an experiment which—though dictated by most compelling considerations—will be as yet untried. They will have put their trust in persons, as yet unknown, who will administer and enforce the Bill of Rights. It would therefore seem proper and desirable that they should safeguard their right to withdraw from the obligations thus contracted in case the machinery of the Bill of Rights should prove unworkable. It is unlikely that such right of withdrawal from a fundamental international enactment of this nature will be lightly resorted to. If exercised, it will leave unimpaired the substantial obligations of the Charter of the United Nations in the matter of human rights and fundamental freedoms.

THE UNIVERSAL DECLARATION AND THE
EUROPEAN COURT

CHAPTER 17

THE UNIVERSAL DECLARATION OF
HUMAN RIGHTS

1. The Proclaimed Importance of the Declaration

THE Universal Declaration of Human Rights, the text of which is reproduced as an annex to this Chapter[1] and which was proclaimed by the General Assembly of the United Nations on 10 December, 1948, has been hailed as an historic event of profound significance and as one of the greatest achievements of the United Nations. It was so described by representatives of various States at the final Session of the General Assembly sitting in Paris and during the debates of its Third Committee. Thus Mrs. Roosevelt, Chairman of the Commission on Human Rights and the principal representative of the United States on the Third Committee, said: ' It [the Declaration] might well become the international Magna Carta of all mankind . . . Its proclamation by the General Assembly would be of importance comparable to the 1789 proclamation of the Declaration of the Rights of Man, the proclamation of the rights of man in the Declaration of Independence of the United States of America, and similar declarations made in other countries.'[2] The last part of the comparison was sufficiently elastic to remove from it a charge of obvious exaggeration. The President of the Assembly admitted that the document to be approved was not

[1] See below, p. 428.
[2] *Official Records of the Third Session of the General Assembly*, Part I, p. 862.

a convention by which States would be bound to carry out and give effect to fundamental human rights. But he believed it to be 'a step forward in a great evolutionary process'. He said: 'It was the first occasion on which the organised community of nations has made a declaration of human rights and fundamental freedoms. That document was backed by the authority of the body of opinion of the United Nations as a whole, and millions of people, men, women, and children all over the world, many miles from Paris and New York, would turn to it for help, guidance and inspiration.'[3] The Rapporteur, the representative of Haiti, described the Declaration as 'the greatest effort yet made by mankind to give society new legal and moral foundations' and as thus marking 'a decisive stage in the process of uniting a divided world'.[4]

The delegate of Pakistan compared the Declaration with the Convention on Genocide previously adopted by the General Assembly and submitted that both documents constituted an epoch-making event.[5] The delegate of Denmark affirmed that 'the universal declaration of human rights made the promises of the Charter a living reality'.[6] The delegate of Syria was equally emphatic:

> 'The Declaration was the achievement of generations of human beings who had worked towards that end. Now at last the peoples of the world would hear it proclaimed that their aim had been reached by the United Nations.'[7]

The representative of Paraguay, while admitting that the Declaration was not perfect, described it as being '. . . the most harmonious, comprehensive and universal that has so far been achieved' and affirmed that 'it would shed a light on the way man had to tread to reach happiness'.[8] While the expansive language of some delegates may be attributed to the native temper of the countries which they represented, no such considerations explain the phraseology used by the Belgian representative. He said:

[3] *Ibid.*, p. 934.
[4] *Ibid.*, p. 854.
[5] *Ibid.*, p. 890.
[6] *Ibid.*, p. 891.
[7] *Ibid.*, p. 922.
[8] *Ibid.*, p. 901.

'In certain circles, it had been said that the declaration of human rights was a purely academic document. That statement was erroneous, for the declaration had not only an unprecedented moral value, it had also the beginnings of a legal value. The man in the street who appealed to the declaration would support his protests with the authority of the unanimous decision of the peoples and Governments of the United Nations.'[9]

He did not elaborate the point that although that vote was a decision upheld by all the peoples of the world (with the exception of the nine States which abstained from voting), it was a decision to which those who proclaimed it were as yet unwilling to give the dignity and the force of an obligation binding upon them in the sphere of law as well as in that of conscience. In the course of the deliberations of the Third Committee the Belgian delegate voiced the view of the vast majority of its members in expressing the hope that the Declaration would be adopted 'both as an homage to France and because it was important for the United Nations to give to the waiting world a tangible proof of its activity and usefulness '.[10] The representative of Iceland expressed his full conviction that 'the universal declaration of human rights would arouse great hopes among peoples who were still deprived of those rights '.[11] With very few exceptions [12] the Delegations of the States represented at the General Assembly voiced their conviction not only of the importance of the Declaration but also of the desirability of avoiding any delay in its adoption.

In his Report to the General Assembly the Secretary-General emphasised, in similar terms, the significance of the Declaration drafted by the Commission on Human Rights. He said: 'This declaration, the first attempt in history to write a " Bill of Rights "

[9] *Ibid.,* p. 880.

[10] A/C3/S.R.91, p. 6.

[11] *Official Records of the Third Session of the General Assembly,* Part I, p. 878.

[12] The delegate of New Zealand was among the very few who, at the very outset, expressed a critical view of the Declaration. She suggested that, at least, the Declaration should be adopted at the same time as the Covenant. 'If the Declaration was adopted first, there was less likelihood that the Covenant would be adopted at all; by the time it was ready for adoption, some States, having already accepted the Declaration, might be unwilling to vote for it' (A/C3/S.R.89, p. 4). She pointed to the fact that that danger was increased by the prospect of many reading into the Declaration more than to which it was entitled. She instanced the view expressed by the French representative before the Economic and Social Council to the effect that the Declaration was an organic act of the United Nations having all the legal validity of such an act.

for the whole world, is an important first step in the direction of implementing the general pledges of the Charter concerning human rights.'[13]

2. The Rejection of the Declaration as a Legal Instrument

The practical unanimity of the Members of the United Nations in stressing the importance of the Declaration was accompanied by an equally general repudiation of the idea that the Declaration imposed upon them a legal obligation to respect the human rights and fundamental freedoms which it proclaimed. The debates in the General Assembly and in the Third Committee did not reveal any sense of uneasiness on account of the incongruity between the proclamation of the universal character of the human rights forming the subject matter of the Declaration and the rejection of the legal duty to give effect to them. The delegates gloried in the profound significance of the achievement whereby the nations of the world agreed as to what are the obvious and inalienable rights of man—so obvious and fundamental that they considered the suggestion of describing them as grounded in nature to impart to the Declaration an undesirable element of controversy and confusion [14]—but they declined to acknowledge them as part of the law binding upon their States and Govern-

[13] *Report to the General Assembly,* 1948.

[14] The proposal to insert the words ' by nature ' in Article 1 was rejected on the suggestion of the Belgian representative for the reason that these words might lead to ' long philosophical arguments ' (A/C3/S.R.96, p. 3). The Belgian suggestion was supported by the Chinese representative whose objection was based on the ground that the phrase ' had a ring of Rousseau and evoked memories of the theory that man was naturally good ' (*ibid.,* p. 6). After a prolonged discussion in the Third Committee the view prevailed that the Declaration should not contain a reference to the origin of rights. The Soviet representative emphasised that equality of rights before the law was determined not by the fact of birth but by the social structure of the State (A/C3/S.R.98). Jacques Maritain, the philosopher, was invoked in favour of the same proposition. However, the true question at issue—which seems to have escaped the Committee—is not that of the origin of rights. The true issue is that of their validity—*i.e.,* the question whether the State is the final arbiter of human rights. The Preamble of the Declaration actually invokes the ' equal and inalienable rights of all members of the human family '. A long discussion took place on the Dutch proposal to insert in the Preamble a reference to the divine origin of man. The Soviet representative opposed it and pointed to the Declaration of 1789 which omitted any mention of deity. He was reminded by the Belgian delegate that the American Declaration of Independence used the words ' endowed by their Creator '. But the Belgian representative admitted that the proposal raised a very delicate philosophical problem and that it would be inconceivable that the Committee should try to solve that question by a vote (A/C3/S.R.165, p. 6).

ments.   They gave occasional expression to the view that any apparent inconsistency between the fact of the general agreement as to what are fundamental human rights and the refusal to recognise them as juridically binding in the sphere of conduct was fully resolved by the acknowledgment of their validity in the realm of conscience and ethics.

The United States, a country whose standing in the world and the perseverance of whose representatives were largely instrumental in the speedy adoption of the Declaration—a course originally resisted by the United Kingdom and other countries of the British Commonwealth [15]—insisted repeatedly and emphatically on the fact that the Declaration was not a legal document and possessed no legally binding force.   Thus the representative of the United States, in the same statement before the General Assembly in which she extolled the virtues of the Declaration, said: ' In giving our approval to the declaration

[15] Thus in the course of the meeting of the Human Rights Commission in December 1947, the Australian representative, Colonel Hodgson, objected to the proposal to adopt a Declaration otherwise than as forming part of a Bill of Rights.   The relevant extract from the Minutes is instructive:

' He was of opinion that the Commission's Terms of Reference did not require it to draft a Declaration of Human Rights.   The Draft Declaration presented by the Drafting Committee was, in his opinion, equivalent to a preamble to a Bill of Rights, and as such it should contain a statement of general principles to cover the whole range of human rights and fundamental freedoms.   He maintained that the Commission's task was to draft a Bill of Human Rights, not a Declaration which, he felt, entailed no legal obligations and would not in any way affect the lives of men and women unless translated into concrete action.   In his opinion, an international Bill was a law in both the domestic and international fields, and no executive or legislative organ of a government would be able to override its provisions.   It was the Bill of Human Rights which should be submitted to Member Governments in order that it might be seen whether its contents were in conflict with national legislation and whether new legislation to comply with its provisions would be necessary ' (E/CN.4/S.R.27, p. 5).

Equally, the British representative, Lord Dukeston, felt that the first task of the Commission was to produce a draft International Bill of Human Rights, which would become a legal document and which would be implemented (*ibid.*, pp. 7, 8).   In February, 1948, the spokesman of the British Government reaffirmed that view in the House of Commons.   In associating himself with the view that it was undesirable to press for the adoption, in 1948, by the General Assembly of a general document relating to human rights, he said: ' We want definition . . . and we want to be quite firm in ensuring that this is not just another pious resolution ': *Hansard*, House of Commons, vol. 447, No. 72, col. 2271 (26 February, 1948).   And see above, p. 396, n. 2, as to New Zealand.   In May, 1948, the Lord Chancellor referred to ' a vague and general statement in the form of a Declaration which will be full of fine-sounding phrases ' and which is ' in itself nothing more than a statement of ideals '.   He said: ' His Majesty's Government feel quite definitely that . . . it would be undesirable to submit this matter to the General Assembly during 1948 ': *Hansard*, House of Lords, 5 May, 1948, vol. 155, cols. 666, 668.

today, it is of primary importance that we keep clearly in mind the basic character of the document. It is not a treaty; it is not an international agreement. It is not and does not purport to be a statement of law or of legal obligation. It is a declaration of basic principles of human rights and freedoms, to be stamped with the approval of the General Assembly by a formal vote of its members, and to serve as a common standard of achievement for all peoples of all nations.' [16]   A general statement, in almost identical terms, had been previously made by the representative of the United States in the Third Committee. [17]   In the course of the discussion, in that Committee, on specific questions the United States consistently affirmed that the Declaration had no legal force. [18]   That emphatic repudiation of the idea that the Declaration was a legal instrument creating legal obligations did not signify a sudden change in the attitude of the United States, as well as of other States.   That attitude was maintained throughout the drafting of the Declaration by the Commission on Human Rights. [19]

[16] *Bulletin of State Department,* 19 (1948), p. 751.

[17] A/C3/SR.89, p. 2.

[18] In the course of the discussion on the Preamble the Soviet Union proposed the wording :' The General Assembly recommends the following " Declaration of Human Rights " to all States Members of the United Nations to be used at their discretion both in adopting appropriate legislative and other measures '. The delegate of the United States urged that the Russian proposal would seriously impair the moral force of the Declaration. She said: ' The fact that the Declaration would not be legally binding upon Governments made it all the more necessary to phrase the Preamble so that it would exercise upon them the greatest possible form of moral " suasion ".' (A/C3/S.R.165, p. 8.) When in the course of the discussion on Article 1 it was proposed to define the duties of States corresponding to the rights of man, the representative of the United States objected on the ground that the exact definition of the duties of States ' was a legal question, which necessarily placed it outside the scope of the International Declaration of Human Rights ' (A/C3/S.R.95, p. 3). When in connexion with the discussion on Article 25 the Soviet representative made proposals elaborating the right to a decent standard of living the United States representative objected to it on the ground that it went beyond the scope of a declaration and altered its legal form: ' The declaration should be a statement of principles. The State's obligations would be laid down in the Covenant' (A/C3/S.R.143, p. 1). Somehow the view prevailed that mere principles need not be obligatory. In the course of the discussion of the question of the right to a nationality, France proposed an additional paragraph laying down that ' it is the duty of the United Nations to approach States for the purpose of preventing statelessness and, where necessary, to concern itself with the fate of stateless persons '. The proposal was objected to by the United States on the ground that the Declaration should be a statement of the rights of the individual and should include no reference to the duties of Governments or the United Nations (A/C3/S.R.123, p. 6).

[19] Thus in the course of the drafting of the Declaration by the Commission on Human Rights in June, 1948, the representative of the United States (Mrs. Roosevelt) said: ' The Declaration should not be in

With isolated exceptions,[20] all delegations which had occasion to express themselves on the subject attached importance to stressing the absence of any element of legal obligation in the Declaration about to be proclaimed by the General Assembly. They did so, to a large extent, in order to draw attention to the necessity of the Declaration being followed by a legally binding instrument—a Covenant—provided with means of international supervision and enforcement. Thus the delegate of Australia said: 'The declaration represented a common ideal to be attained by all peoples of the world; it had no legally binding character. The General Assembly should see to it that the rights listed in the declaration did not remain a dead letter and should ensure effective respect of those rights.'[21]

The British representative at the General Assembly, without wishing 'for a moment to minimise the great moral force' of the document, expressed the very strong feeling of his delegation that 'the Commission on Human Rights should continue its work on the draft covenant and on the measures for implementation of the declaration'.[22] Previously the representative of the United Kingdom stated expressly in the course of the general debate in the Third Committee that, pending the completion of a binding international covenant, the Declaration would have

any sense a legislative document. The General Assembly was not a legislative body. . . . It was clear that the Declaration, as envisaged, did not create legal remedies or procedures to ensure respect for the rights and freedoms it proposed to the world; that ideal would have to be achieved by further steps taken in accordance with international and domestic law. The Declaration would have moral, not mandatory, force'. *Summary Record,* E/CN4/S R.48, p. 7. See also E/CN4/S R.50, p. 8, for similar observations by the Indian representative. At a later stage the United States representative opposed the Russian proposal to refer expressly in the Declaration to a limitation of working hours. She pointed out that the Declaration had 'no juridical value. . . . Consequently mentioning that right in the Declaration was a meaningless gesture' (E/CN4/S R.69, p. 10)—a remark which elicited the answer, on the part of the Russian representative, that the same argument could be raised against all other Articles of the Declaration. And see E/CN4/S R.74 for yet another similar observation of the representative of the United States.

[20] See below, pp. 404-406.

[21] *Official Records of the Third Session of the General Assembly,* Part I, p. 876. In the Third Committee, in connexion with the discussion of the question of asylum, the Australian delegation pointed out that it had previously insisted that formulas implying obligations must be avoided in the text of the declaration of human rights. The Declaration, he said, 'must make no reference to the corresponding obligations of States': A/C3/S.R.121, p. 16.

[22] *Official Records of the General Assembly, Third Session,* Part I, *Plenary Meetings,* p. 883.

'great moral authority, through the proclamation of an ideal, even though it could not impose specific obligations'.[23]   He dissented expressly from the view of the French representative that the Declaration could be considered to have legal authority as an interpretation of the relevant provisions of the Charter. 'No General Assembly resolution', he said, perhaps somewhat sweepingly, 'could establish legal obligations.'[24]   In another connexion he insisted that 'although the Declaration was of great significance, it was a statement of principle devoid of any obligatory character'.[25]   In connexion with the Resolution, discussed in the Sixth Committee, in the matter of Russian legislation relating to marriages of Russian nationals with foreign subjects, the British representative, unlike other delegates, refrained from asserting that the Russian action was illegal. Using language of studied restraint, he confined himself to submitting that the Russian attitude was contrary to the relevant article of the Declaration—an Article against which the Russian representative spoke and voted.[26]

The Indian delegate insisted that as the draft Declaration was not strictly a legal document it was not necessary to examine its wording in detail. He urged the speedy adoption of the draft, for 'although it would not be legally binding, it would have a certain amount of force and might help to dispel pessimism and disillusionment and thus relieve the tension of the present world situation'.[27]   The representative of Norway agreed that the purpose of the Declaration was to set moral standards rather than to impose legal obligations. He suggested that it would be of practical value, 'as it would undoubtedly serve as a basis for the discussion in the United Nations of any question of human rights'[28]—a suggestion the cogency of which is not apparent. The Argentinian delegate similarly observed that the Declaration was 'a document which involved moral obligations only and

[23] A/C3/S.R.93, p. 2.

[24] *Ibid.*

[25] A/C3/S.R.164, p. 8.

[26] Mr. Fitzmaurice (United Kingdom) 'wished to make it clear that he had abstained from discussing the legal aspect of the question. What he said was that even if there was a legal basis for the action of the Soviet authorities, it was none the less an infringement of fundamental human rights' (A/C6/S.R.197, p. 6).

[27] A/C3/S.R.91, p. 4.

[28] A/C3/S.R.89, p. 5.

should be followed by one imposing legal obligations'.[29]   The Mexican delegate stated that the Declaration did not involve legal obligations. He thought, however, that that fact 'would not diminish the value of the document'.[30]

The French and, following him, the Belgian representatives were alone in claiming some legal force for the Declaration—an assertion the merits of which are discussed later in this Section.[31] But even they were unable to adhere to that view with any appearance of consistency. Thus, in connexion with the suggestion that Article 1 and the Preamble should be combined in one article on the ground that they were of equal weight, Professor Cassin, the principal French representative, reminded the Committee that 'the precedent of the Charter did not apply to the Declaration, for the Charter was a legally binding convention, whereas a declaration was a document of a different kind'.[32] When in the course of the discussion bearing on the right of property the Soviet representative proposed an amendment stating that everyone has the right to own property in accordance with the law of the country where such property is situated, the Belgian representative objected to it on the ground that there was no reason for the Declaration, which was only a recommendation and imposed no obligations, to contain a reference to national laws.[33] Similarly, in connexion with the French proposal concerning the right of petition, the Belgian representative expressed doubts as to the legal correctness of including the problem of petitions in a declaration which would not be legally binding upon its signatories.[34]

In the matter of the denial of the legal authority of the Declaration there was no difference between the States which voted in favour of the Declaration and those nine States[35] which

---

[29] *Ibid.* At a later meeting he suggested that the Declaration should also take into account existing constitutions of the various countries so that 'it would have a juridical value as well'; A/C3/S.R.90, p. 7. See also A/C3/S.R.164, pp. 9 and 10 for the statements, respectively, of the Greek and Philippine representatives to the effect that the Declaration imposed moral obligations.

[30] A/C3/S.R.90, p. 3.

[31] See below, pp. 405-408.

[32] A/C3/S.R.97, p. 6.

[33] A/C3/S.R.126, p. 4.

[34] A/C3/S.R.160, p. 2.

[35] Byelorussia, Czechoslovakia, Honduras, Poland, Saudi Arabia, Ukraine, Soviet Russia, South Africa, Yugoslavia.

abstained from voting—although Soviet Russia and the States associated with her repeatedly proposed the insertion of provisions which would give the Declaration some appearance, but no more, of a binding obligation. They resisted with vigour any proposal to make the Declaration an enforceable international obligation. In the Third Committee the Russian representative emphasised that the creation of international institutions for safeguarding human rights would constitute interference in the internal affairs of States in disregard of national sovereignty.[36] 'They would furthermore tend to transform internal disputes into international disputes, thus endangering world peace.' The Russian, and the associate, representatives rejected any notion of a Declaration likely to interfere with national sovereignty, which they considered the cornerstone of international relations.[37] As the degree of the limitation of national sovereignty also represents in any given case the reality of the legal obligation in the international sphere, it became clear that the Russian representatives used the term 'implementation' in a way differing substantially from accepted usage. They insisted throughout that the Declaration, while avoiding scrupulously any reference to international supervision and enforcement, should contain detailed indications of how human rights, especially in the social and economic sphere, should be implemented by the State.[38] They proposed the insertion of an article laying down that 'the human rights and civic rights and fundamental freedoms enumerated in the present Declaration shall be guaranteed by national laws'. These specific and general proposals for implementation by national authorities were rejected on the—unobjectionable—ground that there was no place for provisions

---

[36] A/C3/S.R.92, p. 9.

[37] The Russian representative said at the final meeting of the General Assembly on 10 December, 1948: 'It was an entirely false theory that the principle of national sovereignty was a reactionary and outdated idea, and that the repudiation of that principle was an essential condition of international co-operation. The draft declaration of human rights appeared to endorse that reactionary view directed against national sovereignty and was therefore entirely inconsistent with the principles of the United Nations'; *Official Records of the General Assembly, Third Session, Part I*, pp. 923, 924. The wording of the Russian amendment to the Preamble of the Declaration was: 'The General Assembly recommends the following " Declaration of Human Rights " to all States Members of the United Nations to be used at their discretion both in adopting appropriate legislative and other measures' (A/C3/314/Rev. 1).

[38] See above, p. 298, n. 3.

for enforcement in a document which, by universal consent, was in the nature of a proclamation of principle binding only in the sphere of conscience. At the same time that particular reason for the rejection of the Russian proposals added emphasis —if any further emphasis was needed—to the general view that the Declaration was not intended in any way as implying a legal obligation.

It was only occasionally and by way of rare exception that a delegation showed some lack of appreciation of the fact that the Declaration was not intended to be legally binding. Thus the Canadian delegate in the Third Committee refrained from voting for the Declaration for reasons which could have had validity only if the Declaration were legally binding. He pointed, for instance, to the difficulties created by Article 21 (2), which gives the right of equal access to public employment regardless of political creed and which might therefore be interpreted as an obligation to employ in public service persons aiming at the destruction of those very institutions which it is the object of the Declaration to preserve. Moreover, the Canadian delegation attached importance to the fact that according to the Canadian Constitution various matters covered by the Declaration were within the jurisdiction of the provinces as distinguished from that of Canada.[39] At the General Assembly Canada voted for the Declaration in order not to do anything which might appear to 'discourage the effort to define the rights of mankind'.[40] There is probably no necessity to consider the Canadian hesitation as to Article 21 (2), and the Declaration in general, as implying any suggestion that the Declaration is legally binding. Thus, for instance, the representative of the United States, in her general statement at the final meeting of the General Assembly, while expressly repudiating the notion of the Declaration as a legally binding instrument, attached importance to stating that the binding force—the morally binding force—of the Declaration in respect of Article 21 (2) was qualified by the terms of Article 29 (2) providing for limitations on the exercise of the rights laid down in the Declaration in the interests of morality, public order and general welfare. The delegate of Chile, while

[39] *Official Records of the General Assembly, Third Session, Part I*, pp. 898, 899.
[40] A/PV., 182, p. 91.

agreeing that only the Covenant, to be adopted at a future date, would be legally binding, suggested that the violation by any State of the rights enumerated in the Declaration would mean violation of the principles of the United Nations.[41] This was also the view underlying the observations of the delegate of Lebanon[42] and of an amendment proposed by Soviet Russia and rejected by the General Assembly.[43] The delegate of India, somewhat obscurely, described the Declaration as 'a declaration of obligations'. Apparently, however, she considered the document to be only a declaration of moral obligations, for she emphasised that 'the adoption of the Declaration should not . . . lead to neglect the most important document: the Convention'.[44]

There was, therefore, little justification for the reason adduced by the South African delegate before the General Assembly as the explanation for his abstention. That alleged reason was that in the discussion in the Third Committee the Declaration was treated as a definition of the rights and freedoms mentioned in the Charter, with the result that the adoption of the Declaration 'would entail certain legal obligations for the Governments subscribing to it'.[45] The actual reasons underlying the South African abstention were of a different nature.

The only attempt to claim legal force for the Declaration came from the French and Belgian representatives. As shown above,[46] that attempt was by no means consistent; nevertheless, it merits attention and consideration. In the Third Committee, the French delegate, Professor Cassin, maintained that although the Declaration 'would not possess coercive legal power', it could be considered as an authoritative interpretation of the Charter and as the common standard to which the legislation of all the Members of the United Nations shall aspire.[47] The first part of that statement is considered below.[48] The second part was

---

[41] A/C3/S.R.91, p. 7.

[42] *Ibid.*, p. 8.

[43] 'Any violation or limitation of these rights [of the Declaration], whether direct or indirect, shall be deemed to violate the present Declaration and to be incompatible with the high principles proclaimed in the United Nations Charter'; *Official Records of the General Assembly, Third Session, Part I*, p. 928.

[44] *Ibid.*, p. 894.

[45] *Ibid.*, p. 911.

[46] See above, p. 402.

[47] A/C3/S.R.92.

[48] See below, p. 409.

apparently not intended as an assertion that the States voting for the Declaration were legally bound to effect corresponding changes in their national legislation.   Professor Cassin then proceeded to point out that although the Declaration had no coercive power, it could not be considered as weakening in any way the pledges made by the signatories of the Charter, a statement which is in itself unobjectionable for the reason that the Declaration, not being a legal instrument, can neither add to nor subtract from existing obligations. Yet the remarks that followed tended to introduce into the argument a distinct element of confusion. In the view of France, he said, ' States are compelled by the Charter to recognise the competence of the main bodies of the United Nations in the matter of human rights . . . the competence of the United Nations in questions of human rights is positive '.[49]   That statement he then elaborated in such a way as both to make its meaning uncertain and to infuse legal consequences into the act of adopting the Declaration.   He said: 'The provisions of Article 2, paragraph 7, of the Charter relating to the domestic jurisdiction of member States, could not be invoked against such competence when, by the adoption of the Declaration, the question of human rights was a matter no longer of domestic, but of international concern.' Thus, while the distinguished lawyer was saying, in the first part of his statement, that the competence of the United Nations in the matter of human rights was ' positive ', he proceeded to suggest that such competence was the result of the adoption of a Declaration which practically all Members of the United Nations consider not to have created any legal obligation at all.   The argument is typical of some of the possible effects of the Declaration.   While it is clear that the Declaration does not create legal obligations, the argument—for which there is no legal justification—in support of the contrary view is advanced in reliance on assertions which must cast doubt on the legal validity of the existing obligations of the Charter.

The observations made by Professor Cassin caused the Belgian representative, Professor Dehousse, to reconsider his previous view of the ' purely optional significance of the Declaration '.[50]

[49] A/C3/S.R.92.
[50] A/C3/S.R.108, p. 8.

He pointed out, in the first instance, that the Declaration, being a recommendation of the General Assembly, which was a juridical organ of the United Nations, had an ' undeniably legal character '. He did not substantiate the view that the Declaration would be in the nature of a recommendation. Neither did he elaborate the significance of the statement that the document would have an ' undeniably legal character '. He then proceeded to inquire whether the Declaration, when accepted, would possess a purely optional significance or whether it would have binding effects. He assumed that certain principles of the Declaration were already part of ' the customary law of nations and were, in consequence, recognised in unwritten international law '. The fact that these principles had now been made part of the Declaration would not deprive these rules of their binding character.

It may not be easy to ascribe any ascertainable meaning, in the accepted terminology and principles of international law, to these submissions of the learned delegate. The student of international law may find it difficult to subscribe to the view that it is a rule of customary international law that, to mention some of the least controversial pronouncements of the Declaration, ' everyone has the right to life, liberty and security of person ' (Article 3 of the Declaration); or that ' no one shall be held in slavery or servitude ' (Article 4); or that ' no one shall be subjected to torture or to cruel, inhuman, or degrading treatment or punishment ' (Article 5). Prior to the Charter, apart from the precarious doctrine of humanitarian intervention, international law considered these matters to be within the exclusive domestic jurisdiction of the State. With regard to the other rights enumerated in the Declaration, Professor Dehousse admitted that no State would be under an obligation to make corresponding changes in its national legislation. He said: ' No Member State, even if it had voted for the Declaration, would be legally bound to write into its legislation the principles of the Declaration. But it would assume the obligation to take them into consideration. In other words, the recommendation resulting from the work of the Committee would create the beginning of an obligation for the Member States of the United Nations.'[51] These considerations led Professor Dehousse to the conclusion that

[51] *Ibid.,* p. 109.

' the document would have an incontestable legal value . . .
It would not have any obligatory value strictly so-called; but it
would place an obligation on Member States to consider the
action which should be taken on that recommendation of the
General Assembly '.   After having thus affirmed the ' incontestable legal value ' of the Declaration, the Belgian delegate admitted
' the subtle character of the question with which he had just
dealt ' and expressed the wish that the Legal Department of the
Secretariat should study it closely.[52]

3.   THE ' INDIRECT ' LEGAL AUTHORITY OF THE DECLARATION

The language of the Universal Declaration of Human Rights,
the circumstances and the reasons of its adoption,[53] and, above
all, the clearly and emphatically expressed intention of the States,
Members of the United Nations, who voted for the Resolution
of the General Assembly, show clearly that the Declaration is
not by its nature and by the intention of its parties a legal document imposing legal obligations.   It is now necessary to consider
the view, expressed in various forms, that, somehow, the
Declaration may have an indirect legal effect.

(i) In the first instance, it may be said—and has been said [54]—
that although the Declaration in itself may not be a legal document involving legal obligations, it is of legal value inasmuch
as it contains an authoritative interpretation of the ' human

[52] In his Fourth Annual Report to the General Assembly in 1949 the Secretary-
General made no effort to assert that the Declaration was a binding legal
instrument.   He said: ' It is true that this Declaration is not a law, but neither
have been many of the most influential documents of history.   The United
States' Declaration of Independence, and France's Declaration of the Rights
of Man were not laws when they were proclaimed ' (*Introduction*) *General
Assembly, Official Records,* Fourth Session, Supplement No. 1, p. xiii.   *Sed
quære*: see below, p. 420.   And see Duguit, *Traité du droit constitutionnel,*
2nd ed. (1923), vol. II, p. 159, who, on the question of the legal nature of
the Declaration of 1789, held a view different from that propounded by the
Secretary-General.

[53] See below, p. 425, n. 81.

[54] See above, p. 406.   This apparently was also the view of Dr. Malik, the
Lebanese representative at the General Assembly in 1948, who had been
associated from the outset with the drafting of the Declaration.   He pointed
out that the Declaration defined in detail the human rights and fundamental
freedoms which members of the United Nations had pledged themselves to
promote.   He said: ' Hence every government knew . . . to what extent
exactly it had pledged itself, and every citizen could protest to his Government if the latter did not fulfil its obligations ': *Official Records of the Third
Session of the General Assembly, Part I,* p. 860.

rights and fundamental freedoms' which do constitute an obligation, however imperfect, binding upon the Members of the United Nations. It is unlikely that any tribunal or other authority administering international law would accept a suggestion of that kind. To maintain that a document contains an authoritative interpretation of a legally binding instrument is to assert that that former document itself is as legally binding and as important as the instrument which it is supposed to interpret. A document described and intended as an authoritative interpretation of an already binding instrument may impose upon the parties thereto obligations as far-reaching as the principal convention. It may go beyond that. It may transform what was originally a general and non-committal expression of principle into a tight network of substantial obligations. To say, therefore, that a document is not legally binding and that it embodies, nevertheless, an authoritative interpretation of a legally binding instrument is to make a statement the first part of which contradicts the second. The contradiction can be removed only by dint of the further explanation that 'authoritative' means morally, and not legally, authoritative—an explanation which amounts to an abandonment of the view that the Declaration is legally relevant. But only some such explanation would be consistent with the almost unanimous insistence of the Members of the United Nations that, in adopting the Declaration, they did not intend to assume legal obligations. They did not intend to assume such obligations by the backdoor of an 'authoritative' interpretation of the Charter in the matter of human rights and fundamental freedoms.

(ii) Accordingly, there would seem to be no substance in the view that the provisions of the Declaration may somehow be of importance for the interpretation of the Charter as a formulation, in this field, of the 'general principles of law recognised by civilised nations'. The Declaration does not purport to embody what civilised nations generally recognise as law. It embodies, in the words of its Preamble, 'a common standard of achievement for all peoples and all nations, to the end that every individual and every organ of society, keeping this Declaration constantly in mind, shall strive by teaching and education to promote respect for these rights and freedoms and by progressive measures, national and international, to secure their universal and effective recognition and observance'. The Declaration gives expression to what, in the fullness of time, ought to become principles of law generally recognised and acted upon by States Members of the United Nations. In the course of the discussion preceding the adoption of the Declaration, various delegates admitted that, on specific matters, the laws and practices of their countries were not in accordance with the tenets of the Declaration. They repeatedly denied that they were about to accept a legal obligation to adapt their national legislation to the high aspirations of the Declaration. Some of them have, subsequent to the adoption of the Declaration, repudiated the suggestion that there exists any such obligation. Thus, in the British House of Commons, the Prime Minister, when answering, on 18 January, 1949, the question whether the British Government would accede to the Declaration and what changes it proposed to initiate in British domestic and colonial legislation in order to bring such legislation into line with the principles laid down in the Declaration, explained that, unlike the proposed Covenant, which would be a legally binding Convention, the Declaration 'is a statement of fundamental human rights and freedoms that the General Assembly has proclaimed as a common standard of achievement which all should strive to attain', and that there was 'no question of any separate act of accession by States, or of an obligation to give early legislative effect to any provision with which United Kingdom or Colonial laws may at the moment be at variance'.[55] In reply to a further question as to what action it was proposed to take to give effect to Article 24 of the Declaration which lays down that everyone has the right to equal pay for equal work, the Prime Minister's answer was that 'these declarations contain a great number of rights'

[55] *Parliamentary Debates,* House of Commons, vol. 460, No. 40, cols. 16 and 17. The question of the Declaration, in relation to national legislation and otherwise, has come up repeatedly in the House of Commons: see *ibid.,* col. 334 (20 January, 1949); *ibid.,* cols. 73-74 (24 January, 1949); *ibid.,* cols. 135-136 (26 January, 1949); *ibid.,* vol. 461, cols. 343-4 (9 February, 1949), when the Foreign Secretary, in reply to the question whether ' he will continue to ensure that our delegates do everything possible to proceed with the Covenant which will, at any rate, include provision for reference to an international court ', answered: ' I certainly will press on with it. I think the Covenant is much more important than a mere declaration '.

and that it is not accepted 'that every State will be able at once to realise all these ideals '.[56]

(iii) For the same reason it is doubtful whether the provisions of the Declaration can indirectly benefit the promotion of respect for human rights and fundamental freedoms to the extent of securing recognition as part of the ' public policy ' of the law of the States concerned and of being enforceable as such by their Courts. When, in 1945, in *In re Drummond Wren* [57] a Canadian Court declined to enforce a restrictive covenant for the reason that it was discriminatory on account of race, it invoked Article 55 and other relevant provisions of the Charter of the United Nations which, seeing that Canada had become a Member of the United Nations, had, in the view of the Court, become part of the ' public policy' of the law of Canada. When, in 1948, in *Hurd* v. *Hodge,* the Supreme Court of the United States, by way of a novel and almost revolutionary interpretation of the Fourteenth Amendment of the Constitution, rendered a similar decision in a similar matter, it stated, without referring expressly to the Charter, that prohibition of discrimination was now—for the reason, *inter alia,* of treaties concluded by the United States —part of the public policy of its law.[58] But these considerations can hardly apply to the detailed provisions, as such, of a Declaration which in the view of the States which voted for it

[56] *Ibid.,* vol. 460, col. 18. When, in the course of the discussion of the draft of the Declaration before the Human Rights Commission, it was proposed to include a provision protecting the individual not only against discrimination, but also against ' any incitement to discrimination ', the representative of the United Kingdom objected to the proposal on the ground that in the United Kingdom there had never been any need for legislation to compel the authorities to take action against incitement to discrimination and that if the Declaration were to contain the provision as proposed ' the United Kingdom, feeling morally bound to carry out the provisions of the Declaration, would be obliged to pass laws which experience had shown neither necessary nor reasonable '. *Summary Record of the Fifty-Second Meeting of the Commission,* 28 May, 1948; E/CN4/S.R.52, p. 14.

[57] (1945) 4 *Ontario Reports,* pp. 778, 781.

[58] See the Opinion of Vinson, C.J., in *Hurd* v. *Hodge* (1948), 68 Sup Ct. 847, 853: ' The power of the federal courts to enforce the terms of private agreements is at all times exercised subject to the restrictions and limitations of the public policy of the United States as manifested in the Constitution, treaties, federal statutes and applicable legal precedents.' See also *Namba* v. *McCourt and Neuner,* decided in 1949 by the Supreme Court of the State of Oregon: 204 Pac. (2d), 569. In that case the Court held—quoting, *inter alia,* Articles 55(c) and 56 of the Charter of the United Nations—that the Oregon Alien Land Law discriminated against persons of Asiatic descent and was, accordingly, void as being in violation of the equal protection clause of the Fourteenth Amendment.

implies neither a legal obligation nor a moral duty to adapt their legislation to the principles of the Declaration.

(iv) For identical reasons it is idle to attempt to kindle sparks of legal vitality in the Universal Declaration of Human Rights by regarding it as a recommendation of the General Assembly and by inquiring into its legal effects as such. It is not clear whether the Declaration is in the nature of a recommendation —a term which, in turn, bristles with a multiplicity of meanings. Some of the 'recommendations' of the General Assembly produce a legal effect, for instance, its recommendations, in the form of 'instructions' or otherwise, addressed to the organs of the United Nations—such as the Economic and Social Council, the Trusteeship Council or the Secretary-General—which are placed under the authority of the General Assembly.[59]   Also, when the General Assembly, in pursuance of the authority conferred upon it by the Charter, creates an organ—such as the International Law Commission—its decision produces definite legal effects.   It is not clear that decisions of that nature are 'recommendations'.   They are decisions which the General Assembly is entitled and bound to take in the normal course of the administration of the business of the United Nations.   The Declaration of Human Rights is cast in the form of a Resolution. But the only operative part of the Resolution is to 'proclaim' the Declaration 'as a common standard of achievement for all peoples and nations'.   Significantly, it does not contain a recommendation to Members of the United Nations to observe its principles—an omission which may usefully be compared with the Resolution, adopted at the same time, which 'recommends Governments of Member States to show their adherence to Article 56 of the Charter by using every means within their power solemnly to publicise the text of the Declaration and to cause it to be disseminated, displayed, read and expounded principally in schools and other educational institutions, without distinction based on the political status of countries or territories'. It is probable that some recommendations of the General Assembly, such as those advising the parties to adopt a particular method of pacific settlement, are entitled to respect in the sense not only that a moral duty exists not to disregard them lightly,

---

[59] See Sloan in *British Year Book of International Law*, 25 (1948), pp. 1 *et seq.*

but also that they may be treated by the Security Council as a factor in deciding, according to Article 39 of the Charter, whether there exists a threat to peace or a breach of the peace—with all the legal consequences attaching to such a decision. However, unless violence is done not only to the ordinary connotation of words but also to the fundamental structure of the United Nations, which denies to the General Assembly the power of sovereign decision binding the Members of the United Nations, it is difficult to see how a recommendation can be legally binding. Above all, assuming that the Declaration is a recommendation, it is abundantly clear that that particular recommendation was not intended to be legally binding.[60] There was throughout a solemn and emphatic repudiation of the intention to consider it as such. Any hesitating imputation of a ' nascent legal force'[61] to the

---

[60] In the course of the final discussion before the General Assembly in 1948, Professor Cassin, the French representative, asserted that the Declaration ' while it was less powerful and binding than a convention, had no less legal value, for it was contained in a resolution of the Assembly which was empowered to make recommendations; it was a development of the Charter which had brought human rights within the scope of positive international law '; *Official Records of the Third Session of the General Assembly*, Part I, p. 866. The argument seems to assume that because the Assembly is empowered to make recommendations the latter are somehow legally binding. There is an element of confusion in the distinction between instruments which have legal value and those which have some legal value.

[61] See Sloan, *op. cit., in fine.* There is a disadvantage in reading legal obligations into acts of the General Assembly clearly not intended as such. In May 1949 the Legal Section of the Secretariat expressed the opinion that the proposed United Nations Charter of the Rights of the Child, although not having the same legal effect as a multilateral convention, would not be entirely without force and that ' even from a strictly legal standpoint, one might well conclude that a declaration will have significant juridical consequences ' (E/CN.5/S.R.126, p. 3). The above conclusion was reached on the ground that as in Article 56 of the Charter Members pledge themselves to take joint and separate action in co-operation with the Organisation for the achievement of the purposes set out in Article 55, there is a general obligation on the part of Members to take action ' in co-operation ' in order to achieve the principles approved by the Assembly and that ' the declaration should therefore serve as a strong inducement to Members to continue to be guided by the principles contained in the Children's Charter '. It is not clear what is the nature of the ' strong inducement ' alluded to. The position is different when a Resolution of the Assembly purports to lay down rules of law as in the case of the Resolution affirming the principles of law recognised by the Charter of the Nurnberg Tribunal and its judgment (Resolution 95 (1)) or the affirmation that genocide is a crime under international law (Resolution 96 (1)). It is arguable that such Resolutions are binding upon the States whose representatives voted for them. The difference between the authority of a recommendation when addressed to the organs of the United Nations and when addressed to the members of the United Nations was clearly—and accurately—brought out in the observations of the Polish delegate to the Economic and Social Council in connexion with a request of the Council, in pursuance of a Resolution of the General Assembly, that member States should supply information in connexion with certain economic and social

recommendations of the General Assembly must yield to the clearly manifested contrary determination of the authors of the Declaration.

(v) Finally, it has been maintained that although the Declaration is not binding upon the Members of the United Nations who voted for it, it is, somehow, binding upon the organs of the United Nations charged with the administration of the relevant provisions of the Charter. It is difficult to find any ascertainable meaning in that contention. No organ of the United Nations is entitled to act in a manner amounting to an imposition of obligations upon the Members of the United Nations when no such obligation is grounded either in the Charter or in any binding instrument subsequently accepted by the Members of the United Nations. Thus if the Commission on Human Rights were to assume the powers of investigation and recommendation—as, notwithstanding the restraint which it has imposed upon itself, it is bound and entitled to do—in the matter of complaints of violation of human rights, it could not properly look to the Declaration as a measure of the obligations of the State concerned. Undoubtedly, numerous Articles of the Declaration do not differ, in substance, from what would follow from a natural interpretation of the term ' human rights and fundamental freedoms'. To that extent the Declaration, by incorporating the obligations following from the Charter in an instrument which is not binding, may be said, in a sense, to have subtracted from rather than added to its authority.[62] In so far as the Declaration goes beyond that it provides no authority for an extensive interpretation of the obligations of the Charter.

Undoubtedly the Declaration will occasionally be invoked by private and official bodies, including the organs of the United

matters. He pointed out that the Resolution of the Assembly gave the Council the power to ask for such information but that member governments could refuse to give it (*Economic and Social Council, Fourth Year, Eighth Session*, 18 March, 1949, p. 658). Resolution 119 (II) of the General Assembly enables the latter to review steps taken by Members to give effect to the Charter. That Resolution calls upon Members to carry out all recommendations of the Assembly upon economic and social matters and recommends that the Secretary-General report annually to the Economic and Social Council and the Council report to the Assembly upon the action taken by Members to give effect to the recommendations of the Council and of the Assembly upon matters falling within the competence of the Council.

[62] ' In a sense '—for as a matter of law the Declaration is a neutral and ineffective instrument.

Nations. But it will not—and cannot—properly be invoked as a source of legal obligation. Thus the Third General Assembly in adopting in 1949 a Resolution recommending the Government of Soviet Russia to withdraw the measures preventing Soviet wives of citizens of other nations from leaving the country, relied, *inter alia,* on the Universal Declaration of Human Rights 'formulated' by the General Assembly.[63] However, like the Declaration, the recommendation thus adopted was not of a binding character. The fact that the General Assembly, in a recommendation which is not binding, invokes a previous recommendation which is equally devoid of binding legal force, does not endow the latter with legal authority.[63a]

[63] 25 April, 1949; Doc. A/842. When at the first Session of the International Law Commission its Chairman, Professor Hudson, observed that it was dangerous to proclaim the duty to respect human rights and fundamental freedoms without defining them, the Colombian representative replied that, in his opinion, the Universal Declaration of Human Rights defined the fundamental rights and freedoms referred to in the Charter (17 May, 1949; A/CN.4/S.R.20, p. 17). The Byelorussian representative, speaking in connexion with the Russian Resolution on trade union rights, urged that the Economic and Social Council ' could not ignore the principles enshrined in the Charter and the Universal Declaration of Human Rights' (17 March, 1949, *Economic and Social Council, Official Records.* Fourth Year, Eighth Session, p. 641). In connexion with the case, brought before the General Assembly in April, 1949, of the observance of human rights by Hungary and Bulgaria, Belgium and Panama relied on the Declaration as a reason, or one of the reasons, giving the General Assembly the right to discuss the matter notwithstanding the provisions of Article 2, paragraph 7, of the Charter. The Belgian delegate said: ' The decisive consideration which caused his delegation to overcome its misgivings was the adoption of the Universal Declaration of Human Rights by the General Assembly during the first part of its third Session. He did not think that the Assembly could now refuse to examine certain facts relating to violations of human rights which, rightly or wrongly, were brought to its attention' (A/BUR/S.R.58, p. 18). The representative of Panama was even more emphatic. He did not agree that the Declaration was in no way binding. ' It defined what the rights and liberties set forth in the Charter were and could not be simply set aside as having no juridical force' (*ibid.,* p. 20). This also was the view of the representative of Lebanon. He said: ' The Declaration of Human Rights was essentially quite different from any other resolution adopted by the General Assembly. . . . The other resolutions merely conformed with the Charter from the point of view of form, whereas the very substance of the Declaration of Human Rights was contained in the Charter and was the subject of specific provisions. The Declaration continued and, in a way, supplanted the Charter, and could not therefore be considered a mere resolution': *ibid.,* S.R.59, p. 12. He spoke to the same effect in the Political Committee: A/AC.24/S.R.39, p. 6.

[63a] In addition to the above-mentioned Resolution, the General Assembly and other organs of the United Nations have repeatedly invoked the Declaration. See, for instance, Resolution 265 (III) adopted in 1949 in which the General Assembly, in connection with the dispute between India and the Union of South Africa, invited the Governments of these two countries and of Pakistan to enter into discussions taking into consideration, *inter alia,* the purposes and the principles of the Charter of the United Nations and the Declaration of Human Rights. In a Resolution (315 (IV)) adopted in

Not being a legal instrument, the Declaration would appear to be outside international law. Its provisions cannot form the subject matter of legal interpretation. There is little meaning in attempting to elucidate, by reference to accepted canons of construction and to preparatory work, the extent of an obligation which is binding only in the sphere of conscience. If the obligations of the Declaration are only morally binding, every State is entitled to interpret them not in accordance with the common intention—assuming that there be such—of the States which voted for it, but according to its own lights as to the ethical rights and wrongs of any given situation. There may be a tendency —which ought to be resisted—to indulge in a legal interpretation of what is not a legal instrument for the reason that its adoption was preceded by prolonged discussion often indistinguishable from that which precedes the adoption of a statute or a binding international instrument.[64] It may be idle to interpret the nuance

1949 in the matter of discrimination practised by certain States against immigrating labour, the General Assembly referred to the principle of non-discrimination embodied in Articles 2 and 23 of the Declaration. In a Resolution on educational advancement in Trust Territories the General Assembly declared formally that discrimination on racial grounds as regards educational facilities available to the different communities in the Trust Territories is not in accordance with the principles of the Charter, the Trusteeship Agreements and the Universal Declaration of Human Rights (324 (IV)). In recommending, in the same year, the abolition of corporal punishment in Trust Territories, the Trusteeship Council described such punishment as 'a humiliating practice inconsistent with the spirit' of the Declaration (Doc. A/933, Annual Reports 1 and 3). As to the guidance received from and express reliance upon the Declaration in connexion with the proposed European Court of Human Rights see below, p. 435. On the other hand, there is no reference to the Declaration in Article 3 of the Union Statute of the Kingdom of the Netherlands and the Republic of the United States of Indonesia of November 1949. In that Article the parties to the Union recognise the fundamental human rights and freedoms enumerated in the Appendix to the Statute. These follow closely, in many respects, the Articles of the Declaration. See *U.N. Doc.* S/1417/Add.1, pp. 71, 76-78.

[64] See, for instance, the elaborate argument of the South African delegate with respect to the comprehensiveness, which he considered to be excessive and unrealistic, of the principle of equality (A/C3/S.R.95, p. 12). He also objected to the insertion of the reference to dignity in Article 1 since the various Articles should be devoted to the statement of fundamental rights 'whereas the dignity of the individual was actually a deeper and broader concept than a right' (A/C3/S.R.96, p. 3). The representative of Iraq objected to the affirmation that men are both free and equal, 'for if they were free to develop all their latent possibilities, inequality would result' (A/C3/S.R.96, p. 7). The Egyptian delegate expressed the doubts of Moslem countries with regard to Article 16 which provides for freedom to contract marriages without any limitation due to race, nationality and religion. He pointed to restrictions in Moslem countries upon the marriage of a Moslem woman with a person of another creed. 'These limitations', he said, 'are of a religious character and are born from the very spirit of our religion' (A/PV.183, p. 2). He also expressed anxiety, not shared by the representative

of a meaning of an article when the article as a whole is not binding, when its application is subject to 'just requirements of morality, public order and the general welfare in democratic society', and when every State is the exclusive judge of these requirements.

4. THE QUESTION OF THE MORAL FORCE OF THE DECLARATION

The fact that the Universal Declaration of Human Rights is not a legal instrument expressive of legally binding obligations is not in itself a measure of its importance. It is possible that, if divested of any pretence to legal authority, it may yet prove, by dint of a clear realisation of that very fact, a significant landmark in the evolution of a vital part of international law. Undoubtedly, extreme care must be taken, in respect of a document of this nature, not to gauge by rigid legalistic standards what was intended by many States to be an historic demonstration of loyalty to the ideals of the Charter. Nor would even a suspicion of sterile scepticism or lack of reverence be appropriate in relation to a document which is the result of much faith, patient labour, and devotion. But the determination to refrain from captious criticism ought not to interfere with the duty resting upon the science of international law to abstain from infusing an artificial legal existence into a document which was never intended to have that character. Any attempt to do so must prove abortive in the long run. If made, with temporary appearance of success, it would tend to weaken efforts in the direction of true progress.

For these same reasons it is not improper to devote a brief discussion to the question of the moral authority of the Declaration. That question, which loomed large in the discussions of the General Assembly and its Third Committee, was answered

of Pakistan, as to Article 18, which provided for the freedom of the individual to change his religion. The Article, he submitted, implied an indirect encouragement to proselytising by certain missions in the Orient at the expense of the Moslem creed. Detailed, and occasionally heated, discussions took place on the question of the proper age in relation to the right to marry. The representative of Saudi Arabia insisted on the phrasing 'men and women of legal matrimonial age' as distinguished from 'full age'. He said: 'It was not for the Committee to proclaim the superiority of one civilisation over all others and to establish uniform standards for all the countries in the world' (A/C3/S.R.125, p. 6). Some delegates objected that the provision of Article 25 according to which everyone has the right to holidays with pay was too categorical in relation to the capitalist employer or the housewife.

with an affirmative as emphatic as the repudiation of its authority
as a legally binding instrument. Thus the representative of the
United States attached great importance to the Declaration for
the reason that ' at a time when there are so many issues on which
we find it difficult to reach a common basis of agreement, it is a
significant fact that forty-eight States have found such a large
measure of agreement in the complex field of human rights '.[65]
Yet there was no less profound significance in the fact that these
forty-eight States were equally agreed in their determination not
to be legally bound by the principles which they declared to be
fundamental. The British representative in the Third Committee
spoke in similar terms: ' The moral authority of the document
that would be adopted by the Assembly would serve as a guide
to the Governments in their efforts to guarantee human rights
by legislation and through their administrative and legal practice.'[66] Before the General Assembly the British representative,
in comparing the Declaration with Magna Carta and similar
instruments, said: ' This is, indeed, an historic occasion because,
great as are those documents, never before have so many nations
joined together to agree upon what they consider to be the basic
and fundamental rights and freedoms of the individual.'[67] That
combination of the assertion of the fundamental character of the
rights proclaimed in the Declaration and of the denial of the legal
obligation to respect them raises in itself, in a most acute form,
a cardinal issue of international morality. It also raises the
question of the moral authority of the Declaration—a question

---

[65] *Loc. cit.*, above, p. 399.

[66] A/C3/S.R.93. It was stated in 1949 by Professor Cassin, the French representative on the Human Rights Commission, that his Government had
published the Declaration in the *Journal Officiel* and that it had undertaken
a study of all laws and practices in French territory which might not have
been fully in accordance with the Declaration. ' Such a study ', he said,
' which was tantamount to an examination of conscience, should be undertaken in every country in the world ' (E/CN.4/S R.89, p. 7). It is doubtful
whether, in view of the previous statements by Governments that the
Declaration was not binding, the question of conscience entered into the
matter at all. At the same meeting of the Commission the Indian representative affirmed that the Declaration ' was in no way binding and that its
acceptance by States was not a guarantee that the rights which it proclaimed
would be respected by them ' (p. 10).

[67] A/PV.181, p. 516. The comparison with Magna Carta is omitted in the
final version of the speech as printed in the *Official Records of the General
Assembly, Third Session, Part I*, p. 882. In general it is of interest to compare the texts of the speeches made on that occasion by the various delegates
as printed in the *Procès Verbal* with the more sober version appearing in the
Official Records of the General Assembly.

which, in the context of a legal exposition, requires to be dealt with only very briefly.

The moral authority and influence of an international pronouncement of this nature must be in direct proportion to the degree of the sacrifice of the sovereignty of States which it involves. Thus conceived, the fundamental issue in relation to the moral authority of the Declaration can be simply stated: That authority is a function of the degree to which States commit themselves to an effective recognition of these rights guaranteed by a will and an agency other than and superior to their own. The moral influence of ideas flows from the sincerity of those who proclaim them. Their sincerity is, in turn, evidenced by the degree of sacrifice which they are willing to bear on behalf of the ideas which they propagate. The Declaration does not purport to imply any sacrifice of the sovereignty of the State on the altar of the inalienable rights of man and, through them, of the peace of the world. Its moral force cannot rest on the fact of its universality—or practical universality—as soon as it is realised that it has proved acceptable to all for the reason that it imposes obligations upon none. As suggested by the author of this book in his Report presented in September 1948 to the Conference of the International Law Association: ' A declaration of this nature might possess a moral value if it sprang from bodies whose business it is to propagate views and to mould opinion. When coming from such a source the word of enlightenment and exhortation may be as potent as a deed. When emanating from Governments it is a substitute for a deed. What the conscience of mankind expects from governments is not the proclamation of the idea of the rights of man or even the recognition of the rights of man. What the conscience of the world expects from that quarter is the active protection of human rights and the assumption for that purpose of true and enforceable obligations.' For the same reason there is little persuasive force in the argument that the absence of legal authority emphasises and adds to the moral strength of the Declaration.

Undoubtedly, no Bill of Rights, however rigid may be its legal obligations and however drastic its instrumentalities of enforcement, can prove effective unless, by education and enlightenment, it secures the support of the public opinion of the world. But public opinion in support of such aims cannot be created by pronouncements expressing ' a common standard of achievement '. It is inaccurate, in this respect, to compare the Declaration of 1948 with that of 1789 and similar constitutional pronouncements. These may not have been endowed, from the very inception, with all the remedies of judicial review and the formal apparatus of enforcement. But they became, from the outset, part of national law and an instrument of national action. They were not a mere philosophical pronouncement. It is because of that—and only because of that—that, in the words of Lord Acton, the single confused page of the Declaration of 1789 outweighed libraries and proved stronger than all the armies of Napoleon. There is nothing in the Declaration adopted by the General Assembly which includes—or implies—any legal limitation upon the freedom of States. It leaves that freedom unimpaired. In that vital respect it marks no advance in the enduring struggle of man against the omnipotence of the State. The moral authority of a pronouncement of this kind cannot be created by affirmations claiming for it such authority.[68]   One of .the governing principles of the Declaration—a principle which was repeatedly affirmed and which is a juridical heresy—is that it should proclaim rights of individuals while scrupulously refraining from laying down the duties of States.[69]   To do otherwise, it was asserted, would constitute the Declaration a legal instrument. But there are, in these matters, no rights of the individual except

[68] In the same way—and the observation is pertinent with regard to some formulations of the ' covenant ' and of ' measures of implementation ' discussed by the Commission on Human Rights—a document does not become legal and binding merely because its authors described it as such. Its provisions must, in effect, be such as to bind the signatories. The same applies to ' measures of implementation '. See the writer's observations on this point in his Report to the International Law Association, Brussels Conference, 1948. The Preamble to the Declaration, it will be noted, states that ' it is essential if man is not to be compelled to have recourse, as a last resort, to rebellion against tyranny and oppression, that human rights should be protected by the rule of law '. Yet the Declaration does not purport to be a positive contribution to the rule of law.

[69] In its comments, submitted in 1948, on the draft of the Declaration, the Government of the United States gave clear expression to that view. It said: ' Since it is the proper purpose of the Declaration to set forth basic human rights and fundamental freedoms, as standards for the United Nations, it is inappropriate to state the rights in the Declaration in terms of governmental responsibility. In particular it is improper to state in the Declaration that certain things shall be unlawful ': E/CN.4/85, p. 7.

as a counterpart and a product of the duties of the State. There are no rights unless accompanied by remedies.[70] That correlation is not only an inescapable principle of juridical logic. Its absence connotes a fundamental and decisive ethical flaw in the structure and conception of the Declaration.

Such moral authority as the Declaration may otherwise possess is further impaired by the fact that some of its crucial provisions—while clearly not intended to imply a legal obligation—are couched in language which is calculated to mislead and which is vividly reminiscent of international instruments in which an ingenious and deceptive form of words serves the purpose of concealing the determination of States to retain full freedom of action. Thus few persons—and perhaps few lawyers —reading Article 14 of the Declaration relating to asylum will appreciate the fact that there was no intention to assume even a moral obligation to grant asylum. There was an explicit disclaimer of any such intention. That Article provides, in its first paragraph, that ' everyone has the right to seek and to enjoy in other countries asylum from persecution '. The Committee rejected the proposal that there shall be a right to be granted asylum. According to the Article as adopted there is a right ' to seek ' asylum, without any assurance that the seeking will be successful. It is perhaps a matter for regret that in a Declaration purporting to be an instrument of moral authority an ambiguous play of words, in a matter of this description, should have been attempted. Clearly, no declaration would be necessary to give an individual the right to seek asylum without an assurance of receiving it. The right ' to enjoy asylum ' was interpreted by the British delegation, which introduced the amendment containing these words, ' as the right of every State to offer refuge

[70] In the course of the debate in the Canadian House of Commons on the proposed Bill of Rights a member of the House observed: ' These great traditional rights are merely pious ejaculations unless the individual has the right to assert them in the courts of law ': *House of Commons Debates* (1947), vol. 86, p. 3188. The brief Declaration on the Fundamental Rights of the Individual adopted by the Institute of International Law in 1947 states the same proposition in emphatic terms: 'Affirmer le respect des droits de la personne humaine sans en assurer l'efficacité par des mesures effectives de garantie et de contrôle est insuffisant aussi bien dans l'ordre international que dans l'ordre interne' (Art. IV): *Annuaire*, 1947, p. 259. No such emphasis on—or indeed—any reference to the necessity of international guarantees was contained in a similar Declaration adopted by the Institute in 1929: *Annuaire*, 1929, vol. 1, pp. 730-732.

and to resist all demands for extradition '.[71] But this, with regard
to political offences and persecution generally, is the right which
every State indisputably possesses under international law.[72] That
right gains no accession of strength by being incorporated in a
Declaration. Undoubtedly, the grant to individuals of the right
of asylum would have meant an innovation in international law
(although it would not have been *contrary* to international law
as suggested by the Haitian representative).[73] It would have
necessitated a change in the immigration laws of most countries
and would have amounted to a limitation of the absolute right
of States to regulate immigration—a consideration by reference
to which the proposal was opposed equally by Australia and
Soviet Russia as implying an interference with matters exclusively within the domestic jurisdiction of States.[74] It is even
possible—though highly improbable—that, as suggested by the
British delegate, ' its application might actually lead to persecution by encouraging States to take action against an undesirable
minority and then to invite it to make use of the right of asylum '.[75]
But it would have been more consistent with the dignity of the
Declaration if these considerations had resulted in the elimination of the question of asylum from the Declaration. As it
happened, a formula was accepted which is artificial to the point
of flippancy. The Committee had previously rejected a French

[71] A/C3/S.R.121, p. 5. In the original draft of the article the words ' the right
to seek ' were followed by the words ' and to be granted ' asylum.

[72] For this reason stress on the right of States to grant asylum is merely redun-
dant. This applies to the discussions of the International Law Commission
on the subject in 1949. In connexion with the proposed Declaration on the
Rights and Duties of States, Mr. Yepes insisted that the right of asylum was
' one of the noblest creations of customary international law ', and that ' it
would be inconceivable not to include it ' in the proposed Declaration. At
the same time he urged that ' the recognition of the right of States to grant
asylum did not bind them to grant it to all political refugees who asked for
it ' and that the States themselves were free to decide whether or not asylum
should be given to a political refugee (9 May, 1949, Doc. A/CN.4/S.R.16, p.
16). He suggested—rightly, it is believed—that the duty corresponding to the
right of asylum was not that of granting asylum but that of respect for it on
the part of the State of which the refugee is a national. Both these aspects
of the law relating to asylum form an undisputed part of international law.
It is not certain that their authority is strengthened by being made to form
part of a Declaration the legal nature of which is dubious. What is confusing is the tendency to refer in this connexion to the ' right of asylum '—a
phrase implying that it is a right belonging to the individual. Professor
Scelle expressed in this connexion the view that under Article 14 of the
Universal Declaration of Human Rights States had the right ' and even the
duty to grant such asylum ' (*ibid.*, p. 21).

[73] A/C3/S.R.122, p. 6.

[74] A/C3/S.R.121, p. 16 and S.R.122, p. 3.

[75] A/C3/S.R.121, p. 5.

proposal to give the United Nations some standing in the administration of the exclusive right of States to grant asylum.[76] The proposal was accompanied by a note stating, with much relevance, that 'there is no point in proclaiming a right without at the same time stating whose duty it is to give effect to that right'.

The same purely nominal—and, in effect, deceptive—solution was adopted in the matter of nationality. After stating, in the first part of Article 15, that 'everyone has the right to a nationality', the Declaration proceeds to lay down that 'no one shall be arbitrarily deprived of his nationality'. The natural implication of the principle that everyone is entitled to a nationality would be the prohibition of deprivation—whether arbitrary or otherwise—of nationality in a way resulting in statelessness. None of the States which in the period between the two World Wars resorted to deprivation of nationality, *en masse*, for political or racial reasons would have admitted that such measures were arbitrary. They were, in their view, dictated by the highest necessities of the State. In a pronouncement claiming primarily moral authority there should have been no room for the institution of statelessness which is a stigma upon international law and a challenge to human dignity in an international legal system in which nationality is the main link between the individual and international law. There was no inclination to soften the impact of that incongruous contradiction by the adoption of the principle that persons who, because of statelessness, do not enjoy the protection of any government, shall be the concern of the United Nations. A French proposal to that effect was rejected both by the Human Rights Commission [77] and by the Third Committee of the General Assembly[78].

There is a further element of incongruity in the fact that, on account of the objections raised largely by reference to the exclusive jurisdiction of States, the Declaration, which is a document claiming moral authority, contains no reference to the right of petition—though a special resolution of the General Assembly safeguarded in this respect, somewhat inconclusively, the possi-

[76] The French proposal was to add to the proposal as adopted the words: 'The United Nations, in concert with the countries concerned. is required to secure such asylum for him.'
[77] E/CN.4/S.R.59, p. 11.
[78] See above, p. 399, n. 18.

bility of giving effect to what it described as an ' essential human right '.[79] The same consideration applies to the omission,[80] after considerable discussion, of any reference to the protection of the right of minorities to the preservation and development of their separate entity as distinguished from their protection against non-discrimination which is provided for, in general language, in Articles 2 and 7 of the Declaration. In comparison it was probably an accident of final drafting which resulted in the fact, which some delegates found extraordinary, that the fundamental freedoms of thought, of conscience, of religion, and of expression and opinion, should be relegated to the distant Articles 18 and 19 and placed after the Article affirming the right of property.

5. THE DECLARATION AND THE CHARTER

Any criticism of the Universal Declaration of Human Rights from the point of view of its legal value or moral force must be tempered by the realisation that in the intention of those who urged—or acquiesced in—its adoption the Declaration was but a first step. The proclamation of the Declaration was certainly not intended as a complete fulfilment of the task of adoption of an International Bill of Rights conceived as an instrument embodying binding and enforceable obligations. In fact, the proclamation of the Declaration by the General Assembly was accompanied by a resolution stating that as ' the plan of work of the Commission on Human Rights provides for an International Bill of Human Rights, to include a Declaration, a Covenant on Human Rights and measures of implementation ', it ' requests the Economic and Social Council to ask the Commission on Human Rights to continue to give priority in its work to the preparation

[79] The Resolution requested the Economic and Social Council to ask the Commission on Human Rights to give further examination to the problem of petitions when studying the draft Covenant on Human Rights and measures of implementation ' in order to enable the General Assembly to consider what further action, if any, should be taken at its next regular session ' regarding that matter.

[80] The question was referred, in a separate Resolution, to the Economic and Social Council and to the Sub-Commission on the Prevention of Discrimination and the Protection of Minorities, requiring them to make a thorough study of the problem of minorities ' in order that the United Nations may be able to take effective measures for the protection of racial, national, religious or linguistic minorities '. The Resolution explains that in view of the universal character of the Declaration of Human Rights ' it is difficult to adopt a uniform solution of this complex and delicate question, which has special aspects in each State in which it arises '—an explanation which in view of the general character of the Declaration carries little conviction.

of a draft Covenant on Human Rights and draft measures of implementation '. The question whether that first step was necessary and desirable must remain a matter of controversy. It would be unworthy to attribute it wholly to considerations of internal politics in some States or to a desire, on the part of the Commission on Human Rights, to show some semblance of results after exclusive preoccupation with the drafting of the Bill of Rights to the detriment of other activities entrusted to it.

It must remain a matter for speculation whether the Declaration will prove a stepping stone to a true Bill of Rights—which is what is meant by a Covenant and provisions for implementation—or whether it will become a factor in postponing considerably or abandoning the main instrument for which it was intended to pave the way. For although the Declaration can claim no legal force and, probably, only inconsiderable moral authority, that circumstance does not deprive it altogether of significance or potential effect. Somewhat paradoxically, the realisation of the ineffectiveness of the Declaration *per se* must tend to quicken the pace of less nominal measures for the protection of human rights. It is possible—perhaps probable—that although the Declaration is not in itself an achievement of magnitude, it may, by the realisation of that very fact, prove a potent summons to raising and safeguarding the status of man in the international legal system. It is probable that some of the Governments which urged—or, after initial hesitation, supported —the adoption of the Declaration may have had that possibility in mind. There would, indeed, have been no other justification for adopting the Declaration or for the speed with which it was adopted.[81] But that possibility will not materialise—it will be indefinitely postponed—if we strain both law and fact in order

[81] The view prevailed among members of the Commission on Human Rights that unless definite instruments were submitted to the General Assembly the work already done in the matter of an International Bill of Human Rights would be endangered and that public opinion might begin to regard that question in the light of a purely academic problem. There was probably no justification for such anxiety. The true danger of the situation lay in the possibility that the Commission might consider its work, which was still in the preparatory and exploratory stages, as being in the nature of a mature and final product. To attempt, in the political and psychological atmosphere of international relations following upon the Second World War, to give final shape to a fundamental and historic instrument the essence of which must be some distinct measure of surrender of exclusive rights of sovereignty, was bound to injure the cause of human rights. This is probably a case in which delay would have been preferable to fostering an illusion of achievement.

to find in the Declaration of 10 December, 1948, a juridical and moral reality.[82]

These considerations suggest that the analysis of the Declaration as advanced in this Section may not be purely negative.[83] Moreover, in addition to the principal, and perhaps not wholly unintentional, aspect of its potential usefulness, the discussions and the study preceding the adoption of the various Articles of the Declaration must prove of value for the formulation of the substantive and procedural clauses of a binding and enforceable

[82] Some time before the adoption of the Declaration the writer of this book pointed to the grave disadvantages of an international instrument which is no more than an announcement of principle. It may be useful to quote here the relevant passages: 'A bare Declaration of Rights devoid of the characteristics of legal obligation and enforcement would probably constitute a retrogressive event in relation to the Charter. It would tend to weaken the achievement of the Charter and to impair the possibilities of its progressive development as the protector of the rights of man. It would foster the spirit of disillusionment and, among many, of cynicism. There may be a justification and a necessity for a mere declaratory pronouncement, such as the Declaration of 1789, in time of revolutionary *élan* and defiance. Within the State there may also be reasons for the hope that the Declaration, though not followed by specific legal remedies, will be realised through the organic unity and continuity of national life and tradition. These factors are absent in the case of an International Bill of Rights. . . . What practical guidance can there be in a Declaration which is unavoidably and deliberately of a general and abstract character? No Declaration couched in general terms could illuminate the meaning of those essential human rights and freedoms which have behind them the accumulated weight of the best aspirations of mankind throughout the centuries. The experience of the retrogression of the immediate past, some of the traces of which still survive, has added to their already overwhelming cogency. No general Declaration can remove—though it can obscure or ignore—such differences of opinion or practice as exist or are tolerated. The urgent need of mankind is not the recognition and declaration of fundamental human rights but their protection by the international community. There would be a complete justification for incurring the risks and disadvantages inherent in that attempt, if the Declaration were to constitute progress in a vital respect. That progress would consist in lifting the inalienable rights of man from the august but precarious and controversial sphere of the law of nature—of mere declarations—to the plane of positive law and of the legal sanction of the international community.' *The International Protection of Human Rights* in *Hague Academy. Recueil des Cours,* vol. 70 (1947) (1), Chapter III, § 10.

[83] For a less critical appreciation of the Declaration see Stillschweig in *Friedens-Warte,* 49 (1949), pp. 7-19, and Kunz in *American Journal of International Law,* 43 (1949), pp. 316-323. In his *Preface to the Universal Declaration of Human Rights and Its Predecessors* (1949), Professor van Asbeck admits that the Declaration ' has not the binding character inherent in a convention '. He then states that the Declaration ' stands as an " implementation " of the Charter of the United Nations, a treaty itself, and the Declaration, being such, might eventually happen to be considered, in a legal sense, as supplementary to the treaty law '. For a powerful vindication of the usefulness and authority of the Declaration see Cassin in *La technique et les principes du droit public. Etudes en l'honneur de Georges Scelle,* vol. 1 (1950), pp. 67-91. On the other hand see Holcombe, *Human Rights in the Modern World* (1948), pp. 130 *et seq.,* who considers many of the provisions of the proposed Declaration to be unnecessary and too ambitious, and, to the same effect, Mr. Holman, President of the American Bar Association, in *American Bar Association Journal* of November 1948 and April 1949.

International Bill of the Rights of Man. There is no warrant for the pessimistic assumption that an international enactment of this kind is a matter of the distant future. Its realisation does not depend either upon the unanimity—or even upon a two-thirds majority—of the Members of the United Nations.[84] Moreover, there is no decisive reason why an International Bill of Human Rights between States genuinely resolved to place the rights of man under safeguards independent of their own will and power should not effectively come into being outside the United Nations. This may be the case, for instance, as between members of a regional association of States linked together by a common heritage of which respect for the rule of law and the rights of man is the most precious asset.[85]

In the meantime, so long as circumstances render impossible a universal or general Bill of Rights endowed with judicial and executive safeguards, the cause of human rights and fundamental freedoms is not altogether without legal protection and safeguards. The Charter of the United Nations imposes upon its Members solemn legal obligations in this field. In that sphere the organs of the United Nations, once they have ceased to regard the drafting of a Bill of Rights to be their exclusive function, have a prominent and decisive part to play.[86] The International Bill of Human Rights, when adopted as an effective and enforceable instrument, will complete the historic achievement of the Charter in the

---

[84] See above, p. 308. There is a possibility that the efforts to proceed with a true International Bill of Rights may be impeded by the apprehension that the number of signatories of an effective instrument of that nature might be so small as to invite invidious comparisons with the wide acceptance of the non-committal Declaration. There is no ground for any such apprehension—unless it be the desire to maintain the fictitious authority of the Declaration. It appears that at the time of the adoption of the Declaration there was among the States represented on the Human Rights Commission a substantial number—possibly a majority—of countries willing to lend their support to a binding and enforceable Bill of Rights.

[85] See below, p. 445.

[86] There were indications that, after a not altogether fruitless period of trial and error, that view of the legal situation may prevail. Thus, notwithstanding the Resolution of the General Assembly of 1948, instructing the organs of the United Nations to give priority to the drafting of the so-called Covenant of Human Rights and its provisions for implementation, the Secretary-General, in exercising his undoubted right of initiative, took the important step, in May 1949, of proposing to the Commission on Human Rights the reconsideration of its previous decision, which has no foundation in law, that the Commission ' has no power to take any action in regard to any complaints concerning human rights '. See *Report by the Secretary-General on the Present Situation with regard to Communications Concerning Human Rights;* Doc. E/CN.4/165 (2 May, 1949). And see above, p. 259.

sphere of human rights and fundamental freedoms. Pending that consummation, the Charter, when interpreted in good faith and acted upon by the Members of the United Nations and its organs, is a potent instrument for fulfilling a task which—alongside of that of the preservation of peace—constitutes the crucial purpose of the United Nations and of international law. These tasks are complementary and, upon final analysis, identical.

ANNEX

THE UNIVERSAL DECLARATION OF HUMAN RIGHTS

PROCLAIMED BY THE GENERAL ASSEMBLY OF THE UNITED NATIONS ON 10 DECEMBER, 1948

Whereas recognition of the inherent dignity and of the equal and inalienable rights of all members of the human family is the foundation of freedom, justice and peace in the world,

Whereas disregard and contempt for human rights have resulted in barbarous acts which have outraged the conscience of mankind, and the advent of a world in which human beings shall enjoy freedom of speech and belief and freedom from fear and want has been proclaimed as the highest aspiration of the common people,

Whereas it is essential, if man is not to be compelled to have recourse, as a last resort, to rebellion against tyranny and oppression, that human rights should be protected by the rule of law,

Whereas it is essential to promote the development of friendly relations among nations,

Whereas the peoples of the United Nations have in the Charter reaffirmed their faith in fundamental human rights, in the dignity and worth of the human person and in the equal rights of men and women and have determined to promote social progress and better standards of life in larger freedom,

Whereas Member States have pledged themselves to achieve, in co-operation with the United Nations, the promotion of universal respect for and observance of human rights and fundamental freedoms,

Whereas a common understanding of these rights and freedoms is of the greatest importance for the full realisation of this pledge,

Now therefore the General Assembly proclaims this Universal Declaration of Human Rights as a common standard of achievement for all peoples and all nations, to the end that every individual and every organ of society, keeping this Declaration constantly in mind, shall strive by teaching and education to promote respect for these rights and freedoms and by progressive measures, national and international, to secure their universal and effective recognition and observance, both among the peoples of Member States themselves and among the peoples of territories under their jurisdiction.

Article 1

All human beings are born free and equal in dignity and rights. They are endowed with reason and conscience and should act towards one another in a spirit of brotherhood.

Article 2

1. Everyone is entitled to all the rights and freedoms set forth in this Declaration, without distinction of any kind, such as race, colour, sex, language, religion, political or other opinion, national or social origin, property, birth or other status. Furthermore, no distinction shall be made on the basis of the political, jurisdictional or international status of the country or territory to which a person belongs, whether this territory be an independent, trust, non-self-governing or under any other limitation of sovereignty.

Article 3

Everyone has the right to life, liberty and the security of person.

Article 4

No one shall be held in slavery or servitude; slavery and the slave trade shall be prohibited in all their forms.

Article 5

No one shall be subjected to torture or to cruel, inhuman or degrading treatment or punishment.

Article 6

Everyone has the right to recognition everywhere as a person before the law.

Article 7

All are equal before the law and are entitled without any discrimination to equal protection of the law. All are entitled to equal protection against any discrimination in violation of this Declaration and against any incitement to such discrimination.

Article 8

Everyone has the right to an effective remedy by the competent national tribunals for acts violating the fundamental rights granted him by the constitution or by law.

Article 9

No one shall be subjected to arbitrary arrest, detention or exile.

Article 10

Everyone is entitled in full equality to a fair and public hearing by an independent and impartial tribunal, in the determination of his rights and obligations and of any criminal charge against him.

Article 11

1. Everyone charged with a penal offence has the right to be presumed innocent until proved guilty according to law in a public trial at which he has had all the guarantees necessary for his defence.

2. No one shall be held guilty of any penal offence on account of any act or omission which did not constitute a penal offence, under national or international law, at the time when it was committed. Nor shall a heavier penalty be imposed than the one that was applicable at the time the penal offence was committed.

Article 12

No one shall be subjected to arbitrary interference with his privacy, family, home or correspondence, nor to attacks upon his honour and reputation. Everyone has the right to the protection of the law against such interference or attacks.

Article 13

1. Everyone has the right to freedom of movement and residence within the borders of each state.

2. Everyone has the right to leave any country, including his own, and to return to his country.

Article 14

1. Everyone has the right to seek and to enjoy in other countries asylum from persecution.

2. This right may not be invoked in the case of prosecutions genuinely arising from non-political crimes or from acts contrary to the purposes and principles of the United Nations.

Article 15

1. Everyone has the right to a nationality.

2. No one shall be arbitrarily deprived of his nationality nor denied the right to change his nationality.

Article 16

1. Men and women of full age, without any limitation due to race, nationality or religion, have the right to marry and to found a family. They are entitled to equal rights as to marriage, during marriage and at its dissolution.

2. Marriage shall be entered into only with the free and full consent of the intending spouses.

3. The family is the natural and fundamental group unit of society and is entitled to protection by society and the State.

Article 17

1. Everyone has the right to own property alone as well as in association with others.

2. No one shall be arbitrarily deprived of his property.

Article 18

Everyone has the right to freedom of thought, conscience and religion; this right includes freedom to change his religion or belief, and freedom, either alone or in community with others and in public or private, to manifest his religion or belief in teaching, practice, worship and observance.

Article 19

Everyone has the right to freedom of opinion and expression; this right includes freedom to hold opinions without interference and to seek, receive and impart information and ideas through any media and regardless of frontiers.

Article 20

1. Everyone has the right to freedom of peaceful assembly and association.

2. No one may be compelled to belong to an association.

Article 21

1. Everyone has the right to take part in the government of his country, directly or through freely chosen representatives.

2. Everyone has the right of equal access to public service in his country.

3. The will of the people shall be the basis of the authority of government; this will shall be expressed in periodic and genuine elections which shall be by universal and equal suffrage and shall be held by secret vote or by equivalent free voting procedures.

Article 22

Everyone, as a member of society, has the right to social security and is entitled to realisation, through national effort and international co-operation and in accordance with the organisation and resources of each State, of the economic, social and cultural rights indispensable for his dignity and the free development of his personality.

Article 23

1. Everyone has the right to work, to free choice of employment, to just and favourable conditions of work and to protection against unemployment.

2. Everyone, without any discrimination, has the right to equal pay for equal work.

3. Everyone who works has the right to just and favourable remuneration insuring for himself and his family an existence worthy of human dignity, and supplemented, if necessary, by other means of social protection.

4. Everyone has the right to form and to join trade unions for the protection of his interests.

Article 24

Everyone has the right to rest and leisure, including reasonable limitation of working hours and periodic holidays with pay.

Article 25

1. Everyone has the right to a standard of living adequate for the health and well-being of himself and of his family, including food, clothing, housing and medical care and necessary social services, and the right to security in the event of unemployment, sickness, disability, widowhood, old age or other lack of livelihood in circumstances beyond his control.

2. Motherhood and childhood are entitled to special care and assistance. All children, whether born in or out of wedlock, shall enjoy the same social protection.

Article 26

1. Everyone has the right to education. Education shall be free, at least in the elementary and fundamental stages. Elementary education shall be compulsory. Technical and professional education shall be made generally available and higher education shall be equally accessible to all on the basis of merit.

2. Education shall be directed to the full development of the human personality and to the strengthening of respect for human rights and fundamental freedoms. It shall promote understanding, tolerance and friendship among all nations, racial or religious groups, and shall further the activities of the United Nations for the maintenance of peace.

3. Parents have a prior right to choose the kind of education that shall be given to their children.

Article 27

1. Everyone has the right freely to participate in the cultural life of the community, to enjoy the arts and to share in scientific advancement and its benefits.

2. Everyone has the right to the protection of the moral and material interests resulting from any scientific, literary or artistic production of which he is the author.

Article 28

Everyone is entitled to a social and international order in which the rights and freedoms set forth in this Declaration can be fully realised.

28

Article 29

1. Everyone has duties to the community in which alone the free and full development of his personality is possible.

2. In the exercise of his rights and freedoms, everyone shall be subject only to such limitations as are determined by law solely for the purpose of securing due recognition and respect for the rights and freedoms of others and of meeting the just requirements of morality, public order and the general welfare in a democratic society.

3. These rights and freedoms may in no case be exercised contrary to the purposes and principles of the United Nations.

Article 30

Nothing in this Declaration may be interpreted as implying for any State, group or person any right to engage in any activity or to perform any act aimed at the destruction of any of the rights and freedoms set forth herein.

CHAPTER 18

THE PROPOSED EUROPEAN COURT AND COMMISSION FOR HUMAN RIGHTS

1. THE RECOMMENDATIONS OF THE CONSULTATIVE ASSEMBLY OF THE COUNCIL OF EUROPE

IN September, 1949, the Consultative Assembly of the Council of Europe, at its first ordinary Session, adopted Recommendations to the Committee of Ministers concerning human rights and fundamental freedoms. These Recommendations provided for the adoption, in a separate Convention, of the principle of a collective guarantee of human rights and fundamental freedoms and for the establishment of a European Court of Justice and a European Commission for Human Rights.[1] In the Convention the Member States were to undertake to ensure to all persons residing within their territories various rights in accordance with the relevant Articles of the Universal Declaration of Human Rights adopted by the General Assembly of the United Nations in 1948. It is convenient to reproduce here a list of the rights as enumerated in Article 2 of the Recommendations:

1. Security of the person, in accordance with Articles 3, 5 and 8 of Article 19 of the United Nations Declaration;

2. Exemption from all slavery and servitude, in accordance with Article 4 of the United Nations Declaration;

3. Freedom from all arbitrary arrest, detention, exile, and other measures, in accordance with Articles 9, 10 and 11 of the United Nations Declaration;

4. Freedom from all arbitrary interference in private and family life, home and correspondence, in accordance with Article 12 of the United Nations Declaration;

5. Freedom of thought, conscience and religion, in accordance with Article 18 of the United Nations Declaration;

[1] See *Report on the Proceedings of the First Session of the Council of Europe, Strasbourg, 8th August—8th September, 1949*: Misc. No. 14 (1949), Cmd. 7807, pp. 25-28.

6. Freedom of opinion and expression, in accordance with Article 19 of the United Nations Declaration ;

7. Freedom of assembly, in accordance with Article 20 of the United Nations Declaration;

8. Freedom of association, in accordance with Article 20 (paragraphs 1 and 2) of the United Nations Declaration;

9. Freedom to unite in Trade Unions, in accordance with paragraph 4 of Article 23 of the United Nations Declaration;

10. The right to marry and found a family, in accordance with Article 16 of the United Nations Declaration.

Definite provision was to be made for the right of political freedom—the right to government by consent. According to Article 3 of the Recommendations the Convention was to include the undertaking by Member States ' to respect the fundamental principles of democracy in all good faith, and in particular, as regards their metropolitan territory—

1. To hold free elections at reasonable intervals, with universal suffrage and secret ballot, so as to ensure that Government action and legislation is, in fact, an expression of the will of the people;

2. To take no action which will interfere with the right of criticism and the right to organise a political opposition.'

The fundamental rights and freedoms were to be guaranteed without any ' distinction based on race, colour, sex, language, religion, political or other opinion, national or social origin, affiliation to a national minority, fortune or birth '.[2] It was provided that in order to ensure the observance of the obligations of the Convention as defined above, the latter was to set up a European Court of Justice and a European Commission for Human Rights. These proposals will be surveyed and commented on in the present Chapter. It must be a matter of speculation when and in what manner they will be accepted by Governments.[3] But they will have a place in the history of the efforts to make the effective protection of human rights part of the positive law of nations. To that extent they are of more than transient or purely regional interest.

[2] Article 5.

[3] The Recommendations provided for a report on the question to be laid by the Committee of Ministers before the second Session of the Assembly.

2. THE COUNCIL OF EUROPE AND HUMAN RIGHTS

Before surveying the proposed Bill of Rights and the Recommendations concerning the two principal organs—the Court and the Commission—for ensuring the observance of the proposed Convention, it may be useful to assess the place of human rights and fundamental freedoms in the Statute of the Council of Europe. The latter was adopted, in the traditional form of a treaty,[4] by the Governments of Belgium, Denmark, France, the Irish Republic, Italy, Luxembourg, the Netherlands, Norway, Sweden, and the United Kingdom in May, 1949.[5] The Statute itself did not accept the plan of either a European Court of Human Rights or any other special agency responsible for the international enforcement of human rights and fundamental freedoms. Its provisions constitute nevertheless a landmark in the international legal recognition of these rights. They may not have been altogether uninfluenced by the more ambitious proposals of the European Movement—a private body led by statesmen of distinction. In this, as in many other matters, international institutions are the twin product of the attitude of Governments acting as trustees of national sovereignty and of what public opinion, without anticipating objections on the part of Governments, vigorously formulates and advocates as rational and practicable.

Respect for human rights and fundamental freedoms is the main feature of the Council of Europe conceived as the first step towards the closer integration of European States. In the Preamble to the Statute the Signatory States reaffirm ' their devotion to the spiritual and moral values which are the common heritage of their peoples and the true source of individual freedom, political liberty and the rule of law, principles which form the basis of all genuine democracy '. The aim of the Council as laid down in the first Chapter of the Statute is ' to achieve a greater unity between its Members for the purpose of safeguarding and realising the ideals and principles which are their common heritage and facilitating their economic and social progress '. It is provided that this aim shall be pursued through the organs of

---

[4] Misc. No. 7 (1949), Cmd. 7686. And see Misc. No. 10 (1949), Cmd. 7720, containing an Explanatory Note on the provisions of the Statute.

[5] Iceland, Greece and Turkey were subsequently invited to full, or associate, membership.

the Council by discussion of questions of common concern and by agreements and common action in, *inter alia,* the maintenance and further realisation of human rights and fundamental freedoms.

The recognition of obligations in the matter of these rights and freedoms is the principal—or, perhaps, the only—condition of membership in the Council of Europe. For Article 3 of the Statute provides that 'Every Member of the Council of Europe must accept the principles of the rule of law and of the enjoyment by all persons within its jurisdiction of human rights and fundamental freedoms, and collaborate sincerely and effectively in the realisation of the aim of the Council as specified in Chapter I'. Article 4 lays down that any European State which is able and willing to fulfil the provisions of Article 3 may be invited by the Committee of Ministers to become a Member of the Council of Europe. According to Article 5 the same condition applies with regard to associate membership of the Council. Moreover, a State may retain membership only so long as it fulfils the conditions of Article 3. For Article 8 provides that any Member of the Council of Europe which has seriously violated Article 3 may be suspended from its rights of representation and requested by the Committee of Ministers to withdraw from the Council. If such Member does not comply with this request the Committee may decide that it has ceased to be a Member of the Council.

The provisions of the Articles referred to above explain why, although the Statute nowhere uses a form of words expressly laying down that Members *undertake* to respect and observe human rights and fundamental freedoms, I am referring to the *obligations* of Members of the Council in the sphere of human rights. There ought to be no doubt that the Charter in effect imposes those obligations. No other interpretation can reasonably be put upon Article 3 according to which every Member must accept the principles of the rule of law and of the enjoyment by all persons within its jurisdiction of human rights and fundamental freedoms, or upon Articles 4 and 8 in which compliance with Article 3 is expressly laid down as a condition of membership or of the continuation thereof. In that sphere the provisions of the Statute are clearer and leave less room for controversy than the corresponding Articles of the Charter of the United Nations—although there, too, generally accepted principles of interpretation lead to the same conclusion.[6]

However, while in that respect the Statute of the Council of Europe constitutes an advance upon the Charter of the United Nations, it does not—apart from one exception—provide for express international guarantees of the observance of these obligations other than the distinctly limited powers of discussion and recommendation. That exception, the very limited importance of which is discussed in another part of this book,[7] consists in the sanction of expulsion of a Member who fails to comply with the principles of the Statute in this vital sphere. Thus, for instance, unless the Statute is to become a travesty of its purpose, it is clear that if a dictatorship were established in any of the Member States such régime would be inconsistent, in the words of the Statute, with ' the principles of the rule of law and of the enjoyment by all persons within its jurisdiction of human rights and fundamental freedoms '—of which the right to government by consent is not the least fundamental and one without which other freedoms are, in the long run, impossible. Any such State would be liable to expulsion under Article 8—a measure which does not require the unanimity of the Committee of Ministers and which can be effected by a majority of two-thirds of its members. Moreover, as the power of expulsion cannot be exercised without preliminary discussion and investigation whether the State in question has ' seriously violated ' the Statute, there ought to be no doubt that such right of discussion and investigation is inherent in the Committee of Ministers. Also, in so far as the power of expulsion may be reasonably held to include the power to recommend to the offending State, on pain of expulsion, the cessation of conduct contrary to the Statute, it is probable that such a recommendation in the nature of a warning may be adopted by a two-thirds majority of the Committee of Ministers— although in general, according to Article 15, recommendations of the Committee of Ministers addressed to Member States require the unanimity of all its members. In addition, the Committee must be deemed to have the power under Article 15 to discuss any violation of human rights and to consider action

[6] See above, pp. 145-154.
[7] See above, pp. 293, 294.

thereon apart from the sanction of expulsion. For that Article authorises the Committee of Ministers to ' consider the action required to further the aim of the Council of Europe '. However, such action requires unanimity. As to the Consultative Assembly, Article 23 of the Statute lays down that it shall discuss, and make recommendations upon, any matter within the aim and scope of the Council of Europe which is either referred to it by the Committee of Ministers with a request for its opinion or has been approved by the Committee for inclusion in the agenda of the Assembly on the proposal of the latter. Any matter ' within the aim and scope of the Council of Europe ' includes questions of human rights and the rule of law. Moreover, it would appear that even if a question, including one of human rights, is not referred to the Consultative Assembly by the Committee of Ministers, the former can discuss it as preliminary to a request to the Committee of Ministers for its approval for the inclusion of the subject in the agenda of the Consultative Assembly. But there are obvious limitations to a discussion of that nature.

These, then, are the international guarantees and agencies of supervision of the observance of the obligations of the Statute in the matter of human rights. Apart from the power of expulsion —and the powers incidental to it—the authority and instrumentalities of the Statute would seem, in this respect, to fall below those of the Charter of the United Nations. Under the latter, the General Assembly and its organs—such as the Economic and Social Council and the Commission on Human Rights—possess not only an unlimited power of discussion in their own right, but also the power to make recommendations addressed generally or individually to Members of the United Nations.[8] Such recommendations, not being binding, do not amount to intervention contrary to Article 2 (7) of the Charter—assuming that Article 2 (7) is relevant at all in this connexion seeing that as the result of the provisions of the Charter questions of human rights and fundamental freedoms are no longer matters essentially within the domestic jurisdiction of the Members of the United Nations. Under the Statute of the Council of Europe the Consultative Assembly has no independent power of discussion and recom-

[8] See above, pp. 167-173.

mendation. The powers of the Security Council in the matter of human rights and fundamental freedoms are as wide as those of the General Assembly of the United Nations in all cases in which the violation of human rights constitutes a threat to peace. Neither are these powers qualified by an absolute requirement of unanimity. Moreover, the Charter provides for a Commission on Human Rights. That body, in the initial stage of its activities, has to some extent stultified its purpose by a self-imposed limitation, not grounded in the Charter, of its jurisdiction and by devoting itself, to the practical exclusion of other functions, to the task of drafting an International Bill of Human Rights or its substitutes.[9] However, that recession from the purposes of the Charter is not necessarily of a permanent character.

3. THE BILL OF RIGHTS

In view of the summary and provisional character of the Bill of Rights which the proposed Convention is intended to enforce it is not necessary to comment upon it in detail. Although the question of the nature of the rights to be guaranteed by the Convention was examined by a Committee of the European Movement, as well as by the Legal Committee and the Plenary Meetings of the Strasbourg Assembly, these deliberations were necessarily fragmentary and incomplete. Within the time at their disposal these bodies were unable to examine in requisite detail all the problems involved and to avail themselves of the experience, however limited, accumulated in the work of the United Nations Commission on Human Rights and the deliberations of the Third Committee of the General Assembly which adopted the Universal Declaration of Human Rights. There is, therefore, no occasion to comment on that part of the proposed Convention. What has been said elsewhere in this book on the essential principles of a Bill of Rights and the necessity of prolonged study and preparation of an instrument of this nature,[10] which is of basic constitutional importance, applies with no less force to a regional Bill of Rights. In particular, for the reasons stated,[11] there is objection to resolving the difficulties inherent in the problem of securing

[9] See above, p. 261.
[10] See above, Chapter 13.
[11] See above, pp. 285, 354.

rights in the economic and social sphere by the simple expedient of disregarding them altogether.[12]   Similarly, there is objection to the ingenious limitation, in Article 3 of the Draft Convention, of the obligation 'to respect the fundamental principles of democracy in all good faith, and in particular, as regards their metropolitan territory'.[13]   Fundamental principles of democracy are of general application.   There are other, less objectionable, methods of meeting the case of colonial and dependent territories which have not yet attained a sufficient degree of maturity permitting a full measure of self-government.[14]   Neither can the omission of the question of the effective protection of the right of national and other minorities to the preservation of their distinct entities,[15] as distinguished from protection against discrimination,[16] be regarded as a satisfactory feature of the Draft Convention.

On the other hand, in so far as the Draft Convention shows a tendency to avoid excessive elaboration of the rights to be guaranteed, it is fully in accordance with a sound appreciation of the purposes of an international bill of rights.[17]   The tendency, which found expression in the Draft of the Convention, was that

[12] The problem was not absent from the minds of the members of the Assembly. The reasons, which are controversial, for its absence from the Recommendations are best stated in the following passage from the Report of the Committee on Legal and Administrative Questions: 'Certainly, "professional" freedoms and "social" rights, which have themselves an intrinsic value, must also, in the future, be defined and protected; but everyone will understand that it is necessary to begin at the beginning and to guarantee political democracy in the European Union, and then to co-ordinate our economies, before undertaking the generalisation of social democracy': *Consultative Assembly*, Doc. No. 77, p. 1.

[13] See above, p. 436.

[14] See above, p. 351.

[15] See above, p. 352.

[16] Article 5. The Strasbourg Conference dealt with this matter in a manner not free from a suspicion of evasiveness. The *Rapporteur* of the relevant Commission explained the omission of any reference to the positive protection of minorities by stating, somewhat dialectically, that the intention was not to draw up a list of fundamental rights, but only of those which appeared suitable for inclusion in an immediate international guarantee (see Doc. 77, p. 4). Rights of minorities, in the wide sense stated above, have been in the past the object of international guarantees.

[17] See above, p. 329. Nevertheless, after some discussion, the Assembly decided to include the right to marry within the list of the rights to be guaranteed. But see the observations of Lord Layton on that subject at the 18th meeting of the Assembly: AS/CR.18. Prov. Proposals were also put forward—but not adopted—for prohibition of sterilisation (*ibid.*, pp. 119, 121). They met with objections on the part of Denmark, whose delegates attached importance to the right to sterilise compulsorily sexual criminals.

the detailed application of the general terms of the Bill of Rights should be left to the legislation of the Signatory States provided that such legislation was not inconsistent with the principles of the Bill.[18] That tendency was of substantial assistance in ensuring to a large extent—though not to the full extent—a satisfactory solution of the problem of the so-called general limitation clause.[19] Thus Article 4 laid down that ' subject to the provisions laid down in Articles 5, 6 and 7, every Member State, signatory of the Convention, shall be entitled to establish the rules by which the guaranteed rights and liberties shall be organised and protected within its territory '. Article 5, referred to above,[20] formulated the principle of non-discrimination. Article 7—which is probably of doubtful helpfulness—stated that the object of the collective guarantee of the Convention ' will be to ensure that the laws of each State in which are embodied the guaranteed rights and liberties as well as the application of these laws are in accordance with " the general principles of law as recognised by civilised nations " and referred to in Article 38 of the Statute of the International Court of Justice '. The crucial Article 6 laid down that in the exercise of the rights and in the enjoyment of the liberties guaranteed by the Convention ' no limitation shall be imposed except those established by the law, with the sole object of ensuring the recognition of and respect for the rights and liberties of others, or with the purpose of satisfying the just requirements of public morality, order and security in a democratic society '. Yet while the Convention thus expressly provided that any limitations of the rights guaranteed by it must not only be established by law, but must also satisfy other conditions, it did not lay down that these other conditions must not be inconsistent with the purposes of the Convention.[21] It was claimed by the *Rapporteur* of the

[18] See, *e.g.*, the Report by Professor Teitgen (17th Meeting, 7 September, 1949: AS/CR.17/Prov., pp. 25, 26), who, while stressing that the slow work of tribunals has often played a prominent part in defining and crystallising rules of law, said: ' An international convention will establish a list of guaranteed freedoms, and it will be for each country to fix for itself the way in which these guaranteed freedoms shall be exercised within its territory. Each country will evolve its own rules as to the exercise of its liberties. International collective guarantee will aim at ensuring that, under the pretext of organising the exercise of guaranteed liberties, the State will not actually limit or suppress them altogether.'

[19] See above, p. 366.

[20] See above, p. 436.

[21] See above, p. 369.

Commission in question that the effect of the Articles referred to was that there should be ' no limitation of rights for reasons of State, but that it is competent for the State to act in accordance with its national legislation provided it is in conformity with international principles '.[22]   The wording of the Articles as adopted failed to secure that purpose.   In general, however, that part of the Recommendations must be regarded as taking into account the experience of past efforts in that field—except in so far as its verbal association with the Universal Declaration of Human Rights, which is an instrument devoid of legal force, may prove a source of confusion.

4.   THE EUROPEAN COMMISSION FOR HUMAN RIGHTS

The Recommendations of the Strasbourg Assembly for a European Commission for Human Rights and a European Court of Justice must be considered in the light of the shortcomings, as indicated above,[23] of the Statute of the Council of Europe as compared, in the matter of human rights and fundamental freedoms, with the Charter of the United Nations.   The Recommendations with regard to the Commission and the Court were calculated to remove these defects and to emphasise, in turn, the central place which human rights and fundamental freedoms occupy in the Statute of the Council of Europe.   Although the Court and its organisation figure prominently in the Recommendations, their centre of gravity lies in the Commission.   It was recommended that the Commission shall consist of members elected by the Committee of Ministers and the Consultative Assembly of the Council of Europe by a simple majority of the votes cast in each of those bodies.[24]   Recourse to the Commission was to be open: (1) to any Signatory State which may resort to it in respect of an alleged breach of the Convention by another Signatory; (2) to any person or corporate body which claims to have been the victim of a violation of the Convention by a Signatory State.   The admissibility of such petitions by private persons or bodies was to be

[22] *Loc. cit.,* p. 27.

[23] See above, p. 436.

[24] No provision is made for the case of the impossibility of securing a majority in these two bodies for the requisite number of members to be elected— there are to be as many members of the Commission as Member States signatories of the Convention—but the Recommendations are admittedly of a general nature.

conditional upon the exhaustion of all means of redress within the State concerned—a requirement which, in accordance with the practice of international tribunals in the matter of exhaustion of local remedies,[25] must be interpreted in a reasonable manner. The duty of the Commission is to investigate and enquire into the petitions. It may reject a petition as irregular or manifestly unfounded. It may also dismiss it as the result of a more detailed examination or enquiry. If it does not reject the petition, then the Commission ' shall try to effect a conciliation of the opposing parties ' and ' if conciliation fails, the Commission shall set forth the facts in a report which shall be published '.

The main scheme, as accepted in the Recommendations and as explained during the debates at Strasbourg and by the Committee of the European Movement largely responsible for its initial formulation, for a Commission for Human Rights resembles closely the proposals and the reasoning put forward in the present book and previously advanced by its author.[26] In addition, there are persuasive reasons why complaints of violations of human rights in countries bound by the Statute of the Council of Europe should form the subject matter, in the first instance, of a procedure of investigation and conciliation by a non-judicial body of independent persons. The principal reason is that in the States which were the original signatories of the Statute the courts —and the legislatures—have been in fact the faithful trustees of the rights of man. In relation to those States the need for international guarantees of human rights would seem, in some respects, to be largely in the nature of affirmation of a principle rather than the result of a need demonstrated by daily occurrence. That principle is grounded in the realisation that the State, however firmly wedded to the tradition of human rights and freedoms, cannot be the final arbiter of the rights of man. Admittedly, affirmation of that principle is not a mere symbolic gesture. Even in democratic countries situations may arise in which the individual is in danger of being crushed under the impact of ' reason of State '. The Dreyfus affair in France provided a telling example of that possibility. Examples of more recent date can

[25] See above, p. 380.

[26] See *An International Bill of the Rights of Man* (1945), and his *Report to the Brussels Conference of the International Law Association*, 1948. And see above, pp. 373-381.

be adduced.   A number of constitutional cases decided by English courts shed instructive light on the subject.   Thus in *Liversidge* v. *Sir John Anderson,* Lord Atkin, in a dissenting judgment, uttered a protest against a strained construction being put upon the words of a statute, even in time of war, with the effect of giving the Executive an uncontrolled power of imprisonment.   He said:

> ' I view with apprehension the attitude of judges who on a mere question of construction when face to face with claims involving the liberty of the subject show themselves more executive minded than the executive. . . . In this country, amid the clash of arms, the laws are not silent.   They may be changed, but they speak the same language in war as in peace.   It has always been one of the pillars of freedom, one of the principles of liberty for which on recent authority we are now fighting, that the judges are no respecters of persons and stand between the subject and any attempted encroachments on his liberty by the executive, alert to see that any coercive action is justified in law.   In this case I have listened to arguments which might have been addressed acceptably to the Court of King's Bench in the time of Charles I.' [27]

Lord Atkin remained in a minority.   But that very fact suggests that even in countries in which the rule of law is an integral part of the national heritage and in which the courts have been the faithful guardians of the rights of the individual, there is room for a procedure which will put the imprimatur of international law upon the principle that the State is not the final judge of human rights.   In the case referred to above, Lord Macmillan, speaking as one of the majority of the Law Lords, said: ' The liberty which we so justly extol is itself the gift of the law and as Magna Carta recognises may by the law be forfeited or abridged.'   These are significant words.   Yet the essence of an effective international guarantee of the rights of man is that liberty must not be in the absolute gift of the national State.   There may —and ought to—be a limit to which freedom can be denied or abridged by the State.   The circumstance that decisions of municipal courts—however authoritative and important—on these matters have not always been unanimous and that they have often been exposed to criticism shows that there is no compelling reason for claiming for them unqualified finality.   Undoubtedly,

[27] [1942] A.C. 206 at 244.

an international court or commission may not be unanimous and its decisions may leave the subject matter in the same state of legal or moral uncertainty as the decision appealed against. Similarly, on matters affecting so closely the core of national life— the relation of man to the State—a foreign tribunal not versed in the law, peculiar circumstances, and tradition of the country concerned, may give a judgment which, in that country, will carry little conviction. These arguments are not unanswerable. For may it not be said that although these matters touch the core of national life, they bear at the same time on fundamental human rights proclaimed to be universal in their validity and not inferior in importance to the requirements of the national State?

These conflicting considerations supply a powerful argument in favour of making the international procedure non-judicial in the first instance. It is to be expected that a substantial number of cases brought before the Commission will be on the border-line where the apparently vital necessities of the State and the rights of man converge and conflict.[28] In cases of this description— such as temporary suspension of civil liberties in time of war and the like—in which the political element plays a preponderant part, a procedure by a body which is semi-political and semi-judicial would seem to be indicated in the first instance. That procedure may, in some cases, result in the withdrawal of complaints which are exaggerated or unfounded. In other cases it may bring home to the authorities and Government of the State the propriety of modifying the measures adopted. It would not act by way of formal nullification or repeal of the acts of the national legislature or judiciary.

At the same time it must remain axiomatic that the purpose of that procedure cannot properly be the sacrifice of fundamental human rights to the convenience of governments and, in the absence of most compelling considerations, even to the necessities of the State. The ultimate end of the State is to secure the rights and freedoms of the individual—though it is also true, and this is a relevant factor in the situation, that the State is at present an essential condition for securing these rights. For that reason, in so far as ' conciliation ' is described as the principal task of the Commission, that task cannot properly be interpreted as implying

---

[28] See Lord Atkinson in *Rex* v. *Halliday,* cited above, p. 376, n. 58.

a political compromise, to be invariably achieved at the expense of the individual, between human rights and the susceptibilities of the sovereign State. There cannot properly be any question of 'conciliation' thus conceived when fundamental rights of the individual are flagrantly violated. 'Conciliation' consists in attempts to remove, by non-judicial means and by direct approach to the Government concerned, the ascertained cause of the injury.

For the same reason safeguards must be provided for leaving open to the individual the eventual possibility of a judicial remedy before the Court. The Court of Human Rights must remain as the residuary organ of protection of human rights and fundamental freedoms in the same way as the political authority of the Council of Europe must be available as the ultimate safeguard of human liberties in the countries of Western Europe. If, therefore, any particular system of international protection of human rights were to deprive the individual, without compelling reasons, of the eventual right of judicial remedy, it would be open to serious criticism. Such compelling reasons may consist in the fact that the petition is so obviously ill-founded that to permit it to go before the Court would amount to sanctioning an abuse of its process. But the obviousness, in that sense, of the legal merits— or demerits—of the case must be so clear as to require endorsement by a substantial majority of the Commission.[29] Accordingly, it would not seem consistent with principle if the Commission were to be given the power to decide, by a simple majority, whether to transmit a case to the Court. Yet this is the solution adopted by the Strasbourg Recommendations—except that, apparently, any complaint, whether brought by a State or an individual, must, if not settled by conciliation, be submitted for a legal decision of the Court at the request of any Signatory State.[30] That provision to some extent mitigates the consequences of the denial to the individual, by a bare majority of the Com-

---

[29] As in the case of the proposed Court, so also with regard to the Commission, those opposing the proposal drew attention to what they considered the probability of the Commission being flooded by petitions which are not only unfounded but also deliberately encouraged, for purposes of propaganda, by forces inimical to democracy. For an impressive answer to these objections see the statement of Sir David Maxwell Fyfe (18th Meeting, AS/CR.18/Prov., p. 99). He insisted that the political origin of a complaint is not a sufficient reason for refusing to investigate it and that although democratic methods have been invariably attacked by enemies of democracy this was not a reason for abandoning them.

[30] Article 19 of the Recommendations.

mission, of the right to a judicial remedy. On the other hand, the procedure contemplated is open to the objections inherent in a system which leaves to States a decisive share of the initiative in the protection of human rights.[31]

The Recommendations relating to that part of the proposed Convention did not provide for the obligation of the Signatories to accept the findings and recommendations of the Commission. In fact, apart from the duty to prepare and publish a report seting forth the facts of the case, the proposed Convention did not impose upon the Commission the obligation to make recommendations. Yet, for the reasons stated elsewhere,[32] the entire system may become to a large extent illusory unless, subject to a right of appeal to the Court, there is an obligation to accept and to act upon the recommendation of the Commission and unless sanctions are provided for the case of non-fulfilment of that obligation.

5. THE EUROPEAN COURT OF HUMAN RIGHTS

The proposals, as outlined in the Draft Convention, for a European Court of Human Rights are of significance not only inasmuch as they amounted to a recognition of the principle of international judicial protection of human rights, but also because they implied the possibility of such protection at the instance of individuals—though in the latter case, according to the scheme proposed, the consummation of that possibility depended upon the approval of the majority of the Commission. At the same time it is of importance to note three features of the Recommendations which affect adversely the value of the detailed scheme as adopted. While, in the end, the proposal for a European Court of Human Rights was adopted by an overwhelming majority,[33] the persistent opposition succeeded in leaving its impress upon one of the main aspects of the Recommendations adopted by the Assembly.[33a]

[31] See above, pp. 287-290.

[32] See above, p. 293.

[33] Seventy-six delegates voted in favour; seventeen abstained; sixteen were absent.

[33a] Thus M. Rolin, of the Belgian delegation, questioned the very necessity for a special Court. He said at the 18th Meeting (8 September, 1949:

(1) It was proposed, in the first instance, that although the findings of the Court [31] shall be pronounced in open session (Article 26), 'the deliberations of the Court, like those of the Commission, shall be secret'. While some highly controversial arguments may be put forward in favour of the view that the deliberations of the Commission, which aims at conciliation, need not necessarily be in public, no plausible argument seems possible in support of the secrecy of the deliberations of the Court. The notion of a clandestine judicial determination of fundamental human rights is incongruous, unnecessary, and probably not deserving of a place in any future discussion of the subject.

(2) While it was proposed, in Article 24, that the jurisdiction of the Court shall extend to all violations of the obligations of the Convention, whether they result from legislative, executive or judicial acts, the same Article provided that 'nevertheless, where objection is taken to a judicial decision, that decision cannot be impugned unless it was finally given in disregard of the fundamental rights defined in Article 2 by reference to Articles 9, 10 and 11 of the United Nations Declaration'. The effect of that provision, which is typical of the consequences of achieving what is in essence a purely quantitative compromise in matters

AS/CR.18/Prov.): 'We have to admit that the good will of our Governments to conform to the Convention will be certain, and that if there is a mistake and a report from the Commission of enquiry redress will be given' (p. 75). He doubted whether more than one case a year would come before the Court; the judges would thus hold a sinecure which would be unnecessarily expensive and hardly conducive to the dignity of the Court. He urged that the proposal was useless and illogical, and that if accepted it would be detrimental to the authority of the International Court of Justice inasmuch as it would remove a substantial source of litigation from its jurisdiction (p. 76). He was supported by some British delegates. Thus Mr. Ungoed-Thomas said: '. . . If we allow the right of individuals to petition the Court, we must look at what happened in the United States of America, where there is a law that no person shall be deprived of life, liberty or property without due process of law. A harmless provision of that kind . . . was used in order to prevent States taking action against trusts' (p. 84). But see below, p. 455, for the views of M. Bidault. It is possible that the nature of the arguments advanced in opposition to the proposal for a European Court proved an important factor in securing its acceptance.

[31] The Court was to consist of nine members. It was not to include more than one national of any Signatory State. Its members were to be elected by the Committee of Ministers and the Consultative Assembly of the Council of Europe by a simple majority of votes cast in each of these bodies. The suggested provisions followed largely those of the Statute of the International Court of Justice. Apparently no consideration was given to the need for avoiding the formation of a Court of such a composition as must result from a necessarily haphazard process of political election. For the possibility of a different method see above, p. 384.

of principle,[35] is to sanction the finality of decisions of municipal courts and to eliminate international judicial protection in such matters as security of the person, freedom of conscience, thought and religion, freedom of opinion and expression, and freedom of assembly and association. That unexpected limitation was accepted in deference to emphatic protestations from some delegates who regarded as utterly unacceptable the notion of decisions of the highest tribunals of their countries being questioned before a foreign tribunal.[36] Apparently no such strong objection was

[35] For the proposals for a European Court of Human Rights were not adopted without substantial opposition which relied on the often-invoked argument against conceding to private persons the right to initiate proceedings before an international court. It was urged that ' an accusation before a Court of Justice. called upon to give judgment, involves such grave considerations that it is necessary for the responsibility to be left to the governments of the different Members of the European Council, whether they operate severally or collectively ' (Amendment of M. Rolin and Mr. Ungoed-Thomas: Doc. No. 84). Apparently—though this did not appear clearly from the amendment—the opposition was willing to concede to individuals the right of petition before a Commission for Human Rights provided that it had no power to make a declaration on the merits of a request submitted to it and that its jurisdiction was merely ' to establish the facts and to make them publicly known ' (*ibid.*). The authors of the amendment, which was in fact adopted in relation to the powers of the Commission (see above, p. 449), were confident that ' if our States are, as has been said, really law-abiding States, such a measure of publication would be sufficient to arouse the attention of the Parliaments and to persuade the Governments to make the necessary rectification '. Finally, the authors of the amendment suggested. perhaps with little consistency, that ' in the event of a Member of the Council of. Europe persisting in an attitude condemned by the public opinion of other States, it would be possible for the Parliament of another State to use the report of the Commission of Enquiry as a basis for a request for its own Government to intervene by setting in motion some inter-State form of procedure, whether by means of legal action or arbitration '. There is little consistency in the view that an orderly international judicial procedure is incompatible with the sovereignty of States, but not interference by foreign Governments prompted by a public discussion and vote in their Parliaments.

[36] The desire to meet these objections, while adhering to the principal idea of a European Court of Human Rights, led to some unavoidably obscure and contradictory explanations. See, for instance, the Observations of the *Rapporteur* at the 17th Meeting (7 September, 1949: AS/CR.17/Prov., p. 31): ' The European Court would not act as a final court of appeal dealing with all errors in law or in fact which might be put down as a breach of the national laws, because it is not to be thought that a European Court would be required to censure a legal decision given within a member State. It would only deal with breaches of any one of the fundamental rights maintained in Article 2 of this Declaration. . . . A judgment could not be the subject of international censure if it appeared that only the national law has been violated. But if there is a question of one of the fundamental rights being violated and of all ordinary tenets of law being broken, then the matter could be brought before the European Court so that the Court might state what the position is. But there is no question of referring a matter to the European Court if there has only been an error in law or in fact in the decision of a national court.' See also *Report of the Committee on Legal and Administrative Questions*: ' The Committee observes in this connexion that the Court will not in any way operate as a Supreme Court

raised against the impairment, as the result of the jurisdiction of an international tribunal, of the sovereignty of the national legislature.

(3) There was no provision in the proposed Convention which either rendered binding the decision of the Court or which conferred upon the political organs of the Council of Europe the power to enforce the judgment of the Court.   In this respect the authority of the decisions of the European Court of Human Rights as proposed would fall considerably below that of the International Court of Justice.[37]   The proposed Convention merely provided that the findings of the Court should be transmitted to the Committee of Ministers.   There can be no justification for a system in which judicial decisions in the matter of fundamental rights of man partake of a smaller degree of legal authority and enforceability than decisions of other international tribunals. Thus also in that respect a mechanical compromise, if persisted in, may succeed in affecting adversely what might otherwise become a development of the utmost significance.   While the opposition to the proposal for a European court was defeated in the final voting, it succeeded in reducing to a very considerable —perhaps decisive—degree the scope of the main proposal. There is little substance left in a European Court of Human Rights the protection of which cannot be directly invoked by the individual and which can be denied by a simple majority of a Commission sitting *in camera;* which conducts its deliberations in secret; which has no power of review of judgments of municipal courts except in a limited segment of cases; and whose decisions are neither binding nor enforceable.   As in the case of the Universal Declaration of Human Rights, it is within the legitimate province of legal science to penetrate behind artificiality of language and to draw attention to the possibility that the reality of a European Court of Human Rights may be reduced to vanishing point because of the limitations surrounding its jurisdiction and the binding force of its decisions.   In this as

---

of Appeal having jurisdiction to review any errors of law or of fact which are alleged against the judgment in question. The Court would have power to impugn a judicial decision if that decision had been made in disregard of the fundamental rights laid down in Article 2 of the draft resolution, which is based on Articles 9, 10 and 11 of the United Nations Declaration ' (Doc. 77, p. 7). As mentioned, the limitation referred to in the last-quoted sentence seems arbitrary.

[37] See Article 94 of the Statute of the Court.

in other matters, no achievements of substance can be brought about without actual sacrifices of sovereignty. In so far as attempts may be made to accomplish that result at no expense to national sovereignty, such efforts must, in the long run, prove deceptive, inimical to the authority of international engagements, and injurious to international morality.

6. THE EUROPEAN COURT OF HUMAN RIGHTS AND THE SOVEREIGNTY OF THE MEMBERS OF THE COUNCIL OF EUROPE

For these reasons it is within the province of any legal exposition of the subject to reveal, with all requisite clarity, the large extent of the limitation of the sovereignty of States implied in the notion of an international court—and commission—of human rights, whether on a regional basis or otherwise. The proposal for a European Court of Human Rights—freed from illogical and incongruous limitations—implies such a surrender of sovereignty. It not only gives to international agencies the power to investigate and review judicial decisions of the highest municipal tribunals. It implies in effect the authority to review legislative acts of sovereign parliaments. That power would go substantially beyond that entrusted to the Supreme Court of the United States, where the original Bill of Rights affords protection against Congress and the Union but not against denial of fundamental rights on the part of the States. It is of little consequence whether that faculty of review amounts to a right of formal nullification of judicial and legislative acts or to a mere declaration that they are contrary to human rights and fundamental freedoms as defined by a Bill of Rights. It matters not whether that power of review is limited by any previous obligation on the part of the aggrieved individual to exhaust the legal remedies available within the State. For there are no legal remedies to exhaust against acts of Parliament. Thus the Commission and the Court would possess jurisdiction—to mention only questions which may arise in Great Britain—to entertain appeals against the policy of the Government with regard to the demand for equal pay for women;[38] the practice embodied in the Control of Engagements Order and the legislation on which it is based;[39] the executive and legislative regula-

[38] See above, p. 339, n. 32.
[39] See above, p. 410, n. 55. The Order was repealed in 1950.

tion of the right of assembly, such as the local prohibition of processions; executive or judicial limitation of or interference with the right of meeting; [40] any purported interference with the right of political asylum by executive action or judicial decision; any alleged denial of justice by courts on political grounds—a plausible reason for appeal in trials for treason; any alleged arbitrary imprisonment—it will be noted that the power of imprisonment for contempt by courts and Parliament is, in theory, arbitrary inasmuch as it is not subject to judicial remedy.   In a case decided in 1947 [41] the House of Lords held that an arrest without a warrant can be justified only if it is an arrest on a charge made known to the person arrested—although it found for the appellant, the police, on the ground that the respondent, who was arrested on suspicion that he had stolen or feloniously received a bale of cloth then in his warehouse, in fact knew of the nature of the offence for which he was arrested.   Under the proposed system it would have been open to him to appeal to the international authority on the ground that the arrest was in violation of the safeguards against arbitrary detention.   This would be so although it is clear that the exhaustive judgments of the learned Law Lords in this case are in fact a powerful vindication of freedom from arbitrary arrest.   Thus Lord Simon in his judgment quoted with emphatic approval the statement [42] that ' the liberty of a man is a thing specially favoured by the common law ', and warned against a practice which might revive the French *cachets* or the methods of Nazi Germany.   The range and number of decisions given every year by the Supreme Court of the United States in the field of civil liberties and the Bill of Rights generally are a reminder of the vast—and, to some, alarming—possibilities of international review.   Yet, as mentioned, the jurisdiction of the Supreme Court is limited, for the original Bill of Rights provides remedies only against Congress and the Union, and not against the States.[43]

[40] Such as was expressed in *Thomas* v. *Sawkins* [1935], 2 K.B. 249, where it was held—for the first time in English history, as pointed out by Professor Goodhart (*Cambridge Law Journal*, 6 (1938), p. 22)—that police officers are entitled to enter and remain on private premises if they have reasonable ground for believing that otherwise an offence or a breach of the peace will be committed there.

[41] *Christie* v. *Leachinsky* [1947] A.C. 573.

[42] In Dalton's *Country Justice* (1618), p. 406.

[43] An international procedure for the protection of human rights within the States of the Council of Europe would in many ways be more practicable than the enforcement of the Bill of Rights by the Supreme Court of the

These possibilities must be kept clearly in mind and fully explained to the point of acknowledgment that, in a system of judicial review by international courts the decisions of which are legally binding, a portion of national sovereignty will be vested in the nine persons comprising the European Court of Human Rights. After that has been done—but only then—it may be permissible to urge that some such consummation is inevitable if the proclamation of allegiance to the rights of man is not to remain within the realm of phrases; that, assuming that it is at all permissible to reduce the recognition and protection of human rights to the level of an ideological weapon, such weapon, if it is to be effective, must be made of weightier stuff than mere declarations or even a mere condition of membership or of continued membership;[44] that the operation, within the framework of a regional organisation, of an effective Human Rights Council and Court may provide useful experience for the more general and more difficult task of protection of human rights within the United Nations; and that although it may be true that schemes of this nature amount to some extent to introducing, by a back-door, the idea of a Federation, they may be a convenient step for assisting in the promotion of the integration of Europe by way of functional institutions and organs rather than by the outright and politically impracticable adoption of a formal

United States in relation to the States of the American Union. For the tradition of the rights of man and of the rule of law among the Western European States comprising the Council of Europe is no less strong than in the United States. Moreover, from some points of view the problem is simpler in relation to the States of Western Europe, where there is absent the baffling and perplexing problem of the Negro minority. At the same time it must be remembered that the States of the American Union are less sovereign than the States of the Council of Europe. The States of the American Union have surrendered most of their sovereignty to the Union. That sovereignty is circumscribed by the amendments to the Bill of Rights. It may be further curtailed, and abolished, by constitutional amendment—not to mention decisions of the Supreme Court.

[44] The following passage from the remarks of M. Bidault at the 18th Plenary Meeting of the Strasbourg Assembly in 1949 may be quoted in this connexion: 'What we must do here, is to realise that the European law on the rights of man, which we wish to proclaim here—should be like everything else here—provided with a minimum of enforcement, without which it would be in vain and its proclamation useless. I therefore beg the Assembly to consider that a law without a tribunal is something even worse than the absence of law as it presupposes the existence of force, which is at least better than hypocrisy': AS/CR.18/Prov., p. 82. See also the observations of Professor Teitgen, the *Rapporteur,* at the 17th Meeting (AS/CR. 17/Prov., p. 33), emphasising that there is no true surrender of sovereignty inimical to the independence of States unless such surrender takes place in the interest of an individual State as distinguished from the society of States at large.

federal constitution.   There may be force in the view that until that consummation comes to pass the Council of Europe will be lacking in full reality in relation to what, according to its Statute, is the very essence of its being and to what the authors of the Statute of the Council of Europe have justly described as forming already ' the common heritage of their peoples '.   The association of States of Western Europe provides a starting point for further progress in securing the rights of man in so far as, after the initial achievement of the Charter, that cause may have come to a standstill in the United Nations.   In turn, the cause of human rights offers to the Council of Europe an opportunity which may raise it high above the level of a political expedient and invest it with a dignity and authority which may prove one of the main sources of its strength.

7.   Sovereignty, Federation and the Rights of Man

In this connexion it is fitting to draw attention, by way of general conclusion, to the intimate relation between the three central issues of international law and organisation: the idea of sovereignty, the notion of the *civitas maxima* conceived as a World Federation of States, and the international recognition and protection of the rights of man.   It is the abiding lesson of history and a compelling postulate of reason that a world-embracing Federation—of which regional Federations may be a necessary stage—is, in the words of Immanuel Kant, the only means of attaining perfect internal government, which is, in turn, the essential condition of the realisation of the moral and intellectual capacities of mankind.   If that is so, then the idea of an all-embracing Federation of States must be regarded not as an infinite ideal but as an object of a moral duty of positive action and as a practical standard of human endeavour.

However, it is unlikely that that consummation can be promoted by the determination to adhere in all respects to the accepted features of the federal system.   For most of the Federations, past and present, have not been associations of States differing in historic experience, language, culture, economic development, tradition and law.   The rational solution of the problem of international organisation will be hastened by the acceptance of the view that the differences between the typical

forms of unions of States—such as Federations and Confedera-
tions—are to a large extent a matter of degree; that no such
solution is feasible in so far as it envisages the immediate and
total disappearance of the international personality of States; that,
subject to that condition, there is no obstacle—certainly not
in international law—to the gradual limitation of rights of
sovereignty within an association of States based on the continued
recognition of the distinct international personality of States; and
that there is no contradiction between the notion of sovereignty
conceived as independence in relation to other States of the international society and the gradual approximation to a Federation
of the World properly so called.

In theory, a full-fledged federal system between the nations
of the world would be more conducive to enhancing the
stability of international peace, to the protection of the
rights of man, and to reducing the evils and abuses of national
power than a looser system of Confederation based on the
unrestricted sovereignty of its members. This may be admitted
without conceding all the advantages claimed to be linked with
the federal system.[45] However, as it is highly controversial
whether the political integration of mankind will—or can—be
accomplished by the outright adoption of a world federal constitution,[46] it is necessary to bear in mind the two typical

[45] Thus, for instance, contrary to a widely held view, a federal constitution
does not render unnecessary or juridically impossible the collective enforcement of the federal law against Member States as distinguished from individuals responsible for the actions of those States—a feature of the federal
system which some regard as ethically superior inasmuch as it obviates the
injustice of collective punishment and emphasises the element of individual
responsibility. Yet the Continental theorists of *Bundesexekution* are by no
means agreed that enforcement of the law against a rebellious member
State as such is contrary to the idea of the federal system. We may recall,
as a minor example, the mild Swiss practice of coercing a disobedient Canton
by quartering in it federal troops at its expense, a sanction which has been
described as particularly offensive to the native sense of frugality. In the
United States of America the abandonment, after the Civil War, of the
doctrine of collective enforcement of the federal law against the States as
such was possible only with the help of a daring venture in constitutional
dialectics. It was asserted that an act of a State legislature or of a State
executive in violation of the Constitution or of the acts of the national
executive performed in pursuance of the Constitution is not an act of the
State Government, which cannot, in law, act against the Constitution, but
of persons illegally and falsely assuming to act as the Government, and that
such persons, but not the State, can and must be coerced individually or
as a group. Neither is it desirable to adopt without qualification the view
that sanctions against collective units are invariably immoral and that individuals ought to be able to escape the consequences of their criminal conduct
in so far as they act as a State.
[46] This is not an adequate reason for treating with impatience or lack of
respect individual attempts or organised movements to frame the constitution

characteristics of the federal system and to examine which of these is likely to offer more tangible prospects of realisation.

The first of these features is, in the international sphere, the obliteration of the international personality of the Member States and the substitution for it of that of the Federation as such. This is one of the principal marks of the distinction between a Confederation and a Federal State. Undoubtedly, practice has occasionally disregarded the rigidity of the distinction, in this respect, between the two kinds of association. Thus the American Confederation of 1777 did away with the international personality of the Member States as if it were a Federal State. It denied to them the right to conclude treaties and to send and receive diplomatic representatives. The States of the German Confederation between 1815 and 1866 were international persons, although at the same time the Confederation was a full subject of international law. On the other hand, the German Federal State created in 1871 admitted, and Switzerland and some other Federal States still admit, a certain capacity of the Member States in the domain, largely internal, of the treaty-making power. In 1944 Soviet Russia, in a manner not devoid of artificiality, created a semblance of international capacity for the component Members of the Federation. Nevertheless, the practically complete supersession of the international personality of the Member States must, as a matter of positive law, be regarded as still constituting one of the two main distinguishing features of the federal system. It cannot be expected that governments, or, indeed, the peoples

of the international commonwealth. Such efforts must be regarded as a manifestation of the revolt of the human spirit against the offensive absurdity of civilised communities living, in their mutual relations, in a state approximating to political anarchy. They must be regarded as a constructive protest against the view, insulting to the dignity of man, that the relations of States must for ever remain in a condition of a precarious balance of power and that war—the inevitable upshot of that condition—must for all time be suffered as an enduring factor of human existence and as a decree of blind fate impervious to human will and responsibility. It is unhistoric to interpret history as teaching that war and power must remain paramount in the relations of States—for no other reason than that they have always been so. Equally, it may be deceptive to succumb to the facile wisdom of the warning that it is dangerous and ineffective to create institutions unless they are deeply rooted in the spirit of peoples. For that spirit is the result—and not only the cause—of the protective and civilising influence of laws and institutions which intelligent courage and foresight have brought into being ' in advance of public opinion '. For a searching and fervent estimate, from this point of view, of the significance of the international protection of human rights see McDougal and Leighton in *Yale Law Journal*, 59 (1949-1950), pp. 60-115, in particular pp. 114, 115. And see Glaser in *Revue de droit pénal et de criminologie*, January, 1950.

whom they represent, will be willing to renounce the international personality of their States even in cases in which geographical propinquity seems to favour that course. Thus it may be impracticable to urge a form of European association in which Great Britain or France or Sweden will disappear as international units; in which they will be deprived of the right to send and receive diplomatic and consular representatives; in which, as in the case of Member States of Federal States, they will forfeit the jurisdictional immunities enjoyed by States in foreign courts; and in which they will not be permitted to conclude treaties either between themselves or with other States. It is irrelevant to point to the existing Federal States as showing that separate international personality of the Member States is not essential and that its absence is borne with equanimity and without a sense of loss of a valuable attribute of statehood or of corporate dignity. For these Member States were not, as a rule, international persons prior to having been linked by the bond of federal union. The importance, in the twentieth century, of the distinct international personality of States may be asserted without going to the length of the claim that, as at present constituted, they represent an enduring and indispensable form of political association.

In comparison, the second main distinguishing feature of the federal system, namely, the direct relation between the individual human being and the Federation, offers possibilities which, being less drastic in nature, may become a factor of deep significance in the evolution of the Federation of the World.[47] That direct relation between the individual and the Federation reveals itself in a variety of ways such as the operation of the federal law upon individuals and the participation of individuals in the creation of the federal legislative and other organs. It would manifest itself even more conspicuously through the recognition and protection, in relation to Member States, of the fundamental rights of man. Inasmuch as such recognition and protection of the rights of man implies—as it clearly does—a restriction of their sovereignty in its vital aspect, it would add emphasis to the fact

---

[47] This, in fact, was the distinguishing characteristic of the federal system as seen by the authors of *The Federalist*. ' The great and radical vice in the construction of the existing Confederation is the principle of *Legislation* for *States* or *Governments,* in their *Corporate* or *Collective Capacities,* and as contradistinguished from the *Individuals* of which they consist' (*The Federalist,* No. XV, Hamilton).

that no integration of international society is possible without far-reaching limitations of the sovereignty of its component units. At the same time such limitations of sovereignty, profound as they are, can be achieved without interference with their international personality and status.

It must be borne in mind, in this connexion, that the idea and the historic experience of Federations have, in a different way, tended to impair the authority of the notion of sovereignty conceived as the highest and indivisible source of authority. For it is not only that the phenomenon of the Federal State was called in to show that a single and undivided sovereign will as propounded in Austinian jurisprudence is not essential to the State— where, it was asked, is the sovereign according to the Constitution of the United States of America? The way in which legal writers, largely moved by political motives, juggled with the conception of sovereignty in order to find a solution suitable for their purposes has done much to demonstrate the relativity and divisibility of the rigid notion of an absolute, exclusive and sacrosanct ' competence to determine all competencies '. In the United States, the authors of the *Federalist,* anxious to smooth the path of the transition from a Confederation to a Federal State, developed the theory of the division of sovereignty between the Union and the Member States. Tocqueville planted the doctrine in European soil. German writers, such as Waitz, adapted it for German consumption with the added embellishment of the distinction between the substance of sovereignty (which, they taught, was indivisible) and the attributes of sovereignty (which could be portioned out). That was the moderate theory when contrasted with that of Calhoun, the protagonist of the right of secession, who insisted on the indivisibility of sovereignty but asserted that it was fully retained by the Member States and not at all impaired by the delegation of some of its prerogatives to the Federation. The other extreme was represented, in particular in Germany, by those believers in national unity who regarded sovereignty both as indivisible and as essential to the State, with the result that, in their view, the Members of the Union could not properly be regarded as States. The bitter pill was sweetened by writers such as Laband who served the causes both of the unity of the Federation, which they considered to be exclusively sovereign, and of the separate individuality of the Member States by means of the demonstration that sovereignty is not at all essential to statehood. They were supported by the high authority of Jellinek, who, while buttressing national unity by insisting on the complete subordination of the Member States to the Federation and on the absence of the right of secession, flattered the vanity of the Member States by arguing that they took part in the life of the Union in their capacity as States and that they were not without some status in international law. On the other hand, Duguit, while urging that the Members of the Federation are States as distinguished from decentralised provinces, insisted that statehood cannot be comprehended by reference to the traditional notion of sovereignty—in which fact he found yet another argument in support of his criticism of the accepted notion of the sovereign State.[48] Similar consequences follow from the view that the essence of the federal system consists in the limitation of the competence—of the sovereignty—of the Federation and of the Member States to their respective spheres.[49] It is that feature of the federal system which represents its principal contribution to the main theme of political thought and practice: the combination of self-government with the paramount necessity of order.

These, then, are some of the aspects of the inter-relation between the three central issues of international law: the political integration of mankind in the direction of the Federation of the World, the curbing of the pretensions and aberrations of the doctrine of sovereignty, and the effective protection of human rights as part of the constitution of international society. The very idea of federation, inasmuch as it postulates a direct relation with the individual human being, receives a decisive accession of strength from the recognition, through effective institutions, of the rights of man. At the same time the notion and the experience of the federal system have acted as a powerful solvent of the doctrinal and political absoluteness of sovereignty. So have the ideas of the natural and inalienable rights of man which, when embodied in the safeguards and institutions of positive law—municipal and international—constitute a significant challenge to the unbridled sovereignty of the omnipotent State. In both senses

---

[48] For a penetrating survey of the various theories from this point of view see Kunz, *Staatenverbindungen* (1929), pp. 597-621. See also Mouskhély in *La technique et les principes du droit public. Etudes en l'honneur de Georges Scelle,* vol. I (1950), pp. 397-437, and Giraud, *ibid.,* pp. 253-266.

[49] See *e.g.,* Wheare, *Federal Government* (1946), p. 15.

—by their positive association with what is the essence of the federal system and by their negative effect on the mystic powers of sovereignty—the rights of man have played, and are increasingly bound to play, a significant part in the development towards a comprehensive Federation of the States of the earth.

That advance towards the goal of federal integration can be visualised in accordance with two differing patterns of development. In the first instance, in terms of geography, it may be a combination of and a compromise between the essentially complementary principles of universality and regional association. The claim of the latter to moral authority increases in proportion as it is intended to serve or is capable of serving as a link in the chain of the evolution leading ultimately to a true Federation of the World under the rule of law. Subject to that condition, regional organisations of States are justified and may be beneficent. This is so in particular in the sphere of protection of human rights in cases in which, within a limited number of States bound by an affinity of a geographical or other character, the respect for human rights and the rule of law based on the principle of government by consent have become part of the national heritage of the States in question not only in name but also in fact.[50] Given that affinity, the essence of such regional associations need not necessarily be compromised by what has been described as ' disgusting alliances '.[51] For the effective recognition of the rights of man by and in the association at large is likely to exercise, in the long run, a sustained and potent influence—provided that the acknowledgment and protection of these rights within the association is ensured not by verbal declarations but by binding obligations and working institutions. Such obligations and institutions represent in themselves a powerful reality calculated to bridge any discrepancy between the proclaimed purpose of the association and any defective practices within the territories of any of its members.

Secondly, the advance towards the final integration of international society can be accomplished not only by the formal and deliberate adoption of a comprehensive federal constitution. It

[50] A condition which is non-existent in States governed by a dictatorship or in which violent revolutions have traditionally replaced the method of choosing the government by constitutional means more adequately expressive of the consent of the people.
[51] See above, p. 109, n. 29.

can also be achieved by the gradual acceptance of institutions which are naturally congenial or essential to the federal system. Of these institutions the protection, within an association of a federal nature, of the rights of man, acknowledged and effectively guaranteed by the association, seems to offer more distinct prospects of realisation than schemes based on the renunciation of the international personality of States. In so far as regional experience is a stage in the evolution towards the more complete integration of international society, such recognition and protection of human rights may in itself become a significant contributory factor in the consummation of the organised *civitas maxima,* with the individual human being in the very centre of the constitution of the world. It is also for that reason that these regional developments in the matter of the protection of the rights of man must leave intact the authority and not disdain the inspiration of both the achievements and the potentialities inherent in the law on the subject as already enshrined in the Charter of the United Nations.

INDEX